THE COMPLETE POETRY OF CICELY FOX SMITH

Cicely Fox Smith,
from *The Bookman*, p. 274;
photograph by Emil Otto Hoppé

2nd Edition
(Fully revised)

Edited by

Charles Ipcar and James Saville

Poetry Books by Cicely Fox Smith:

Songs of Greater Britain, 1899.
The Foremost Trail, 1899.
Men of Men, 1900.
Wings of the Morning, 1904.
Lancashire Hunting Songs & Other Moorland Lays, 1909.
Songs in Sail, 1914.
Sailor Town: Sea Songs and Ballads, 1914
The Naval Crown, 1915.
Fighting Men, 1916.
Small Craft, 1917 & 1919.
Rhymes of the Red Ensign, 1919.
Songs and Chanties: 1914-1916, 1919.
Ships and Folks, 1920.
Rovings, Elkin Mathews, 1921.
Sea Songs and Ballads 1917-22, 1923 & 1924.
Full Sail: More Sea Songs and Ballads, 1926.
Sailor's Delight, 1931.
All the Other Children, 1933.
Here and There in England with the Painter Brangwyn, 1945.
Country Days and Country Ways Trudging Afoot in England, 1947.
Ship Models, 1951.

Other books written, co-authored, or edited by Cicely Fox Smith:

The City of Hope (novel set in Alberta), 1914.
Singing Sands (novel set in Vancouver Island, BC), 1918.
Peregrine in Love (novel set in Victoria, BC), 1920.
Sailor Town Days, 1923.
A Book of Famous Ships, 1924.
The Return of the Cutty Sark, 1924.
Ship Alley: More Sailor Town Days, 1925.
Tales of the Clipper Ships, 1926.
A Book of Shanties (traditional sea songs), 1927.
A Sea Chest: An Anthology of Ships and Sailormen, 1927.
Ancient Mariners, 1928.
There Was a Ship: Chapters from the History of Sail, 1929.
Ocean Racers, 1931.
True Tales of the Sea, 1932.
Anchor Lane, 1933.
Peacock Pride (with Madge S. Smith), 1934.
Adventures and Perils, 1936.
Three Girls in a Boat (with Madge S. Smith), 1938.
All the Way Round: Sea Roads to Africa (travel), 1938.
The Ship Aground: A Tale of Adventure, 1940, 1942, & 1958.
The Voyage of the Trevessa's Boats, 1940.
The Story of Grace Darling (biography), 1940.
Thames Side Yesterdays, 1945.
Painted Ports (with Madge S. Smith), 1948, 1965.
Knave-Go-By: The Adventures of Jacky Nameless (with Madge S. Smith), 1951.
Seldom Seen (with Madge S. Smith), 1954.
The Valiant Sailor (with Madge S. Smith), 1951, 1955, & 1959.

Copyright © 2012 & 2015 Charles Ipcar and James Saville

All rights are reserved under International and Pan-American Copyright Conventions. Except for brief passages quoted in a newspaper, magazine, radio or television review, no part of this book may be reproduced in any form or by any means, electronic or mechanical, including photocopying and recording, or by any information storage and retrieval system, without permission in writing from the editors or the publisher.

First Edition 2012
Second Edition 2015
1 2 3 4 5 6 7 8 9 10 LSI 20 19 18 17 16 15

Cover and Book Design: Michael John Linnard, MCSD
Book set in: Arial, Times New Roman, Trajan Pro

A good faith effort has been made to identify and appropriately attribute all the photographers, illustrators, cartoonists and other artists whose work has been used to illustrate the poems in this book.

Photograph on page 770 (top) is of Charlie Ipcar introducing the C. Fox Smith Workshop, June 12, Greenmanville Church, Mystic Sea Music Festival 2011, taken by Judy Barrows and reprinted with kind permission. Photograph on page 770 (bottom) is of James Saville and reprinted with kind permission.

The front cover painting is titled "Shipwreck-1854" by Ivan Aivazovsky (1817-1900).

The back cover photograph is of Cicely Fox Smith by Emil Otto Hoppé from *The Bookman*, September, 1923, p. 274

Library of Congress Cataloging-in-Publication Data

Smith, C. Fox (Cicely Fox), d. 1954
  The complete poetry of Cicely Fox Smith / edited by Charles Ipcar and James Saville. — 2nd ed.
    p. cm.
  Includes bibliography references, glossary and index
  ISBN 978-1-935656-38-8 (pbk. : alk. paper)
  I. Ipcar, Charles. II. Saville, James. III. Title.
  PR6037.M35 2012
  821'.912--dc23
                    2015017847

Little Red Tree Publishing, LLC,
635 Ocean Avenue,
New London, CT 06320.
website: www.littleredtree.com

CONTENTS

Foreword by Charles Ipcar and James Saville   vi
Introduction by Marcia Phillips McGowan, Ph.D.   xii

Biography of Cicely Fox Smith by Charles Ipcar and James Saville   xvii

Book 1—The Early Poems: 1896 to 1913   1

Contains poems from the following books:

Songs of Greater Britain (1899)
The Foremost Trail (1899)
Men of Men (1900)
Wings of the Morning (1904)
Lancashire Hunting Songs and Other Moorland Lays (1909)
Miscellaneous Poems from Magazines and Newspapers

Book 2—The Major Poems: 1914 to 1931   203

Contains poems from the following books:

Songs in Sail (1914)
Sailor Town (1914)
The Naval Crown (1915)
Fighting Men (1916)
Small Craft (1917)
Sailor Town (1919)
Rhymes of the Red Ensign (1919)
Ships and Folks (1920)
Rovings (1921)
Sea Songs and Ballads 1917-1922 (1923)
Full Sail (1926)
Sailor's Delight (1931)
Miscellaneous Poems in Magazines or Manuscripts

Book 3—The Later Poems: 1932 to 1953   565

Contains poems from the following books:

True Tales of the Sea (1932)
All the Other Children (1933)
Anchor Lane (1933)

Oxford Book for Boys (1938)
Here and There in England with the Painter Brangwyn (1945)
Country Days and Country Ways (1947)
Ship Models (1951)
Miscellaneous Poems (magazines by date of publication)

Book 4 - Unpublished Poems 687

Miscellaneous Poems

Appendix A: Reviews (1899-1931) 729
Appendix B: Discography—Poems Recorded as Songs 741
Appendix C: Cicely Fox Smith Bibliography 744
Appendix D: Bibliography of Nautical Artwork 746
Appendix E: Graphic Artists 747
Appendix F: Autobiographical and Biographical References 748

Glossary 749
Index of Poem Titles 755
About the Editors 770

Foreword—1st Edition

On the Trail of Cicely Fox Smith

My own interest in Cicely Fox Smith as a nautical poet was triggered by a sea music concert by Danny and Joyce McLeod (UK) presented at the Maine Maritime Museum in Bath, Maine, in the summer of 2000. Before then she was only familiar to me as footnotes in *Shanties of the Seven Seas* by Stan Hugill and *Songs of American Sailormen* by Joanna Colcord. Little did I realize at the time what an amazing journey I was to embark upon.

In the 1990s Danny and his singing friends had adapted over a dozen of Cicely Fox Smith's poems for singing and I found the songs compelling, full of fascinating nautical characters and their intriguing stories. I felt as if I were listening to sailors talking among themselves in the foc'sle of a ship or at a table in some sailortown dive over a hundred years ago, and maybe I was. Danny had also pulled together a basic biography of her, with a long list of her publications. Danny's work was the initial inspiration and guide for my journey.

My picture of Cicely Fox Smith at that time was a highly romantic one, of a young British poet who had traveled alone to the wild shores of British Columbia, befriended deep-water sailors, and may have even become one herself aboard some tall sailing ship. Her real life story, as far as we have determined, still seems highly romantic but some of the details are quite different from that initial short biography. And we know there is still much more to be learned about her life.

I lost little time collecting a set of Cicely's long out of print poetry books and set about adapting more of her poems to music. By 2004 I was able to join Danny and Joyce at a Cicely Fox Smith workshop at the Mystic Sea Music Festival as a presenter. And I became even more committed to finding out the details of her life and work.

I learned from Cicely Fox Smith's writings that she had been resident in the Victoria, British Columbia, area in the early 20th century. Here for example is her vivid description of Victoria Harbour from *Sailor-Town Days*:

> "You can sit on the edge of the Outer Wharf at Victoria, and fish for black bass with a bit of cotton rag, and watch the great ships come in from the sea with the wonder of the East in their holds.
>
> Over across the Strait of Juan de Fuca the summits of the ranges of the American mainland are flushed with faint rose, for it is only at sunset that the black bass bite. There is a smell of forest fires in the air, and a glow on the flanks of the remote mountains,

and a light wisp of cloud that means miles of ravaged woodland and an inferno of smoke and flame in which men are fighting, parched and blackened like demons. The light on Brotchie Ledge has just begun to wink leisurely, and far out on Race Rocks the lighthouse answers it with his occulting beam.

The sun has gone down into the China Seas in a great fiery golden pomp, like the sea-burial of an old Norse king, and a splendid afterglow, slow and solemn as a funeral march, goes flooding up to the zenith like the glow of a funeral pyre; and on the edge of it hangs a lonely star. A small moon drifts like a feather dropped from an archangel's wing. A riding-light has begun to glimmer in the rigging of the anchored windjammer in the Royal Roads."

So in the summer of 2005 I found myself walking the streets of Victoria's waterfront. Standing at the site of one of her favorite haunts the Outer Wharfs, now identified as Shoal Point, I too watched the "old sunset glory setting all the clouds aflame" and "the snow-crowned peaks that gleam" of the Olympic Mountains across Juan de Fuca Strait. What a heavenly sight! And the sight is still to be enjoyed by anyone who walks there.

However, as she feared "The ports I knew grown strange" is an apt description for what has happened to Victoria's inner harbor. Most of the old buildings there have been torn down and replaced with high-rise hotels and condominiums. Only a dozen or so remnants survive of the buildings she would have remembered from where she worked. In *There Was a Ship* she described her law office as being "up two flights of stairs in Wharf Street… next door but one from a ship-chandler's establishment." One of those shops nearby during her residency was most likely McQuade's Ship Chandlers, a business which later moved a block north to the Yates Block currently occupied by the famed Chandlers Sea Food Restaurant.

Outer Wharfs—2005

Some of the other buildings she described in the neighborhood that she would see during her lunch break included the Occidental Hotel, the Panama Saloon, and the junk shops in nearby Chinatown. Further north, up Store Street, was likely one of her other favorite haunts the Rock Bay Lumber Mills, where she'd watch the longshoremen loading lumber into tall ships. This arm of the Inner Harbour was also where the tugboats would berth and the old sealing schooners she was so fond of were moored. Just below Wharf Street were warehouses and the shipping offices for many single ship firms such as the clipper ship *Antipode*, identified by their modest white on black sign boards. And on the block where she worked there was an abundance of wholesale grocery shops, hotels and saloons.

Chandlers Seafood Restaurant -2005

Much to my dismay I found no evidence at the time in the BC Royal Archives that she published any poems in the local newspapers while she was resident there. It was five years later that I was able to confirm that she published "The Long Road Home" and her short story "The Supreme Moment" in *The Daily Colonist* in 1911. In my defense I should say that I only had a day or two to scan through years of microfiche at the Archives, and at that time everyone had assumed she had been resident in Victoria from 1905 to 1913.

She never returned to Victoria but there is evidence in her later poems such as "Pacific Coast" that she never forgot this beautiful harbor. I in turn made efforts to insure that the Victoria Folk Song Society members were aware of her stay by singing them several of her poems at their monthly sea music gathering.

In 2006 I flew to England to see what additional poems I could find in the British Library, having exhausted what was available from the used books I was able to purchase on-line. There I was able to copy some of the pre-1914 poetry books. I also was able to meet my co-editor of this book, James Saville, for the first time. Jim and I had discovered our mutual interest in this poet as we began posting hundreds of her poems on a classical poetry website.

In 2007 I revisited Australia for a concert tour and to see if I could interest anyone there in tracking down the only surviving copy of Cicely's romantic novel *The City of Hope*, loosely based on her residency in Lethbridge, Alberta, from the fall of 1911 to the spring of 1912. One of my musical friends there, Margaret Walters, was later able to access the book via inter-library loan from its repository in Tasmania and send me a copy.

When I returned to Victoria in 2009 I was able to do more research and present more songs based on Cicely's Pacific Coast poems. I also recruited several volunteers, Bill Huot and Aziza Cooper, who did critical follow-up research; these volunteers were able to eventually find on-line newspaper files at the University of British Columbia, including files of city directories and insurance maps. We eventually determined the street address of where she lived in the James Bay neighborhood, and the fact that she was not living there alone but with her mother and sister.

Our research in Victoria became more focused after one of our British volunteers, Jake Wade, was able to document from barely legible steamship passenger lists when she voyaged between Liverpool to Canada, and when she was actually resident in England from the Census records. We determined that she, with her mother and sister, had traveled to Alberta in 1911. They lived with her older brother Richard from the fall to the spring and then moved on to Victoria. They left Victoria to return to England in the fall of 1913.

In 2010 my wife and I revisited England to do more music and research. Our first stop was at the National Maritime Museum in Greenwich, where I had learned there was a collection of Smith's papers that her sister delivered there after the poet's death in 1954. It's there with the help of Chris Roche that I finally found some high quality photos of the poet, as a young girl and as a young woman. I also found a proof copy of the excellent *Bookman* literary review, which we are so delighted to include in this book. In addition we found a few unpublished poems, a lot of clipping files, and reams of nautical research material, which may be of interest to other scholars.

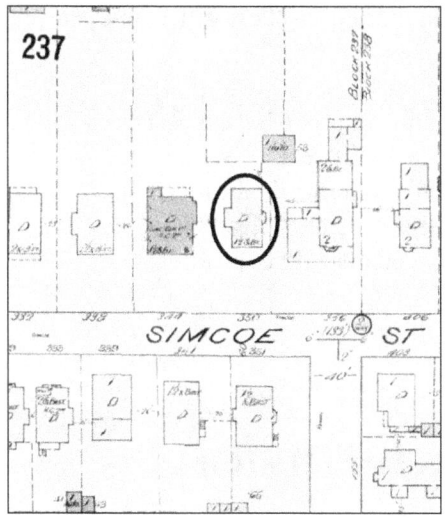

350 Simcoe St., James Bay Neighborhood, Victoria, BC, Canada, 1913 Insurance Map.

Our next trip was to the Manchester area where she resided as a teenager, to photograph one of the houses that her family resided in, but more importantly to locate the Navigation Inn. The Navigation Inn is mentioned in "The Jolly Bargeman" and the one in the Manchester area is located at Buxworth. I had contacted Ian Bruce who lives in the neighboring town of Stockport and is a collector of canal boat songs. Bruce was nice enough to reserve a room for us at the Inn and deliver us there by narrowboat. And we got to regale the taproom crowd with the song.

Next we drove over to Yorkshire where I co-coordinated a Cicely Fox Smith workshop with James Saville at the Otley Folk Festival, It's there I got to meet two of our best UK research volunteers, Jake Wade and Barrie Mathers. Barrie was primarily responsible for making copies of all the poems published in *Punch* magazine from 1923 to 1954, none of which was available on-line because of copyright issues; he also copied *Peregrine in Love* for us, a romantic novel which has detailed descriptions of 1911 Victoria from the perspective of a young adventurous woman.

Since 2010 we have learned a few more details about Cicely's life and her publications. As more and more newspaper archives come on-line we are discovering just how widely she was published. Surprisingly, even in the pre-1914 period her poems and short stories were regularly appearing in the Australian and New Zealand newspapers. And her poems were also being recited at that time by professional entertainers in that part of the world.

However, we still do not have a full picture of this intriguing woman's life. We are convinced she kept a journal and if it ever surfaces it will make fascinating reading. Until then we will have to piece together her life from what we can harvest from her literary works and the historical archives. We do wish that she had been rediscovered sooner while her sister Madge was still alive but unfortunately that did not happen. And there seems to be no other close relatives who are still living in the UK or Canada who can fill in the details.

Perhaps, it's best to imagine Cicely's life than to fill in the details, some of which are undoubtedly mundane. But the search has been so rewarding. One of her sailor philosophers summed up this conundrum in "Port o' Dreams" in this fashion:

> "An' I'll never fetch that harbour, but it's maybe for the best,
> For I daresay if I found it, it'd be like all the rest,
> An' I like to think it's waitin', waitin' all the while for me,
> With the red wine an' the white wine an' the dancin' an' the spree,
> An' the firefly gleamin' golden in the palms I'll never see!"

Charles Ipcar
Richmond, Maine. 2012

Foreword—2nd Edition

It is three years on since the first edition and a lot has happened. We have been inundated with new research and information. Surprisingly, thanks to the efforts of our small army of researchers and supporters, we have been able to increase the body of published and unpublished work previous attributed to Cecily Fox Smith. In all we have increased her published work by 23, to stand at 660 poems, contained in Book 1, 2, and 3. This pushes her earliest published poetry back to 1896, when she was just 14 years of age. We have also, primarily through the efforts of Jake Wade and Danny McLeod, been able to include 51 previously unknown and unpublished poems in a new Book 4.

We are particularly pleased to include a wonderful introduction by Dr. Marcia Phillips McGowan, which lends an air of academic credibility to this book that was sadly never afforded Cecily Fox Smith in her life time. Marcia, quite rightly in our view, scolds the academic community for refusing to relocate Cecily Fox Smith to her rightful place in the canon of British women literary figures of the 20th Century.

We have also taken this opportunity to fully revise and edit the entire book. We have been able to add a number of lengthy reviews missing from the first edition, which greatly expand the reference points and responses to her work from the media at the time of their publication.

Charles Ipcar,	James Saville
Richmond, Maine. 2015	Bradford, UK. 2015

Acknowledgments

This book could not have been completed without the encouragement and hard work of dozens of people all over the world. First of all we recognize Danny McLeod of the United Kingdom (UK) who has played such a principal role as a performer and researcher in reintroducing Cicely Fox Smith as a nautical poet to the world. Other major researchers include Alan Hardy (UK), A. B. Blackmore (UK), W. H. Webb (UK), John Edgar Mann (UK), Ian "Nobby" Dye (UK), and Bob Zentz (US).

Alan Fitzsimmons (UK) deserves special mention for first adapting so many of the poems that have been sung by McLeod and his bandmates. Other singers who have played a major role in adapting Smith's poems for singing include Bob Roberts (UK), Sarah Morgan (UK), Dick Miles of Ireland, Bob Zentz (US), Gordon Morris and Peter Massey (UK), William Pint and Felicia Dale (US), Dave Webber and Anni Fentiman (UK), Barrie Temple (UK), and Tom Lewis (UK).

In addition there are web-based resource groups that were also of great assistance. Project Gutenburg deserves special mention for its on-line archives of *Punch* magazine (up to and including 1922). The Mudcat Café is a website for those interested in folk music whose forum has provided spirited discussion of Smith's work, clues for further research, and in some cases invaluable volunteers from all over the world. Our new facebook page, since the publication of the first edition, has been a focal point for all those interested in CFS, and growing daily.

There are the many volunteers who conducted research, photocopied or scanned hundreds of pages from exceedingly rare books or periodicals which could not be readily purchased in the used book market. Major work was done by Jenna Ipcar (US); Margaret Walters of Australia; Aziza Cooper and Bill Huot of Canada; Chris Roche, and Barrie Mathers of the United Kingdom. A special thanks to Jake Wade for his transcription of handwritten poems and enumerable pieces of valuable research.

We are particularly thankfully to Marcia Phillips McGowan, for her diligent research and for writing such an important introduction to this second edition, sadly lacking in our first edition.

Finally, we would like to thank our publisher Michael Linnard, introduced to us by Joanie DiMartino, who had the courage and determination to see that this vast inventory of poems was republished in as complete and comprehensive form as possible.

We cannot personally thank everyone who has been of assistance in this project but know that your work was greatly appreciated.

Introduction

Cicely Fox Smith was a young, respectable, middle class woman at the turn of the nineteenth to the twentieth century. For someone in her social position, she possessed a rather unique talent: she was able to master the dialect of seagoing men and then reproduce it in enchanting poetry that has lent itself readily to the rhythms of sea chanteys. While this in itself is fascinating to me, I will instead focus on why Smith, once a celebrated narrative poet, has been in our day, largely forgotten. Despite a large body of significant work, Smith's name is missing both from the standard literary canon and from the one that has been so extensively revised by feminist critics from the 1980s to the present.

In the first edition of *The Complete Poems of Cicely Fox Smith*, poet Joanie Di Martino remarks upon the fact that Smith's work was critically acclaimed in her generation yet has been neglected since her death. Di Martino acknowledges that Smith "eschewed the literary movements of her generation" such as "Modernism, Imagism and the Free Verse Movement, which abandoned structure and rhyme" (xi) and mentions that the experimentalism of the avant-garde is missing in Smith's work. I would like to posit that it is this missing element that accounts, at least partially, for the unjustifiable neglect of her work. In addition, Smith's adherence to Victorian era values during a time of post-WWI disillusionment that was experienced by a large majority of the British population—most notably Modernist poets, writers and artists—undoubtedly influenced this neglect. Like her contemporaries John Masefield, Joseph Conrad, and Rudyard Kipling, Smith was attracted both to the sea and to traditional modes of narrative expression. She chose to ignore Ezra Pound's famous dictum to "make it new." In a time of social upheaval and inevitable movement towards rights for women, the Cicely Fox Smith who so purposefully mastered the language and rhythms of men ironically chose to remain an "old fashioned girl," one who valued and celebrated the past in a time which insisted on looking to the future.

In fact, there is in Smith's diction and poetry little acknowledgement of the changes wrought in post-WWI women's lives. Perhaps as a result, when she is mentioned at all by feminist critics, it is only to refer to her as a "jingoist" writer, one who unquestioningly accepted her womanly role of supporting the disastrous war which cost at least ten million men their lives, virtually wiping out a whole British generation. In contrast, other women poets such as H. D. (Hilda Doolittle), Mina Loy, and even Edith Sitwell, reacted rather strongly in their poetry not only to Victorian formalist patterns and images, but to the values these patterns and images preserved. Whereas H. D., for instance, attempted to reconstruct gender norms in her poetry, Cicely Fox Smith seems to have accepted them, following the rhythms and images of the great male masters of Romantic and Victorian balladry such as Sir Walter Scott and Samuel Taylor Coleridge, Alfred Lord

Tennyson and Rudyard Kipling. The Modernists' distrust of Victorian positivism, evinced by such writers as Wyndham Lewis, May Sinclair, Ezra Pound, T. S. Eliot and Mary Borden, to name a few, continues to this day, as does the influence of Sigmund Freud, Carl Jung and Henri Bergson. Smith, however, eschewed these influences and remained a positivist writer. Perhaps the popularity of her poetry in her own time is largely due to her rejection of what she may have seen as negative influences on her own writing and her celebration of the traditional cultural values of Imperial Britain. Smith's poetry reaffirms the value of the past and, as Rosa Maria Bracco notes, offers us "an important insight into middle class ideology" (203). Like many middle class writers addressing a predominately middle class audience, Smith knew what her public wanted and gave it to them.

However, Smith's acceptance not only of the rhythms and carefully rhymed stanzas of Victorian poetry but of the very cultural values and gender norms that kept women out of the literary canon have done her no favors with the literary critics of the latter half of the twentieth century and the first part of the twenty-first. The fact that Smith, like many others of her generation, felt a need for affirming life and faith rather than destabilizing it, as did the Imagists, Vorticists, Surrealists and adherents to other revolutionary literary movements, should not condemn her to obscurity. We must remember that she was born in a time when women used synonyms or initials to sign their work because literature was considered a male purview; Marian Evans used the pseudonym George Eliot, and the Bronte sisters used the male pseudonyms Acton, Currer and Ellis Bell in order to gain the opportunity to be published. Smith was born into a world which showed her, until gender norms began to change and her work was well-established, that the use of the initials C. F. S. or the name C. Fox-Smith would bring credibility to a genre—the sea poem—long considered to be the privilege of men. However, the confluence of the first wave of the Women's Movement with women's contributions to the Great War effort from 1914-1918 led to the subsequent enfranchisement of British women over thirty in 1918. Women's work in the war effort brought them access to professions hitherto restricted to men. Although women writers in general continued to struggle to maintain professional standing and respect, new opportunities brought self-awareness and a destabilization of gender norms.

In fact, many feminist critics have noticed a transition away from self-concealment to self-awareness and assertion in post-WWI women's poetry. I detect an increasing self-assertion in Smith's 1930s poems such as "I Have Seen," from *Anchor Lane*, or in the tongue-in-cheek *Punch* poems such as "The Misanthrope," "Sale By Auction," "Tea in the Garden," and "County Pleasures"—arguably the wittier poems of the 1930s. Smith's sense of humor is evident in much of her poetry, but nowhere as much as in her underestimated *Punch* poetry. When poems framed in the first person appear, relating her own experiences, we are introduced to a new voice, one which asserts that everyday life as well as heroic deeds are not only worthy of note, but may be gently satirized. These poems are less conventional, more Dorothy Parker-like. This voice appears as well in Smith's children's poems, which are sheer joy to read. Such poems are a far cry from the better known sea poems and the hortatory poems celebrating the glory of empire.

There is a new ease in them—a sense of fun that perhaps could only come with the relative freedom felt by women between the two world wars.

This sense of ease was absent when Smith began to write in the late nineteenth century. The preface to *The Poets and the Poetry of the Nineteenth Century: Christina Rossetti to Katharine Tynan* (1907), edited by Alfred H. Miles, includes poems by Smith and mentions, in typical Victorian fashion, that her father was a Balliol man and the Arnold prize winner of his year (447). The fact that he became a barrister on the Northern Circuit and that her mother was a clergyman's daughter must have instilled in Smith the upper middle class values that are immediately evident in her early poetry. She seems never to have questioned those solidly Christian values against which many of her contemporaries rebelled. Yet it is interesting that as late as 2006 she is included in the *Home Front Encyclopedia: United States, Britain and Canada in World Wars I and II*, wherein her volume of war poems, *Fighting Men* is mentioned as a "significant collection" (372). However, the definitive feminist critics of women's writing during the Great War barely mention her except to note her jingoism. The writers most lauded by feminist critics are those who served either in the hospitals, at home, or the ambulance units near the front, and related the horrors of war that these positions revealed to them. In *Women's Poetry of the First World War*, Nosheen Khan mentions Smith among writers like Katharine Tynan and Alice Meynell, who were of "established reputation" (5). However, Khan groups Smith with Jessie Pope as a "popular" writer whose "war verse is primarily jingoistic" (5). Khan does mention, however, that "despite modern unwillingness to admire the heroism that existed," such verse is of relevance to the whole story of the years 1914-18. She admits that the anti-war view, so celebrated in the works of other feminist critics, "cannot fully explain the poetry of the First World War" (5). I agree and deplore the fact that Smith's name does not appear in such seminal academic studies as Margaret Higonnet's *Women Writers of WWI* or Claire M. Tylee's *The Great War and Women's Consciousness*. However, as Tylee does note, during and after the Great War, "...many women were unable to grasp the descriptions offered them in place of the blindfolds fabricated by the government's propaganda apparatus..." (55). She adds that everyone not at the battlefront "was subjected to linguistic constructions which it was difficult to resist" (55). The points of view of women on the home front have been denigrated since Siegfried Sassoon's bitter war poem "Glory of Women" (1918). Perhaps it is time to put such derision to rest. In truth, despite the experimental prose and verse of such writers as Mary Borden, who led ambulance units during both world wars, the poetic idiom of the soldier poets themselves is either primarily Georgian (think of Rupert Brooke's sonnets) or a continuation of conventional Victorian verse (think of John McCrae's "In Flanders Field").

In addition, I would argue that Smith's reputation and that of her sea poetry over the years suffered because of the institutional sexism of twentieth century reviewers and anthologists alike. Until she began to write sea songs, the genre was rife with masculine privilege. Like the written work of women writers that emerged from the Great War front lines, which was ignored for decades because of alleged inauthenticity, Smith's sea songs, appearing as they did in successive volumes, suffered critically by comparison to those of such "authentic" male writers as John Masefield, Rudyard Kipling, and ironically, Joseph Conrad, who praised her work generously (Publisher's Circular 259). Fox Smith's gender led one reviewer, for instance, though she admired the poems in *Sailor Town* and *Small Craft* immensely, to speak of an author who writes "with glamour about the life before the mast" (Plaisted 729). I would venture to say that glamour is a word that has never been coupled with the works of the great male writers of sea poetry.

Moreover, the same reviewer diminishes Fox Smith's "little volumes" by saying they "are not great in the sense that Masefield's sea poems and some of the descriptive prose-poetry of Conrad are great" because of the narrowness of theme and confinement to the "seaman's vocabulary and point of view" (729). So what is, perhaps, most remarkable in Smith's work, her mastery of the language and experience of the seaman, is denigrated rather than praised. This is the same fate that many of her contemporary women writers and artists suffered. It is only in the last twenty or so years that the work of Mary Cassatt, for instance, has been recognized as equal to that of male Post-Impressionists to whom she was so often compared or that the work of Edith Wharton, which had always suffered by comparison to that of her friend and fellow writer Henry James, has been recognized as great in its own right. Ironically, after assuring the reader that these poems are "not great" (i.e. not worthy of being preserved in any literary canon), the reviewer goes on to praise the realism of Fox Smith's poetry, "the feeling of a ship with the wild sea beneath it, the keen zest of battling for life against famine, cold, and shipwreck" (729). And she grants that "the sailorman himself would not be ashamed to roar them out on a gala night with such chanteys as 'Home, dearie home' and 'Ah, fare you well'" (729).

One final insight into the virtual disappearance of Smith's poetry before the appearance of this volume was suggested to me through reading Rosa Maria Bracco's *Merchants of Hope: Middlebrow Writers and the First World War*. Bracco challenges prevailing views of a "modern" revolution in literature. Although she recognizes the "separateness" of men's realities at the front from those of women at home, she argues that as England is "synonymous" with tradition (128), it is "middlebrow" writing that offers its readers "an anchor of meaning within the confusing and contradictory world of the 1920s and 1930s" (199). Though Bracco is speaking mainly of fiction, her assertion that middlebrow writing "reaffirmed historical continuity and the coherence of faith" (12) may be applied to poetry of the period, including that of Cicely Fox Smith.

At present Smith continues to be recognized principally as the fine maritime poet that she is. There can be no higher tribute than her early recognition by Joseph Conrad (see Appendix A, p. 729.) as "the quintessence of the collective soul of the latter-day seaman." Her mastery of the vocabulary of the sea and the rhythms of its men are perhaps without peer. How Smith attained this mastery as a conventional, even evangelical, woman of the late nineteenth and early twentieth centuries remain a mystery. But as so many of her ballads lend themselves to musical expression perhaps she will be perceived, at last, not only as a master of verbal phrasing that is musical both in sound and intent but as a versatile poet whose voice, if not convictions, changed over time. The past was not dead to those, like Cicely Fox Smith, who sought to preserve British conservative values. It was to be cherished, and its poetry was to sustain and celebrate it. Whatever our own politics, it must be acknowledged that it is this singleness of purpose as well as the skillful use of rhyme, rhythm and diction that have enabled the well wrought poems of Cicely Fox Smith at last to be included in their own volume.

Marcia Phillips McGowan, Ph.D.
Distinguished Professor Emerita of English
Eastern Connecticut State University

Works Cited:

Bracco, Rosa Maria. *British Middlebrow Writers and the First World War.* Providence: Berg, 1993

Ciment, James, Mary Hickey and Thaddeus Russell. *The Home Front Encyclopedia: United States, Britain and Canada in World Wars I and II. Vol. 1.* Santa Barbara: ABC CLIO, 2006.

Conrad, Joseph. "Conrad's Great Tribute to Miss C. Fox-Smith." *The Publisher's Circular and Booksellers' Record* (August 23, 1924).

Khan, Nosheen. *Women's Poetry of the First World War.* Lexington: University of Kentucky P, 1988.

Miles, Alfred H., ed. *The Poets and the Poetry of the Nineteenth Century. Vol. IX: Christina Rossetti to Katherine Tynan.* London: Routledge, 1907.

Plaisted, Martha. "Sea Songs by a Woman." *Bookman* (August 1919). Reprinted in the Appendix A, p. 729.

Tylee, Claire M. *The Great War and Women's Consciousness.* Iowa City: U of Iowa P, c. 1990.

BIOGRAPHY OF CICELY FOX FMITH

Cicely Fox Smith was born February 1, 1882, into a middle class family in Lymm, near Warrington, England during the latter half of the reign of Queen Victoria. Her father Richard Smith was a barrister and her mother Alice Wilson Smith was a housewife. Cicely well might have been expected to have a brief education and then to settle down to life as a homemaker either for her family or her marriage partner. Thankfully that did not happen.

Cicely Fox Smith as a young girl, circa 1892

Cicely was well-educated at The Manchester High School for Girls from 1894 to 1897, where she described herself later as "something of a rebel,"[1] and started writing poems at a comparatively early age. In an article for the school magazine she later wrote "I have a hazy recollection of epic poems after Pope's *Iliad,* romantic poems after Marmion stored carefully away in tin tobacco boxes when I was seven or eight."[2] All of that early work is lost unfortunately. She published her first book of verses when she was 17 and it received favorable press comments.

Wandering the moors near her home she developed a spirit of adventure. She would follow the Holcombe Harriers hunt on foot as a girl, no mean feat.[3] She had a fierce desire to travel to Africa but in time settled for a voyage to Canada.

She sailed with her mother and sister Madge in 1911 on a steamship to Montreal. They then traveled by train to Lethbridge,[4] Alberta, and stayed for about a year with her older brother Richard Andrew Smith before they continued on to British Columbia (BC).[5] From 1912 to 1913 the three of them resided in the James Bay neighborhood of Victoria, 350 Semco Street[6], at the southern tip of Vancouver Island. Cicely described herself working as a typist for the BC Lands Department and later for an attorney on the waterfront. Her spare time was spent roaming nearby wharves and alleys, talking to residents and sailors alike. She listened to and learned from the sailors' tales until she too was able to speak with that authoritative nautical air that pervades her written work.[7]

The Manchester High School for Girls

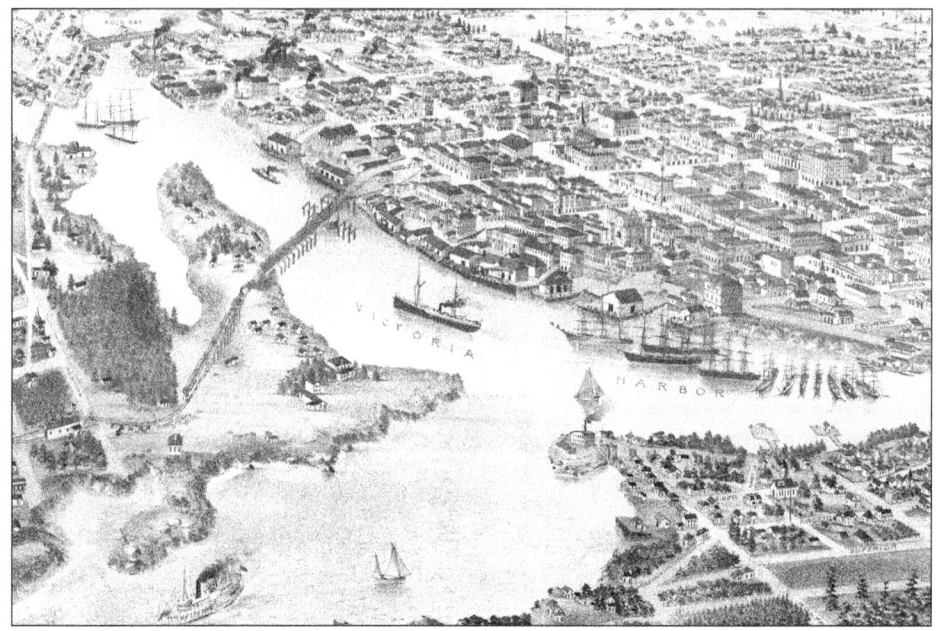
Inner Harbour, Victoria, British Columbia, 1889

On November 23, 1913, Cicely, together with her mother and sister, arrived home in Liverpool aboard the White Star Dominion Line steamer *Teutonic* on the eve of WWI.[8] She and her family then settled in Holcombe Cottage, Boothroyden. They then moved to Bury, Lancashire, and after the end of WWI to Hampshire. Her final residence was in West Halse Bow, Crediton, North Devon from about 1950 to 1954.

She soon put her experiences to use in a great outpouring of poetry, some of it clearly focused on supporting England's war efforts. Much of her poetry was from the point of view of the sailor. The detailed nautical content of her poems made it easy to understand why so many readers presumed that Cicely was male. One correspondent wrote to her as "Capt. Fox Smith" and when she tried to correct him he wrote back "You say you are not a master but you must be a practical seaman. I can always detect the hand of an amateur."[9] He was almost correct. She was familiar with life at sea as few armchair amateurs would ever be. It was only when she was well-established that she started routinely using the by-line "Miss C. Fox Smith" or "Cicely Fox Smith."

S. S. *Teutonic*, circa 1900

Initially she was able to publish her poetry in a wide variety of magazines and newspapers such as *Blackwood's Magazine, Blue Peter, Canada Monthly, Country Life, Cunard Magazine, Daily Chronicle, Grand Magazine, Holly Leaves, Outlook, Pall Mall Gazette, The Daily Mail, The Dolphin, The London*

Mercury, The Nautical Magazine, The Spectator, The Sphere, The Times Literary Supplement, Westminster Gazette, White Star Magazine, The Windsor Magazine, The Daily Colonist (British Columbia), *The Register* (Australia), *Nelson Evening Mail* (New Zealand), and last but hardly least *Punch* magazine for which she wrote many poems between 1914 and her death in 1954. She later re-published most of these poems in her poetry books.

Other literary works by her included three romantic novels, numerous short stories and articles, as well as several books describing "sailortown." She also published a book of traditional sea shanties that she had collected, and edited a collection of sea poems and stories primarily by other authors. In 1937 she finally realized a childhood dream by sailing around the coast of Africa, as a guest of the Union-Castle Mail Steamship Co. Ltd., stopping in the harbors along the way. She wrote of her experiences in *All the Way Round: Sea Roads to Africa.* In the 1940's she began writing children's sea stories with her sister Margaret (Madge) Scott Smith, other travel books, history books, a book about ship models, at least one biography titled *Grace Darling*, and contributed to and edited many collections. She also contributed many literary reviews for *Punch* magazine and the *Times Literary Supplement*.

The fine art work of her older brother Philip Wilson Smith, known at the time for his etchings of Elizabethan architecture and oil paintings, illustrates many of her poetry and prose books. Her brother was also a veteran of WWI. He died May 7, 1954.

Her literary achievements were such as to persuade the Government to award her, at the age of 67, a modest pension for "her services to literature."

She kept writing to the end of her life about many things and many places but always with the accuracy and knowledge of an expert. She even chose her own gravestone epitaph, an extract from one of Walter Raleigh's poems:[10]

> *But from this earth*
> *This grave*
> *This dust*
> *My lord shall raise me up*
> *I trust.*

Cicely Fox Smith died on April 8th, 1954, in the village of West Hasle Bow, Devon, where she'd been living with her sister Madge. Madge lived on another 19 years, dying in September of 1973.

She is now gaining a wider audience as more and more musicians are putting her poems to music and producing many fine songs, primarily in the nautical folk song tradition; over 80 of her poems have so far been adapted for singing and have been recorded. It is hoped that the present book will help further such interest in the creative work of this fine writer.

Charles Ipcar and James Saville,
May 1, 2015

Notes:

1. *All the Way Round*, Cicely Fox Smith, published by Michael Joseph, London, UK, 1938, p. 13
2. "Cicely Fox Smith of Bow," A. B. Blackmore, in Devon Life, UK, May, 1977, p. 28.
3. "Cicely Fox Smith," by W. A. F., *The Bookman*, published by Hodder & Stoughton, London, UK, Volume 64, September, 1923, p. 274
4. *Later English Poems* 1901-1922, J. E. Wetherell, published by B. A., McClelland & Stewart, Limited, Toronto, Canada, 1922, pp. 35-36
5. *1911 British Census; Later English Poems 1901-1922*, pp. 35-36 and 1908 Passenger List (Montreal/Quebec)
6. *Henderson's Greater Victoria City Directory, 1913*, on p. 799; she is listed as "writer" "r" (resident) at 350 Simcoe Street; her sister is noted on p. 802 as is her mother on p. 803.
7. *Sailor Town Days*, p. 163-182; *Peregrine in Love* pp. 86-87; *A Book of Famous Ships*, p. 160
8. 1913 Passenger Lists (Liverpool)
9. *Songs and Chanties: 1914-1916*, Elkin Mathews, London, UK, 1919, p. 232.
10. "Cicely Fox Smith of Bow," A. B. Blackmore, in *Devon Life*, UK, May, 1977, p. 29; in *All the Way Round*, p. 216, the poet quotes the entire Raleigh verse after musing beside the grave in Rhodesia of one of childhood heroes, Leander Starr Jameson, who was one of Cecil John Rhodes' principal assistants:

> "Even such is Time, that takes in trust
> Our youth, our joys, our all we have,
> And pays us but with age and dust;
> Who in the dark and silent grave,
> When we have wandered all our ways,
> Shuts up the story of our days!
> But from this earth, this grave, this dust,
> The Lord shall raise me up, I trust."

There is no doubt in our minds that she chose part of this verse as her own epitaph in memory of her childhood hero.

BOOK 1

THE EARLY POEMS: 1896 TO 1913

Prince's Dock, Hull, by Moonlight, painted by Atkinson Grimshaw
from *The Art of Nautical Illustration*, by Michael E. Leek,
published by Quantum Books, London, UK, 2005, p. 93

Beside the Pool

Beside the pool tall alders grow,
Like stately columns, row on row,
And on the bank long grasses blow
      Beside the pool.

Beside the pool the livelong day
The whispering branches seem to say;
"Come, rest and dream the hours away
      Beside the pool."

Beside the pool at ease I lie;
No cloud is in the clear blue sky,
No sound except the breeze's sigh
      Beside the pool.

Beside the pool we hear no more
The restless city's ceaseless roar—
Only the swallows cry and soar
      Beside the pool!

❖ ❖ ❖ ❖ ❖

From *Hearth and Home: An Illustrated Weekly Journal for Gentlewomen*, Issue 276, August 27, 1896, p. 587.

This is the first poem published by this poet in a commercial publication.

Battle of Isandhlwana (Isandula)

Isandula-1

Hark to my pitiful tale—a story of slaughter and woe,
A tale of how Englishmen fought, and were slain by a barbarous foe.
The morning dawned sunny and clear, when our gallant but ill-fated band
Drew up to combat the foe by the hill of the "Little Hand."
Slowly the impis crept on; and slowly they girded us round:
Nearer and nearer they came—still nearer, yet never a sound.
And we knew that our doom was come; we knew it, but would not flee,
For we thought on what Britons would say in our country far over the sea;
And we thought on our dear ones at home—and our courage came back to us then:
Though win we could not, we knew—at least we could perish like men.
Then with a roar and a rush, and a yell like hyenas at bay,
On came the Zulus in waves, resolved to be slain or to slay.
And they mowed down our column like grass—they flowed o'er the place where we stood,
While we volleyed them, back to back—unflinching as Englishmen should.
Step by step we drew back; then panic seized on us at last,
And we rushed for the river, like leaves driven on by a merciless blast.
One of us, bearing the flag, reached the water; but all was in vain;
There he turned on the foe; and there with the colours was slain.
But yet he fell not alone—his friend had run to his side:
Together they fought their last fight, and together those valiant ones died.
And when we returned to the spot, we found on the scene of their stand,
Fourteen brave warriors and strong, that they battled with, hand to hand.
There they lie, side by side (thank Heaven that their end was swift)—
Coghill and Melville, the brave ones—the heroes of Fugitives Drift.
'Twas useless to hope to win—had been madness, I know it full well—
But I would to heaven I had stayed there, and stood by the brave men that fell!
But the enemy drove us like sheep; that we feared them it is not true;
But a straw cannot stem the torrent; they were thousands—and what could we do?
Great was the wailing that night in the camp where the Zulu held sway,
For many they valued highly had fallen in battle that day.
And of those that we left on the field not one had escaped with his life,
But they fought for the honour of England, and they bore themselves bravely in strife.
Thus was the battle lost; thus perished that valiant band;
Thus Englishmen fought and died at the hill of the "Little Hand."

❖ ❖ ❖ ❖ ❖

From *Hearth and Home: An Illustrated Weekly Journal for Gentlewomen*, Issue 302, February 25, 1897, p. 628.

Isandula, older spelling Isandhlwana, is an isolated hill in the KwaZulu-Natal province of South Africa, located 105 miles north by northwest of Durban. The Battle of Isandlwana on January 22, 1879, was the first major encounter in the Anglo–Zulu War between the British Empire and the Zulu Kingdom and was a decisive victory for the Zulus and caused the defeat of the first British invasion of Zululand. About 22,000 Zulu warriors defeated a contingent of approximately 1,350 British and Native troops.

Our Colonial Troops

In this moment of our joy and exultation
From far distant shores they come,
To join in glad reunion with the nation
Whose land they call their home.
Theirs no banner all emblazoned with their glory,
But, tho' hid from mortal ken,
In fadeless hues is writ the noble story
On the hearts of Englishmen!

In other climes they fight, perchance to perish,
They were bred 'neath other skies;
But 'tis England's age long glory that they cherish,
It is England's fame they prize.
They love the land to all our hearts the nearest.
As only Britons can,
And the honour that to them is far the dearest
Is the name of Englishman!

They have proved their worth in many a hard-fought battle,
On valley, hill, and plain,
When the savage war-cry drowned the musket-rattle
'Mid the dying and the slain.
They have made our land the greatest known in story
Since time and earth began,
True heirs, indeed, to all old England's glory,
And the name of Englishman!

❖   ❖   ❖   ❖   ❖

From *Hearth and Home: An Illustrated Weekly Journal for Gentlewomen,* Issue 329, September 2, 1897, p. 675.

Gordon Avenged!

September 2nd 1898

Glory for these glad tidings, far and near,
That come today across the plunging main:
Shattered the Dervish host, broken their spear,
Their mad fanatic turned to fear,
Avenged is Gordon slain!

Glory to those who, killed in glorious fray,
Lie where they fell upon the Egyptian plain:
From the fair 'scutcheon of our fame away
Strong English hands have wiped the stain to-day;
Avenged is Gordon slain!

Glory to those who, ere the set of sun,
Fought their first fight, and fought it not in vain:

Major-General Charles Gordon

Twining their flag with blood stained laurels won
When our great work of years at length was done,
Avenged is Gordon slain!

The men who shed his life-blood long before
Of their dark deed now reap the bitter grain:
Now their short hour of triumphing is o'er,
Shattered the reign of blood for evermore—
Avenged is Gordon slain!

With painful toil have we redeemed the past:
Our soldiers marched to triumph once again:
Now brought to nought that army, then so vast,
Scattered the Dervish host—at last, at last,
Avenged is Gordon slain!

❖ ❖ ❖ ❖ ❖

From *Hearth and Home: An Illustrated Weekly Journal for Gentlewomen*, Issue 389, October 27, 1898, p. 924.

This poem is a tribute to Major-General Charles George Gordon who was slain in the gallant defence of Khartoum, Sudan, in 1885. It is also a tribute to General Sir Herbert Kitchener who led the British relief forces that eventually reached the City, two days after its fall, and defeated the rebel army of Abdullah al-Taashi, the successor to the self-proclaimed Mahdi, Muhammad Ahmad.

A Birthday Greeting

Long years be thine, dear Editor,
'Mid loving girls and boys,
Sorrowing with all their childish griefs,
Rejoicing with their joys.
As swiftly thro' the days and years
Time's hurrying footsteps wend,
Still may'st thou be, in all their hearts,
A loved tho' unseen, friend.

And as the years roll on apace,
With freight of joy or woe,
Shall we forget the kindly friend
Who loved us long ago?
Nay—each, when years have passed away,
May turn old pages o'er,
Remember how the world went then,
And be a child once more!

❖ ❖ ❖ ❖ ❖

From *Hearth and Home: An Illustrated Weekly Journal for Gentlewomen*, Issue 393, November 24, 1898, p. 108.

This issue of Hearth and Home contained one other poem and a letter congratulating the editor on his birthday!

Red, White, and Blue

Sons of the seagirt land,
Strong round the banner stand
    Steadfast and true!
Honour and loyalty
Ever our watchword be!
Flutter o'er land and sea
    Red, white, and blue!

Red for the life-blood shed,
When for their country bled
    Brave men and true!
White for our stainless name,
Blue for our faith and fame,
Guarding from every shame
    Red, white, and blue!

Britons, while earth endure,
Keep we our 'scutcheon pure
    Centuries through!
Long may Britannia's fane
Inviolate remain—
Ever without a stain
    Red, white, and blue!

❖ ❖ ❖ ❖ ❖

From *Songs of Greater Britain*, edited by Cicely Fox Smith, published by Sherratt & Hughes, Manchester, UK, 1899, pp. 1-2. Set to the music of "God save our Queen," the British National Anthem.

This poem was published when the poet was only 17 years of age and composed shortly after she, like the rest of Great Britain, had undergone the mass celebrations for Queen Victoria's Diamond Jubilee in 1897. It is hardly surprising that this last mass celebration of the British Empire at its height inspired the young Cicely to such patriotic outpourings.

Spanish Treasure Ship taken by Anson's "Centurion," 1743

How We Took the Great Galleon

Eighty men of Devon stood out to sweep the sea,
To plough the Spanish Main, my boys, to plough the Spanish Main,

Eighty men of Devon, staunch and true and free,
And it's many a month shall pass ere we come home again.

All on an April morning we sailed from Plymouth Sound,
All in the early morning, boys, before the sun was high;
The seagulls they were crying and calling all around,
And the moon hung white and pale in the pure blue April sky.

We left our homes to slumber upon the brown hillside,
We left the quiet farm, my boys, and drowsy market-town,
We left the tranquil harbour where ships at anchor ride,
And went to fight our battles for country, faith, and crown.

By noon the cliffs of England were a grey mist far behind,
And it's farewell to your homes, my boys, and ho for the Spanish Main!
And many a league to westward we sped before the wind,
To reap our share of plunder from the argosies of Spain.

Far o'er the wild Atlantic we steered our westward way,
Where never voice is heard, my boys, save wail of bird and breeze,
And the cold dead fog it whelmed us and held us night and day
Till a wind came down from northward and tore the oily seas.

And many a mile to southward before the gale we fled,
And so the voyage went, my boys, for many a livelong day
Ere we moored beneath the palm-trees, when the eastern sky was red,
And lay to wait the galleons as they went their homeward way.

Ah, long and long we waited and fretted to be free,
We lay and chaffed in vain, my boys, like bandogs on the chain,
Till there came a mighty galleon, high tow'ring o'er the sea,
And at her masthead flaunted the golden flag of Spain.

And when we saw her colours, a ringing cheer arose
From eighty British hearts, my boys, prepared to fight and win.
For we thought with rage and horror on these our nation's foes,
The hated Holy Office and our tortured English kin.

Out from the shadowy thicket, across the line of spray,
We ran our gallant ship, my boys, beneath the lofty prow,
And when they saw our mettle, fast, fast they fled away,
With the golden image shattered that decked their mighty bow.

We chased her south from Flores the livelong summer day,
We hung upon her heels, my boys, like hounds upon the deer,
Till underneath a cliff-side we brought the foe to bay,
And grappled her and boarded with a rousing English cheer.

We swarmed up sides and bulwarks and gave them blow for blow,
And all night long we fought, my boys, 'mid the dying and the dead,

Till our young Captain's broadsword had laid their leader low,
And at the masthead floated St. Georges Cross of red.

Long may the Cadiz merchants watch for their sailors bold,
Ere they see that galleon proud, my boys, come o'er the Western main,
With silk and fruit and spices and stores of gems and gold
For great Castilian nobles and haughty dames of Spain.

All in the early morning we sighted England's shore,
With wealth and fame and glory, boys, from far across the main;
We'd ploughed the seas and conquered for full twelve months and more,
And on a fair May morning we reached our homes again.

❖ ❖ ❖ ❖ ❖

From *Songs of Greater Britain*, edited by Cicely Fox Smith, published by Sherratt & Hughes, Manchester, UK, 1899, pp. 3-9; first published in *Hearth and Home: An Illustrated Weekly Journal for Gentlewomen*, Issue 380, August 25, 1898, p. 602, under the title "The Gordon Highlanders at Dargai."

The header graphic is titled *"Spanish Treasure Ship taken by Anson's 'Centurion,'" 1743* and is from *Nautical Illustrations*, edited by Jim Harter. published by Dover Publications, Mineola, New York, 2003, p. 23.

The Fight of the *Caroline*

It was the good ship *Caroline*,
That ploughed the Channel foam,
All for the sake of England's fame,
Of country, king, and home.
Staunch northern men were her mariners,
From the mouth of noble Tyne,
And a braver man than her captain true,
And a stouter ship, and a better crew,
Ne'er sailed the ocean brine.

It was the French ship *Guerriere*,
A league from the Breton shore,
Ship of the line of eighty guns,
Four hundred men and more,
That saw far off the English flag
Float free o'er the waters grey;
And their hearts beat fierce when they saw the foe,
The little craft that had harassed so
Their commerce many a day.

Glad grew the hearts of the English men,
When they saw the fight draw near,
And up from eighty English throats
There rose a dauntless cheer.
"Make ready, make ready," the captain cried,
"Make ready, mariners mine;
Fire straight, fire straight, my gunners,

Fire straight, and spare not of your ball,
Or farewell to the *Caroline*."

The two ships grappled then and there,
And the battle's din grew loud,
And the shot of the gallant *Caroline*
Tore every sail and shroud.
Up o'er the side they came in scores,—
Our men were staunch and bold,
But the Frenchmen swarmed o'er the side like bees,
And the English crew that had swept the seas,
It was eighty men all told.

But straight, straight had our gunners fired,
And soon, a riddled wreck,
Down sank the hull of the *Guerriere*,
With half her crew on deck.
There was but time to cut her loose,
Ere she sank beneath the brine,
And left the crew of the *Guerriere*,
To join in battle, fierce and fair,
On the deck of the *Caroline*.

Grimly, grimly, the whole day long,
The deadly fray went on;
Grimly, grimly, the whole day long,
Till the last of the light was gone.
And the dense sea-fog o'er the fight came down,
And hid heaven far and near,
And the lightning gleamed like a fiery sword,
And the masts and the rigging were gone by the board,
And there was none to steer.

Grimly, grimly, the whole day long,
They fought on the slippery deck,
Drifting, drifting, the whole day long,
Floated the shattered wreck.
And the dead and the wounded lay in a ring,
Around ten dauntless men—
Men of the brave old bulldog breed,
That has done for England many a deed,
And can do now as then.

And then from the French, that fought on the deck,
Went up a desperate groan,
For over the din of the deadly fight
They heard the breakers moan,
Where, over the waves of the narrow seas,
The cliffs for ever frown,

And there, unbeaten to the last,
With the British flag still nailed to the mast,
The *Caroline* went down.

Once more as the sinking ship went down,
'Mid the cries of rage and fear,
Above the wail of the drowning foes,
Rose up a British cheer.
There, with the ship that they held to the end
They lie 'neath the Channel brine.
Bravely they fought for their country then:
God rest their souls, for they died like men,
The crew of the *Caroline!*

❖ ❖ ❖ ❖ ❖

From *Songs of Greater Britain*, edited by Cicely Fox Smith, published by Sherratt & Hughes, Manchester, UK, 1899, pp. 10-15.

The reference is to an incident in the war against Napoleon and revolutionary France. The *Guerriere* and the *Caroline* were on opposing sides in the war at that time but it was the English ship, *Blanche*, that captured the French *Guerriere* in June of 1806.

The Stand of Wilson's Patrol

Beside the Shanghai river,
Alone with the veldt and sky,
The heroes of Wilson's patrol
By the shrines of the heathen lie,
The sons of a strong young nation
By the halls of a creed gone by.

Slowly the foes drew round them,
And those who might have fled
Preferred to stand by their fellows
And die at their posts instead,
To be numbered for ever and ever
With England's glorious dead.

The day dragged slowly onward,
As dwindled their little store,
Till spent was the last of the powder
And the sound of the fight gave o'er,
Till the rifles ceased their clamour,
And the guns spoke out no more.

But ere the band lay silent
By the silent Maxims there,
The hymn of a loyal nation
Rose up on the startled air,
Telling the wondering foemen
How the "palefaced" English dare.

The anthem of loyal England
Ne'er rang more true and high
Than there 'mid the dead and dying,
Under an alien sky,
When the sun and the flowing river
Saw Wilson's patrol die.

Beside the Shanghai river
The Briton thinks with pride
How the men of Wilson's patrol
Fell fighting side by side,
With the name of the Queen they fought for
On the lips of the last that died.

❖ ❖ ❖ ❖ ❖

From *Songs of Greater Britain*, edited by Cicely Fox Smith, published by Sherratt & Hughes, Manchester, UK, 1899, pp. 16-18.

Although no record has currently been found to precisely locate this incident it is possible that it relates to an incident in the Opium Wars of the mid 19th Century involving Arthur Knyvet Wilson.

Then and Now

O fair to see, scudding with gull-like motion,
Or hovering poised on shadowing wings of snow;
The ships that won the empire of the ocean
A hundred years ago!

What could yon vessel tell of combats glorious,
That now so calmly at her anchor rides,
When the deep voice of England's guns victorious
Spoke from those oaken sides?

Those that ne'er bowed to man, to Time surrender,
And, as the passing years at last prevail,
Gone are the tapering masts, the rigging slender,
And snow-white spread of sail.

Gone—once the terror of the pirate-rover;
But, following on the steps of such as these,
We forge wherewith to bridge the ocean over,
A sword to cleave the seas.

That—a memory of the struggles of our nation,
When England staunchly stay'd Napoleon's plan;
This—emblem of a younger generation
And the wondrous art of man.

And, tho' beneath that banner, famed in story,
No snow-white sails across the seas are blown,
Our ocean-greyhounds boast a new-won glory,
A beauty all their own.

Sped forward by their hearts' fierce palpitations,
White foam from those resistless bows far-hurled,
They watch upon the highway of the nations,
And the markets of the world.

And should the cannon's roar and broadside's rattle
Call Britain's bulwarks to defend her shore,
They will bear themselves right bravely in the battle
Tho' wooden walls no more!

❖ ❖ ❖ ❖ ❖

From *Songs of Greater Britain*, edited by Cicely Fox Smith, published by Sherratt & Hughes, Manchester, UK, 1899, pp. 19-21.

In the harking back to Napoleonic times it is obvious that, even at this early age, the poet's thoughts were on naval matters and on the wooden ships rather than the newer ironclads of her own time.

The British-Born

England, our England, thou whose sway
Spreads o'er broad lands and boundless sea,
Tho' thro' the wide world far they stray,
Thy children's hearts are shrin'd in thee.
Let others cherish, if they will,
The splendours of the Southern morn,
Flash'd o'er blue lake and snow-clad hill,—
But England for the British-born!

The roll of her imperial seas
Beating vast rhythms on England's strand;
The flutter of a soft-wing'd breeze
Laughing o'er English pasture-land;
The happy brooklet's bubbling flow,
The sweep of wind thro' ripening corn,
Than all the gorgeous East can show
Are dearer to the British-born!

In vain the East, the West, the South,
Unfold their charms to English eyes;
They long amid the desert's drouth
For our mild sun, our show'ry skies.
When Britain's children lonely stray,
Aliens in alien lands forlorn,
Turning their eyes untouched away,
Still homeward look the British-born.

❖ ❖ ❖ ❖ ❖

From *Songs of Greater Britain*, edited by Cicely Fox Smith, published by Sherratt & Hughes, Manchester, UK, 1899, pp. 22-23.

The Colonists

We have heard a voice that calls us—
A voice that bids us go—
A voice that bids us waken
From the narrow world we know.
We go to do our duty,
Unfearing toil and pain,
For the flag, the flag of England,
The flag that rules the main!

There are fairer meads in England
Than these, so parched and sere;
The wild bird's song in England
Is sweeter far than here.
We may not dwell in England,
For we have work to do
For the land, the land of England,
The land we love so true!

Still, still the sons of England
Pursue the onward track,
Tho' men who look not forward
Strive hard to hold them back.
Still, still the word is "Onward!"
With hearts that fear not blame,
On the way, the way of Britons,
The way that leads to fame!

❖ ❖ ❖ ❖ ❖

From *Songs of Greater Britain,* edited by Cicely Fox Smith, published by Sherratt & Hughes, Manchester, UK, 1899, pp. 24-25.

The Song of the Sword

This is the Song of the Sword,
A proud and a ringing song,
The song of the tempered blade
That has lain in the sheath too long.
"It's oh for the strong right hand,
And the hiss of the wheeling brand,
To make honour a power in the land,"
Saith the sword.

The vigour rusts in men's hearts
As the sword rusts there on the wall,
And they go on their selfish ways
And hear not their country's call.
And their hearts grow sickly and fade,

But their lives would be newly made
By a flash from the broad bright blade
Of the Sword.

"Oh, love of the land is there,
It is but hidden away.
The lion in English heart
Is asleep and waiting the day
When tales of how brave men fall
Shall ring like a trumpet-call
Thro' the hearts of each and all,"
Saith the Sword.

Draw ye the sword from the sheath;
It has rusted overlong,
And all that the pen can do
Is powerless to right the wrong.
And "It's oh for a circling brand
In the grip of a strong right hand
To make honour a power in the land,"
Saith the sword.

From *Songs of Greater Britain,* edited by Cicely Fox Smith, published by Sherratt & Hughes, Manchester, UK, 1899, pp. 26-28.

Britannia Triumphans

Mother of five mighty nations, on her island throne she sits serene,
She who in her right hand proudly wields the sceptre of the Ocean Queen.
Over continents and islands flies her ocean-ruling flag unfurled:
Unto all her roaring markets flows the streaming trade of half the world.
Still the vigour of her children, courses thro' her Empire's every part,
Still the Titan pulse of Empire throbs for ever at her mighty heart.
Still triumphant, still unfearing, goes she ever on her conquering way;
Hers the hope of young To-morrow, hers the glorious promise of To-day.
Hers the laurels of Trafalgar—hers the deathless fame of Waterloo;
Hers the boon that builds up Empire—strong men's hearts to queen and country true.

Onward, onward, sons of England, ever slaying evil, bringing good,
Hewing down the ghastly fetish from its altar black with human blood;
Conquering fever-swamp and jungle; staying not tho' Death stand face to face:
Peace and plenty following ever on the footsteps of the English race.
Onward, onward, sons of Britain, onward by the same old glorious way,
Owning still that dogged courage that can hold the banded world at bay.
Looking backward thro' the ages on an unstained history's spotless page,
Knowing that the name of Briton is the wide world's proudest heritage.

From *Songs of Greater Britain*, edited by Cicely Fox Smith, published by Sherratt & Hughes, Manchester, UK, 1899, pp. 29-31.

"Mother" refers to Queen Victoria.

The Song of the Greatest Isle

A health to our soldiers and sailors true
That guard Britannia's throne;
To England under the southern blue,
To the flag that the English own.
To the honoured names of our English dead;
To our Empire's strong-built pile;
To the men that have girded the earth with red,
To the sons of the Greatest Isle!

There's never a nook on the wide world's face
But with her fame has rung,
And the farthest home of the farthest race
Has heard the English tongue.
Where the white bear roams and the Pole-star gleams,
Where the tropic islets smile,
Where the dank, dim plain in the noonglare steams,
Sleep the sons of the Greatest Isle!

And ever it's over the seas away
In the teeth of a whistling wind,
Full steam ahead thro' the smoking spray,
With the bonny, brave Isle behind.
Go forth, go forth, on the forward track,
O'er the ocean many a mile,
Thro' the Southern sands and the Polar pack!—
And here's to the Greatest Isle!

❖ ❖ ❖ ❖ ❖

From *Songs of Greater Britain*, edited by Cicely Fox Smith, published by Sherratt & Hughes, Manchester, UK, 1899, pp. 32-33.

England in China: 1897-98

Grey gloom the storm-clouds in the Orient far,
Foreshadowing dark and anxious hours to be,
Where Britain's rivals to her commerce bar
The golden portals of the Eastern Sea.
Now in the hour of her trial be her mien
Brave and serene and calm—worthy an Ocean Queen.

Reason prevails not with our envious foe;
They hate to think 'tis justice that we speak;
Yet tell it wide, that all the world may know
No base monopoly is this we seek,
But all the myriad ports of China thrown
Open to all the world—not yours or ours alone.

Ay, howl your fill—our day will come ere long,
The Lion watches from his island throne
Prepar'd to stand in arms against the wrong;
Not against you, save to defend his own.
Then fling yon harbours wide to all the world,
Or the mad blast of war across the globe be hurl'd.

If reason serve not, then let Force prevail;
War's dire arbitrament the right will show.
Our guns are heard where meek-ey'd Peace doth fail,
And, if the foes of England will it so,
Speak, cannon, tell them in your echoing roar,
We fight as well to-day as e'er we fought of yore.

❖ ❖ ❖ ❖ ❖

From *Songs of Greater Britain*, edited by Cicely Fox Smith, published by Sherratt & Hughes, Manchester, UK, 1899, pp. 34-35.

The Gordons at Dargai

Gallant Gordons! Evermore on your rugged native shore
Shall your valour honoured be,
For a fight well fought and won 'neath the burning Indian sun
Far away across the sea.
All the days of long ago no more glorious deed can show
Than the deed your arms have done.
When your children's sons are old, still the story shall be told
How the Dargai heights were won!

On a fair October day they made ready for the fray,
And their leader spake them brave:
"Ours to take the heights or die—onward now to victory
Or to find a soldier's grave!"
At the word the gallant band, foot to foot and sword in hand,
Cheering, broke into a run.
Every heart aflame with hope, dashed they onward up the slope
To the heights that must be won!

Hiss'd the bullets then like hail; but not theirs to shrink and quail,
Struggling onward up the hill;
While the pibroch shrilling high drown'd the foeman's battle-cry,

And the shouts of "Strike and kill!"
What tho' half their number fell? What cared they for shot and shell,
So their duty once was done—
So they earned a brighter fame for the Gordons' honoured name
And the distant heights were won?

As a wave upon the shore breaks the waveworn boulders o'er
Rushed our redcoats on the foe,
And they battled hand to hand, Khyber knife and Highland brand,
Battled, raining blow on blow,
Till the dark ranks, feebler grown, slowly, slowly, backwards thrown,
Saw the deadly fight was done,
Hung a moment on the verge, as the foam crest on the surge,
Faltered, and the heights were won!

❖ ❖ ❖ ❖ ❖

From *Songs of Greater Britain*, edited by Cicely Fox Smith, published by Sherratt & Hughes, Manchester, UK, 1899, pp. 36-38. First published in *Hearth and Home: An Illustrated Weekly Journal for Gentlewomen*, January 13, 1898, under the title: "The Gordon Highlanders at Dargai."

This refers to a famous incident in the long undeclared conflict between Britain and Russia which was actually fought in Afghanistan. Although she refers to Khyber knife and Highland brand it is more likely the rifles that made the difference. The British had the new Martini-Henry breechloader and the Afghans the older Jezail matchlocks.

Our Jubilee Visitors

In this moment of our joy and exultation
From distant lands they come,
To join in glad reunion with the nation
They love to call their home.
Theirs no banner all emblazoned with their glory,
But, hid from mortal ken,
In fadeless hues is writ the noble story
On the hearts of Englishmen!

In other climes they fight, perchance to perish;
They were bred 'neath other skies;
But 'tis England's agelong glory that they cherish,
It is England's fame they prize.
They love the land, to all our hearts the nearest,
As only Britons can:
And the honour that to them seems far the dearest
Is the name of Englishman.

They have proved their worth in many a hard-fought battle
On valley, hill, and plain,
When the savage war-cry drowned the rifle-rattle
'Mid the dying and the slain.
They have made our land the greatest known in story

Since Time and Earth began:
True heirs indeed to all old England's glory,
And the name of Englishman!

❖ ❖ ❖ ❖ ❖

From *Songs of Greater Britain*, edited by Cicely Fox Smith, published by Sherratt & Hughes, Manchester, UK, 1899, pp. 39-40.

Omdurman

September 9, 1898

Glory for these glad tidings, far and near,
That come to-day across the plunging main;
Shattered the Dervish host, broken their spear,
Their mad fanatic frenzy turned to fear,
Avenged is Gordon slain!

Glory to those who, killed in glorious fray,
Lie where they fell upon the Egyptian plain:
From the fair scutcheon of our fame away
Strong English hands have wiped the stain to-day,
Avenged is Gordon slain!

Glory to those who, ere the set of sun,
Fought their first fought it not in vain,
Twining their flag with bloodstained laurels, won
When our great work of years at last was done,
Avenged our Gordon slain!

The men who shed his life-blood long before
Of their dark breed now reap the bitter grain;
Now their short hour of triumphing is o'er,
Broken the reign of blood for evermore,
Avenged is Gordon slain!

Now once again have we redeemed the past,
Our armies marched to triumph once again,
Now brought to nought that army, once so vast;
Shattered the Dervish host; at last, at last,
Avenged is Gordon slain!

❖ ❖ ❖ ❖ ❖

From *Songs of Greater Britain*, edited by Cicely Fox Smith, published by Sherratt & Hughes, Manchester, UK, 1899, pp. 41-42.

This poem refers to the British victory on 1898 over the forces of Mahdi Mohammed Ahmed, Abdullah al-Taashi following the defeat and death of General Gordon at Khartoum, Sudan, in 1885.

A Song of the Day

Queen of the waves of ocean,
Sister to stars and dew,
Flung wide to the sun and tempest,
A splendour of scarlet and blue:
Bulwarked by brave men's courage,
Knowing not stain of shame,
Flag of the strong-souled English,
Long may thy lot be fame!

After long years of silence,
After long years of calm,
The thunder afar off warns us
To guard the old flag from harm.
The clouds are piled on the skyline;
The air is heavy with fray:
Sons of the strong-souled English,
Look to your arms to-day!

There are hearts that are bitter with envy
To think of our power's increase;
And a dagger's hid in the fingers
That hold the branch of peace.
There's many a wrong to be righted
When dreamers have said their say;
Sons of the strong-souled English,
Come to the flag to-day!

We have dallied too long with their treaties,
And promises made to break.
When will the play be over,
And the Lion at last awake?
The day draws nigh for our action.
Let them answer us, yea or nay!
Sons of the strong-souled English,
Stand by your guns to-day!

❖ ❖ ❖ ❖ ❖

From *Songs of Greater Britain,* edited by Cicely Fox Smith, published by Sherratt & Hughes, Manchester, UK, 1899, pp. 43-45.

The Bugle-Call

"Beware! Beware!"
The shrilling bugles blare.
"Lest you waken unaware
The lion form his lair,
Beware, beware, beware,
When the British bugles blare."

"O come! O come!
Sons of Britain to the drum.
There's glory wait for some
Ere the battle's din is dumb.
O come, O come, O come
To the bugle and the drum!"

"Come one, come all!"
The thrilling bugles call,
"Some may triumph, many fall,
But all are in my thrall;
Come one, come each, come all,
When you hear the bugle call!"

❖   ❖   ❖   ❖   ❖

From *Songs of Greater Britain*, edited by Cicely Fox Smith, published by Sherratt & Hughes, Manchester, UK, 1899, pp. 46-47.

Britannia Africana

Where the Cape frowns out o'er the waters,
Staunchly she takes her stand,
With the flag that the English follow
Held firm in her upraised hand.
High o'er the land it flutters,
Unfurled in the breaking dawn;
Flame-bright in her right hand glitters
The sword that is always drawn.

Beneath her upon the cliff-side
Shatter the waves in spray.
But the foes that strike at her stronghold
Are not less vain than they.
As the sea draws back from the cliff-side,
Where the dark caves gloomy yawn,
They gather their shattered squadrons
From the sword that is always drawn!

Forward, O *Queen* of the Ocean,
Leave nought of thy task undone:
For thro' toil and trouble and warfare
Was our English Empire won.
Go on thy ways and conquer,
Scorning to cringe and fawn,
Defending thine own broad banner
With the sword that is always drawn!

❖ ❖ ❖ ❖ ❖

From *Songs of Greater Britain*, edited by Cicely Fox Smith, published by Sherratt & Hughes, Manchester, UK, 1899, pp. 48-49.

Our Country

O England, merry England!
The whole wide world can show
No land so sweet as England
Where'er the four winds blow.
Fair scenes of rural England
How sweet to English eye
The stretch of wide brown fallow,
The dome of wide free sky
Where the lark pours forth, rejoicing,
His carol long and loud;
Hanging, a sunlit shadow,
'Mid windy wings of cloud.

The sweep of English uplands,
The sigh of English trees,
The laugh of English rivers,
Or breath of English breeze;
The scent of purple clover
Off English meadows blown—
These, these to me are dearest,
For they are England's own.
Others, in search of beauty,
May roam o'er land and sea;
But the land, the land of England,
Our own dear isle for me.

❖ ❖ ❖ ❖ ❖

From *Songs of Greater Britain*, edited by Cicely Fox Smith, published by Sherratt & Hughes, Manchester, UK, 1899, pp. 50-51.

To Arms

"To Arms!" the maddening bugles call;
Make ready—ready for the fray.
Be true to Britain, one and all,
We fight for life or death to-day.
Who speaks to Britain's sons of shame?
Nay, war, if war must be, we wage
For England's name, and England's fame,
And England's royal heritage!

Is it forgotten with the years,
That lesson learnt with shame and woe,
With dark defeat and bitter tears,
When Nelson conquered, long ago?
The storms that looms above today
Shall break in thunders mightier far;
The flag that holds the seas in sway
Floats o'er a later Trafalgar!

Form as thou standest Ocean Queen,
Resistless on thy inviolate strand,
Far o'er the watching world are seen
The gleaming of thy half-drawn brand.
High o'er the shrine of Britain's fame
Floats thy broad banner wide unfurled;
The flag that knows no stain of shame,
The victor-flag of half the world!

The thunder of thy battle-line
Shall echoing sound from deep to deep,
For, challenged o'er the Channel brine,
Thy couchant lion wakes from sleep.
Go forth against thy vaunting foe;
Go forth—exulting in thy might;
And let the voice of battle show
That right is might, and might is right!

❖   ❖   ❖   ❖   ❖

From *Songs of Greater Britain*, edited by Cicely Fox Smith, published by Sherratt & Hughes, Manchester, UK, 1899, pp. 52-54.

The Vanguard

We the vanguard of a nation in the lands of desolation,
We who live and die unknown,
We who spend our days in sorrow for the people of to-morrow,
And the land we call our own.
For the bearing of our burden do we win no worthy guerdon—

For our labour and our pain?
Do we battle unavailing, struggling, triumphing and failing—
Live our lives out all in vain?

Nay: tho' in the noble story of Old England's deeds of glory
Honoured names we have not won;
Tho' the seed that we are sowing be not ready for the mowing
Ere our days on earth be done,—
In the jungle's tangled fastness, lonely bush and desert vastness,
Boundless veldt and steaming plain,
Do the vanguard of a nation for a future generation
Toil and suffer—not in vain!

For the seed we sow in sorrow shall be garnered on the morrow
By the people yet unborn,
And across the darkness breaking, all the land to hope awaking,
Flushes up the rose of morn.
Each may do what will not perish for the land that Britons cherish
Ere he take his journey hence;
And the British banner flying o'er the spot where he lay dying,
Is the soldier's recompense!

❖ ❖ ❖ ❖ ❖

From *Songs of Greater Britain*, edited by Cicely Fox Smith, published by Sherratt & Hughes, Manchester, UK, 1899, pp. 55-57.

Minden Day

All morning rang the gardens where grew the roses sweet
With sound of drum and bugle, and tramp of marching feet;
And each man plucked a blossom as he went his onward way,
And gaily bloomed the roses in their caps on Minden Day.

But many a flower was faded ere sank the summer sun,
And many a man lay gasping before that day was done;
When the ranks of foot charged madly on mounted squadrons gay,
The rose of merry England was in the van that day,

The foemen see and wonder: their staggering squadrons reel,
Flung back ere yet they know it, before that wall of steel.
But many a crimson blossom on the ground all trampled lay,
For men fell like leaves in Autumn on glorious Minden Day.

❖ ❖ ❖ ❖ ❖

From *Songs of Greater Britain*, edited by Cicely Fox Smith, published by Sherratt & Hughes, Manchester, UK, 1899, pp. 58-59.

"Minden Day" is named in celebration of the Battle of Minden on August 1, 1759. It is now celebrated as Yorkshire Day by all true Tykes and it is ironic that a Lancasterian such as Smith should honour the "enemy" county in this way.

A Norseman

Beneath the golden eagle's shade
Gleam restless eyes of steely grey,
That look out calmly, unafraid,
From brows deep-tann'd by salt sea-spray,
Thro' many a year of sun and breeze,
Spent toiling over unknown seas.

Ah, dreaded! when that burnished helm
Flash'd back the glare from blazing farms,
And the red glow o'er all the realm
Awoke the peaceful land to arms,
And the fierce tumult drawing near
Palsied the listening monks with fear.

So childlike, when the work of years
In frolic thou wouldst swift destroy;
So manlike, when at clash of spears
Shivered a swift and sudden joy
Thro' all thy mighty frame, to feel
A foe man worthy of thy steel.

And now, when battle draweth nigh,
'Neath modern culture's slight veneer,
The Briton feels his heart beat high,
Showing that Viking blood is here.
The manlike destined still to last,
The childlike buried in the past.

❖ ❖ ❖ ❖ ❖

From *Songs of Greater Britain*, edited by Cicely Fox Smith, published by Sherratt & Hughes, Manchester, UK, 1899, pp. 60-61.

The Grey Wolf

The grey wolf stood in the ruin hoar,
The wolf that hunts alone:
His shadow lay along the floor,
Athwart the cold hearthstone.
The winding of the hunter's horn
Fell on his listening ear,
Far on the whistling tempest borne,
And filled his heart with fear.
Lone wolf, grey wolf, heed not hunter's holloa,
Nor the baying of the hounds, ranging far and near!
It is other game they follow, thro' the thicket, in the hollow,
And the grey wolf need not fear!

Who may they be and what their prey,
That hunt at dead of night,
When the winds are loose and the woods are grey
In the silvery cold moonlight?
Nor fox nor red-deer seek the band;
What means such headlong pace?
'Tis the stain of blood on a murder's hand
That calls them to the chase!
Lone wolf, grey wolf, heed not hunter's holloa,
Nor the baying of the hounds, ranging far and near!
It is other game they follow, thro' the thicket, in the hollow,
And the grey wolf need not fear!

He slew Lord Ronald in the night.
Ah! black and base his deed!
And these have sworn to do the right
That he may have his meed.
The hounds are belling in the woods:
The broad stream flows before;
And safety waits across the flood,
Upon the farther shore.
Lone wolf, grey wolf, heed not hunter's holloa,
Nor the baying of the hounds, ranging far and near!
It is other game they follow, thro' the thicket, in the hollow,
And the grey wolf need not fear!

He leapt into the cold, dark wave,
And like was he to drown,
For strong the darkling current drave,
The eddies dragg'd him down.
But swiftly tho' the river glides,
The bank is won at last,
And in the ruin grey he hides,
His deadly peril past.
Lone wolf, grey wolf, hoary midnight rover,
Dweller in the ruin'd hall, 'mid the moonlight clear,
Tho' he deems his peril over, other dangers round him hover,
He hath other foe to fear!

As 'neath the ivied wall he crept,
Cold, wet, but still elate,
Full at his throat the grey wolf leapt,
With one deep growl of hate.
A moment and the fight was o'er,
And hush'd hid dying groan:
His blood is red upon the floor,
Athwart the cold hearthstone.
Lone wolf, grey wolf, heed not the hunter's holloa,
Nor the baying of the hounds, ranging far and near!

It is other game they follow, thro' the thicket, in the hollow,
And the grey wolf need not fear!

❖ ❖ ❖ ❖ ❖

From *Songs of Greater Britain*, edited by Cicely Fox Smith, published by Sherratt & Hughes, Manchester, UK, 1899, pp. 65-69.

Guido Sebaldi

Guido Sebaldi the mason
Worked at a house of stone:
Guido Sebaldi the mason
Sang at his work alone.

Till a stranger, he said unto him
As he hammer'd the stone one day:
"Guido Sebaldi the mason,
Hark to the words I say!"

"Leave thou this work, fit only
For oxen that draw the plough:
No longer Sebaldi the mason,
Guido the sculptor thou!"

Then Guido Sebaldi the mason
Look'd on his work in shame.
And "Lo," he said, "I am lusty,
I will build me a noble name."

Guido Sebaldi the sculptor
Toil'd till his heart grew sore.
Guido Sebaldi the sculptor
Sang at his work no more.

Vainly Sebaldi the mason
Hammer'd the senseless stone.
Vainly Sebaldi the mason
Sigh'd at his work alone.

His hands were ready and skillful,
And his days with toil were rife,
But the soul of the master was needed
To waken the stone to life.

Sadly Sebaldi the mason
Went back to the house of stone;
And his brow once more grew cheery
As he sat at his work alone.

But yet he was always thinking
Of hopes that were long since o'er;
And Guido Sebaldi the mason
Sang at his work no more.

❖ ❖ ❖ ❖ ❖

From *Songs of Greater Britain*, edited by Cicely Fox Smith, published by Sherratt & Hughes, Manchester, UK, 1899, pp. 70-72.

Autumn

Stern Time hath banished with a frown
The summer, now grown wan and old;
In grief the woodlands lay adown
Their crowns of gold.

No more the copses echo round
With stockdove's moan and woodwren's lay;
To gladden distant shores with sound
They wing their way.

The wild winds shudder thro' the trees,
Where late the redstart's carol rang;
The torn nests wanton with the breeze
Where sweet birds sang.

The sere, sad leaves, their glory done,
Fall from the bough to meet the wave;
The stream they shadowed from the sun
Gives them a grave.

❖ ❖ ❖ ❖ ❖

From *Songs of Greater Britain*, edited by Cicely Fox Smith, published by Sherratt & Hughes, Manchester, UK, 1899, pp. 73-74.

The Rally Round the Flag

The rally round the mother-land
Is spreading far and near,
For to every loyal Englishman
That mother-land is dear.
Although the salt sea rolls between,
All hearts may still be one
In that vast empire which beholds
The circuit of the sun.

Where rich Canadian homesteads
Stand 'neath the forest oak,
Where on New Zealand's pine trees
Is heard the woodman's stroke;

And where Australia's goldfields
Give forth their wealth untold,
All are as truly English
As e'er they were of old.

True to our peerless England;
True to our noble Queen—
The ruler of the greatest race
That ever yet has been;
True to the stainless banner
That floats o'er half the world,
As when, in long-past ages,
That flag was first unfurled.

Though, from the sea-girt island,
Where the empire had its birth,
The English name has spread so far
It circles all the earth,
Yet 'tis a wider England
To which this isle has grown;
Tho' her sons be scattered far and wide,
Their hearts are still her own.

❖   ❖   ❖   ❖   ❖

From *Songs of Greater Britain*, edited by Cicely Fox Smith, published by Sherratt & Hughes, Manchester, UK, 1899, pp. 75-77.

Diamond Jubilee

Clang out, wild bells, your glad acclaim:
Roar, deep-mouthed cannon, honour to her name!
To her whom England loves to hail
Oldest and noblest of our noble kings,
Roar loyalty and love till Heav'n's vault rings.
Flare, ye red beacons, till the stars grow pale;
Carry o'er England's plains to ocean's wave
The exultation of a nation's voice;
Of thousands that as one rejoice
To honour her whom God has pleased to save.

Victoria, sixty years a queen!
But eighteen summers hadst thou seen,
When, 'midst thy mourning for a kinsman dead,
The nation placed upon thy sorrowing head
The burden of a crown,
And in thy young hands laid
The priceless jewel of the land's renown.
Since then Time's feet have swiftly flown;
The head that bears the diadem with age is silvery grown,
The wondrous tale of sixty years hath blest thine honoured throne!

And now once more the wild glad bells peal out,
Once more is heard the universal shout,
Once more thy broad realms ring with joy for thee,
Once more thy world-wide Empire joins to hail thy Diamond Jubilee!
Now let the brazen trumpet blare,
And let our cheering rend the air,
And let the long loud roar of shouting rise
With glory, glory, glory, to the skies;
For sixty years of power without a stain,
Sixty years of one long glorious reign,
Sixty years of peace with honour, sixty years of glorious gain!

❖ ❖ ❖ ❖ ❖

From *Songs of Greater Britain*, edited by Cicely Fox Smith, published by Sherratt & Hughes, Manchester, UK, 1899, pp. 78-80.

The Diamond Jubilee for Queen Victoria was celebrated on the 20th and 21st of June, 1887.

The Witch-Wife

The Witch-wife dwells by the Northern Sea
And it's oh but the wind pipes shrill!
Alone on the waveworn shore sits she,
Where the boisterous winds blow wild and free
From the icefields drear and chill.

She sits by the reef where seamen drown
When the sea-mist's swirling grey,
And she wears on her brow a golden crown,
For she rules the seals from the North Cape down
To the coast of Noroway.

Over her shoulders her dank locks stream
And it's oh but the wind blows cold!
And she sits as one who is lost in a dream;
But the curl of her lip and her eye's cold gleam
Bodes ill for the sailor bold.

King Eric has sailed from Noroway,
O'er the wintry sea he roves,
And he's hunted the seals for a month and a day
Over the icepack cold and grey,
The seals that the Witch-wife loves.

And over the sea to his home he steers,
His long, long hunting o'er,
And "Lo!" he cries, "the light appears,
That ever my longing vision cheers
When I near my native shore."

The good ship steers for the welcome light
And it's oh but the waves roll cold!
Lured to her doom in the dead of night
By the treacherous lamps so calm and bright
That the weird sea-maidens hold.

She leaps on the rocks like a hunted thing,
And the waves now leap above.
Such was the fate of Eric the King,
Who hunted the seals to his ruining,
The seals that the Witch-maids love!

❖ ❖ ❖ ❖ ❖

From *Songs of Greater Britain*, edited by Cicely Fox Smith, published by Sherratt & Hughes, Manchester, UK, 1899, pp. 81-83.

The Ballad of Rosalie

There came a knight to the river-side—
Ah, Rosalie!
With his false cousin at his side—
Ah, Rosalie!
And o'er the ford he fain would ride
To see his bride, fair Rosalie!

His cousin rode with purpose fell—
Ah, Rosalie!
For oh! He loved the bride full well—
Ah, Rosalie!
And his envy was deep as the flames of hell.
Alas, alas for Rosalie!

Amid the stream they spurred amain—
Ah, Rosalie!
The false, false traitor knew his gain—
Ah, Rosalie!
And seized her true knight's bridle-rein.
Alas, alas for Rosalie!

The stream runs deep and the stream is wide—
Ah, Rosalie!
Where from the ford he reels aside—
Ah, Rosalie!
And never again he'll see his bride.
Alas, alas for Rosalie!

She came at sunset to the ford—
Ah, Rosalie!
Where the stream runs deep and the stream is wide—
Ah, Rosalie!

And there she saw her own true lord.
Alas, alas for Rosalie!

She laid her down upon the strand—
Ah, Rosalie!
And reached and caught him by the hand—
Ah, Rosalie!
And drew his body to the land.
Alas, alas for Rosalie!

She combed his locks of ruddy gold,—
Ah, Rosalie!
She kissed his cheeks so lily-cold,—
Ah, Rosalie!
And lapped him in her mantle's fold:
Alas, alas for Rosalie!

Of rushes green she made his bed:
Ah, Rosalie!
With sweetest flowers beneath his head—
Ah, Rosalie!
And crooned sad dirges o'er her dead.
Alas, alas for Rosalie!

They could not draw the maid away:—
Ah, Rosalie!
She watched beside him night and day:—
Ah, Rosalie!
And to herself would softly say,
"Alas, alas for Rosalie!"

Upon the ground she made her bed—
Ah, Rosalie!
And strewed his couch with roses red—
Ah, Rosalie!
Till by his side they found her dead.
Alas, alas for Rosalie!

❖ ❖ ❖ ❖ ❖

From *Songs of Greater Britain*, edited by Cicely Fox Smith, published by Sherratt & Hughes, Manchester, UK, 1899, pp. 84-88.

A Castle in Spain

On a hill-top brown it stands:
One side, open tablelands
Stretch to meet the sky:
On the other, winding dales,
Prospects fair of hills and vales
All unfolded lie.

And within are colonnades;
Cool, dim aisles whose groin'd roof shades
From the noontide ray.
Silent courts and echoing halls
Where a fountain calls and calls
All the night and day.

And a tower my castle crowns,
Looking over breezy downs,
Uplands broad and free,
With its casements small and quaint
Open to the murmurs faint
Of the distant sea.

Best of all the dark alcove
With its view of park and grove:
Where the hum of bees
Floats into the low-ceil'd room
With the roses' sweet perfume
Borne upon the breeze.

And the gardens, fair and wide,
Stretch upon the sunny side
Many a terrace-ledge.
Yew-walks, ghostly, grey, and dim:
Ordered lawns and flower-beds trim,
To the streamlet's edge.

Such my castle in the air:
Yet I doubt if half so fair,
Were it true, 'twould seem.
Beauteous is, yet not so dear
As the world we live in here,
That of which I dream.

❖   ❖   ❖   ❖   ❖

From *Songs of Greater Britain*, edited by Cicely Fox Smith, published by Sherratt & Hughes, Manchester, UK, 1899, pp. 89-91.

The Skylark

Winged seraph of the summer heaven,
Whose wondrous rapture, wild and long,
A hundred bards in vain have striven
To prison in a song!

How can they tell, with all their art,
What passions make thy glad throat swell,
That, throbbing at thy fiery heart,
Thou feel'st but canst not tell?

How can we picture in our dreams
The joys that thro' thy paen glow,
That joy that sours so high it seems
About to break in woe?

Sing on, wild bird, thy wild glad song,
That fills our eyes with sudden tears,
While back upon the fancy throng
Memories of vanished years!

Sing on, sing on, for ever free!
We cannot know what thou dost sing,
And better it should ever be
An undiscovered thing.

❖ ❖ ❖ ❖ ❖

From *Songs of Greater Britain*, edited by Cicely Fox Smith, published by Sherratt & Hughes, Manchester, UK, 1899, pp. 95-96.

A Contrast

I wandered in a garden-square,
By pathways walled with straight-clipt yew,
And over-arched by jasmine fair,
Wet with new-fallen dew.

And all about the order'd beds
Wandered the South wind's listless breath,
Where roses droop'd their weary heads
And lilies white as death.

The heavy air was all-too sweet
With perfume of unnumbered flowers,
And dark wet mould beneath my feet
Fresh-wet with recent showers.

O'er the wide plain, with ne'er a hill,
I heard a lonely swallow call,
And I grew weary of the still
Sad glamour of it all.

I wandered on the lone moorside
When Summer's fern was tinged with gold,
And all around me, waste and wide,
Spread sweeps of purple wold.

A voiceful wind, instinct with life,
Swept its wild harp's exultant strings,
And all the scented air was rife
With whir of cleaving wings.

Above, fresh blue without a cloud,
Below, blue plain and fertile vale,
Around, the happy moorland, loud
With stir of strong-wing'd gale.

O perfect day without alloy!
O song of breeze and wild bird's wing!
It was an ecstasy of joy
To be a living thing.

❖ ❖ ❖ ❖ ❖

From *Songs of Greater Britain*, edited by Cicely Fox Smith, published by Sherratt & Hughes, Manchester, UK, 1899, pp. 92-94.

Calm before Storm

There is silence on yon fair valley,
And calm on yon purple hill:
But the trees are moaning together
With a sigh that is never still.

The wold and the fertile farmlands
Lie under a stifling haze,
And the cattle are winding slowly
Home by the well-known ways.

The world is still in the gloaming,
The winds are at rest on the fell;
And up thro' the golden twilight
Floats the chime of an evening bell.

But the trees are bending together,
And whispering each to each,
With a sorrowful rustle of branches
And a sigh that is almost speech.

And the birds in the sheltering gable
Draw closer in vague affright;
For the heart of the earth is heavy
With the storm that will come to-night.

❖ ❖ ❖ ❖ ❖

From *Songs of Greater Britain*, edited by Cicely Fox Smith, published by Sherratt & Hughes, Manchester, UK, 1899, pp. 97-98.

Ultima Thule

The tides roll white and pale
On a shingly, stormy strand,
And the seabirds sweep and wail
In the swing of the seaborn gale
Over the sand,

In Thule, Ultima Thule,
The lonely land.

Sometimes the icepack white
Sails by, all silent and grand,
And sometimes the lightning bright
Pierces the heart of the night
Like a fiery brand,
In Thule, Ultima Thule,
The lonely land.

Fronting the waters grey,
The halls of the ancients stand,
Fallen and gone to decay
With those who dwelt on a day,
A valiant band,
In Thule, Ultima Thule,
The lonely land.

Once they were kings on the sea;
Their ships now rot on the sand,
Fall'n is their high roof-tree,
And the fox and the wolf roam free
In those ruins grand,
In Thule, Ultima Thule,
The lonely land.

❖ ❖ ❖ ❖ ❖

From *Songs of Greater Britain*, edited by Cicely Fox Smith, published by Sherratt & Hughes, Manchester, UK, 1899, pp. 99-100.

The Last Race

They brought her to the crowded paddock,
The red sun glinting on skin like jet,
Lightning, the winner of twenty races,
The mare that had never been beaten yet;
And the people who deemed that her lot was failure
Gave a pitying glance as they sauntered past,
Saying: "Her racing days are over,
Pity to bring her to lose at last!"

Over the hurdles they go together—
(Has she forgotten her old-time skill?)—
And her master stoops in the saddle to whisper,
"Courage, old lass, and we'll beat them still!"
One more fight—'tis the last, last struggle,
The last, last time that the welcoming cheer
Will rise from the crowd as she forges onward,
Growing in strength as the end draws near!

She is up with the first—now they stride together,
The old horse striving with might and main,
As she spurns the turf she has trod so often,
The course she never will tread again.
Flank to flank, not an inch to part them;
Was there ever a race that was run so well?
But with one great bound past the post she galloped,
Won by a neck—then she staggered and fell.
Gallant old racer: she died in action!
Her triumphs are over, her work is done.
Better to go to her death, unbeaten,
In the last, last race she will ever run!

❖ ❖ ❖ ❖ ❖

From *Songs of Greater Britain*, edited by Cicely Fox Smith, published by Sherratt & Hughes, Manchester, UK, 1899, pp. 101-102.

After the Storm

O the calling of the waves on the pebbled beach below,
And the seagull sweeping o'er the waters grey!
O the weeping on the quay! O the bitter, bitter woe
For the mariners that perished yesterday!

The ruddy rose will blow and the winter snow will fall,
And the varying year bring round the crops again,
And the nesting birds in spring from the cottage eves will call,
But they sleep sound beneath the sleepless main!

In vain the buoy-bell clangs where the beetling cliff looks down,
And in vain for them the harbour lights will burn:
There are broken hearts to-day in the little fishing town
For the sailors who will nevermore return.

They are lying far below 'neath the sad Atlantic swell,
Where the pale light gleams and flickers overhead;
Where the seabirds dive and soar and the surges toll a knell,
They will sleep until the sea gives up her dead.

And far below their heads will steer the careless crews,
And far above the liners come and go;
And fifty fathoms deep, in the mid-Atlantic ooze,
The deep-sea cable throbs with joy and woe.

And the sea keeps on its moan where the silent cliff looks down,
And the gull its ceaseless call across the bay,
And hearts must bear and break in the little fishing-town
For the mariners who perish day by day.

❖ ❖ ❖ ❖ ❖

From *Songs of Greater Britain*, edited by Cicely Fox Smith, published by Sherratt & Hughes, Manchester, UK, 1899, pp. 103-105.

One Summer's Day

High on the bank the tall trees idly dream,
Bough and green leaf against an infinite sky,
And fleck with sun and shade the dappled stream
Soft flowing by.

A cool wind breaths across the peaceful scene,
Sweet with subtle scent of new-mown hay:
And far behind the fertile stretch of green
Fades into grey.

Look—there a trout rose in yon silent pool,
With leap and splash, and gleam of silver side,
Where in the shadow, clear and dark and cool,
Deep waters glide.

First a white breadth of shingle—then a height
Of tree on tree piled up to meet the sky,
Behind, blue hills, a haze of purple light,
In slumber lie.

O joy! to hear some skylark's carol strong
Sweet-blended with the river's murmuring—
To lie and listen to the pleasant song
The waters sing.

And far from here perchance we oft may dream,
When in the town November's skies are grey,
Of long hours spent beside the flowing stream
This summer's day.

❖ ❖ ❖ ❖ ❖

From *Songs of Greater Britain*, edited by Cicely Fox Smith, published by Sherratt & Hughes, Manchester, UK, 1899, pp. 106-107; first published in *Hearth and Home: An Illustrated Weekly Journal for Gentlewomen*, Issue 384, September 22, 1898, p.729.

The Caged Monarch

Prison'd king! what worlds of woe
In thy weary, gold-brown eyes—
Thoughts of roaming long ago
Under Africa's sultry skies,
Of the wood, the waste, the flood,
And the night-wind's harmonies!

Dost thou dream of times no more,
There behind the prison-bars,
When the thunder of thy roar,
Throbbing to the silent stars,

Drove the deer half-mad with fear,
Cowering to the rocks and scars?

Dost thou dream of hunts of old,
In the spangled tropic night,
When, unconquered, uncontrolled,
Roving in thy unchecked might,
Beasts would shrink that came to drink—
Shrink and shudder with affright?

Ev'n, perchance, as now hast thou,
Couch'd beside thy mangled prey,
Look'd beneath thy lordly brow
When, in freedom's glorious day,
In his lair would hunters dare
To bring the king of beasts to bay.

Claws of steel and locks of gold,
Captured, prison'd, left to pine,
All thy grief we may behold
In those golden eyes of thine,
All thy woe for long ago—
Flying herds and slaughtered kine!

❖ ❖ ❖ ❖ ❖

From *Songs of Greater Britain*, edited by Cicely Fox Smith, published by Sherratt & Hughes, Manchester, UK, 1899, pp. 108-109.

The Workers

Tho' the days of the drowsy hamlet,
Of arrow and bow, be done,
Tho' we live 'mid forges and foundries,
And fight with the Gatling guns,
Are we not men and Britons
As the people of England then?
Can we not fight the battles
And do the deeds of men?

We may not slumber our lives out
In sweet Arcadian ease,
Hearkening the gentle music
Of the birds on the forest trees.
Tho' these be drowned in the clamour
'Mid the engines' smoke and smell,
Patience and toil and courage
Are the tales the engines tell.

Man's skill, man's labour, man's triumph
Seeking some unknown thing,
And the wondrous art of the ages,

Are the songs that our engines sing.
We honour the days that are vanished,
Nor look on the past in scorn,
And we do, in our generation,
The work to which man was born.

❖ ❖ ❖ ❖ ❖

From *Songs of Greater Britain*, edited by Cicely Fox Smith, published by Sherratt & Hughes, Manchester, UK, 1899, pp. 110-111.

Mariners Born

Often I think of my man that's dead,
When I look o'er the salt sea-foam;
It was forty years since the day we were wed,
But the deep sea called him home.
I had three sons and I loved them dear,
Ruddy and strong and tall,
And I cherished them well for many a year,
But the deep sea took them all!

For one by one they would yearn to roam,
As they grew from childhood's days,
And one by one they went from our home
To go on their seabound ways.
They went from our home on the seaward hill,
And left me to make my moan;
For who can keep a man from his will
When the deep sea calls her own?

I have given my kith to the eager tide,
My kin to the cruel blast,
And I know that with never a one by my side
Must my last days be past.
The orphan child of my eldest son,
I have left but him alone,
And I know he will go as the rest have gone
When the deep sea calls her own!

I saw him stand on the cliff last night,
Where the wind blows cold from the sea,
And my heart leapt up to my throat at the sight
For the grief that arose in me.
And often I wake and shudder in fear
In the night-time all alone,
For I know that the day is drawing anear
When the sea will call her own!

❖ ❖ ❖ ❖ ❖

From *Songs of Greater Britain*, edited by Cicely Fox Smith, published by Sherratt & Hughes, Manchester, UK, 1899, pp. 112-114. A youthful poem that will come back to haunt the poet in her later life, as the fears so vividly described here are played out during her residence in the harbor town of Victoria, British Columbia.

Penmaenmawr

Betwixt twin forts by Nature planned
Slumbers the little drowsy town,
While wooded heights, serene and grand,
Slope down to meet the sweep of sand
From uplands wild and brown.

Far out to sea the vessels lie,
Where wild white steeds are leaping free,
And far as roves my wandering eye
There is no cloud in yon clear sky,
No shadow on the sea.

Peace, sweetest peace this summer's day,
Save when, upon the laughing breeze,
There floats across the gleaming bay
A sound of children at their play
Beside the sunny seas.

Peace, sweetest peace on sea and land,
Lulling to rest the wearied brain,
Amid the mountains calm and grand,
Grey cliff, and sickle-sweep of sand,
And everlasting main.

❖ ❖ ❖ ❖ ❖

From *Songs of Greater Britain*, edited by Cicely Fox Smith, published by Sherratt & Hughes, Manchester, UK, 1899, pp. 115-116. "Penmaenmawr" is in North Wales, west of Llandudno, UK.

Duty

Thorny the ways that lead to Duty's shrine,
Thro' grim ravines, o'er iron crags they pass,
And sandy wastes with never a blade of grass,
And densest forests where no sun can shine.
But he who lays unmurmuring at her feet
All earthly joys that make life sweet to live,
And says: "I give thee all I have to give,"
Shall find the memory of good deeds more sweet
Than years of useless pleasure; and for him
Shall those stern eyes with sudden love grow dim,
And she shall stoop, all mercy, from her throne,
And clasp him in her arms, and say: "Well done!"

❖ ❖ ❖ ❖ ❖

From *Songs of Greater Britain*, edited by Cicely Fox Smith, published by Sherratt & Hughes, Manchester, UK, 1899, p. 117.

At Eventide

Red shines the sun thro' the purple gloaming
Across the sea and athwart the sand,
Where the weary billows moan upward foaming,
Sobbing aloud on the pebbled strand.
A night-black curtain of cloud descending,
Hangs o'er the rift where the sinking sun
Shines out once more ere the daylight's ending,
One short hour ere the day be done.

Many a ship on the tooth'd reefs leaping
Will go to her doom 'mid the cold salt spray,
Ere the early dawn, o'er the skyline creeping,
Sadly gleam o'er the waters grey.
The fishers come into the peaceful haven;
Faintly the foam on the bar gleams white;
Dark is the sky as the wing of raven:
God speed all sailors at sea to-night!

❖ ❖ ❖ ❖ ❖

From *Songs of Greater Britain*, edited by Cicely Fox Smith, published by Sherratt & Hughes, Manchester, UK, 1899, pp. 118-119.

The Foremost Trail

We've drunk our fill of pleasure,
Of town-bred ease and mirth;
Our hearts are fain to wander
The utmost ends of earth.
The oft-sung songs ring hollow;
The well-known ways grow stale;
We're off to lead the vanguard,—
To tread the Foremost Trail!

It's oh to leave behind us
The Railhead of the Past,
To roam, where none have trodden,
Thro' hopeful lands and vast!
The fruitless feast is over;
The lamplight's glare grows pale;
And "Outward ho!" 's the watchword,—
To tread the Foremost Trail!

O some may drive to eastward,
Stem on into the day,
And some steer out to westward,
Where sunset skies grow grey.
It's "hey the flowing furrow

And ho the swelling sail!"
We're outward bound for action,—
To tread the Foremost Trail!

❖   ❖   ❖   ❖   ❖

From *The Foremost Trail*, by Cicely Fox Smith, published by Sampson Low, Marston & Co., London, UK, 1899, pp. 1-2.

Saint Paul's

From where the City's seething tide
Rolls on unceasing, day by day,
To yonder soaring dome aside
A little turn, a little stay,
And find, if thou art England's son,
The secret—that is hid from none.

There read the tale that is your own,
The records of your birthright scan,
And learn from yonder sculptured stone
What means the name of Englishman,
With tears—not sprung from grief or shame,
But joy and pride in such a name.

Read yon proud roll of glorious days,
Of captured towns, and combat won!
What need have we of wordy praise
To gild the fame of Wellington,
When every name's a deathless fray,
And every fight a crown of bay?

Here, Nelson's name; who held our fate
In his one hand to make or mar;
And saved his land and made her great,
Before he fell at Trafalgar,
With conquering England's victor-cheers
Loud-ringing in his dying ears.

And here they sleep at last; but these
Whose names you read on yonder wall,
They fought for England overseas
And met swift death at duty's call;
"Comrades," the simple legend saith,
"In arms, in glory, and in death."

Here sleeps, a placid form in stone,
Our eyes upon some image fall,
That brings to mind some hero's deed,
His country's flag at last his pall,

Who, living, served his country well,
And "in his country's service" fell.

And here, where stand in lasting stone,
Brought to the roll-call far and near,
The names of men who lived unknown,
And left no name. Save only here,
Look from the tale of England's dead;
The flags of England wave o'erhead.

Gone now their gallant days of yore,
When, while the rending bugle rung,
Against the shrieking blast of war
Staunchly by stalwart hands upflung,
Proud as the crest that crowns a wave
Swept on the flag that leads the brave.

Shattered and rent by shot and shell,
They watch the daylight wax and wane,
And hear the long Te Deum swell
Along the aisles of England's fane,
When England's sons, in later days,
Win o'er again their fathers' bays.

Silent, they speak; their folds are stirred
That droop, as one whose strength is spent,
And whisper each to each unheard
Above some hero's monument
High dreams of unforgotten years,
That wake our pride, and wake our tears.

❖ ❖ ❖ ❖ ❖

From *The Foremost Trail*, by Cicely Fox Smith, published by Sampson Low, Marston & Co., London, UK, 1899, pp. 3-5.

In the Museum of the Royal United Service Institution

Seized from strong foes by England's might,
Gleaned from the world's-end far and wide,
The trappings and the pomp of fight
Around us lie on every side:
The trophies of the ringing fray;
The flag that draped a sailor's bier;
The little things of every day
That draw a mighty name so near.

The sword-knot that a hero wore;
The sword that struck for England well;
The coat a Russian sabre shore;
The timber rent by shot and shell;

A shred of cloth, a tarnished lace,
A helmet with a drooping plume,
Bring all the wild heroic days
Resounding thro' the silent room.

Sounds thro' the stillness, clear and strong,
The midnight bugle's startled call;
Speaks yon grim cannon, voiceless long;
Waves yon torn ensign on the wall,
As when beneath it went to war
The best earth held of strong and brave,
Amid the veiled fight's clang and roar,
The thunder o'er the shot-lashed wave.

Here lie Omdurman's victor-sword,
And hauberks wov'n of tempered rings;
Light Maxims; brazen cannon stored
In armouries of Eastern kings;
The flags Napoleon's bravest bore;
The tribesman's knife, the Dervish spear;
From wars a hundred years before,
And frontier fight of yester year.

Ah! more than weapons strong to slay,
For these in danger's hour may fail,
The heart that beats as brave to-day,
'Neath coat of red as coat of mail.
These records, uncompleted yet,
Of England's might on shore and sea,
Tell us the tale we ne'er forget
Of what has been and still shall be.

❖ ❖ ❖ ❖ ❖

From *The Foremost Trail*, by Cicely Fox Smith, published by Sampson Low, Marston & Co., London, UK, 1899, pp. 6-7.

It is easy to surmise that this poem was written after a visit by the young poet to this museum in London. In those days the Museum would have had a large and varied set of exhibits from the military (Army and Navy at that time) extolling Britain's military and scientific prowess. The impression these exhibits made on the young Cicely is clear from this poem and others from this book.

Pro Patria

Rise up, strong men of England;
On outward journeys wend,
To fight the fight of heroes,
And chance what Fate may send,—
To the house that's always building,
By the road that hath no end!

Rise up, rise up, my brothers,
Rise up and go your way!
What heed the feast and drinking,
The gaming and the play?
Imperial England's fortunes
Have need of men to-day.

Because she gave us glory,
The strength to do and dare,
The high seat 'mid the nations,
The laurell'd name we bear,
We who were born her children
Give heart and hand to her.

From her we got our birthright
Of fame and ancient pride,
The rule of teeming ocean,
Dominion rich and wide;
For us her best have suffered,
For us her bravest died.

Of toil, as of her glory,
We too must take our share,
And hold our proudest guerdon
With willing hearts to wear
The self-sought yoke of freemen,
The chains we joy to bear.

Then go ye forth, my brothers,
Where'er her flag hath flown,
Or white man's speech is heard of,
Or white man's bugle blown;
Our own is England's glory,
Her peril, too, our own!

❖ ❖ ❖ ❖ ❖

From *The Foremost Trail*, by Cicely Fox Smith, published by Sampson Low, Marston & Co., London, UK, 1899, pp. 8-9. First published in the *Manchester Evening Chronicle*.

Roving Men

Take the boat to the bounds of the ocean,
Away to the ends of the earth:
We've a heritage no one may plunder,
A right that is ours from our birth!
Wooers of fortune the fickle,
Bondsmen of limitless sea,
Brothers in soul from the cradle,
Blood of the Vikings are we!

Since our fathers sailed with Drake,
Alien lands to find and take,
In the misty days of yore,
Forth our hopeful way we wend,—
Tramp the world from end to end,
Roam the ocean and the shore.
Tho' men say the earth is old
And can nothing new unfold,
And that all her songs are sung,
Yet our burning steps pass on
Where the men of old have gone,
As it was when earth was young.

We have jested with the earth
In the fullness of our mirth
In her silent sanctity:
We have wrestled long with Death
'Mid the poisonous fever breath,
Which should gain the mastery.
Southern Cross and Northern Light
Know our manhood and our might,
And our folly and our sin:
On the lonely untrod lands
Lightly have we laid our hands,
Set and sealed them for our kin.

In our days the war and dearth
Heralding a nation's birth,
From our ranks death's harvesting;
Yet we stay not to behold,
As the passing years unfold,
All the fruit our toil may bring.
Other folk may follow on
Where our fleeting steps have gone,
Sow and reap where we have trod:
But our restless footsteps turn
To the wilds for which we yearn,
Unknown way and untilled sod!

Take the boat for the bounds of the ocean,
Away to the ends of the earth:
We've a heritage no one may plunder,
A right that is ours from our birth!
Little we ask for our guerdon;
Nought save to roam and be free;
Bound for the tents of the nomad,
Blood of the Viking, are we!

❖ ❖ ❖ ❖ ❖

From *The Foremost Trail*, by Cicely Fox Smith, published by Sampson Low, Marston & Co., London, UK, 1899, pp. 10-12. "Guerdon" in this context means reward.

Lords of the Sea

Great captains of the bygone days,—
Whose spirits 'mid our spirits lurk,—
Who fearless trod the ocean ways,
Look down and see your handiwork!

The Lion from his island height
Sways all the sea from Pole to Pole:
On outer deep and inmost bight
He sees his armoured fleets patrol.

Eastward and Westward, North and South,
His vessels ply 'twixt alien strands,
Bearing from every harbour-mouth
The garnered wealth of many lands.

Little of riches did you reck,
Small meed you asked for toilsome years,
But death upon some reeling deck,
The noise of battle in your ears.

For you,—who full on France and Spain
Your smiling scorn defiant hurled;
The roving kings of trackless main,
The landless lords of half the world,—

For you the young heart throbs with joy,
For you the victor-soul awakes,
For you, in many an English boy
The flame of patriot fervour breaks.

Reading the tales of long ago,
When Drake and Grenville sailed and slew,
In kindred souls the kindred glow
Leaps up to win such fame anew.

Ours, ours the thrash of trampled seas,
Where Howe and England's Nelson fought:
God grant us strength of such as these
To guard the fame our fathers sought.

❖ ❖ ❖ ❖ ❖

From *The Foremost Trail*, by Cicely Fox Smith, published by Sampson Low, Marston & Co., London, UK, 1899, pp. 13-14.

The Lion in the second verse is a personification of England, especially in its more martial aspects.

In the fourth verse "reck" means to take heed of and "meed" means rewards.

Sons of the English

Why do you smile so glad, sons of the English?
Why do your eyes gaze forward, happy and glowing?
"Only we know that the battle cometh upon us,—
Joy in the knowing."

Whitherward trend your ways, sons of the English?
Where go ye forth to-day, stalwart and cheery?
"Outward thro' alien lands take we our journey,
Lands that are dreary."
Where have ye won your bays, sons of the English,
Bays that ye clasp in your fingers dripping and gory?
"Swift from the hands of Death, bleeding and breathless,
Grasped we our glory."

When will you cease to roam, sons of the English,
Out over perilous seas no longer forth faring?
"Never while earth has foes for our hands to conquer,
Deeds for daring."

Were it not happy to rest, sons of the English,
Travail and wounds and pain no longer pursuing?
"Rest—when the very blood that throbs in our pulses
Drives us to doing?"

What will the end of it be, sons of the English,
You who go forth to war, fearing no omen?
"Death if need be: red death in the flush of the foray,
Face the foeman!"

❖ ❖ ❖ ❖ ❖

From *The Foremost Trail*, by Cicely Fox Smith, published by Sampson Low, Marston & Co., London, UK, 1899, pp. 15-16.

The King's Kraal

Daily the sound of the drums and trumpets' braying
Tolled out a victim's knell:
Daily above the bosom bared for slaying,
The grim knife rose and fell:
Daily the blind eyes of their craven devils
Watched the red life-blood flow:
Daily, above the sound of savage revels,
The King's Kraal rang with woe.

Came from the southward, conquering and freeing,
The lifters of the yoke,
When, the last time, the idols stood unseeing

On alters wreathed in smoke.
And, 'mid the ruins of a kingdom vanished,
With strong-voiced loud acclaim,
Symbol of gloomier days for ever banished,
The King's Kraal sank in flame.

No more is heard the sound of victims' wailing
For heedless gods that die;
No more from earth for vengeance, unavailing,
The slaughtered thousands cry,
And o'er the spot, with meaning felt so keenly
Once named "The Place of Blood,"
Strong hands have set the English flag serenely,
Where late the King's Kraal stood.

❖ ❖ ❖ ❖ ❖

From *The Foremost Trail*, by Cicely Fox Smith, published by Sampson Low, Marston & Co., London, UK, 1899, pp. 17-18.

Note by the Poet: "The kraal (compound) of Lobengula, King of the Matabele, occupied the site on which the present Government House, Buluwayo, now stands. It was destroyed by the Chartered Company's forces in 1893."

Lobengula was a Zula king who was tricked into signing over his kingdom to Cecil Rhodes' Chartered Company. When the King resisted the takeover, he was defeated and died in the retreat. This is a classic example of ethnocentric rationalization by this young poet.

Her Majesty's Forces

To-day, as when the musket-rattle
O'er Belgian lowlands spoke,
And 'mid the rush and roar of battle
The famed Grand Army broke,
Should the dense storm-cloud, dark with omen,
Fling forth its freight of war,
Gladly against the marshaled foemen
Would Britons march once more.

Whether thro' parching deserts straining,
Or stagnant, steaming fen,
They do their duty uncomplaining,
They live, they die like men.
Tho' nameless in our story's pages,
In glorious graves they lie,
Attesting unto all the ages
How Britons dare and die.

Outward from every harbour wending
Go our proud navies forth,
Strongly on all the seas defending
The Island of the North.
Outward o-er every ocean faring,

Unchecked, they go their ways;
Steadfast in purpose, swift in daring,
As e'er in bygone days.

Whether from strong bows staunchly flinging
The crash of plunging seas,
Or idly at the anchor swinging,
Kissed by a soft south breeze;
Whether 'mid lifeless desolation,
Or thronging harbour-mart,
Right bravely for the Empress-nation
They play their mighty part.

When o'er the wakened nations ringing,
The bugles blare once more,
And foreign foes defiance flinging,
Assail our English shore,
Silent and steadfast, calm and steady,
To meet the foemen then,
Will stand, for all invaders ready,
The soldier-citizen.

E'en now, perchance, the storm is nearing,
E'en now half-drawn the blade;
But it shall find us all unfearing,
Prepared and unafraid.
Each true to his appointed station,
Shoulder to shoulder stand,
The forces of a mighty nation,
A firm, united land.

❖   ❖   ❖   ❖   ❖

From *The Foremost Trail*, by Cicely Fox Smith, published by Sampson Low, Marston & Co., London, UK, 1899, pp. 19-21.

The opening two lines refer to the Battle of Waterloo in 1815, which makes the phrase "soldier-citizen" a little odd as the French Revolutionary Forces were known as "citizen" not the British.

The Path of the English

When the racing sea-tides flow,
And the strong ships seaward go,
When the voice of the ocean's crying,
And the wind's wild bugles blow,
Go forth—for the order's sped,
And the way lies clear ahead;
Go forth, where the salt spray's flying,
On the way that the English tread.

Be strong to dare and fulfill,
When the trumpet's blaring shrill,

Tho' the foe stand close in the hollow,
And the shot fly straight from the hill.
Go forth! May you know not dread,
Nor halt where the vanguard's led,
For strong must they be who follow
On the way that the English tread.

Go forth! For the Empress-land
Be the work of each strong young hand.
Tho' your name may never be written
Where the names of the mighty stand;
Tho' the light that is bright ahead
Be the glare of a sunset red,
Go forth, as befits a Briton,
On the way that the English tread.

For is it not the best of all
In the front of the fight to fall,
Tho' you're leaving your life's young beauty
To answer the ringing call?
To know, when the swift death's sped,
And your strength is well-nigh fled,
That at least you have done your duty
On the way that the English tread.

❖ ❖ ❖ ❖ ❖

From *The Foremost Trail*, by Cicely Fox Smith, published by Sampson Low, Marston & Co., London, UK, 1899, pp. 22-23; first published in *Hearth and Home: An Illustrated Weekly Journal for Gentlewomen*, Issue 411, March 30, 1899, p. 842.

Stand Firm!

Beware! The sword of England
Is in your hand to keep:
Look that it be not tarnished
Nor pilfered in your sleep.
As you shall dare or falter
You mould our England's fate;
We charge you, lead our people
To keep their country great!

Beware! Lest in your blindness,
Your folly and your pride,
You fling the strength that guards us
All wantonly aside:
Lest, when you turn for safety
To vaunted sword and shield,
Your arm, so strong aforetime,
Be grown too weak to wield.

The traveller armed for combat
May tread the bandit's cave;
The hunter with his weapons
The snarling pack may brave;
But if unarmed and helpless
He dares his way to wend,
The thief shall bind and rob him,
The wolf shall turn and rend.

Beware! Lest in your striving
To make your might secure,
You win for lasting portion
The shame that shall endure:
The scorning and the spurning
Of ages yet unborn;
The wrath of strong men helpless,
The curse of Samson shorn.

By England and her honour,
Her people and her Throne,
By all she is, and has been,
We charge you hold your own.
By all you hold most holy,
By all your burdening powers,
Be true to those who follow,
Keep faith with us and ours!

❖ ❖ ❖ ❖ ❖

From *The Foremost Trail*, by Cicely Fox Smith, published by Sampson Low, Marston & Co., London, UK, 1899, pp. 24-25. First published in the *Manchester Evening Chronicle*.

A Cavalry Soldier

With loud talking and laughter,
And a long, careless stride,
He paces the crowded pathway,
With head high in pride.
And mean men passing beside him
Shrink, as from one unclean,
From the strong son of England,
The servant of the Queen.

In the forefront of battle
I think I see him ride,
With the drawn sabre gleaming
That swings at his side;
With a bearing erect and stalwart,
And a look calm and keen,
The strong son of England,
The servant of the Queen.

When the drums beat to battle,
With a quick-leaping breath,
'Mid the rush and hurry of warfare
He rides down to death.
And the waiting and toil and hardship
Are as if they had not been
To the strong son of England,
The servant of the Queen.

When the wild charge is over
And the safe ground they gain,
He may hear a cry from behind him
Of a comrade in pain.
And back on his way of mercy
To the smoke-mantled scene
Goes the strong son of England,
The servant of the Queen.

❖ ❖ ❖ ❖ ❖

From *The Foremost Trail*, by Cicely Fox Smith, published by Sampson Low, Marston & Co., London, UK, 1899, pp. 26-27.

Man the Conqueror

To the home of primal Nature, to her woodlands wild and bright,
Came a race of alien folk,
And the virgin forests echoed from day-dawn to the night
With the ringing axe's stroke.
Long they toiled, with weary labour,—cleft a pathway clear and wide
Thro' the forests fever-fraught;
And the Jungle-Spirit whispered: "Would they thrust my bars aside?
I will make them toil as nought."

To the dwindled torrent came they, where the stream slept dull and dead
That had leapt the banks last year:
And for long they toiled unceasing in the sluggish river's bed,
Drove the pile and laid the pier.
And the drowsy River-Spirit reared his dripping lily-crown,
Laughing loud in scornful glee:
"Would they yoke me? Would they bind me? Wait until the flood comes down,
I will sweep them out to sea!"

To the bison's proudest pasture, where the four winds wander free,
Came the busy toilers forth:
And they cleft it with their highway far as eye of man could see,
From the South unto the North.
And the monarch of the bison shook the splendour of his mane,
Looked, and lowed in utter scorn:
And he spake: "A little longer! We will sweep them from the plain,
With the might of hoof and horn!"

But in vain the creeping jungle flings her arms across the way,
And the full flood-torrent roars;
For there comes a Lord of Conquest and a mightier one than they,
Brought afar from alien shores.
And the bison plunge in panic from the ringing road of steel,
And the light along the sky,
Where the cleft air shrieks and flickers, and the blind stars swim and reel,
As the engines thunder by!

❖   ❖   ❖   ❖   ❖

From *The Foremost Trail*, by Cicely Fox Smith, published by Sampson Low, Marston & Co., London, UK, 1899, pp. 28-29.

Wreck of HMS *Birkenhead* 1852

The Loss of the *Birkenhead*

Silent they stood upon that stranded wreck
Fast on a hidden shoal,
Drawn up in line upon the leaning deck
For their last muster-roll.
There was no wailing heard of wild affright,
No cry of those who drown:
All silent, in the darkness of the night,
The *Birkenhead* went down.

Many there were that hour who sank below,
Drown'd in the dark cold brine,
Who ne'er had tried their worth against the foe,
Nor stood in battle-line.
But bravely, truly, as in front of fight,
Each won a hero's crown,

When the staunch *Birkenhead* at dead of night
Off Danger Point went down.

Where lives the man dare say that all in vain
Those hero lives were spent?
Ever their proud example shall remain
A deathless monument.
Ever the tale of sacrifice shall shine
In England's long renown,
How, strong and still, drawn up in steadfast line,
Five hundred souls went down.

❖   ❖   ❖   ❖   ❖

From *The Foremost Trail*, by Cicely Fox Smith, published by Sampson Low, Marston & Co., London, UK, 1899, pp. 30-31.

The *Birkenhead* was a British paddle-wheel frigate of 1400 tons. On the 26th of February, 1852, she struck a submerged rock off Danger Point, South Africa. This disaster has secured a place in history due to the gallantry of her soldiers who, in the face of great danger, urged the women and children to escape in the boats before trying to save themselves. In the tragedy 445 People lost their lives. 193 people, including all the women and children, survived. This disaster is seen as the start of the naval tradition "Women and children first!"

The header graphic is a painting titled *Wreck of the "Birkenhead"* by Charles Dixon, from *Britannia's Bulwarks* published by George Newnes, London, UK, 1901.

The Roll-Call

Who hath heard the legions tramping?
Who hath heard the chargers champing?
Who hath looked upon the arming of the band?
Who hath seen the squadrons muster?
Who hath seen the standards cluster?
When the Sons of War ride forth to rouse the land.
None hath heard the marching feet, the harness rattle;
None hath seen the blazoned banner broad unfurled:
But the sons of Britain gather to the battle,
And their tramp shall shake the world.

Who hath heard the bugles blowing?
Who hath seen the banners flowing?
Who hath heard the war-drums rolling for the fray?
Who hath heard the trumpets blaring?
Who hath seen the camp-fire flaring
At the bivouac of the armaments today?
None hath heard the drums command us ready;
None hath seen the fire's red glow within his ken:
But an unseen watchfire burneth clear and steady
In the hearts of Englishmen.

Who hath seen the sabers gleaming?
Who hath seen the pennons streaming?

Who hath seen the ordered ranks together close?
Who hath heard the cannon roaring?
Who hath seen the standard soaring
O'er the field that we must never yield to the foes?
None hath heard the clash of arms, the trumpet's shrilling,
Nor the voice that crieth loud to one and all;
But far and near the watchful land is thrilling
With a silent bugle call.

❖ ❖ ❖ ❖ ❖

From *The Foremost Trail*, by Cicely Fox Smith, published by Sampson Low, Marston & Co., London, UK, 1899, pp. 32-33.

This was written at a time when Britain was entering a second war with the Boers in Africa, a war which would last for 3 years and cost 22,000 lives.

The Last Trek

Across the veldt the homeless wind goes wailing,
O'er leagues of heath and grassland wild and brown,
And the broad pale band of saffron sky is paling
Where the sun went down.
He is lying still and silent in the gloaming,
The hunter of the waste, whose race is run:
He has come unto the end of all men's roaming,
And the last trek's done.

He has looked on many things, in many places:
From earth and open sky he gleaned his lore:
He has trod with Death in many chases;
He will ne'er hunt more.
For the eyes are closed that used to glance so keenly,
And stiff and cold's the hand that held the gun,
And the lion now may roam his realm serenely,
For the last trek's done.

Give his body to the kindly earth's safe-keeping:
He sleeps so sound he will not hark nor heed,
Tho' the lion wake the echoes where he's sleeping,
Where the springbuck feed.
In the lands he loved so let him rest profoundly,
Unheeding beating rain and blinding sun,
For he who loved to roam will sleep full soundly
Now the last trek's done.

❖ ❖ ❖ ❖ ❖

From *The Foremost Trail*, by Cicely Fox Smith, published by Sampson Low, Marston & Co., London, UK, 1899, pp. 34-35.

At an early age this poet was fascinated with Africa and the great explorers. However, it wasn't until the 1930's that she got to visit some of the places she used to write about as a school girl.

The Men Who May Not Sleep

When the deer have gone to covert, and the wild bird chirp their last,
And the rabbits play at twilight down the dale,
When the water-meads grow ghostly and the dews are rising fast,
And the misty river shows a fleecy trail,
When the white moon hangs her shield o'er the drowsy clover-field,
And the English night draws down on vale and steep,
Look awhile across the billow ere you rest upon your pillow,
And remember then the men who may not sleep.

In the stifling tropic midnight they are lying open-eyed,
With watchful ears thro' sleepless nights grown keen,
And a hand that rests unceasing on the pistol close beside,
For they know not what the foes that lurk unseen.
God help them if they doze, or their lives are with their foes,
So slowly, slowly through the night they creep,
And they wake from homesick dreaming but to see the dagger gleaming,
But to know the time is come when they may sleep.

Thro' the breathless, fog-rolled ocean, at the dense mid-dark of night,
On their slow and cautious way the liners go:
And the watchers dare not think on the closely-looming plight
Of the heedless, helpless folk who sleep below.
Slow they creep by blindfold ways thro' the white, unlifting haze,
And the fog-horn wails its woe o'er all the deep;
And with wide eyes outward straining, all unflinching, uncomplaining,
Stand strong and stern the man who may not sleep.

It is easier far to battle when the bugles sound alarm,
To charge with never time to draw a breath,
Than to live with hand on pistol and an ear that lists for harm,
And night by night to stand full face with Death.
To wait the night-time's end, one 'mid foes, with ne'er a friend,
When the camp-fire flickers low and shadows creep;
Strong his heart must be and ready, pulses cool and senses steady,
Who would live as live the men who may not sleep.

❖ ❖ ❖ ❖ ❖

From *The Foremost Trail*, by Cicely Fox Smith, published by Sampson Low, Marston & Co., London, UK, 1899, pp. 36-38.

Empire-Makers

Heavy the yoke of Empire: hard its ways
For weakling feet to know;
Filled with fierce war and danger all our days,
Temptation and sore woe.
Haply we turn from noble ways that tire,
More selfish scenes to scan;
Haply we grope for glory in the mire;
Else were we more than man.

Not ours to turn from danger's face away,
Nor e'er for rest to long;
Schooled to await our death from day to day
With steadfast hearts and strong.
By ways before untrod blindfold we go,
Unknowing where to turn;
Yet not unfruitful all our pain and woe;
At every step, we learn.

Oh, well for you whose lives are set and plann'd,
Hedged in on every side:
Yet, did you stand as we, in unknown land,
On trackless wastes and wide,
And seek to find which pathway leads to fame,
And which to deepest hell,
And win for sin applause, for virtue blame,
Say, would ye know so well?

But are your lives the happier, you who dwell
In peaceful paths apart,
Striving the structure of your mind to tell,
Searching your own sad heart:
Or ours,—who hear in accents sweet and clear
The Voices call our name
And win for guerdon but an unknown bier,
Of haply, deathless fame?

❖ ❖ ❖ ❖ ❖

From *The Foremost Trail*, by Cicely Fox Smith, published by Sampson Low, Marston & Co., London, UK, 1899, pp. 39-40.

The Bugle

Oh, the flute it tells of parting, and all things sweet and sad,
And the gay guitar of frolic, and song and laughter glad:
But the bugle tells of daring, of chargers' champ and neigh,
The sounding voice of warfare, the clangour of the fray.

It holds the host from combat, when hand-held war steeds fret;
It sounds to ringing charges the world will ne'er forget:
When foemen creep from ambush, it rends the trembling night,
And makes the sleeping bivouac a fiery swathe of fight.

Its voice is hope and courage, and all that's young and brave,
Full filled with high ambition, with strength to slay and save;
It nerves the flagging footstep to struggle toward the goal;
It drives men forth to action; it wakes the rover's soul.

It's oh the strenuous yearning that thrills you thro' and thro',
When you hear it calling, calling, and you know it calls for you;
And it's oh the eager longing, the longing nigh to pain,
When your feet must keep from roving, and the bugle call in vain!

❖ ❖ ❖ ❖ ❖

From *The Foremost Trail*, by Cicely Fox Smith, published by Sampson Low, Marston & Co., London, UK, 1899, pp. 41-42.

The Charge of the 21st Lancers

"Charge!"
And down to the clash and the flashing of spears,
To the heart of the seething tumult of savage Emirs,
Cleaving a pathway thro' weapon and armour and targe,
Thundered the headlong rush of the cavalry charge.

Lo, on a sudden,—all hidden and lurking unseen,—
Leapt into life from the hollow ravine
Foemen in rank on rank, where before there were none!
"Are they hundreds or thousands?"
What matter when fame's to be won?

It was conquer or die! Did one fall from the saddle in pain,
'Twas farewell to the sunlight he never should look on again;
Hacked and hewed from the semblance of man by the pitiless foes;
For the Red Cross never can save from such foemen as those!

Back to the world from the hurry and heat of the fray:
But the blood of the brave went to winning the laurels of that day.

"Form!" And they formed at the order (the muster was four
Where, ere the winning of spurs, there was numbered a score);
Blinded with blood, black with powder, and maddened with pain;
Ready to charge for old England—again and again!

❖ ❖ ❖ ❖ ❖

From *The Foremost Trail*, by Cicely Fox Smith, published by Sampson Low, Marston & Co., London, UK, 1899, pp. 43-44.

Note by the poet:

"At the battle of Omdurman, September 2nd, 1898, the 21st Lancers were ordered to clear off a number of Dervishes who were harassing the British troops. The number was much greater than was believed when the order was given, owing to a depression in the ground which sheltered a large force. The loss of life among the Lancers was very heavy. In B troop, only four men out of twenty rallied at the further side."

Sir Winston Churchill, then a supernumerary lieutenant with the 21st, took part in this action and there are two chapters about it in his book "The River War," which was published in the same year [1919] as this poem. Three Victoria Crosses were issued after this action.

Good Hope

Good Hope! Since white men's banners
First met the seaward breeze,
Since first the keels of Europe
Swept round to unploughed seas,
Fated through generations
With strong-limb'd foes to cope,
Your lot has been for ever
To live and work in hope.

Good Hope! Though wild and weary
The pathway through the years,
Paven with grief and labour
And dim with mists of tears,
Go forth, go forth and conquer,
Though ways be dark and long;
Be true, as ye are stalwart;
Be brave, as ye are strong!

Good Hope! O far-off kindred,
Strive onward, heart and soul,
Welding the severed fragments
To one imperial whole!
Good Hope! Through flying vapours
Red dawns the distant light:
Strike home—for Queen and Empire,
And God defend the right!

❖ ❖ ❖ ❖ ❖

From *The Foremost Trail*, by Cicely Fox Smith, published by Sampson Low, Marston & Co., London, UK, 1899, pp. 45-46. First published in the *Manchester Evening Chronicle*.

For England

Who's for merry England? the gallant isle of England,
The little isle we love.
The distant thunder's booming, the dark-brow'd storm-cloud looming,
And it's "Who's for merry England" when the skies are dark above!

We're for brave old England; the freeborn sons of England,
When storm and stress come nigh!
The voiceful tempest's crying, the salt sea-spume far-flying,
And it's all for brave old England when the cloud-wrack's dark on high!

Who's for merry England? The noble name of England,
The queen of half the world;
The sword is bared for battle; the war drums moan and rattle;
And it's "Who's for merry England?" when the flag of war's unfurled.

We're for dear old England! The distant sons of England,
Her children overseas.
For the flag that we too cherish, we conquer or we perish,
And it's "Stand by dear old England" when the flag of war flies free.

All for merry England—live and die for England,
Her welfare dearest meed!
That England's age-long story may glow with greater glory,
It's all for merry England in the hour of England's need!

❖ ❖ ❖ ❖ ❖

From *The Foremost Trail*, by Cicely Fox Smith, published by Sampson Low, Marston & Co., London, UK, 1899, pp. 47-48.

The word "meed" in the final verse is now considered archaic but it meant a reward.

Franklin

No drum-beat nerved them to the fight;
They heard no bugle blare:
No sword or lance-point glittered bright,
No standard floated there;
Only the streaming Northern Light
Shook, high in air.

They had no hope of victory
Against their unseen foe;
They had no hope of fame to be
That they might live to know:
Nothing before them could they see
But frost and floe.

They died; in death was not foregone
The old high English pride:
They died: till many a year was done
They slumbered side by side,
To show the folk who follow on
How brave men died.

❖ ❖ ❖ ❖ ❖

From *The Foremost Trail*, by Cicely Fox Smith, published by Sampson Low, Marston & Co., London, UK, 1899, p. 49.

Most likely this poem is a tribute to the ill-fated Sir John Franklin Arctic Expedition of 1845-48 in search of a northwest passage from the Atlantic to the Pacific. Franklin and his crew were trapped in the ice and none survived. Eleven years later from a lonely cairn of stones, the expedition's log was recovered.

Out and Away

Follow, follow, you who sicken where the throngs pulsate and thicken,
Leave your doubting and your dreaming and your lazy, listless ease,
Leave the oft-trod streets of town for the springy, bracing down,
For the heather-scented moorland and the open, singing breeze.
For there's plenty left to live for that 'twere well your life to give for,
While the bell-voiced hounds are baying, and the ringing guns are playing,
And the sturdy sons of England are English sportsmen still.

Follow, follow, fast and fleetly, where the hounds are chiming sweetly,
Where the air blows keen and merry, and your horse is going strong,
Till you feel the swift blood flow that was wont to run so slow,
And the days that dragged so weary never seem an hour too long.
Over fence and into hollow, never falter, ever follow,
Never swerving for a moment, straight ahead o-er brook and brake,
For the lessons learned to-day may be needed far away,
In a strong cross-country gallop when there's life and death at stake.

Though the prize be but a trifle, prey of fishing-rod or rifle,
On the sultry moor in August, by the Highland stream in May,
Win your battles where you can; take misfortune like a man,
For he's never brave in earnest who isn't brave in play.
Tho' the real fight be weary, in some valley strange and dreary,
With the tribesmen sniping round you over every mound and hill,
Do your duty, friend and friend; struggle stubborn to the end,
And fight like English sportsmen and like English soldiers still.

❖ ❖ ❖ ❖ ❖

From *The Foremost Trail*, by Cicely Fox Smith, published by Sampson Low, Marston & Co., London, UK, 1899, pp. 50-51.

The Ship of State

The Ship of State is strongly built,
Seaworn and seasoned well
By ages gone of storm and stress,
And foeman's shot and shell.

The Ship of State needs seamen bold
To weather out the gale,
For there are tempests dark above,
Would make a weak man quail.

Black, jagged rocks and hidden shoals
Upon her passage wait;
Currents and headwinds, gales and calms
Waylay the Ship of State.

God grant her men whose steadfast souls
Are by no fears distraught,
To steer her thro' the gathering storm
And bring her safe to port.

❖   ❖   ❖   ❖   ❖

From *The Foremost Trail*, by Cicely Fox Smith, published by Sampson Low, Marston & Co., London, UK, 1899, p. 52.

True Blue (Song for Music)

On the scroll of our island's proud story,
Where brave deeds shine brightly as stars,
You may read of the power and the glory
We owe to our gallant Jack Tars.
Of slander Britannia's no lover:
She can give a brave foeman his due:
But there is not a force the world over
To match with old England's True Blue!

Then here's to each ship and each crew;
To the flag that they float under too;
May the brave and the free ever rule o'er the sea,
And here's to old England's True Blue!

Long ago, all the force unavailing
Of the vaunted Armada of Spain,
From the harbour of Cadiz forth sailing
To conquer us came o'er the main.
In the roar of the battle's commotion
They soon learnt their rashness to rue:
Their fleet fled afar o'er the ocean,
When they met with old England's True Blue!

Then here's to each ship and each crew;
To the flag that they float under too;
May the brave and the free ever rule o'er the sea,
And here's to old England's True Blue!

Tho' departed is Nelson the fearless,
And wooden walls guard us no more,
Our sons on the sea are still peerless,
As they were in the days that are o'er.
And if to the power of our nation
You are seeking a tangible clue,
You may find it without hesitation,
In the ranks of old England's True Blue!

Then here's to each ship and each crew;
To the flag that they fought under too!
May we never forget all the glorious debt
We owe to old England's True Blue!

❖ ❖ ❖ ❖ ❖

From *The Foremost Trail*, by Cicely Fox Smith, published by Sampson Low, Marston & Co., London, UK, 1899, pp. 53-54.

Song for Saint George's Day

St. George for merry England!
Fair 'fall the cross of red,
Beneath whose folds, unyielding
In fight our forebears bled.
The four wild-winged angels
Have seen it steadfast soar,
The forefront of the armies
When strong men ride to war.

St. George for merry England!
On all breezes blown,
We give it loyal greeting;
We hail it for our own:
The flag whose name is honour,
That floats not o'er the slave;
Liege-lord of all the navies
That climb the crested wave.

St. George for merry England!
God guard the cross of red,
The pride of England's servants,
The pall of England's dead!
And when our wrath shall bid it
Shake forth its folds on high,

May England's flag triumphant
Lead on to victory!

❖ ❖ ❖ ❖ ❖

From *The Foremost Trail*, by Cicely Fox Smith, published by Sampson Low, Marston & Co., London, UK, 1899, p. 55.

Our Distant Kin

Strong sons of Britain overseas,
Strong, brave and true, as on that day
When first, in ages passed away,
Your fathers' vessels felt the breeze!

Brave sons of Britain far away,
Ne'er be your arms in battle shamed;
And may the Empire you have framed
Grow great and prosper, day by day!

True sons of Britain, oft of yore
We faced the banded world for you:
Forget not whence your strength you drew,
True sons of Britain evermore!

❖ ❖ ❖ ❖ ❖

From *The Foremost Trail*, by Cicely Fox Smith, published by Sampson Low, Marston & Co., London, UK, 1899, p. 56. Adapted (extra stanza) as song "Strong Sons of Britain," published by L.C. Vincent, London, 1900:

> The garnered years long heritage, the kingdom of Imperial sea
> The fame of valorous name of free, be yours and ours for age on age.

With Chorus: Strong sons of Britain overseas, strong, brave and true as on that day
When first in ages passed away, we flung our banner to the breeze.
Brave sons of Britain overseas, strong and brave and true.

Westminster Tower

In the seagirt land of the North,
By the endless ebb and flow of the streaming tide,
The tower keeps silent watch from the riverside
Over the lands of the English far and wide;
And the darkness of trampled peoples is turned into light,
And tyrants are flung from their thrones in a day and a night,
When the first of the nations leaps up in her wrath and her might,
And the word of the land goes forth.

Let the word of thy strength go forth!
The people hang on the word 'neath the southern stars,
Where the air is thrilling and throbbing with rumours of wars,
While ye who are strong for the shaking of Empires and kings,
Jangle and wrangle and jar over little things.
Be true to the old-time fame of your name and your pride,

You who have power o'er the English, the whole world wide,
From the tower that keeps its watch by the riverside,
O'er the rush and thunder and roar by the streaming tide
In the Empress-isle of the North.

❖   ❖   ❖   ❖   ❖

From *The Foremost Trail*, by Cicely Fox Smith, published by Sampson Low, Marston & Co., London, UK, 1899, pp. 57-58.

The Rhyme of the Four Strong Men

In lands that are now forgotten,
In the old wild days of yore,
The Four Strong Men made compact
That they should fight no more.

They fashioned their swords into ploughshares,
Their spears into pruning-hooks;
And to make the compact stronger
They wrote it in parchment books.

And two should sit at the judgment
When two fell out in speech;
To hold them from bloody warfare
And to do the right to each.

And no man should wrong his neighbour,
And each should have his own,
And the clash and clamour of fighting
Should never again be known.

Now one was a breeder of oxen;
And one had fields of wheat;
And one he owned rich vineyards
Where grapes grew large and sweet.

And one had pastures and meadows
Stretching o'er leagues of plain,
Where fed his wild fierce horses
That none but he could rein.

Now two of the Strong Men quarreled
With word that were far from sweet;
For one said his neighbour's oxen
Had trampled his growing wheat.

And they took the strife to their brothers,
That they might set it straight,
And healed be the wounds of warfare,
And bridged the gulf of hate.

But the lord of the peerless horses
Held back from the wordy fray;
For he asked: "What need of my judgment?
Here have I nought to say."

"What know I of your quarrel,
And the truth of its right and wrong?
Leave I all to your neighbour,
Him who hath watched you long."

Their neighbour he heard them witness,
And set them a day apart;
And for hours he sat in silence
To ponder it in his heart.

And as he was musing and brooding,
Came a knock at his outer door,
And his neighbour the owner of oxen
Entered and stood before.

He stood for a minute in silence,
Crimson of cheek and mute,
Twisting his fingers together,
Shifting from foot to foot.

Then spoke: "O judge, on the morrow
Thou wilt give us thy verdict true:
Great is the trust thou holdest:
See thou give each his due."

"Neighbour," he said, "thou knowest
How fair are my herds of kine.
So ponder thy verdict a little;
And—the half of a herd is thine!"

And he whose crops had been trampled
Mourned o'er his bitter fate:
And the victor, the owner of oxen,
Went on and waxed more great.

While the judge he sat in his vineyard,
Watching his wealth increase;
And folk said to one another:
"Great is the boon of peace."

Now the judge and the owner of oxen
Had trouble upon a day:
For the second laid claim to the oxen
His word had given away.

"Lo," he said, "it is falsehood;
By the mark on their foreheads fine,—
By their horns with the golden circlets,
Of a truth they are surely mine."

They went at last to the neighbour
They had robbed of his right before:
Once he was strong and wealthy,
Now he was weak and poor.

He thought on his fallen fortunes;
He thought on his neighbour's might;
He weighed their power in the balance,
And gave no thought to the right.

And he said: "Full strange is thy story:
Lacking of truth i'wis;
Give back the kine to thy brother:
Of a truth they are surely his."

And the two that were kept from combat
Met daily with looks askance:
And the bystanders nudged and whispered,
At the sight of their vengeful glance.

While the time grew longer and longer
Since they vowed that wars should cease;
But the cry of the crowd grew fainter:
"Great is the boon of peace!"

Now the three were sorrowful-minded,
Because he grew so strong
Who ruled the windy pastures,
Where the sun shone all day long.

His horses grazed in the pastures;
His horses fed in the hay:
Strong and slender and willful,
White and sable and gray.

Fain were his kin to harm him,
Fain from their heart and soul:
Severed in purpose and nature;
Only in hatred whole.

Yet they would not strive by the judgment
To drag his pride in the dust:
For each had bartered his honour;
None could his brethren trust.

This one thro' greed of riches,
That one thro' fear of pain:
And as it had been aforetime,
They knew it might chance again.

So they gathered in secret council,
Far from people's sight,
Planning and plotting together
To steal his steeds by night.

But as they counseled in secret,
They lifted their voices high,
And he whom they sought to ruin
Came riding unnoticed by.

He heard them speak of his horses,
He heard them name his name;
And the warm swift blood in his pulses
Leapt to his cheek like flame.

With a heart quick throbbing in anger
Swiftly he lighted down,
And he stood in the midst of his rivals,
With a smile that was half a frown.

"Well is it done, my masters,"
(High was his scorn and great,)
"That, ev'n as the stinging serpents,
By stealth would ye wreak your hate."

"Enough of this unseen warfare,
Folly and lies and spite,
Anger that fears the trial,
Envy that dares not smite."

"Have done with your secret scheming,
Cunning and plot and plan;
Come forth—to a fair-fought combat;
Stand up—as man with man!"

And the peaceful vineyards and meadows
Woke from their slumbers sweet
To the rush of the reeling foray,
The stamp of the straining feet.

The strong men warring together,
They fought with their naked hands,
For the weapons they once had wielded
Were taken to till their lands.

Long was the fight and mighty,
For their pride was galled with sores,
With the smart of unvenged insults,
The hate of the unfought wars.

And at last when the victor and vanquished
Went on their ways again,
Gone was the hidden hatred,
Healed the old wounds and pain.

And the mists of secret and falsehood
Parted, that each might know
Who was his friend and ally,
And who his lifelong foe.

And the village rang with the clangour
Of hammers that strike on steel,
Forging new weapons of warfare
For the strong men to guard their weal.

And one kept watch o'er his oxen;
One o'er his fields of wheat;
One o'er the fertile vineyards
Where grapes grow large and sweet;

One o'er his proud wild horses,
His horses strong and fleet,
All day long by his pastures
Pacing his sleepless beat.

And truth was greater than falsehood,
And right was right once more;
In the lands that are lost and forgotten,
In the old wild days of yore.

❖ ❖ ❖ ❖ ❖

From *The Foremost Trail*, by Cicely Fox Smith, published by Sampson Low, Marston & Co., London, UK, 1899, pp. 59-67.

A Coral Island

Girded by wastes of sounding foam,
Slumbers unseen the fruitful isle;
Day in, day out, the cloudless dome
Looks down with its unending smile,
And night by night the voiceful tide
Flashes one glory far and wide.

Never by plash of cleaving oar
The dreary long lagoons are stirred;

The rollers on the sun-bleached shore
Beat out their mighty songs unheard.
The rounding fruit in plenty here
Ripens untended, year by year.

High set upon the western hill,
Twin lofty palm-trees watchful stand,
That keep unending vigil still
O'er silent cliff and untrod sand.
Nightly they show, when daylight dies,
Dark spires against the saffron skies.

Where dense the hanging tendrils grow
The remnants of a galleon lie
(The only monuments to show
How humankind has e'er come nigh);
Some vessel seeking gems and gold
In wild adventurous days of old.

The waters of the dark lagoon
Lap softly round her mouldering keel,
And creepers hang in wild festoon
From broken mast and lichened wheel,
And in the gilded figure-head
Bright-breasted songsters make their bed.

Deep in the darkness of the hold
Where beams and nails have fallen away,
Flash gleams of light from hard-won gold,
And one great ruby's crimson ray,
That seems as if some tropic bloom
Had budded in the faint-lit gloom.

The white bones lie about the deck
Of those who trod it long ago,
And little, lying there, they reek
Of that forgotten hoard below;
Their lifelong quest of wonders past;
Their joys, their sorrows ceased at last.

❖ ❖ ❖ ❖ ❖

From *The Foremost Trail*, by Cicely Fox Smith, published by Sampson Low, Marston & Co., London, UK, 1899, pp. 68-69.

This poem is the first in a set of "Miscellaneous Verses" that were included in this book.

The poem might be viewed as a precursor to a whole set of tropical island poems including "Port o' Dreams" and "Sailor's Farewell" that the poet would later compose, or maybe it simply shows a familiarity with Robert Louis Stevenson's *Treasure Island*.

The Four Buglers

In the high halls of morning,
Where the red dawnlights glow,
On the threshold of sunrise
Four buglers stand arow,
In the high halls of morning,
Where the wind-bugles blow.

And ever one or another
Sends forth a mighty blast,
Till the vaults ring and echo
With the sound against them cast,
And the red dawnlights shiver
At the breath sweeping past.

When one sets lip to bugle
The fishermen go not forth:
When one sets lip to bugle
The floes come out of the North:
Great is the power of either,
And who shall weigh their worth?

When one sets lip to bugle
The lands are eased of drouth:
When one sets lip to bugle
The birds come back from the South:
And which shall be known for stronger
When the bugle is to his mouth?

From the four gates of morning
The sounds of the bugles go,
Each with its freight of summer,
Tempest or rain or snow;
From the high halls of morning
Where the red dawnlights glow.

❖ ❖ ❖ ❖ ❖

From *The Foremost Trail*, by Cicely Fox Smith, published by Sampson Low, Marston & Co., London, UK, 1899, pp. 70-71. The second in a set of poems included at the end of this book as "Miscellaneous Verses."

Songs of the City

Hushed is the midnight rush and roar,
At rest the pulse that all day long
Throbbed onward like the endless song
Of waves upon a rockbound shore.

Another day is with the past:
Its joy and sorrow, work and play,
Have followed on the accustomed way,
And the great city sleeps at last.

Far off across the silent town,
The first faint flush of golden green
Across the housetops dimly seen,
Drives the dun vapours flickering down.

Sleep on, great city, rest thy fill;
Forget thy toil in soothing dreams
Of dewy uplands, rippling streams,
Broad, fertile plain and sun-kissed hill.

Now that the long wild round is run,
Before the great bell's thundering bass,
Slumber in peace a little space
Betwixt the shadow and the sun.

Amid the hurrying city's strife
How strange to think that, long ago,
The farmer watched his harvest grow
Where now the long street teems with life!

There where a lofty warehouse towers,
Mayhap, a peaceful homestead rose,
With barn and haystack girded close,
'Mid fertile meadows rich in flowers.

Yet, mighty city, mourn not thou
Thy rustic glories, long since flown;
Thou hast a glamour of thine own,
Tho' all thy flowers are faded now.

A nobler lot is thine—to breed
The soldier, singer, statesman, sage,
The guardians in a future age
Of England in her hour of need.

Therefore, regret not days gone by,
Nor suffer grief thy head to bow:

A nobler garland binds thy brow
Than all the flowers of Arcady.

For o-er the roofs the young moon glows,
Pale gold amid the rising mist,
By the last gleam of sunset kissed
With fading hues of faintest rose.

Along the street, forlornly grey,
The gas lamps show a feeble spark,
Bright isles of light amid the dark
Dim close of this October day.

Ah, strange, sad, solemn twilight time—
Vague sorrow brooding over all
The great town 'neath the murky pall,
With all her splendour, all her crime!

Dark is the West where sank the sun:
The thunder from a hundred towers,
Now chiming forth the fleeting hours,
Proclaims aloud—the day is done.

The sky flames high with lurid light:
The darkness reigns on earth no more,
The twilight mystery fades before
The radiance of the city night.

❖   ❖   ❖   ❖   ❖

From *The Foremost Trail*, by Cicely Fox Smith, published by Sampson Low, Marston & Co., London, UK, 1899, pp. 72-75. The third in a set of Miscellaneous Poems in this book.

The Lament of Maeldune

Over the hills of heather
Wakens the windy morn,
In the island of Inisfalen
Where my fathers were bred and born.
Round me, grey in the glooming,
The though of the troublous seas,
Spangled with spray far flying,
Lashed white by a boisterous breeze.

And oh! But it's long I've left it,
Following fame and strife,—
For great it grew in my bosom,
The pride and the love of life,—
Since I went from the misty meadows
High up on the hill that lie,

Gladly to greet all dangers,
Gladly to dare and die.

Perchance, in the land I long for,
Round the rooms that I loved of old,
The winds are wailing in sorrow
In the halls of my forebears bold.
And it's oh for the scent of the seaweed,
In the land that I loved of yore,
In the island of Inisfalen,
Grey billow and shingled shore.

❖ ❖ ❖ ❖ ❖

From *The Foremost Trail*, by Cicely Fox Smith, published by Sampson Low, Marston & Co., London, UK, 1899, pp. 76-77.

Early Spring

Swiftly along these woodland ways,
Where squirrels scud and thrushes sing,
From the long trance of wintry days
Wakes the warm heart of spring.

Gleaming with April sunshine's gold,
The bare trees glow with hope of green,
With glimpses of the wide brown wold
And pale pure blue between.

On a keen breeze from heath-clad hills
Floats shrill and sad a curlew's cry;
And here the bell-voiced blackbird trills
His random minstrelsy.
The sweet scent from the trampled sod,
The very song the wild birds sing,
Remind me of the paths I trod
In some forgotten spring.

Somewhere I knew this spring-tide scene;—
Ah! when and how I cannot tell,—
These ways where I have never been,
And yet—I know so well.

❖ ❖ ❖ ❖ ❖

From *The Foremost Trail*, by Cicely Fox Smith, published by Sampson Low, Marston & Co., London, UK, 1899, pp. 78-79.

The 5th in a set of poems entitled "Miscellaneous Verses" in this book.

The Maids of the Northern Lights

In the hidden lands of utter cold, in the ice-realms weird and white,
Where straight o'erhead the Pole-star hangs, in the cold sky burning bright,
The Maidens Three of the Northern Lights sit weaving thro' the night.

Ever they sing their ancient song amid the ice and snow,
The song of hidden lands of frost where mankind may not go,
The song of the seal and the cachalot, of the iceberg and the floe.

They weave the rainbow and the cloud, long as the seasons roll;
With weft and warp they weave all night, up there by the silent Pole;
They take the threads from the sun and snow, and make the fabric whole.

They weave the glistening gossamer, and the sunset wings that soar,
The light that glints on the fallen dew, and the mist-wreaths white and hoar;
Laughing they cast it to the winds, and think of it no more.

Last, at the waning of the night, when the lamps of Heav'n burn low,
All in the frozen Polar morn, where the red cock may not crow,
They weave by the cold grey light of dawn the things that work for woe.

They weave the lights that dead men bear down the feared and haunted glen,
And the phantom lights that dance o' nights over the luring fen,
And the fires that flare on stormy seas to trap seafaring men.

Far in the land of the lonely Pole, where the lights flash to and fro,
The Maidens Three they sit and weave, high over the drift and floe,
Singing the while the mystic song they fashioned long ago.

❖ ❖ ❖ ❖ ❖

From *The Foremost Trail*, by Cicely Fox Smith, published by Sampson Low, Marston & Co., London, UK, 1899, pp. 80-81.

The Clouds

All day the clouds sail by,
Out of the west, whose tears are scarcely dried,
Where the veiled sun, 'reft of his crimson pride,
Glows gold athwart the sky.

All day they come and go,
Fresh from the waste where ailing petrels sweep,
The shouting tumult of the outer deep,
Where wild sea breezes blow.

What are the tales they tell?
Bowed down by thoughts of moonlight glancing, pale,

Fitful, upon the harvest of the gale
Rolled on the stormy swell.
They tell of a storm-thrashed main,
Of ships deserted flung to rot forlorn,
Of mastless hulks defiant to the morn
That brings no hope again:

Of ships that drive a way
Thro' wild waste leagues of rollers plunging free,—
Of sheer cliff-sided cleavers of the sea
That spurn the striving spray.

They tell of wild affright,
Shrill shuddering cries when ship and iceberg meet,
Clanging of bells, and tramp of hurrying feet,—
Then silence, and the night.

They tell of hungry waves
That leap and leap about some staggering keel,
Where stalwart men, their hands upon the wheel,
Sink silent to their graves.

Thither, tho' homes may mourn,
They go to draw the veil o'er heav'ns that smile;
Out of the deep they come a little while,
Unto the deep return.

❖   ❖   ❖   ❖   ❖

From *The Foremost Trail*, by Cicely Fox Smith, published by Sampson Low, Marston & Co., London, UK, 1899, pp. 82-83.

A Worshipper

Against the oaken pew he leant,
A child of summers three or four,
And smiled to see each stained-glass saint
Cast by the sunlight on the floor.

He wondered why the folk should look
So sad and stern on either hand.
His thoughts were wandering from the book,
The prayers he could not understand.

Yet, when the organ's thunder filled
The dim-lit aisles in praise and prayer,
Sweetly his baby treble trilled,
Happiest of all who worshipped there.

The sunshine made his heart rejoice;
And who shall chide him? Who declare
God did not hear the childish voice
That sang because His world was fair?

❖ ❖ ❖ ❖ ❖

From *The Foremost Trail*, by Cicely Fox Smith, published by Sampson Low, Marston & Co., London, UK, 1899, p. 84.

The Rock

Here the inscrutable purpose of my God
Set me, to be to men a thing of hate,
Watching the way where the weary steamers plod,
Doomed to the end to slay and desolate.

Passive I stand and slay thro' the shouting night,
When doomed ships drive against my stirless frame,
And windy seas, lashed mad to a shimmer of white,
Curtain my brows as if to hide my shame.

Yet, when the sea rolls calm to the skyline's edge,
Fading, a magic realm, in sunset's glow,
And the seabirds bask and nestle on hollow and ledge,
Almost I dream It will be always so.

Almost I dream that the seas will never awake,
Tossing their manes of foam against the sky,
Where now, 'neath the trail of smoke that the liners make,
Men look on me, and know the land is nigh.

Tho' mine be a name of sorrow, a word of fear,
Even on my brows the wandering seabirds rest;
And, when men see me heralding home so near,
Even the race I slay salute me blest.

❖ ❖ ❖ ❖ ❖

From *The Foremost Trail*, by Cicely Fox Smith, published by Sampson Low, Marston & Co., London, UK, 1899, pp. 85-86.

His Going Forth is from the End of Heaven

Over hill and valley, flame, O king of morning,
Before thee in thy glory the hoary vapours scud,
Bring forth thy plunging coursers, the dewy meadows scorning,
And streak the gates of morning with foamflakes dashed with blood.

Over field and forest, blaze, O king of noontide,
Drive forth thy red-maned horses o'er all the fertile plain,
Make bounteous of fulfillment the promise of the Junetide,
That the fruit may round and ripen, and the garners teem with grain.

Over shore and sky-line, gleam, O king of even,
In the mystic, twilight ocean let thy burning axles sink,
Till the glow has died to dimness and the far light fades in heaven,
Where the chariot stays its journey and the steeds go down to drink.

❖ ❖ ❖ ❖ ❖

From *The Foremost Trail*, by Cicely Fox Smith, published by Sampson Low, Marston & Co., London, UK, 1899, p. 87.

Oom Paul's Hat

Over the veldt in Pretoria town
Kruger sits in his fortress, I hold,
Where the German guns o'er his country frown,—
Bought for Paul with the strangers' gold.
Cannon are thundering far away,
Cannon that tell of the dawning day,
When over the grasslands wide and brown
Come British guns to Pretoria town.

Take his hat from off the rack,
Take it down and bring it back;
Kruger's hat for your booty take,
And send it round for the soldiers' sake.

Over the veldt in Pretoria town
The President sits while his burghers bleed
Bluffing a land of old renown
With bible texts for a tyrant's greed,—
Gold flung forth by a secret hand
To poison the heart of an English land,—
Plots and plans that as dust go down,
When our guns boom over Pretoria town.

Paulus Kruger's brought to book;
Take his hat from off the hook,—
Kruger's hat for your booty take,
And send it round for the soldiers' sake.

Yea! tho' yet ere the reckoning day
Tarries the host at the doors awhile;
Tho' many may fall in a doubtful fray,
And it's far to come from the distant Isle,
Nearer and nearer draws the day,
The doom that nothing shall turn away,
When the points of steel and the coats of brown
Clear the way to Pretoria town.

Take his hat from off the rack,
Take it down and bring it back;
Kruger's hat for your booty take
And send it round for the soldiers' sake

❖ ❖ ❖ ❖ ❖

From *The Manchester Courier and Lancashire General Advertiser*, December 19, 1899.

To the Mac Cailen More, Duke of Argyll

I send to you,—whose sires have held
Their firm unwavering stand,
For far-seen light and honest faith
Amid a raging land,
Fearless upon the scaffold steps
Or field of Sheriffmuir,—
These lays of long-past fights of Spain
And Britain's latest war,

Knowing that one who loves as you
This isle serene and strong
Will something see of noble aim
In my weak flight of song,
And, tho' that Titan strife of Spain
Some mighty singer needs,
Will read with no unkindly heart
Poor songs of deathless deeds.

❖ ❖ ❖ ❖ ❖

From *Men of Men*, by Cicely Fox Smith, published by Sampson Low, Marston & Co., London, UK, 1900, p. v.

This poem dedicates this early volume of poetry to the Duke of Argyll whose ancestors are featured in some poems.

The Quest of the Queen

All on a windy morn in lusty March,
Rode Godwin hawking thro' his father's woods
And singing as he rode: stalwart was he,
Knit worthily for deeds of high enterprise:
Ruddy his cheeks were, and his eyes were bright
And wild as his own falcon's: but as yet
Never those sinewy limbs had stretched themselves
To aught of purpose; never those wild eyes
Had roved beyond the boundaries of his home,
Or snatched its hidden magic from the sea,
Or hardened resolute in a perilous hour;
Swiftly the gallant days of youth went by
With hawking, hunting, coursing, sport and joy;
So mightily grew Godwin to his prime.

Wildly the wintry gale off leagues of sea
Rioted thro' the trees, that, stirred by storm,
Flung up bare arms against a steely sky:
Far off the thunder of the boiling surf
Boomed deeply in the caves: and Godwin rein'd
His steed and stood a moment, where one tree,
A giant of the forest, lay a wreck
Blasted by lightning, and its place was clear.
And as he stood there, breathing fast and hard,

(For swiftly had he galloped up the woods)
There came towards him slowly thro' the trees
An old, old, feeble man: stooping with age,
And scored by time, and hoary as the frost:
Slowly he drew along the woodland ways,
And set his hand on Godwin's bridle-rein,
And looked into his face with brave blue eyes,
Open and young and hopeful as a boy's,
And cried to him aloud: "Where is thy sword,
O Godwin? Where the shield upon thy arm?"
And as the lad gazed wondering, once again
He spake: "O come thou, come unto my Queen,
For she has sent me forth into the woods
To bring her loitering champion." And he turned,
Still keeping hold upon the bridle-rein,
And Godwin stayed him not: and so the twain
Went on among the arches of the wood
Where the brown mould was fretted by the sun
Filtered thro' forest rafters: far above
Sweetly the quiring birds made melody,
Last came they out upon a ledge of rock
Over against the rollers of the deep:
There, home of gulls, and beat by wildwing'd storm,
The last jagged remnant of a mighty keep
(Built by grim kings in mystic days of old)
Clasped the stern cliff with stubborn feet of stone
Welded to rock of ages. Far below
The sea-caves and the surf made harmony.

There,—like a pillar set upon the cliff
To guide the wanderer over 'wildering foam,—
Stood, with her hair blown backward by the breeze,
And parted lips, and eager seaward gaze
Straining across the deep, a wide-eyed Queen.
And Godwin passing silent to her side,
Look'd in those eyes, and knew himself her slave,
And still with face turned seaward, thus she spake.
"I—I am she whose throne is based on rock,—
Whose feet are bathed in illimitable sea,—
Whose garment sweeps the edges of the earth.
O follow, follow, thou whose heart is strong,
Thou who wast bound to serve me from thy birth,
O follow to the edges of the earth.
Follow my lamp, and thy shall find reward,—
Follow where I shall lead until the end,—
Ay, follow to the edges of the earth.
Here is the sword that shall be thine to wield,
A gleam to light the world with victory,
A glory to the edges of the earth.

There lies the way whereon thy feet shall tread,
Whose path is o'er the everlasting sea,—
Whose goal is at the edges of the earth!"

So rang her song: and as her burning voice
Died echoing, came a mighty gust of wind
That beat the forest backward from the sea,
And flung the spray up to the topmost cliff
And made the grim rock quiver: and it seemed
That the great Queen went forth upon the wind
Over the shouting tumult of the sea;
And the bright lamp she held above her head
Clear in the darkening sunset like a star
Gleamed: and she passed in glory o'er the sea.
Then Godwin, looking round him, found himself
Alone upon the rock: and slow and dazed
He wended homeward, through the stormy woods.
His falcon all unheeded on his wrist
Sat cowering: in his hand the naked sword
Gleamed like a moonbeam: and amid his dreams
Clear as a clarion rang the wild refrain:
"O follow to the edges of the earth!"
And with the morn he rose, and bade farewell
To weeping mother and to mourning sire,
And buckled on the falchion of his Queen,
And so set forth.

The woods were wet with dew:
The budding bracken thrust up-curling fronds;
And all the world was wild with wild birds' song,
And fresh with winds of morning.
And his heart
Gave one wild throb of pain at leaving all,—
Leaving the olden home where he was born,
Leaving the merry woods he held so dear,
Leaving the scenes so full of yesterdays,
And dear old sights of childhood. But again
Sprang to his mind the image of his Queen,
With "Godwin, follow, follow!" and he past,
Rejoicing, to the port, and there took ship
To set himself down upon a desolate shore
Full of wild war and peril, fire and sword.

Low hung the clouds above a troubled sea
When Godwin came to land. A score poor huts
Straggled beside the shore, where dwelt a few
Who chaffered with the heathen round about:
And, far behind, the wild, waste, homeless land
Stretched in long sweeps of wood and sand and marsh

Up to the high-piled wall of purple crag
Faint in the distance, leagues on leagues away.
And Godwin stood there lonely, knowing not
Whither to seek the lady with the light,
And saw the wide waste land; and sick of soul
His boy-heart yearned for home.
And those who dwelt
In the poor huts beside the barren shore
Pressed him with friendly words to stay with them,
And laughed his eager questionings with scorn,
Saying: "Why wander out into the wilds
Where you shall surely die?" And when he told,
Shaking his head, how his fair Queen had called:
"Follow my lamp, and thou shalt find reward!"
They cried: "Here surely is enough reward:
Here we get gold and gems from the wild folk;
Here has your lady led you: false were she
To lead you to your death: here lies your goal."
And Godwin's heart was lonely and he stayed.

Now while he held high revel with his friends
His Lady's image faded in his breast,
And slowly passed her message from his brain.
And there beside the moaning of the surf,—
Drowning sad dreams of home in revelry,—
Sped the swift months, and Godwin loitered still.
But as he sat and feasted in the night,
And gave no thought to those brave dreams of old,
He heard a voice above the roaring sea,
And saw a light against the window-pane:
And, rising, left the merry-making crew,
And took his rusting sword from off the wall,
To follow on the voice he once had heard,
The lamp that once had led him.

Far behind
Faded the lights that showed the haunts of man:
He heard the lion roaring in the dark:
He saw the stars thro' streaming veils of cloud
Glint on wide pools and quagmires left and right:
But following on the light that went before
Ever his feet were firm upon the way,
And he sped on, and knew not any fear.
So day and night he followed thro' the wilds,
And often was he drenched with rain and dew,
And wasting dearth and fevers sapped his strength
Till he was nigh failing: and more pale
Shone now the guiding star; more faint the voice
Peal'd on before him.

Seven long weeks he toiled:
And yet his straining footsteps seemed to draw
Not any nearer to the fleeting flame.
Till as the pale light of the trembling dawn
Lay faint and glimmering, like a sleeping ghost,
Along the distant ridges, close before
He saw his Queen: for here the winding road,
That led his footsteps thro' the bog and brake,
Swept looping round, and well-nigh joined between
Stretched but a little space of tangled ground.
O, but a few short strides, one swift, bold rush,
And all the grief were over! Who so dull
As drag slow feet along the curving road,—
Die a dog's death, perchance, beside the way,—
When this fair chance held out enticing hands
And bade him on and conquer? So he sprang
Shouting, from off the causeway where he stood,
And struggling onward, gasping. And it seemed
That the far voice broke into passionate sobs,
And the faint light died down to nothingness.
Then treacherous bogs snatched at his weary feet,
And brambles caught and held his struggling limbs:
And as he stumbled, mired, came shouting crowds
That fell upon him in his weariness
And smote his useless sword out of his hand.
Hither and thither in the quaking bog
Reeled the wide tide of combat. Dim and strange,
Veiled by his streaming wounds, saw Godwin then
His lady watching him afar.
Red were her eyes with many tears but stern
She look'd and moveless, like a carven queen.
Then those fierce foemen bound him hand and foot
And led him to her, jeering; and they went
With fiendish scorn and mockery, out of sight,
And left him lying near her: but she turned
And passed with veiled eyes: and he knew she wept.

The time grew long since that dark day of grief,
And Godwin's wounds were healed: but now no more
He saw in darkest night the light that led:
No more the trumpet voice that cheered him on
Made smooth the hill and hollow: so he went
And built himself a lonely tower
On the far border of his ladye's land,
There to do battle for her with the foe,
And make her desert places fair with flowers,
And so perchance, be pardoned. And alone
He dwelt between the desert and the sky.

The years went by: not years of stain and strife,
Full of high hope and resonate renown,
Loud with victorious battles dear to men:
But slow sad years that make a young men old,
Weary with weight of unrewarded care,
And long with thankless toil of little things.
And at the eve he often climbed the stair,
And looked across the rolling desert-land,
And sayw the level sunset light the sea,
Far out to the westward: and his heart grew high
With lingering thoughts of home and beautiful woods
And far-off, dear green places
And, at last,
He saw a light upon the twilight hills—
A light that was not sunset,—and it seemed
As that sweet star, his lady, came to him
To give him pardon; yet again he looked,
And saw the light glint from a score of spears,
And knew the foemen came,
And once again
He felt the joy of battle in his blood,
And the wild light fired up his weary eyes,
And strength returned with peril.
And he went,
Full-armed and glittering like the evening star,
And stood with drawn sword at the castle gate
To await the onslaught.
Fiercely then and loud
Swept down the rush of horsemen from the hill.
And Godwin, with his back against the wall,
Struck down the foremost rider, horse and man,
And they fell, clattering.
Rang along the halls
The clash of arms and the clang of falling men,
And Godwin struck and struck with weakening arm
And knew no more of sorrow.
But at last
They pressed him backward slowly from the gate,
Till in the darkening hall he stood at bay
For one last bout of battle.
Once again
Thro' the high traceried windows, all at rest
He saw the golden moon, the glimmering mere,
And hills on fire with sunset.
Then again
Came the wild shout and rush of fighting men,—
And Godwin, with the sunset on his face,
Struck one wild cleaving stroke that snapped his sword,
And hurled the fragments from him with a cry,

"I follow, I have followed to the end."
And so he fell.

And even as he passed
There came a shouting from the outer gate,
And many men came riding from afar,
Led by a lady with a burning torch,
And fell upon the foemen in the hall
Till all within were slain.
And the stern Queen
Came swiftly unto Godwin as he lay,
And knelt beside him on the blood-stained floor,
And took his hands, and kissed his damp chilled brow,
Whispering sweet words of love.
And Godwin woke,
And looking saw who knelt beside him there:
And spoke with failing voice: "O lady mine,
I am done with dark defeat and toil and care:
I shall not look upon my home again:
But, for this glorious hour of victory,
'T were well to toil, nor rest, a hundred years,—
To follow to the edges of the earth.
O more than all that peaceful lives can give,
O more than boundless riches, boundless ease,
Lo, I have found thee, and I find thee sweet."
And as the rose-lipped sunrise kissed the hills,
Smiling, he sank to sleep: and far away
Beyond the high cloud and the morning star
God's bugles rang reveille.
So at last
Triumphantly came Godwin to his end.
And those who fain would seek his monument
Shall find a lonely grave across the seas,
Where, in the realm he kept secure from foes,
The wilderness has blossomed like the rose.

❖   ❖   ❖   ❖   ❖

From *Men of Men*, by Cicely Fox Smith, published by Sampson Low, Marston & Co., London, UK, 1900, pp. 1-18.

This long allegory is most likely the poet's tribute to the British adventurers who settled and held South Africa, before the Boar wars. Afterwards the British Empire controlled vast portions of Southern, East and West, Africa for more than half a century. One particular adventurer, Leander Starr Jameson, attracted her youthful admiration and decades later she even visited his remote grave in what was then called Southern Rhodesia; Jameson is best known as Cecil Rhodes' right-hand man.

Peninsular Ballads: Prologue

This is the lot of the English;—in many a page it is written,—
To weep for a loved one that sleeps in a grave that is far o'er the wave;
Fighting far over the seas the perilous battles of Britain,
Winning her way thro' the years with the blood of her dear and her brave.

Land of a glory forgotten,—a ruin our children may pity,—
Tho' dead as thy Moorish invaders the fame of thy empire may be,
Still shall the names of thy mountains, of valley and river and city,
Whisper of honour and pride to an isle in the midst of the sea.

Not for thy gardens and vineyards, thy olives, thy pomegranates glowing,
Not for the gold of the sun, or seas like the blue of the sky,
Not for thy white-walled towns, or the scent of thy orange-groves blowing,
Quickens the blood in the pulses, glistens the tear in the eye.

No! for the fame of our forebears that hangs o'er the scenes where they perished,
Honour we greatly the places once loud with the roar of the fray,
Holding them dear to our hearts as the earth that our childhood has cherished,
Keeping the names of their victors still green with a garland of bay.

Shall not the names of our honour, the names that are sweet in the telling,
Speak to the hearts of the English,—for are they not truly our own?
Names that are bright on our banners, the roll of our victories swelling,
Names that are known to the English wherever those banners are blown.

Dear are ye, dear to us all, O fields of our fathers victorious,
Fights of the pass and the valley, the glacis, the trench, and the ford,
Names that are strange to our lips, yet part of our heritage glorious,
Bought for us out of the ages by purchase of blood and the sword.

This is the lot of the English;—tho' oceans from England may sunder,
Never to feel as a stranger, with nothing to hail as his own,—
Since there is not a land of the world but the bones of his kindred lie under,
Never a wind but upon it the fame of our fathers is blown.

❖   ❖   ❖   ❖   ❖

From *Men of Men*, by Cicely Fox Smith, published by Sampson Low, Marston & Co., London, UK, 1900, pp. 21-23.

The prologue of a set of poems focused on the British forces in the Peninsular War of Spain and Portugal during the late 18th and early 19th centuries.

The Charge of the 23rd Light Dragoons at Talavera

O, hearts leapt up lightly, and steel flashed out ready,
When the Light Dragoons formed for combat that day,
To charge on the columns that, ordered and steady,
Lay stretched out before them in battle array.
And their spirits grew higher as their squadron swept nigher,
And swifter their stride,— when, all suddenly seen
As they charged on like thunder,—the foemen to sunder,
A swift, hidden hollow yawned cleaving between.

Perchance it were wiser to hold them, and spare them
From splendour of peril and glory of death;
But they heard in the tumult the wild bugles dare them,
None stay to draw rein, and none stood to draw breath.
For when battle is brewing and brave deeds are doing,
And English blood is aflame and alight,

O who then shall stay them and who shall gainsay them,
And who shall withhold them from sport or from fight?

And eager, as oft on some winter far morning,
When the glad-sounding horn carols out "Gone away!"
They spurred on unheeding, the obstacle scorning:
And spurning the turf as they sped to the fray,
Their hoof-thunder shook it, full gallop they took it,
That stern steel-fringed gully before them; and soon
Seemed all the grim hollow a welter and wallow
Of fallen charger and Light Dragoon.

Scattered and spent from the din of that valley,
Up from the depth of the seething ravine,
Panting and breathless, they drew to the rally,
Still fresh for the onset, and eager, and keen.
And, ne'er drawing bridle, their scabbards swung idle,
And, sweeping whirled sabers the pathway to clear,
They met, wildly closing, the foemen opposing,—
Those horsemen that nothing could stop in career.

One line broke before them, and on all unstaying,
They flung their fierce wave on the foemen before,
And hither and thither the combat rolled swaying,
And the fight in its fury raged more and yet more.
But down to the rattle and clash of the battle
Fresh masses of foemen came swift to the fight,—
Came thronging and swarming, their line freshly forming,
And falling to onslaught to left and to right.

Then, baffled and weakened and broken and scattered,
The stern stubborn squadrons drew back from the fray,
Like a wave of the ocean whose fury is shattered;
And few rallied safe to the colours that day.
Yet honour and glory is bright in their story
So bravely who fought and so bravely who died,
For half of their number there found their last slumber
Who galloped to death in that glorious ride.

❖ ❖ ❖ ❖ ❖

From *Men of Men*, by Cicely Fox Smith, published by Sampson Low, Marston & Co., London, UK, 1900, pp. 24-27.

Basaco

The watchfires died away from the bivouac on the hill,
And o'er the mountain-tops the dawn crept cold and slow,
And in the morning sky the stars were shining still,
When up the steep hillside came the columns of the foe.

They saw but as they came sweeping onward, wave on wave,
The Rifles on the slope and the guns along the height,
But on the hollow hill, the bravest of the brave,
Grim and stern and still, waited eager for the fight.

Gaily, gaily streamed the foe from the misty dark ravine,
On with gleam of waving swords and with beating drums they pressed,
Till they topped the nearest ridge, that, dipping down unseen,
Held the Light Division hid in the hollow of the crest.

Closer still they came, and their leaders cheered them on,
And the Rifles from the rush drew back sullenly and slow,
And, glorying all too soon in the fight they deemed was won,
Up and o'er the hill came the columns of the foe.

"Charge! Charge! Hurrah!" rang the voice of Craufurd then,
"Remember gallant Moore that was slain but yesteryear!"
And hot-foot to the fight charged the leader and the men,
With a glint of British steel and a rousing British cheer.

Close against the foe thrice the ringing volleys spoke,
Lashed against their ranks the stinging storm of lead;
And the bayonet behind glittered grimly thro' the smoke;
Once they stood to fire: then they staggered, broke and fled.

Beaten, broken, flung from their foothold on the height,
Driven down like sheep to the reddened stream below,
Huddled, swept and torn from the fury of the fight,
Down and down the hill reeled the columns of the foe.

❖ ❖ ❖ ❖ ❖

From *Men of Men*, by Cicely Fox Smith, published by Sampson Low, Marston & Co., London, UK, 1900, pp. 28-30.

Fuentes D'Onor

Squadron on squadron came galloping on,
Furiously charging, and sweeping the field,
The squares were hard pressed and the cavalry gone,
And Ramsay cut off! He must die or must yield!
None dared to hope for the battery then,
None dared to dream they would see them again:
Little they deemed that the guns and the men
Would follow the flag in the battles of Spain.

Tho', in their thousands engirding them there,
French swords were gleaming and French plumes were tossed,
There were no weaklings to whine and despair,
Not yet awhile was the battery lost.
Never a man but would scorn to surrender,
Trapped at the first in so gallant a fray:
Surrounded, outnumbered, their chance was but slender,
But where there's a will there is surely a way.

A stir and a rush and a sudden uproar,
A flashing of steel 'mid the dust and the smoke;
With a shout and a cheer from their captors they tore,

Forth from the throng at the gallop they broke.
Breakneck the pace as the open they won,
Cleaving the foe as a wave of the sea,
Straining and spurring and thundering on,
Madly the battery raced to be free.

Shaken the squadrons went reeling aside;
To left and to right they were scattered away;
Back came the guns from the desperate ride,—
Saved at the sword's point in hand to hand fray.
What did they heed tho' their chances were slender?
Courage and hardihood saved them the day.
Theirs was the valour that brooks no surrender;
Theirs was the will—and it found them a way.

❖ ❖ ❖ ❖ ❖

From *Men of Men*, by Cicely Fox Smith, published by Sampson Low, Marston & Co., London, UK, 1900, pp. 31-33. The "battery" described here was a set of field cannons that were transported from place to place by a team of horses.

The Die-Hards: Albuera

Close-locked in fight,—beat by battle's raging passion,
A stern wall of steel on a hillside drenched with rain,
They held the height in the grim old English fashion,
And where was the man that should lose their hold again?
There was shot running short, and half were down and dying,
And the line raked and rent by shell and shard,
But clear rang a voice thro' the clash of combat crying:
"Stand firm, Fifty-seventh, die hard!"

Did e'er a sign or a thought of fear come o'er them?
Was there a word or murmur of retreat,
Tho' the foe pressed them hard, and the day was dark before them,
And the grape tore their ranks, and the bullets showered like sleet?
Stern set for death, thro' the clamour heard they dimly,
Staunch as steel on the ground they stood to guard,
Brave was the call,—and they answered to it grimly,—
"Stand firm, Fifty-seventh, die hard!"

A fierce chain of steel, and a rank that wavered never,
Holding the hill in the tumult and the rain,
True to the call that shall be a word for ever,
Firm to the last, 'mid the hundreds of slain,—
Dead in their ranks, where they fought and won their glory,—
Lying face to the foe,—nobly scarred;
Telling the world with their silent stirring story,
How the brave Fifty-seventh died hard.

❖ ❖ ❖ ❖ ❖

From *Men of Men*, by Cicely Fox Smith, published by Sampson Low, Marston & Co., London, UK, 1900, pp. 34-35. This poem is the poet's tribute to the Middlesex Regiment that was cut down to the last man defending a hilltop in Spain during the Napoleonic Wars.

Ciudad Rodrigo

"Who's for the breach?" they said,
At the chill dark close of a wintry day,
"For the Light Division who leads the way?"
Never a man for a moment stayed;
Never a man hung back afraid:
Forth from the ranks stepped one and all,
Keen to lead on for the shot-rent wall,
Or a place with the glorious dead.

They might not load nor cheer;
Tho' bullets were pelting wild and fast,
Hand to hand it must be at the last:
Hand to hand they must win their way;
Silent must charge through the darkness grey:
And with empty muskets and ready steel,
And clenched teeth set for the shock and reel,
They went on their wild career.

Never a shot was there
As they sped at the double upon their way,
Over the ditch with never a stay,
Raced up the slope thro' the furious fire,
With hearts that fear not nor spirits that tire,
Filled with the joy that brave men feel
In close-fought clashing of cold white steel
And battle-play fierce and fair.

Then Napier, leading them on,
With a shattered arm he staggered and fell;
But still, as he lay, 'mid the storming shell,
"On with the bayonet, on!" he said,
And on with an answering cheer they sped,—
Scaled the breach with a wild hurrah,
Reach'd the rampart and leapt the bar,
And the fight was over and done.

Thro' the cannon's thunder and peal,
Thro' spurting volley and bursting shell,
Tho' they might not fire and their leader fell,
Silent and stern and stubborn and true,
They did the deed they were told to do,
By the headlong valour that none withstand,
And the strong heart nerving a strong man's hand,
And the push of the cold white steel.

❖ ❖ ❖ ❖ ❖

From *Men of Men*, by Cicely Fox Smith, published by Sampson Low, Marston & Co., London, UK, 1900, pp. 36-38.

The Burial of General Craufurd at Ciudad Rodrigo

They laid him down,—the soldier slain in war,—
Fresh from the midnight flame, the midnight roar,
To sleep his last proud sleep of victory
Beside the wall new-won:
The comrade of the bivouac and the field,
For ever swift to strike and slow to yield,—
Gone to a grave well meet for such as he
Now his last fight was done.

Hard was he, hard and harsh in word and deed,
The sturdy stuff the northern islands breed,
He, English of the English, man of men,
Foremost, where all were brave,
His keen, high voice, so full of fire and pride,
Rang out the clearest in the hour he died,
Cheering the men he ne'er should lead again,—
Who bore him to his grave.

They knew him,—from Corunna's dark retreat,
When o'er the bare, bleak highways swept with sleet
He urged them on, in cold, curt, soldier way,
From shame and rout and death,
To that wild hour, when, as he stood serene,
Proudly alone in that tumultuous scene,
In the forefront of fierce victorious fray
He yielded up his breath.

His eyes were closed on victory and defeat;
Called from the midst of all he held so sweet,
He had not heard the thunder of their cheers
Ring o'er the walls they won,
When those he used to lead in fields of fight
Followed him to his grave upon the height,
With stern eyes wet with unaccustomed tears
For a brave soldier gone.

❖   ❖   ❖   ❖   ❖

From *Men of Men*, by Cicely Fox Smith, published by Sampson Low, Marston & Co., London, UK, 1900, pp. 39-41.

Major-General Robert Craufurd (5 May 1764–23 January 1812) was a Scottish soldier and Member of Parliament (MP). After a military career, which took him from India to the Netherlands, he was given command of the Light Division in the Napoleonic Peninsular War under the Duke of Wellington. Craufurd was a strict disciplinarian and somewhat prone to violent mood swings, which earned him the nickname "Black Bob." He was mortally wounded storming the lesser breach in the Siege of Ciudad Rodrigo on 19 January 1812 and died four days later.

South Africa—1899

Throned like an empress on the south-most height,
Keen, clear and brave, her eyes gaze northward far
To where, still foremost in the endless fight,
Restless and swift and strong, her English are.

Gladly she gives, by manlike men possessed,
Her long-stored wealth of teeming reef and fold,
Pouring against the portals of the West
From open hands, largess of fleece and gold.

Long, long she slept, with idle, nerveless hands,
Dreaming strange dreams beside her unploughed deep,
Till the strong wanders out of alien lands
Beheld her wealth afar, and broke her sleep.

Still men from far off, as in days of old,
Flock swiftly to the splendour of the spoil,
Building great nations on a base of gold,
Sorrow and joy, success and fruitless toil.

Strengthened with blood and wealth of former time,
Stalwart and swift her wakened steps go forth,—
The beauty and the bounty of her clime
Made fruitful by the vigour of the North.

Her hair is twined with gems; her old-time lords
Toil 'mid the wealth they passed unheeding by:
Her hand is on the key whose twisted wards
Unlock the secret of her destiny.

Wounded in furious conflict oft and sore
By those fierce children of the younger days,
Her hands must battle for her own once more,
Nor yet may rest beside her hard-won bays.

With fearless feet, and brave eyes blind with tears,
She treads the path to conquest; far away
The promise of the unrecorded years
Breaks like red dawn across her clouded day.

Behold the queenly head serenely rise
That storm and stress have not availed to bow;
The splendour of the sunlight in her eyes,
The glory of the morning on her brow.

❖ ❖ ❖ ❖ ❖

From *Men of Men*, by Cicely Fox Smith, published by Sampson Low, Marston & Co., London, UK, 1900, pp. 45-47.

The Word of the English

Hearken, hearken, hearken!
Give ear, O ye nations, from afar
To the voice of the children of the Lion,
As they gather from the world's end to the war,
O'er the seas and the desert and the mountains,
From the rising to the setting of the sun,
Runs the sound of the watchword of the English:
"We are brothers—we are Britons—we are one!"

For they hear o'er the seas the word of battle
And their hearts leap within them for the fray,
And they send forth their mankind to the combat,—
To stand by their fellows far away.
For they say: "Shall our kindred do their duty
And their brothers hang unheeding from the fight?
Shall we dwell in our safety here ignobly,
While they do battle yonder for the right?"

"They have hewed out their fortunes, e'en as we have;
Their souls are of the stuff that England breeds;
Their lips are tuned to our own Northern language:
Their hearts have throbbed to hear of English deeds.
Shall we idly stand aside and watch the battle,
And see the work of English strength undone?
Nay! tho' far-rolling leagues of sea divide us,
We are brothers—we are Britons—we are one!"

Hearken, hearken, hearken!
Give ear, O ye nations, to the call:
We have sworn by the ancient fame of England,
Who would trample down the one, must conquer all.
From the Northmost to the Southmost of the ocean,
From the rising to the setting of the sun,
Goes the word of the English to the English:
"By the love of the English for the English,
On the faith of the English to the English,
We are brothers—we are Britons—we are one!"

❖ ❖ ❖ ❖ ❖

From *Men of Men*, by Cicely Fox Smith, published by Sampson Low, Marston & Co., London, UK, 1900, pp. 48-50.

Farewell (1900)

Daughter of old England!
Buckle on his sword:
Forth to fight for England
Goes your king and lord,—
Goes to battle's thunder,
Goes, perchance to fall:
Happy homes to sunder,
Hark! The bugle's call!

Tho' our hearts be cheerless,
Shall we cling and cry,
When our menfolk fearless
Go their ways to die?
Shall we,—wrong enacting
By the love we claim,—
Foolish, weak, exacting,
Drag them back from fame?

Tho', as well it may do,
Seems the waiting long,
Let us, e'en as they do,
Suffer and be strong:
Yet awhile unshrinking,
Let our smiles be glad,
Lest they grieve in thinking
That they have left us sad.

Dies the bugle's thrilling,
Calling to the fray;
Fades the brown and silver
Down the cheering way.
Now awhile our weeping
May in secret flow:
Hold them, Heav'n keeping!
Let us turn and go!

❖ ❖ ❖ ❖ ❖

From *Men of Men*, by Cicely Fox Smith, published by Sampson Low, Marston & Co., London, UK, 1900, pp. 51-52.

Boot and Saddle

Gather ye, galloping cross-country riders,
Saddle your horses and arm for the right;
Show now the scoffers and fireside deriders
First across country is first in the fight.

Far from the voice of the pack, chiming cheery
Over the fields to the sound of the horn,
Onward by yeomen who faint not nor weary,
Now must the banners of England be borne.

Far o'er the seas where the bullets are flying,
Trumpets are shrilling their glorious song:
"Come ye, O come ye," the bugles are crying,
"England has need of the gallant and strong."

Come ye, O come ye from the low and the high lands,
Saddle your horses and arm for the fray:
Far comes the call to the men of the islands:
England has need of her children today.

Gather ye, strong-hearted gentlemen-riders,
Saddle your horses and arm for the right;
Show by your valour the scorners and chiders
Straight at the fences is straight to a fight.

❖   ❖   ❖   ❖   ❖

From *Men of Men*, by Cicely Fox Smith, published by Sampson Low, Marston & Co., London, UK, 1900, pp. 53-54.

Whom the Gods Love

Oh, sweet is life in living,
And earth is fair and sweet,
When limbs are strong and supple,
And youth's swift pulses beat.
Oh, fair the years unfolding,—
The gallant deeds in store
For hearts keen-set on glory,
When all the world before.

High hopes of fame and honour
Along the dawning years;
Young hearts that leap to action;
Brave brows unbent by fears;
Strong souls that march exulting
Full face to meet the foe,—
To work the fate allotted,
As time and tide may show.

Oh, sweet the death of heroes
Upon some ringing field,
Who go to war determined
To none but death to yield.
No time have they for shriving,
No time to shrink and pray:
Before the God of Battles
They go the soldier's way.

O strong and true and gallant!
O life serenely flung
Upon thy country's altars
So nobly and so young!
O chosen heir of honour,
Scarce past thy boyhood's span,
At one brave step fulfilling
The proudest hopes of man.

O for the grave and lonely,
Beneath a stranger sky,
Where lies a lad who, living,

Learnt well the way to die.
O fair the tale of glory
He leaves to gild his name!
O light along the ages
To lead young feet to fame!

❖ ❖ ❖ ❖ ❖

From *Men of Men*, by Cicely Fox Smith, published by Sampson Low, Marston & Co., London, UK, 1900, pp. 55-56.

The Search-Light, Kimberley, 1899-1900

Dark night upon the leaguered town,
And on the hidden foe;
Anxious the distant nation waits
For news of weal and woe.
Like ghastly dawn across the sky,
In glimmering streaks and pale
The white light on the midnight sky
Gasps out its silent tale.

Strained eyes across the lonely veldt
Watch the white gleams afar,
The cold white light whose pallid glare
Pales the warm Southern star.
What tells the message of the night?
Of loss or hard-won gain,
Wild sudden sortie of the dark;
Fierce onslaught pressed in vain?

Swift veers the finger o'er the heav'ns;
(Too slow it moves—too slow!)
How fares it with the leaguered town?
How fares it with the foe?
Fast as it may the aid draws nigh:
Still say they: "All is well!"
Yet speed ye! Speed! For who can know
What next night's dark may tell?

❖ ❖ ❖ ❖ ❖

From *Men of Men*, by Cicely Fox Smith, published by Sampson Low, Marston & Co., London, UK, 1900, pp. 57-58.

In 1899-1900 the South African town of Kimberly held by the British was besieged for 124 days by the Boer Forces before the British successfully relieved the town.

The Eve of Battle

We're a score of men together
To drink to the days of yore,
To the little joys and sorrows
That were our lives before.
We're a nobler lot to live for;

We're a prouder death to dare:
Yet once, for we fight to-morrow,
A glass to the days that were!

To the things that we loved so dearly
In the careless days gone by;
To the beat of hoofs at the hurdles,
To the sound of the hounds in cry.
To the feast and the game and the frolic,
We were but children then,—
God grant, now the game's in earnest,
We play our parts like men!

Good-bye to the careless revel,
Farewell to the fruitless past:
In the roar of the fight to-morrow
There'll be work for men at last.
Here's a health to the fight's survivors,
And here's to the men who fall!
To the death that is sweet and goodly,
To the sword on the soldier's pall!

We're a score of men together,
And one more glass we'll drain:
Hands round ere our ranks be thinner;
There'll be gaps ere we meet again.
Here's luck in the fight to-morrow:
Here's a chance of fair renown:
Here's a gallant race and a stirring pace,
Ere the Last Fence brings you down!

❖ ❖ ❖ ❖ ❖

From *Men of Men*, by Cicely Fox Smith, published by Sampson Low, Marston & Co., London, UK, 1900, pp. 59-60.

Jack Ashore—Ladysmith

Ten thousand British, twenty thousand foe;
Boers on a hilltop, shelling all they know:
Navy men with navy guns, quick and cool to aim,
Fit and fresh from off the seas to play at Tommy's game.
On shore, off shore, a man in fighting trim;
Jack ashore and Jack afloat, it's all the same to him,
Jack afloat and Jack ashore, the same thro' thick and thin,
On the sea and off the sea, he always fights to win.

Bluejackets cheery, hearty, true, and strong,
Come to fight for England and bring the guns along.
Lords of all the outer deep, bold in word and deed,
Full of fight from off the seas to help in Tommy's need.

On shore, off shore, a man in fighting trim;
Jack ashore and Jack afloat, it's all the same to him,
Jack afloat and Jack ashore, the same thro' thick and thin,
On the sea and off the sea, he always fights to win.

Silence of the hilltop, guns that shell no more,
Show that Jack the sailor's a man of war ashore.
Here's to him by land and sea—men and guns and all—
Hearts of oak from off the seas to come at Tommy's call.
On shore, off shore, a man in fighting trim;
Jack ashore and Jack afloat, it's all the same to him,
Jack afloat and Jack ashore, the same thro' thick and thin,
On the sea and off the sea, he always fights to win.

❖ ❖ ❖ ❖ ❖

From *Men of Men*, by Cicely Fox Smith, published by Sampson Low, Marston & Co., London, UK, 1900, pp. 61-62. According to the poet's note this event happened in South Africa on October 30, 1899.

Rhodesia

Brave land of young To-morrow!
In hope and strength arise!
Draw forth our teeming thousands
To dwell 'neath wider skies,
That those who strive and struggle
In seething, stifling town,
May tread the paths of honour,
May haply reach renown.

In place of hopeless weaklings,
Of stunted limbs and brain,
Of vigor cramped and helpless,
Wan cheek and bloodless vein,
Breed up the pride of manhood,
The form erect and whole,
Swift blood and steady pulses,
Strong body and strong soul.

Brave land of young To-morrow!
In hope and strength arise!
Draw forth our teeming thousands
To nobler destinies!
That so men may not perish
Unknowing hope and pride,
Because they lived unheeded,
Nor knew the world was wide!

❖ ❖ ❖ ❖ ❖

From *Men of Men*, by Cicely Fox Smith, published by Sampson Low, Marston & Co., London, UK, 1900, pp. 63-64.

Faugh-A-Ballagh (Clear the Way!)

O far o'er the ocean and far from old Ireland
Stubborn the work that is doing today:
All for the rose and the shamrock and thistle
Forward together and clear the way!
Where's the man of us all would fear?
Give them the steel and charge with a cheer!
All for the rose and the shamrock and thistle,
Forward to victory—clear the way!

On to the trenches, tho' darkly behind them
Gather the foemen that wait for the fray:
Who would not lead where the battle is hottest?
Who'll be the foremost to clear the way?
Where's the man of us all would fear?
Give them the steel and charge with a cheer!
All for the rose and the shamrock and thistle,
Forward to victory—clear the way!

Madly the bugles are crying us onward:
Sweet to our ears is the music they play:
Charge—for the rose and the shamrock and thistle!
Home with the bayonet—clear the way!
Where's the man of us all would fear?
Give them the steel and charge with a cheer!
All for the rose and the shamrock and thistle,
Forward to victory—clear the way!

❖   ❖   ❖   ❖   ❖

From *Men of Men*, by Cicely Fox Smith, published by Sampson Low, Marston & Co., London, UK, 1900, pp. 65-66.

The poem title is the motto of the Royal Irish Fusiliers. The poet would have us sing this poem to the tune "St. Patrick's Day."

Honour the Brave!

England! Not vainly yet
Thine eyes with sorrow wet
For solace crave:
Still in hearts true as gold,
And, like their fathers, bold,
Beats the swift blood of the old:
Honour the brave!

Yet, ere victorious days
Set all thy heart ablaze,
Fear not tomorrow!
Soon shall thy strong men's might
Make thy proud 'scutcheon bright,

Therefore, tho' dark the night,
Smile thro' thy sorrow!

Wail, pipes of Scotland, wail,
For those who, doomed to fail,
Went to the grave:
Tho' theirs no victor's crown,
Well were their lives laid down:
Cherish their fair renown!
Honour the brave!

Honour, too, those who fell,
Plunging thro' storms of shell
Their guns to save:
Forget not how they died
(By their cause sanctified):
Oh, stoop not from thy pride!
Honour the brave!

From *Men of Men*, by Cicely Fox Smith, published by Sampson Low, Marston & Co., London, UK, 1900, pp. 67-68.

The poet notes that this poem was composed in January of 1900.

Majuba Day

Majuba Day! Majuba Day!
Here's a health to Bobs and his force to-day!
For the wiped-out shame from Britannia's fame,
And the work they wrought on Majuba Day!

Your burghers held high festival
Because of what has been, they say,
With gleeful sports and pastimes, Paul,
In honour of Majuba Day.
Or did you think amid it all
Of what was passing far away?
O did you even wonder, Paul,
How Cronje spent Majuba Day?

You'll struggle yet to dupe them all,
With scheming heart, and lips that pray:
Perhaps you hope a little, Paul,
To keep away the reckoning-day.
Of this be sure,—whate'er befall,
Whate'er you hide, what e'er you say,
Your hour of triumph's over, Paul,
Your glorying in Majuba Day.

We stumbled; but we did not fall:
A bitter debt we've had to pay:
We've deeply drunk of sorrow, Paul,
Since that first dark Majuba Day.
Our turn has come, in spite of all,
Our time to wipe the stain away:
O well you speak so proudly, Paul,
When next comes round Majuba Day?

Majuba Day! Majuba Day!
Here's a health to Bobs and his force to-day!
For the wiped-out shame from Britannia's fame,
And the work they wrought on Majuba Day!

❖ ❖ ❖ ❖ ❖

From *Men of Men*, by Cicely Fox Smith, published by Sampson Low, Marston & Co., London, UK, 1900, pp. 69-70.

The poet notes that this poem was composed February 27, 1900.

At Last!

Mafeking (May 16th, 1900)

Flag that has flown o'er a thousand fields victorious,
Flag that art first on the land and the seas,
When hast thou known of a victory more glorious?
Old the country is that bore them; but the men that went before them,
All the gallant, great and good, on sea or land,
Fighting-men, whose names are written on the glory-roll of Britain,
They shall joy to grip their kinsmen by the hand.

There's a little lovely town that the rolling plains environ,
And it bears no name of glory, and England's far away,
And a stranger sky looks down on its straggling roofs of iron:
It will tell a tale of fame to an English heart for aye.
For the fights that have been fought there, and the work that has been wrought there,

Shall we in world-wide England e'er forget?
Seven month they held it fearless, tho' the days were dark and cheerless,
And the flag of England's flying o'er them yet.

Men who have fought with a courage uncomplaining,
Men who have laughed at the bitterness of death,
Men who have smiled when the star of hope seemed waning,
Know ye the joy that your triumph wakeneth?
When shall England know again braver leader, braver men,
Staunch to save her, staunch to serve thro' good and ill?
Long your struggle was and splendid,—
God be thanked that it is ended,
And the flag of England flying o'er you still.

Men who are dead 'neath the ground you died in keeping,
Men who are gone from the glory and the pain,
Will the thunder of our cheers reach your ears where you are sleeping?
Will you not rejoice that you perished not in vain?
When the guns no more are speaking, or the shells above you shrieking,
And o'er your graves the shouting throng goes by,
For a moment will you waken and rejoice that unforsaken
Is the cause for which you deemed it good to die?

By the flag they have battled for so long,
By the fame they have suffered so to save,
Honour be and praise to the gallant and the strong,
Honour to the bravest of the brave!

❖ ❖ ❖ ❖ ❖

From *Men of Men*, by Cicely Fox Smith, published by Sampson Low, Marston & Co., London, UK, 1900, pp. 71-73.

The long siege by Boer troops of the British occupied town of Mafeking in South Africa was relieved on May 16th, 1900.

The header graphic is an illustration titled *At Last!* as drawn by Linley Sandvarnes, *Punch* magazine, Volume 118, March 7, 1900, p. 167. However, the cartoon actually depicts Sir Redvers Buller relieving besieged Sir George White at Ladysmith on February 28, 1900.

The Bond of Brotherhood

Not for their grandsires' homes they fell,—
For names passed down from sire to son;
Not for the soil whereon they dwell,
The earth their fathers' strength has won.
Far o'er the deep their dust is blown
Thro' lands their fathers have not known.

O ye who ask why thus they go
To fight and fall in nameless lands,—
And why, against so far a foe,
Strong brother by strong brother stands,
Shall roaming sea and wheeling sun
Make sundered hearts that beat as one?

The names that once had nought to tell,
They bid our hearts beat high today:
And every scene where Britons fell
Shall live in glory far away,
And every spot where flowed their blood,—
High-altar of our brotherhood.

O watcher of the pine-clad West,
O dwellers in the East or South,
Thro' their strong limbs your shores are blest
Who lately left the harbour-mouth.
Be proud, be joyful, while you mourn
For those who never shall return.

Whether from East or South or West
Wander the brothers of the breed,
The names they know shall e'er attest
In that far land a home indeed,
Since there men's hearts may leap with pride,
To think how "hence our kindred died."

❖ ❖ ❖ ❖ ❖

From *Men of Men*, by Cicely Fox Smith, published by Sampson Low, Marston & Co., London, UK, 1900, pp. 74-75.

Composed during the second Boer War in South Africa.

Resurrexit (June, 1900)

The old flag's flying from the rampart,
The old flag's blown upon the breeze,
And the old shame's blotted from the 'scutcheon,
And the old rule's come from overseas.
Oh, serenely shall the flag of England soar
Where in sorrow and in shame it sank before:
We have paid a heavy toll of blood and treasure;
We have given of our bravest without measure:
It shall fly, where once it flew, for evermore.

"I shall arise!"
So they swore it long ago,
When the sky was dark with woe,—
Hopeful in the dearest day,
Found our kindred heart to say:
"I shall arise!"

"I have arisen!"
Flag that bids the land be free,
Brought at last from oversea,
Death and danger proudly through,
Waves thy scarlet and thy blue:
"I have arisen!"

"It has arisen!"
Brought from its shameful grave,
Bought with blood of great and brave,
It has fallen but to rise:
Bugles, sound it to the skies:
"It has arisen!"

For the old flag's flying there serenely,
The old flag's floating on the breeze,
And the old shame's blotted from the 'scutcheon,
And the old rule's come from overseas.
Oh, serenely shall the flag of England soar
Where in sorrow and in shame it sank before:
We have paid a heavy toll of blood and treasure;
We have given of our dearest without measure:
It shall fly where once it flew, for evermore.

❖   ❖   ❖   ❖   ❖

From *Men of Men*, by Cicely Fox Smith, published by Sampson Low, Marston & Co., London, UK, 1900, pp. 76-78.

This poem was composed during the second Boer War in South Africa. As the poet explains, "After the retrocession of the Transvaal in 1881, the English residents of Pretoria buried the Union Jack, inscribing over it the word 'Resurgam.'"

To the South African Guild of Loyal Women

When the thunder of the battle rolls no more,
And the last bugles blow o'er the plain,
They'll be many in old England mourning sore
For the men who must remain;
Yet when they think upon their glorious dead,
They shall know that their memory shall not fade,—
That sacred, where their dear ones fought and bled,
Is the ground where they are laid.

They need not know in bitter yearning long
For a spot their tear-dimmed eyes may never see,
Where unheeded and alone the weeds may throng
And the wild things wander free.
Tho' in a stranger land our soldiers sleep,
And far away is all they held so dear,
Yet kindred hands their glorious graves shall keep
Tended from year to year.

When, as the years bring round the time again,
Beneath their names our tribute wreaths we lay,
Who sleep full sound in some Southern plain
From their Isle far away,
Tho' they rest afar across the sundering foam,
'Neath a turf never wet with English showers,

We grieve not, since we know that, far from home,
Their graves are glad with flowers.

❖ ❖ ❖ ❖ ❖

From *Men of Men*, by Cicely Fox Smith, published by Sampson Low, Marston & Co., London, UK, 1900, pp. 79-80.

Hymn of Thanksgiving after Victory

Lord of Hosts, before whose frown
Nations in their might bow down,
Thou who bidd'st the strong man's might
Work Thy will in blood-red fight,
Lord of Hosts on land and sea,
Gloria tibi, Domine!

God of Battles, throned in might,
Thou whose arm is strong for right,
For the strength that Thou hast given
In the fight where we have striven,
Hear the soldier's thanks for Thee:
Gloria tibi, Domine!

God of Victory, Thou who made
Stalwart men and unafraid,
Ere in sweet repose we lie,
Ere we lay our harness by,
Stained with fight, we bow the knee:
Gloria tibi, Domine!

❖ ❖ ❖ ❖ ❖

From *Men of Men*, by Cicely Fox Smith, published by Sampson Low, Marston & Co., London, UK, 1900, p. 81.

This "thanks for victory" hymn was composed after the British had defeated the Boers in South Africa in 1900.

The Happy Dead

Happy the dead on some resounding field,—
Dead with the joy of battle in their hearts,—
Dead—with the bays of battle earned in death.
They shall not head, tho', with the sinking sun,
Roll back the fruitless fight that raged so long,
And leave them lying silent where they fell.

Happy the dead on some tumultuous field,
Who, fighting their wild battle in the dark,
Full-breasted meet their death and know no more.
They shall not know the pang of dark defeat,
The bitter sting of duty vainly done:
Happy the dead: for none shall do them wrong.

Happy the dead who lie in lonely graves:
Knelled by the sound of England's mournful guns,
And shrouded by the standard that they loved.
Only they know the self-forgetting joy
And the strong spur of courage, and the pride
Of battle, and the noblest victory.

❖ ❖ ❖ ❖ ❖

From *Men of Men*, by Cicely Fox Smith, published by Sampson Low, Marston & Co., London, UK, 1900, pp. 82-83.

Men of the Marches

We in our citied ease,
Far from the noise of war,
Often we think on you,
Sentries by gates afar,
Under your sweltering skies
And sun that parches,
Say, shall we pity you,
Men of the Marches?

Men of the olden time,
Forging their weary way
Far from their native land,
Hold we full high to-day;
Even as the roving men
Of England's child-days,
So to our children, you,
Men of the wild days.

Shall we not see the past
Living again in you,
Who in the wilderness
Found the old world anew,
Danger and drought and death
Gallantly scorning?
O for the life you lead,
Men of the morning!

For yours to tread the first
Over the ways unknown,
Grasping from Time's vast hoard
Prizes we all may own;
Whatever storm and stress
Over your way break,
Who would not strive by you,
Men of the daybreak!

❖ ❖ ❖ ❖ ❖

From *Men of Men*, by Cicely Fox Smith, published by Sampson Low, Marston & Co., London, UK, 1900, pp. 84-85.

The Gift

What have we to give
To one who stands
Waiting with open hands,
Mother of many sons in many lands?
Who holds o'er land and main
Her easeless, restless reign,—
Who oft hath called her own,
and ne'er hath called in vain.

What is best to give
When comes her call?
Courage that fears no fall,
And brave-eyed youth that dreadeth not at all;
Hearts strong on hope to cling,—
Hope for what years may bring,
And service void of ease,
and faith unquestioning.
What hath she to give,—
What last reward
For loyal heart and sword?
What crown of victory, what princely hoard?
Honour and strength and pride,
And toil with joy allied,—
Glory and hope and fame,
for which her best have died.

Toast To Absent Friends

❖ ❖ ❖ ❖ ❖

From *Men of Men*, by Cicely Fox Smith, published by Sampson Low, Marston & Co., London, UK, 1900, p. 86.

The header graphic is a cartoon titled To "Absent Friends!" commemorating the end of the Boar War, as drawn by Swains, from Punch magazine, December 26, 1900, p. 459.

The Broken Brigade

We who are gone from the lands that are dear to us,
We who were merry in days that are dead,
Shall we not hope that the dawn may be near to us?
Shall we lament that our folly has fled?
Tho' in life's spring we have squandered the best of it,
Gallant careers that we deemed we might win,
Honour and glory and wealth and the rest of it,
(Such is the price we have paid for our sin),—
Greater the value of joys in their scarcity;
Many the lessons from sorrow to learn:
Truer the friends that are found in adversity;
Sweeter the praise that is harder to earn.
Yea, tho' we go, and our comrades may rue us not,

Dead be the past as a song that is sung:
Out in the open, in countries that knew us not,
Find we the honour that left us so young.
Yea, tho' at times for the old days we hunger,
Fortune and glory may meet us at last:
Hope is in lands that are wider and younger,
Hope for the fallen to conquer the past.
Yea, tho' we die, and the earth bear no trace of us,
Nought save a grave that none careth to tend,
Haply the devil that wrought the disgrace of us
Proveth the angel disguised in the end!

❖ ❖ ❖ ❖ ❖

From *Men of Men*, by Cicely Fox Smith, published by Sampson Low, Marston & Co., London, UK, 1900, pp. 87-88.

Nec Aspera Terrent

Hark, the bugles call us out!
Hark, the chargers restless neigh!
Who will tread the beaten track?
Who will dare the shorter way?
Failure, say they? Who would fear
When the world is wide before,

And the skies are wide above,
And a strong man's heart is sure?
When was ever kingdom made,
Glory bought, or empire won,
When was might guerdon gained
But a mighty risk was run?

If we count the risk too great,—
Shrinking, keep the safer way,
Should we not for many a year
Mourn the chance we lost to-day?

Ne'er again such chance will be:
Not to take it, this were sin:
Think not what we stand to lose:
Think what waits us if we win!

Worth the dreary afterdark,
Lost career and bitter blame,
But an hour to stand alone,—
Fight and fail for such an aim.

❖ ❖ ❖ ❖ ❖

From *Men of Men*, by Cicely Fox Smith, published by Sampson Low, Marston & Co., London, UK, 1900, pp. 89-90.

Fife and Drum

Fife, fife and drum, and the feet along the highway,
Crying: "Follow, O my masters, to the field of death and fame:
Young are you, and strong and true, here is mighty work to do
On the pathway of the ages that is evermore the same."

Fife, fife and drum, and the sad wild music thrilling,—
Sad with tears that fall for heroes, wild with courage all afire,
Still the marching feet of men, in their unison triumphant,
Tread their way along the ages to the tune of your desire!

Fife, fife and drum, and the feet along the highway!
Not of fear and death their speech is to the gallant and the brave;
But a gift that's worth the giving, and a life that's worth the living,
And a death that's worth the dying, and a light beyond the grave.

Fife, fife and drum! O the sad, wild music shrilling,
Far and fair and hopeful ever,—soaring skyward all afire!
And it's oh, to follow on to the end whereto thou callest,—
Follow down to death or glory on the feet of thy desire!

❖   ❖   ❖   ❖   ❖

From *Men of Men*, by Cicely Fox Smith, published by Sampson Low, Marston & Co., London, UK, 1900, pp. 91-92.

Messmates All

Who will drink a health with me?
Drink together, messmates all!
To the men who sat aforetime
Where we sit to-night;
Brothers they, in peace and war-time,
Field of sport and field of fight:
Scattered now o'er land and sea,
Messmates all!

Stand up and drink with me!
Drink together, messmates all!
To the men who lie in glory
On the field they won,
Beating out an Empire's story,
Warring with Napoleon,—
Men who died to keep us free,
Messmates all!

To our brethren far and lone!
Drink together, messmates all!
To the men who lie forgotten
Far from all they knew,
'Mid the jungles dank and rotten,—

'Twixt the sand-glare and the blue;
Men who died and made no moan,
Messmates all!

To the near and far away!
Drink together, messmates all!
Bound in unity the race is
By the sword they drew,
Whether in the nameless places,
Paardeberg or Waterloo!
Years ago and yesterday,
Messmates all!

❖ ❖ ❖ ❖ ❖

From *Men of Men*, by Cicely Fox Smith, published by Sampson Low, Marston & Co., London, UK, 1900, pp. 93-94.

A timeless drinking song for soldiers at home and abroad. This poem was first adapted for singing by Mike Kennedy in 2010.

A Song of the Open

Mother Earth, who bred us stalwart,
Bred us lusty, bred us free,
She hath spread her nets to take us,
She has lured us warily
To the wind across the open,
And the restless, roaming sea.

She hath sent her winds to whisper
Of the far lands whence they roam,
Sent her shouting storms to call us
From the green field of our home,
With a dream of far wild places
And the roving, racing foam.

She hath sung to us divinely
In the moaning of her tides,
Of some ship that waits our coming,—
That for us at anchor rides,—
Set us longing for the sea-song
Of the wave-wash on her sides.

By the roving hearts within us
Hers for good and ill are we,
By the vigour she hath sent us
Hers while youth and strength shall be,—
Bondsmen of the boundless open
And the restless, roaming sea.

❖ ❖ ❖ ❖ ❖

From *Men of Men*, by Cicely Fox Smith, published by Sampson Low, Marston & Co., London, UK, 1900, pp. 95-96.

This poem is one of the first precursors of the many nautically themed poems to come

The Outposts

The sun and the clouds above them
Their lights and shadows weave,
And nought on earth shall glad them
And nought on earth shall grieve;
Gone home to dust, are lying
By deepest sleep possessed,
The eyes that loved not slumber,
The feet that knew not rest.

Above them, all unheeded
The great days wax and wane,
With burning floods of sunshine,
And bounteous showers of rain;
And fearless herds go plunging
And trampling overhead,
And lordly beasts come hunting
That little heed the dead.

They marched with eyes full forward,
They worked while there was light,
And is earth nought to them
Wherein they took delight?
O when the men who follow
Fulfill the work begun,
Will *they* not joy together
To know their task is done?

And if good fights go by them,
And shots fly fast above,
Their dust shall thrill, responsive
To deeds they used to love;
And if new nations' voices
Some day shall call them blest,
Those sounds shall surely move them,—
Shall surely reach their rest.

O, if those gone remember
At all the world they leave,
The joys of earth shall glad them,—
The tears of earth shall grieve;
Shall now be all forgotten
The toil you deemed the best,
O, eyes that watched till even,
O, feet that roved to rest?

❖ ❖ ❖ ❖ ❖

From *Men of Men*, by Cicely Fox Smith, published by Sampson Low, Marston & Co., London, UK, 1900, pp. 97-98.

God's Gift

Out of the sword's swift lightning,
And the cannon's withering breath,
And the legions stern and eager,
And the headlong ride to death,
Out of the clash and the clang,
And the war-smoke's eddying drift,
Unto the race of man
God giveth a gift.

He giveth man, for a solace
In all the evils that be,
The glory of strong resistance,
Tho' it hopes not for victory;
To fighters of losing fights
He giveth pride to defend,
Strength and courage and faith,
Going on to the end.

Wounded, never to whimper,—
Beaten, not to repine,—
Clasping toil as a lover,—
Drinking death like a wine:
A gallant and goodly fight,
A short and a glorious shrift,—
Unto the strong of soul
God giveth a gift.

Never to leave the colours,
Not to shrink at the last,
Not to dread for the morrow,
Not to weep for the past:
When the day dies down on defeat
And every hope gone by,
Still to hold for the cause,—
So, fighting, to die.

Out of the sword's swift lightning,
And the cannon's gasp of red,
And the charging squadron's thunder
And the steel-barbed legion's tread,
Out of the flash and the flame
And the war-smoke's eddying drift,
Unto the race of man
God giveth His gift.

❖ ❖ ❖ ❖ ❖

From *Men of Men*, by Cicely Fox Smith, published by Sampson Low, Marston & Co., London, UK, 1900, pp. 99-100.

Westminster Boys

Where at the central pulse of England's might
The Abbey towers stand stately, rears its head
One column, to the memory of the dead
On forgotten fields of glorious fight;
It stands before the gates that saw them go
In fullness of strong years to yield their breath,—
Some the sword's toil, some sickness'; all, we know,
Bravest and best, and over young for death.

Yet it may chance that some, who boys to-day,
Treading the path to manhood, shall speed forth,
To stand as these stood, 'neath a stranger sky
In some life-crowning foray far away,
Remembering that proud pillar in their North,
May with a joyful soul go forth to die.

❖ ❖ ❖ ❖ ❖

From *Men of Men*, by Cicely Fox Smith, published by Sampson Low, Marston & Co., London, UK, 1900, p. 101.

Tramp Freighter

An Ocean Tramp

To-morrow and to-morrow,
O the slashing of the foam along the furrow!
We'll loosen from the jetty when the tide has ceased to flow.
East, West, North and South we're going, boys,
Out where the salt winds are blowing, boys,
Along the ocean highways where the little traders go!

I have rocked in Pacific harbours,
I have fought the Polar seas,
I have bowed to the Northern tempests,
I have laughed to the South Sea breeze:
I have driven far to the Northward,

Through tempest and strain and toil,
To trade with the fur-clad people
For their sealskin and their oil.
Iceberg and floe and storm-wind,
They pass me scathless by;
For why should the mighty ocean
Wage war on such as I?

I have run in the dark of the night-time
Where the cruisers guard the bay,
Into the leaguered harbour
Making my unseen way:
I have lain by the plague-swept city
Where a ceaseless death-bell toil'd,
When the sailors die in the foc's'le,
And the cargos rot in the hold.

I have sought the palm-fringed islets
Where the liners come naught nigh,
Trailing the smoke of my funnels
Over a stainless sky.

And ever I'm tramping, tramping,
Over the world-wide main,
Ever out from the haven
To seek new ports again.

Lagos and sweltering Aden,—
I know them one and all,—
Manila's princely harbour,
The heights of Montreal,
The shallow roads of Durban,
And Riga's fortress strong,
The guarded bay of Capetown,
The island of Hong Kong,
The swarming docks of Melbourne,
The markets of Bombay,
And virgin South Sea harbours,
And drowsy Mandalay.

To-morrow and to-morrow,
O the slashing of the foam along the furrow!
It's out to one or other of the thousand ports I know;
East, West, North and South we're going, boys,
Out where the salt winds are blowing, boys,
Along the ocean highways where the little traders go!

From *Men of Men*, by Cicely Fox Smith, published by Sampson Low, Marston & Co., London, UK, 1900, pp. 102-104.

Another precursor to the many nautical poems this poet will compose. The nautical language does not ring quite true at this point in her literary career but the romance of the sea is there.

First adapted for singing by Mike Kennedy, as recorded on *A Dog's Life*, 2015

The header graphic is an illustration titled *Tramp Steamer circa 1900* from *Oars, Sail and Steam*, edited and illustrated by Edwin Tunis, published by The World Publishing Co., Cleveland, Ohio, US, 1952, p. 57.

The King's Grief

The king was lonely, the king was sad,
Sad in his youth, when the world was glad:
Sick at heart on his lonely throne
For a friend and a brother to call his own;
There were wise old statesmen, and trusty lords,
And grey-haired prelates with saintly words,
Guiding and training his manhood's spring,—
Never a friend for a lonely king.

But a fair frank face that was void of guile
Won his heart with a song and smile,
And fearless laughter and reckless joy
Rang passing sweet to a weary boy;
Comrade in sport and comrade in play,
(Together sorry, together gay,)
Ready a jest and a laugh to fling,—
Brother and friend to the lonely king.

But faintly at first thro' the palace walls
Dark whispers came to the king's high halls;
Of a crushed realm bleeding for one man's gain,
And a people that called to their king in vain,—
Of licensed murder, and unbound shame,
And foul wrong wrought in a king's pure name,—
Fire and torment, to wrest and wring;
Alas! and alas for the lonely king!

King Ferdinand of Serena.
Ramon, his friend.

KING: Count Ramon,—since tomorrow thou must die,
And seeing thou hast been nearer to our heart
Than any other,—we have called you here
To bid thee farewell—

RAMON: Ferdinand,—my brother!

KING. Nay, Ramon! Not thy brother, but thy king,—
Who has so loved thee,—whom thou hast so wronged,—

Whom thou hast blinded with thy winning ways,
And led along false paths of carelessness,—
Glad roads that lead to ruin.

RAMON: O my king!
When have I wronged thee? When has not this heart
Been true as steel to thee? O wert thou lone,
Throneless,—forlorn,—with none to give thee aid,—
This hand should still be thine; this hand should bleed
To its last drop, to save thee!

KING: Ah, my Ramon!
If one should lead a shepherd from his flock,
And win his soul to sweet forgetfulness,
And while he slept, call up the ravening wolves
To pray upon his charge,—were this a friend?
Ramon, I am the shepherd of this realm,
And who wrongs this, wrongs me: there lies your sin;
O, were I throneless, saidst thou?
Were it so,
We might have lived together, happy boys,
And led rejoicing lives from day to day
And never dreamed of sorrow. But alas!
Thou hast come nigh and won a lonely king,—
After thy kind, thou has been true to me:
And yet I cannot save thee: if I could,
I would not.

RAMON: Yet this hand has lain in thine;
Thy lips have called me brother:
Ferdinand,
Look from the window yonder!
Dost thou not
See how the sunlight glances off the sea
Where we have sailed, such summer days as this,
And sworn strong vows of friendship: we have row'd,
Hawk'd, hunted, roamed together: in this room
We have play'd and feasted in the winter eves:
Ferdinand, I am young:—we both are young;—
You will not let me die.

KING: Ay,—so saw I
But yesterday: mine eyes are opened now:
There lies Serena with her thousand roofs,
And there my duty: where I used to see
A world made fair for me to revel in,
I see a thousand deeds and destinies
That I have fail'd to watch o'er:—broken laws

That I have fail'd to guard:—and trampled rights
That I have fail'd to keep: and this for thee:

Oh, Ramon, Ramon, you have taught a king
To make his realm a playground,—led away
Him who should be a guardian to his realm
To paths free lads may play in: and my people
Call'd me all vainly from my dalliance;
I am more theirs than they are mine: farewell,
Farewell for ever! I must let thee die:
Thou hast drunk of power and place, and sat with kings:
Thou hast duped me,—wronged my people bitterly:
Therefore, farewell!

RAMON: Hast thou not also sinn'd,
Who hast made merry with me,—given thy power
To me, and when the hour of reckoning comes
Puttest me by?

KING: Ah, bitter, bitter truth!
Mine, doubly mine, the sorrow and the sin,—
Who set a slight thing in the place of princes
Because his ways were winsome.
Yet farewell,
Thou who wast once my friend!

RAMON: False, false indeed!
Such is the faith of kings.

KING: Ah! such that soon
When they strike off that dear, dear head of thine,
My heart will go down bleeding to thy grave
Where I would fain lie with thee: and whene'er
I look on happy scenes we used to know,
My heart will ache for thee: and I shall hold
A silent sorrow on my lonely throne;
Such is the faith of kings: and such their grief.

The king grows old upon his throne,—
Steadfast in justice, strong of will,
Tender to hear a wrong'd one's moan,
And stern to ill;
None knows how, since his boyhood's day,
Old grief dwells 'neath that smile serene;
None knows how, in his heart, for aye
A grave is green.

❖ ❖ ❖ ❖ ❖

From *Men of Men*, by Cicely Fox Smith, published by Sampson Low, Marston & Co., London, UK, 1900, pp. 107-113.

The Fairies' Child

She lived beside the edge of a sweep of heather
In a lone cot by the rill,
Where the wold and the fertile farmland came together,
And the winds ne'er are still:
Her hair was like ripening corn with the sunlight in it;
Her feet were swift as the deer;
And her voice was glad and sweet as the song of a linnet,
And her laugh was crystal-clear.

But once on a day the air was filled with wailing,
And grief long and sore,
For she came not home when the evening light was failing,
And they ne'er saw her more;
Forth in the early morn she had hastened fleetly
Over the leaping rill,
At the sound of a fairy's laughter ringing sweetly,
And a call from the hill.

Gone, she was gone thro' the close-barr'd gates of Faerie,
That magic eve in June;
But still, when the winds are loose and the moor is eerie,
In the light of a fitful moon,
On the edge of the moor she wanders calling, calling,
She more than mortals fair,
And she dries the tears that will keep falling, falling,
With her long, streaming hair;
And mothers shudder and clasp their children nearer,
When the wind's sounding shrill,
Lest they hear the voice of the lost one ringing clearer,
And the call from the hill.

❖   ❖   ❖   ❖   ❖

From *Men of Men*, by Cicely Fox Smith, published by Sampson Low, Marston & Co., London, UK, 1900, pp. 114-115.

A Seaside Church

A gray-roof'd church on a hill, set in the sound of the waves,
Hearing them all day long on the shingle murmuring,
Looking out from the slope with its tiny acre of graves,
Over the smiling sea, gold-green like a peacock's wing.

Many a mile to the West, deep-blue to the noonday sky
Stretches the waste of waters, wide and windy and free,
Flecked with dashes of white where the swift-winged seagulls fly,
Singing down on the shore the endless song of the sea.

Calm it is now: last night the waves were wild enough,
Trampling up on the shingle like colts in the fields at play;
By the white crests out on the sea you can tell that the night was rough,
Where the breakers leap on the bar, far out in the sunlit bay.

See, by the shadowy porch. A poor dead bird on the ground,
Too weak to cope with the wind, that thundered so wild and high,
Beaten hither and thither, drenched and 'wildered and drowned,
Driven home from the sea to its Father's house to die.

Poor little broken wing! Poor draggled feathery breast!
Flung with thy happy life by the might of the western blast
To the little church on the hill where the seaboard people rest—
Men who have followed the sea till the great sea took them at last.

Here at our feet they lie, where the salt winds merrily blow,
Telling their tales of the ocean, wide and windy and free,
Here where the rollers sound on the shingle far below,
Singing down on the shore the olden song of the sea.

❖ ❖ ❖ ❖ ❖

From *Men of Men*, by Cicely Fox Smith, published by Sampson Low, Marston & Co., London, UK, 1900, pp. 116-117.

The Lay of the White Heifer

Home from the fields the kine came slowly winding,
Thro' the soft summer twilight, calm and still,
Up the steep lanes, between the hanging hedgerows,
To the little lonely farmstead by the hill.

Slowly they came, the black and brown and dappled,
And with them pacing to the open door,
With nostrils breathing scent of sweetest clover,
A snow-white heifer none had seen before.

Unknown it came up from the evening meadows;
No trace of whence it wandered could be found;
No one had ever known so fair a creature—
So white and sleek, in all the country round.

Within the farm the aged wife lay dying,
The grey old witch the village held in fear:
And sudden, in the silence of the midnight,
She started up some distant sound to hear.

"O lassie, don't you hear my baby calling,
My baby that I buried long ago:
Calling across the meadows: 'Mother, mother,'
Calling and calling ever, soft and low?"

"Oh no, it's but the snow-white heifer lowing,
Across the upland meadow, far away,"
Answered the trembling village maiden
That watched beside her to the break of day.

"Oh no, I hear my little baby calling:
I know her voice across the weary years;
She's come to take me where she went aforetime,
And left me with my sorrow and my tears."

"I lived my life unloved, and all unloving,
Because my heart was hardened by my woe;
But yet I think they'll let me see my baby,
My little baby that left me years ago."

Loud howled the wind around the quaint old gables,
Fierce on the shaken casement beat the rain;
And in the dark was heard above the tempest
A hand that tapped against the window-pane.

They spoke of wondrous happenings in the night-time,
A finger on the latch—a fair white form—
One flitting swiftly thro' the darkened chamber,
Two passing hand-in-hand into the storm.

The old wife died before the dawn came creeping
Over the eastern uplands veiled in rain:
They said she smiled in death: and since that morning
None saw the snow-white heifer there again.

❖   ❖   ❖   ❖   ❖

From *Men of Men*, by Cicely Fox Smith, published by Sampson Low, Marston & Co., London, UK, 1900, pp. 118-121.

The Little Serving-Boy

Thou, mounted on thy gallant steed,
A mighty man dost ride,
And I, thy little serving-boy,
Run singing at thy side.

Thou thinkest I who follow thee
Am but a thoughtless boy,
That warbles, like the forest birds,
From fullness of my joy.

Yet does my careless caroling
Bring to thy lips a smile,

My feet run lightly at the thought
For many a weary mile.

Oh, didst thou know how oft my feet
Were aching as I ran,
Tho' I am but thy serving-boy,
And thou a mighty man,

Thou wouldest lift me from the ground
And set me on thy knee,
And glad me with thy noble smile,
And let me ride with thee.

So thou, thy shield upon thy arm,
O'er hill and dale dost ride,
And I, thy little serving-boy,
Run singing by thy side.

❖ ❖ ❖ ❖ ❖

From *Men of Men*, by Cicely Fox Smith, published by Sampson Low, Marston & Co., London, UK, 1900, pp. 122-123.

The *Bride* of Leith

The *Bride* o' Leith swings out to sea,
Breasting the snow-white foam,
And the pier is thronged with waving hands,
For she has far to roam;
Her sails are white in the morning light:
God send her safely home!

The captain's wife is lone at home,
She spins full wearily,
And night and morn she kneels and prays,
(So slow the moments flee),
"God prosper all good mariners
That sail upon the sea!"

The *Bride* o' Leith steers home again,
Not lightly does she ride,
There's goodly cargo in her hold,
There's blood upon her side:
In the trough of the sea her laden keel
Rolls in the plunging tide.

There are folks who watch for a ship that ne'er
Comes up within their ken,
Who watch for a goodly merchantman
That shall ne'er come home again:
There are maids in Portsmouth town to-day
That weep for murdered men.

The night was dark and the waves ran high,
And loud the storm-wind's roar,
And white and aghast, with one accord
The frighted seamen swore
They saw thro' the mist-rack and the rain
A ship that went before.

No lights shone out from her looming side,
No lamp at her masthead;
No hail came over the boiling surf
From the vessel of the dead;
And a dead man stood at the helm and steered,
And the waves in her wake were red.

And, cowering down on the wave-swept decks,
Betwixt the night and morn,
They saw the hull of a drifting ship
Close on them swiftly borne,
That the *Bride* o' Leith robbed days agone,
And left to sink forlorn.

The *Bride* o' Leith lies sunken deep,
The avenger lieth nigh,
Thro' rotting spar and sail and rope
The shuddering tides drive by,
And none shall know till the judgment day
Where those who manned her lie.

❖ ❖ ❖ ❖ ❖

From *Men of Men*, by Cicely Fox Smith, published by Sampson Low, Marston & Co., London, UK, 1900, pp. 124-126.

Conall's Daughter

Wind from the eastward whose breath goes seaward surely
Over the cold grey rollers that hold me apart,
Would I were a white gull to hasten wither thou goest,—
To sail on wide wings to the isle of my heart;
Home to the lightning lough with a far glimpse of the ocean,
To the hills that surely forget not Conall's daughter,—
Home to the white strand, and Fanad, and green Inisowen,
And the woods down to the water.

The soaring curlews over the glimmering bog-pools,
Rising and falling across the twilight moor,
Crying and calling like ghosts in the rose-red light of the sunset,
Do they tell the same sad tale they told of yore?
My little white goats that crop the short grass of the forelands,
Do they ever bleat for their mistress, Conall's daughter,
Far from the white strand, and Fanad, and green Inisowen,
And the woods down to the water?

Often in dreams of the night I see them clearly,
I see the dark hill and the cornlands fertile and fair,
I smell the blue turf smoke going up from the valley,
And all the same as it was when I wandered there;
Dreams of the night,—but yet like wounded birds I clasp them
Warm in the hungry heart of Conall's daughter,
Far from the white strand, and Fanad, and green Inisowen,
And the woods down to the water.

❖ ❖ ❖ ❖ ❖

From *Men of Men*, by Cicely Fox Smith, published by Sampson Low, Marston & Co., London, UK, 1900, pp. 127-128.

Brandan's Isle

Far in the West lies sleeping
Brandan's Isle in the sea;
The wind and the waves together
Moan round it ceaselessly.

Only on clear calm evenings,
When the sun is low in the West,
You can see on the far horizon
Saint Brandan's Isle of the Blest.

The winds keep guard there ever,
Watching, with folded wings,
To drive from the dreaming islet
All touch of earthly things.

And if any vessel come there,
The winds blow out from the shore,
And at morn, when the wind abateth,
The Isle is seen no more.

In the Isle of unending summer,
Under the stainless blue,
Lie in their patient slumber,
The Saint and his faithful few.

They sleep till the last loud trumpet
Shall break their age-long rest,
And the sea shall pass, and the sunset,
And Brandan's Isle the Blest.

❖ ❖ ❖ ❖ ❖

From *Men of Men*, by Cicely Fox Smith, published by Sampson Low, Marston & Co., London, UK, 1900, pp. 129-130.

The Calling of the Birds

Have you heard the seagull calling, the seagull out at sea?
And sorry is its voice, though its wings are wide and free!
Though the wind blows to the land, and the waves laugh on the strand,
There are tears, there are tears in the calling on the sea.

The waters of the wide lough are racing cheerily:
The white waves leap and lighten for the joy of open sea:
The clouds pass over lightly, and the sun glints on it brightly,
And the strong ships spread their wings out and sail for open sea.

Have you heard the curlew calling, the curlew on the hill?
And sorry is its voice o'er the moorland floating shrill:
Though the day is fair and fine, and the breeze a draught of wine,
There are tears, there are tears in the calling on the hill.

The sun is shining fair,—is shining on the hill,
On the cabin by the bog, and the water lying still,
On the heather blooming sweet, and the gold-green windy wheat,
And the brown bog and the turf-stack and the purple on the hill.

❖ ❖ ❖ ❖ ❖

From *Men of Men*, by Cicely Fox Smith, published by Sampson Low, Marston & Co., London, UK, 1900, pp. 131-132.

Rhodalind

In the palace garden-close
Many a flower buds and blows,—
Many a lily, ne'er a rose;
And, when on the purple fells
Hum the bees in heather bells,—
Dreamy eyes and listless mind,
Wandered there Queen Rhodlind.

When the sun drew toward the West,
There she walked, in splendour drest,
And her head drooped on her breast,
And her pale lips never smiled
As the summer hours she whiled,—
Pluckt the lilies, passing by,—
Heedless, let them fall and die.

But as once she wandered slow
Where the flowers bud and blow,
In the summer sunshine's glow,
Close against the eastern wall
Where the slanting sunbeams fall,
Scenting all the sleepy air,
Lo! a rose-tree blossomed there.

And to pluck its flowers she sped
Till her snowy hands were red
With the blood its thorns had shed;
And she reveled 'mid her bowers,
Till her lips were like her flowers,
Ruddy as the reddest rose,
Blooming in her garden-close.

❖ ❖ ❖ ❖ ❖

From *Men of Men*, by Cicely Fox Smith, published by Sampson Low, Marston & Co., London, UK, 1900, pp. 133-134.

The Witch of Mull

"Witch of Mull, the strangers here
Come to wreak their vengeance drear:
Call the wind and call the wrack;
Drown them, drive them, beat them back!"
Wind and wave are wild in Morvern.

"Gormla, speed! Their magic powers
Calm the deep and baffle ours:
Aid us, thou who know'st full well
Strongest brew and blackest spell!"
Wind and wave are wild in Morvern.

Magpies twelve upon the mast
Call aloud to wave and blast"
"Bonnily on Morvern shore
Shall we feast when all is o'er!"
Wind and wave are wild in Morvern.

Harried seaward, fast they flee
Wind and wrack and raging sea:
Hard and grey the rocks before,—
Hard their bed on Morvern shore!
Wind and wave are wild in Morvern.

Bonny dead men on the sand,—
Dead and drowned on Morvern strand,—
Broken mast and battered hull,—
Glad the witches are in Mull!
Wind and wave are wild in Morvern.

❖ ❖ ❖ ❖ ❖

From *Men of Men*, by Cicely Fox Smith, published by Sampson Low, Marston & Co., London, UK, 1900, pp. 135-136.

Hic(ks) Jacet

Go, heap against your native race
Slander on slander, lie on lie;
Go, trumpet in God's sacred places
Your brazen throated blasphemy,

Go, turn to your own coward ends
The Church in whose proud name you preach;
The shelter that the pulpit lends
Gives licence to your traitor speech

Sacred, the savage bloodstained rule
Sacred you hold the Dervish might
Sacred, the traitors hireling tool
The Fenian slaying in the night.
Yet, when your trampled kindred call,
You bid us stretch no hand to save:
The God who sees the sparrow fall
Sees not, you deem an English slave.

Go, gloze a tyrant's vices o'er;
Say true is false and false is true:
Go, plunge the reeling world in gore
That all mankind may speak of you.
Go pander to the mean and vain
To make your earthly place secure
Not all the mitres man can gain
Can make a craven's honour pure.

❖ ❖ ❖ ❖ ❖

From *The Manchester Courier and Lancashire General Advertiser*, Wednesday, 24 January, 1900. This early poem was prefaced with a reference to Canon Hick's sermon: "Manchester Cathedral, January 21st 1900."

The title, "Hic Jacet" is Latin and translates as "here lies" or an "epitaph" and the poet is making a play on words. The column heading over the poem is "RADICAL CLERICS AND THE WAR." For the poet to call the poem "HIC(KS) JACET" indicates that she is directing the poem towards Canon Hicks, of Manchester Cathedral, who was criticized by three other correspondents to the paper for remarks he had made—from the pulpit—concerning the Boer War. The poet was an ardent supporter of the British in their war against the Boers of South Africa. She followed the campaign closely in the newspapers and wrote many poems in tribute to the victorious British troops.

The Lesson of Manchester North

"Three cheers for Kruger"—far away
Anxious he waits for England's voice
To give him heart once more to say:
"A Liberal's in—rejoice, rejoice!"
Wire the good news to Afric's shore
One seat for Kruger's safe once more!

By shuffling speech and half-told lie
Spouted galore from tub and stump,
By issues shunned and elbowed by,
And pratings of the parish pump,
By turncoat lies and two-faced play,
One seat for Kruger's saved to-day.

You learnt what decent minds detest:
You learnt and shuddered in your shoes:
The principles you last professed

You knew too well we would not choose.
You heard your seat's sure death-knell toll:
You dropped them like a red-hot coal.

You trapped men blindfold to your end,
You drugged their doubts, you hushed their fears,
You swore you were the soldier's friend;
You kept the truth from English ears:
What heed you your chameleon past?
One seat for Kruger's safe at last.

O men of England, hark and heed:
Be warned in time "lest you forget;"
Shall fear and hate, in word and deed,
Treason and spite, be bygones yet?
Well can they lie, and cringe, and bow:—
"Three cheers for Kruger:"—hear them now!

❖ ❖ ❖ ❖ ❖

From *The Manchester Courier and Lancashire General Advertiser*, Manchester, UK, April 10, 1900, p. 6.

False Colours

O, preacher of a craven creed!
Some meeker pupils you must find:
Your days are in the yellow "leaf,"
You are not to a Briton's mind.
Yet, since you chose the coward's part,
Pipe your old tune, as best you can:
Play fair, (if such a thing you know),
And show your colours like a man!

O, preacher of a craven creed!
We know you glad to run and hide,—
To set, for your own safety's sake,
Some foolish lady by your side.
True pupil of your brother Boer,
Cautious, you slip behind your back
Your quondam flag of craven white,
And hide—behind the Union Jack!

O, preacher of a craven creed!
Pack up your carpet-bag again:
That flag you shame upon your door
Will prove a falsehood all too plain,
Go, share with Paul his headlong fall:
Reap—as you once were fain to sow:
Pray heaven for a manly heart,
And let Old England's ensign go!

From *The Manchester Courier and Lancashire General Advertiser*, Manchester, UK, May 17, 1900, p. 7.

The Old Love and the New

To the leaderless party 'twas Bannerman spoke:
"If our sails be not trimmed, there are seats to be broke:
Let us haste, ere too late, our old courses to rue;
It's off with the old love, and on with the new!"

Chorus: They've done with Oom Paul, they've done with the Boer,
              They swallow the words they have spoken before;
              Now show them full plainly, you good men and true,
              They're off with the old love—not on with the new.

Remember their hopes to give England a fall,
Their Boer Committees, their letters to Paul:
Remember the ends they so loved to pursue,
Ere they fled from the old love to plead with the new.

His hope to the end, they must topple with Paul,
Their Monds and their Brunners, their Lawtons and all;
They reap as they sowed—and for all they can do,
They're off with the old love, not on with the new.

So show them your meaning, you good men and true,
Your hearts are true British, your colours True Blue;
When the polling day comes, oh, what will they do,
If they're off with the old love—not on with the new?

❖ ❖ ❖ ❖ ❖

From the Manchester *Courier and Lancashire General Advertiser*, Manchester, UK, September 29, 1900, p. 14.

Here the young poet has composed another satirical song about the critics of the Boar War. Set to the music, of the Air: Bonnie Dundee

---

Dr Clark's 'Plaint

I'm sick of the sound of "pro-Boer,"
And everyone will call me so;
Can you tell me of a safe seat in Britain,
To which a pro-Boer can go!

Chorus: Wrap me up in that old borrowed banner,
              And say a pro-Boer lies low, lies low;
              There isn't a safe seat in Britain, Britain,
              To which a pro-Boer can go.

They've sent us all flying in Glasgow,
And Manchester's got a new school;
We're too late for a seat with the Welshmen,
Where it's always so safe as a rule.

There's Scott and myself and the small fry,
I fear we'll be getting a fall.
Oh! is there no plan to invite us,
Where there won't be a contest at all?

I fear they won't have me in Caithness
And England won't have me I know;
I would I were sitting with Labby,
For the place where the bootmakers grow.

They've kicked out Sir Wilfred and Stanhope,
They've laid out my friends in a row, a row;
And if they won't have me in Caithness
Oh! Where shall the pro-Boer go?

❖ ❖ ❖ ❖ ❖

From *The Manchester Courier and Lancashire General Advertiser*, Manchester, UK, October, 8, 1900, p. 6.

The poet added this note with reference to Mr. Balfour's speech: "The pro-Boer party hide their rags and tatters under the ample folds of the Union Jack." Set to the music, Air: "The Tarpaulin Jacket."

Victoria the Well-Beloved

Glorious her crown came to her: and more proud
It goes to him who follows: not in grief
Wholly, as those who have no hope, to-day
The Great Queen's ships draw shoreward, and the guns
Thunder along the oceans: and the flag
That never dipp'd its folds before a foe
Droops low in sorrow: not in grief alone
Goes forth the last proud martial pageantry
Meet for a soldier's daughter — England's Queen.
Her name shall live for ever: she who reign'd
Not like the stalwart warrior-kings of old,
Far-off, alone, and dreaded; but whose life,
Tender and true and womanly thro' all,
Made throne and people one in links of love:
Most royal and most loyal, who so knew
And loved her people, that her fame and theirs
Go hand in hand along the ringing years
One glory to the end of humankind:
Who thro' a long life of sweet sacrifice
So kept the path of honour and of truth
That tho' all crowns beside shake to their fall
The throne she held shall tremble not: her name
Stands starlike on the brows of history,
Last light in that Imperial diadem,
The waxing glory of a thousand years
From Alfred to Victoria: now at last,
True to the call of duty till the end,
Gone, full of years and honour, to repose.

We may not bow too long before the tomb,
While on the thundering road of centuries
The wheels of Empire run, and may not rest.
Yea! from her grave whose first and noblest thought
Was ever Duty, Duty points the way
To where. Beside the throne she kept so pure,
Steady amid all lights that leap and wane
Burn the twin fires of Loyalty and Love.

❖ ❖ ❖ ❖ ❖

From *The Manchester Courier and Lancashire General Advertiser*, Manchester, UK, February 4, 1901, p. 5.

The poet's tribute to Queen Victoria.

The Crown of Gold

There was grief in the land,—
Fear and ill-omen:
The foe was at hand
With his spears and his bowmen.
Famine was in the town,
Sorrow and crying,
And the sun seemed going down
On the land and her renown,
And the Queen was dying.

Dying 'mid want and war
In her youth and beauty,
She who had striven so sore
With a royal duty,—
Dying, poor widowed one,
In a time of sorrow,
Leaving her little son
To a dark to-morrow.

She lay near to death
In a twilight room:
Faintly came her breath:
In the gathering gloom
She lay with closed eyes now
As if a trance had bound her,
With still mouth and white brow
And her gold hair round her.

And she woke suddenly
With a great cry of fear,
And the waitingmaids drew near,
For they thought her like to die.
And she spake out hastily:
"Lo, I have dreamed a dream,
Loves are not true to me
Nor friends what they seem.
There's nought true at all

Nor hope for to-morrow,—
Nothing but tears to fall
And nought i' the world but sorrow."

"Go forth now, hither call
My vassals one and all;
Bid them to ask of me
What most they crave,
Yea, and whate'er it be
I will give cheerily,
Eere I go to the grave."

And they went forth weeping
And called in, as she bade,
Lords and courtiers, great and small,
From courtyard and hall,
And serving-man and maid.
And her old hound came creeping,
Creeping to her side,
Laid his head down, calm and grand,
In her listless hand,
And lay there satisfied.

"Lo," she said, "speak out, I pray,
O my servants, tried and true!
Fear not, but say your say
What you will that I should do:
Nought will I say you nay
That I may grant you!"

O and swift the answers came:
Nought of faltering, nought of shame
As they spake their hearts' desire,—
Wealth and power,
A fortune for a dower,
Or the half of a shire.
Then the Queen cried out again,
And there stood a mist of tears
In her eyes of blue:
"O my dream was true,
Nor false were my fears,
Nor my doubtings vain.
There's nought i' the world but sorrow:
O what shall my babe do
In the dark to-morrow?"
And there came in tramping then
All her great grim fighting-men,
With their weather-beaten faces
Scarred and seamed with war's rough traces,
Cap of steel, and sword on thigh.
Then one spake up huskily"
"Lady Queen, this boon we pray.
Little wealth, we know indeed,

Have these hard times left us now.
Therfore since we must to-day
Somewhat ask for—we (behold!)
Ask, our one and only meed,
Even the drown of gold
From off thy brow."

Bitter flowed the salt tears down.
"Yea, take my golden crown,
And let me die.
Glad of an end am I,
For there's nought i' the world true,
Nought i' the world but sorrow;
Yet what shall my babe do
In the hard to-morrow?"

Swiftly came they then,
All her great grim fighting-men
Who had served her thro' long years.
Spur on heel and sword on thigh,
Half-smiling thro' their tears
Came they nigh.
Forth swept each cold blue blade
As a rough brown hand was laid
On her locks of gold.
And they passed one by one,—and behold
Each in his strong finger twining
Held, as it were wealth indeed,
The Queen's last meed
A lock of golden hair, gleaming and shining!

And she smiled again at last
Ere her spirit passed,
And her sea-blue eyes were glad
'Neath her sweet shorn brows serene.
And thus sake the Queen:
"O no longer sad
Am I for the morrow!
For I know in time of sorrow
While yet in all the realm
One bears in his helm
The guerdon that I gave,
My son shall never vainly crave,
Tho' ill days betide him,
A true sword to defend him,
A true heart to befriend him,
A true friend beside him!"

❖ ❖ ❖ ❖ ❖

From *Wings of the Morning*, edited by Cicely Fox Smith, published by Elkin Mathews, London, UK, 1904, pp. 1-6.

The Wayfarers

Now farewell, you kindly folk,
For our rest is ended:
Out into the wind and rain
Go the roving men again,
Whom ye have befriended.

We have sat beside your hearth,
Feasted with you gladly;
We whose way is on the seas,
We have stayed to take our ease,
Yet we go not sadly.

When the ropes are white with rime
Oft we shall remember,
How we sat at Christmas-tide
Honoured guests your hearth beside
In the bleak December.

When against the plunging keel
Crested seas are pouring,
Haply we shall deem that ye
Think of mariners at sea
When the gales are roaring.

We shall wander far and near
(Yet we shall remember)
Out into the driving rain
Go the sailor-men again
In the bleak December.

Now farewell, you homely folk,
Sisters, wives and mothers,
Out into the wind and rain
And the salt-spray of the main
Go your roving brothers.
We have talked with sailor-men
While the casements rattle,
Heard them tell strange tales by whiles
Of mysterious Eastern isles,
Kings of Ind, and battle.

They have told us wondrous tales,—
Tales of death and daring,
Seas no other seaman knew,—
Shown us signs to prove them true,
Mighty shoulders baring.

So farewell, you kindred all;
Yet we shall remember
Oft the firelight on the pane
Shining thro' the driving rain

In the bleak December.

Now farewell, you roving men,
Seaward from us faring,
In whose hearts the sailor-folk
Roused adventure when the spoke
Words of death and daring.

Haply, after many years,—
Swarthy, sturdy, free men,
Ye will come to us again,
Come as came the sailor-men
Who have made you seamen.

When the winter hurricane
Sets the doors a-shaking,
In the nights when wind and rain
Beat against the window-pane,
We shall shudder, waking.

When about the twilight room
Firelight shades are fleeting,
Often we shall sit and watch
For a hand upon the latch
And a voice of greeting.

O remember on the deep,
When you come, returning
Home from off the seas again
Out of wind and driving rain,
Bright the fire is burning.

❖ ❖ ❖ ❖ ❖

From *Wings of the Morning*, edited by Cicely Fox Smith, published by Elkin Mathews, London, UK, 1904, pp. 7-9.

The King's Shame

Hear now the tale of Rodolf, and the grief
Of Osric, and the sorrow of the isles.

Osric the bold, a prince of the far North,
Long-limbed, and brown with buffeting salt-sea winds,
Once trod the busy streets of Istamboul;
And there black hair and eyes and ruddy lips
And slim sweet limbs took hold of his soul
And led his fierce heart captive. So it chanced
That, steering Northward from his voyaging,
He carried to his stormy realm a bride,
And set a slave upon the throne of queens,
And all his wild sea-captains drank to her.
But when the wind was high on winter eves,

And surges boomed all night along the shore,
Ever her heart went pining to the South
From the high chamber where she sat alone
Hearing the shouting revel of the King,
And clung and cried above her crying babe
Till the wild night was waning; and the light
Passed from her eyes, the roses from her mouth,
And left her but a pining, palefaced thing,
White with dark hair about her, like a ghost.
Yet her sad heart took solace in her boy,
The grim King's darling, Rodolf. Strong and straight
He grew up like his sire, but lithe and slim,
The mirror of his mother, when she glowed
With all the fiery beauty of the South.
Light on his feet and nimble as the deer,
Often the grey old King would watch with pride
The heir the heavens had granted. And at last,
When autumn hills were purple, in the morn
The courtyard rang with armed men and steeds;
And trembling, half in fear and half in joy,
The fierce old warrior buckled on the sword
At his son's side, and, standing by the door,
His brave blue eyes a mist of rising tears,
Sent out the pride and pillar of his house
To win his spurs in battle. And he stood
Gazing, until the last glint of their arms
Flashed farewell from the skyline: while above
A white face from the window saw them go
With sad eyes red with tears: then the old King
Went in unto his seat beside the hearth,
And sat all day there, gnawing at his beard
And eating out his proud heart silently.

. . . .

The hall grew dark, and red across the floor
Lay the last streak of sunset, where the King
Dozed in his seat besides the fading fire,
And dreamed like an old hound of chases done
And fights long faught and ended. All at once
There came a hurrying and a rush of tongues
Out of the silent court, and cries of grief
Sounded about the gateway; and there broke
Before the startled King a wild-eyed man
Splashed head to heel with battle and with mire,
Crying: "O King, thine army is no more—
Thy men are slain and scattered in the fight!"
Then the old warrior, rising to his feet,
Shrunk not nor wavered at the bitter tale,
Saying: "Speak on." And faltering in his speech

Spoke on the courier: "In the woods it chanced
That as we rode on straggling carelessly
The foemen fell upon us unawares."
Still the old warrior said: "Speak on, nor fear!
How died the flower of Norway?" And the man
Looked up and down the chamber restlessly,
Ere yet he spake: "Red lie the ranked dead
Beside the fallen banner of the King."
Then fiercely rang the question: "Once and for all,
How died my son?" Unwilling came the truth:
"Fled at first shock of battle for his life,
And none was there could stay him."
Reeled and shook
The old King, as a lordly stag might reel
Struck in the chase: then cried to those around
With grey-fringed lips twitching in gasps of rage:
"Fools we ha' bred, good lack, and knaves a few,
But never was there reared a coward yet
To shame the throne we fought for. Bring my horse,
Bring me my sword and shield: tho' I be old,
I am not yet too old to rid my realm
Of such a ruler." So with quivering hands
He girded on his sword, and took his way
To where his old charger stamped and pawed
And neighed to hear his footstep. But a cry
Rang shivering thro' the chamber as he went,
And that wan woman, calling on his name,
Ran to him, pleading for the son she bore
By all the love he ever vowed to her
Beside blue Southern waters. Blind with rage
He heeded not at all her misery:
He felt her drenching tears about his feet,
He heard her wild voice crying out to him,
But nothing said he save one bitter curse:
"Slave,—mother of slaves, let go!" So, spurning her
He went, and heeded not her last wild cry,
And all her fading beauty lying there,
And the scared crowd of frightened serving-maids
Crying and wailing that the Queen was dead.
All the long night hot-foot he rode and spurred
Across the ridges, thro' complaining woods
And blown pines black against the stormy sky
Low-streaked with dead-gold levels,—till he spied
Far on before a dark form on the road
And felt his fierce heart flame again, to know
That there his son fled in vile panic dread
From battle, death and honour. And he spurred
More fiercely, and more fierce was his resolve
For vengeance for his shame. The night was spent,

The dawn came up forlornly from the east
And glimmered on a lone lake of the hills,
When that wild fugitive heard fast and close
The drum of hoofs along the frosty road
And turning saw the fierce face at his back,
And pitiless arm and keen avenging sword,
And knew his life was ended.
And the sword
Drove past the outstretched hands, and the wild cry
Died on the parted lips, and the eyes closed,
And the small graceful head drooped like a flower
Even as he fell and lay. And his lorn sire
Dismounted and stood by him where he lay,
And spoke aloud his sorrow and his scorn:
"Blind fool that I have been, ever to dream
There could come aught but shame, or hope to see
The fire of princes in the souls of slaves!
When was there ever any good of it?
Did e'er the wild bull seek the fields of men,
The eagle leave his eyrie for the plain?
Had I so shamed the beast that nourished me,
Would she, mine own stern mother, so have sought
To save the coward from his fate? Nay, more!
She would have struck me down with her own hand
If none beside would do it—never wept
And prayed so for a craven." His voice broke,
For, on a sudden, something in the pose
Of the dead boy, and something in the face
Caught at his heart and sent it aching back
To memories of his youthful voyaging,
And joys and dear dead loves of long ago
Under the orange groves of Istamboul.
And like a sudden fire his fury died,
So that the red sword left his nerveless hand,
And, bowing down besides the son he slew,
He clasped and chafed and kissed the loose white hands
And the cold brow whereon remorseful tears
Fell slow and sorrowful. And he broke out,
Forgetting all his rage and bitterness,
And the lost honour of his royal line,
At the sight of the dark hair and ruddy lips
So like to those whereon his kisses burned
When first he loved the slave-girl, long ago:
"Heart of my heart, my white dove from the south,
Mine, mine, alone the blame! Forgive, forgive!
O ere I go back to my lonely hall,
Let me but dream again a little while
Of old unclouded days of long ago,
And call back all the treasured tenderness

Forgotten with your beauty." So awhile
He sat there with his head upon his hands,
And in an hour rose up, and mounting rode
Back to the stricken stronghold of his sires,
Slowly, and no man knew that he had wept.
And never gave he utterance to his grief
Save to send spearmen forth along the way,
Bidding them bring the body of the Prince
And give him burial worthy of a King.

❖   ❖   ❖   ❖   ❖

From *Wings of the Morning*, edited by Cicely Fox Smith, published by Elkin Mathews, London, UK, 1904, pp. 10-16.

The Comrade

"Father, I gave my gold and gear,
Cattle and goods full tale,
To save my soul from utter dark:
May this at all avail?"

"Son, ere I know what sin was thine
Surely I may not say:
Yet, for the sake of thy great gifts,
Thy Mother Church will pray."

"Father, a comrade had I once,
Yea, truest friend to me;
Friends were we when we both were young:
He died on the gallows-tree."

"Son, for the hot in of thy youth
Thou shalt be freely shriven:
Yea, tho' your friend's soul burn in hell,
Thou art indeed forgiven."

"And if that friend's soul burn in hell,
There shall mine burn also:
And whither his dear soul hath gone
Thither I too would go."

"Not in the place of souls accurst
Shall we two meet again:
Surely he hath reward of Thee,
O Christ, who died for men!"

"Mine was the neck that should have felt
The hangman's rope that day,
And mine the feet that should have trod
Along the shameful way."

"All for my sake that death he died
And bore the black disgrace,
Nor spoke the word should set him free
And bind me in his place."

"He let them bind him hand and foot,
Gazing on me the while:
No blame in those unfearing eyes
And that serenest smile."

"And when that stainless soul of his
Passed upward to God's gate,
My manhood that had left me then
Came to me all too late."

"Fain would I have flung aside
With one releasing blow,
The worthless life he bought with his,—
The life I hated so!"

"Yet—that my blame might be atoned
From year to bitter year—
I, aching for the death I shunned,
Lived out my penance here."

"Somewhere across the lonely stars
His spirit wakeneth;
And love that gave its life for me
Clings to me still in death."

"I think he listens for my voice
All through the seraph-song,
And watches by the golden gate,
Hoping I come ere long."

"I thin he waits to welcome me
Unto God's glorious aisle,—
To greet me with those steadfast eyes
And that serenest smile."

"Would I not give my gold and gear,
Yea, unto seven times seven,
So I might hope to grasp again
My comrade's hand in heaven?"

❖ ❖ ❖ ❖ ❖

From *Wings of the Morning*, edited by Cicely Fox Smith, published by Elkin Mathews, London, UK, 1904, pp. 17-20.

Queen Radegund

Between the dark and the day,
To the King's room where he lay
With crucifix and winding-sheet,
And chanting brethren two or three,
Queen Radegund came silently.

And she laid aside her crown
And let her dark hair fall adown,—
Fall about her white wan face
And he royal figure's grace,
And her wild eyes, strange and wide.

And she knelt down at his side,
Murmured to him soft and low,
Full of love and full of woe.

Sand the monks by his bed:
"Lord have mercy on our dead!"
"O my love, like a star
Very dear and very far,
Loving-hearted, leal and true!
I have lived, nor ever knew
What the hero heart you gave
To be slighted like a slave."

"Fool, I deemed it good and meet
Thou shouldst worship at my feet,
Give thy great heart's priceless treasure
For a heedless woman's pleasure,
I, unworthy to be thine,
Love of mine, love of mine!"

Not a serf in the realm
But mourns for him who held the helm.

"Wake, love, wake and live;
All thou cravedst, now I give;
Gone the wanton heart's disdain
Never more to give thee pain;
Gone the fickle coquetry
And the heart that roved from thee.
See, my kiss is on thy brow!
Are my lips not fair enow?"
Cold and still, cold and still
Lay the dead King, pale and chill.
"Little heart have I to live:

This atonement would I give,
I who, living, deemed to live
Greatest prize the world can give,—
I would give the years to be
Here to die and follow thee.
Yet I know,—yet I know
Thou wouldst never fly the woe,—
Thou wouldst ever bear the cross
Of bitter sorrow, bitter loss;
I will lay my baubles by,
All the sunshine's gaiety,
Lonely in a convent cell,
Dreaming of the past, to dwell,—
Thro' the long years silently
Dream of thee, dream of thee."

Cold and stark, cold and stark,
Lay the dead that would not hark.

"Love of mine, love of mine,
Coward am I so to pine:
Shall I live for ever so,
Selfish joy and craven woe?
Better, now thy race is run,
Do the deeds thou wouldst have done,—
Live a life more worthy thee,
Haply thou shalt smile to see,—
Serve the cause for whose fair pride
Thou hast toiled and fought and died,—
Play the part that once was thine,
Love of mine, love of mine!"

Came the sun o'er the wold,
With a flood of glorious gold,
Lit the hangings' broidered sheen,
Sleeping King and weeping Queen;
On the snow-cold face it gleamed,
So that for a while it seemed
Thro' the tears that fell like rain
That the dead lips smiled again.

❖ ❖ ❖ ❖ ❖

From *Wings of the Morning*, edited by Cicely Fox Smith, published by Elkin Mathews, London, UK, 1904, pp. 21-24.

Merchant Men (1904)

Ere the word of Kings went over on the pathway of the rover,
To the lands of hope and promise at the breaking of the day
Came a foreword of fulfilling thro' the untold future thrilling,—

Came a people born to conquest to the clearing of the way.
O the race of gallant men!
(Yet they were but merchant men!)
O the hearts, the hearts of heroes 'neath the name of merchant men!
Yea, they followed lightly after with a ready jest and laughter,
And their hearts went forth exulting, hopeful, heedless, one to ten,—
Risk they chose and bitter faring,—O the goodly deeds for daring
When they paved the ways before us in the name of merchant men!

Frontier forts on hills they knew not where the flag of England blew not,
Lonely laager on the upland, lonely watches in the night,
Friendless plains and bleak hills swelling, these they chose to be their dwelling
With the stars of Heaven above them and the camp fires burning bright.
O the lives of merchant men!
O the gallant lives of men!
Life and death in grip together on the ways of merchant men.

Yea, they knew the midnight leaguer and the dark hosts pressing eager,
And the slowly-failing powder—was your gold so mighty then?
And the lone grave in the far land, where was never stone or garland,
They who walked with Death undreading in the ways of merchant men.
O they made the road to follow,—leveled hill and raised the hollow!
(O the bones that rot and whiten in the forest and the fen!)
Wilson by the Shangani River, Clive at Plassey, names for ever,
Fought and conquered, fought and perished in the name of merchant men.
O the wars of merchant men,—
Little wars of merchant men!
O the freedom and the fighting and the lives of merchant men!

Yea, they knew the clash and glory of the battlefields of story:
Swarthy hordes of Indian Rajahs and the impis of Lo Ben,
Stalwart Sikh and fierce Mahratta saw they tremble, melt and scatter,
When they broke the hosts of princes in the name of merchant men.

Yea! Men grudge their dole of glory,—yet they set their seal on story
From the Ganges and the Goomtee to the shores of Hudson's Bay.
Leave, ah, leave the free sky o'er them and the open road before them,
Leave them room, ay, room to live in and the brave old rover's way.
O the lives, the lives of men!
O the gallant lives of men!
When the ruled and held and conquered in the name of merchant men!

Yea, O kin who half forget them and the perils that beset them,
And the hardships and their warfare in the lands beyond your ken,
Laugh! Their memory crumbles never! Scorn! Their work endures for ever—
Theirs who led the van of Empire in the name of merchant men!

❖   ❖   ❖   ❖   ❖

From *Wings of the Morning*, edited by Cicely Fox Smith, published by Elkin Mathews, London, UK, 1904, pp. 25-28.

A Farewell (1904)

The frost is on the pane and the rime's on the ground
And pitch-dark the morn,
And a bitter wind comes up with a weary piping sound
Thro' the bare trees forlorn.
God keep my father's house when I am gone,
God keep the fields that first my eyes looked on,
And the cattle in the byre, and the old dog by the fire,
Till I come home again
From off the main.

My mother'll weep for me, and my father'll rave and rage
That his eldest-born should roam,
But my heart is pining like a seagull's in a cage,—
I cannot abide at home,
And sow and reap and sit beside the fire,
And live for herd and harvest like my sire,—
With the sea's song in my blood, be it ill or be it good,
I must take the road and go
For weal or woe.

There's no one stirring yet as I draw the bolts aside,
And the wind blows off the wold,
And I hear the curlew's cry off the moorlands dusk and wide
And the lamb's bleat from the fold.
God keep the little homestead safe from harm,
The sheep on the brown hillside, and the upland farm;
While I am far and free on the wild waste perilous sea,
God grant them while I roam
Till I come home.

❖ ❖ ❖ ❖ ❖

From *Wings of the Morning*, edited by Cicely Fox Smith, published by Elkin Mathews, London, UK, 1904, pp. 29-30.

In 1904 the poet was already longing to travel overseas, to Africa or anywhere beyond the suburbs of Manchester.

The Dust of the Way

I'm weary of the summer lanes, and of the blackbird's lay;
I'm weary of the red cock that crows at dawn of day:
I'm longing for the windy deck,—the blue that fades to gray,
And the dust of the way, my boys, the dust of the way.
The dust of the way that has neither fence nor turning,
The dust of the way that has neither rail nor end,
So it's farewell to you all, for I hear the ship-bells call,
Down beside the harbour whence the windy highways trend.

I'm weary of the bustling street, the endless tramp and roar,
I'm weary of the gaudy glare from every gin-shop door:

I'm longing for the royal way where never gaslamp glowed,
And the lights on the road, my boys, the lights on the road.
The lights on the road that has never fence nor turning,
The lights on the road that watch o'er us lest we stray:
Round the world and home again, so they watch us o'er the main,
The lamps that hang for mariners for ever and a day.

I'm weary of the weary winds that, mazed from off the main,
Go gasping down the stifling street and up the wooded lane:
I'm longing for the smell and sound of sea and salt and spray,
And the winds on the way, my boys, the winds on the way.
The winds on the way that has neither fence nor turning,
The winds on the way that has neither rail nor end:
So it's farewell to you all, for I hear the ship-bells call
Down beside the harbour whence the windy highways trend.

❖ ❖ ❖ ❖ ❖

From *Wings of the Morning*, edited by Cicely Fox Smith, published by Elkin Mathews, London, UK, 1904, pp. 31-33; published earlier in *The Deseret Evening News (Utah)*, July 6, 1901, p. 19..

The line "I'm weary of the gaudy glare from every ginshop door" occurs in similar fashion in "Old Fiddle" and several other later poems.

A Mighty Hunter before the Lord

When the last of my hunts is over and done,
And I go to my rest with the sinking sun,
And horse and hound are forsaken,
Will all we loved be vanished and vain,
And the years of our life be as nought again
In that land where at last we waken?

I think that sure, tho' the teachers tell
That the joys of heaven and the pangs of hell
Are as things that are veiled and hidden,
We shall not forego the joys of the spoil,
Nor the good glad fields, not the smell of the soil
On the plains where we oft have ridden.

The Lord he shall bridle us steeds of might;
We shall ride great rides in the Lord God's sight
From the morn till the fall of even;
We shall hear the echoes our hoof-beats rouse,
We shall feel the cool keen wind on our brows

Blow fresh from the fields of heaven.
To the end of the earth we shall hunt the wrong;
Nor weary at all tho' the chase be long:
We shall joy in the speed and striving:
We shall sweep foul things from the face of the ground

With whip and spur and with horse and hound,
In panic before us driving.

And when all the hunting is over and done,
And the last wild course is ended and run,
We shall rest, and be weary never,
And tell old tales of the earth and sky,
And mighty hunting in days gone by,
And the horse and the hound for ever.

❖ ❖ ❖ ❖ ❖

From *Wings of the Morning*, edited by Cicely Fox Smith, published by Elkin Mathews, London, UK, 1904, pp. 34-35.

The Charge up Wagon Hill

Caesar's Camp

Not for the wealth of thy teeming markets,
Roaring factory, thronging way,
Stern strong city of toil and commerce
Under thy veil of smoke-cloud grey,
Stands thy name with the great in story,
Glows and glories and lives for aye.

Ringed with foemen and weak with famine,
Sick at heart with a hope long fain,
Far from home and the aid they longer for,—
All night long in the dark and the rain
Grit of the Northland struck for England,
Fought for the right when the fight seemed vain.

Weary and wan the dawn came creeping
O'er shell-swept hollow and rain-swept hill,
Over the slopes where the fight was ended,
And the silent ridge where the dead lay chill,
Sealed and bought with the blood of the English,
Dead on the hill that was English still.

There was never a one stood by to praise them,
No voice to cheer them nor tongue to tell,
No light to guide and no lead to follow,
No helping hand for the men who fell;
Lone in the darkness they won the guerdon
That wealth can buy not nor weakness sell.

So rejoice, O Queen of the Northland,
Ever the tale our hearts shall thrill,
How in the Southland far from England,
By shot-swept hollow and thundering hill,
Men of the Northland held for England
Whose fame should live tho' thy streets were still.

So do honour to dead and living,
Who, few and fearless, from dark to day,
Won a gift for thee and for England
No time nor sorrow can steal away;
Wealth may pass, but the deeds of heroes
Keep and hallow thy name for aye.

From *Wings of the Morning*, edited by Cicely Fox Smith, published by Elkin Mathews, London, UK, 1904, pp. 36-37.

"Caesar's Camp" was a British defended strong point in one of the first major battles in the Boer War on Wagon Hill overlooking Ladysmith.

"The first battle of 1900 in South Africa took place on January 6, when Boer forces, commanded by General Joubert, tried to drive the British from their positions inside Ladysmith. Ten thousand British troops, commanded by General Sir George White, defended the besieged town, which they had held for more than two months."

The header graphic is an illustration from the *London Illustrated News* showing the charge up Wagon Hill held by the British contingent at Caesar's Camp, artist unknown.

A Lancashire Sunset

It is the close of day:
Over the hill and town
The sun goes down:
Clearly from hillside fields with evening gray
I hear the men at work among the hay:
From the plain far away
Goes up the smoke of town and mine and mill:
And looking down
On field and town,
And teeming, thriving plain and distant hill,
Spreading, for all who read, their goodly page,
My heart leaps up to cry:
"Glory to God on high,
Who giveth us a goodly heritage!"

Just now in some far clime
Even at this time,
The darkness dies away,
As now our English daylight fades to gray:
And the sun comes up to the toil and clamour of day.
And o'er the misty plains,—thatched hamlets, rising smoke,
And the strange sunny street
Busy with wakening tread of hurrying feet,
And dark-skinned alien folk,
Strange beach and bay and feathery-forested hill,
Drums that are mine and thine waken and thrill:
"Yea! I have a goodly heritage!"
So, howe'er sore bested,
With neither stick nor stone
To call my own,
Nor roof above my head,
Still could I stand
On English land
And hold my head up with my peers,
Full-armed with pride against all alien jeers,
Saying: "Mine own from immemorial years;
Mine thro' all floods that whelm, all storms that rage:
Yea! I have a goodly heritage!"

❖ ❖ ❖ ❖ ❖

From *Wings of the Morning*, edited by Cicely Fox Smith, published by Elkin Mathews, London, UK, 1904, pp. 38-39. First published in *The Manchester School* magazine in 1902.

The poet was a scholarship student at The Manchester High School for Girls on Dover Street from 1894 to 1897; see "Dover Street" for more details.

St. Katharine Docks

London Pool

London Pool's in London town,
Ay, boys! O boys!
London Pool's in London town,
Where the great ships anchor down!
O to shake the canvas free,
Hear the cordage cheerily
Whistling to the open sea
Down from London Pool, O!

London Pool's a crowded place,
Ay, boys! O boys!
London Pool's a crowded place,
Crafts and crews of every race!
O to hear the clanking chain
Trail along the wharf again,—
Hear the tautening ropes astrain
Down from London Pool, O!

London Pool's a gallant sight,
Ay, boys! O boys!
London Pool's a gallant sight,
Toil by day and glare by night!
O to shake our heels and go,—
Feel the four free winds ablow,
Hail the lights of long ago
Down from London Pool, O!

❖ ❖ ❖ ❖ ❖

From *Wings of the Morning*, edited by Cicely Fox Smith, published by Elkin Mathews, London, UK, 1904, pp. 40-41.

An early nautical poetry to be composed by this poet over the next 30 years. She hasn't found her "sailor's voice" quite yet, some of the wording doesn't ring true, but she will! This is also an example of a poem with a chorus, demonstrating her early interest in the traditional shanty songs.

The header graphic is titled *The Opening of St. Katharine Docks, Saturday the 25th October, 1828*, painted by Edward Duncan.

The Death of Galahad

It was before the hour of dawn,
Ere the birds 'gan to sing,
There came to Galahad's chamber
The herald of the King.

All at the midnight hour he came
And stood at the bedside:
O and his eyes were calm and still
Like pools at eventide.

"Rise up, rise up, Sir Galahad,
Rise up and walk with me:
Bide not at all for any man,
Thy King hath called thee."

"I am not clad in fine raiment,
In purple and in pall,
And I am shamed that thus I go
Unto a great King's hall."

"I have no cloak to my shoulders,
No shoon to my bare feet,—
Surely in sorry plight am I
For a great King to meet."

"Thou shalt not come in fine raiment,
In purple and in pall,
Barefoot shalt go through the cold night,
Nor weary be at all."

"At Whinny Muir thou shalt not shrink
Nor any scath shalt find;
Nor shiver 'neath the starry skies
At the cold shuddering wind."

"Take thou no heed for feet unshod
Nor want of mantle fine,
For fair enow in thy King's sight
Is that white soul of thine."

❖ ❖ ❖ ❖ ❖

From *Wings of the Morning*, edited by Cicely Fox Smith, published by Elkin Mathews, London, UK, 1904, pp. 42-43.

Bewitched

O none may share the sorrow,
And none may break the spell,
For I ha' crost the weird water
An' drunk o' Weeping Well.

And I ha' plukt the bitter fruit
Of Elfinland forlorn,
An' spoke wi' the wan woman
Beneath the twisted thorn.

An' I ha' bought dark wisdom
For the heart within me sold,
An' I ha' gi'en my livin' soul
For a mint o' fairy gold.

The stream runs on i' the old way,
The birds sing on the trees,
An' the sun shines on the hill side,
But I know nought of these.

There is no man dare speak wi' me,
No home where I may dwell,
For I ha' crost the weird water
An' drunk o' Weepin' Well.

❖   ❖   ❖   ❖   ❖

From *Wings of the Morning*, edited by Cicely Fox Smith, published by Elkin Mathews, London, UK, 1904, pp. 44-45.

The poet has several other poems about witches and spells. This is one of her earliest

No Surrender

Souls of the strong, whose glory lives for aye,
Whose names are stars on unforgotten fields,
Who found not in the bitterest dark of day
Despair that yields,—

Say, was it well, victorious over fears,
So to give up young glory for the grave?
Do ye ne'er hunger for your unlived years,
Souls of the brave?

"Life, and the pride of life,
We found them ere our prime;
Strife, and the joy of strife,
These knew we in our time.
Earth, and the lands of earth,
Where'er our ways might trend,

Dear to us from our birth
Seems dearest at the end."

"Men, ay, and sons of men,
Not ours for life to whine,
Bartering, tho' one to ten,
The honour of our line.
Life—what were life to buy,
Yielding to save our skin?
Life—that we held so high
We could not stoop to win."

"Death, and the crown of death,
Ye buy not for a price,—
Hope that nought conquereth
And pride of sacrifice.
We looked our last on earth
Nor, dying, shirked the shot,
Holding the prize well worth
The years we grudged not."

So speak the deeds you did, souls of the slain,
Dead in the name of fame on land and sea,—
Turning the grief to joy, the loss to gain,
Defeat to victory.

❖ ❖ ❖ ❖ ❖

From *Wings of the Morning*, edited by Cicely Fox Smith, published by Elkin Mathews, London, UK, 1904, pp. 46-47.

The Fairy Shepherd

When stars come gleaming one by one,
And fold and farm are still,
O I go out to keep the sheep
All night upon the hill.
My master deems me chill and cold
When he lies warm in bed,
But I run leaping with my flock,
And lightly goes my tread.
I drive them to the fairy ring
Beneath the fairy thron,
And they lie sleeping, one and all,
Like little clouds at morn.
O then I go by secret ways
That ever turn and twist
Among the knotted gorse-bushes
Thick as a grown man's wrist,—
I go amid the weird white stems,
That grow so close and high,
I see thicket all around

And then the starlit sky.
And underneath the wan white moon
Amid the furze and whin,
O I sit down upon the ground
And whistle for my kin.
I whistle with the tune I know,
The tune of Faerie,—
You hear it not by light of day,
Either by land or sea,—
And soon I hear across the night
My kin that answer me.
O first it's like the fitful wind
That whistles down the hill,
And then it's like the curlew's cry
Across the moorland shrill,
And then it's like a bugle-horn,
A-blowing clear and thin,
And they are round me suddenly,
The Little Folk my kin.
My master knows not who am I,
Nor where by night I go;
But I make merry all the night
In fields he cannot know.
And when the starlight flickers low
And birds begin to stir,
My kin go from me suddenly
And leave me sitting there.
O there is dew upon my shoes
That's from no mortal hill,
When I go homeward at the dawn
Across the upland chill.
O I sit down and drowse all day,
I heed not wind or rain:
But I go out when day is dead
To keep the sheep again.

❖ ❖ ❖ ❖ ❖

From *Wings of the Morning*, edited by Cicely Fox Smith, published by Elkin Mathews, London, UK, 1904, pp. 48-50.

The Siren

Dear, O homeland, and dear, O sweet land of mine,
Dear, yea, very dear, O land of my birth;
But O strong and strange the voice that comes singing
With a wild song and a young song of wide ways of earth.

Wakens the voice, when comes the time of quickening field and tree,
The time that brings the bud and bloom, the swallow o'er the sea,
When white upon the orchard-trees the blossom lies like foam,
The stranger voice of singing winds across the fields of home.

O wayward word of wandering, of far lands fair and vast,
Day long desire of dreaming eyes across the sky line cast;
O rover from the roving sea, and far untrodden shore,
Whence knew the trees your olden song, the wild birds of your lore?

Her speech is full of hope and strength, and hot-foot young desire,
Strong is her soul as the salt sea, and fierce her heart like fire;
O seagull's cry and seawind's song, and sunlit seas agleam,
O wakening of the heart's desire and youth's eternal dream!

❖ ❖ ❖ ❖ ❖

From *Wings of the Morning*, edited by Cicely Fox Smith, published by Elkin Mathews, London, UK, 1904, pp. 51-52.

A poem is inspired by the poet's continued desire to travel and explore the world beyond the suburbs of Manchester.

Last Post: "Death is swallowed up in victory"

When all was o'er and done
At the sinking of the sun,
And the last shots had sounded
Above the graves new-mounded,
Over the sunset plain
The bugles spoke again.

Singing of hope and glory,
And youth, and feet that roam,
And fields of fame and honour
More dear than fields of home,—
Of goodly deeds unguerdoned
And great fights fought in vain,
And tears that fall for heroes
And praises of the slain.

Tho' hopes be born to perish
And battles lost in vain,
Is there lot naught but sadness
Who weep the nobly slain?
O dead brows bound with laurel!
O harvest of the years!
Was ever crown of triumph
More glorious than such tears?

"Lights out!"
The plain is still:
The light dies lingering from the hill.
But yet by night and day
Over the world for aye
One lamp burns clear and high,—
Even the flame of fame, that shall not die.

❖ ❖ ❖ ❖ ❖

From *Wings of the Morning*, edited by Cicely Fox Smith, published by Elkin Mathews, London, UK, 1904, pp. 53-54.

Green Ribands

There's a word i' the winds o' mornin',
There's a song i' the standin' corn,
For they tied my sleeves wi' green ribands
The day that I was born.

My brothers and my sisters
They call me daft an' queer,
For all the goodly world that's mine
They may not see nor hear.

They cannot tell the bird's talk
Nestin' i' the eaves,
Nor see the wee sly faces
A-peekin' thro' the leaves.

They know not what the stream says
Bubblin' by the stones,
Nor what the wind would tell them
In strange sweet undertones.
O my merry playmates!
My friends I know fu' well!
Dry leaves i' the autumn woods,
Winds upon the fell!

My blessin' on the careless nurse,
My blessin', night an' morn,
Who tied my sleeves wi' green ribands,
The day that I was born!

❖ ❖ ❖ ❖ ❖

From *Wings of the Morning*, edited by Cicely Fox Smith, published by Elkin Mathews, London, UK, 1904, pp. 55-56.

"Green ribands" were a 19th century Irish symbol for solidarity with the earth, among other things.

Isandula-2

Ever the story liveth of the fight on the far hillside,
Fraught with the ancient sorrow that is brother born of pride:
Holds thy heart unforgetting the name of a far-off grave,
Wet with thy tears, O England—ay, red with the blood of the brave,
Who found, by a far stream's tide, 'neath the sky of a stranger land,
Death and glory in one at the Hill of the Little Hand.

Dark like a cloud they came, the hosts of the Zula king,—
Yea, and still as a cloud: silent they drew in a ring
Round the doomed camp white in the sun, and the soldiers scattered and few,
Darkling the impis came on: and the Englishmen, what could they do?
God! Will it ever be told? It were all too bitter to tell,

Dark wave pouring on wave, and savage yell upon yell,
Fights unseen and unknown none liveth to hand to fame:
Brave men dead by the guns they spiked ere the spear-stroke came:
Eddies drowned in the tide,—swirls in a pitiless flood,
And the remnant swept to the river—the river red with their blood.

Yet, O God of the heroes, thanks and praise unto Thee,
Who givest a gift that is greater than an easy victory,
Since from the stream of slaughter by the lonely mountain roll'd,
Young hands grasped there the laurels that death shall not withhold:
Yea, a crown that is fairer than the victor's crown of fame,
A star in the years that shall be, and an everlasting flame.

Swift they raced for the river—for there was that they bore
They must hold for, strike for, strive for till life shall be no more,—
Only to save the colours—tho' all beside be lost
Still this is left to die for—(O is it worth the cost?
Is it worth a young life's glory—its promise and its pride?
Hear in their deed the answer—hear how for this they died!)

Shoulder by shoulder they spurred—reached the river—and one at the last
Came unhurt to the shore, and haply his peril were past;
Yet—what of safety, of life? There are greater, things to lose,
There are nobler, goodlier guerdons for a hero-heart to choose.
Back to midstream he turned, to the foe and the purple tide,
To stand by the friend he loved so—to die at a comrade's side,
And the dead men round in a ring bore witness how they died.
So by the lonely river, under the lonely sky,
Dwells by the graves of heroes the dream that shall not die:
By the flow of a far stream's wave, 'neath the sky of a stranger land,
Death and glory in one at the Hill of the Little Hand.

❖ ❖ ❖ ❖ ❖

From *Wings of the Morning*, edited by Cicely Fox Smith, published by Elkin Mathews, London, UK, 1904, pp. 57-59.

On January 22, 1879, Isandlwana was the site of the Battle of Isandlwana, where over 20,000 Zulu warriors defeated a contingent of British soldiers in the first engagement of the Anglo-Zulu War. Almost the entire column of about 1,200 British soldiers was killed, and the regimental colours were lost.

The Lighthouse Builders

On head and height their stars are bright
Where sails and steamers go,
Where southward flares the Dondrah light
Or the twin Maidens glow.
Praise be to those who set them there
Above the 'longshore foam,
Wishing luck to men who fare where the welcome watch-lights glare,
And a fair voyage home.

To some the pride of arches wide,
Statue and sculptured urn;
To these the guarding lights that guide
At night when no stars burn,
A far-seen hand upheld on high
Above the wandering foam,
Wishing luck and victory to the vessels going by
And a fair voyage home.

All seamen know the lights that glow
And, seeing, bless their name
Who set wherever ship may go
A column crowned with flame,—
A pillar on some hero's grave
Far-seen across the foam,
Wishing luck across the wave to the seaward-faring brave,
And a fair voyage home.

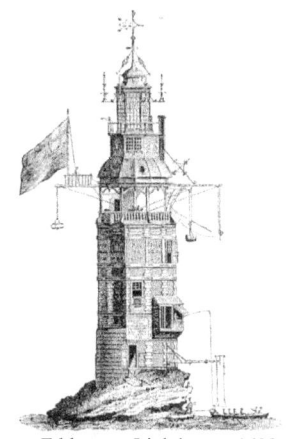

Eddystone Lighthouse, 1698

❖ ❖ ❖ ❖ ❖

From *Wings of the Morning*, edited by Cicely Fox Smith, published by Elkin Mathews, London, UK, 1904, pp. 60-61.

The header graphic is an illustration of Henry Winstanley's Lighthouse at Eddystone Rock, Plymouth, 1698 to 1703, from *The Complete Book of Maritime Design*, edited by Nicki Marshall, published by Gramercy Books, New York, US, 1998, p. 163.

Jack o' Lanthorn

O bat's cry and mist-rack and dark o' the moon!
O roving of wayfarers and wetting of gay shoon!
Fen-pool and quagmire and pathways white wi' fog,
And Jack o' Lanthorn dancing, a-dancing in the bog!

Ho! You tramping sailor-lad, fresh from off the foam,
Here's the flash of fire-light, here's the blink of home!
Ho! You courting farmer's lad, foolish, fond and fain,
Here's the lamp a-gleaming from your true love's window-pane!

Long, long and weary the way that you go:
Short to tread and swift to tread the road that I show:
Turn, O lover from the plough, and lad from the sea,
Here's the lamp of your desire, turn and come to me!
O bat's cry and mist-rack and dark o' the moon;
O roving of wayfarers and wetting of gay shoon!
Fen-pool and quagmire and pathways white wi' fog,
And Jack o' Lanthorn dancing, a-dancing in the bog!

❖ ❖ ❖ ❖ ❖

From *Wings of the Morning*, edited by Cicely Fox Smith, published by Elkin Mathews, London, UK, 1904, pp. 62-63.

Afoot

Afoot

Long is the road 'twixt town and town that runs,
Travelled by many a lordly cavalcade,
With trappings gay, and rich caparisons,
Jester and squire, and laughing knight and maid;
With gallant clash and stir they go their way:
I trudge afoot through all the drouth of day.

For me, the misty meadows fresh with morn,
The tramp thro' noontide heat to evening grey,
The far-seen smoke from the day's goal upborne,
The halt, the friendly greeting by the way,
The distant hill behind far hill descried,
The road by day, the rest at eventide.

I know each wayside wood, each moorland brown,
Each hidden byway and reposeful nook,
Where I may linger when the sun goes down,
Dipping tired feet in some cool-flowing brook;
I know the free hill and the glooming glen,
And kindly fires, and humble homes of men.

❖ ❖ ❖ ❖ ❖

From *Wings of the Morning*, edited by Cicely Fox Smith, published by Elkin Mathews, London, UK, 1904, p. 64. Reprinted in *Country Days And Country Ways: Trudging Afoot in England,* by Cicely Fox Smith, published by F. Lewis, Ltd., Leigh-on-Sea, UK, 1947, p. 11; first published in the *Spectator* in 1902.

There is a delightful book of poems, edited by E. V. Lucas, entitled *The Open Road* in which this poem appears along with a note of thanks to the poet from the editor dated 1905.

This is one of the few very early poems that the poet ever reprinted in one of her later, and in this case much later, works.

The header graphic is drawn by E. A. Cox, R. B. A., and accompanies this poem as it was reprinted in *Country Days And Country Ways*, 1947, p. 11.

A Bird's Call

Over the upland fields, where free and strong
The fresh hill-breezes swept,
I heard a wild bird calling all day long,
Calling as if it wept.

And the wild voice brought back delights and tears
From time's forgotten hoard,
Cleaving the dead cold mist of bygone years
Like a two-edged sword.

And speech forgotten sprang up word for word,
Unfolding like a scroll
At the wild mandate of a lonely bird
Calling like a lost soul.

O sad sweet cry beneath the skies of gray!
O tale of perished years!
O everlasting hope for the new day,
The joy beyond the tears,

When we, who striving to the light must go,
Whom toils and trammels bind,
Somewhere the purport of our days shall know,
Somewhere at last shall find

God's treasure-house of lost loves found again,
Of torn hearts healed anew,
Sorrow grown joy, and pleasure after pain,
And all dear dreams come true.

❖ ❖ ❖ ❖ ❖

From *Wings of the Morning*, edited by Cicely Fox Smith, published by Elkin Mathews, London, UK, 1904, pp. 65-66.

Lancashire from the Hills

There is a glow of sunset down
The wet rut and the gleaming lane,
And runlet fresh with rain.
And there, beyond the bare trees seen,
Over the hillside's shoulder brown
And furrows flushed with springing green,
Lo, pomp of hiving factory, thriving town,
Under the purple reek sun-kissed with fire,
The throbbing heart of England,—Lancashire!

These for thy glory and dower,
(O land that sent me forth!)

Strength and purpose and power,
Thronging shire of the North!
Thine to speak the English word,
Not spoken low, nor faintly heard,
Nor paltering weakly, fearfully,
With the might God giveth thee,—

The wind of a mighty people speaking sure
Speaking the speech of Empire more and more;—
O not thine the rural beauties
That to fairer shires belong,
But thine the lordlier destiny,
Rugged, resolute, stern and free,
The wider end, the mightier duties,
O living, strenuous, strong!

❖ ❖ ❖ ❖ ❖

From *Wings of the Morning*, edited by Cicely Fox Smith, published by Elkin Mathews, London, UK, 1904, pp. 67-68.

The Jonah

He brought the bad luck with him when first he came aboard;
That night we dragged the anchor in the roads where we were moored:
We sailed upon a Sunday, 'twas Friday that he came,
And we left our luck behind us, but we liked him all the same.

A wild nor'-easter started when we left the harbour first,
And all the weary voyage through we'd weather of the worst,
He'd tales to tell of hurricanes, and shipwrecks many a one,
And we thought there'd be another before the cruise was done.

But he left us at the last, when the seas and skies were blue,
In his bunk at break of day, as a common man might do:
And we'd weather fair as fair could be, but still we all were fain
To have our poor old Jonah and the bad luck back again.

❖ ❖ ❖ ❖ ❖

From *Wings of the Morning*, edited by Cicely Fox Smith, published by Elkin Mathews, London, UK, 1904, p. 69.

The poet is hitting her stride in this early poem, adding a twist to an old tale and some empathy for old Jonah who has evidently passed on. She would return to a similar "Jonah" in a much later poem titled "Mike."

Hesperus

Across the plain the daylight dies,
Where in red pomp the sun went down:
A lone star climbs the darkening skies
Above the smoke of town.

Where flapping home by twos and threes,
The clamorous rooks return again,

There shines amid the leafless trees
Red sunset on the pane.

A cool west wind blows fresh and free
Across the glittering plain afar,
And like a lamp burns steadily
One lone and lovely star.

O diadem of lights that gleam
The wide land o'er, beyond my ken!
O lone star brooding like a dream
Above the homes of men!

❖ ❖ ❖ ❖ ❖

From *Wings of the Morning*, edited by Cicely Fox Smith, published by Elkin Mathews, London, UK, 1904, p. 70.

"Hesperus" is the personification of the evening star, the planet Venus.

Whalemen Ashore on a Spree

The Fight on the Island

Thro' the roaring dark of the tempest
We had struggled the whole night long,
With seas that broke on the bulwarks
And headwinds stubborn and strong,
When we came with the wind behind us
To an isle of slumber and song.

And we sailed thro' the scented palm-trees
Up an oarless beautiful reach,
And we lay to rest from our faring
On the sunbaked glittering beach,

And dwelt with the shy strange people
With their soft sweet languorous speech.

Till once in the grand calm twilight
When the beaches were loud with glee,
Brothers, by right of peril
Of the fight and the stormy sea,
Rose up and cursed one another
By all the names there be.

And one reached out for a pistol
And one for a knife to hurl,
All for the sake of a woman,—
A brown-skinned slip of a girl
With a voice like the distant surges
And teeth as white as a pearl.

And we buried the dead man sadly
Where the breakers plunge and comb,
In the sound of the sea's old crooning,
Over against the foam,
With the face on his still heart smiling
Of a girl he had loved at home.

We were sick of the wild shy people,
We knew we had dreamed too long:
And a slain man sat at the revel
And the beach was bitter with wrong,
And we sailed with the wind against us
From the isle of slumber and song.

❖ ❖ ❖ ❖ ❖

From *Wings of the Morning*, edited by Cicely Fox Smith, published by Elkin Mathews, London, UK, 1904, pp. 71-72.

The theme of the romantic tropical island where things go bad is one this poet returns to years later in "Sailor's Farewell."

The header graphic is an illustration titled *Whalemen from the offshore grounds ashore in Lahaina, Hawaiian Islands, 1830's,* drawn by Stan Hugill, from his book *Sailortown,* published by E. P. Dutton & Co., New York, US, 1967, p. 53.

The Shadow

By thronging mart and lonely hill,
By bridle-path and broad highway,
I, follower of the shadow, still
Follow a shadow night and day.

The planets light me on my way,
The bounteous suns arise once more,

And stars by night and sun by day
Still show the fleeting form before.

What heed—tho' men by crowded ways
Jeer at the aim they cannot know,
Tho' wayside loafers stand to gaze
And, turning, mock me as I go?

Have I not heard o'er pool and pine
The brave voice call across the wild?
Have I not held that hand in mine
And gazed into those eyes that smiled?
Tho' mine no life of fireside ease,
Tho' blind men jeer and fools revile,
Need I e'er ways more smooth than these
Or guerdon greater than that smile?

❖ ❖ ❖ ❖ ❖

From *Wings of the Morning*, edited by Cicely Fox Smith, published by Elkin Mathews, London, UK, 1904, p. 73.

In Great Waters

Ho, ye valiant mariners, ho, my merry men,
Sought ye gems of Ophir, or gold of Darien?
Sank ye in the outer deep of waters cold and green,
Fighting for a king's sake, or serving for a queen?

"O not in royal service we sailed the seas for gain
Nor laden with rich treasure that's dug in reef and vein:
We serve a harder mistress, we earn a poorer fee,
Salt wind, an' storm-wrack, an' silver o' the sea."

"Ye make no tomb to our fair name, no song to our renown,
When the northern gales destroy us, and the icebergs drive us down.
For us no sod is holy, for us no death-bell tolls,
Nor children keep our graves gay for resting of our souls."

"O the white flowers above us are flowers o' the foam,
The foam that's salt with women's tears that fishers leave at home;
O deeper than the deepest mine we lie full lonesomely,
Who delve at peril of our lives for silver o' the sea."

❖ ❖ ❖ ❖ ❖

From *Wings of the Morning*, edited by Cicely Fox Smith, published by Elkin Mathews, London, UK, 1904, p. 74; published earlier in *The New York Tribune*, November 15, 1902.

Perhaps, a tribute to the fishermen who seek to harvest fish, "the silver o' the sea."

The Lost Land

Widershins and round about
Among the gorse and whin!
Open, gates o' Fairyland,
Ope and let me in!
Cold and cold the world's way,
And the road's hard and weary:
Back I come to the lonely hill
And the old land o' Faerie!

Cold wind on the heather,
Gold light in the sky!
Open, gates o' Fairyland,
Ope and let me by!
Where's the trick I used to know?
Elfin bells a-ringing,—
Where's the way to the elfin-land,
And the wide gate swinging?

Widershins and round about
Among the gorse and whin!
Open, gates o' Fairyland,
Ope and let me in!
Gold fetters on my feet
And gold chains bind me;
Lone I stand on the cold hillside,
And the gates barred behind me!

❖ ❖ ❖ ❖ ❖

From *Wings of the Morning*, edited by Cicely Fox Smith, published by Elkin Mathews, London, UK, 1904, pp. 75-76; published earlier in *The New York Tribune*, March 8, 1903.

Who has not lamented the loss of fairyland, once so readily accessible when one was young?

The Enchanted Forest

The gnarled boughs hang darkling down,
And biers sweep my knees;
The moon is low, like a gold lamp,
Behind the twisted trees.

O dark and still are the wet fern
And trees where no birds nest;
What need have I for night or day
Who ride a livelong quest?

There is no cockcrow in the dark,
No bleat from a far fold,

When the Forest Folk begin to stir
Under the starlight cold.

Rend your wild hair, you elfin things,
That peep from bush and tree;
I know what strangling arms you reach
Athwart the dusk to me.

Twist your fierce lips, you false fair things,
I know what dance you tread
To what drear tune 'neath the cold moon
O' nights wi' the sheeted dead.

❖ ❖ ❖ ❖ ❖

From *Wings of the Morning*, edited by Cicely Fox Smith, published by Elkin Mathews, London, UK, 1904, p. 77.

From the Sea

I sat by the fireside alone an' wearily:
I heard the rain beat an' the wind moanin' by
A hand came to the shakin' door, and one came in to me,
An' my boy stood by me once again, my boy I lost at sea.

He tirled not at the pin, he made no cry nor moan:
But he lifted the latch, and he stood by the hearthstone;
The wet weed was about him from his heel to his crown,
An' drippin' to the floor did the salt streams run down.

He said: "O weep not, mother, tho' I come not again:
I grieve to hear your tears fall as slow as autumn rain;
O far above my drowned bones the stormy waters roll,
For the sea hath my body, but Christ hath my soul.

Christ who called fishermen all to follow Him,
Christ who stilled the stormy winds when moon an' stars were dim,
Christ who walked so wondrously on waves of Galilee,
Saved my soul from drownin' deep in hollows o' the sea.

O fathoms under water my bones are white as snow:
My soul by Him that saved me is washen white also:
O weep not that above me winds blow an' waters roll,
For the sea hath my body, but Christ hath my soul."

❖ ❖ ❖ ❖ ❖

From *Wings of the Morning*, edited by Cicely Fox Smith, published by Elkin Mathews, London, UK, 1904, pp. 78-79.

This poem's theme is similar to old ballads, known as "night visiting songs," which have the ghosts of sailors appearing in the bedroom of their love ones after they've been lost at sea.

Ring o' Bells Pub Sign

Ring o' Bells

If I might leave this harbour, if I might cross the sea,
'Tis I that know full well where a little while I'd be—
Sittin' in the window-nook a-lookin' to the quay,
At the Ring o' Bells,
The pleasant Ring o' Bells,
All among the old faces, an' the tar an' seaweed smells.

In the hot reekin' city, it's there my heart longs
To be far from strange harbours an' drunken dusky throngs,—
To be hearin' old voices a-singin' old songs
At the Ring o' Bells,
The pleasant Ring o' Bells,
Ah it's there I once was merry, and it's there my heart dwells.

Just the catch of a tune in a gaudy, glaring bar,
And back leagues on leagues my heart goes leapin' far,
Where the gay garden posies an' the English lasses are,
At the Ring o' Bells,
The pleasant Ring o' Bells,
All among the old faces, an' the tar an' seaweed smells.

❖ ❖ ❖ ❖ ❖

From *Wings of the Morning*, edited by Cicely Fox Smith, published by Elkin Mathews, London, UK, 1904, pp. 80-81.

This poem might best be characterized as another precursor of the experience the poet will later have in her stay in the harbour of Victoria, British Columbia, and the volumes of poems that she would then produce. In this poem she imagines herself abroad and being nostalgic for a familiar old sea-side inn. But when she composed this poem she was still in Manchester, England.

"Ring o' Bells" is a reference to a typical sea-side inn. Compare with her later "Old Fiddle" in which she also refers to "gaudy, glaring bars."

The header graphic is a photograph of the Ring O' Bells Tavern, St. Leonards Square, Middleton, near Manchester, by Jim Newell, 2007.

The World's Way

My heart was wide to all the world,
Nor any thought at all I had,
Save that who e'er should pass that way
Should come and enter and be glad.
The cold world on its trampling way
Turned for a while to glance within,
And flouted at my open heart
And all the little loves therein.

If I had shut and barred the door,
And dark and bare the rooms had grown,
If I had left the fires to die,
And all the flowers to fade alone,
And one had come to this locked house
To seek a solace in distress,
Whose were the fault, you jeering ones,
If there were nought but emptiness?

From *Wings of the Morning*, edited by Cicely Fox Smith, published by Elkin Mathews, London, UK, 1904, p. 82.

Perhaps at this point in her life the poet was feeling under appreciated by her friends and family, or perhaps thwarted by a lover. It was years later, however, that she took sail from England to reside and explore Canada.

An Angel Unawares

Ye gave me your broken meat
And of your lees o' wine,
That I should sit and sing for you
All at your banquet fine.

Ye gave me shelter from the storm
And straw to make my bed,
And let me sleep through the wild night
With cattle in the shed.

Ye know not from what lordly feast
Hither I come this night,
Nor to what lodging with the stars
From hence I take my flight.

But there's such wine that warms my blood
As yet you never knew,
So that I heed not wet nor cold,
Nor rags the winds blow through.

If I might sing the song I heard
Ere I came to your door,

Ye should set down the brimming cup
Nor heed the banquet more.

Ye may not hear the songs I hear,
Nor share the feast o' mine,
To whom ye gave your broken meat
And of your lees o' wine.

❖   ❖   ❖   ❖   ❖

From *Wings of the Morning*, edited by Cicely Fox Smith, published by Elkin Mathews, London, UK, 1904, pp. 83-84.

Liverpool

Thro' the dead dark water under skies aglow,
Thro' the shaken shadows silently and slow,
Thro' the looming dock-gates like a thief we glide,
Dropping down the Mersey on the midnight tide.

No crowd at the gangway, no clanging of the bells,
No crying out of women, or shouting of farewells,
Only sound of rising wind through the spars that strains,
And the coughing of the tide in the anchor-chains.

Fainter now behind us die the dock-lamps down;
Flaring like a furnace lies the light of town,
Fades the shore-line into dusk far on either hand,
And the stars burn out above us for the far lights of land.

❖   ❖   ❖   ❖   ❖

From *Wings of the Morning*, edited by Cicely Fox Smith, published by Elkin Mathews, London, UK, 1904, p. 85; also published in the *School Magazine*, Manchester High School for Girls, Manchester, UK, April, 1904.

This setting out poem anticipates the poet setting sail years later on a steamer from Liverpool to Montreal, Canada. Or, perhaps, the poet again made use of her time-machine. Compare this early poem with "Rathlin Head."

Twelve Tree Barrow

When the moths are flitting, and the fields are still,
'Ware the darkling shadows on the haunted hill,
'Ware the ghosts with axe and spear and flint-headed arrow,
Trooping thro' the summer night,
Trooping when the moon is bright
On the Twelve Tree Barrow.

What remembrance of red streams, what furious fray,
Makes the grass grow rich and rank on the mound to-day?
You may see the dead men's bones turned by harrow,
Skulls and thighs of mighty men
Slain in bloody battle then
At the Twelve Tree Barrow.

Draw the curtain closer, bar your windows tight,
Set no foot on yonder hill, tread not there to-night.
Ill for him who dares the spear and flint-headed arrow,
When the warriors wake by night,
Trooping when the moon is white
On the Twelve Tree Barrow.

❖ ❖ ❖ ❖ ❖

From *Wings of the Morning*, edited by Cicely Fox Smith, published by Elkin Mathews, London, UK, 1904, pp. 86-87.

The Ancient Singer

I brood not now upon the printed page,
A nobler voice is in mine ears to-night,
A voice in every land and every age,
Singing strange songs upon its world-wide flight,
And of all music primal harmony.

Thou wert before Pan's pipes or Psalmist's lyre,
Ere Troy town was at all, or Sappho's lay,
Thou, wilder than all dreams of young desire,
And younger than the tears of yesterday,
Older than woeful croon of hidden doves
Thro' the noon-dark of Aphrodite's groves.

Waking by night o'er empty moor or dale,
Thou, with thy ranging voices soft and strong,
First to our mute forefathers didst unveil
The immemorial mystery of song,
All sweetest sadness in thy wordless rune,
To all sublimest speech, sufficient tune.

❖ ❖ ❖ ❖ ❖

From *Wings of the Morning*, edited by Cicely Fox Smith, published by Elkin Mathews, London, UK, 1904, p. 88.

Davy Jones's Locker

Shipmates o' mine, are you sleeping fair an' sound,
Mates fair an' foul, friend an' foe,
Lyin' where lost ships are, sunken deep an' drowned
In Davy Jones's locker down below?
In wide seas an' narrow, deep seas an' shoal,
There's no stone above you an' no bell to toil:
O rest for your body an' peace to your soul,
Shipmates a-sleepin' down below.

Shipmates o' mine, are you sleepin' fair an' sweet,
Where's never sun to burn or wind to blow,
Slid over side wi' the shot at head an' feet
To Davy Jones's locker down below?
Jock fro' Skye an' Stornoway, Mick o' Donegal,

Davy Jones Seated on His Locker

Black skin an' white skin that answer the call,
Rip an' rogue an' honest man, room for 'em all,
Shipmates a-sleepin' down below.

Shipmates o' mine, are you sleeping fair an' sound
While we're a-trampin', trampin' to an' fro,
Do you heed us home-returnin', do you bless us outward bound,
In Davy Jones's locker down below?
Do you dream e'er so little o' the ship an' the crew,
O' ship-bell, an' chantey, an' sea still an' blue,
An' the hoot o' the syren, an' the thresh o' the screw,
Shipmates a-sleepin' down below?

❖ ❖ ❖ ❖ ❖

From *Wings of the Morning*, edited by Cicely Fox Smith, published by Elkin Mathews, London, UK, 1904, pp. 89-90.

This poem seems a precursor of the many nautical poems to come. For example some of the lines foreshadow lines in "Shipmates." But the feeling of loss is all romantic musing, rather than being based on real loss.

The header graphic is a drawing by John Tenniel (of *Alice In Wonderland* fame) of Davy Jones on his locker, from *Punch* magazine, Volume 103, December 10, 1892, p. 272, with the caption "Aha! So long as they stick to them old charts, no fear o' my locker bein' empty!!"

Pixie-Led

A breath on my forehead,
A laugh in my ear,
A shrill sound of fairy pipes
Blowing near and clear.
Away from home and kindred
And out of street and town,
I wandered with the fair folk
Towards the mountain brown.

They led me through the livelong day
By field and moorland wide,
With a pattering of wee feet
Running close beside.
And when I thought I saw them,
O nothing could I find,
Only a dry leaf on the road
Dancing in the wind.

The light was dead suddenly,
And hills shut me in:
The curlews cried in the grey dusk
Across the gorse and whin,
Between the wild waste of the moor
And the great lonely sky,
And the stream upon its cold stones
Sobbing wearily.

❖ ❖ ❖ ❖ ❖

From *Wings of the Morning*, edited by Cicely Fox Smith, published by Elkin Mathews, London, UK, 1904, pp. 91-92.

Sleep

Thy kiss is for the weary, child of God,—
Gliding out of the dusk with silent feet
Thro' fields of languorous poppies heavy-sweet
Thou tell'st of lands wherein we have not trod,
Thou leadest us thro' every longed-for clime,
Thou blottest out the struggle and the strain,
Thy veiled hand turning back the wheel of Time
Makes youth's dream true, gives age its youth again.

Thou conquerest time and distance and the grave:
Clinging of dear ones' hands we find with thee,
Glad garnering of the troublous years' increase,—
Thou friend who comest unto price and slave
With thine Archangel presence silently,
And swaying of great wings, and a sweet peace.

❖ ❖ ❖ ❖ ❖

From *Wings of the Morning*, edited by Cicely Fox Smith, published by Elkin Mathews, London, UK, 1904, p. 93.

The Smell of the Sea

I'd tramped the whole day long on the weary roads ashore,
I was tired as a dog, and my heart was sick and sore,
By strange towns, and long roads, I'd plodded wearily
With ne'er a soul to call my friend, and far from the sea.

I climbed a hilly road in the driving, drenching rain;
There was mist like a fleece lying thick upon the plain,
And a wet west wind came blowing, came blowing fresh and free,
With a damp feel on my forehead and a smell of the sea.

O how should I mistake it, or how name it wrong,
What the heart of me was sick for all the weary road along?
The white fog was before me as thick as it could be,
But I knew my way was coastward, and my face to the sea.

O the chill breath a-blowing, and the salt on my lips,
From the seaport, and the roadstead, and the straining sails of ships!
O the sharp scent of the golden weed about the grey stone quay,
And the heart of me a-leaping at a smell of the sea!

❖ ❖ ❖ ❖ ❖

From *Wings of the Morning*, edited by Cicely Fox Smith, published by Elkin Mathews, London, UK, 1904, pp. 94-95.

Even before she sailed to Canada, this poet had a strong affinity for the sea, as is evidenced by this poem.

Hodson of Hodson's Horse

Not his the lifelong loud renown,
The head with weight of years grown gray:
But his a gallant glorious day
Of tented field and 'leaguered town,

Of swift surprise and breathless ride:
A short adventurous life, wherein
Like some death-courting paladin
Greatly he dared, and greatly died.

And his a name to rouse again
Memories of battles, wild or sad,
Of stricken camps his smile made glad,
And roaring fights on hill and plain,

Old forays of the field and ford,—
Brave echoes from brave years that were,
A trumpet-call, a clinking spur,
And chiming of a swinging sword.

❖ ❖ ❖ ❖ ❖

From *Wings of the Morning*, edited by Cicely Fox Smith, published by Elkin Mathews, London, UK, 1904, p. 96.

"Hodsom's Horse" is a reference to a cavalry regiment raised at Delhi by William Stephen Raikes Hodson in 1857 from Sikhs, Muslims and Afghans of the Punjab.

Afterglow

Wet, streaming sand, and the tide going down;
Boats on the beach, and the sails patched and brown,
And the heath-smoke hanging blue up above the drowsy town.

Strong scent of weed blowing off the harbour-bar,
A liner's trail of smoke on the skyline faint and far,
And the bell-buoy clanging, and a lonely star.

Wet, gleaming shore, and the sea-gull sweeping free,
A swinging lamp alight in the ropes by the quay,
And the wind singing low of a ship that waits for me.

❖ ❖ ❖ ❖ ❖

From *Wings of the Morning*, edited by Cicely Fox Smith, published by Elkin Mathews, London, UK, 1904, p. 97.

The last line may be an additional reference to the poet's compelling urge for exploration, beyond the shores of England.

The Image

Brooding he dreams his age-long dream:
He sees not London's pouring stream
Around him, with these eyes that seem

As if for aye his memory dwells
'Mid lone, sand-smothered citadels,
Where in long waves the desert swells

O'er fallen arch and colonnade,
Stairway and tomb and balustrade
By hands of mighty builders made,—

'Mid fights long fought, and banquets fled,
Where softly falls the lion's tread
O'er ashes of the ancient dead.

❖   ❖   ❖   ❖   ❖

From *Wings of the Morning*, edited by Cicely Fox Smith, published by Elkin Mathews, London, UK, 1904, p. 98.

This poem might have been inspired by a Middle Eastern exhibit the poet viewed at the Royal Services Museum in London.

School

What's the use of books and schooling,
Sum and slate and such like fooling?
Master drones and drones away
Like a bee the livelong day.

It's to-day the boats are sailing
To the North Sea for the whaling:
To the high seas and the wide
They are going on the full tide.

O the wind—the wind a-blowing
On the seas where they are going;
Can I sit and mind my book,
Seeing every time I look

Through the little window yonder
All the wide world and the wonder,
And the wind in the tree,
And the sky, and the sea?

❖   ❖   ❖   ❖   ❖

From *Wings of the Morning*, edited by Cicely Fox Smith, published by Elkin Mathews, London, UK, 1904, p. 99.

This poem seems likely inspired by her final days at The Manchester High School for Girls, when the young poet was restless to be on her own and exploring "All the wide world and the wonder."

Fata Morgana

So I at last attain
All I have longed to gain;
The fairy fleeting shade,
The bliss so long delayed,—
Now stress and strife are past,
I seize at last.

Yet is it well at all?
I trod her echoing hall,
I clasped her robe, and caught:
Lo, is it this I sought,
This hollow sprite I see
That gibes at me?

I took her magic cup,
I drank the charmed wine up.
Where was the sweetness then,—
The fabled prize of men?
Lo, bitterness was there
And dark despair.

O for the road again,
The unrewarded pain,
The hard, rough, wayside bed,
The stars above my head,
Hope like a springing fire,
Doubts, dreams, desire.

❖ ❖ ❖ ❖ ❖

From *Wings of the Morning*, edited by Cicely Fox Smith, published by Elkin Mathews, London, UK, 1904, pp. 100-101.

This poem of personal reflection seems similar to a later poem "Morgan le Fay" in which the poet also sums up her feelings.

"Fata Morgana" is an Italian phrase derived from the latin for "fairy" and the Arthurian sorceress Morgan le Fay, and describes a distorted mirage or a ghostly image.

The King's Jester

It's oh to bear a weary heart
Among the shine and show!
The little streams run cheerily,
Adown the hills I know.

Men brought me from my distant home
Because my jests were bright,
And clad me in a motley coat
To be the King's delight.

And now my heart aches while I smile,
Mine eyes are dim with woe.
The gallant wind goes merrily
Across the hills I know.

What heed! tho' smiles be far from me,
And hearts be rent with pain,
The jester's bells must chime their glee,
My lord must smile again.

It's oh to wear the motley coat
Above a heart of woe!
The birds are calling all day long
About the hills I know.

❖ ❖ ❖ ❖ ❖

From *Wings of the Morning*, edited by Cicely Fox Smith, published by Elkin Mathews, London, UK, 1904, p. 102.

Love Lies Bleeding

Boy Love is dead:
His little wings are torn,
And broken is his bow.
And none hath wiped away the tears of woe,
The tears he lately shed,
Upon his cheek forlorn.

Boy Love is dead,
Tho' he was loth to die.
Lay him to sleep forgot,
Where laughter of new loves may grieve him not,
Nor their rejoicing tread
Awake him, passing by.

❖ ❖ ❖ ❖ ❖

From *Wings of the Morning*, edited by Cicely Fox Smith, published by Elkin Mathews, London, UK, 1904, p. 103.

Possibly in memory of a youthful love episode.

Shipwrecked

The Lost Galleon

Her decks are drowned in sea-wrack, her guns are sunk in sand,
Where she lies in the still water, hard by the Irish strand.
There are dead in her gilded cabins, there are white bones in her hold,
With the coffins rotting plank from plank, brimming o'er with gold.

Broad o' beam they built her, that they might load her deep:
They sowed a goodly harvest for the fierce salt seas to reap:
They freighted her with merchandise, with gold they weighed her well,
Ere they steered slowly to her bourne their castled citadel.

God rest their souls where they lie low,—where she swirled down of yore
With chanting priest and shrieking slave, a stone's throw from the shore,
Nor all their piled-up ingots, nor all their gold could save,—
Under the cliff together, the Don and the chained slave.

Far o'er the gray-green waters goes sound of gull and gale;
White caps are on the breakers, and the sun on a patched sail:
But she lies lost and mouldered, with her captains swart and bold,
Dead in her gilded cabins, and weighted down with gold.

From *Wings of the Morning*, edited by Cicely Fox Smith, published by Elkin Mathews, London, UK, 1904, pp. 104-105; first published in *The Outlook* and subsequently in *The Evening Post*, Volume 66, Issue 136, NZ, December 5, 1903, p. 11.

The header graphic is a painting the *Santa Maria* being wrecked in 1492 by Gustave Adolf Closs in 1892.

Journey's End

When the long day's tramp is over, when the journey's done,
I shall dip down from some hilltop at the going down o' the sun,
And turn in at the open door, and lay down staff and load,
And wash me clean of the heat o' day, and white dust o' the road.

There shall I hear the restless wind go wandering to and fro
That sings the old wayfaring song—the tune that the stars know;
Soft shall I lie and well content, and I shall ask no more
Than just to drowse and watch the folks turn in at the open door.

To hail the folk I used to know, that trudged with me in the dust,
That warmed their hands at the same fire, and ate o' the same crust,
To know them safe from the cold wind and the drenching rain,
Turn a little, and wake a little, and so to sleep again.

❖ ❖ ❖ ❖ ❖

From *Wings of the Morning*, edited by Cicely Fox Smith, published by Elkin Mathews, London, UK, 1904, pp. 106-107; also published in the *Sunday Times*, Perth, Australia, March 20, 1904, p. 10.

The Elf-Child

I know not in what freakist hour
My kindred strange and wild
Did cast me out from Elfinland
To be a human child.

For I have dwelt in homes of men
So many 'wildering years,
And had my part of happiness
And sorrowed with their tears.

I cannot find the road I came
Across the wood and wild,
And lilt away by moor and brae
To be an elfin child.

Yet many a time the willful soul
I brought from Faerie,
Runs riot in my elvish blood,
And breaks the heart in me.

O they wrought grief that brought me here,
A wanton thing and wild,
To drink the cup for mortals brew'd
Who am an elfin child.

❖ ❖ ❖ ❖ ❖

From *Wings of the Morning*, edited by Cicely Fox Smith, published by Elkin Mathews, London, UK, 1904, pp. 108-109.

Rosemary

Rosemary for remembrance,—
O gentle memories
Of hours whose fragrance is like flowers
In olden pleasaunces!
When all the birds go South again
And all the laughter's o'er,
Rosemary for remembrance
Of days that are no more!

Rosemary for remembrance
Of summer posies done,—
And scarlet for midsummer joy
And gold for noonday sun.
God grant us in autumnal days,
When brighter flowers have died,
Rosemary for remembrance
And dreams for eventide!

❖ ❖ ❖ ❖ ❖

From *Wings of the Morning*, edited by Cicely Fox Smith, published by Elkin Mathews, London, UK, 1904, p. 110.

The poet is reflecting on the seasons of change and what is eternal. This poem was dedicated to the Lady Phyllis Windsor-Clive (1886-1971).

This poem was set to music by Charles Willeby, published by John Church Co., Cincinnati, US, 1906; British Library reference: bib ID 2713170. Willeby also did a musical setting for "Crossing the Bar" by Alfred Lord Tennyson.

For'ard On!

Now the last meet is over, the last hunt is done,
And the last farewell spoken at set of the sun,
And the ghost of a voice in the waft of a cry
Seems to ring far away 'twixt the fields and the sky:
    "For'ard on!"

Hey, Bugler, hey, Bever, and hounds one and all,
That sped at his bidding and came to his call,
Nevermore shall you hark to the voice you knew well,
When he cheered on the pack, e'en the hour that he fell,
    "For'ard on!"

O well for the huntsman, the cheery, the true,
At the close of the day in the good fields he knew!
Even so, not a doubt, he'd have chosen to die
Within sight of the hounds, to the sound of the cry,
    "For'ard on!"

In the wind and the rain, ere we leave him to rest,
Once again sound the horn in the call he loved best:

From the days that are over, the good years gone by,
Half fancy there answers the ghost of a cry:
    "For'ard on!"

❖ ❖ ❖ ❖ ❖

From *Lancashire Hunting Songs and Other Moorland Lays*, edited by Cicely Fox Smith, published by J. E. Cornish, Ltd, Manchester, UK, 1909, pp. 9-10, and first published in the magazine *Country Life*.

"For'ard on!" is the traditional cry to start the hounds on a trail.

This poem was written in memory of John Jackson, late huntsman to the Holcombe Harriers, who fell dead in the hunting-field. A few minutes before his death he had been calling to the pack, "For'ard on!"

Little Waxy

Wake, little Waxy! Hunting-time again,
The short days and goodly, the clean Autumn rain:
In the old North country, in the grey open weather,
Hounds upon the moorland chiming all together.

This year in clough and hollow the stream's song sounds the same:
On every windy hillside the grasses burn like flame:
Where the empty air is loud with the peewit's lonely crying
And the call o' the moorland gale to the bird's call replying.

Wake, little Waxy! Voices that you know
Set the upland ringing where the hill-breezes blow;
In the brave North country, in the grey open weather,
Up and Join the chorus, hound and horn together!

Ah, little Waxy! Hunting days are done,
Nevermore the brown field and the rain and the sun—
Only the memories left, o'er the Autumn fields that hover,
Of the brave runs ended, lass, the good days over!

❖ ❖ ❖ ❖ ❖

From *Lancashire Hunting Songs and Other Moorland Lays*, edited by Cicely Fox Smith, published by J. E. Cornish, Ltd., Manchester, UK, 1909, pp. 11-12, and originally published in the magazine *Country Life*.

Royal Music

Sweet in the leafy woods the round
Of singing birds in June;
And sweet on wintry hills the sound
Of hounds that chime in tune—
The sound that is the very soul
Of cleanly upland days,
Where men still walk the kindly earth
In the old kindly ways.

Whether beneath the scurrying wrack
The heartening cry is borne

By snatches down the piping gale,
Or breaks the windless morn,
No heart but answers to the call,
That once, through sun and shower,
Has followed far o'er dale and hill
For hour on flying hour.

Now where from moorlands drenched with mist
The streams run noisily,
Some cleft amid the lonely hills
Brims o'er with melody:
Now where the open hillside sweeps
To the free skyline's bound,
Adown the bare brown fields they drive,
A living wave of sound.

"To Mindful, hark!"—and true as bells
Across a wintry sky
Each voice takes up its wonted note
In well-accustomed cry.
Now Fencer, Fairmaid fill the strain
With challenge shrill and keen,
And steady as a church-bell's note
Old Mindful chimes between.

No fiddler's note that sets the tune
For lads' and lasses' feet
E'er left to haunt the years to come
A memory half so sweet
As here this music fit for kings
Beneath God's open sky,
Where horn and hound hunt care away
And the good winds go by.

❖ ❖ ❖ ❖ ❖

From *Lancashire Hunting Songs and Other Moorland Lays*, by Cicely Fox Smith, published by J. E. Cornish, Ltd., Manchester, UK, 1909, pp. 12-14. First published in the *English Illustrated* magazine.

Parting: The Eve of the Puppy Show

Yo were but a little un, Crowner my lad,
When th' huntsman he said yo'd be t' spit o' yo'r dad,
An' now yo're a big un, an' Spring comin' round,
Time's come for partin', lad!—mak' a good hound!

I thowt I'd ne'er rear yo, lad, six month ago,
But I'se warrant to-day yo'll be pick out o' t' show.
Yo're wick an' yo're gradely, as ever was found,
An' time's come for partin', lad!—mak' a good hound!

There's noan o' our folk but'll miss yo to-neet,
Th' owd slat o' your tongue, lad, an' pat o' your feet,
An' th' childer'll fair cry for thee, marlockin' round;—
But time's come for partin', lad!—mak' a good hound!

Eh, t' pots 'at yo've brokken, lad, tongue cannot tell,
But yo're reet sort o' stuff, lad, we know it fu' well:
Yo'll stand up wi' t' best on 'em, ay, I'se be bound,
An' time's come for partin', lad!—mak' a good hound!

❖ ❖ ❖ ❖ ❖

From *Lancashire Hunting Songs and Other Moorland Lays*, by Cicely Fox Smith, published by J. E. Cornish, Ltd., Manchester, UK, 1909, pp. 15-16, and originally published in *Country Life* magazine.

The breeder would raise the puppies and then put them up for sale at the local fair (in this case a spring fair). Only the biggest of Hunts would have a single pack under the charge of a paid houndsman.

In the modern tongue we believe this would be:

> You were only a little one, Crowner my lad,
> When the huntsman he said you'd be the image of your dad,
> And now you're a big one, and the spring coming round,
> Time's come for parting, lad! Make a good hound!
>
> I thought I'd never rear you, lad, six month ago,
> But I'll warrant to-day you'll be the pick of the show.
> You're fast and you're good, as ever was found,
> And time's come for parting, lad! Make a good hound!
>
> There's none of our folk but will miss you tonight,
> The old lick of your tongue, lad, an' pat of your feet,
> An' the children will loudly cry for you, prancing around;
> But time's come for parting, lad! Make a good hound!
>
> Oh, the pots that you've broken, lad, tongue cannot tell,
> But you're the right sort of stuff, lad, we know it full well:
> You'll stand up with the best of them, aye, I'll be bound,
> And time's come for parting, lad! Make a good hound!

Hunting the Hare

Hark for'ard, hark for'ard, hark for'ard, to hills where October
Lingers awhile in his vesture resplendent yet sober,
Where, salt with the breath of the ocean, the Autumn wind passes
With a sigh o'er the heather's lost purple, the yellowing grasses.

Hark for'ard, hark for'ard, hark for'ard! in morning's young glory
The hound and the horn lead us out through the meadowlands hoary,
By the grey little farms with their scanty hill-pastures about them,
And the thorns crouching low to the ground from the storm-winds that flout them.

Hark for'ard, hark for'ard, hark for'ard! rejoicing we follow,
By the swift little brook that runs pattering deep in the hollow,
By the pool with grey reeds at its rim where the wild duck rise whirring,
And the long moorland grass in the breeze's breath sighing and stirring.

Hark for'ard, hark for'ard, hark for'ard! till daylight be dying
And leaving the hill to the stars and the peewit's lone crying
And the huntsman who rides down the wind, with a ghostly hallooing
His deer o'er the moorland by midnight forever pursuing.

And oft when the wind murmurs low, round the gable-end roaming,
Its song of old voices we knew, in the wild winter gloaming,
When white on the moorland lie drifted the snows of December
In dreams to brave days that are ended, hark back and remember!

❖ ❖ ❖ ❖ ❖

From *Lancashire Hunting Songs and Other Moorland Lays*, by Cicely Fox Smith, published by J. E. Cornish, Ltd., Manchester, UK, 1909, pp. 16-18.

Written when the poet was still a girl in Lancashire and published later under her own name when she was still in her twenties, this is part of a remarkable country collection by someone who would become much better known for her sea poems.

The Hunting of the Witch

I rose up one bright Autumn morning
My heart was as heavy as lead:
I thought I'd go mope in the garden,
But I followed the hounds instead.
To hear the halloo in the valley
You'd ha' thought they were hunting a hare,
But as soon as I heard, I knew better—
'Twas a weary old witch called Care.

At dusk she lay down by my pillow,
At dawn she was haunting me still:
No bell, book and candle could fright her,
No silver bullet could kill;
But she ran from the voice of the huntsman,
She fled from the twang of the horn,
And the sound of the hounds' merry music
Afar on the windy morn.

By fold and by clough and by moorland
We hunted her all the day long,
And I swear that the countryside over
There was never a hare so strong.
Whoop! tear her! good hounds, now you've got her!
You thought you were hunting a hare:
But I know all the while that you've rid me
'Twas a weary old witch called Care!

❖ ❖ ❖ ❖ ❖

From *Windsor* magazine, Vol. XXXI, 1909, p. 110. Later published by J. E. Cornish, Ltd., in *Lancashire Hunting Songs and Other Moorland Lays*, pp. 19-20, in the same year.

This poem was probably composed in the early 1900's. It is known that as a girl the poet followed on foot the local hunts. This poem expresses the pleasure she gained from this pastime and how it would lift her spirits.

Otter Hunting in Ribblesdale

Through yon little planting, by yonder streamside,
Where Ribble's sweet waters flow softly and wide,
While the dew's on the meadows it's up and away,
A-hunting the otter at break o' the day.

Come rise up full soon, come rise up and go,
The mist's on the hill and the river runs low:
While the dew's on the meadows it's up and away
A-hunting the otter at break o' the day.

O hear the glad music of horn and of hound;
O hear how they welcome in day with the sound:
O hear how the valley is loud with the strain
And the woodlands give answer with echo again.

Now Ribble, sun-chequered, slides joyfully down
Which late thro' the bridges roared foaming and brown:
Now hot lies the scent, and the morning is still,—
Hark for'ard, good hounds, to a view and a kill!

A health to good fellowship fill we now high,
You true-hearted sportsmen afar and anigh,
Here's many a good chase when the morning is grey,
A-hunting the otter at break o' the day.

❖ ❖ ❖ ❖ ❖

From *Lancashire Hunting Songs and Other Moorland Lays*, by Cicely Fox Smith, published by J. E. Cornish, Ltd., Manchester, UK, 1909, pp. 20-22. First published in *Country Life*.

The second stanza is clearly a repeatable chorus if sung to the music of "The Bonnets of Dundee."

At the Dawning of the Day

By Ribble's gleaming river
The morning mists are grey,
Where the dew-drowned copses quiver
With the deepening green of May.
And it's hey to be there, and hieing
Where the hound and the horn are crying
And the echoes loud replying
At the dawning of the day.

O the scent of the dewy grasses
In the daybreak calm and cool,
Where the skimming swallow passes
From pool to darkling pool,
And the startled birds go winging
Through the wakened woods a-ringing
With the pack its challenge flinging
At the dawning of the day.

Too soon, we know, will fly us
These hours of morning's gleam,
And the years of our strength drift by us
Like leaves on an autumn stream:
And the din of cheery noises
Which now our hearts rejoices
Grow faint as ghostly voices
Heard once in an olden dream.

Yet when, in a dark December,
The frosty woods are grey,
By whiles we shall still remember
What years steal ne'er away,—
This golden hour undying
When the hound and the horn are crying,
And the echoes loud replying
At the dawning of the day.

❖ ❖ ❖ ❖ ❖

From *Lancashire Hunting Songs and Other Moorland Lays*, by Cicely Fox Smith, published by J. E. Cornish, Ltd., Manchester, UK, 1909, p. 22-23.

Mist

Between the grey hill and the sky
The chill west wind goes wandering by
Where mists upon the moorland lie,

White as wool, from the far-off sea,
Salt as tears on stone and tree,
Drifting and driving silently.

Awhile the lifting mist-wreaths show
Dim shadowy shapes that come and go,
Hound, horse and rider, to and fro,—

Like ghosts from some forsaken hall
Where the winds pipe, and the rains fall
On broken roof and crumbling wall.

And down the clough, where all alone
You heard the hidden streamlet's moan
Sobbing over grass and stone,

Floats, as from elfin hunting-grounds
Beyond the world's remotest bounds,
The faint lost music of the hounds.

❖ ❖ ❖ ❖ ❖

From *Lancashire Hunting Songs and Other Moorland Lays*, by Cicely Fox Smith, published by J. E. Cornish, Ltd., Manchester, UK, 1909, p. 24-25.

From the North

I wish't I was in Lancashire huntin' o' the hare
All across the wide moorlands an' the hollows brown an' bare,
Hearkenin' to the good hounds' cry, hearkenin' to the horn,
Far away in Lancashire on a windy morn.

I wish't I was in Lancashire along o' folks I know,
Rangin' o'er the countryside in all the winds that blow
As they blew when I was yet a lad, in the place where I was born,
Far away in Lancashire on a good huntin' morn.

There's gradely hounds in Lancashire, as such there always were:
There's gradely hills in Lancashire as how they're bleak an' bare:
There's jannock lads in Lancashire, and that I tell yo true,
An' I wish't I was in Lancashire all the day through!

❖ ❖ ❖ ❖ ❖

From *Lancashire Hunting Songs and Other Moorland Lays*, edited by Cicely Fox Smith, published by J. E. Cornish, Ltd., Manchester, UK, 1909, pp. 25-26.

"Jannock" is a rather archaic word meaning fair, straightforward, genuine.

This poem was first adapted for singing by Gary and Vera Aspey, as recorded on *From the North*, 1975.

A North Country Hound (Old Style)

Now hark, all good hunters, I'll sing you the praise
Of a brave hound and goodly, that's worth many lays,—
As gallant a creature as God made for man
Since the hound and the horn on this old earth began.

He's strong and he's straight, lads, his tongue like a bell,
And the stout heart that's in him, lads, tongue cannot tell,
For to breast the steep hillsides where faint hearts must fail,
And to sweep the wide moors in the teeth of the gale.

Oh goodly to see him a-brushing the dews
With his ears fine and flowing, his deep drooping flews;
Let him seek and he'll find, and he needs no halloo,
For he knows what he's hunting, lads, better than you.

Oh goodly to hear him, when, viewing her nigh,
He makes the moors ring with the depth of his cry!
Oh goodly to follow, with fortune for friend,
Till at last with " Who-oop," lads, the best run must end.

Such hounds do they breed in the brave North Countrie
(Where lasses be bonny, and men they be free);

And many a good hound in this land may be found,
But he's second to none, lads, the North-country hound!

❖ ❖ ❖ ❖ ❖

From *Lancashire Hunting Songs and Other Moorland Lays*, edited by Cicely Fox Smith, published by J. E. Cornish, Ltd., Manchester, UK, 1909, p. 26-28.

Set to music by Barrie Temple.

A Lancashire Hare

O brown are the moors in the grey morning lying
Where the west wind comes singing o'er wide sea and plain;
O blithe on the hills when the autumn is dying
The hound and the horn wake the echoes again.
Here's to the hills bleak and bare:
To the winds that give challenge to care!
Here's to the sound of a Lancashire hound,
And the speed of a Lancashire hare!

O hark, and O hark, to the sound of the hollo,
Afar on the hills, in the fall o' the year!
O hark, and O hark, to the hounds that we follow,
How their full-throated chorus swells tuneful and clear.
Through the bent and the heather they revel and rally,—
Their voices all chiming out gallant and gay
A quest by the brookside, a view in the valley,
Then over the hilltop and for'ard away!

O gone are all burdens of sorrow and yearning,
O fast fly the hours that were made for delight,
Till red in the West like a torch dimly burning,
The last gleam of day gives the hunter good-night.
Here's to the hills bleak and bare,
To the winds that give challenge to care!
Here's to the sound of a Lancashire hound
And the speed of a Lancashire hare!

❖ ❖ ❖ ❖ ❖

From *Lancashire Hunting Songs and Other Moorland Lays*, edited by Cicely Fox Smith, published by J. E. Cornish, Ltd., Manchester, UK, 1909, pp. 29-30. First published in *Country Life*.

Set to music by Barrie Temple.

A Stave at Parting

Good-night! the horn's faint music
Through the twilight fades away:
The cold night mists come creeping
O'er the fields we've ranged all day.
Now red o'er the hill-tops smoulders
The last of the wintry sun,

And here's a stave at parting
For the gallant day that's done!

A chill wind moans from the sunset:
There's a thresh of rain from the west,
And horse and hound and rider
Jog homeward now to rest,—
To rest and drowsy dreaming
Of many a long-past run,
And the wind on the well-loved moorland
And the gallant day that's done!

❖ ❖ ❖ ❖ ❖

From *Lancashire Hunting Songs and Other Moorland Lays*, edited by Cicely Fox Smith, published by J. E. Cornish, Ltd., Manchester, UK, 1909, p. 31. First published in the *English Illustrated* magazine.

Hollinshead Hall

Silent the ruined house, slowly rotting and falling;
Empty the great barns, dumb and lifeless and blind;
But for the thin voices out of the stillness calling,
But for the light shadows blowing by like a wind,—
But for the trees' murmur, but for the birds' crying,
Sounding, faint as a dream to a phantom call replying:—
"Hey, boon companions, in the grey dust lying,
Do ye not remember how this earth was kind?"

"Ah, but we lived then," say the whispering shadows,
"Knew life in its fullness that did not canker nor cloy:
Tasted the keen wind, the sweet o' the Spring meadows,
Felt the earth's blood leaping like the heart of a boy.
Ah the good horses in their speed extended!
Ah the hoofs on the upland in those mornings splendid,—
Hey, gallant comrades, though they all be ended,
Should we not remember them, God's gifts of joy?"

"God made the sunlight and the young earth's glory,
Made His good creatures for man's clean delight:
Gave him flowers of remembrance for fields growing hoary,
Lit him torches of memory for the dark of night.
No strong arm but must falter, no blood but grows colder,
No stout beam and rafter but at last must moulder;
Ho, boon companions, though the earth be older,
Shall we not remember when the sun shone bright?"

Yea, though graves be green, yea, though homes be forsaken,
Though barren the granary, and waste gardens lie,
From the years in God's garner new life have they taken,
New life that passeth not 'twixt the earth and sky.
The flower fades, the hours pass,—never Memory's ember:—

Spring unto Spring calls o'er snows of December,—
"Hey, boon companions, shall we not remember
All the good yesterdays that can never die?"

❖ ❖ ❖ ❖ ❖

From *Lancashire Hunting Songs and Other Moorland Lays*, by Cicely Fox Smith, published by J. E. Cornish, Ltd., Manchester, UK, 1909, pp. 32-34.

The poet was always painfully aware that much of the traditional world she loved and valued was passing away before her eyes.

The Clough Among the Hills

I know a clough where nightly
My spirit goes in dream,
Where wind-bent trees grow scantly
Beside a brawling stream,
And there, by gorse and heather,
Grey moorland and grey stone,
The ghost of the years forsaken
Walks in the hills alone.

There in the shy North springtime
Our first late cuckoo calls,
And last on yellowing leafage
The touch of Autumn falls.
There first the budding willows
Break forth in golden pride,
And the snow lies there the longest
In all the countryside.

The upland winds there wander:
The brown moor broods above
Like a stern-seeming mother
Whose heart is filled with love:
And more than banks and moorlands
A hundred times more fair
I love its few late flowerets
And treetops, early bare.

For through yon scattered planting,
Beside yon hurrying stream,
All times and tides forgetting,
My spirit walks in dream,
Where the quiet clough unchanging
With sun or shadow fills,
And the soul o' the past dwells lonely
In the silence of the hills.

❖ ❖ ❖ ❖ ❖

From *Lancashire Hunting Songs and Other Moorland Lays*, edited by Cicely Fox Smith, published by J. E. Cornish, Ltd., Manchester, UK, 1909, pp. 35-36.

After Preston Fight

Twelve o' the clock! the nightmare hours
Crawl through my brain like years;
All the hot sleepless night I hear
The rain drip down like tears,—
Hoarse challenge flung from ward to ward,
Dull tramp o' the sentry's feet,
And the dim, hungry, homeless hum
Nightlong from the restless street.
Far-ah, how far from yon hive of sin
The moorland winds are strong,
And streams from lone brown-bosomed hills
Run down with a sound like song.
Far-ah, how far!—the healing air
For which my torn heart fills,—
Under the cool dark of the sky
The dusk rest of the hills.

Hills—O my hills that I love well!
For which I hunger now
As for the face of an old friend,
Or a kind touch on my brow.
I shall not walk where dreams o' my youth
Like mists at morning cling;
I shall not hear my good hounds' cry
Mate all the uplands ring;
I shall not look on the fields I know,
The farms windy and grey,—
The little things that tug at my heart
Such leagues–such lives away!
They say when a soul goes out to God
Wide should the casements be,
Along its path to the lonely stars
To set the loosed soul free:
And—so God keep me from my death
Within these walls of stone—
Not all the powers of London town
Shall hold me from mine own.

The sky which on Tower Hill looks down
Looks on my hills also:
The winds which round this prison yearn
Are those that hillmen know.
I will turn my face to mine own country,
Mine eyes to my good North;
I will forget the shadow of death
Or ever my breath goes forth.

I shall forget the block and the bonds
And the fierce crowd looking on,—
Yea, as a pigeon hastes to its cote
My soul will leap to be gone,
From the red axe and the bloody dust
And the hot heart grown so cold,
And take its grief to the kind hills
That are old as Earth is old,—
This grief that is like a brand on the brow
And a hot wind through the brain,—
That has seared away the desire of tears
And left a dry sick pain.

I am all too weary for hope, good Lord!
It is all my tired heart's cry:
"Home, home—ah God!—to the North Country
Where I were fain to die!"

❖ ❖ ❖ ❖ ❖

From *Lancashire Hunting Songs and Other Moorland Lays*, edited by Cicely Fox Smith, published by J. E. Cornish, Ltd., Manchester, UK, 1909, pp. 37-39.

"Preston" is located in Lancashire, England. This poem refers to The Battle of Preston, 9-14 November 1715, also known as "The Preston Fight" during the first Jacobite Rising.

York and Lancaster

In Eden ground God bade to blow
Hys roses white and red,
Ere yet man knew to hate hys foe
Or pile thys earth with dead.
Then why, when Earth like Eden seems,
Soe sweet the air with flowres,
Should princes sunder for their dreams
Two hearts soe locked as ours.

Now Eden ground soe distant is,
And man soe stubborn grown,
That not to gain lost Eden's bliss
Will we to errour own:
Yea, thys I know, my heart shall break,
And love itself lie dead,
Ere you your rose of white forsake
Or I forswear the red.

Therefore within thys garden-close
So glad with gold and green,
White bud by red this summer blows
As nought had come between.
And God so spare the rose of white,

And God so speed the red,
I may not hate thy conquering might,
Nor, conquering, mourn thee dead.

❖ ❖ ❖ ❖ ❖

From *Lancashire Hunting Songs and Other Moorland Lays*, edited by Cicely Fox Smith, published by J. E. Cornish Ltd, Manchester, UK, 1909, pp. 40-41.

The Wool-Gatherer

Where hast thou been in the wind and rain?
"Gathering wool on a far plain.

"Four shepherds keep those flocks afar
In pastures where no hedgerows are.

"They own no lord, they take no hire,
They warm their hands at no man's fire.

"When one has driven the flocks all day,
At no far fold they make their stay.

"For one comes hot-foot o'er the plain
And drives them hurrying back again.

"Though the yield should fill the world's wains full,
Never to market comes the wool.

"They cast it all, those wastrel herds,
To naked stars and screaming birds.

"It makes no rug nor coat of frieze:
It makes men shrouds in stormy seas."

❖ ❖ ❖ ❖ ❖

From *Lancashire Hunting Songs and Other Moorland Lays*, edited by Cicely Fox Smith, published by J. E. Cornish Ltd, Manchester, UK, 1909, pp. 41-42. First published in *The Academy* and subsequently in *The New York Tribune*, January 7, 1906.

Barguest

All in the wild and windy night
I heard the treetops moan,
I heard the drift of scurrying leaves
Through the bleak garden blown.
Across the bare and empty fields,
Adown the lonely moor,
Came Barguest padding through the dark
And whining at the door.

Grey as a wreath of autumn mist
Or smoke that skyward rolled
From moorland altars long ago
To strange dim gods of old:
Dark as the dark and starless night
Where loud the storm-winds wail,
Came Barguest through the waste of years,
The midnight and the gale.

All in the mid mirk o' the night
I heard the wild wind cry
The burthen of its ancient song
Between the moor and sky,—
The wind that knows if good or ill
It bodes to me or mine,
That thus I hear beside my door,
The Grey Dog snuff and whine.

❖ ❖ ❖ ❖ ❖

From *Lancashire Hunting Songs and Other Moorland Lays*, edited by Cicely Fox Smith, published by J. E. Cornish, Ltd., Manchester, UK, 1909, pp. 43-44.

The Grey Comrades

Out of the dust of cities and the din of men
I come to the clean spaces of the wide windy moors,
Saying: "Glad, O my kindred, I come hither again,"—
Saying: "Hail me, my comrades, for my heart is yours."

O voices calling and crying in the shadows grey,
Telling the dear tales over that were long since told;
Keepers of sweet memories from a bygone day,
Kind bountiful bosoms and brows wise from of old!

Centuries long they have listened to the four winds' rage;
They hearken the puny plaining of a little world's annoy;
They have known earth in the making, they live from age unto age,
Yet remember an hour's sorrow and a moment's joy.

"Here," they say, "were you happy on a morn of Spring,
Here sang your heart like a harp that the wind swept;
Here are paths that are holy by the dreams they bring,
Here in a grey gloaming you lay down and wept."

"Years go by with their burden of what once has been,
Here is never forgetting on the grey breast of the moors:
Ah the voices of friendship that were here yestreen,
Ah the footstep beloved keeping time with yours."

O wise hills and tender! aglow with beacons afar
That kindle fires of the past from embers faded and grey,
Keeping our heart's lamp burning through the dark hours that are
Between to-night's twilight and to-morrow's day!

❖ ❖ ❖ ❖ ❖

From *Lancashire Hunting Songs and Other Moorland Lays*, edited by Cicely Fox Smith, published by J. E. Cornish Ltd, Manchester, UK, 1909, pp. 44-46. First published in *The Academy* and subsequently in *The Inter Mountain Catholic*, Dec 23 1905.

Hallowe'en

All Hallows Eve—when ghosts do walk the earth:
All Hallows Eve—O light and fireside mirth!
Ah, leave the gay revel and the merry din,
Set the door upon the latch and let the ghosts in.

There comes no dream-lover stepping from the lane,
No pitiful white creature a-beating at the pane:
There is no herb to be gathered nor spell to be said,
And still in the grey graveyard lie the waiting dead.

When the shadows gather, in a room apart,
To the still glow of the firelight, to the dreaming heart,
Far from the loud frolic and the dancers' din,
Friendly out of the gloaming the Dear ghosts come—

Come, when the wind wakens like an olden song,
With smiles half-forgotten and voices lost long,—
With a well-beloved footstep lingering at the door,
Hands full of old posies that smell sweet as of yore . . .

All Hallows Eve—when dreams do rule on earth!
All Hallows Eve—O the feasting and the mirth!
Ah, leave the loud laughter and the dance and din,
Set the door upon the latch and let the ghosts in.

❖ ❖ ❖ ❖ ❖

From *Lancashire Hunting Songs and Other Moorland Lays*, edited by Cicely Fox Smith, published by J. E. Cornish, Ltd., Manchester, UK, 1909, pp. 47-48. At this stage of the young poet's life the ghosts were more abstract. Later they would become more personal.

The Horseman in the Night

In the hedgerow, in the hollow, between the brown hills,
When all with dark and shadows the silent valley fills,
'Tis there that I go trembling when the fields lie white with dew,
And see the lonely horseman that waits there all night through.

All the night long he waits there, in a gap by a broken rail,
Whether by moon or star shine, in the fog or the driving hail:
He bows not his head to the storm-wind, of the rain he takes no heed,—
A shadow against the shadow, dark rider and dark steed.

Why waits he, stark and silent, until the dawn of day?—
Was he slain in a fight forgotten, or hanged by the King's highway,
That without word of challenge, spur-clink or lift of rein,
Lonely he keeps his vigil till daylight comes again?

I went there as the sun rose, and nothing did I see
But a gnarled thorn in the hedgerow where the rider used to be:
I came again at nightfall when the frost in the air was keen,
And lo! the shadowy rider where the twisted thorn had been!

Nightly the spell is worked there, nightly the change comes down
When none is by but the peewit that cries o'er the moor-grass brown:
Sudden, at sound of cock-crow, swiftly, at dawn of day,
Rider and horse from the hedgerow melt like the mists away.

❖ ❖ ❖ ❖ ❖

From *Lancashire Hunting Songs and Other Moorland Lays*, edited by Cicely Fox Smith, published by J. E. Cornish, Ltd., Manchester, UK, 1909, pp. 49-50.

A Place of Dreams

In a dear land, in a dim land,
By well-remembered streams,
Bare trees in moorland hollows stand
Where a lost sunset gleams;
There joy and memory hand-in-hand
Wander: its flowers are dreams.

There often, waking or asleep
My lingering spirit strays,
There where the wild winds sigh and sweep
Along the wintry ways,
And footfalls rustle in the deep
Dead drift of yesterdays.

❖ ❖ ❖ ❖ ❖

From *Lancashire Hunting Songs and Other Moorland Lays*, edited by Cicely Fox Smith, published by J. E. Cornish, Ltd., Manchester, UK, 1909, p. 51. First published in the *Windsor* magazine.

Grey Grisold

All on the misty mountain
In the driving rain,
There saw I Grey Grisold
Bowed under his chain.
The fairies have bound him
With his knees up to his chin,
All in the grey weather
Weeping for his sin.

He lives on the lone mountain
Sitting on a grey stone,
Where the wind pipes sadly
O'er the moorland lone.
I saw his gnarled fingers
And his bent bald crown;
I heard his tears falling,
Falling endless down.

They have fallen so long
To a stream they have grown
They have worn two furrows
In the grey stone.
Through the rocks and the heather
They go flowing down,
Where the plovers fly wailing
Over bog-lands brown.

Grey Grisold was taken
From his bags of gold,
The red gold he got
For the soul that he sold.
To a grey stone they bound him
With his knees up to his chin,
All on the high mountain
Weeping for his sin.

❖ ❖ ❖ ❖ ❖

From *Lancashire Hunting Songs and Other Moorland Lays*, edited by Cicely Fox Smith, published by J. E. Cornish, Ltd., Manchester, UK, 1909, pp. 52-53. First published in *The Academy*.

The Piper

I will not lift the door-latch, I will not step in
From the dark fields and the starlight and the bent and whin:
All about the stone gables, in the dusk alone
You shall hear my pipe playing by your own hearth-stone.

I have no joy of your banquets nor your lighted halls:
I flute not for your dancing at gay routs and balls.
When the last guest has departed, and the lights have died,
Come I with my shrill piping up the lone hillside.

I bring no sheaf of ballads of wars and dead wrongs:
All across the wide world God has taught me my songs,—
Old tunes and unwritten, wrought in far years,
In a strange tongue and tender, with a burden of tears.

O hearts that are restless, O hearts that repine,
Knowledge; of all sorrows and of all dreams is mine.

With a song of dim longing and of lost delight
I will catch at your heart-strings in the dark of the night.

❖ ❖ ❖ ❖ ❖

From *Lancashire Hunting Songs and Other Moorland Lays*, edited by Cicely Fox Smith, published by J. E. Cornish, Ltd., Manchester, UK, 1909, pp. 54-55. First published in *The Outlook*.

Troll's Gold

O I stood by the waterside
And heard the stream run by.
I saw the gnarled trees stand dark
Against the pale gold sky.
And I saw at the grey twilight
In the dusk o' the lone glen
The Trolls, with their earthy faces,
That buy the souls of men.

They have not known man's laughter,
They have not seen sunshine,
They have not heard through the spring wood
The blackbird whistle fine.
They have not heard the sea's song
Nor the wind through the young corn;
They have not looked on the good day
Since the hour that they were born.

All in the dun dusk o' the night
The stream ran noisily;
A weary wind came moaning up
Beside the grey thorn tree.
With their strong kists upon their backs
And faces grey wi' mould,
The Trolls came up out o' the earth
That buy men's souls for gold.

❖ ❖ ❖ ❖ ❖

From *Lancashire Hunting Songs and Other Moorland Lays*, edited by Cicely Fox Smith, published by J. E. Cornish, Ltd., Manchester, UK, 1909, pp. 55-57. First published in *The Academy*.

Old Graybeard

About the shaking window,
Across the bleak brown hill,
Old Graybeard wanders lonely
Beneath the starshine chill.
And ever, as he walks there,
In a thin old voice he croons
Snatches of songs forgotten
And staves of ancient tunes.

He cannot mind them rightly:
He cannot sing one through:
All his old memory clings to
Are gusty notes and few,—
A scrap of a roystering chorus,
A catch from a lost refrain,
Like ghosts of dear dead faces
Half seen in dreams again.

And best he loves to sing you
When the fire burns red and low,
Such airs as lads and lasses
Might tread to, long ago,—
And now he stirs old sorrow
And now he wakens tears,
With a lilt that the dead dance back to
Across the waste of years.

About the drowsy farmstead,
Adown the empty moor,
Old Graybeard wanders piping
And lingers by the door.
Across the fields where sadly
All night a moor-bird cries,
Old Graybeard's fitful music
In snatches wakes and dies.

❖ ❖ ❖ ❖ ❖

From *Lancashire Hunting Songs and Other Moorland Lays*, edited by Cicely Fox Smith, published by J. E. Cornish, Ltd., Manchester, UK, 1909, pp 57-58.

Gilly

Where have you been, Gilly, where have you been?
Shooting at a mark with the lads upon the green?
Or out on the moor where the yeomen do rally?
"Oh I played at the bowls all in yonder green alley."

If the Spanish ships should come, Gilly, how would it be?
"How should they come, and our good ships at sea?"
If a mist wrapped the waters or a great wind blew,
And so they crept in, Gilly, what would you do?

What should we do if it fell upon a day,
Our sailors all at sea, our yeomen all away,
The foemen all streaming from carrack and galley,
And you playing bowls all in yonder green alley?

"I would up and fight," says Gilly, "I would up and die!"
What better were you then, what better were I?
What worse were the foemen for all your brave ending,
Who could not lift a sword for your own home's defending?

Take the old sword, Gilly, rusting on the wall,
And lead out the horse, too, that frets in the stall:
Go out to the moor where the yeomen do rally,
And let the bowls moulder in yonder green alley!

❖   ❖   ❖   ❖   ❖

From *Lancashire Hunting Songs and Other Moorland Lays*, edited by Cicely Fox Smith, published by J. E. Cornish, Ltd., Manchester, UK, 1909, pp. 59-61. First published in *The Spectator*, March 6, 1909, p 17.

First in a set of "Territorial Ballads."

A Ballad of the Time

A man there was, called—what you will; he came of an ancient breed:
Sprung from the loins of the grey North, his sires were men indeed;
And they were lords of all the seas, and, dreaded in all lands,
Years ago and years ago, for they were strong o' their hands.

All in a rich and easy land suddenly dawned a day
When the talk was not of football—that he watched but could not play,
When streets were loud with marching feet, and loud the ringing quays
With more to swell the bloody toll of the war-harrowed seas,—
And a strange thing waked in this man's soul with the shrill trumpet's cry:
"Has England need of men?" he said, "Lo, brothers, here am I!"

Somewhere, far in the ages, somewhere, back in the past,
His fathers heard the bellying sail strain at the long-ship's mast:
Somewhere across the tumbling wave whipt by a stinging breeze,
Eyes that the town-smoke had not dimmed scanned the uncharted seas.

Somewhere, ages before him, in centuries long gone by,
His forbears heard the singing shaft on its fierce errand fly
When the strong arms that learned their skill on every English green
Unto a sterner target drove their arrows swift and keen.

Somewhere in fight or foray, somewhere by sea or shore,
His fathers—they were men of might—used the great craft of war:
Nought had he kept of Cressy field or red Trafalgar's tide,
But the great heart within him and his blind unspoken pride!

Out of the ranks of the fighters they put him grimly aside;
He had never handled a rifle, he could neither shoot nor ride;
There with the babes and women they sternly bade him stay,
Fretting in shame and sorrow the bitter hours away,—

To watch the midnight skyline for a redder dawn than day,
To dream of the gaunt grim sea-wolves swinging over the foam,
The trampled fields of England, and the shambles that was home!

❖ ❖ ❖ ❖ ❖

From *Lancashire Hunting Songs and Other Moorland Lays*, edited by Cicely Fox Smith, published by J. E. Cornish, Ltd., Manchester, UK, 1909, pp. 61-64. First published in *The Manchester Courier*.

Second in a set of "Territorial Ballads."

The Quest (Horses for the Army)

Too good for the knacker, too poor for the lurry!
Let him go to the army that buys in a hurry!
Too good for the kennels, too poor for another,
Let him carry thy destiny, England my mother!

What seek you, what seek you, anear and afar?
"Steeds for my merry men riding to war:
From the pastures of England I ask in my need
The stout heart for labour, the fleet foot for speed.

"Grimly my guns lie: the drivers beside
Yearn for the sight of the teams they must ride:
Loaded my wains are with war's heavy freighting;
All booted and spurred there my yeomen stand waiting."

Have you sought the land over? "Yea, truly have I;
Broad lie the good pastures beneath the grey sky;
I heard the wild wind and I heard the birds' crying,
But never a neigh to my heart's call replying.

"Where were the stallions, all courage and fire,
To beget the clean limbs and the hearts that ne'er tire?
Where were they, the mares that should bear the brave sons
For rush o' the squadrons and roar o' the guns?"

For the fate of an empire, her life and her fame,
The laggard, the stumbler, the faint heart, the lame!
For the red stricken field whereon nations depend,
The splint and the spavin and bellows to mend!

Too good for the knacker, too poor for the lurry,
Let him go to the army that buys in a hurry!
Too good for the kennels, too poor for another,
Let him carry thy destiny, England my mother!

❖ ❖ ❖ ❖ ❖

From *Lancashire Hunting Songs and Other Moorland Lays*, edited by Cicely Fox Smith, published by J. E. Cornish, Ltd., Manchester, UK, 1909, pp. 64-67. First published in *The Manchester Courier*.

Third in a set of "Territorial Ballads."

During the 18th and 19th centuries the army would often need horses in a hurry for either the Cavalry or for gun horses. Cavalry officers often bought their own mounts but the trooper would get what he was given. In times of need the army conscripted horses as well as men but they usually paid for the horses and as it was a seller's market they took whatever they could get at a relatively good price.

The Red Rose

"The sword of the Lord, and of Gideon."

Through the years—from the far day of Flodden,
From the gardens of Minden, the trodden
Red Inkerman snow;
Where Quebec keeps remembrance undying,
Where the dead under strange stars are lying
'Mid names that we know, –

Down the loud-ringing years of our story,
To the day of our yesterday's glory,
Our yesterday's pride—
Come the names of the true, the unfearing,
Stern sons of the grey mother's rearing,
Who conquered and died;

Ungrudging who gave full surrender
Of life, in its high noon of splendour,
Both near and afar;
Not last, on the highway of daring,
With the Red Rose of Lancaster wearing
The red rose of war.

The flower which, flame-bright where it springs on
The tramplings of captains and kings, on
The red-trampled sod,
Men gather to blossom forever—
The crown of all strife and endeavour—
In gardens of God.

What more? A torn standard, whose tatters
The breath of the years' passing shatters,
To dust falling down?
A memory scarce known from the deedless?
A statue high-set o'er the heedless,
Fierce tide of the town?

A name men remember, and wonder
A moment what ghost of war's thunder
It stirs in the brain?
A vision, a glory that passes—

As the light wind that stirs the long grasses
O'er graves of the slain?

Not so! For the spirit which brooks not
The name of dishonour, and looks not
On shirking nor shame,
Still lingers, to wake with the shrilling
Of the trumpets' high challenge note thrilling—
Forever the same.

We know not what battles lie hidden
Till the noise of their thunder is bidden
No longer be dumb—
What winepress of nations must redden
What terrible, vast Armageddon,
In days that shall come.

We know not; yet should the day find us
When a hand should be put forth to bind us
In fetters abhorr'd,
Or some lie under Heaven foully creeping
Call aloud for the terrible, sweeping,
White truth of the sword,

It may be we shall not be found wanting!
Not as children with loud words of vaunting,
But strong as of yore;
Not last, on the highway of daring,
With the Red Rose of Lancaster wearing
The red rose of war!

❖ ❖ ❖ ❖ ❖

From *Lancashire Hunting Songs and Other Moorland Lays*, edited by Cicely Fox Smith, published by J. E. Cornish, Ltd., Manchester, UK, 1909, pp. 67-70. First published in *The Manchester Courier*.

Fifth in a set of "Territorial Ballads."

The ancient symbol of the County of Lancashire is a "Red Rose." That of Yorkshire is a "White Rose!" The two Noble Families, who once ruled the counties, also used them as badges to identify troops. This is the origin of The Wars of the Roses when the two sides fought for the Crown of England.

Voices of the Hills

Dusk on the grey moors and a large silence that fills
Earth, and the wide skies, and the great peace of the hills—

Only my heart hears in the night, softly and low,
Over the fields call thro' the dark voices I know—

Voices of birds crying aloud, each unto each,
Cries with a strange mournful refrain, sadder than speech—

Voices of the wind—keen from the salt seas of its birth—
Singing of wild hopes and desire old as the earth;
Voices of lost youth—of the dear days that are done,
Moments of glad life in the good rain and the sun,

Dreams that we dreamed, faces we loved, laughter and tears,
Hither they come, out of the mist of the years—

Come with their dear burthen of sweet pleasure and woe,
Here at your far crying, O kind voices I know!

❖   ❖   ❖   ❖   ❖

From *The Nelson Evening Mail*, Volume 43, Nelson, New Zealand, May 17, 1909, p. 1; previously published in the *Westminster Gazette*.

BOOK 2

THE MAJOR POEMS: 1914-1931

*In Honour of the British Navy
to commemorate the surrender of the German fleet*,
by Bernard Partridge from *Punch* magazine,
Volume 155, November 27, 1918

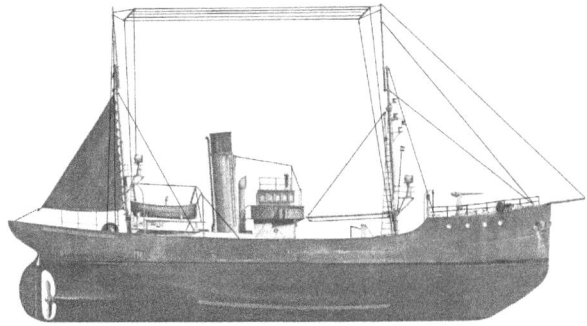

Armed Trawler

Admiral Dugout

He had done with fleets and squadrons, with the restless, roaming seas,
He had found the quiet haven he desired,
And he lay there to his moorings with the dignity and ease
Most becoming to Rear-Admirals (retired);
He was reared 'mid "Spit and Polish," he was bred to "stick and string"—
All the things the ultra-moderns never name:
But a wind blew up to seaward, and it meant the Real Thing,
And he had to slip his cable when it came.

So he hied him up to London, for to hang about Whitehall,
And he sat upon the steps there soon and late:
He importuned night and morning, he bombarded great and small,
From messengers to Ministers of State;
He was like a guilty conscience, he was like a ghost unlaid,
He was like a debt of which you can't get rid,
Till the Powers that Be, despairing, in a fit of temper said,
"For the Lord's sake give him something"—and they did!

They commissioned him a trawler with a high and raking bow,
Black and workmanlike as any pirate craft,
With a crew of steady seamen very handy in a row,
And a brace of little barkers fore and aft;
And he blessed the Lord his Maker when he faced the North Sea sprays,
And exceedingly extolled his lucky star,
That had given his youth renewal in the evening of his days
(With the rank of Captain Dugout, R. N. R.).

He is jolly as a sandboy, he is happier than a king,
And his trawler is the darling of his heart,
(With her cuddy like a cupboard where a kitten couldn't swing,
And a scent of fish that simply won't depart);
He has found upon occasion sundry targets for his guns,
He could tell you tales of mine and submarine,
Oh the holes he's in and out of, and the glorious risks he runs
Turn his son (who's in a Super-Dreadnought) green.

He is fit as any fiddle, he is hearty, hale and tanned;
He is proof against the coldest gales that blow;
He has never felt so lively since he got his first command,
(Which is rather more than forty years ago);
And of all the joyful picnics of his wild and wandering youth,
Little dust-ups 'tween Taku and Zanzibar,
There was none to match the picnic, he declares in sober sooth,
That he has as Captain Dugout, R. N. R.

❖ ❖ ❖ ❖ ❖

From *Sea Songs and Ballads 1917-22*, edited by Cicely Fox Smith, published by Houghton Mifflin Co., New York, US, 1924, p. 125-127. First published in *Punch* magazine, Volume 152, April 4, 1917, p. 224. Also printed in *Small Craft*, 1917.

A tribute to the old retired admiral, who during WWI successfully persuaded the Admiralty to let him do his bit in the war, even if it's as the captain of a modest warship such as an armed trawler. This Admiral was most likely John Locke Marx (1852-1939); his first command was the *Stephen Furness* and he later commanded a 'Q' ship.

Gordon Morris (UK) first adapted this poem for singing, as recorded with Peter Massey on *Full Sail: Inside the Lid*, 2002.

The header graphic of an armed trawler is from *War Ships & Sea Battles of WWI*, edited by Bernard Fitzsimons, published by Beekman House, New York, US, 1973, pp. 138-139.

After Dark

Under the blue sky,
And the white clouds sailing high,
Where the gallant wind went by,
A bird sang on—sang on
Till the day (too soon) was done.

And the daylight died
From the fields and the hillside,
And the moorland bare and wide . . .
But the bird sang on—sang on
Long after the light was gone—

Like a voice that said:
"Oh, you who weep your dead,
Be comforted—be comforted!
For the deed lives on, lives on
Long after the life is gone!" . . .

❖ ❖ ❖ ❖ ❖

From *Sailor Town: Sea Songs and Ballads*, edited by Cicely Fox Smith, published by George H. Doran Co., New York, US, 1919, p. 136. First published in *The Naval Crown* by Elkin Mathews, 1915 and subsequently in *The Evening Public Ledger*, June 4, 1919.

Composed during the first year of WWI, this poem may reflect on the loss of life in the war that would grind on for another three years. But it may also represent a personal reconciliation with death, the death of a loved one that the poet had met in British Columbia a few years before or her father who died in 1905. Smith often used the countryside where she grew up as a place to retreat to and reflect. See her set of poems entitled "Songs of Home" in *Small Craft*, 1919.

Foredeck of the abandoned *Luther Little*

Age (Millwall Dock)

It's 'ard on a ship when she's old—
An' her riggin' a sin to be'old,
An' there's nobody left for to care
As 'er paintwork's all blistered and bare,
An' 'er brasses as glittered like gold,
They're all over tarnish an' mould...
Oh, it's 'ard—
'Ard on a ship when she's old!

It's 'ard on a man when 'e's old...
An' 'is ships are all broke up an' sold,
An' there ain't nothin' left for 'im much
But trampin' around in the slutch
For a job o' shipkeepin' or such,
An' thinkin' o' foolin' an' fun
An' things as 'e's seen an' 'e's done
Where there's somethin' like 'eat in the sun,
An' 'is stren'th's like a tale as is told
In the mud, an' the rain, an' the cold...
Oh, it's 'ard—
'Ard on a man when he's old!

❖   ❖   ❖   ❖   ❖

From *Full Sail: More Sea Songs and Ballads*, edited by Cicely Fox Smith, published by Houghton Mifflin Co., New York, US, 1926, pp. 106-107.

There is an acute awareness in many of Smith's poems that the Great Age of Sail is passing, the ships as well as the shellbacks. This poem dwells on that.

This poem forms a set with "Poor Old Ship (Regent's Canal Dock)." Word "slutch" means mud.

The header graphic is a photograph of the capstan on the fore deck of the abandoned four-masted schooner *Luther Little*, Wiscasset, Maine, in 1957 as photographed by Robert Ipcar.

All Hallows

All on the autumn woods the mist lay white and chill;
And I heard the rising wind come piping down the hill,
And the stream sigh o'er the shallows
On the Eve of All Hallows
When the house was still.

I did not set the door wide, no meal did I spread,
Neither a cup of water nor a platter of bread,
They came without my calling
When the night was falling,
From the days that are dead.

No dogs barked at their passing from the silent fold;
There was no step on the doorsill nor print on the damp mould
To tell the world to-morrow
I supped with love and sorrow
Ere the hearth grew cold.

Dear dreams of years departed, kind ghosts of vanished days,
Slipped in then to the firelight, stretched their hands to the blaze,
Lost voices whispered nigh me,
Loved footsteps lingered by me
Ere they went their ways.

I heard a bird crying along the lonely hill,
I heard the stream sighing and the wind piping shrill
Across the frosty fallows . . .
On the eve of All Hallows
When the house was still.

❖ ❖ ❖ ❖ ❖

From *Small Craft: Sailor Ballads and Chantys*, edited by Cicely Fox Smith, published by George H. Doran Co., New York, US, 1919, pp. 124-125. First published in *Songs of Sail*, 1914.

The last and most haunting poem in a set called "Songs of Home" published shortly after the poet's return to England from British Columbia on the eve of WWI. Was she thinking of those who had departed from the world she had known in Canada, or those who would be lost in the war to come?

Types

All Sorts

"It takes all sorts to make a world, an' the same to make a crew;
It takes the good an' middlin' an' the rotten bad uns too;
The same's there are on land," says Bill, "you meet 'em all at sea . . .
The freaks an' fads an' crooks an' cads an' ornery folks like me."

"It takes a man for every job—the skippers an' the mates,
The chap as gives the orders an' the chap as chips the plates—
It takes the brass-bound 'prentices (an' ruddy plagues they be)
An' chaps as shirk an' chaps as work—just ornery chaps like me."

"It takes the stiffs an' deadbeats an' decent shellbacks too,
The chaps as always pull their weight an' them as never do,
The sort the Lord as made 'em knows what bloomin' use they be,
An' crazy folks, an' musical blokes . . . an' ornery chaps like me."

"It takes a deal o' fancy breeds—the Dagoes an' the Dutch,
The Lascars an' calashees an' the seedyboys an' such;
It takes the greasers an' the Chinks, the Jap an' Portugee,
The blacks an' yellers an' 'arf-bred fellers . . . an' ornery folks like me."

"It takes all sorts to make a world an' the same to make a crew,
It takes more kinds o' people than there's creeters in the Zoo;
You meet 'em all ashore," says Bill, "an' you find 'em all at sea . . .
But do me proud if most of the crowd ain't ornery chaps like me!"

❖ ❖ ❖ ❖ ❖

From *Rovings: Sea Songs and Ballads*, edited by Cicely Fox Smith, published by Elkin Mathews, London, UK, 1921, pp. 51-52. First published in *Punch* magazine, Volume 159, July 21, 1920, p. 46.

A vivid picture of how an old sailor might have described his messmates aboard one of those tall sailing ships at the close of the 19th century. The crew of a ship was not exactly a "melting

Along the Prairie Trail

I know it's only dreaming, and it never may be more,
But I'm thinking, as I have done many and many a time before,
That some day I'll be standing here and leaning on the rail,
And look, and see you coming along the prairie trail.

Oh, first I'd think perhaps I took some other one for you,
And then I'd be afraid to wake and find it wasn't true,
And there'd be sweet flowers everywhere, and singing on the gale,
When I went out to greet you along the prairie trail.

I'd have my hands in yours then, and you'd have hold of mine:
I'd look, and look again, and drink the sight of you like wine,
And ah! We'd have so much to say that all our words would fail
When you came up to meet me along the prairie trail.

I daresay dreams are folly (but sometimes they come true),
And after all is said, it's just a pleasant thing to do,
To stand, as I do now, and watch the sunset sky grow pale,
And think you're coming yonder along the prairie trail.

❖   ❖   ❖   ❖   ❖

From *Small Craft: Sailor Ballads and Chantys*, edited by Cicely Fox Smith, published by George H. Doran Co., New York, US, 1919, pp. 133-134. Earlier published in Songs of Sail, 1914.

The third of a set of poems entitled "Songs of the Wild." Perhaps, the poet is showing an influence here from prior poems by the Australian poets Henry Lawson and A. B. "Banjo" Paterson.

The Anchor Watch

O shipmates all, as you lay sleeping
Blow, boys, blow!
Across the world the day came creeping
Blow, boys, bully boys, blow!
With a cold wet wind the shrouds were shaking,
And in all the port was no one waking,
In the morning watch and the grey dawn breaking
Blow, boys, bully boys, blow!

I saw a ship come down the river
Blow, boys, blow!
In the morning light her sails did shiver
Blow, boys, bully boys, blow!
I saw the sun on her royals gleaming
And her gilded trucks in the dawn a-gleaming,
And the bubbled foam of her bow-wave streaming—
Blow, boys, bully boys, blow!

I heard the gulls all round her calling
Blow, boys, blow!

I heard the watch on the braces hauling
Blow, boys, bully boys, blow!
I heard their voices over the water—
"O Shenandoah, I love your daughter"—
And the dash o' the tide on her weather quarter
Blow, boys, bully boys, blow!

Then like a cloud she broke and lifted
Blow, boys, blow!
Her spars did melt, her sails they drifted
Blow, boys, bully boys, blow!
And all that I saw was a white mist flying,
All that I heard, the grey gulls crying,
And the tide's sob and the wind's sighing. . . .
And one far call out of dreams replying
Blow, boys, bully boys, blow!

❖ ❖ ❖ ❖ ❖

From *Rhymes of the Red Ensign*, edited by Cicely Fox Smith, published by Hodder & Stoughton, London, UK, 1919, pp. 69-70.

This poem seems inspired by the traditional shanty "Congo River."

Anchors

Anchors

In a breaker's yard by the Millwall Docks,
With its piled-up litter of sheaveless blocks,
Stranded hawsers and links of cable,
A cabin lamp and a chartroom table,
Nail-sick timbers and heaps of metal
Rusty and red as an old tin kettle,
Scraps that were ships in the years gone by,
Fluke upon stock the anchors lie.

Every sort of a make of anchor
For trawler or tugboat, tramp or tanker,
Anchors little and anchors big
For every build and for every rig,
Old wooden-stocked ones fit for the Ark,
Stockless and squat ones, ugly and stark,
Anchors heavy and anchors small,
Mushroom and grapnel and kedge and all.

Mouldy old mudhooks, there they lie!
Have they ever a dream as the days go by
Of the tug of the tides on coasts afar,
A Northern light and a Southern star,
The mud and sand of a score of seas,
And the chuckling ebb of a hundred quays,
The harbour sights and the harbour smells,
The swarming junks and the temple bells?

Roar of the surf on coral beaches,
Rose-red sunsets on landlocked reaches,
Strange gay fishes in cool lagoons,
And palm-thatched cities in tropic noons;
Song of the pine and sigh of the palm,
River and roadstead, storm and calm—
Do they dream of them all now their work is done,
And the neaps and the springs at the last are one?

And only the tides of London flow,
Restless and ceaseless, to and fro;
Only the traffic's rush and roar
Seems a breaking wave on a far-off shore,
And the wind that wanders the sheds among
The ghost of an old-time anchor song:—

"Bright plates and pannikins
To sail the seas around,
And a new donkey's breakfast
For the outward bound!"

❖   ❖   ❖   ❖   ❖

From *Rovings: Sea Songs and Ballads*, edited by Cicely Fox Smith, published by Elkin Mathews, London, UK, 1921, pp. 26-27. First published in *Punch* magazine, Volume 161, July 27, 1921, p. 75.

This poem is focused on the poet's fondness for wandering, or as she used to describe it "dock-walloping," along the Thames. It was prompted by what she observed in the Millwall Docks.

The header graphic is an illustration titled *Anchors* drawn by Edward William Cooke showing several old anchors and an old sailor by the quayside, 1829, from *Sailing Vessels in Authentic Early Nineteenth-Century Illustrations*, reprinted by Dover Publications, New York, US, 1989, p. 7.

Gunnery Practice

Armed Merchantmen: an Old Song Re-Sung

By the Liverpool Docks at the break of the day,
I saw a flash packet, bound westward away;
And well did I mark how each new-mounted gun
Like silver did gleam in the first morning sun.

Bound away, bound away,
Where the wide waters flow,
She's a Liverpool packet—
Oh, Lord, let her go!

For thieves be abroad on the ocean highway
To harass our traders by night and by day,
But let such attempt her, to take or assail,
They may find to their cost she's a sting in her tail.

She's a crack ocean liner—now catch her who can!—
Her crew are true British and game to a man;
The pirates of Potsdam had best have a care—
She's the Navy's stepdaughter, and touch her who dare!

Bound away, bound away, with a bone in her mouth,
She passes the Bar light, she turns to the south,
A Liverpool packet that stays for no foe—
Safe, safe on her journey, oh, Lord, let her go!

Bound away, bound away,
Where the wide waters flow,
She's a Liverpool packet,—
Oh, Lord, let her go!

From *Songs and Chanties: 1914-1916,* edited by Cicely Fox Smith, published by Elkin Mathews, London, UK, 1919, pp. 153-154. First published in *The Naval Crown* in 1915.

A WWI poem with a chorus modeled after the traditional 19th century sea shanty "Liverpool Packet."

"The pirates of Potsdam" is a reference to the German naval forces.

The header graphic is an illustration titled *Merchantmen at Gunnery Practice* as drawn by Muirhead Bone, from *Merchantmen-at-Arms*, by David M. Bone, published by Chatto & Windus, London. UK, 1919, frontispiece.

Mexico Dance Hall

Back to Hilo

There's a dark an' dirty wineshop on a waterfront I know,
An' a cross-eyed Dago keeps it—or he kep' it years ago—
Where the sailormen an' greasers sit them down to dice and dine—
An' I wish I was back again in Hilo—
        In Hilo—
Drinkin' old Jacinto's wine!

There's the blessed Andes standin' up behind it like a wall,
An' there's dust, an' stinks, an' insecks, an' there ain't much else at all,
An' them sulky Dago wenches, they was never much my line—
But I wish I was back again in Hilo—
        In Hilo—
Drinkin' old Jacinto's wine.

For my mind it keeps on turnin'—an' I ask you, ain't it queer,
When the stuff we used to get there warn't a bloomin' patch on beer?—
To that dirty Dago's wineshop an' them old-time pals o' mine—

An' I wish I was back again in Hilo—
          In Hilo—
Drinkin' old Jacinto's wine.

❖   ❖   ❖   ❖   ❖

From *Rovings: Sea Songs and Ballads*, edited by Cicely Fox Smith, published by Elkin Mathews, London, UK, 1921, p. 45.

A favorite topic for yarns and fo'c'sle ballads were the taverns that sailors had visited in the sailortowns around the world. The ethnic slurs would have been typical for the sailors of that day. The poem itself seems reminiscent of an earlier one by Masefield titled "A Night at Dago Tom's."

First set to music by Michael Head (1900-1976) in 1949, as published in *Six Sea Songs*.

The header graphic is an illustration titled *Mexico Bar* as drawn by shantysinger and sea songs collector Stan Hugill, from his book *Sailortown*, p. 234.

Jack Ashore

A Ballad of Old and New

As I went down through Portsmouth Town, with my bundle in my hand,
I met a chap in a pigtail rig, just newly come to land;
I met a fellow of an old-style build, with a look both bold and free,—
With varnished hat and buckled shoes, like the men of the Old Navee.

"What news, what news, young fellow," he said, "of rigging loft and yard;
What ships are new, and what are built this year at Buckler's Hard?
And is the cry, 'More frigates,' still, as I mind it used to be?
Do England's oaks build ships this day like the ships of the Old Navee?

"And when these things you've answered all, why, then, lad, tell me true,
Who stands this day where Nelson stood (if any so may do),
What prizes late our Fleet has won, what victories gained at sea;
Does England hold what she fought for of old, in the days of the Old Navee?"

"By Tyne and Clyde and Merseyside our ships lie keel by keel,
And a man must stop his ears to hear the hammer on the steel;
By Buckler's Hard nought now you hear but song of bird and tree,
But the ships of grey will be first in the fray like the ships of the Old Navee.

"Dogger and Bight and Falklands fight, and one or two beside,
And Jutland Bank shall one day rank with the names of Nelson's pride;
But that's a tale is all too hard for simple lads like me,—
Not word, but deed, is the sailor's creed, as it was in the Old Navee.

"But when the time for deeds is come, we've fighting lads a few,
Can hit and hold, both swift and bold, the same's they used to do,
Can hunt the pirate submarine from broad and narrow sea,
And strike the raider in his lair as they did in the Old Navee.

"So let the Navy have her fling, she'll show in the Navy's way
Our frontier is the foeman's shore, to-day as yesterday:
For the fights that are fought on blue water will win or lose the sea,
As it was when Hawke and Nelson sailed in the ships of the Old Navee.

"And all we ask is to finish our task some day with a free sky o'er us,
A day fair and fine, with a clear skyline, and a foe that will stand before us:
We've a man from Wexford that we know full well for as good as any may be,
And the bulldog's grip that never slip, as it was in the Old Navee!"

As I went down through Portsmouth Town, a cold rain falling fast,
I saw the flap of old *Victory's* flag, where she dreams of victories past,
And this was the word the salt wind bore that blew from the English sea:
"Be it steam or sail, you weather the gale by the New as the Old Navee!"

❖ ❖ ❖ ❖ ❖

From *Small Craft: Sailor Ballads and Chantys*, edited by Cicely Fox Smith, published by George H. Doran Co., New York, US, 1919, pp. 17-20.

One of this poet's patriotic poems for reinforcing national pride during WWI.

The header graphic is an illustration drawn by George Cruikshank, from *Dibdin's Sea Songs*, edited by Thomas Dibdin, published by Henry G. Bohn, London, UK, 1854, facing p. 76.

The U-Boat and Its Prey

The Ballad of the *Dinkinbar*

It was the steamship *Dinkinbar*,
From the Gulf of Mexico
For Liverpool in time of war
With a thousand mules below,
And a bunch of polyglot muleteers
To tend on them also.

A swarthy breed from Eagle Butte,
And a greaser from Brazil,
And Daly of the broken nose,
And Ike, and Texas Bill.

In divers tongues that yarned and swore
And wrangled o'er their play,
As they dealt their deck of greasy cards
To pass the hours away.

And talked of how to burn good pay
And play the blooming fool
Among the wenches and the sharks
In the port of Liverpool.

But Texas Bill a bitter laugh
He'd laugh and shake his head:
"It's me for a new style jamboree
When I strike land," he said.

"My brother lies in deep water
Not over far from here,
Where a U-boat sank both ship and men,
A bit beyond Cape Clear."

"They left him to drown with his drownin' mules
In the light of open day,
An' I guess I'll not sleep easy o' nights
While that score's yet to pay."

"So I'm goin' in for a khaki suit
When I gets in from sea,
I kin shift my birthplace north o' the line
As handy as kin be,
An' . . . I guess there'll sure be a fightin' job
For a big long thing like me!"

It was the steamship *Dinkinbar*,
At the stormy end o' the year
That came in sight of the Bull and Cow
Which are beside Cape Clear.

And soon as rang the lookout's cry
That hailed the sight of land,
Oh, they were aware of a U-boat there
That signaled them to stand.

She fired a shot across their hawse
And they had to heave-to then,
For she could make her fifteen knots,
And the *Dinkinbar* but ten,
And she had her machine gun ready to fire
On all but unarmed men.

Her captain he came over the side,
A cold-eyed swaggering Hun
That wore the Iron Cross on his breast
To tell of murders done,—

And his squarehead crew brought up their bombs
To send the ship below
With the poor living things she bore
That knew not a friend or foe.

It was a British ship of war
Was swiftly drawing near,
For she had heard of a submarine
Was lurking off Cape Clear.

She came from the South with a bone in her mouth,
Her shot sang over the sea,
And straight for the pirate's conning tower
It sped like a hiving bee,
It struck—it smashed it like a shell—
That down like a stone went she.

Then the pirate captain ran to the rail
To signal to his crew,
But all he saw was a smear of oil
On the water's face that grew.

And first he swore and gnawed his lip,
And glanced around in fear,
Till a thought came into his mind again
That brought him better cheer.

"Are not the English easy folk
With pirates ta'en in war?
And my luck is good that safe I stand
On the deck of the *Dinkinbar*."

He turned—he saw the muleteers
Come surging from below,
(Like a rustlers' crowd you see on screen
At a moving picture show).

And once he looked on Texas Bill,
And then he turned and ran,
For the look he saw it was not good
To see on the face of man.

Then in and out among the boats,
By hatch and alleyway,
Hunter and hunted, to and fro
In deadly chase sped they.

And through the engine-room where stilled
Was now the engine's clang,
On steel ladder and steel grating
Their footsteps slipped and rang.

Till in the screw shaft's stifling dark,
With spent and grasping breath
The U-boat's captain turned at last
To pay his dues to death . . . .

And twice Bill lifted his hand to strike,
And twice he turned aside,

But his brother's blood it called so loud
It would not be denied,
And down in the dark (like those he slew)
The U-boat captain died.

The cruiser's boat came under the side,
They hailed her with a cheer,
And Texas Bill looked over the rail
And called both loud and clear,
"Come up, come up, now, Lootenant,
But you'll find no prisoner here."

"For Texas law is life for life
Alike in peace and war,
And life for life has paid this day
On board o' the *Dinkinbar*."

From *Small Craft: Sailor Ballads and Chantys*, edited by Cicely Fox Smith, published by George H. Doran Co., New York, US, 1919, pp. 46-51.

A poem from WWI which brutally illustrates that the old adage, "an eye for an eye," had not lost its punch. Such is war!

The header graphic is an illustration titled *The German Submarine and Its Prey*, from WWI, artist unknown.

On the Bridge

The Ballad of the *Eastern Crown*

I've sailed in 'ookers plenty since first I went to sea—
An' sail or steam, an' good or bad, was all alike to me;
There's some 'ave tried to starve me, an' some 'ave tried to drown—
But I never met the equal o' the *Eastern Crown*.

'Er funnel's like a chimley, 'er sides is like a tub,
An' pay is middlin' scanty, an' likewise so is grub;
She's 'ard to beat for steerin' bad, she's 'ard to beat for grime,
An' rollin' is 'er 'obby—oh, she's rollin' all the time!

Rollin' down to Singapore—rollin' up to Maine—
Rollin' round to Puget Sound, an' then 'ome again!
A long roll, an' a short roll, an' a roll in between,
An' the crew cursin' rosy when she ships it green!

We sailed from Philadelphia, New York an' Montreal,
Dischargin' general cargo at our various ports o' call;
We knocked about a year or so 'tween Callao an' Nome,
An' then to Portland, Oregon, to load with deals for 'ome.

She's met with accidents a few (which is 'er usual way);
She scraped a bowsprit off a barque in San Francisco Bay;
She's shed propeller blades an' plates wherever she 'as been . . .
An' last she's fouled 'er bloomin' screw on a German submarine!

Rollin' in the sunshine—rollin' in the rain—
Rollin' up the Channel—an' we're 'ome again!
A long roll, an' a short roll, an' a roll in between,
An' the crew cursin' rosy when she ships it green!

As on the 'igh an' draughty bridge I stood my wheel one day,
"If we sight a submarine" (I 'eard the Old Man say)
"I'd do as Admirals retired an' other folks 'ave said,
I'd run the old Red Duster up an' ring 'full speed ahead';

I'd sink before I'd 'eave 'er to or 'aul my colours down;
By Gosh, they'll catch a Tartar if they catch the *Eastern Crown*!
I've thought it out both 'igh an' low, an' this seems best to me—
Pursoo a zig-zag course" ('e says) "an' see what I shall see!"

Rollin' through the Doldrums—rollin' in the foam—
Rollin' by the Fastnet—an' we're nearly 'ome;
A long roll, an' a short roll, an' a roll in between,
An' the crew cursin' rosy when she ships it green!

'E said it, an' 'e meant it, an' acted as 'e said
When sure enough we sighted one abeam o' Lizard 'Ead;
You should 'ave 'eard the engines grunt—you should 'ave seen 'er roll!
She was beatin' all the records as they shoveled on the coal!

They missed us by a spittin' length—'er rollin' served 'er well,
But it served 'er even better after, as you're goin' to 'ear me tell;
For she some'ow rolled 'erself atop o' the bloomin' submarine . . .
An' oil upon the water was the last of it we seen.

Rollin' up to London Town (an' down by the bow);
Rollin' 'ome to Surrey Docks—ain't we 'eros now?
A long roll, an' a short roll, an' a roll in between,
An' the crew cursin' rosy as she ships it green!

From *Songs and Chanties: 1914-1916*, edited by Cicely Fox Smith, published by Elkin Mathews, London, UK, 1919, pp. 119-122. First published in *The Spectator,* April 10, 1915, p. 15; also Timaru Herald, New Zealand, Vol. CII, issue 15668, May 29, 1915, p. 3.

A poem composed during the first two years of WWI in tribute to the Merchantmen's battle with the German U-boats.

First adapted for singing by Bob Zentz (US), as recorded on *Closehauled on the Wind of a Dream*, 2007.

The header graphic is an illustration titled *The Bridge of a Merchantman* as drawn by Muirhead Bone, from *Merchantmen-at-Arms*, p. 7.

The Elixir of Hate

The Ballad of the Hun King's Dream

About the dead dark o' the night,
Ere the first cock clapped his wing,
The Hun Lord's soul had wandered far—
A shrunk and wizened thing—

Beyond Polaris and the Plough,
And the cold Northern Crown,
Where white in space the Milky Way
O'er the lip of space pours down.

East o' the Sun, West o' the Moon.
In a twilit land walked he,
The same where vagrant souls do range
When sleep has set them free—
And a shadowy guide went at his side
Whose face he might not see.

And first there was a place of thorns,
And then a salt sea-shore,

And then a river dark and wide
That no man might cross o'er;
And the wind blew, the wind blew
As it could blow no more.

"What thorns be these, so long and keen,
That bites me to the bone?" . . .
Oh, these be thorns of hate and lies
Which you on earth have sown.

"What sea is this before my feet
That has so salt a tide?"
Oh, that is the flood of women's tears
That fall and are not dried;
They weep, and, weeping, name his name
Through whom their dear ones died.

"What stream is this so dark and deep
That laps me to the chin?" . . .
Oh, that is the river of men's blood
Who perished by your sin.

There is no boat shall ferry you,
No ford shall bring you through
The red river that runs always
Between your God and you.

There was no light in all the land
But the far glare of Mars;
And the wind blew, the wind blew,
It shook the fixed stars.

And in that wind the shivering soul
Like a dry leaf was driven . . .
"What wind is this, what fearful wind,
That rocks the stars in Heaven?"

Oh, that is the breath of a dead mother
With a dead babe at her side,
Beneath your iron heel who lay,
And cursed you as she died!

❖ ❖ ❖ ❖ ❖

From *Sailor Town: Sea Songs and Ballads*, edited by Cicely Fox Smith, published by George H. Doran Co., New York, US, 1919, pp. 105-107. Earlier published in *The Naval Crown* by Elkin Mathews in 1915.

A WWI poem composed early in the War, the "Hun King" being a cartoon characterization of Kaiser Wilhelm II of Germany.

The header graphic is a cartoon titled *The Elixir of Hate* as drawn by L. Raven-Hill, from *Punch* magazine, May 5, 1915, p. 343.

Limping Home

The Ballad of the *Matterhorn*

By Casey's Occidental Rooms, when the sun is getting low,
The chattering crowds of Chinatown along the pavements go,
And then you'll hear the wrangling gulls about the harbour-side,
And see the ships come in which use the oceans deep and wide,
And smell the smell o' the waterfront, the shipping and the tide.

And there do meet all brands o' folk which on the Coast are found,
From Behring Strait to Mexico, from Frisco and the Sound,
The Dago and the Dutchman there, with all queer breeds that be,
Stand up to drink with Jap and Chink beside the sunset sea.

And there do swear and fight and lie and leave their pay behind
The whalers and the tugboat men and the loggers rolling blind;
And there the Siwash and the Sikh go jostling side by side,
And sailormen blow out and in like driftlogs tide by tide.

By Casey's Occidental Rooms, as I was strolling by
And thinking over this and that, and things both far and nigh,
There chanced to meet me face to face a man I used to know;
That sailed with me in the *Matterhorn*, in a day that's long ago.

And "Oh, Lord love you, Mike," I said, and took him by the hand,
"Do you sail yet in the *Matterhorn*, and are you long for land?
It's good to see your face again, these longshore lads among,
To 'mind me of the *Matterhorn* and the time when I was young."

"If I had sailed in the *Matterhorn* it is not here I'd be,
And thirsty as the hob of hell as I am now," said he,
"A bitter drink I'd sup among the cold and clammy dead
If I had signed in the *Matterhorn* when last she sailed," he said.

"She's gone, and none but old Cape Stiff can tell the when or how,
And them that watched the lists for her, they're tired o' watching now;

Far down, far down in Dead Man's Bay both ship and men do lie,
And the *Lutine* bell has rung for her this many a day gone by."

"I saw her sail from Salthouse Dock—the sun was risin' red,
And 'See you next in Callao' my friends aboard her said;
'Tween Callao and Liverpool a many ports there be,
And many men I'll meet again—but them I shall not see."

"Well, safe we got to Callao, but we were long a-going,
The old tub leaking like a sieve, old Horn his hardest blowing;
The big seas swept her fore and aft; the sails they cut like steel;
Our bodies to the yards they froze, our hands froze to the wheel."

"And them that sailed before us came, and most that since did sail,
They came all battered with the seas and broken with the gale;
And one that had been missing long, with sticks all snapped and shorn
Limped in to tell her tale ashore, but not the *Matterhorn*."

"So last we knew that she was gone, as best and worst may go,
The good ship and the bad likewise, the fast ship and the slow;
A fast ship was the *Matterhorn* when all them kites was spread,
A fast ship and fine she was—" "Ay, she was fast," I said.

From course to skysail up she soared like a midsummer cloud;
In all the earth I have not seen a thing more brave and proud;
And she is gone as dreams do go, or song sung long before,
Or the golden years of a man's youth when they are his no more.

And all the shining moons of youth, and all the stars of dream
Were tangled in her topmast spars and through her shrouds did gleam;
Now thundering like a North Sea gale, now humming faint and low,
Came singing with her down the years the winds of long ago.

By Casey's Occidental Rooms a bitter thing I heard,
With a heavy heart I turned away, and long I spoke no word;
I bared my head there where I stood, "God rest her soul," I said,
As if a woman I had loved in a far land was dead.

❖   ❖   ❖   ❖   ❖

From *Songs and Chanties: 1914-1916*, edited by Cicely Fox Smith, published by Elkin Mathews, London, UK, 1919, pp. 73-77. First published in *Blackwood's Magazine*, Vol. 195, June, 1914, p. 812. Also published in *Sailor Town* both in the UK and US in 1919.

There was an "Occidental Hotel" across from the lawyer's office in Victoria, British Columbia, where the poet worked as a typist during part of her stay from 1912 to 1913. The hotel was on the edge of Victoria's flourishing Chinatown and its waterfront.

Compare with "The Old Fiddle" for another take on this neighborhood in Victoria and the theme of time slipping away.

The header graphic is a photograph of the four-masted barque *Hougomont* limping into Port Adelaide, Australia, after being dismasted in 1932, Nautical Photo Agency, from *Last of the Wind Ships*, #194.

The Ballad of the Only Love

Oh, have you been to Rio Grande, or yet to 'Frisco town,
Or west away to Mobile Bay where they roll the cotton down?
Oh, have you been in any place where sailors come from sea,
And saw you there my only love that sends no word to me?

Oh, does he walk with a yaller gal forgetting to be true,
Or drink with pals in sailor-town as many sailors do?
Does he with strangers fill his glass and to them sing his song,
And never think of his only love—
His only love, his only love—
And never think of his own true love that waits for him so long?

"Yes, I have seen your only love, and spoken with him also,
And it wasn't very far away nor very long ago;
He said, 'Oh, tell my gal at home to forget me if she can
And she'd better get another love that ain't a sailorman'"

"But he doesn't walk with no yaller gal, I tell you straight and plain,
And there's never a pal in sailor-town 'll drink with him again;
We buried him out of an open boat a hundred miles from shore,
And you'd better get another love—
Another love, another love—
Oh, you'd better get another love, for he'll come home no more."

"Our ship was sunk in the light of day, as plenty more have been,
In the North Atlantic homeward bound by a pirate submarine,
And we was drifting many a day and food and drink had none,
When a cruiser picked us up at last at the rising o' the sun."
"Your man was first to go, poor chap, he was crazed-like in his head,

Along o' drinking sea-water, for all the captain said,
'I'll marry my lass with a ring,' he'd say, 'when I get in from sea,
And she shall be my only love—
My only love, my only love—
Oh, she shall be my own dear love, for I know that she loves me.'"

Oh, cold, cold are the Atlantic deeps, and very wide the sea,
With all its weight of stormy waves between my love and me;
And wide and deep the tide o' time a-rolling year on year,
But there'll be no parting after death for us that loved so dear.
 Oh. Many a sailor will come home, and many a ship from sea,

But never a ship on any tide will bring my lad to me,
And the long, long days they'll come and go, and the lonely years pass by,
But I will keep my only love—
My only love, my only love—
Oh, I will keep my only love until the day I die!

From *Sailor Town: Sea Songs and Ballads*, edited by Cicely Fox Smith, published by George H. Doran Co., New York, US, 1919, pp. 30-33. The poem first appeared in an earlier edition of *Sailor Town* published by Elkin Mathews in 1914, p. 30.

The poet provides several alternative ways that her favorite shantyman "Dan" died, the "Lee Fore Brace" being only one alternative. Perhaps, she never really learned what happened to him. But there can be little doubt that she loved him (see "Shipmates") and there is no evidence that she ever later fell in love with anyone else.

Torpedoed but Still Afloat

The Ballad of the Resurrection Packet

Oh, she's in from deep water, she's safe in port once more,
With shot-'oles in 'er funnel which were not there before;
Yes, she's 'ome, dearie, 'ome, an' we're 'alf the sea inside!
Ought to 'ave sunk, but couldn't if she tried!

An' it was "'ome, dearie, 'ome, oh, she'll bring us 'ome some day,
Rollin' both rails under in the old sweet way!
Freezin' in the foul weather, fryin' in the fine,
The resurrection packet of the Salt 'Orse Line!"

If she'd been built for sinkin' she'd 'ave done it long ago;
She's tried 'er best in every sea an' all the winds that blow;
In 'uricanes at Galveston, pamperos off the Plate,
An' icy Cape 'Orn snorters which freeze you while you wait.

She's been ashore at Vallipo, Algoa Bay likewise,
She's broke 'er screw shaft off Cape Race an' stove 'er bows in ice,
She's lost 'er deck-load overboard an' 'alf 'er bulwarks too,
An' she's come in with fire aboard, smokin' like a flue.

But it's "'ome, dearie, 'ome. Oh she gets there just the same,
Reekin', leakin', 'alf a wreck, scarred an' stove an' lame;
Patch 'er up with putty, lads, tie 'er up with twine,
The resurrection packet of the Salt 'Orse Line!"

A bit west the Scillies the sky was stormy red;
"Tonight we'll lift Saint Agnes Light if all goes well," we said;
But we met a slinkin' submarine as dark was comin' down,
An' she ripped our rotten plates away an' left us there to drown.

A bit west the Scillies we thought 'er sure to sink,
There was 'alf a gale blowin', the sky was black as ink;
The seas begun to mount an' the wind begun to thunder,
An' every wave that came, oh we thought 'twould roll 'er under!

But it was "'Ome, dearie, 'ome, an' she gets there after all—
Steamin' when she can steam, an' when she can't she'll crawl,
This year, next year, rain or storm or shine,
The resurrection packet of the Salt 'Orse Line!"

We thought about the bulk-'eads, we wondered if they'd last,
An' the cook 'e started groanin', an' repentin' of the past;
But thinkin' an' groanin', oh they wouldn't shift the water,
So we got the pumps a-workin', same as British seamen oughter.

If she'd been a crack liner she'd 'ave gone down like stone,
An' why she didn't sink is a thing as an't be known;
Our arms was made o' lead, our backs was split with achin',
But we pumped 'er into port just before the day was breakin'!

An' it was "'Ome, dearie, 'ome, oh she'll bring us 'ome some day,
Don't you 'ear the pumps a-clankin' in the old sweet way?
This year, next year, rain or snow or shine,
She's the resurrection packet of the Salt 'Orse Line!"

❖   ❖   ❖   ❖   ❖

From *Songs and Chanties: 1914-1916*, edited by Cicely Fox Smith, published by Elkin Mathews, London, UK, 1919, pp. 183-186. First published in *Punch* magazine, Volume 149, November 3, 1915, p. 377.

Another WWI ballad commemorating the danger and difficulty that merchantmen had in trying to slip through the German submarine blockade of England. This badly wounded ship successfully makes her way home.

This poem was first adapted for singing by Mike Kennedy in 2010.

The header graphic is a photograph of the American freighter *S.S. Westward Ho* soon after she was torpedoed by the German submarine *U-62*, on August 8th, 1918. She was successfully towed into a French port, repaired and re-launched, photographer unknown.

Grand Republic

Beauty

I've been north an' south (said Bill),
I've been east an' west,
An' seen lots o' sights, I 'ave,
As some folks reckon best . . .

'Bergs like big cathedrals
Sailin' stately by . . .
Coral islands where the sea's
Bluer 'n any sky . . .

Flyin' fish like rainbows
Flashin' through the spray . . .
Dawn on Fujiyama's crest
Like apple-trees in May . . .
But I reckon as the grandest sight
Ever I see
Was a right racin' clipper
Under canvas, runnin' free—

Was a flash flyin' clipper
With her kites both large an' small,
With 'er low sails and 'igh sails
From water-sails to skysails—
Ringtail, jib-o-jib, Jamie Green and all!

I've been 'ere an' there (said Bill),
I've been up an' down,
An' many a fine thing I've seen
In many a foreign town . . .

Temples full o' carvin's
In jade and ivory . . .
A thumpin' golden Buddha
Sittin' smilin' out to sea . . .

Blob-shaped domes all shinin'
Same as bubbles in the sun . . .
Pyramids an' what not—
I've seen 'em every one.

And I reckon as the finest thing
A man ever made
Was a slim slashin' clipper
Swingin' down the Trade—

Was a right racin' clipper,
Taut an' trim and tall,
With 'er low sails and 'igh sails
From water-sails to skysails,
Ringtail, jib-o-jib, Jamie Green and all!

❖   ❖   ❖   ❖   ❖

From *Sailor's Delight*, edited by Cicely Fox Smith, published by Methuen & Co., London, UK, 1931, pp. 88-90; first published in the magazine *Holly Leaves*.

There are not many sailors alive today who could name the various supplemental sails a true clipper ship could array.

The header graphic is a painting of the four-masted clipper ship *Grand Republic* with all sails set by Charles Robert Patterson, 1924, from *Sailor-Painter*, by Robert Lloyd Webb, published by Flat Hammock Press, Mystic, Connecticut, US, 2005, p. 156.

Bill

His age on the ship's books is fifty-four:
It's stood at that this twenty years or more.

He's had no schooling, so he makes his mark
With a fist that's gnarled and hard and brown as bark.

He remembers the great days of the tea clippers
Back in the 'fifties, when the racing skippers

Cracked on to glory—served in great old ships
That were lost or burned or wrecked or gone to chips

When we were in our cradles. Ay, he knew
Once Captain Forbes of the *Marco Polo* too—

"A sandy bloke he was—ginger for pluck
As the saying goes—but sp'iled by too much luck."

He makes square sennet better than all the rest:
Even our bosun's got to give him best.

❖ ❖ ❖ ❖ ❖

From *Full Sail: More Sea Songs and Ballads*, edited by Cicely Fox Smith, published by Houghton Mifflin Co., Boston, US, 1926, pp. 25-26.

It was not uncommon for old sailors to lie about their age when signing aboard ship. Captain "Bully" Forbes was a notorious skipper of the Canadian built sailing ship, the *Marco Polo*, at one time the fastest ship afloat.

Bill

Bill Brewster

In Burke's Saloon, among the crowd,
I heard Bill Brewster boasting loud,
Boasting loud and boasting long
A lot of longshore stiffs among.
And oh! The tales Bill Brewster told
About his deeds both brave and bold,
And how he tamed on his last trip
A tough-nut, hard-case, blue-nose ship,
Damned the skipper, licked the mate,
And downed a bosun twice his weight,
And had 'em eating from his hand,
Within a week from losing land . . .
And how he'd fought a whole saloon
Of jealous Dagoes, to some tune,
Armed to the teeth with guns and knives,
And sent 'em howling for their lives,
And all because the girls, you know,
They just love Bill Brewster so!

And somewhere else, off his bat
He'd laid out six policemen flat,—
For "Boys," said he, "no fetal error,
But when I'm roused I'm sure a terror!"

So off he swaggered with his din
To find more greenhorns to take in,
And all his bunch of stiffs did follow
With all their mouths stretched wide to swallow
The guff Bill handed 'em, like beer . . .
And sure enough Bill's yarns to hear
You'd think no skipper'd stand his ground
For half-an-hour when Bill was round,
Nor any mate that sails the sea
Would dare lay hands on such as he,
Nor port from Bombay to Brazil
But trembles just to hear of Bill.

And yet when Bill's out at sea,
Why, quite a different chap is he,—
For he's the sort that likes to shirk
Such nasty things as jobs of work,
The sort that never tries to earn
The pay he well knows how to burn,
Or stand his trick, or pull his weight,
Fair and fair like a good shipmate.
The kind of thing that suits Bill more
Is hanging round the galley door,
And licking pots, and peeling spuds,
And dobying other people's duds,
And eating up the cabin scraps,
And sneaking things off other chaps.
And yet you'd never think how quick
He'll stir himself to dodge a kick,
Nor yet how smart aloft he'll shin
At the sight of a belaying-pin.
For Bill afloat's like plenty more
That talk so big when they're ashore,
And once at sea, you'll quickly find
His valour's mostly . . . in his mind!

❖ ❖ ❖ ❖ ❖

From *Ships and Folks*, edited by Cicely Fox Smith, published by Elkin Mathews, London, UK, 1920, pp. 41-42.

Here we have a braggart sailor brilliantly nailed!

The header graphic is an illustration drawn by Charles Pears, from *Salt-Water Poems and Ballads*, John Masefield, published by The Macmillan Co., New York, US, 1912. facing p. 36.

Bill the Dreamer

"Some day when I'm rich (said Bill) I'm going to leave the sea,
Sail an' steam alike 'll see the livin' last o' me;
And 'bout ship or heave her to, they'll rouse me out no more,
In a clean quiet cottage like I've often seen ashore,
With hen-and-chickens, daisies growing by the door."

"Quiet will the days come and easy will go,
Smoking of my pipe there and workin' with a hoe,
And thinkin' of poor mates o' mine toiling in the cold
That hadn't sense to leave it an' they growing old."

"For when all's said and done, lads, it's little short o' sin
To spend your money foolish that's bitter hard to win;
I'll save my pay a year or two, and then I'll sail no more,
Sitting down so easy in my little place ashore."

And so went his yarn on and so would he say—
Round the Horn with hurricanes blowing all the way,
All the way from Callao trudging home again
To the Bar light shining in the cold and rain.

But who's to keep from share and share with friends o' the best?
And girls along the waterfront, they'll help to spend the rest;
And the cottage and the garden and the daisies by the door,
They went the way of many dreams when sailors come to shore.

And he's rolling down to Rio with a drunken Dago crew,
And the deadheads under hatches till they get their groaning through;
Yes, he's rolling down to Rio as he's often done before,
And will do till the day comes for Bill to sail no more,
When the ninth wave, the last wave, shall bring him to shore!

❖ ❖ ❖ ❖ ❖

From *Sailor Town: Sea Songs and Ballads*, edited by Cicely Fox Smith, published by George H. Doran Co., New York, US, 1919, pp. 18-19. An earlier edition of *Sailor Town* was published by Elkin Mathews in 1914; earlier published in *The Evening Post*, Volume 87, Issue 85, Wellington, NZ, April 11, 1914, p. 13 but first published in *The Spectator*.

Compare this poem with one titled "Hell's Pavement" by John Masefield for similar sentiment.

Bill's Choice

"All that sort o' guff," said Bill, "they may keep
About 'ow nice it is bein' buried at sea,
For I don't want no rest in the rollin' deep,
Nor yet no blinkin' fishes a-nibblin' me."

"I never could see no sense in slingin' a rhyme
Over a bolt o' sail an' a dollop o' lead,

An' sailormen get salt water enough in their time
Not to be wantin' the taste of it after they're dead."

"An' if I was goin' to be buried, the place for me
'Ud be some snug port or other, I don't mind where,
Somewhere within the sound an' smell o' the sea,
East or West or South—well, I won't much care."

"So long's I can lay quiet an' hear the ships
Goin' an' comin' . . . an' sailormen 'avin' their fun . . .
A song an' a laugh an' a drink an' a girl's red lips . . .
An' a bit of a shellback's yarn when the long day's done."

❖ ❖ ❖ ❖ ❖

From *Rovings: Sea Songs and Ballads*, edited by Cicely Fox Smith, published by Elkin Mathews, London, UK, 1921, p. 44.

There have been many debates on the somber subject of burial at sea or ashore, especially so since sailors didn't like sailing with a corpse on board. The second stanza objects to romantic poems about sea burial.

A Battle with the Foresail

Bill's Christmases

"Christmas," said Bill, "on Christmas cards, it's winders all aglow,
An' lots o' stuff to eat an' drink an' a good three feet o' snow,
An' a bunch o' bouncin' girls to kiss under the mistletoe.

Holly an' robin redbreasts too, as rosy as can be,
An' waits an' chimes an' all such gear as you never get at sea,
But it's different things as Christmas means to a ramblin' bloke like me.

The first I ever 'ad at sea I was 'ardly more 'n a nipper,
An' I'd took an' signed, bein' young an' green, in a dandy Down-east clipper
With a bullnecked beast of a bucko mate an' a rare tough nut of a skipper.

An' we dined 'andsome, so we did, off biscuits an' salt 'orse,
An' finished up with scraper duff an' sand-an'-canvas sorce,
An' them as growled got seaboot soup by way of an extry course.

I've 'ad my Christmas 'ere an' there, I've 'ad it up an' down,
I've 'ad it sober on the seas an' drunk in sailor-town,
I've 'ad it where the folks are black an' where the folks are brown,

And under many a tropic sky an' many a foreign star,
In Perim, Portland, Pernambuck, Malacca, Malabar,
Where the rum bird-'eaded totem poles and the gilded Buddhas are.

I've 'ad it froze in Baltic cold an' burned in Red Sea 'eat,
I've 'ad it in a Channel fog as busy as a street,
An' once I 'ad it off the 'Orn, an' that was sure a treat.

I was in the clipper *Sebright* then—a big ship, 'eavy sparred,
With every sort o' flyin' kite an' a seventy foot mainyard,
An' 'andlin' 'er in a gale of wind, I tell you, it was 'ard!

We come on deck for the middle watch, an' save us, 'ow it blew!
A night like the devil's ridin' boots, that never a star shone through,
An' the seas they kep' on poopin' 'er till we 'ad to 'eave 'er to.

We snugged 'er down, we 'ove 'er to, an' there all night lay she,
With one mainyard arm pointin' to 'eaven an' one to the deeps o' the sea,
Dippin' 'er spars at every roll in the thunderin' foam alee.

Till the wind an' sea went down a bit an' the dawn come cold an' grey,
An' we laid aloft an' loosed the sails an' squared the ship away,
An' a chap beside me on the yard says, 'Bill, it's Christmas Day!'"

❖   ❖   ❖   ❖   ❖

From *Sea Songs and Ballads 1917-1922*, edited by Cicely Fox Smith, published by Houghton Mifflin Co., New York, US, 1924, pp. 22-24. Earlier published in *Sea Songs and Ballads*, 1922. First published in *Punch* magazine, Volume 161, December 21, 1921, p. 495.

There were few holidays, if any, on sailing ships, and even if there were a modest plan for something special for Christmas what happened was subject to the weather and the captain's whim.

First adapted for singing by Bob Zentz (US), recorded on *Closehauled on the Wind of a Dream*, 2007.

The header graphic is an illustration titled *A Battle with the Foresail* as drawn by Gordon Grant from his book *Sail Ho!*, facing p. 92.

A Forecastle Yarn

Bill's Enemy

"There's a bloke I sometimes want to kick the worst way in the world,"
Said Bill, while from his short black pipe the dog-watch smoke-wreaths curled,
"'E's a decent sort o' blighter, an' 'e mostly means me well,
But the 'arm that feller's done me it'd take a week to tell."

"'E spends my 'ard-earned cash on beer an' wine an' fancy gals,
'E gets me fightin' with cops an' scrappin' with my pals:
'E takes an' pawns my sea-chest when 'e's been an' burned my pay,
And' I've never got the bloomin' guts to up an' say 'im nay."

"'E's lost me every chanst I've 'ad o' getting' on in life:
If it 'adn't been for 'im I'd 'ave a public an' a wife:
I've run my ship along of 'im an' wished I 'adn't after:
Cut off my nose to spite my face an' what could you 'ave dafter?"

"There ain't no other chap alive I'd stand it from," said Bill,
"But we've allus sailed together, an' I guess we allus will:
'E's a sort o' blessed inkybus or Old Man o' the Sea,
An' there ain't no shakin' of 'im off—for why? Because 'e's me!"

❖ ❖ ❖ ❖ ❖

From *Full Sail: More Sea Songs and Ballads*, edited by Cicely Fox Smith, published by Houghton Mifflin Co., New York, US, 1926, pp. 81-83.

"Bill" is one of the poet's favorite sailor philosophers, along with Mike Murphy and a few others.

First adapted for singing by John and Joy Rennie of Dogwatch as recorded on *Adventures*, 2006.

The header graphic is an illustration titled *A Forecastle Yarn*, 1880, artist unknown.

Sinking Merchantman

Billy's Yarn

"Oo seen her off?" . . .
        "Me," says the tide,
"I 'ad to, for why, there was no one beside;
For sailor-folks' women, they're busy enough,
'Thout 'angin' round pier-'eds to see their chaps off.
The gulls all about 'er they wrangled an' cried,
An' I seen 'er off," says the Liverpool tide.

"Oo waved 'er good-bye?" . . .
        "Me said old Tuskar,
"When the sun it went down an' the light it got dusker,
(With a sea gettin' up an' the wind blowin' keen).
An' the smoke of 'er funnels could 'ardly be seen,
An' the last of the sunset was red in the sky . . .
With the first of my flashes I waved 'er good-bye."

"Oo seen 'er sink?" . . .
        "Me," says the sun,
"At the top o' my climbin' I seen the thing done . . .
I seen 'er 'eave to, an' I seen 'er 'ull shiver,
Settle, an' stumble, an' tremble, an' quiver,
An' 'er stern it went up, an' 'er bow it went down,
An' the most of 'er people they just 'ad to drown,
An' I'd never a cloud for to shut out the sight,
So I seen 'er sink," says the sun in 'is might.

"Oo seen the last of 'er?" . . .
        "Us," says the crew,
All that was left out o' twenty-and-two,
"We seen the last of 'er—floatin' around
On a bottom-up boat among dead uns an' drowned—
We seen 'er waterways runnin' with blood—
We seen poor mates of ours shot where they stood—

But them chaps as done it, I tell you now true,
They ain't seen the last of us yet," says the crew,
"No, you bet your sweet life," says what's left o' the crew.

❖ ❖ ❖ ❖ ❖

From *Small Craft: Sailor Ballads and Chantys*, edited by Cicely Fox Smith, published by George H. Doran Co., New York, US, 1919, pp. 42-43. An earlier edition of *Small Craft* was published in 1917.

A classic WWI vintage poem in tribute to the merchantmen who fell victim to the German submarine blockade of the British Isles, but who resolved to get their revenge.

The header graphic is a photograph of a sinking merchantman in WWI after being torpedoed by German U-boat, photographer unknown.

Blue Anchor Lane

Blue Anchor Lane

If, tired of to-day, for some corner you sigh
That Change has forgotten and Progress passed by,
From the road that leads dock-wards, its bustle and hurry,
Its clanging and banging of tramcar and lorry,
By a junk-store and then by a chip-shop turn down,
Keep on past the "Dolphin"—or is it the "Crown"?—
And it may be you'll find (if indeed it remain)
The place that I think of as Blue Anchor Lane.

There's a row of old houses where sailor-folk dwell,
With here a ship model and there a pink shell;
There's a crazy old pub that was kept long ago
By some peg-legged old salt that had sailed with Benbow;
And the barges go by with their brown sails a-flapping,
And on the worn stairs comes the high tide lap-lapping,
And, grey days and blue days, in sunshine or rain,
Time lies there at anchor off Blue Anchor Lane.

But just where to find it—ah, that I can't tell!
I have lost the road to it, its right name as well,
And I cannot remember them, try as I may,
Through Dockyard's mean streets though I ramble all day,
By chip-shops unnumbered turn hopefully down,
Pass whole schools of "Dolphins" and "Crown" after "Crown,"
And, footsore and weary, still search for in vain
The turning that took me to Blue Anchor Lane.

And it may be the tide that, resistless and strong,
Sweeps empires like straws on its current along
Has swept, like Assyria and Ur in their day,
Its quaintness and queerness for ever away,
Its sailormen's homes with their pink tropic shells,
Its slanty old pub and its waterside smells,
And only the gulls and the river remain
Where the Past used to linger in Blue Anchor Lane.

❖ ❖ ❖ ❖ ❖

From *Sailor's Delight*, edited by Cicely Fox Smith, published by Methuen & Co., London, UK, 1931, pp. 121-124.

Gordon Morris (UK) first adapted this poem for singing as recorded on *The Long Road Home*, 2005.

The header graphic *Blue Anchor Lane*, drawn by Phil W. Smith, was used to illustrate this poem in the above book, facing p. 122.

Outward Bound

The Blue Peter

Last night when I left her my true love was weeping
For sorrow at parting, but parting must be:
What use for her tears, and what use to be keeping
A lad by the fireside, that follows the sea?

For the cold day's a-breaking, the town hardly waking,
The moon like a ghost in the pale morning sky,
And the Blue Peter's blowing, to tell ye we're going,
And the gulls in the river all calling good-bye!

The last hawser's cast and the tug-whistle's blowing,
The shore growing dim in the mist and the rain:
And wide, very wide, is the world where we're going
And long, very long, till ye see us again!

Farewell and adieu to ye—still we'll be true to ye,
Still we'll remember wherever we be,—
Hope we'll be meeting ye, hope you will be greeting
Someday your sailor home from the sea!

All in the cold morning, all in the grey weather,
On the sheds and the shipping the rain slating down,
All hands to the capstan bars, roaring together
A stave for farewell to the folk of the town:

Hong Kong and Vancouver, Callao and Suva,
The Cape and Kowloon, it's a very far cry
From the slow river creeping by houses all sleeping,
And the gulls in the wake of us, calling good-bye!

❖   ❖   ❖   ❖   ❖

From *Small Craft: Sailor Ballads and Chantys*, edited by Cicely Fox Smith, published by George H. Doran Co., New York, US, 1919, pp. 98-99. Earlier appeared in *Songs in Sail* published by Elkin Mathews, 1914.

First adapted for singing by Bob Zentz (US), as recorded on *Closehauled on the Wind of a Dream*, 2007, using the traditional sea tune "Farewell and Adieu to You Spanish Ladies."

The header graphic is a lithograph of the East Indianman *Sutlej* flying the Blue Peter from her foremast as she sets out to sea from Portsmouth, having just dropped off her pilot in the cutter to the left; lithograph by Thomas Goldsworth Dutton, circa 1847, from the collection of the National Maritime Museum, Greenwich, UK.

Pulling Away from a Blazing Tanker

The Boats of the *Albacore*

"Five boats there was," says Bristol Tim, "in the steamship *Albacore*—
She used to sail on the Far East run 'tween Hull an' Singapore—
Four under davits an' one on chocks, you couldn't ask no more."

"But one was smashed at the davits, an' the same shell killed 'er crew,
An' one got tangled up in the falls an' stove, an' that was two,
An' the one as was lashed went down with the ship, she couldn't 'elp but do."

"There was nine got clear in the captain's boat, but we missed 'em by an' by,
For there wasn't a light in the whole black night, nor a star in the bloomin' sky,
An' the Lord He knows where them chaps went, an' the sea as saw them die."

"An' seven men in the quarter boat there was as went away,
Seven men in an open boat a-driftin' around the Bay,
In the rain an' wind that bit to the bone an' freezin' dollops o' spray."

"Seven men in an open boat with neither oars nor sail—
We done our best with a len'th o' spar an' a rag of an old shirt-tail,
An' we took it in turns to watch, an' steer, an' sleep a bit, an' bale . . .

"Seven men in an open boat, an' the fifth day dawnin' red—
When a drifter picked 'er up at last due South o' Lizard 'ead,
Seven men in an open boat, two livin' an' five dead."

"An' the two that was livin' they 'd signed again afore a month was through,
They'd signed an' sailed for to take their chance as a seaman's bound to do;
An' one went West when the *Runnymede* was mined with all 'er crew . . .
"An' God 'elp Fritz when we meet," says Tim, "for I was one o' the two!"

❖   ❖   ❖   ❖   ❖

From *Rhymes of the Red Ensign*, edited by Cicely Fox Smith, published by Hodder & Stoughton, London, UK, 1919, pp. 33-34. First published in *Punch* magazine, Volume 155, September 11, 1918, p. 161.

This poem is a commemoration of a merchantman lost in WWI, and what became of her crew.

The header graphic is a painting titled *Pulling Away from a Blazing Tanker* by Anton Otto Fischer, from *Anton Otto Fischer Marine Artist*, edited by Katrina Sigsbee Fischer, published by Mill Hill Press, Nantucket, Massachusetts, US, 1984, p. 246.

Bosun

Sixteen stone
Of beef and bone,
Sort o' beggar to hold his own
With a foc's'le full of fighting drunks
And haul and hustle 'em out of their bunks.

Made of spunyarn and Stockholm tar,
The same as all good bosuns are:
Can't read, can't write,
But he can holler and he can fight,
And swear—why, no one can come near him!
I tell you it's a treat to hear him!
He can cuss in Spanish and Portugee,
Eye-taliano, Chinook, Chinee,

A dash of Yank and a smatter of Greek,
And as many besides as there's days in the week,
And keep it up from the Nore to Dover,
And never use a word twice over!

❖ ❖ ❖ ❖ ❖

From *Full Sail: More Sea Songs and Ballads*, edited by Cicely Fox Smith, published by Houghton Mifflin Co., New York, US, 1926, pp. 13-14.

The "bosun" was typically an experienced sailor who was promoted by the captain to directly oversee the crew, while the captain and his officers issued the orders. He was a "hands-on" man, with little ambition to become an officer.

Cabin Boy

Boys

"B'ys is the divvle," says Chips, says he,
"Plaguey young varmints as ever I see,
Nothin' but bother wherever they be;
B'ys is the divvle—the divvle!" says he.

"Monkeys is noisy an' parrots is worse;
Pigs while they're livin' 'ud make a man curse;
Wild beasts an' tame, you can keep 'em for me,
But b'ys, they're the divvle—the divvle!" says he.

"Pilgrims is quarrelsome, coolies as bad,
Passengers' questions 'ud drive a man mad;
Wherever there's wimmen there's trouble at sea,
But b'ys, they're the divvle—the divvle!" says he.

❖ ❖ ❖ ❖ ❖

From *Sailor's Delight*, edited by Cicely Fox Smith, published by Methuen & Co., London, UK 1931, pp. 35-36.

"Chips" is the nickname for the ship's carpenter, one of the few members of the crew who didn't share a watch, and who worked only during the day unless there were an emergency.

The header graphic is a painting titled *The Stowaway* by Anton Otto Fischer from his book *Focs'cle Days*, published by Charles Scribner's Sons, New York, US, 1947, p. 13.

Dazzle

British Merchant Service—1915

Oh, down by Millwall Basin as I went the other day,
I met a skipper that I knew, and to him I did say:
"Now what's the cargo, captain, that brings you up this way?"

"Oh, I've been up and down (said he) and round about also…
From Sydney to the Skager-rack, and Kiel to Callao…
With a leaking steam-pipe all the way to Californ-i-o"…

"With pots and pans and ivory fans and every kind of thing,
Rails and nails and cotton bales, and sewer-pipes and string…
But now I'm through with cargoes, and I'm here to serve the King!"

"And if it's sweeping mines (to which my fancy somewhat leans)
Or hanging out with booby-traps for the skulking submarines,
I'm here to do my blooming best and give the beggars beans!"

"A rough job and a tough job is the best job for me,
And what or where I don't much care, I'll take what it may be,
For a tight place is the right place when it's foul weather at sea!"

There's not a port he doesn't know from Melbourne to New York;
He's as hard as a lump of harness-beef, and as salt as pickled pork…
And, he'll stand by a wreck in a murdering gale, and count it part of his work!

He's the terror of the fo'c's'le when he heals its various ills
With turpentine and mustard leaves, and poultices and pills…
But he knows the sea like the palm of his hand, as a shepherd knows the hills.

He'll spin you yarns from dawn to dark—and half of 'em are true!
He swears in a score of languages, and maybe talks in two! …

And he'll lower a boat in a hurricane to save a drowning crew.
A rough job or a tough job—he's handled two or three—
And what or where he won't much care, nor ask what the risk may be …
For a tight place is the right place when there's wild weather at sea!

❖ ❖ ❖ ❖ ❖

From *Sailor Town: Sea Songs and Ballads*, edited by Cicely Fox Smith, published by George H. Doran Co., NY, 1919, pp. 85-87. Also in *Songs and Chanties 1914-1916*, 1919. First published in *The Naval Crown*, 1915.

The header graphic is an illustration titled *Dazzle* as drawn by Muirhead Bone showing an armed merchantman painted in the cubist camouflage pattern that was typical of WWI Navy and civilian ships, from *Merchantmen-at-Arms*, p. 163.

On the job of victory

The Builders

Not here the grace of the sonnet's flow,
The blithe ballade and the smooth rondeau,
The minstrel's tale and the wooer's sighs,
And the lovelorn lay to a layde's eyes . . .

Here shall a lordlier rhythm be found
In the throb and beat of the hammer's sound,
A rugged chant with a bold refrain,
A rougher rhyme and a sterner strain.

The ancient rune of the venturer man,
Builder of ships since the world began,
To brave the perils and dare the ways
Of the sea that serves him, the sea that slays.

Centuries gone, it was shaped and sung,
Centuries gone when the world was young,
When first he launched on the trackless tide
His cockleshell craft of boughs and hide—

The same old song that is always new
(Be it liner, longship or bark canoe),
The same to-day in a world grown old
As it was when they sailed for the fleece of gold:

A song of strength and a song of speed,
Of the dream made true and the word made deed,
In bow and bulwark and ribs and keel
An epic in iron, an ode in steel.

❖ ❖ ❖ ❖ ❖

From *Sea Songs and Ballads 1917-22*, edited by Cicely Fox Smith, published by Houghton Mifflin Co., New York, US, 1924, pp. 25-26. First published in *Punch* magazine, Volume 161, September 14, 1921, p. 218.

This poem was prefaced with this quote from *The Times*: "There is not much poetry in a shipyard as a rule."

The header graphic is a WWI poster titled *On the job for victory!* painted by Jonas Lie, circa 1917, published by United States Shipping Board Emergency Fleet Corporation.

Bullington

It was in the high midsummer, and the sun was shining strong,
And the lane was rather flinty, and the lane was rather long,
When—up and down the gentle hills beside the stripling Test—
I chanced to come to Bullington and stayed a while to rest.

It was drowned in peace and quiet, as the river reeds are drowned
In the water clear as crystal, flowing by with scarce a sound,
And the air was like a posy with the sweet haymaking smells,
And the roses and Sweet Williams and Canterbury Bells.

Far away as some strange planet seemed the old world's dust and din,
And the trout in sun-warmed shallows hardly seemed to stir a fin;
And there's never a clock to tell you how the hurrying world goes on
In the little ivied steeple down in drowsy Bullington.

Small and sleepy, there it nestled, seeming far from hastening Time
As a teeny-tiny village in some quaint old nursery rhyme;
And a teeny-tiny river by a teeny-tiny weir
Sang a teeny-tiny ditty that I stayed awhile to hear.

"Oh, the stream runs to the river, and the river to the sea,
But the reedy banks of Bullington are good enough for me;
Oh, the lane runs to the highway, and the highway o'er the down,
But it's better here in Bullington than there in London town."

Then high above an aeroplane in humming flight went by,
With the droning of its engines filling all the cloudless sky,
And like the booming of a knell across the perfect day
There came the gun's dull thunder from the ranges far away.

And while I lay and listened, oh, the river's sleepy tune
Seemed to change its rippling music, like the cuckoo's stave in June;
And the cannon's distant thunder, and the engine's war-like drone
Seemed to mingle with its burthen in a solemn undertone.

"Oh, the stream runs to the river, and the river to the sea,
And there's war on land and water, and there's work for you and me!
On many a field of glory there are gallant lives laid down
As well for tiny Bullington as might London town!"

So I roused me from my daydreams, for I knew the song spoke true
That it isn't time for dreaming while there's duty still to do;
And I turned into the highway where it meets the flinty lane,
And the world of wars and sorrows was about me once again.

❖ ❖ ❖ ❖ ❖

From *Small Craft: Sailor Ballads and Chantys*, edited by Cicely Fox Smith, published by George H. Doran Co., NY, 1919, pp. 62-64. First published in *Punch* magazine, Volume 153, August 1, 1917, p. 83.

A moment of calm is captured here during WWI in a quiet country setting, only to be brought back to the task at hand as an "aeroplane" and the sound of distant guns impinge on the "peace and quiet" of this remote place.

The *Cutty Sark* in the Old Pagoda Anchorage

By the Old Pagoda Anchorage [1924]

By the old Pagoda Anchorage they lay full fifteen strong,
And their spars were like a forest, and their names were like a song.
Fiery Cross and *Falcon* there
Lay with *Spindrift*, doomed and fair,
And *Sir Lancelot* of a hundred famous fights with wind and wave,
Belted Will and *Hallowe'en*
With *Leander* there were seen,
And *Ariel* and *Titania* and *Robin Hood* the brave . . .

Thyatira of the lovely name and proud *Thermopylae*,
By the old Pagoda Anchorage when clippers sailed the sea—
Racing home to London River—
Carry on for London River—
Crack her on for London River with her chests of China tea!

By the old Pagoda Anchorage (it's many a year ago!)
A sight it was to see them with their decks like drifted snow,
And their brasses winking bright,
And the gleaming gold and white
Of the carven kings and maidens on each slim and soaring bow,
And the high and slender spars
Humming shanties to the stars,
And the hulls whose speed and staunchness are a dead man's secret now,—

The ships so brave and beautiful that never more shall be,
By the old Pagoda Anchorage when clippers sailed the sea—
Racing home to London River—
Crack her on for London River—
Carry on for London River with her chests of China tea!

❖ ❖ ❖ ❖ ❖

From *The Return of the Cutty Sark*, by Cicely Fox Smith, published by Methuen & Co., London, 1924, p. 8.

The Pagoda Anchorage at Mawei was twenty-five miles from the entrance to the Min River and twelve miles below the City of Foochow in China.

The header graphic is a painting titled *The Pagoda Anchorage* by Montague Dawson, 1973, which featured the clipper ship *Cutty Sark* in the center.

By the Old Pagoda Anchorage [1926]

By the old Pagoda Anchorage they lay full fifteen strong,
And their spars were like a forest, and their names were like a song,
Fiery Cross and *Falcon* there
Lay with *Spindrift*, doomed and fair,
And *Sir Lancelot* of a hundred famous fights with wind and wave:
Belted Will and *Hallowe'en*
With *Leander* there were seen,
And *Ariel* and *Titania* and *Robin Hood* the brave:
Thyatira of the lovely name and proud *Thermopylae*,
By the old Pagoda Anchorage when clippers sailed the sea,
Racing home to London River—
Carry on for London River—
Crack her on for London River with her chests of China tea!

By the old Pagoda Anchorage (it's many a year ago!)
A sight it was to see them with their decks like drifted snow,
And their brasses winking bright,
And the gleaming gold and white
Of the carven kings and maidens on each slim and soaring bow,
And the high and slender spars
Humming shanties to the stars,
And the hulls whose speed and staunchness are a dead man's secret now—
The ships so brave and beautiful that never more shall be,
By the old Pagoda Anchorage when clippers sailed the sea,
Racing home to London River—
Crack her on for London River—
Carry on for London River with her chests of China tea!

By the old Pagoda Anchorage the clippers lie no more,
There is silence on the river, there is quiet on the shore,
And the silted channels seem
Still to murmur as in dream
Of the tea ships in their glory, lifting sea-ward on the tide,
All the strong and fair and fleet,
By those shores that used to meet,
And the valiant master mariners that walked their decks in pride,
By the old Pagoda Anchorage when clippers sailed the sea,
Logging fourteen on a bowline, ay, and seventeen running free,
Racing home for London River—
Crack her on for London River—
Carry on for London River with her chests of China tea!

❖ ❖ ❖ ❖ ❖

From *Full Sail: More Sea Songs and Ballads*, edited by Cicely Fox Smith, published by Houghton Mifflin Co., NY, 1926, pp. 84-87. Other, less complete, versions of this poem may be found in an earlier edition of *Punch* magazine and in Smith's own *The Return of the Cutty Sark* published in 1924.

This poem was first adapted for singing by Charles Ipcar in 2009, as recorded on *Sailortown Days*, 2009.

The Call

There's an office back in London, and the dusty sunlight falls
With its swarms of dancing motes across the floor,
On the piles of books and papers and the drab distempered walls
And the bowlers on their pegs behind the door.
There's an office-stool in London where a fellow used to sit
(But the chap that used to sit there's oversea);
There's a job they're keeping open till that fellow's done his bit,
And the one that job is waiting for is—Me!

And it may be black ingratitude, but oh, Good Lord, I know
I could never stick the office-life again,
With the coats and cuffs and collars and the long hours crawling slow
And the quick lunch and the same old morning train;
I have looked on Life and Death and seen the naked soul of man,
And the heart of things is other than it seemed,
And the world is somehow larger than the good old office plan,
And the ways of earth are wider than I dreamed.

There's a chap in the Canadians—a clinking good chap too—
And he hails from back o' nowhere in B. C.,
And he says it's sure some country, and I wonder if it's true,
And I rather fancy that's the place for me.
There's a trail I mean to follow and a camp I mean to share
Out beyond the survey, up in Cassiar,
For there's something wakened in me that I never knew was there,
And they'll have to find some other chap to fill that vacant chair
When the boys come marching homeward from the war.

❖ ❖ ❖ ❖ ❖

From *War Verse*, edited by Frank Foxcroft, published by T. Y. Crowell, New York, US, 7th edition, 1918, pp. 344-345. First published in *Punch* magazine, Volume 155, August 21, 1918, p. 120. Also reprinted in the same form in *The Literary Digest*, December 7, 1918, pp. 39-42. A more complete version of this poem can be found in the poet's own book *Rhymes of the Red Ensign*, Hodder & Stoughton, 1919, p. 43, and is printed next as "The Call 2."

Composed just before the end of WWI, this poem focused on the thoughts of the soldiers about to return to civilian life.

The Call 2

There's an office back in London, and the dusty sunlight falls
With its swarms of dancing motes across the floor,
On the piles of books and papers and the drab distempered walls,
And the bowlers on their pegs behind the door.
There's a row of clerks a-sitting at their desks there day by day,
While the muffled roar of London thunders by;
With their eyes upon their ledgers they are growing bald and grey,
And if something hadn't happened—so would I!

But après la guerre—après la guerre—
They'll have to find another chap to hang his hat up there ;
They'll have to get some other lad to climb that office stair,
For I'm going to ramble round a bit—après la guerre!

There's an office-stool in London where a fellow used to sit
(But the chap that used to sit there's oversea!)
There's a job they're keeping open while that fellow does his bit
(And the one that job is waiting for is—Me!)
There's a spotty fly-blown window and a dusty dim wire blind,
There's a view of dingy bricks and smoky sky;
But I've cut the whole connection and I've left the lot behind,
And I'm never going back there—no, not I!

There's a chap in the Canadians, a clinking good chap too,
And he hails from back o' nowhere in B. C.,
And he says it's sure some country, and I wonder if it's true,
And I rather fancy that's the place for me,
For he talks about the gorges where the glacier meets the pine,
And the hosts of heaven go marching star by star,
Over leagues of silent ranges where the lone lakes gloom and shine,
Out beyond the survey, up in Cassiar!

And it may be black ingratitude, but oh, good Lord, I know
I could never stick the office life again,
With the coats and cuffs and collars, and the long hours crawling slow,
And the quick lunch, and the same old morning train;
I have looked on Life and Death, and seen the naked soul of man,
And the heart of things is other than it seemed,
And the world is somehow larger than the good old office plan,
And the ways of earth are wider than I dreamed.

And après la guerre—après la guerre—
Though a thousand jobs await me, by my living soul I swear
If the God of Battles spares me I'll be anywhere but there
When the boys go marching home again—après la guerre!

❖   ❖   ❖   ❖   ❖

From *Rhymes of the Red Ensign*, edited by Cicely Fox Smith, published by Hodder & Stoughton, London, UK, 1919, pp. 43-45. Titled in the poet's manuscript as "Après la Guerre." This is a more elaborate version of this poem than was published in the 7th edition of *War Verse*, 1918, pp. 344-345.

Composed just before the end of WWI, this poem focused on the thoughts of the soldiers about to return to civilian life.

The Cape Horner

The Cape Horner

I never was in clipper ships when they was in their prime:
The tea fleet an' the wool fleet, they was done afore my time:
The ship I knowed the best was a big Cape Horner,
Thrashin' to the westward round that stormy corner,
Loaded down with Cardiff coal for Californio,
Rollin' round to 'Frisco—forty year ago!

When it was "Round the Horn and 'ome again, that's the sailor's way,"
'Crost the road to Newcastle, back to 'Frisco Bay,
Up the Coast to Oregon, down to Callao,
Round the Horn and 'ome again—forty year ago!

She was 'ard-run, undermanned, 'ungry as you please,
She wallowed both rails under in the thunderin' Cape Horn seas:
With three thousand ton inside her she was like a 'ouse to steer,
She didn't carry flyin' kites nor suchlike fancy gear—
But reefin' upper topsails was a picnic in a blow,
Rollin 'ome to 'Frisco—forty year ago!

She was only meant to carry, she was nothin' of a clipper,
But the Old Man was a snorter of an old-style racin' skipper:
The seas they kep' on poopin' 'er, 'e wouldn't 'eave 'er to,
'E 'ung on to 'is topsails and 'e run till all was blue:
It was "Keep 'er movin', Mister!" every time 'e went below,
An'—we beat the fleet from 'Frisco—forty year ago!

But time 'e keeps on movin' too, an' them ol' days are past,
An' the ol' ship's gone for ever, like we all must go at last,
Like the ships that made a forest on the 'Frisco waterside,
The slashin' big fourmasters from the Mersey an' the Clyde,
An' the Yankee skysail yarders with their plankin' scoured like snow,
Loadin' grain at 'Frisco—forty year ago!

Law's ships, De Wolf's ships, Castles, Counties, Glens,
Potter's fleet and Leylands, Halls, and Clans and Bens,
Cities, Ports, and Passes, Falls an' Lord knows what—
All of 'em are gone now, and most of 'em forgot,
Rotten ships and good 'uns, speedy ships and slow,
That used to load at 'Frisco—forty years ago!

When it was "Round the Horn and 'ome again, that's the sailor's way,"
'Crost the road to Newcastle, back to 'Frisco Bay,
Up the Coast to Oregon, down to Callao,
Round the Horn and 'ome again—forty year ago!

❖   ❖   ❖   ❖   ❖

From *Sailor's Delight*, edited by Cicely Fox Smith, published by Methuen & Co., London, UK, 1931, pp. 3-6; first published in *Punch* magazine, Volume 181, August 5, 1931, p. 136.

"Newcastle" is a reference to the coal port in Southeast Australia.

Alan Fitzsimmons first adapted this poem for singing, as recorded by Pinch o' Salt on *Sea Boot Duff & Hand Spike Gruel*, 2000.

The header graphic titled *The Cape Horner* is drawn by Phil W. Smith to illustrate this poem in the above book, facing p. 6.

Cape Stiff

Cruel is the sea, and the hardest thing of all
Is her taking and her leaving, and the way it seems to fall,
How always it's the best men who have to hear the call—
Ah, Cape Stiff, and the big seas pouring!

And of all good sailormen that use the deep sea
Where would you find a better or a truer lad than he
That we lost in the dirty weather from the four-mast barque *Tralee*,
By Cape Stiff, and the great gale roaring?

It was all hands on deck that night, to heave her to;
The sails were frozen hard, the cold wind bit you through,
You couldn't hear a man beside you speak, so loud it blew,
Near Cape Stiff, and her yards dipping under!

The night was black as hell—never saw him go…
It wasn't till the dawn broke I'd time to ask and know
The sea that swept us out and back had rolled him far below,
By Cape Stiff, in the great seas' thunder.

And fair weather or foul weather it's all one to him,
Though the sea's in the half-deck and the empty bunk aswim,
It's a long watch below for weary head and aching limb,
By Cape Stiff, and the loud wind crying!

And now we're rolling home before the good Trade Wind,
But I'm thinking night and day how we've left him far behind…

Him that was so merry, him that was so kind,
By Cape Stiff, in the cold deeps lying!

❖ ❖ ❖ ❖ ❖

From *Small Craft: Sailor Ballads and Chanteys*, edited by Cicely Fox Smith, published by George H. Doran Co., NY, 1919, pp. 105-106. Previously published in Songs in *Sail,* 1914.

This seems a sister poem to the poet's "Lee Fore Brace" and "News in Daly's Bar," mourning as it does the loss of a shipmate.

The header graphic is a painting titled *The "Gwydyr Castle" off Cape Horn* by Anton Otto Fischer, from his book *Foc's'le Days*, p. 29.

Captain Joseph Johnson

Captain Joseph Johnson
Is the nicest man I know:
He was captain of a clipper ship
A long time ago.
He lives past the coastguard,
In a little white house,
With a flagstaff and a figurehead
From a wrecked ship's bows.

Captain Joseph Johnson
Has the jolliest king of things,
Whale's teeth and flying fish,
And a big shell that sings,
And a ship inside a bottle—
If you tried to ever so,
You couldn't guess till Christmas
How it got there—but I know!

Captain Joseph Johnson
He knows an awful lot,
He's showing me square sennet
And a Matthew Walker knot.
"Stick to it, my sonny,"
Is what Captain Johnson says
"And you'll make a first-class sailorman
One o' these days!"

❖ ❖ ❖ ❖ ❖

From *Round the Mulberry Bush*, edited by Rose Fyleman, published by Dodd, Mead & Co. New York, US, 1928, p. 26.

Captain Paul Jones

Cap'n Paul Jones was a Britisher born,
    he hailed from the Solway shore,
But he struck a snag with his folks at home,
    as many have done before;

He shook the old land's dust from his feet,
    and he gave her a piece of his mind,
But he never knew that he'd somehow
    left a bit of his heart behind.

Cap'n Paul Jones was a skipper of fame,
    and a darned good sailorman too,
And a bit of a bucko, as I've heard tell,
    in the way he handled his crew:

He learned 'em to drill and he learned 'em
    to shoot and to jump at the word o' command,
The same as he knew how they learned 'em
    to do in the ships of his native land.

Captain John Paul Jones

Cap'n Paul Jones was a Britisher born,
    though he changed his flag and his name,
In his *Ranger* frigate he led us a dance,
    but we honour him all the same;

We used to call him a pirate then,
    and he certainly wasn't our friend,
But he sailed and he fought as a Britisher ought,
    which is what matters most in the end.

Cap'n Paul Jones was a Britisher born,
    which is why, now the time is come,
He knows the tug of the Solway tide,
    and the rattle of Drake's old drum;

He is back to the sea in the old, old way,
    a sailorman smart and bold,
And the flag o' the *Ranger* is flying to-day
    by the flag that she fought of old.

❖ ❖ ❖ ❖ ❖

From *Sailor Town: Sea Songs and Ballads*, edited by Cicely Fox Smith, published by George H. Doran Co., NY, 1919, pp. 103-104. First published in *The Naval Crown* by Elkin Mathews in 1915. Also published in *The London Spectator*, June 16, 1917, p. 671 and in *The New York Tribune*, July 15, 1917.

Composed in anticipation of the United States joining forces with England and her allies in WWI against Germany and her allies. The United States did not in fact enter the War until 1917.

The header graphic is an illustration, artist unknown, from *The Life and Character of John Paul Jones, a Captain in the United States Navy, During the Revolutionary War*, by John Henry Sherburne, Adriance, Sherman, & Co., New York, 1851, frontispiece.

Casey an' Me

First I knowed Casey him an' me was young,
An' many a yard we h'isted, an' many a stave we sung
In Macfarlane's clipper *Merlin*, skysail-yarder, her as come
Round in ninety days from 'Frisco, first of all the grain fleet 'ome.

An' I wish she was a-sailin' for 'Frisco once again
With a sandy Glasgow skipper an' a kickin' mate from Maine,
With a Finn an' a Frenchy, an' a woolly Portugee,
A Scotchman, a Dutchman, an' Casey an' me!

She was 'ard an' she was 'ungry, she was wet an' she was wild,
An' the bread was mostly weevils, an' the duff was mostly sp'iled,
An' the mate 'e was a terror, an' the bosun e' was worse,
An' the crowd o' greasers forrard they'd 'a' made an angel curse.

First I knowed Casey—Lord! It's long since then:
The old *Merlin* went a-missin' nineteen-nine—or was it ten?
An' I last crossed 'awse with Casey once ashore in Callao,
But I couldn't say when that was—years an' donkeys' years ago.

But I wish I was a-haulin' outer Salthouse Dock this day,
With the Mersey gulls a-pipin' an' the mornin' breakin' grey,
Sweatin' up the topsail yards, roarin' out in chorus,
All the bloomin' world to see, all our years afore us…

In the skysail clipper *Merlin*, bound for 'Frisco once again,
With a sandy Glasgow skipper an' a kickin' mate from Maine,
With a Finn an' a Frenchy, an' a woolly Portugee,
A Scotchman, a Dutchman, an' Casey an' me!

❖   ❖   ❖   ❖   ❖

From *Full Sail: More Sea Songs and Ballads*, edited by Cicely Fox Smith, published by Houghton Mifflin Co., NY, 1926, pp. 64-66.

A Dog-watch Concert

Casey's Concertina

There are lights a-flashing in the harbour
From the ships at anchor where they ride,
And a dry wind going through the palm-trees
And the long-low murmur of the tide …

And there's noise and laughter in the foc's'le,
And the bare feet beating out the tune
To the sound of Casey's concertina
Underneath the great gold moon—
Creaky old leaky concertina
Underneath the great gold moon.

There's a milky glimmer on the water,
And the lonely glitter of the stars,
And a light breeze blowing up the roadstead,
And a voice a-sighing in the spars,
A-sighing, crying in the backstays,
And the furled sails sleeping overhead,
And the sound of Casey's concertina,
Singing of a time that's fled—
Leaky old creaky concertina
Singing of a dream that's dead.

❖ ❖ ❖ ❖ ❖

From *Ships and Folks*, edited by Cicely Fox Smith, published by Elkin Mathews, London, 1920, p. 52.

From a set of poems entitled "The Way of the Ship" which were set to music by Easthope Martin, and published as *Five Chantey Songs*, Enoch & Sons, London, UK, 1920.

The poet deftly captures the spirit of the anchor watch entertaining themselves on the fosc'le deck in some tropical harbor.

First adapted for singing by John and Joy Rennie of Dogwatch as recorded on *England Expects*, 2004. An alternative setting for singing by Bob Zentz (US) was recorded on *Closehauled on the Wind of a Dream*, 2007.

The header graphic is an illustration titled *A Dog-watch Concert* drawn by Gordon Grant, from his book *Sail Ho!*, facing p. 58.

A Channel Rhyme

Start Point and Beachy Head
Tell their tale of quick and dead.

Forelands both and Dungeness
See many a ship in dire distress.

The Lizard and the Longships know
Oft the end of friend or foe.

And many and many a seaman's knell
Has been rung by Manacles bell.

Gull and Dodman ask aright
A wide berth on a dirty night.

Bolt Head and Bolt Tail
Are ill spots in a Channel gale.

Over nigh to Portland Bill
In Channel fog it's just as ill.

And Wolf Rock and Seven Stones
Rest their feet on sailors' bones.

But from Nore Light to Cape Cornwall
Goodwin Sands are worst of all!

❖ ❖ ❖ ❖ ❖

From *Sea Songs and Ballads 1917-22,* edited by Cicely Fox Smith, published by Houghton Mifflin Co., New York, US, 1924, p. 118. Earlier published by Hodder & Stoughton, 1919, in *Rhymes of the Red Ensign,* p. 63.

This poem presents an interesting list of some of the major navigational danger points for ships cruising the English Channel. First set to music by John Warner (Australia) as recorded on *Days of Brine*, 2008, by his group The Roaring Forties.

The Archibald Russell *in the London Docks*

The China Sea

Did you see the poor old hooker, by the ocean wharf she lay?
Her decks are foul with harbour grime, she hasn't long to stay,
With her cargo all aboard her and the Peter flying free,
And a seagull on her foretop a-looking out to sea.

She's loaded up to the fairleads and down to the Plimsoll line,
Her bilges choked and her bulkheads sprung, and the pumps tied up with twine,
And it's fare you well, good comrades all, for aboard her we must be:
A call or two we've got to pay, a call or two upon the way,
From Liverpool to Frisco Bay,
And all across the China Sea.

Oh, think of us, if you will, you friends we leave at home,
A-listing like a log in the lone Atlantic foam;
Oh, think you of us now and then, ill-fitted and worse found,
A-hanging on the skirts of luck this weary world around.

They've changed her name and register, they'll never change her soul;
For rolling of her innards out and eating up of coal
There is no ship that sails the seas can far or near compare
With this weary worn old packet from the port of God knows where!

She'll drown us if she can, the jade, she's drowned her man before;
She'll fling her rusty bones and ours to roll 'tween shore and shore,
Or chartless on her drunken way go tumbling tide by tide
To trip the feet of merchantmen which use the oceans wide.

They rouse us not by night or day to spend our watch below
In getting leaky lifeboats out and teaching cooks to row;
And if the worst should come, why then let ship and all go down,
For we be only sailormen, and we are paid to drown.

Oh, turn you right and round about upon the English shore;
Oh, look you long on England, lads, you may not see her more;
And when we're out of soundings and the Biscay gales do blow,
God help us if the cargo shifts, for then we're bound to go.

And she's loaded up to the fairleads, and down to the Plimsoll line,
Her bilges choked and her bulkheads sprung, and the pumps tied up with twine;
And it's fare you well, good comrades all, for aboard her we must be.
A call or two we've got to pay, a call or two upon the way,
From Liverpool to Frisco Bay,
And all across the China Sea.

❖ ❖ ❖ ❖ ❖

From *Songs and Chanties: 1914-1916*, edited by Cicely Fox Smith, published by Elkin Mathews, London, UK, 1919, pp. 92-94.

Here we have a classic old rust bucket sailing out for maybe her last voyage.

The header graphic is a photograph titled *The "Archibald Russell" in the London Docks* by Alan J. Villiers from his book *Last of the Wind Ships*, #193.

Ship's Carpenter

Chips

Chips
Learned his trade in the Blackwall ships,
Learned it from A to Z,
From rudder trunk to foc's'le head.

Square and hard as a baulk of teak
Or the quid he stows in his starboard cheek,
He rules his life by Blackwall fashion,
Work's his pleasure and his passion.

If you took and shoved old Chips ashore
With just his adze and nothing more,
He'd make no raft of skins, not he,
Nor botched-up job of a scooped-out tree:
He'd start right in and fix a slip,
And lay his keel, and build his ship,
And rig up sheers for masts and all,
The blooming same as old Blackwall:

And last he'd finish her off with lots
Of fancy twiddles and ropes and knots
And flowers and flourishes worked in wood
As large as life and twice as good.

A makeshift job, be it large or small,
Is a thing he can't abide at all,
For he learned his trade in the Blackwall ships,
Did Chips.

❖ ❖ ❖ ❖ ❖

From *Full Sail: More Sea Songs and Ballads*, edited by Cicely Fox Smith, published by Houghton Mifflin Co., Boston, US, 1926, pp. 11-12.

The header graphic is a photograph of ship's carpenter A. G. Traill aboard the *Port Jackson* in 1913, photographer unknown, from *Sail & Steam*, p. 19, Archives of the National Maritime Museum, Greenwich.

Furling the Mainsail

Christmas Night

We shipped a sea on Christmas night—
On Christmas night, on Christmas night!—
From stem to stern the decks were white . . .
"One more like that," the mate did say,
"And she'll not last till the break of day,"
So deep she rolled, so ill she lay,
All the night long till the morning.

It was black dark, and the gale screamed,
On Christmas night, on Christmas night . . .
Like gushing wounds her swing-ports streamed;
All ice the yard was where we clung,
The frozen shrouds shrill carols sung,
Like harps the twangling backstays rung
All the night long till the morning!

We called all hands, we hove her to,
On Christmas night, on Christmas night;
And nothing then was left to do
But hang on all, and wait, and pray
For nothing else to carry away,
So she might last till the break of day,
All the night long till the morning.

And one big roaring sailorman
A sort of rambling yarn began
About a place nigh Wexford town,
And the river Slaney flowing down
By the farm where he was born an' rared;
"And my old mother—she's not heard
A word o' me this many a year . . .
But I've got stuff and I've got gear
Stowed in my sea-chest all for her—
I think I see them old eyes stare—
A lump o' coral like a tree
Them nigs dive after in Feejee,

A Spanish shawl and a carved fan,
And a little tea-set from Japan
That's blue and white, and wee and small,
If this black gale don't break it all . . ."

But the night passed, and the great gale
Went down at dawn ... and we made sail,
And sent the yards to the masthead,
The watch sung out to wake the dead . . .
"Them tea-things is all right," Dan said.

❖   ❖   ❖   ❖   ❖

From *Rhymes of the Red Ensign*, edited by Cicely Fox Smith, published by Hodder and Stoughton, London, UK, 1919, pp. 71-72.

Although it comes to an abrupt end this is still an excellent illustration of how the poet can encapsulate a commonplace scene of sailing life in a few short lines.

The term "nigs" is not meant in a pejorative sense but merely as a common term used between sailormen of various nationalities and with the reference to Fiji (Feejee); it is unlikely to have the same meaning as it does in these "more enlightened" times.

The repeated refrain makes one think that she had a particular tune in mind for this piece, perhaps the old winter Solstice song "Christmas Day in the Morning."

First adapted for singing by Charles Ipcar, as recorded on *Never Turn a Blind Eye to the Storm*, 2015.

The header graphic is an illustration titled *Furling the Mainsail* by Anton Otto Fischer, from *Anton Otto Fischer*, p. 163.

Lethbridge Circus Parade

The Circus in the West

All through the little prairie town
'Mid dusty levels broad and brown
I saw the Circus pacing on;
I felt its vague barbaric spell,
I smelt the queer old circus smell
As old Rome or Babylon.

The tinsel gleamed, the big drum rolled,
The ponies pranced and caracoled
In gaudy gilt caparison;
And still beneath it was the strange
Sad undertone of Time and Change,—
As erst in vanished Babylon.

I saw where, wrinkled, grey and wise,
With swaying gait and brooding eyes,
The elephants went pacing on,
Unmoved amid the gaping throng,
As if they only thought: "How long—
How far from here to Babylon?"

No longer than this restless hour,
Its lust and folly, pride and power,
To-day as in the ages gone:
No further than this feverish, queer,

New town which was not yesteryear
Need mankind seek for Babylon.

New towns in strange new lands arise;
But old as earth and stars and skies
The Circus of the world goes on;
Still traveling on its ancient round
Where'er man's dust of dreams is found—
Here—now—to-day—in Babylon.

❖ ❖ ❖ ❖ ❖

From *Small Craft: Sailor Ballads and Chantys*, edited by Cicely Fox Smith, published by George H. Doran Co., New York, US, 1919, pp. 140-141; reprinted in *Evening Post*, Volume CXI, Issue 19, Wellington, NZ, January 23, 1926, p. 22.

The seventh in a set of poems entitled "Songs of the Wild," possibly inspired by the poet's year long stay in Lethbridge, Alberta in 1911.

The header graphic is a photograph of the Ringling Brothers and Barnum & Bailey Circus Elephants parade along 4th Avenue South in Lethbridge, Alberta, circa 1930s, photographer unknown.

Clare's Brigade

Men of the old grievous battles, men of Clare's Brigade,
Do ye hear the troops marching through the land where ye are laid,
Far from the clear running brooks, the dappled sun and shade
On the fair green hills of holy Ireland?

Ah, but not in the old fashion (men of Clare's Brigade!),
Not in the sorrow of exile your kinsmen draw the blade,
For the old trouble's ended now, its grey ghost is laid
On the fair green hills of holy Ireland.

There shall be pride and love there where sorrow dwelt before;
Kind peace shall be her portion, ay, peace from shore to shore,
And Patrick's plant springing there, springing ever more
On the fair green hills of holy Ireland!

❖ ❖ ❖ ❖ ❖

From *Sailor Town: Sea Songs and Ballads*, edited by Cicely Fox Smith, published by George H. Doran Co., NY, US, 1919, p. 128. Earlier published in *The Naval Crown* by Elkin Mathews in 1915.

Composed during the first year of WWI in tribute to this Irish brigade that fought for England, and the promised freedom of Ireland. References to "Clare's Brigade" can be traced back in poetry of Emily Lawless to 1745.

Clipper Ships at Sea

The Clyde-Built Clipper

A ship there was, and she went to sea
Away O, my Clyde-built clipper!
In eighteen hundred and seventy-three,
Fine in the lines and keen in the bow,
The way they've forgotten to build 'em now,
Lofty-masted and heavily sparred,
With stunsail booms to every yard,
And flying kites both high and low
To catch the winds when they did blow
And away, my Clyde-built clipper!

Fastest ship on the Colonies run—
Away O, my Clyde-built clipper!
That was her when her time begun;
Sixteen knots she could easily do,
And thirteen knots on a bowline too;
She could show her heels to anything made
With skysails set in a favouring trade,
Or when she was running her easting down
From London River to Hobart Town
And away, my racing clipper!

Old shellbacks knew her near and far
Away O, my Clyde-built clipper!
From Circular Quay to Mersey Bar,
And many a thundering lie they told
About her runs in the days of old;
But the time did come and the time did go,
And she grew old as we all must grow,
And the most of her gear was carried away
When caught aback in a gale one day
And away, my old-time clipper!

Her masts were sprung from fore to mizen
Away O, my Clyde-built clipper!
And freights was poor and dues had risen,
And there warn't no sense in rigging her new,
So they laid her up for a year or two;
And there they left her, and there she lay,
And there she might have been laying to-day,
But when cargoes are many and ships are few
A ship's a ship be she old or new
And away, my poor old clipper!

So in nineteen hundred and seventeen
Away O, my Clyde-built clipper!
They've rigged her new and they've scraped her clean,
And sent her to sea in time of war
To sail the seas as she sailed before;
And in nineteen hundred and seventeen
She's the same good ship as she's always been;
Her ribs are as staunch and her hull's as sound
As any you'd find the wide world round
And away, my brave old clipper!

The same as they were when she went to sea
Away O, my Clyde-built clipper!
In eighteen hundred and seventy-three,
Fine in the lines and keen in the bow,
The way they've forgotten to build 'em now,
Lofty-masted and heavily sparred,
With stunsail booms to every yard,
And flying kites both high and low
To catch the winds when they did blow—
And away, my Clyde-built clipper!

❖ ❖ ❖ ❖ ❖

From *Rhymes of the Red Ensign*, edited by Cicely Fox Smith, published by Hodder & Stoughton, London, UK, 1919, pp. 15-17. First published in *Punch* magazine, Volume 153, December 19, 1917, p. 414.

The poet added this note of introduction when this poem was published in *Punch*:

"Many of the fast-sailing clippers, which were making fine passages in the Australian wool trade in the seventies and onwards, were laid up or turned into hulks before the War. Recently, however, several have been re-fitted for sea and are once more doing good service."

Some of the finest steel or iron sailing ships were built at the Clyde shipyard in Scotland near the end of the 19th century and a few years after.

The header graphic is titled *Clipper Ships at Sea* as drawn by Gordon Grant, published by the Seamen's Bank for Savings as a limited edition set of four prints, circa 1930.

The Coast of Barbary

My lad is on the water and far away from me,
And I pray God be good to him wherever he may be,
Up the sea and down the sea,
And along the coast of Barbary.

Oh, night and day ships come in, the ships both great and small,
But never one among them brings a word of him at all,
From Port o' Spain and Trinidad, from Rio or Funchal,
And along the coast of Barbary.

If I must think he comes no more across yon seas forlorn,
If I must think there is no tide may bring him night or morn,
I'd curse the light that I look on, and the day that I was born,
And the cruel coast of Barbary.

But well I know that soon or late he'll come back blithe and brown,
When the fire's a good thing to see, and the dark drawing down,
From many a wild and stormy sea, and many a foreign town,
And along the coast of Barbary.

With a green silk handkerchief and a parrot red and green,
And shells and bits o' things to show from the places where he's been,
Up the sea and down the sea,
And along the coast of Barbary.

❖ ❖ ❖ ❖ ❖

From *Songs and Chanties: 1914-1916*, edited by Cicely Fox Smith, published by Elkin Mathews, London, UK, 1919, pp. 16-17. This poem has the same title as a later but different poem by Smith.

In this poem, perhaps, the poet is not sure that her dear friend "Dan" is lost at sea and she's still hopeful that he will return.

Coastwise

The ships that trade foreign, to London they bear
Their cargoes unnumbered both common and rare,
Their bales and their gunny-sacks, tea-chests and cases,
From all kinds of countries and all sorts of places,
Their copra and teakwood, their rum and their bacca,
Their rice and their spice from Rangoon and Malacca,
Their sugar and sago from far Singapore,
And lumber, and logwood, and manganese ore.

But they that trade coastwise unceasing do ply
On lawful occasions to Ramsgate and Rye,
To Lowestoft and Lymington, Padstow and Poole,
And Falmouth and Fowey and Gorleston and Goole,
the North-country colliers, smutty and small,

Coastwise

The barges and bawleys and schooners and all,
The *Janes* and *Elizas* and *Belles* and the rest,
Two Brothers, *Trafalgar*, and *Pride of the West*.

The ships that trade foreign, wide oceans they know,
Far down to the South'ard they see the whales blow,
Great bergs like cathedrals they likewise behold,
And flying fish shining all silver and gold:
They know the far islets of pearl and of pine,
The Trades and the tempests from Leeuwin to Line,
From the Horn to the Hooghly their smoke-trail is curled,
And their bow-wave is white on the seas of the world.

But they that trade coastwise, they know the salt seas
That surge evermore round the grey mother's knees,
The tide-rips and swatchways, the deeps and the shoals,
Each eddy that dimples, each current that rolls
By Longships and Lizard, by Bishop and Clerk,
And the fangs of the Manacles, deadly and dark,
By reef and by sandbank, by headland and holm,
And Scilly's lone outposts of thunder and foam.

The ships that trade foreign see cities afar,
Where the black and the brown and the yellow folk are,
The tin towns and timber towns, mud towns and all,
From the Straits of Le Mair to the Bay of Bengal.
Of Rio and Sydney the charms they compare,
And others name Frisco than either more fair,
The lordly St. Lawrence they mark in his flow,
And Fraser and Hudson and mighty Hwang-ho.

But they that trade coastwise know little stone quays
With old salts a-smoking and taking their ease,
The smell of the seaweed, the nets in the sun,
The snug little tavern where old yarns are spun,
The coastguard, the flagstaff, the boats in the bight,
The herring gulls mewing by day and by night,
The flash of the lighthouse that flings forth its ray
To ships trading foreign that pass on their way.

❖   ❖   ❖   ❖   ❖

From *Sea Songs and Ballads 1917-22*, edited by Cicely Fox Smith, published by Houghton Mifflin Co., New York, US, 1924, pp. 51-53. Earlier published in *Rovings*, 1921. Later re-printed in *Here and There in England with the Painter Brangwyn* in 1945. First published in *Punch* magazine, Volume 161, August 17, 1921, p. 130.

The graphic header from *Rovings*, facing p. 28, and was drawn by Phil W. Smith especially for this poem in 1921.

Commodore (North Atlantic Mail Service)

Twice twenty thousand tons of steel obey his sole command:
He rules, a king whose lightest word is law from land to land:
And he'd give it all to be fisting down a topsail once again,
With the mate at the bunt a-cursing his best and the skipper raising Cain,
Or bracing yards to each baffling breath in the wayward Doldrum weather,
Or tarring down in the North-east Trades, his chum and he together,
Or sand-and-canvassing down the poop till the planks shone white as snow—
A care-free young brassbounder outward bound to Callao—
A long watch ago.

In harbour trim from head to heel, each day he goes arrayed
With buttons bright as burnished gold and rows of gleaming braid:
And he'd chop the blessed lot, Lord knows! for a suit of dungarees
All paint and pitch, with a patch on the seat, and his trousers up to his knees,
For the feel of the planking warm to his toes and his sun-tanned skin aglow,
A lively young brassbounder outward bound to Callao—
A long watch ago.

He dines in state with glass and plate and a steward by his chair,
A band to play his victuals down and fancy foreign fare:
And he'd swop it all for a greasy kid of pork both salt and tough,
And a lump of leathery harness beef and a slab of the doctor's duff,
And the hot sweet taste of the galley tea and the coffee's nameless flavour,
With the wine of youth to wash 'em down and the salt of youth to savour,
And the cabin tarts he collared that, by gum! he relished so,
A lively young brassbounder,
A care-free young brassbounder—
A hungry young brassbounder outward bound to Callao,
A long watch ago.

❖ ❖ ❖ ❖ ❖

From *Full Sail: More Sea Songs and Ballads*, edited by Cicely Fox Smith, published by Houghton Mifflin Co., Boston, US, 1926, pp. 38-40.

Nurse with Convalescent

The Convalescent

We've billiards, bowls an' tennis courts, we've teas an' motor-rides;
We've concerts nearly every night, an' 'eaps o' things besides;
We've all the best of everything as much as we can eat—
But my 'eart—my 'eart's at 'ome in 'Enry Street.

I'm askin' Sister every day when I'll be fit to go;
"We must 'ave used you bad," she says, "you want to leave us so;"
I says, "I beg your pardon, Nurse, the place is 'ard to beat,
But my 'eart—my 'eart's at 'ome in 'Enry Street."

The sheffoneer we saved to buy, the clock upon the wall,
The pictures an' the almanac, the china dogs an' all,
I've thought about it many a time, my little 'ome complete,
When in Flanders, far away from 'Enry Street.

It's 'elped me through the toughest times—an' some was middlin' tough—
The 'ardest march was not so 'ard, the roughest not so rough;
It's 'elped me keep my pecker up in victory an' defeat,
Just to think about my 'ome in 'Enry Street.

There's several things I'd like to 'ave which 'ere I never see,
I'd like some chipped potatoes an' a kipper to my tea;
But most of all I'd like to feel the stones beneath my feet.
Of the road that takes me 'ome to 'Enry Street.

They'll 'ave a little flag 'ung out—they'll 'ave the parlour gay
With crinkled paper all about, the same as Christmas Day,
An' out of all the neighbours' doors the 'eads'll pop to greet
Me comin' wounded 'ome to 'Enry Street.

My missis—well, she'll cry a bit, an' laugh a bit between;
My kids'll climb upon my knees—there's one I've never seen;
An' of all the days which I 'ave known there won't be one so sweet
As the one when I go 'ome to 'Enry Street.

❖ ❖ ❖ ❖ ❖

From *Songs and Chanties 1914-1916*, edited by Cicely Fox Smith, published by Elkin Mathews, London, UK, 1919, pp. 198-200. Earlier published in *Fighting Men*, Elkin Mathews, 1916. First published in *Punch* magazine, Volume 150, May 17, 1916, p. 329.

The poet in her volunteer work during WWI would have made the acquaintance of many wounded soldiers. Gordon Morris (UK) first adapted this poem for singing, as recorded on *Full Sail: Inside the Lid*, 2002.

The header graphic is a cartoon drawn by Major George Denholm Armour, from *Punch* magazine, September 11, 1918, p. 173.

British and French Soldiers Advancing into Battle

The Conversation Book

I 'ave a conversation book, I brought it out from 'ome;
It tells the French for knife and fork, an' likewise brush an' comb;
It learns you 'ow to ast the time, the names of all the stars,
An' 'ow to order hoysters, an' 'ow to buy cigars.

But there ain't no shops to shop in, there ain't no grand hotels,
When you spend your days in dug-outs, doin' 'olesale trade in shells;
It's nice to know the proper talk for theatres an' such,
But when it comes to talkin', why it doesn't 'elp you much!

There's all them friendly kind o' things you'd naturally say
When you meet a feller causal-like an' pass the time o' day—
Them little things as breaks the ice an' kind o' clears the air,
Which, when you turn the phrase-book up, why, them things isn't there.

I met a chap the other day a-roosting in a trench,
'E didn't know a word o' ours nor me a word o' French;

An' 'ow it was we managed, well, I cannot understand,
But I never used the phrase-book, though I 'ad it in my 'and.

I winked at 'im to start with; 'e grinned from ear to ear;
An' 'e says "Tipperary" an' I says "Sooveneer";
'E 'ad my only Woodbine, I 'ad 'is thin cigar,
Which set the ball a-rollin', an' so—well, there you are!

I showed 'im my wife an' kids—'e up an' showed me 'is,
Then little funny Frenchy kids with 'air all in a frizz;
"Annette," 'e says, "Louise," 'e says, an' 'is tears begun to fall;
We was comrades when we parted but we'd 'ardly spoke at all.

'E'd 'ave kissed me if I'd let 'im, we 'ad never met before,
An' I've never seen the beggar since, for that's the way of war;
An' though we scarcely spoke a word, I wonder just the same
If 'e'll ever see them kids of 'is—I never ast 'is name!

❖ ❖ ❖ ❖ ❖

From *Songs and Chanties: 1914-1916*, edited by Cicely Fox Smith, published by Elkin Mathews, London, UK, 1919, pp. 205-207. First published in *Punch* magazine, Volume 149, December 8, 1915, p. 470. A standard English version with alterations for an American audience was also printed in Everybody's Magazine, Vol. XXXVII-B, December 1917, p.112, attributed to, A Solider at the Front, not Cecily Fox Smith. :

> I HAVE a conversation book—I brought it out from home—
> It tells the French for knife and fork and likewise brush and comb;
> It learns you how to ask the time, the names of all the stars,
> And how to order oysters and how to buy cigars.
>
> But there ain't no stores to buy in, there ain't no big hotels,
> When you spend your days in dugouts doing wholesale trade in shells.
> It's nice to know the proper talk for theatres and such.
> But when it comes to talking, why, it doesn't help you much.
>
> I met a chap the other day a-roostin' in a trench.
> He didn't know a word of ours nor me a word of French.
> And how it was we managed, well, I can not understand,
> But I never used my French book, though I had it in my hand.
>
> I winked at him to start with; he grinned from ear to ear;
> An' he says, "Bong jour, Sammy," an' I says "Souvenir;"
> He took my only cigaret; I took his thin cigar,
> Which set the ball a-rollin'; and so-well, there you are!
>
> I showed him next my wife an' kids; he up an' showed me his—
> Them funny little French kids with hair all in a frizz;
> "Annette," he says, "Louise," he says, and his tears begin to fall;
> We was comrades when we parted, though we'd hardly spoke at all.
>
> He'd have kissed me if I'd let him; we had never met before,
> And I've never seen the beggar since, for that's the way of war;
> And though we scarcely spoke a word. I wonder just the same
> If he'll ever see them kids of his—I never asked his name.

The poet hosted many a London party for service men on leave during WWI and no doubt heard an ironic story like this, which haunted her until she transformed it into a poem. It captures a moment, amidst unbearable chaos, when people from different cultures can still connect as simple human beings.

Peter Massey (UK) first adapted this poem for singing, as recorded on *The Long Road Home*, 2005.

The header graphic is a cartoon titled *Well Met!* showing two British and French soldiers as drawn by L. Raven-Hill, from *Punch* magazine, August 19, 1914, p. 101.

Sailors Wondering What They've Been Served

Cook

Slushy's a Dutchman, he's a crackerjack at music,
He can play the ocarina,
And the German concertina,
But the sort of grub he dishes out 'ud make a kangaroo sick.

He's greasy and he's lazy and he's frowsy and he's fat,
His face is large and dirty and his feet are large and flat,
And he knows no more of cooking than the steward's ginger cat.

His duff is tough as leather and his bread 'ud break your jaw;
His hash is burnt to cinders—if it isn't, why it's raw;
You can tell his tea is meant for tea because it's warm and wet,
And the taste of Slushy's coffee is a thing you won't forget.

If you want to know the secret of its extra special savour,
He drops a dozen beetles in to give the stuff a flavour.

❖ ❖ ❖ ❖ ❖

From *Full Sail: More Sea Songs and Ballads*, edited by Cicely Fox Smith, published by Houghton Mifflin Co., Boston, US, 1926, pp. 17-18.

The cook on a sailing ship seldom knew anything about cooking, seldom had more than a few basic things to cook and those of dubious quality and scant quantity. It should not be surprising that he became the focus for much of the crew's irritation and ridicule on a long voyage. He had many nicknames. "Slushy" was one of the more printable ones.

The rhyme scheme is somewhat irregular in this poem and may be an experiment.

The header graphic is an illustration titled *Grub* as drawn by Gordon Grant from his book *Greasy Luck*, p. 49.

Sinking Schooner

Copper Ore

The *Jane Price* of Swansea
Thirty days out,
With copper ore from Carrizal
And sinking . . .

Drifting,
With her cargo shifting
And her steering gear gone:
And the pumps clanking on
The whole day through
And the whole night too,
And the water gaining
Spite of all we can do,
And no use complaining
And no use thinking . . .

In the *Jane Price* of Swansea
Thirty days out,
With copper ore from Carrizal
And sinking . . .

Drifting,
Like a log, and lifting
To the big green seas
That crash aboard like thunder,
With her lee rail under

And the water to our knees
And all the while mounting,
And we've got past caring,
And we've got past counting,
And the mate's quit swearing,
And the Old Man's drinking . . .

In the *Jane Price* of Swansea
Thirty days out
With copper ore from Carrizal
And sinking . . .

❖ ❖ ❖ ❖ ❖

From *Sailor's Delight*, edited by Cicely Fox Smith, published by Methuen & Co., London, UK, 1931, pp. 141-142.

This is one of the most dramatic poetic descriptions of a ship sinking and the impact on the ship's crew as they gradually realize that they must abandon ship.

First adapted for singing by Alan Fitzsimmons as recorded by Pinch o' Salt on *Sea Boot Duff & Hand Spike Gruel*, 2000.

The header graphic is a photograph of the sinking of the four-masted schooner *Marjory Brown* in the Atlantic, October 20, 1913, off the coast of Long Island, as photographed by a German crewman on the German ship *Berlin*, from *Shipwrecks Along the Atlantic Coast*, by William P. Quinn, Commonwealth Editions, Beverly, Massachusetts, US, 2004, p. 64.

Curios

"I've 'ad," said Dan, "a sight o' curios,
But where they've gone, Lord knows!
The junk I've packed around, alive an' dead,
The parrots green an' red,
Models o' ships whittled in bone or wood,
An' sperm-whale teeth tattooed:"

"An' walkin'-sticks cut out o' sharks' backbones,
An' beads, an' coloured stones,
An' bacca pouches made o' seabirds' feet
You catch wi' bits o' meat,
An' sennet mats (I'll learn you, son, the way
To make them mats one day):"

"Coral, an' bottled flowers, an' singin' shells,
An'—ah, Lord knows what else!
But there, I've giv' 'em all to fancy gals,
Or sold 'em to my pals:
There ain't no sense in keepin' curios, see,
For ramblin' blokes like me."

❖ ❖ ❖ ❖ ❖

From *Full Sail: More Sea Songs and Ballads*, edited by Cicely Fox Smith, published by Houghton Mifflin Co., Boston, US, 1926, pp. 52-53.

Sailors would often collect curios in foreign ports or make craft items during their watch below. And when they got to the next port they would give them away to new friends or sell them for liquor.

Cutty Sark Leaving Shanghai

The *Cutty* Comes Back (1924)

What says the Lizard,
Swinging high his shining spear? . . .
"Pass along, my lady,
I've known, ye many a year!"

Ay, many a time he's seen her,
All splendid from the sea,
Come swaying up from south'ard
With chests of China tea,
Or, loaded to her hatches
With Riverina, bales,
Lead home the racing wool fleet
Rip-roaring for the sales!

What says the wind's song
That lifts her on her way?
"Blow along, my sweetheart,
I've known ye many a day!"

Ay, many a day he's known her,
The salty Channel breeze,
And all his gusty brethren
That range the ridged seas,
But most of all the west winds
Whose stormy marches roll
A bleak and bitter kingdom,—
The Forties to the Pole . . .

The winds that drove the clippers
Like flying deer along,
The winds that break the weakling,
The winds that prove the strong!

What says old Atlantic
That crusts her bows with brine!
"Roll along, my beauty,
For you're a friend o' Mine!"

Ay, well old ocean knows her.
And well she knows him too,
His charging Biscay rollers,
His sunwarmed Tropic blue.
Both deep and shoal she knows him,
She knows him storm and shine,
Lashed white when typhoon rages,
Flat calm athwart the Line,
The swell that lift's the ice-pack
In fogbound seas forlorn,
The long Agulhas combers
And greybeards of the Horn.

❖ ❖ ❖ ❖ ❖

From *The Return of the Cutty Sark*, by Cicely Fox Smith, published by Methuen & Co, London, UK, 1924, p. 49-50.

The famous British tea clipper *Cutty Sark* is on permanent display at the drydock in Greenwich, England, as part of the National Maritime Museum displays. The poet sailed on this ship when she was towed to Greenwich in the 1920's.

The poet revisited this poem and a longer version was published two years later in *Full Sail*.

The header graphic is a painting of the *Cutty Sark* leaving Shanghai on July 17, 1872, with the *Thermopylae* and a sidewheel tug in the background, by Francis Smitherman.

The *Cutty* Comes Back (1926)

When the old *Cutty Sark* goes to sea again,
Crowding on her flying kites once more,
With the Duster at the peak flying free again,
Lizard light'll hail her as of yore,
The Channel breeze'll greet her gustily,
And the old Atlantic give her welcome lustily,
When the old *Cutty Sark* goes to sea again
With the Duster at the peak of yore.

What says the Lizard,
Swinging high his shining spear? . . .
"Pass along, my lady,
I've known, ye many a year!"

Ay, many a time he's seen her,
All splendid from the sea,
Come swaying up from south'ard
With chests of Foochow tea,
Or—loaded to the hatches
With Riverina bales—
Lead home the racing wool fleet
Rip-roaring for the sales!

What says the wind's song
That lifts her on her way?
"Blow along, my sweetheart,
I've known ye many a day!"

Ay, many a day he's known her,
The salty Channel breeze,
And all his gusty brethren
That range the ridged seas,
But most of all the west winds
Whose stormy marches roll
A bleak and bitter kingdom,—
From forty to the Pole . . .
The winds that drove the clippers
Like flying deer along,
The winds that break the weakling,
The winds that prove the strong!

What says old Atlantic
That crusts her bows with brine!
"Roll along, my beauty,
For you're a friend o' Mine!"

Ay, well old ocean knows her,
And well she knows him too,
His charging Biscay rollers,
His sunwarmed Tropic blue,
Both deep and shoal she knows him,
She knows him storm and shine,
Lashed white when typhoon rages,
Flat calm athwart the Line,
The swell that lifts the ice-pack
In fogbound seas forlorn,
The long Agulhas rollers
And greybeards of the Horn.

❖ ❖ ❖ ❖ ❖

From *Full Sail: More Songs and Ballads*, edited by Cicely Fox Smith, published by Houghton Mifflin Co., New York, US, 1926, pp. 100-102.

This is a longer version of the previous poem, with an introductory verse.

Shantying while Hauling on the Lee Fore Brace

Dan

Dan—
Beats the band as a shantyman.
On the tip-top concert platform Dan'd never be the rage.
He wouldn't cut much ice upon the operatic stage.
He couldn't do his courting like a fat Italiano
Bawling fit to bust at the principal soprano.
Maybe his words wouldn't always stand repeating,
Maybe his language 'ud shock a mothers' meeting.
But there's not a doubt about it, he's an A-1 shantyman,
Is Dan.

It's "Pipe up, Dan," when it's looking kind of blue
For a half-drowned ship and a half-dead crew,
When your heart's in your sea-boots and the cold is in your bones,
And you don't care a darn how soon she goes to Davy Jones,
And it's dark as the devil and blowing all it can—
Oh, he's worth ten men on a rope, is Dan!

Ten men heaving round the capstan bars,
Ten men furling aloft among the stars,
Ten men singing out, sheeting home the sail,
Ten men shouting down a Cape Horn gale . . .
With "Poor Old Reuben Ranzo" and "Lowlands Away,"
"Sally Brown" and "Paddy Doyle" and "One More Day,"
"Rio Grand" and "Stormalong" and "Blow, Boys, Blow,"
And "Leave Her, Johnnie, Leave Her" when it's time for us to go!

From *Full Sail: More Sea Songs and Ballads*, edited by Cicely Fox Smith, published by Houghton Mifflin Co., Boston, US, 1926, pp. 27-29.

"Dan" was most likely a close friend of the poet. He was also likely one of her prime informants for traditional songs of the sea, including the sailor worksongs known as shanties. He may have been lost at sea in a Cape Horn gale as described in another of her poems "The Lee Fore Brace."

This poem was first adapted for singing by Eddie Stewart (UK) and presented at the Mystic Sea Music Festival (US) by Stewart along with Danny and Joyce McLeod in June of 2008.

The header graphic is an illustration drawn by Gordon Grant and shows a group of sailors hauling on a halyard while singing a shanty, from *Songs of American Sailormen*, by Joanna C. Colcord, Bramhall House, New York, NY, 1938, p. 47.

Making a Fine Departure

Dan's Dream

Here's the dream I had, boys, an' I tell you true,
I saw the old *Fulmar* plain as I see you—
I saw the old *Fulmar* as she used to be
Many an' many a year since, when I was first at sea.

Just the bloomin' same, lads, as I've seen her look
Crackin' on with all she'd stand, bound for Pernambuck;
Every stitch a-drawin'—flyin' kites an' all—
An' the crowd all haulin', tallyin' on the fall.

All her swellin' canvas shinin' as she came,
Rosy in the sunset, with all her gilt trucks aflame,
With a bone between her teeth, under royals runnin' free,
I saw the old *Fulmar* swingin' out to sea.

I saw the old man there, as life-like as you please,
With his old white whiskers blowin' in the breeze,
An' the mate in the waist, an' the look-out at the fore,
An' old Slush standin' just inside his galley door.

All the crowd was there, boys, all the chaps I knew,
Dagoes, Dutch an' British, good an' bad uns too,
The seamen an' the sojers, the worst an' the best,
An' myself there among 'em, haulin' with the rest.

That's the dream I had, boys, an' so I tell you true,
I saw the old *Fulmar*—I saw her an' I knew—
Knew her to a gantline as I ought to know—
Me as served aboard her forty years ago.

❖ ❖ ❖ ❖ ❖

From *Ships and Folks*, edited by Cicely Fox Smith, published by Elkin Mathews, London, UK, 1920, p. 63.

This poem seems another take on the poet's "Sea Dream" which I think is a more powerful poem. But the poet's old shipmate "Dan" puts in another appearance.

The header graphic is a painting titled *Making a Fine Departure* by *Anton Otto Fischer*, from Anton Otto Fischer, p. 170.

Dan's Epitaph

Dan, he's dead, as I used to know
In the ol' *Thermopylae* years ago;
Nobody'll trouble to fix no stones
Nor plant no plants over ol' *Dan's* bones,
Nor print no cards with a black edge round,
Nor shove wax flowers atop of 'is mound;
But I reckon there's chaps both near an' far,
In Charley Brown's or the Paragon Bar,
From London River to Hobson's Bay,
As'll set their drinks down a minute an' say:—

"Wot, ol' Dan dead as I used to know
In the *Thermopylae* long ago
(or the *Star o' Greece*, or the *Heir o' Linne*,
Or some other o' them as Dan was in)?
'E was a decent shipmate too,
Darned good shipmate 's ever I knew;
'E earned 'is whack an' 'e earned it straight,
'E stood 'is trick an' 'e pulled 'is weight;
An' I don't think ever I seen the man
Could make long splices the like o' Dan."

Well, I 'ope they'll say when I come to die
As much for me as for Dan, say I!

❖ ❖ ❖ ❖ ❖

From *Sailor's Delight*, edited by Cicely Fox Smith, published by Methuen & Co., London, UK, 1931, pp. 80-81.

This is another tribute by the poet to one of her favorite sea shanty and yarn sources, "Dan," and possibly close personal friend, who was lost at sea.

Toasting the Crowd

Dan's Fortune

"I've made my fortune once," said Dan,
"A nice little pile for a sailorman,
Along o' salvin' a Dago barque
We picked up once on the edge o' dark
The time I was bound from 'Frisco 'ome
In Clay's old 'ooker *Eurynome*:
The mess she was in 'ud make you shudder,
But we rigged 'er up a jury rudder
An' brought 'er 'ome in a beast of a gale
Under what could be spared o' the mate's shirt-tail:
An' they treated us 'andsome, so they did,
For they dished us out a 'undred quid,
Bill an' Ginger an' Shorty an' me—
An' that was the end o' that," said he.

"An' I thought as I'd marry a gal I knowed,
An' set up shop off o' Redriff Road,
An' call it 'The Occidental Bar,'
Or 'The Sailor's Delight,' or 'The Baltic Star,'
With a winder full o' chops an' steaks,
An' pickled cabbage an' fancy cakes,
An' the model I'd made o' the *Eurynome*
For to make old shellbacks feel at 'ome:
An' chaps from Boston an' Bombay
They'd say: 'If ever you're London way
You just drop in at Dan's,' they'd say,
'For the best o' grub both cold an' 'ot
You'll get it all at Dan's, that's what.'"

"But I blowed the lot on a nine-day's spree,
Both ends an' the bight of a jamboree:
It went in bowlers an' blue serge suits

An' stick-up collars an' square-toed boots,
An 'orseshoe tie-pin fit for a king,
A watch an' drops an' a diamond ring:
It went in treatin' an 'undred pals,
Blouses an' brooches an' fun for the gals,
Beer an' whisky an' cheap champagne,
Drinks for the crowd an' drinks again,
An' just another afore we go—
An' where the rest went *I* dunno!"

"But I come to myself 'alfway down Channel,
With an 'ead like lead an' a tongue like flannel,
An' a down-east mate with a face like a foot
Ticklin' my ribs with the toe o' 'is boot:
An' I 'adn't no watch an' I 'adn't no pin,
An' I 'adn't no tie for to stick one in,
An' the sharks an' the lubbers you bet they was gay
A-lickin' their chops on Ratcliff 'Ighway
Over one more fool of a sailorman—
An' that was the end o' that," said Dan.

❖ ❖ ❖ ❖ ❖

From *Full Sail: More Sea Songs and Ballads*, edited by Cicely Fox Smith, published by Houghton Mifflin Co., Boston, US, 1926, pp. 48-51.

Clearly "Dan" blew his fortune in a classic sailortown spree, and was only "lucky" in the sense that he survived to be shanghaied aboard an outward bound ship rather than being knifed in a tavern brawl or back alley.

The header graphic is an illustration titled *The Ship, a Sailors' Tavern, 1850*, most likely portraying a favorite watering place on the San Francisco waterfront; artist unknown.

Dan's Odyssey

"I've sailed in a deal o' ships," said Dan,
"Since first my sailorin' days began:
For I never could stick, the way I'm made,
To the same ol' ship an' the same ol' trade,
An' the same ol' places time an' again,
No better'n a bloomin' railway train.
Fact of it is, I'm a bit of a roamer,
The same as that there bloke in 'Omer . . .
I was in a barque, the *'Omer*, once,
Bit of a thing, five 'undred tons,
And 'omeward bound, I well recall,
With a cargo of ore from Carrizal;
The very day we made the Lizard
There came away a beast of a blizzard
As kep' us beatin' to an' fro
For more'n a week in sleet an' snow,
And thinkin' o' the Christmas dinners
Waitin' ashore for us poor sinners."

"Lord, what a fleet them ships 'ud be
If you could see 'em all!" said he.
"Fust o' the lot, the old *Johore*—
Parsee-built in 'forty-four—
She was a good old has-been too,
Malabar teak right through an' through,
With a galleried stern and big bluff bows
An' six glass stern-ports just like an 'ouse:
An' she'd got that old an' she got that leaky,
When we loaded nitrates 'ome from Iquique;
We pumped all night an' we pumped all day
Like pumpin' the blessed sea away,
Round the 'Orn and up to the Line,
An' we blessed the stars as the passage was fine,
An' a shore gang 'ad to take her on
An' start to pump afore we was gone
Or else she'd 'ave sunk in the New South Dock . . ."

"Next was the clipper *Inchcape Rock*:
She was a beauty, she was a queen,
Loveliest thing as ever I seen!
Why did I leave 'er? *I* dunno—
I was tired of 'er—I 'ad to go."

"Then came the *Stromness*, Colonies clipper,
Wot 'ad ol' Bully Baynes for skipper:
It was a treat to 'ear 'im swear!
You bet I wasn't long in 'er.
I run 'er in 'Frisco for a spouter,
A reg'lar ol'-time out-an'-outer
As went up North to the Behring Sea:
That was too blinkin' cold for me."

"Next, Gow's old packet *Inisfail*:
I tell you, that old ship could sail!
The *'Omer,* 'er I spoke of first,
The *Tees* ol' shellbacks said was cursed
Because she always killed 'er man:
The *Star of Peace*, the *Gulistan*,
Nor them ain't all by chalks," said Dan.
"Fact of it is, it seems to me
A sort o' bloomin' Uly-see
Is wot I've allus been," said he.

❖ ❖ ❖ ❖ ❖

From *Full Sail: More Sea Songs and Ballads*, edited by Cicely Fox Smith, published by Houghton Mifflin Co., New York, US, 1926, pp. 55-58. First published in *Punch* magazine, Volume 167, November 12, 1924, p. 546.

"Nor them ain't all by chalks" may mean that "Dan" hasn't "chalked up" or totaled all the ships that he's served in.

The Day's Work

"A woman's work is never done,
Or so I've heard," said Dan;
"But if that's true of anyone,
That one's a sailorman."

"The folks ashore think life at sea's
All leaning on the rail
To smoke your pipe an' take your ease
An' watch the hooker sail."

"I'd like to 'ave 'em 'ere, that's all,
In this 'ere watch with me,
To take their turn at pullyhaul,
Like all the rest," said he.

"I'd like to see 'em splashin' round
On the slantin' streamin' decks,
An' tallyin' on a brace 'arf drowned,
With water to their necks;"

"Or layin' out on a tops'l yard,
Some dark night, shortenin' sail,
With the canvas frozen iron-'ard,
In a shrickin' Cape 'Orn gale."

"An' then, when to their bunks they crawl,
Their eyes ain't closed afore
'All 'ands!' they hear the bos'n bawl,
An' tumble up once more."

"But times like that ain't what I mind;
It's when it's fine it's worse;
The jobs o' work of every kind
'Ud make a parson curse."

"There's soogy-moogy, tar and ile,
There's 'olystones an' paint,
An' the Chief Mate fussin' fit to rile
A blushin' plaster saint."

"There's rattlin' down an' slushin' too,
There's endless shiftin' sail,
An' chippin' plates till all is blue,
Nor that ain't 'arf the tale."

"For, calm or storm, and rain or sun,
You can take this 'ere from me,
A sailor's work is never done,
An' that's a fact," said he.

❖   ❖   ❖   ❖   ❖

From *Sailor's Delight*, edited by Cicely Fox Smith, published by Methuen & Co., London, UK, 1931, pp. 15-17.

You couldn't ask for a better description of what a deep-sea sailor was expected to do on a day-to-day basis aboard one of those romantic looking old windjammers.

The Vimy Memorial

The Dead for England

Where rest the dead for England? . . .
In fields of France afar,
And shell-torn plains of Flanders,
Once loud with England's war.

And many a desert silence,
And many a wandering wave,
Have given the dead for England
Their glory and their grave.

How sleep the dead for England? . . .
A quiet sleep and sound;
They could not sleep the sweeter
At home in English ground

Than yonder far from England
Beneath a stranger sky,
With the salt seas streaming over,
And the armies marching by.

What gave the dead for England? . . .
All gracious things in life
They gave and, giving, grudged not,
The kiss of child and wife,

Love's dream and dreams' fulfilment,
Small joys and peaceful ways,
The strength of youth exulting,
The length of mellowing days.

What leave the dead to England,
For England's sake who died? . . .
Their dear ones for our caring,
Their memory for our pride.

Their trust to hold unswerving,
To end their task begun,
And a fairer, sweeter England
To build when war is done!

❖ ❖ ❖ ❖ ❖

From *Rhymes of the Red Ensign*, edited by Cicely Fox Smith, published by Hodder & Stoughton, London, UK, 1919, pp. 53-54.

Composed by the poet near the end of WWI.

The header graphic is a photograph of *The Vimy Memorial* overlooking the Douai Plain from the highest point of Vimy Ridge, about eight kilometers northeast of Arras, photographer unknown.

The Bow of the Abandoned *Luther Little*

Dead Man's Bay

I thought I heard the Old Man say,
　　Leave her, Johnnie, leave her!
"Her course is set for Dead Man's Bay
　　And it's time for us to leave her!

Dead Man's Bay where old ships lie
    Leave her, Johnnie, leave her!
When deepsea days are all gone by!
    And it's time for us to leave her!"

Time for us to leave her, Johnnie, time to go!
The same seas'll toss us, the same winds blow;
We'll have our fun and folly, dreaming and desire,
And she gone to ashes on a landward fire.

Ah, the grand old days, Johnnie!—wind and weather,
Days of sun and nights of storm we knew together,—
The game we played with old Cape Stiff, and our lives the stake . . .
Turn and say good-bye, Johnnie, for old sake's sake!

Long and long after, far and far away,
Maybe you'll remember, maybe then you'll say,
When you hear an old name spoken or an old song sung:
"Ay, once we sailed in her, when she and we were young."
Old men nodding by a hearth ashore . . .
Old ships decaying that use the sea no more . . .
That's the way it goes, Johnnie, since the world begun,
And it's time for us to leave her, for her day is done!

And to Dead Man's Bay she's bound at last
    Leave her, Johnnie, leave her!
Where storm and shine alike are past
    And it's time for us to leave her!
No more labour, no more laughter,
    Leave her, Johnnie, leave her!
One more watch and a long sleep after
    And it's time for us to leave her!

❖ ❖ ❖ ❖ ❖

From *Songs and Chanties: 1914-1916*, edited by Cicely Fox Smith, published by Elkin Mathews, London, UK, 1919, pp. 107-108.

"Dead Man's Bay" is where the old ships are taken, to be broken up or burned by the marine salvagers.

The chorus "Leave her, Johnnie, leave her!" is from a traditional sea shanty of the same name.

First set to music by Mike Kennedy, 2010.

The header graphic is a photograph by Robert Ipcar of the abandoned four-masted lumber schooner, the *Luther Little*, 1957, which rotted away along the Wiscasset waterfront in Maine.

British troops resting in support trench

A Declaration of War

This is the yarn that M'Larty told by the brazier fire,
Where over the mud-filled trenches the star-shells blaze and expire—
A yarn he swore was a true one; but Mac was an awful liar.

"Way up in the wild North country, a couple of years ago,
I hauled Hank out of a snowdrift—it was maybe thirty 'below'—
And I packed him home to my shanty, and I took and thawed him with snow."

"He was stiff as a cold-store bullock, I might have left him for dead,
But I packed him along, as I've told you, and melted him out instead,
And I rolled him up in my blankets and put him to sleep in my bed."

"So he dwelt in my humble shanty while the wintry gales did roar,
While the blizzards howled in the passes and the timber wolves at the door,
And he slept in my bunk at night-time while I stretched out on the floor."

"He watched me frying my bacon, and he said that the smell was grand,
He watched me bucking the stove-wood, but he never lent me a hand,
And he plaid on my concertina the airs of his native land."

"And one month grew into two months, and two months grew into three;
And there he was sitting and smiling like a blooming Old Man of the Sea,
Eating my pork and beans up, and necking my whiskey and tea."

"You say, 'Why didn't I shift him?'—For the life of me I dunno,
I suppose there's something inside me that can't tell a fellow to go
I hauled by the heels from a snowdrift at maybe thirty 'below.'"

"But at last when the snows were going, and the blue spring skies were pale,
Out after bear in the valley, I met a chap on the trail,
A chap coming up from the city, who stopped and told me a tale."

"A tale of murders and hold-ups all over the land and sea,
And when he was through I was laughing, for the joke of it seemed to be
Hank's folks had been acting that way while Hank was rooming with me."

"So I hiked to the shanty, and never a word I said,
I floated in like a cyclone, I yanked him out of my bed,
And I grabbed the concertina and I smashed it over his head.

"I shook him up for a minute, I stood him down on the floor,
I grabbed the scruff of his trousers and I ran him along to the door,
And I said, 'This here, if you get me, is a Declaration of War!'"

"And I gave him a hoist with my gum-boot, a kind of lift with my toe,
But you can't give a fellow a hiding, as any one sure must know,
You hauled by the heels from a snowdrift at maybe thirty 'below.'"

❖ ❖ ❖ ❖ ❖

From *Sailor Town: Sea Songs and Ballads*, edited by Cicely Fox Smith, published by George H. Doran Co., New York, US, 1919, pp. 62-65. First published in *Punch* magazine, Volume 153, October 17, 1917, p. 274.

In the context of the time, the beginning of WWI, "Hank" is a surrogate for all Germans. Although Hank is apparently oblivious that the War has begun, he gets evicted from his comfortable abode by his savior when M'Larty learns of the War, and an entirely innocent concertina gets destroyed. Still M'Larty is somewhat constrained by the fact that he saved Hank's life and doesn't bash his head in.

The header graphic is a photograph titled *British troops resting in support trench*, WWI, photographer unknown.

Deep Water Jack

O it's "Ah fare ye well," for the deep sea's crying,
You thought you could forget it, but it's no use trying,
Trying to forget it when it calls you so! . . .
Hey, Deep Water Johnnie, kiss your girl and go!

Here's warmth and soft living, and an easy bed!
It's toil, and much peril, that you're going to instead,
Hard life, and bitter faring, and a poor man's fee
Are all of a man's portion that follows the sea.

But it's "Ah fare ye well," the deep sea's calling
Back to cold and hunger and heaving and hauling,
To decks awash and frozen yards, as very well you know:
But ah! Deep Water Johnnie, kiss your girl and go!

Sailor's Farewell

How can a man help it, when the God that made him
Set his feet to follow where the four winds bade him?
How should a man help it, when his heart goes jigging
To the sea's song and the sail's song and wind through the rigging?

And it's "Ah fare ye well," for the deep sea's crying!
You thought you could forget it, but it's no use trying,
Trying to forget it when it calls you so! . . .
Hey, Deep Water Johnnie, kiss your girl and go!

❖   ❖   ❖   ❖   ❖

From *Songs and Chanties: 1914-1916*, edited by Cicely Fox Smith, published by Elkin Mathews, London, UK, 1919, pp. 23-24. Earlier published in *Songs in Sail* in 1914.

Another poem of a girl left behind to reconcile herself as to why her sailor lover is returning to the sea.

The header graphic is an illustration titled *Poor Jack* by George Cruikshank, from *Dibdin's Sea Songs*, frontispiece.

Jackdaw

The Defaulter

The regimental jackdaw 'as a bright an' beady eye;
'E sits upon the tent-pole an' 'e winks both bold an' sly:
'E says: "You bloomin' idiot, you, to go an' get C.B.!"
An' I wish I was the jackdaw, an' I wish that 'e was me!

The regimental jackdaw, 'e is like a bloomin' lord,
'E 'ops it when 'e thinks 'e will, an' no one speaks a word:
'E takes 'is 'ook without no pass, 'e don't come 'ome to tea,
An' I wish I was the jackdaw, an' I wish that 'e was me!

The regimental jackdaw, 'e can always speak 'is mind:
'E tells the Colonel what 'e thinks when thus 'e feels inclined,
'E sauces of the Adjutant as 'andy as can be,
An' I wish I was the jackdaw, an' I wish that 'e was me!

The regimental jackdaw, 'e 's the jolliest thing I've seen,
'E 'as no pack to carry an' 'e 'as no pipe to clean,
'E 's breakin' rules the 'ole day long an' never gets C.B.—
An' I wish I was the jackdaw, an' I wish that 'e was me!

❖   ❖   ❖   ❖   ❖

From *Small Craft: Sailor Ballads and Chantys*, edited by Cicely Fox Smith, published by George H. Doran Co., New York, US, 1919, pp. 53-54. Also published by Elkin Mathews, London, 1917. First published in *Punch* magazine, Volume 151, November 16, 1916, p. 342, as "The Happy Defaulter." Another WWI era poem, but in a lighter vein than most.

The header graphic is a lithograph by Maurice Ernest Jessop, from *Ye Jackdaw of Rheims*, by Rev. Richard Harris Barham (aka "Thomas Ingoldsby"), Eyre & Spottiswoode Printers, London, UK, 1837.

The Derelict *Three Mary's*

The Derelict

(Notice to Mariners: "North Atlantic Ocean, Derelict reported")

"We left 'er 'eaded for Lord knows where, in latitude forty-nine,
With a cargo o' deals from Puget Sound, an' 'er bows blown out by a mine;
I seen 'er just as the dark come down—I seen 'er floatin' still,
An' I 'ope them deals'd let 'er sink afore so long," said Bill."

"It warn't no use to stand by 'er—she could neither sail nor steer
With the biggest part of a thousand mile between 'er and Cape Clear;
The sea was up to 'er waterways an' gainin' fast below,
But I'd like to know she went to 'er rest as a ship's a right to go."

"No one to tend 'er binnacle lamps an' light 'er masthead light,
That's worked her traverse an' stood 'er trick an' done 'er best in 'er day,
To be driftin' around like a nine-days-drowned on the Western Ocean swell,
With never a hand to reef an' furl an' steer an' strike the bell."

"No one to tend 'er binnacle lamps an' light 'er mast'ead light,
Or scour 'er plankin' or scrape 'er seams when the days are sunny an' bright;
No one to sit on the hatch an' smoke an' yarn when work is done,
An' say, 'That gear wants reevin' new some fine dogwatch, my son.'"

"No one to stand by tack an' sheet when it's comin' on to blow;
Never the roar of 'Rio Grande' to the watch's stamp-an'-go;
An' the seagulls settin' along the rail an' callin' the long day through,
Like the souls of old dead sailor-men as used to be 'er crew."

"Never a port of all 'er ports for 'er to fetch again,
Nothin' only the sea an' the sky, the sun, the wind an' the rain;
It's cruel 'ard on a decent ship, an' so I tell you true,
An' I wish I knew she 'ad gone to 'er rest as a good ship ought to do."

First published in *Punch* magazine, Volume 153, November 21, 1917, p. 356. It was later published under the shorter title "The Derelict" in *Rhymes of the Red Ensign*, Hodder & Stoughton, London, UK, 1919, pp. 11-12, in a more colloquial and, in my opinion, a more poignant form.

During the dark days of WWI the Admiralty put out many such warnings, each one with its own story. Here the poet gives the thoughts of a sailor who might have made the original alert.

This poem was first adapted for singing by Mike Kennedy in 2009.

The header graphic is an illustration titled *The Derelict* as drawn by Charles J. A. Wilson, from *Ships*, by William A. Baker, published by Barre Publishers, Barre, Massachusetts, US, 1971, p. 77.

Sailor Leading Song in Pub

A Dog's Life

"Oh, a sailor's life's a dog's life, an' that's the truth," says Bill,
"A sailor's life's a dog's life, look at it 'ow you will;
You break your back with workin' for 'arf a coolie's pay,
An' a sailor's life's a dog's life, look at it 'ow you may."

"There's mates to kick an' 'aze you (an' you dursen't 'it 'em back);
There's cold to freeze your innards an' there's 'eat as burns you black;
There's junk as tough as green 'eart an' weevils in the bread,
An' fistin' frozen canvas till you're wishin' you were dead."

"But you bet I'm goin' to quit it, nex' time I jump ashore;
As soon as I strike ol' 'Frisco, you won't see *me* no more;
I'll set a course sou'westward to an island as I know,
Where we laid once loadin' copra—might be twenty year ago."

"I'll lay out on the beach there, where the sun is good an' 'ot,
An' I won't need no more trousis, when I've wore out them I've got;
With a gunny round my middle, an' a soul to call my own
I wouldn't change my fortune for the King's upon 'is throne."

But when we'd finished loading and sailing day came round,
With the pilot-boat alongside and the mudhook off the ground,
And the towboat cast the hawser off and left us with a cheer,
Why, there'd be Bill a-growling as he'd done for twenty year.

"Oh a sailor's life's a dog's life, an' that's a fact, my son;
'Is pay's no more'n a coolie's, 'is work is never done;
But you bet I'm goin' to quit it fust chance as comes my way,
For a sailor's life's a dog's life, look at it 'ow you may."

❖ ❖ ❖ ❖ ❖

From *Sailor's Delight*, edited by Cicely Fox Smith, published by Methuen & Co., London, UK, 1931, pp. 37-39; first published in *Punch* magazine, Volume 180, May 27, 1931, p. 574.

Once again there's the dream about retiring from sea-faring to some island in the Pacific, a theme that is more fully developed in "Port o' Dreams."

First set to music by Michael Head (1900-1976) in 1949, as published in *Six Sea Songs*. More recently adapted for singing by Bob Zentz (US), as recorded on *Closehauled on the Wind of a Dream*, 2007, using the traditional tune "Three Drunken Maidens."

The header graphic is from an illustration by Veronica Whall, from *Sea Songs and Shanties*, by Captain W. B. Whall, published by Brown, Son & Ferguson, Glasgow, UK, 1927, p. 20.

Doldrums: One of Murphy's Yarns

Day after day the sun stared widely
Over the wide and windless seas;
Against the masts the sails drooped idly,
Unhanded, waiting for a breeze.

It seemed we should lie there for ever,
As if no wind till Judgment Day
Would set her royal clews a-quiver
And speed her southward on her way.

"I heard onst of a barque," said Murphy.
"Becalmed, that couldn't get a breath,
Till all the crowd was sick with scurvy
An' the skipper drunk himself to death."

Doldrums

"So then they'd scoffed the last stale biscuit
An' the scuttle butt was all but dry,
They reckoned it was time to risk it,
An' tuk t' the boats an' said 'Good-bye.'"

"An' there they left the ol' barkey layin',
An' there, most like, she's layin' now,
With weeds like Noah's whiskers swayin'
Along her keel from stern to bow."

"All her bright-work green an' spotted,
All her paint-work bleached an' bare,
All her canvas black an' rotted,
An' not a living soul to care."

"Square the mainyard!" the silence breaking,
Like Gabriel's trumpet rang the word;
Out of the dawn the wind came, waking
The sleeping sails, so long unstirred.

The jibs were filled, they pulled like horses,
The gear ran twittering through the sheaves,
The reef points on the tautened courses
Pattered again like falling leaves.

Southward she sped, her keen bows cleaving
Steady and strong the watery ways,
Like some strange dream behind her leaving
The breathless nights, the gasping days.

And somewhere that old ship forgotten,
With all her paintwork weathered bare,
And all her canvas black and rotten,
And sea-birds fouling everywhere;

All her idle gear decaying,
Not a soul to tend her wheel,
And weeds like Noah's whiskers swaying
Fathoms long below her keel.

❖ ❖ ❖ ❖ ❖

From *Sailor's Delight*, edited by Cicely Fox Smith, published by Methuen & Co., London, UK, 1931, pp. 25-27; first published in *Punch* magazine, Volume 180, May 13, 1931, p. 511.

A sailing ship can be trapped in the "Doldrums" for a few days or weeks, or forever as in Murphy's yarn.

The header graphic is a painting titled *Doldrums* by Anton Otto Fisher, from his book *Foc's'le Days*, facing p. 24.

Ducklington

"To Ducklington," the signpost read;
And "That's the way for me," I said,
For that (I thought) must surely be
A pleasant kind of place to see,
Where downy and delightful things
With yellow feet and cherubs' wings
And busy bills and bobbing heads
Will dip and dive in oiser-beds,
Or dabble by the brooklet edge
And hunt for tadpoles in the sedge,
Or, heedless of the careful clucks
Of such poor hens as mother ducks,
True infant Drakes, put out to sea
On the broad pond's immensity.

Alas the dream! The year was old;
The rickyards brimmed with Autumn's gold;
Low bowed the weighted fruit-trees down,
The green was parched and bare and brown,
And all the ducks that quacked beside
The pond that drought had all but dried
Were old and sober, staid and sage,
Forgetful in their riper age
That they, in some sweet April gone,
Were ducklings once at Ducklington.

But time will come and time will go,
And this year's follow last year's snow,
And Spring come back to Windrush side
With swallow-flight and mating tide,
With fleeting sun and flying shower,
The colt's-foot and the cuckoo flower,
With bloom in spate on orchard trees
And faint frail scent of primroses,
And running brooks and ponds abrim
Where downy broods shall dive and swim
As broods like them, since Time began
And grass grew green and water ran,
From year to year have surely done
At duckling time in Ducklington.

❖ ❖ ❖ ❖ ❖

From *Sailor's Delight*, edited by Cicely Fox Smith, published by Methuen & Co., London, UK, 1931, pp. 130-132.

Exploring or re-exploring the small rural towns in England was also a favorite theme and past-time for this poet.

Eight Bells

Eight Bells

Eight bells chimed from the fo'c'sle
Back to the chime from the poop;
Out tumbled the port watch, cursing;
The cock crowed loud from the coop.

The sea was bright as a mirror,
The moon was shiny as steel,
When Ginger limped aft at midnight
For to relieve the wheel.

He spat on his hands as he took it
And the course, which was "Full an' by,"
And "'Appy New Year," says Ginger,
And "Same to yourself," says I.

"'Ere's a bit more meat in the lobscouse,
A few more plums in the duff,
A few less kicks wi' the 'alfpence,
A bit more smooth wi' the rough."
"'Ere's grub whenever you're 'ungry
An' drink whenever you're dry,
An' a ''Appy New Year,'" says Ginger,
And "Same to yourself," says I.

❖ ❖ ❖ ❖ ❖

From *Sailor's Delight*, edited by Cicely Fox Smith, published by Methuen & Co., London, UK, 1931, pp. 78-79.

This gruff interchange between sailors changing watches, seems to ring true, especially when holidays come and go while the routine of sailing the ship carries on.

Bob Zentz (US) adapted this poem for singing as recorded on *Closehauled on the Wind of a Dream*, 2007. An alternative setting was first done in 1995 by Alan Fitzsimmons (UK) as recorded on *Seaboot Duff & Handspike Gruel* by Pinch o' Salt in 2000.

The header graphic is titled *Eight Bells* as drawn by Phil W. Smith to illustrate this poem, from *Anchor Lane*, by Cicely Fox Smith, published by Methuen & Co., London, UK, 1933, facing p. 136.

Epilogue: Cape Horn Days

Thousands of years, before the ships came by,
He watched the uncounted sunsets flame and die,
Saw on the southern ocean's wind-racked grey,
Thousands of years, come up the ungreeted day,
And heard the tumult of a million tides
Fret with their ebb and flow his sea-scarred sides.
No life, no voice, but seas rising and falling,
And the seals barking, and the seabirds calling,
And blowing whales, ungallied yet of man,
Travelling the salt roads, theirs since Time began:
Till, through the chartless waste of unsailed sea,
Bluff-bowed, slow-wallowing, small incredibly,
Climbing the mile-long crests, the Dutchmen came,
Marked the great headland, named him by his name . . .

They came—deep-rolling treasure fleets of Spain,
Bold raiders, flushed with plunder of the Main,
Trader, explorer, whaler, buccaneer,
Tall skysail clippers flying like hunted deer,
Staunch little copper ore barques, and Clyde fourposters
Crammed to the coamings with grain: and old West coasters
Laden with guano or nitrate, or piled with lumber—
Ships of all flags, all ports—ships without number—

They came, they passed . . . and now draws near the day
The last Cape Horner goes the old sailor's way:
No more, no more, on the wind's pauses drifted
Shall come a sound of seamen's voices lifted
In some old thundering chorus, raising the shout
At sheets or braces, or maybe singing out
With short sharp cries, stowing the frozen sail,
Like seabirds' voices crying down the gale:
No more the seaman, fighting his weary way,
Struggling to make his westing, day by day,
Peering 'neath lashes stiff with salt and rime
Through the thick weather for the thousandth time,
Shall sight afar the well-known peak at last,
Smite his cold palm, and say "Old Cape Horn is past!"

Then shall the ancient solitudes return,
Unwatched, immense, the dawns and sunsets burn:
Only the snow, the sleet, the driving rain,
The berg, the floe, the empty seas remain—
The cold and unremembering sea whose lips
Mumble the bones of men, the ribs of ships,
Beauty, and strength, and swiftness, who shall know
How watched, how wept for, years on years ago . . . ?

From *Sailor's Delight*, edited by Cicely Fox Smith, published by Methuen & Co., London, UK, 1931, pp. 40-43.

"Cape Horn" was named by Dutch explorers Jacob le Maire and Willem Schouten, who first mapped this region of the world in 1616, in honor of their chief financial backer's home town Hoorn.

This poem is a tribute to Cape Horn and the sailing ships and crews which made the perilous journey around that tip of South America.

The Eternal Feminine

"Why are ships wimmen?" says Billy Magee;
"'Ere's a few reasons as looks good to me."

"There's good uns an' bad uns, an' wild an' contrary,
An' stubborn an' stupid an' devil-may-care-y;"

"There's some that ain't nothin' but varnish an' paint,
There's some 'as got tempers 'ud bother a saint;"

"There's some steers a course an' there's some as just won't,
There's them fellers sticks to an' them as they don't."

"An' this 'ere's a fact about wimmen and 'ookers—
The best uns to live with ain't all the best lookers."

"'Umour an' coax 'em, you'll get your own way with 'em;
'Andle 'em wrong, there's the divvle to pay with 'em."

"Larn all your life, you won't know all about 'em—
An' wot 'ud the world be for us chaps without 'em?"

❖ ❖ ❖ ❖ ❖

From *Sailor's Delight*, edited by Cicely Fox Smith, published by Methuen & Co., London, UK, 1931, pp. 86-87.

First adapted for singing by Bob Zentz (US), as recorded on *Closehauled on the Wind of a Dream*, 2007.

The Fair Hills of Ireland

The fair hills of Ireland they're the sweetest hills I know,
With the silver skies above them and the soft rain dropping slow,
And Saint Patrick blessed the little hills because he loved them so;
     The fair green hills of Holy Ireland
And long as Ireland's skies endure and Ireland's hills shall stand,
The blessing of Saint Patrick be upon the Irish land—
     The fair green hills of Holy Ireland.

The green fields of Ireland, they are greener than the rest
And green the shamrock growin' thereon so close to Ireland's breast,
And Saint Patrick bless'd the little fields because he loved them best;
     The small green fields of Holy Ireland,
And long as Ireland's grass is green and Ireland's waters run,

The blessing of Saint Patrick be upon them everyone—
    The small green fields of Holy Ireland.

The true hearts of Ireland, they're the warmest hearts on earth;
There's never gold will buy their love nor treasure tell their worth,
And Saint Patrick bless'd the little homes, in sorrow and in mirth,
    And the true kind hearts that are in Ireland,
And long as Ireland's heart is sound and Ireland's faith is one
The blessing of Saint Patrick be upon her evermore,
    And the true kind hearts, true kind hearts, that are in Ireland.

❖ ❖ ❖ ❖ ❖

From *The Fair Hills of Ireland: Song*, English words by Cicely Fox Smith; Welsh words by E. Lewis; music by Charles Villiers, Stanford (1852-1924); published by Enoch & Sons, London, UK, 1918. Transcribed at the British Library.

ANZAC Cove, Gallipoli, Turkey, 1915

Farewell to ANZAC

Oh, hump your swag and leave, lads,
The ships are in the bay—
We've got our marching orders now,
It's time to come away—
And a long good-bye to Anzac Beach—
Where blood has flowed in vain
for we're leaving it, leaving it,
Game to fight again!

But some there are will never quit
This bleak and bloody shore—
And some that marched and fought with us
Will fight and march no more;
Their blood has bought till Judgment Day
The slopes they stormed so well,
And we're leaving them, leaving them,
Sleeping where they fell.

Leaving them, leaving them—
The bravest and the best—

Leaving them, leaving them,
And maybe glad to rest!

We did our best with yesterday,
Tomorrow's still our own—
But we're leaving them, leaving them,
Sleeping all alone.

Ay, they are gone beyond it all,
The praising and the blame
And many a man may win renown,
But none more fair a fame;
They showed the world Australia's lads
Knew well the way to die;
And we're leaving them, leaving them,
Quiet where they lie.

Leaving them, leaving them
Sleeping where they lie—
Leaving them, leaving them,
In their glory and their pride.
Round them sea and barren land,
Over them the sky—
Oh! We're leaving them, leaving them,
So quiet where they lie.

❖ ❖ ❖ ❖ ❖

From a book of WWI poetry called *War Verse*, edited by Frank Foxcroft, published by Thomas Y. Crowell Co., New York, US, 1918, pp. 153-154, and first printed in the *The Spectator*; January 15, 1916, p. 10, also reprinted in several New Zealand newspapers in 1916.

This poem focuses on the abandonment of the disastrous Gallipoli campaign in 1916. Thousands of Australian and New Zealand troops, among others, were mowed down by the Turks, and there were bitter recriminations resulting from this failed invasion.

First set to music by Martyn Wyndham-Read as recorded on *Back to You*, 2010.

The header graphic is a photograph titled *ANZAC Cove, Gallipoli, Turkey, 1915*, photographer unknown.

Fiddler John: a Country Tale

Fiddler John he used to dwell
A long while since, so I've heard tell,
In an old thatched house with a leaning wall
That always looked just ready to fall . . .
And wherever you went, both far and near,
When people did meet to make good cheer,
Why, every time you'd find in the middle
Old bent John and his old cracked fiddle . . .

With a catch, a round, and a country dance,
A fine new tune *à la mode de France*,

The Old Fiddler

A stave for sorrow, a stave for mirth,
This for a wedding, that for a birth,
"Ground for the Floor" and "The Green Grass Grows" . . .
"Man's Life's a Vapour and full of Woes" . . .
An alehouse glee when the full quarts foam,
And a right jolly lilt for a harvest home.

Fiddler John, he grew so old
He kept his bed, so I've been told,
He kept his bed and there he lay
In his old thatched house for many a day;
And the lads and lasses loitering by,
On summer nights they 'ud linger nigh
To hear him play by the light o' the moon
On his old cracked fiddle each, old tune.
A catch, a round, and a country dance,
A fine new tune *à la mode de France*,
A stave for sorrow, a stave for mirth,
This for a wedding, that for a birth,
"Ground for the Floor" and "The Green Grass Grows" . . .
"Man's Life's a Vapour and full of Woes" . . .
An alehouse glee when the full quarts foam,
And a right jolly lilt for a harvest home!

Fiddler John, he is dead and gone;
His green, green grave the grass grows on—
Fiddler John, he lies in the ground,
And the green grass grows all around, all around;
His bones are dust and his fiddle's rotten,
And his old, old tunes they are all forgotten.
And the old thatched place where he used to dwell
It leaned some more and down it fell . . .
But still, they say, when the moon's at the full,
And the mist on the common's as white as wool,
When the river's loud on the distant weirs,
And they're all abed at the "Crook and Shears,"
By Fiddler's Field if you're homeward going,
You'll see what looks like a garden growing . . .
Ranks of carrots and beans and peas,
Plums and apples on gnarled old trees,
Tall white lilies as straight as arrows,
Sprouts and cabbage and big green marrows,—
And out of the house that stands in the middle
You can hear the sound like an old cracked fiddle . . .

With a catch, a round, and a country dance,
A fine new tune *à la mode de France,*
A stave for sorrow, a stave for mirth,
This for a bridal and that for a birth,

"Ground for the Floor" and "The Green Grass Grows" . . .
"Man's Life's a Vapour and full of Woes" . . .
An alehouse glee when the quart mugs foam,
And a right jolly lilt for the last load home!

❖   ❖   ❖   ❖   ❖

From *Ships and Folks*, edited by Cicely Fox Smith, published by Elkin Mathews, London, UK, 1920, pp. 72-74.

A ghostly tribute to the old traditional fiddlers who provided such an essential service within rural English villages for centuries. Fist adapted for singing by Mike Kennedy, as recorded on *A Dog's Life*, 2015

The header graphic is by Michigan artist Kathryn L. Darnell, © Kathryn L. Darnell 1982, used with permission..

Schooner Attacked by U-Boat

The Fighting Merchantmen

As I looked over the water—
As I looked over the foam,
I saw an old-time packet-ship
Come cheerily plunging home;
I saw the holes in her riddled sails,
And the shine of a little brass gun
On either side of her battered poop
In the light of the westering sun.

I hailed her over the water,
I hailed her over the tide:
"What news of war down Channel,
What news from the ocean wide?"
And from her shadowy bulwarks
A shadowy voice replied:
"Oh, homeward from the Indies bound,
Abeam of the Tuskar light,
We met a saucy privateer—

She bid us strike or fight;
And we sent her home with a pain in her ribs,
And her main topmast shot down,
To l'arn her to meddle with his Majesty's mails,
Bound home to Falmouth town!"

Frigate or sloop or chasse-marée,
Let 'em bang us if they can,
They will maybe find not much to their mind
In a fighting merchantman!

As I looked over the water,
As I looked over the foam,
I there did see a ship's longboat
Come wearily labouring home;
I saw the crew bend to their oars,
Like tired men they rowed,
As gunwale deep in the sunset tide
She wallowed with her load.

I hailed her over the water,
I hailed her over the tide:
"What news of war down Channel,
What news from the ocean wide?"
And in her stern sheets standing,
A bull-voiced mate replied:
"Oh, homeward bound from the River Plate,
Abeam of Tuskar light,
We met a pirate submarine
At the coming on of night,
She knew her game was safe to play,
As safe 'twill be again
When the game is not with fighting craft,
But peaceful merchantmen."

"They raked us first with shrapnel fire
Above deck and below,
They slipped a tin-fish into our bilge
And left us sinking slow;
We left our skipper on the bridge
With a bullet in his head;
We've our wounded here in the boat's bottom,
And most by now are dead."

"Our foes, they say, when war is done,
Shall pay us ton for ton;
But better now is shot for shot
And gun to answer gun;

Give England's ships their fighting chance—
Then let him catch who can,
He will maybe find not much to his mind
In a fighting merchantman!"

❖ ❖ ❖ ❖ ❖

From *Small Craft: Sailor Ballads and Chantys*, edited by Cicely Fox Smith, published by George H. Doran Co., New York, US, 1919, pp. 39-41. An earlier edition of Small Craft was published in 1917 by Elken Mathews, London, pp. 36-38.

The header graphic shows a schooner badly shot up in WWI, with a small dog the only apparent survivor barking defiantly at the adjacent German U-boat, as painted by Anton Otto Fischer from *Anton Otto Fischer*, p. 41.

Figureheads

Figureheads

"You never see a decent figure'ead—
Not now," Bill said,
"A fiddlin' bit o' scroll-work at the bow
That's the most now . . .
But Lord! I've seen some beauties, more'n a few,
An' some rare rum uns, too.

"Folks in all sorts o' queer old-fashioned rigs—
Fellers in wigs—
Chaps in cocked 'ats an' 'elmets—lords an' dukes—
Folks out o' books—
Niggers in turbans—mandarins an' Moors—
An' 'eathen gods by scores.

"An' women in all kinds o' fancy dresses—
Queens an' princesses—
Witches on broomsticks, too—an' spankin' girls

With streamin' curls—
An' dragons, an' sea-serpents—Lord knows what
I've seen an' what I've not.

"An' some's in breakers' yards, bleached bare with time
An' thick with grime;
An' some stuck up in gardens here an' there
With plants for 'air;
An' no one left as knows but chaps like me
How fine with paint and gold they used to be
In them old days at sea."

❖ ❖ ❖ ❖ ❖

From *Sea Songs and Ballads 1917-1922*, edited by Cicely Fox Smith, published by Houghton Mifflin, Boston, US, 1924, pp. 94-95. Earlier published in *Ships and Folks*, 1920. First published in *Punch* magazine, Volume 158, May 26, 1920, p. 386.

The header graphic titled *Figureheads* is drawn by Phil W. Smith, from *Sea Songs and Ballads*, 1924, facing p. 95, and was used to illustrate this poem.

The Apprentice's First Voyage

First Voyage

The barque lay in the Sou'-West Dock, her cargo all aboard;
Up came a young apprentice just as smart as any lord;
His cheeks were round and rosy and his buttons shone like gold,
His uniform and cap-badge were a picture to behold;
As proud as twenty Admirals, as perky as you please,
The little first voyager joined the *Southern Seas*.

The mate he was a Bluenose and as hard as pickled pork;
Says he: "Mind what I say, my lad, you've come to sea to *work*;
This hooker ain't a dancing-class nor yet a ladies' school,
When I say 'Jump' you've got to jump, for discipline's my rule;
So sharp now, spit upon your fists, unship that brassbound rig,"
And the little first voyager he cleaned out the pig.

There was fog in the Channel and a fine cold rain,
The ship crawled through it wailing like a thing that was in pain;
The crowd had got their shore heads still, they couldn't raise a stave,
And everyone on board her was as cheerful as the grave.
The decks were running wet and his bunk was chill and clammy,
And the little first voyager cried for his mammy.

Clear from the Channel chops and rolling down the Bay
The big seas from the westward came plunging cold and grey;
The Old Man kept her moving under everything she'd carry,
She stood it like a good 'un, but she rolled like Old Harry,
She rolled both rails under with a heavy cargo in her,
And the little first voyager said "No" to his dinner.

But all things have an end in time, and 'twasn't very long
Till she picked her North-East Trade up, blowing steadily and strong,
Royals, skysails, flying jib—all were set and filling,
Every sheave-block chirruping, every backstay thrilling,
Thrilling like a fiddle-string, humming like a hive,
And the little first voyager was glad he was alive.

The barque she was a hungry ship, as hungry as could be,
You couldn't find her like for it in all that sailed the sea;
There was sawdust in the coffee, there were weevils in the bread,
If you couldn't chew the junk you carved it into ships instead;
He scoffed his whack of crackerhash, it wasn't half enough,
So the little first voyager he swiped the cabin duff.

Running down the tropics in a whole-sail breeze,
She curvetted and sidled to the dancing glancing seas,
She fretted at her bridle like a mare brought in from grass,
Till "Easy" said the helmsman—"easy now, my bonny lass!"
Her weight upon the tiller was a thing a man could feel
And the little first voyager he took the lee wheel.

In the high south latitudes it blew up cold and hard,
The spray froze on men's faces as the sails froze on the yard;
"Aloft and furl them topsails," came the mate's bull-throated roar,
"And jump, ye sons of sodgers, if you never jumped afore!"
You couldn't hear the next man shout, the gale it screamed so loud,
And the little first voyager was furling with the crowd.

The skipper taught him some things and the mate he taught him more,
And Old Stiff he taught him several that he hadn't known before;
He learned a lot from bo'sun and he learned a lot from Chips,
The way to make square sennet and the way to bottle ships;
They said they'd make a seaman of him yet afore they quit,
And the little first voyager began to know a bit …

Romping up the Channel with Dungeness in sight,
"We'll burn our pay," the foc'sle said, "in Sailortown to-night;
We 'aven't seen old England's shores for three-'n-a-quarter years,"
Then sent their pannikins afloat and gave the tug three cheers;
She'd sailed the wide world all around to end where she began—
And the little first voyager came home a sailorman.

❖ ❖ ❖ ❖ ❖

From *Sailor's Delight*, edited by Cicely Fox Smith, published by Methuen & Co., London, UK, 1931, pp. 18-24; first published in *Punch* magazine, Volume 180, April 15, 1931, p. 416.

A vivid description of what a young apprentice sailor would experience on his first voyage. The "apprentice" is probably shipping aboard one of the Blackwall cargo "frigates" where the training was more formalized than in regular merchant ships.

The header graphic is an illustration titled *The Apprentice's First Voyage*, from *The American Neptune*, Pictorial Supplement 13, "Life between decks under Sail," plate 25, published by the Peabody Museum, Salem, Massachusetts, US, 1971, artist unknown.

The Five Ricks

Five ricks in a row
Stand in my father's field, I know,
Five ricks beside the hedge
That marks the long field's topmost edge . . .
There they stand; from there you see
Coppice, cottage, field and tree,
The shining vane on the church steeple,
And houses full of decent people
I've known since I was a little chap,
Good folks that sometimes say, mayhap,
"I wonder, now, what young Jim's doin'
Out there in all that noise and ruin" . . .

Five ricks in a row
Stand in my father's field, I know,
And over them there's a blue sky
Where small white clouds go floating high,
Like shell-bursts round a battle-plane . . .
But night'll come and the light'll wane,
Bats'll flit, and not a sound
Be heard in the fields around,
But a hunting owl, and a little breeze
That makes a rustling in the trees,
And by the ricks and round about
The lean grey rats slip in and out,
Here and there on every hand,
Like snipers out in No Man's Land.

If times was what times used to be,
What sport there for old Vic and me!

The same old girl, the same old dear,
That's been my pal now many a year,
Since first I bought her, one Spring fair,
A six week's pup from a gipsy there . . .
But now she's growing old and grey
At home, and I am far away,
And there ain't no games for her, I reckon,
Though the night seems just about to beckon
For little dogs to hunt their fill
Of rats and such-like things to kill;

And so Vic shakes herself, and sighs, turns three
Times round and down she lies,
And stretches out before the blaze
Her old rheumatic bones, and lays
Between her paws her grizzled head
And torn ears, waiting for my tread.

❖ ❖ ❖ ❖ ❖

From *Small Craft: Sailor Ballads and Chantys*, edited by Cicely Fox Smith, published by George H. Doran Co., New York, US, 1919, pp. 60-61.

A WWI poem that portrays a soldier at the front thinking about the peaceful family farm that he grew up on. Having grown up on such a family farm I find this one particularly haunting.

Spring in the Trenches

Flanders' Woods

England's woods are green to-day;
Every day and all day long
In among the trees do stray
The birds' song and the winds' song.

Last year's leaves beneath our feet
Light do sigh and soft do stir,
As if they kept remembrance sweet
Of young dead lovers walking there . . .

In Flanders' woods on hurrying wings
Every day and all day long
The seeking bullet flies and sings
Thin and shrill its bridal song.

All the summer leaves are brown,
And all the boughs of summer bare;
And many a gallant lad lies down
With glory for his sweetheart there.

❖ ❖ ❖ ❖ ❖

From *Songs And Chanties 1914-1916*, edited by Cicely Fox Smith, published by Elkin Mathews, London, UK, 1919, p. 228; also published in *Fighting Men* by Elkin Mathews in 1916. First published in *The Winsdor Magazine*, Volume 42, June-November, 1915, p. 648.

A WWI poem comparing the quiet of the English woods with that on the Flanders' front.

The header graphic is a painting titled *Spring in the Trenches*, Ridge Wood, 1917, by Paul Nash, from *The War Poets*, by Robert Giddings, Orion Books, New York, US, 1988, p. 176.

Flying Kites

"It was them there flyin' kites of 'ers done it," said he,
"Runnin' down the Tropics a sight she was to see
A pictur' to see with 'er sails both large and small,
An' 'er pretty skysails atop of 'em all."

"Bill was on the stunsail boom workin' on the gear,
Somethin' or another as wasn't runnin' clear;
She was loggin' all o' sixteen, an' me at the wheel an' all,
An' I 'eard a feller shoutin', an' then I see Bill fall."

"The wind was on the quarter an' freshenin' to a gale,
An' you dursen't shove the hellum down with all that press o' sail:
The ol' man done 'is best, but it warn't no good to 'im—
She was loggin' sixteen steady, an' Bill, 'e couldn't swim."

"So we squared 'er off afore it like a tower o' cloud,
Runnin' down the Tropics so lofty an' so proud,
Runnin' down the Tropics a sight she was to see,
But—it was them there flyin' kites of 'ers drowned Bill," said he.

❖ ❖ ❖ ❖ ❖

From *Full Sail: More Sea Songs and Ballads*, edited by Cicely Fox Smith, published by Houghton Mifflin Co., New York, US, 1926, pp. 90-91.

Working high in the rigging was always a dangerous job, especially when the ship had all sails set and with a brisk wind was tearing along at 16 knots. There was no safe way to stop such a ship and turn around quickly to search for a sailor who had fallen from the rigging. If such a sailor survived the fall, it was also unlikely that he'd know how to swim and he would quickly drown.

The Flying Fish Sailor

The Flying-Fish Sailor

"The Western Ocean rolls and roars
From Sandy Hook to Europe's shores,
From Fastnet Light to Portland, Maine,
And Newport News and back again,
With Boston, Salem, Montreal,
And plenty o' ports both large and small,
And them that like may keep 'em all,
Not me," says the flying-fish sailor.

The Western Ocean roars and rolls
With all its deeps and all its shoals
And many a thundering wintry gale,
And many a storm of rain and hail,
And let who likes have sleet and snow,
And driving fog and drifting floe,
For South away and Eastward Ho!
Is the road for the flying-fish sailor.

In Blackwall Dock a ship is moored,
Her hatches on and her stores aboard,
In Blackwall Dock she lies to-day,
And she will sail when the morning's grey
For Sunda Strait and Singapore,
And Palembang and plenty more,
And many a swarming Eastern shore
That's known to the flying-fish sailor.

The girls they'll cry and the lads'll shout
When the blooming tugboat warps her out:
We'll drop the pilot off the Nore
With fond farewells to take ashore
To mothers, wives and sweethearts too—

Love to Sally and love to Sue—
And that's the last for a year or two
You'll see of the flying-fish sailor.

We'll drop the tug and we'll bear away
Down the Channel, across the Bay;
The Western Isles we'll leave behind
And make the Line with the good Trade wind:
We'll see the dolphins sport and play,
(And haul our yards ten times a day),
While South'ard still we beat our way,
The way of the flying-fish sailor.

And forty south when we have passed,
Her easting down she runs at last,
Where the white whale swims in the far South Sea,
And the brave West winds blow full and free:
The good old winds they bluster and blow
The same as they used to years ago,
And the good old stars that well we know
Look down on the flying-fish sailor.

The darned old hooker 'll log sixteen,
She'll ship it heavy and ship it green,
She'll roll along with her lee-rail under,
While the big seas break aboard like thunder:
The pots and pans they'll carry away,
And the cook go down on his knees and pray,
But let the seas roar as they may,
All's one to the flying-fish sailor.

At Sydney next a call we'll pay,
And meet a pal on Circular Quay;
We'll glance at Java Head also,
And Fuji's crest of frozen snow,
And slant-eyed girls in far Japan,
Wun Lee, Wang Ho and little Yo San,
With braided hair and twinkling fan,
Will smile on a flying-fish sailor.

And last of all the day'll come round
When the blooming mudhook leaves the ground,
And to old England we return,
Our pockets filled with pay to burn,
With a painted fan and an ivory comb
From foreign towns beyond the foam,
And a golden ring for the girl at home
That waits for the flying-fish sailor.

From *Sea Songs and Ballads 1917-22*, edited by Cicely Fox Smith, published by Houghton Mifflin Co., New York, US, 1924, pp. 3-5. Earlier published in *Sea Songs and Ballads*, 1922. First published in *Punch* magazine, Volume 161, November 2, 1921, p. 357.

This poem hits the major ports on a sailing voyage from England to Japan.

First adapted for singing by Charles Ipcar, as recorded on *Uncommon Sailor Songs*, 2004.

The graphic header is titled *Ocean Express* from an original "Ship Sailing Card" republished in *Other Yankee Ship Sailing Cards* by State Street Trust Co., Boston, Massachusetts, 1949, p. 66.

Follow the Sea

"What is it makes a man follow the sea?
Ask me another!" says Billy Magee:
"Maybe it's liquor and maybe it's love—
Maybe it's likin' to be on the move—
Maybe the salt drop that runs in his blood
Won't let his killick lie snug in the mud:
What is it makes such poor idjits as me
Follow the sea—follow the sea? . . .
Jiggered if I know!" says Billy Magee.

"What is it keeps a chap rollin' around
All his life long from the Skaw to the Sound?
Samplin' the weathers from Hull to Rangoon—
Doldrums an' westerlies, Trade an' typhoon—
Hurricane, cyclone an' southerly buster—
In any old drogher as flies the Red Duster?
What is it makes a chap follow the sea—
Follow the sea—follow the sea—
Bust me if I know!" says Billy Magee.

"What is it makes a man stick to the sea?
Ah, you may ask me!" says Billy Magee.
"Stick to it hungry and stick to it cold,
Stick to it after he's broken and old,
Freeze in the Forties an' sweat on the Line,
Shiver an' burn in the rain an' the shine,
Stick it until he can't stick it no more—
Curse it an' leave it for something ashore—
Chuck up his shore job an' follow the sea—
Stick to an' live by an' die by the sea—
Search me if I know!" says Billy Magee.

❖ ❖ ❖ ❖ ❖

From *Sea Songs and Ballads 1917-22*, edited by Cicely Fox Smith, published by Houghton Mifflin Co., New York, US, 1924, pp. 20-21. First published in *Punch* magazine, Volume 162, May 24, 1922, p. 410.

This poet wrote a lot of sentimental and nostalgic poetry but she was also an expert at humour when she wanted to be. Anyone who contributed to *Punch* magazine for over 40 years would have to have a humorous side. This is an excellent example of the poet combining the sea experience and humour extremely effectively.

Alan Fitzsimmons first adapted this poem for singing as recorded on *Seaboot Duff and Handspike Gruel* by Pinch o' Salt, 1995.

Fraser River

Fraser river's flooding high,
Cold and deep and cruel flowing,
All lonely stand the hills nearby,
And man may drown and no one knowing.

Oh, if you heard a shot by night,
Heed not, for it nothing strange is:
What but a hunter should it be
Scaring the wolves along the ranges?

And if beside a mountain trail
One man less a camp is sharing,
No way new is it for men
To come and go and no one caring.

Oh, let you ask now near and far:
Oh, let you ask both here and yonder:
What was he but a roving man,
And who can say where such may wander?

If a thing be gone it comes no more!
If a thing's lost there's none shall find it
Where Fraser river's roaring down
With the weight of all the snows behind it.

And Fraser river's full in flood,
Deep and cold and cruel flowing,
All lonely is the land thereby,
And a man may drown and no one knowing . . .

❖ ❖ ❖ ❖ ❖

From *Small Craft: Sailor Ballads and Chantys*, edited by Cicely Fox Smith, published by George H. Doran Co., New York, US, 1919, pp. 129-130. An earlier edition of *Small Craft* was published in 1914.

The Fraser River referred to flows past Vancouver, British Columbia. From a set of poems called "Songs of the Wild."

Fulfilment

The last grim fight was over, the last red trench was won
About the taken and re-taken hill,
And far beyond the dead-strewn slopes the battle's noise rolled on,
Far on . . . and left the soldier lying still.

He knew no more the din, the reek, the darkness and the slime,
The strangling poison-cloud that hid the sky;
He heard no more the devil's forge beat out its fateful chime,
And shells like birds of slaughter screaming by.

He walked, a whole and care-free boy, in fields he loved of old—
He breathed again the jolly breeze of morn . . .
He heard the pigeons clap their wings above the old grey fold
In the country far away where he was born.

He saw the blossom lie like foam on every hedge and tree,
And the sunlight breaking golden through the cloud;
He heard a hundred streams run down rejoicing to the sea,
And all the birds of Spring-time singing loud.

He saw, in bright battalions ranged, the embattled hosts of God,
Stand rank on rank high up the rifted skies . . .
And souls set free that sprang and soared above the blood-stained sod,
His comrades with the splendour in their eyes.

❖ ❖ ❖ ❖ ❖

From *Songs and Chanties 1914-1916*, edited by Cicely Fox Smith, published by Elkin Mathews, London, UK, 1919, pp. 224-225. First published in *Fighting Men* by Elkin Mathews in 1916.

Composed in the middle of WWI, in tribute to the dying soldiers.

The Furrow

An old horse to the furrow—an old man to the plough—
For the young horse and the young lad, they're needed yonder now—

The horse, so young and mettled he scarce had known the rein,
That shook his feathered fetlocks and tossed his streaming mane—

The lad that used to drive him, so strong and straight and tall,
That dressed him fine with ribbons and groomed him in the stall.

Ah, there as here, old Captain, we know, both I and you,
He'll drive a straight furrow as he always used to do!

The clods before the ploughshare fall heavily apart,
But never a clod among them so heavy as my heart—

To smell the clean earth breaking and the kind country smells,
And think o' the stink and reek there, and the bursting o' the shells.

An old horse to the furrow—an old man to the plough—
And the young horse and the young lad . . . how fare they yonder now?

❖ ❖ ❖ ❖ ❖

From *Sailor Town: Sea Songs and Ballads*, edited by Cicely Fox Smith, published by George H. Doran Co., New York, US, 1919, pp. 134-135. Earlier published in *The Naval Crown* by Elkin Mathews in 1915.

Composed during the first year of WWI. The poet was intimately familiar with rural farm life in England, and its the details she provides which make the imagined horrors of war at the front even more powerful.

Gerrans Churchtown

The spire at Gerrans Churchtown, it stands up bold and high,
It stands above the harbour and sees the ships go by;
It sees the long tides breaking from the Gull to Lizard Head,
The blue-lights and the searchlights, the living and the dead.

The lads of Gerrans Churchtown, a roving breed are they,
With their mothers' milk they tasted the salt wind and the spray;
The sea was first their playmate, he licked their feet with foam,
The lads of Gerrans Churchtown that could not bide at home.

The lads of Gerrans Churchtown, they're where they're wanted now,
They cleave their fathers' furrow, their grandsires' field they plough,—
A field of many acres from Scapa Flow to Nore,—
And the old men pull the lifeboat, and the young lads watch the shore.

And will they come at long last? . . . Ay, surely they will come,
Some day—a day to dream of—that brings the Grand Fleet home—
From peril, toil and glory, and battles overpast,
The bells of Gerrans Churchtown shall ring them home at last.

Will all them come together? . . . Not those whose hearts are still
In a wider green God's-acre than lies on Gerrans hill;
It's a brighter sun they look on than sets in yonder West,
And a sweeter bell than Gerrans' has rung them to their rest.

❖ ❖ ❖ ❖ ❖

From *Sailor Town: Sea Songs and Ballads*, edited by Cicely Fox Smith, published by George H. Doran Co., New York, US, 1919, pp. 23-24. An earlier edition of *Sailor Town* was published by Elkin Mathews in 1914. It also appears in *Small Craft* also published by Elkin Mathews, Cork Street, London 1917, pp 20-21.

Composed in the first months of WWI, and focuses on the war's effect on the coastal communities as well as the nation. First adapted for singing by David Watts (UK) with collaboration from other members of Elsie's Band, 2007.

A Garden in the North

Yestreen I walked where wind and tree
Called all the lost years back to me,
Where shaken leaf and waft of bird
Spoke to me each its well-known word.

I knew—ah, well I knew of old
The wet earth and the sky's pale gold,
The light wind stirring restlessly
The brown leaf on the beechen tree.

I knew the far grey line of hills
Behind the barn—the daffodils
Beneath the bare bough putting forth
Their spears' brave challenge to the north.

What more? Only the joy, the pain,
Shadows and dreams that waked again
(As in these barren boles the Spring
Wakes at the west wind's summoning):

Only the drift of thorn leaves dry
That stirred and sighed as I went by,
As if some page I turned and read
There an old tale of years long fled.

And the wise wind that keeps alway
The lost sweet soul of yesterday
Brought to me on its whispering breath
Love, hope, remembrance—Life and Death!

❖   ❖   ❖   ❖   ❖

From *Small Craft: Sailor Ballads and Chantys*, edited by Cicely Fox Smith, published by George H. Doran Co., New York, US, 1919, pp. 120-121. First published in *Songs of Sail*, 1914.

This poem may reference the poet's feelings after the death of her father.

Shadows of Ships

Ghosts in Deptford

If ghosts should walk in Deptford, as very well they may,
A man might find the night there more stirring than the day,
Might meet a Russian Tsar there, or see in Spain's despite
Queen Bess ride down to Deptford to dub Sir Francis knight.

And loitering here and yonder, and jostling to and fro,
In every street and alley the sailor-folk would go,
All colours, creeds, and nations, in fashion old and new,
If ghosts should walk in Deptford, as like enough they do.

And there'd be some with pigtails, and some with buckled shoes,
And smocks and caps like pirates that sailors once did use,
And high sea-boots and oilskins and tarry dungaree,
And shoddy suits men sold them when they came fresh from sea.

And there'd be stout old skippers and mates of mighty hand,
And Chinks and swarthy Dagoes, and Yankees lean and tanned,
And many a hairy shellback burned black from Southern skies,
And brassbound young apprentice with boyhood's eager eyes,

And by the river reaches all silver to the moon
You'd hear the shipwrights' hammers beat out a phantom tune,
The caulkers' ghostly mallets rub-dub their faint tattoo—
If ghosts should walk in Deptford, as very like they do.

If ghosts should walk in Deptford, and ships return once more
To every well-known mooring and old familiar shore,
A sight it were to see there, of all fine sights there be,
The shadowy ships of Deptford come crowding in from sea.

Cog, carrack, buss and dromond—pink, pinnace, snake and snow—
Queer rigs of antique fashion that vanished long ago,
With tall and towering fo'c'sles and curving carven prows,
And gilded great poop lanterns, and scrolled and swelling bows.

The Baltic barque that foundered in last month's North Sea gales,
And last year's lost Cape Horner with the wonder on her sails,
Black tramp and stately liner should lie there side by side—
Ay, all should berth together upon that silent tide.

In dock and pond and basin so close the keels should lie
Their hulls should hide the water, their masts make dark the sky,
And through their tangled rigging the netted stars should gleam
Like gold and silver fishes from some celestial stream.

And all their quivering royals and all their singing spars
Should send a ghostly music a-shivering to the stars—
A sound like Norway forests when wintry winds are high,
Or old dead seamen's shanties from great old days gone by,—

Till eastward over Limehouse, on river, dock and slum,
All shot with pearl and crimson the London dawn should come,
And fast at flash of sunrise, and swift at break of day,
The shadowy ships of Deptford should melt like mist away.

❖ ❖ ❖ ❖ ❖

From *Rovings: Sea Songs and Ballads*, edited by Cicely Fox Smith, published by Elkin Mathews, London, UK, 1921, pp. 9-11.

The Deptford Royal Navy Yard, next to Greenwich, was one of the major navy yards in England.

The header graphic is an illustration titled *Shadows of Ships* as drawn by Phil W. Smith, from *Anchor Lane*, facing p. 50.

Ghosts in the Garden

It needs not in the owl-light grey
Hither to creep with mystic rune,
Nor yet in shuddering stealth to pay
Lip-service to the freakish moon.
Here is no spell to sing or say;
Ghosts in the garden walk by day.

Where spreads its wide and plumy wings
The stormy sunset's weeping gold,
To those lone walks their presence clings,
Their footsteps stir the last year's mould
Whose vapour, faint like incense, brings
The fragrance of forgotten Springs.

It may be, nought is seen or heard
Save sights and sounds that well may be
But passing of a vagrant bird,
But shadow of a shaken tree:
By presence seen, or spoken word,
The haunted stillness is not stirred.

Yet o'er the leaf-drift wet and brown,
E'en now, some lingering footfall past,
And where yon late-blown rose's crown
On Summer's forehead clung the last,
The waft of some dead lady's gown
Brought the sweet ruin shattering down.

❖ ❖ ❖ ❖ ❖

From *Small Craft: Sailor Ballads and Chantys*, edited by Cicely Fox Smith, published by George H. Doran Co., New York, US, 1919, pp. 122-123. First published in *Songs of Sail*, 1914.

The fourth poem in a set called "Songs of Home" published shortly after the poet's return to England after three years in Canada and as WWI was just beginning.

The Gipsy Soldier

The gipsy wife came to my door with pegs and brooms to sell
They make by many a roadside fire and many a greenwood dell,
With bee-skeps and with baskets wove of osier, rush and sedge,
And withies from the river-bed and brambles from the hedge.

With her stately grace like Pharaoh's queen (for all her broken shoon),
You'd marvel one so proud and tall should ever ask a boon;
But "livin's dear for us poor folk," and "money can't be had,"
And her "man's in Mespotamia," and "times is cruel bad."

Yes, times is cruel bad, we know, and passing strange also,
And it's strange as anything I've heard that gipsy men should go

To lands through which their forebears trod from some unknown abode
The way that ended long ago upon the Portsmouth Road.

I wonder if the Eastern skies and Eastern odours seem
Familiar to that gipsy man as memories of a dream;
Does Tigris' flow stir ancient dreams from immemorial rest
Ere ever gipsy poached a trout of Itchen or of Test?

Does something in him seem to know those red and arid lands
Where dust of ancient cities sleeps beneath the drifted sands?
Do Kurdish girls with lustrous eyes beneath their drooping lids
And Eastern babes look strangely like the Missis and the kids?

I wonder if the waving palms, when desert winds do blow,
In their dry rustling seem to sing a song he used to know,
Or does he only curse the heat, and wish that he were laid
Beneath the spread of Rufus' oaks or Harwood's beechen shade?

Well, luck be with the gipsy man, and lead him safely home
To the old familiar caravan and ways he used to roam,
And bring him, as it brought his sires from their far first abode
To where the gipsy camp-fires burn along the Portsmouth Road.

❖ ❖ ❖ ❖ ❖

From *Small Craft: Sailor Ballads and Chantys*, edited by Cicely Fox Smith, published by George H. Doran Co., New York, US, 1919, pp. 65-67. First published in *Punch* magazine, Volume 153, July 11, 1917, p. 24.

Seems a sister poem to "The Portsmouth Road" but with more focus on the gipsies.

The Glory of the Marne

The rivers broaden to the sea
In power and wealth and pride,
And stately ships from all the world
Do berth on every tide . . .
But Marne hath never port nor pier,
Warehouse nor wharf nor quay,
And the very name of her is lost
Before she finds the sea.
The rivers run rejoicing down
And singing as they flow,
In rain or sun their course assigned
Pursuing, swift or slow . . .
But Marne goes weeping all day long,
And is not comforted,
Her trampled banks and bloodied pools,
And shallows choked with dead.

Yet hath she glory of her own
'Mid rivers great and small,

And nobler dower than pride or power
Is hers among them all,
Poor Marne hath seen the hosts of Hell
Turned backward from their goal,
And the stormy dawn of Hope arise
On earth's war-darkened soul,
And Marne hath fame for evermore
While the floods of Time shall roll.

❖ ❖ ❖ ❖ ❖

From *Rhymes of the Red Ensign*, edited by Cicely Fox Smith, published by Hodder & Stoughton, London, UK, 1919, pp. 51-52.

Dutch Galliot Unloading

The *Good Intent*

They built her in the olden days,
They built her strong, they built her stout,
In Farmer George's golden days
It must have been or thereabout.
They knew no rush or hustle then,
They drove no rivets racing time:
A sort of pleasant bustle then
Filled up the hours from chime to chime.

With care and pains they'd linger on
Each chisel touch and mallet stroke,
And lay a loving finger on
Her curving sides of Devon oak.

As so they worked, and so she grew
From garboard unto gunwale strake,

And if uncommon slow she grew
They built to last and no mistake.

Well, finish her they did at last;
Sparred, rigged and fitted, forth she went,
And out to sea she slid at last—
The ketch of Plymouth, *Good Intent*.

She went—and Lord! she's going still,
The same old sea's beneath her bow,
The same old winds are blowing still,
The same old skies behold her now.

A stout West-country crew she had,
And paid then at the capstan head:
A seasoned skipper too she had,
Whose sons—and grandsons—all are dead.

The coast from north to south she knows,
Its tiny ports and sleepy piers
From Hull to Avenmouth she knows,
She's used them for a hundred years.

The Channel lights they wink at her
(They've done it at her cargoes too):
The friendly stars they blink at her
The way they always used to do.

Old *Temeraire* she might have seen,
And curtseyed to the *Victory*,
And many a ding-dong fight have seen,
For those lively days at sea.

The packets in their day were new,
And many a bluff East Indiaman;
She saw them all when they were new,
Since first her sailing days began.

She saw, she waved them on their way,
Trim brig and plunging seventy-four,
And one and all they've gone their way,
Like clouds that pass and are no more.

Frigate and sloop and battleship,
She's seen 'em come, she's seem 'em go,
Red tramp and reeking cattleship
And China clipper winged like snow.

And still her old luck nods to her,
And, be it peace or be it war,

It doesn't make much odds to her—
She's lived in rousing times before.

....

They might not count as skilled to-day
In her old hull whose lesson's hid:
"God send our shipwrights build to-day
As honest as their granddads did!"

❖   ❖   ❖   ❖   ❖

From *Sea Songs and Ballads 1917-22*, edited by Cicely Fox Smith, published by Houghton Mifflin Co., New York, US, 1924, pp. 110-112. Later reprinted in the same form in *Rhymes of the Red Ensign* in 1919, pp. 59-62. First published in *Punch* magazine, Volume 155, October 9, 1918, p. 237.

"Farmer George" is a reference to King George III of England the reigning monarch (1760-1820) when the *Good Intent* was built.

The poet added this note: "The ketch *Good Intent*, built at Plymouth of British oak 128 years ago, is probably the oldest (1919) British merchant-vessel afloat."

This poem was first set to music by Michael Kennedy in 2010.

The head graphic is an illustration of a similar ketch titled *Dutch Galliot Unloading, Great Yarmouth*, as etched by Edward William Cooke, 1829, from *Sailing Vessels in Authentic Early Nineteenth-Century Illustrations*, reprinted by Dover Publications, New York, US, 1989, p. 42.

Prayer after Vimy Ridge Victory

Good Luck

The hour was near for starting
Ere Vimy ridge was won,
And we said "Good luck" at parting
As we had often done
In folly, sport or fun.

(For love and pride and passion
With speech accord but ill,

And if we had skill to fashion
Brave words to speak our fill,
We should be speaking still).

All dreams men strive and sigh for,
Or lose beyond recall,
The things men live and die for,
The great things and the small—
Our "Good luck" meant them all.

"To each his dear ambition
As unto each seems best,
Love's crown or fate's fruition,
The fame, the medaled breast . . .
And to the dead their rest!"

❖   ❖   ❖   ❖   ❖

From *Small Craft: Sailor Ballads and Chantys*, edited by Cicely Fox Smith, published by George H. Doran Co., New York, US, 1919, p. 52. Previously published by Elk Mathews, London, 1917.

The capture of "Vimy ridge" in WWI cost tens of thousands of lives on both sides.

The header graphic is an illustration from *Punch* magazine during WWI, artist unknown.

The Great Pyramids

The Grand Tour

I always wished to see the world, I 'ad no chanst before,
Nor I don't suppose I should 'ave if there 'adn't been no war;
I used to read the tourist books, the shippin' news also,
An' I 'ad the chanst o' goin', so I couldn't 'elp but go.

We 'ad a spell in Egypt first, before we moved along
Acrost the way to Suvla, where we got it 'ot an' strong;
We 'ad no drink when we was dry, no rest when we was tired,
But I've seen the Perramids an' Spink, which I 'ad oft desired.

I've what 'll last me all my life, to talk about an' think,
I've sampled various things to eat an' various more to drink;
I've strolled among them dark bazaars, which makes the pay to fly
(An' I 'ad my fortune told as well, but that was all my eye!)

I've seen them little islands too—I couldn't say their names—
An' towns as white as washin'-day, an' mountains spoutin' flames;
I've watched the sun come lonely up on miles an' miles of sea,
Why, folks 'ave paid a 'undred pound an' seen no more than me!

The sky is some'ow bluer there—in fact, I never knew
As any sun could be so 'ot or any sky so blue;
There's dates an' figs an' suchlike things all 'angin' on the trees,
An' black folks walkin' up an' down as natural as you please.

I always wished to see the world, I'm fond o' life an' change,
But Abdul got me in the leg; an' this is passin' strange,
That when you see old England's shore, all wrapped in mist an' rain,
Why, it's worth the bloomin' bundle to be comin' 'ome again!

❖   ❖   ❖   ❖   ❖

From *Songs & Chanties: 1914-1916*, edited by Cicely Fox Smith, published by Elkin Mathews, London, UK, 1919, pp. 211-213. Earlier published in *Fighting Men* by Elkin Mathews in 1916. First published in *Punch* magazine, Volume 150, January 26, 1916, p. 70.

During WWI the poet hosted many London parties and had the opportunity to talk with many wounded vetrans. She certainly got the ironic military chatter down.

"Suvla (Bay)" refers to the ill-conceived and unsuccessful campaign by the British to wrest control of the Dardanelles Strait from Turkey in 1915-1916.

The header graphic is a photograph of sailors from the U. S. S. Cruiser *Raleigh* with guides, circa 1900, in front of the Great Pyramids of Egypt, from Detroit Publishing Co., photographer unknown.

The Green Thicket

All in a green thicket I heard a bird sing,
And blithe though his song was it made the tears spring,
To hear a bird sing as he swung on his spray,
All in a green thicket at break of the day.

All in a green thicket his song it did pour
That told of the Springs that shall come nevermore,
That sang of sweet blossoms, now faded and dry,
All in a green thicket in Aprils gone by.

All in a green thicket that morning in Spring,
I smelt the sharp scent of each young growing thing,
I smelt the sweet herbage all drowned with the dew,
And the time that's gone from me was with me anew.

All in a green thicket at break of the day
It was like the dear voice of a friend far away,

It was like the kind touch of a hand that I know,
And the smile and the tears of dead Aprils ago,

All in a green thicket one morning in Spring,
For to smell the young woodland and hear the bird sing,
Oh, long did I loiter and dream by the way,
All in a green thicket at break of the day.

❖   ❖   ❖   ❖   ❖

From *Sailor Town: Sea Songs and Ballads*, edited by Cicely Fox Smith, published by George H. Doran Co., New York, US, 1919, pp. 60-61. An earlier edition of *Sailor Town* was published by Elkin Mathews in 1914.

The poet has returned to her native England after three years in Canada.

The Half Loaf

The Half Loaf

There ain't the tall windjammers like we knew when we was young,
With their masts as made a forest every water-front along;
But I know a smutty cargo tramp that's loadin' at Millwall,
An' any ship's a better ship than no darned ship at all . . .
When she's outward bound—an' the same ol' seas'll hustle 'er—
Outward bound—an' the same ol' winds'll bustle 'er—
South away to Singapore, North away to Nome,
An' round the world an' back again is one way 'ome.

There ain't the good old 'ouse-flags every shellback used to know
In the tea-fleet an' the wool-fleet an' the grain-fleet years ago,
But there's still the same ol' Duster an' the same ol' Peter too,
An' I reckon them two's good enough for blokes like me an' you . . .
When we're outward bound—an' the same ol' stars'll wink at us—
Outward bound—an' the same ol' lights'll blink at us—
South away to Singapore, North away to Nome,
An' round the world an' back again is one way 'ome.

There ain't no capstan chorus now, there ain't no mate to bawl,
"Are ye men or are ye corpses? Give it lip now, heave an' pawl!"
But the bloomin' gulls all round 'er an' the wind that's blowing strong
In cargo gear and funnel stay, they sing the same ol' song:
"Outward bound—an' the same ol' seas 'll bury 'er—
Outward bound—an' the same ol' winds 'll worry 'er—
South away to Singapore, North away to Nome,
An' round the world an' back again is one way 'ome!"

❖ ❖ ❖ ❖ ❖

From *Sailor's Delight*, edited by Cicely Fox Smith, published by Metheun & Co., London, UK, 1931, pp. 108-110.

Alan Fitzsimonds (UK) first adapted this poem for singing, as recorded by Pinch o' Salt on *Seaboot Duff & Handspike Gruel*, 2000.

The header graphic titled *The Half Loaf* illustrated this poem and was drawn by Phil W. Smith, from *Sailor's Delight*, facing p. 110.

"Go past the post-office and sharp to the left afore you come to the church."

Half-Past Eleven Square

There's a town I know in Flanders, an' there ain't much else to say,
But it's pretty much like most towns when the war 'as passed their way;
There's tumbled shops an' 'ouses, an' there's brickbats everywhere,
An' a place that British soldiers call "'Alf-past Eleven Square."

There's a silly clock stuck up there that's forgot the way to chime,
With its silly fingers pointin' to the same old bloomin' time;
An' the world it keeps on turnin', but it makes no difference there,
For it never gets no later in 'Alf-past Eleven Square.

There's a stink o' gas a-crawlin' where the people lived before,
That it used to tell the time to when there 'adn't been no war,
In the day the whizz-bangs bustin', in the night the starshells' glare,
An' 'oo cares what the time is in 'Alf-past Eleven Square?

You could walk for 'arf a day there, an' there's not a soul to meet
In the empty smashed-up 'ouses an' the empty sandbagged street;
They've packed their traps up long since an' they've gone for change of air,
For you bet it ain't no 'ealth-resort—'Alf-past Eleven Square.

An' it only wakes up sometimes, when the armies come an' go,
With the transport an' the wounded an' the big guns crawlin' slow;
But let 'em come or let 'em go, the clock don't seem to care
If it's Fritz or Tommy marchin' through 'Alf-past Eleven Square.

But it's waitin'—waitin'—waitin' till the world goes on once more,
An' the folk come back to live there as they used to live before,
An' open wide the broken door an' climb the broken stair,
An' move along its fingers in 'Alf-past Eleven Square.

Yes, it's waitin'—waitin'—waitin', just the same as you an' me.
For the same world, only better than the old one used to be;
An' I've got a barmy notion that I wish I might be there
When twelve o'clock is strikin' in 'Alf-past Eleven Square!

❖ ❖ ❖ ❖ ❖

From *War Verse*, edited by Frank Foxcroft, published by T. Y. Crowell, New York, US, 1918. pp. 304-305. First published in *Punch* magazine, Volume 155, July 24, 1918, p. 56. An identical version also appears in the poet's own book *Rhymes of the Red Ensign*, published by Hodder & Stoughton, 1919, pp. 47-49.

This haunting poem was composed near the end of WWI and paints a stark picture of the devastation of typical small town square, with the hope that it will someday be put back together again.

The header graphic is a cartoon drawn by G. L. Stampa, from *Punch* magazine, Volume 152, August 29, 1917, p. 165.

Hans Dans an' Me

Hans Dans an' me was shipmates once, an' shared the wind an' weather,
An' many a job o' work in them old days we done together;
I've stood my trick with Hans afloat an' drunk with him ashore,
But—never no more, Hans Dans, my lad, Lord love you, never no more!

Hans Dans an' me was shipmates once, we couldn't 'elp but be,
'E'd shoved 'is bloomin' nose in every ship as sailed the sea!
For Hans'd sign for three pun' ten when union rates was four,
But'—never no more, Hans Dans, my lad, you bet yer, never no more!

Hans Dans an' me was shipmates once, an' if 'e'd fought us clean,
Why, shipmates still when war was done might Hans an' me 'ave been,
The truest pals a man can have are them 'e's fought before,
But—never no more, Hans Dans, my lad, d' ye get me, never no more!

Hans Dans an' me was shipmates once, but long's I sail the sea,
There'll be no foc's'le big enough to hold Hans Dans an' me,
For all the seas an' all the years won't wipe out Hans's score,
Nor do away the dirty work 'e 's done an' called it war,
No, never no more, Hans Dans, my lad, so 'elp me, never no more!

❖ ❖ ❖ ❖ ❖

From *Rhymes of the Red Ensign*, edited by Cicely Fox Smith, published by Hodder and Stoughton, London, UK, 1919, pp. 35-36. A verse first appeared in *Punch* magazine, Volume 155, September 4, 1918, p. 158.

The strong anti-German sentiment in this poem is a direct response to the anti-German propaganda efforts of England and her allies during WWI. The propaganda efforts of the Germans were, of course, similar.

The Happy Warrior (April 23rd)

I

Here, a soldier plain, I kneel,
Sword on thigh, spur on heel.

If I fall or if I stand,
Lord, my times are in Thy hand.

Three things beneath the sun,
These I'll ask, and so have done.

Clean hand, clean sword,
And a clean heart to serve Thee, Lord!

II

When Spring's turned and Winter's done,
Life in every bough does run.

Very sweet the Spring sky . . .
Shall a man desire to die,

Die, and be no more seen
Where streams run and fields are green,

And the birds do sing shrill
Mating songs in April?

Should a man not fear to fall,
Lord, Lord . . . if life were all? . . .

❖ ❖ ❖ ❖ ❖

From *Sailor Town: Sea Songs and Chantys*, edited by Cicely Fox Smith, published by George H. Doran Co., New York, US, 1919, pp. 112-113. Earlier published in *The Naval Crown* by Elkin Mathews in 1915; also published in *The Register*, Adelaide, South Australia, June 5, 1915.

Composed in the first year of WWI.

Tall Ships Loading Lumber at Hastings Mill

Hastings Mill

As I went down by Hastings Mill I lingered in my going
To smell the smell of piled-up deals and feel the salt wind blowing,
To hear the cables fret and creak and the ropes stir and sigh
Shipmate, my shipmate! as in days gone by.

As I went down by Hastings Mill I saw a ship there lying,
About her tawny yards the little clouds of sunset flying;
And half I took her for the ghost of one I used to know
Shipmate, my shipmate! many years ago.

As I went down by Hastings Mill I saw while I stood dreaming
The flicker of her riding light along the ripples streaming,
The bollards where we made her fast and the berth where she did lie
Shipmate, my shipmate! in the days gone by.

As I went down by Hastings Mill I heard a fellow singing,
Chipping off the deepsea rust above the tide a-swinging,
And well I knew the queer old tune and well the song he sung
Shipmate, my shipmate! when the world was young.

And past the rowdy Union Wharf, and by the still tide sleeping,
To a randy dandy deepsea tune my heart in time was keeping,
To the thin far sound of a shadowy watch a-hauling,
And the voice of one I knew across the high tide calling
Shipmate, my shipmate! and the late dusk falling.

❖ ❖ ❖ ❖ ❖

From *Sailor Town*, edited by Cicely Fox Smith, published by George H. Doran Co., NY, 1919, pp. 56-57.

Hastings Mill was the primary lumber mill and lumber shipping wharf for Vancouver, British Columbia. The "rowdy Union Wharf" was adjacent. After her work as a typist in a law office, Smith used to walk along Store Street on the Victoria waterfront to a similar lumber yard and muse over the ships being loaded there for faraway ports.

First adapted for singing by Charles Ipcar, as recorded on *More Uncommon Sea Songs*, 2005.

The header graphic is a photograph of tall ships tied up at the Hasting Mill lumber wharf at Vancouver, British Columbia, in the early 1900's, photographer unknown, from *Light on the Water*, by Keith McLaren, Douglas & McIntyre, Vancouver, 1998, p. 41.

Hay Harvest: 1916

I saw the mowers swinging
Their scythes in the English hay . . .
What swathes of dead are lying
In fields of France this day!

The mowers mow in the sunshine,
Their scythes flash all together—
Even as flash the bayonets
Out there in the golden weather.

The mowers mow in the sunshine,
The sweat stands on each brow . . .
It is blood, not sweat, our bravest
Spend in war's windrows now.

I see the mowers swinging
Their scythes in the grass and flowers . . .
Ah God! What price has bought it,
This English peace of ours!

❖ ❖ ❖ ❖ ❖

From *Songs and Chanties 1914-1916*, edited by Cicely Fox Smith, published by Elkin Mathews, London, UK, 1919, p. 231. First published in *Fighting Men* by Elkin Mathews in 1916.

The human cost of WWI, at the end of its second year, is reflected in this "peaceful" rural hay harvest. But there is no escaping the impact of the more deadly harvest across the Channel in France.

Flying Fish

High Noon

It's rummy, the way things come back to you . . . down by the Docks
I'd stopped at a junk store, all rusty old hinges and locks,
Old shoes, and false teeth, and odd chessmen, and broken-up innards of clocks.

And, chucked in a heap with a lot of such litter, there lay
A badly stuffed flying-fish, dingy and dusty and grey,
That had gleamed like a rainbow long since as it flitted through sunshine and spray.

And, Lord! How it brought it all back to me! Clear as could be,
High noon once again in the Tropics—the ship running free,
And the blue old Pacific a-shining as far as a fellow could see . . .

The sway of the masts and the slow dip and lift of the rail:
The mate with his eye cocked aloft at the set of the sail,
And the bosun, the ugly old image, his mouth opened wide in a hail:

Old Sails with his palm and his needle, cross-legged on the hatch,
A-stitching away at a bolt-rope, or putting a patch
In a fair-weather topsail, and spinning his endless old yarns with the watch:

Old Slush at the door of his galley, and Chips with his chest:
The barefooted man at the wheel in his trousers and vest,
The flash of the rings in his ears and the sea-snake tattooed on his breast.

High noon in the Tropics—the white and the gold and the blue,
The glitter of flying-fish scattering spray as they flew,
The songs that we sang and the tales that we told and the shipmates we knew!

Then it passed like a dream: I was back here in Poplar again
With my collar turned up to my ears in the cold and the rain,
And the ships as they groped through the river mist wailing like creatures in pain.

❖ ❖ ❖ ❖ ❖

From *Full Sail: More Sea Songs and Ballads*, edited by Cicely Fox Smith, published by Houghton Mifflin Co., New York, US, 1926, pp. 61-63.

This is the poet at her best! The memories of years ago come flooding back, triggered by the nautical junk shop, only to be followed by the shock of the last verse as we're brought back to a present reality.

Compare with "The Old Fiddle" and "A Sea Dream."

First adapted for singing by Mike Kennedy, as recorded on *A Dog's Life*, 2015

The header graphic is from a set published in London by Abraham Rees in the period 1797-1820; many of these prints were engraved from artwork by Sydenham Edwards.

Home Along

When days are getting' short an' cold, an' the long nights begin,
With waves like mountains rollin' high, an' the norther blowin' thin,
Oh, then my thoughts do stretch their wings an' fly across the sea,
Home along, home along, to the place where I would be!

Home along, home along, there's deep an' leafy lanes,
Where kind an' warm's the summer sun an' soft the autumn rains;
An' many a ship to harbour comes, an' sailor home from sea,
Home along, home along, in the West Countrie!

I wonder how they're farin' now, the young folks an' the old,
An' if they think at all o' me, when nights are cold;
An' what's the tale on Market Strand, the news on Fish Strand Quay,
Home along, home along, in the West Countrie!

Home along, home along, 'tis maybe not the same
Wi' no one left but old men there, the faint 'earts an' the lame;
Who'll pull my oar to lifeboat now, when the blue lights burn at sea,
Home along, home along, in the West Countrie?

I wish that 'Igh Kiel fleet would come, the waitin's cruel slow,
An' when I get my bit o' leave, oh, I know where I will go,
To sit me down beside the fire, or stroll beside the quay,
Home along, home along, in the West Countrie.

Home along, home along, an' I'd like to see it now,
The ruddy furrow white wi' gulls behind my father's plough—
A friend to greet, an' a girl to meet, an' a score o' folks to see,
Home along, home along, in the West Countrie!

❖ ❖ ❖ ❖ ❖

From *Songs and Chanties 1914-1916*, edited by Cicely Fox Smith, published by Elkin Mathews, London, UK, 1919, pp. 196-197. First published in *Fighting Men* by Elkin Mathews in 1916.

A WWI poem from the perspective of a sailor thinking about what he'd like to do on his home leave.

"'Igh Kiel fleet" is a reference to the German High Seas Fleet. Eventually the Germans did venture out in 1916 and did bloody battle with the British Grand Fleet at the Battle of Jutland.

Home for Christmas—Old Style

"I'm goin' to get 'er 'ome
For Christmas," said the skipper
O' the clipper
Flyin' Foam . . .

Built on the Clyde, an' built to go,
By Bell an' Burnie for Keith an' Co.,
She was a beauty, she was a mover,
An' our ol' man was the man to shove 'er!

We cleared the 'Eads the fust of October:
It was "All 'ands aft," afore we was sober,
An' "Boys," says 'e, "on board this packet
You'll 'ave to jump or else stand the racket . . . "

"'Cos I mean to get 'er 'ome
For Christmas," said the skipper
O' the clipper
Flyin' Foam.

Off o' Cape Stiff it blowed a teaser—
A reg'lar snorter, a beast of a freezer—
It blowed bad, an' it blowed bitter,
With lumps o' seas that froze when they 'it 'er,

With hail as stung like shot in our faces,
An' ice like iron on sheets an' braces:
But 'ailin' an' freezin' an' snowin' an' blowin',
'E stuck to 'is topsails, 'e kept 'er goin'—

'Cos I mean to get 'er 'ome
For Christmas, did the skipper
O' the clipper
Flyin' Foam.

She took 'er Trade an' she run from the South
With everything set an' a bone in 'er mouth,
She snored along with 'er lee rail under,
An' 'er main to'gal'ntsail bust like thunder!

It was breezing up an' the sea a smother,
But we laid aloft an' we bent another—
For 'e says, says 'e, "By the Great Lord Harry,
She must darn well drag what she can't darn carry,"

"But I'm goin' to git 'er 'ome
For Christmas," said the skipper
O' the clipper
Flyin' Foam.

We 'adn't 'ardly struck the Channel
When a fog come down as thick as flannel:
You couldn't see, an' you couldn't 'ear,
An' all you could do was stand an' steer.

An' where we was, well, there warn't no knowin',
But we blowed the 'orn an' we kep' on goin',
Till all of a suddent the fog got thinner,
An' there was the Foreland, as I'm a sinner . . .

An' 'e'd got 'er 'ome
For Christmas, 'ad the skipper
O' the clipper
Flyin' Foam.

❖ ❖ ❖ ❖ ❖

From *Sailor's Delight*, edited by Cicely Fox Smith, published by Methuen & Co., London, UK, 1931, pp. 56-59; first published in *Cunard* magazine.

This poem traces a voyage from Australia's Sydney Heads, round Cape Horn, to England. The captain really "cracks it on" and does make it home by Christmas.

Alan Fitzsimmons (UK) first adapted this poem for singing as recorded by Pinch o' Salt on *Seaboot Duff & Handspike Gruel*, 2000.

British Horse-drawn Artillery

Homeward

Behind a trench in Flanders the sun was dropping low,
With tramp, and creak and jingle I heard the gun-teams go;
And something seemed to 'mind me, a-dreaming as I lay,
Of my own old Hampshire village at the quiet end of day.

Brown thatch and gardens blooming with lily and with rose,
And the cool shining river so pleasant where he flows,
White fields of oats and barley, and elderflower like foam,
And the sky gold with sunset, and the horses going home!

Home, lad, home, all among the corn and clover!
Home, lad, home when the time for work is over!
Oh there's rest for horse and man when the longest day is done
And they go home together at setting of the sun!

Old Captain, Prince and Blossom, I see them all so plain,
With tasseled ear-caps nodding along the leafy lane,
There's a bird somewhere calling, and the swallow flying low,
And the lads sitting sideways, and singing as they go.

Well gone is many a lad now, and many a horse gone too,
Off all those lads and horses in those old fields I knew;
There's Dick that died at Cuinchy and Prince beside the guns
On the red road of glory, a mile or two from Mons!

Dead lads and shadowy horses—I see them just the same,
I see them and I know them, and name them each by name,
Going down to shining waters when all the West's a-glow,
And the lads sitting sideways and singing as they go.

Home, lad, home . . . with the sunlight on their faces!
Home, lad, home . . . to those quiet happy places!
There's rest for horse and man when the hardest fight is done,
And they go home together at setting of the sun!

❖   ❖   ❖   ❖   ❖

From *Songs and Chanties 1914-1916*, edited by Cicely Fox Smith, published by Elkin Mathews, London, UK, 1919, pp. 216-218; also published in *Fighting Men* by Elkin Mathews in 1916. First published in *The Windsor Magazine*, Volume 45, December-May, 1916-1917, p. 118.

During the WWI, horses were conscripted as well as men! This poem is written from the view-point of a soldier lying in a trench one evening in Flanders. He hears the sound of harnessed horses pulling gun carriages and is reminded of his peace-time life in Hampshire (Southern England) when he would hear the same evening sounds but of horses carrying the labourers back from the fields. He mourns "both horse and man" but also the passing from peace to war. Note the slight changes in the refrain verse.

Sarah Morgan (UK) first adapted this poem for singing (retitled "Home Lads Home"); Morgan found a version of the poem called "Going Home Together" in the magazine *This England* in 1984, as contributed by a soldier who considered the poem anonymous. Morgan recorded this song on *Bread & Roses,* 1987. One of the first groups to re-record Morgan's song was Cockersdale on *Doin' the Manch*, 1988. It has since been recorded by at least a dozen other groups and is probably the poet's most frequently recorded poem.

The header graphic is a photograph of a British horse-drawn artillery unit passing a burning village bombed by enemy aircraft during WWI, from *War of the Nations*, New York Times Co., New York, US, 1919, photographer unknown.

Hoodoo

"Don't you sign in that 'ooker,
Reid's *Gulistan*;
She's a fust-class looker,
But she kills 'er man."

"There's nothin' much faster
Than 'er sails the seas;
I've known none go past 'er
In a wholesail breeze."

"I done a round trip in 'er
Nine years back or ten,
But I ain't goin' to ship in 'er
Never again."

"Sometimes it's a sheet takin'
Charge o' the watch,
Or a footrope breakin',
Or an open hatch."

"You may watch night an' mornin',
But, watch 'ow you can,
She don't give no warnin';
She kills 'er man."

"The grub as they gave you
Was the best I ever scoffed;

But good grub don't save you
If you fall from aloft."

"They treat chaps fine in 'er,
Take it all round,
But I wouldn't sign in 'er
For a thousand pound."

"Not in that there 'ooker,
Reid's *Gulistan*;
She's a lovely looker,
But she kills 'er man . . ."

❖   ❖   ❖   ❖   ❖

From *Sailor's Delight*, edited by Cicely Fox Smith, published by Methuen & Co., London, UK, 1931, pp. 31-33; first published in *Punch* magazine, Volume 181, July 1, 1931, p. 718.

Traditional sailors were a superstitious lot and a "hoodoo," an unlucky ship, was one to be avoided at all costs.

First adapted for singing by Alan Fitzsimmons as recorded on *Seaboot Duff & Handspike Gruel* by Pinch o' Salt, 1995.

Horn Weather

When Admiral Drake came round the 'Orn,
A good long while afore we was born,
The ships 'e 'ad, they was bluff an' chubby,
Their sterns was 'igh an' their spars was stubby,
An', take 'em all round, from fore to mizen,
They was rum sort o' craft, them ships o' his'n . . .
An' it rained an' it blowed,
An' it hailed an' it snowed,
One at a time an' all together—
For the ships they go an' the ships they come,
An' whether they're ornery or whether they're rum
Don't make much odds to the Cape 'Orn weather!

They 'adn't no jibs not yet no staysails,
Royals nor stunsails nor none o' they sails;
They'd a sort of a Jimmy Green set forrad,
An' as for the topsails, their cut was 'orrid;
There warn't no reef-points nor no such gear,
But they clewed up their courses uncommonly queer . . .
An' it rained an' it froze,
There was fogs, there was floes,
One at a time an' all together—
For ships bein' women, why, as you suppose,
They change their rig same as women their clo'es;
But there ain't no change in the Cape 'Orn weather!

They 'ad lamp-posts stickin' up port an' starboard,
But port in them days warn't port but larboard;

They 'ad charts as 'ud make our Old Man shudder,
An' a sort of a pole as worked the rudder;
There warn't no wheel nor yet no chronometer,
An' they shot the sun with a wooden barometer . . .
But it 'owled an' it roared,
An' the seas come aboard,
One at a time an' all together—
For whether they're ol' ships or whether they're new,
Or Drake or just fellers that's like me an' you,
It's the same for 'em all is the Cape 'Orn weather!

❖   ❖   ❖   ❖   ❖

From *Sailor's Delight,* edited by Cicely Fox Smith, published by Methuen & Co., London, US, 1931, pp. 12-14; first published in *Punch* magazine, Volume 180, April 1, 1931, p. 360. Later published in *True Tales of the Sea,* 1932, pp. 13-14.

Composed as a tribute to the harsh conditions that ships faced trying to sail round Cape Horn at the tip of South America. Sir Francis Drake is said to have sighted Cape Horn in 1577.

Lady Melville Passing Through Icebergs

Ice: the Bosun's Story

"Ice," said the bosun, sniffing like a dog across the rail to wind'ard in
    the Cape Horn fog,—
"Ice," said the bosun, "wot sunk the *Skerryvore* time I sailed on board
    'er back in 'seventy-four."

"The Ol' Man was a looney—worst I ever knew; 'e cracked on to
    blazes when it was thick as stew;
'E bunged through it blindfold—fourteen knots we ran till we fouled a
    berg bigger 'n the blinkin' Calf o' Man."

"We run our bows on it in the middle o' the night, an' a fallin' spar
    killed 'im—an' dam well sarve 'im right!
We took to the longboat, and it was jump or drown; she'd 'ardly
    touched the water when the ol' ship went down."

"We made land at daybreak—ice an' sand an' stones, an' seabirds
    wailin' an' a wind that chilled your bones;

An' for two blessed months there we lived like fightin'-cocks on the
    winkles an' seaweed we gathered off the rocks."

"Till a spouter chanced to sight us, cruisin' round that way, or else
we'd be stiff 'uns layin' there to-day;
An' ice," said the bosun, sniffing once again, "is a thing I've had no
    use for, no, never since then."

❖ ❖ ❖ ❖ ❖

From *Sailor's Delight*, edited by Cicely Fox Smith, published by Methuen & Co., London, UK, 1931, pp. 28-30; first published in *Punch* magazine, Volume 180, June 17, 1931, p. 653.

Running into an iceberg while rounding Cape Horn was a nightmare for any deep-water sailor who survived such an encounter.

First adapted for singing by Bob Zentz (US), as recorded on *Closehauled on the Wind of a Dream*, 2007.

The header graphic is a painting by Thomas Goldsworth Dutton showing the clipper ship *Lady Melville* passing through icebergs on her homeward voyage from Melbourne on May 21, 1863.

The *Implacable*

She sailed agin Lord Nelson–
Away-ay-oh!
All taut from truck to keelson–
John Franswaw!
The bloke whose name she carried
Our ships had oft been harried.
He was a dandy fighter
Likewise was non politer;
A regular true blue 'un,
The Admiral Duguay-Trouin!
She sailed agin Lord Nelson
Oh, she was there with bells on!
But she didn't have no luck there;
A prisoner she was took there.
Her name and flag she chang-ed,
But still the seas she rang-ed,
Until the fighting nations
Sought peaceful occupations.
She kept on gettin' older;
Her ribs began to moulder
She's due for overhaulin'
To fit her for her callin'
Of learnin' their duty
To England, Home and Beauty,
So may we soon be'old her
Afore she gets much older.
As taut from truck to keelson–
Away-ay-oh!
She sailed agin Lord Nelson–
John Franswaw!

❖ ❖ ❖ ❖ ❖

From *Punch*, Volume 170, Jan 20, 1926, p. 58

In Drydock

The staunchest vessel built of men
Has got to drydock now and then;
And men who use the sea, like her,
Need overhauling and repair.
Good luck to one and all—may they
More fit for sea be, day by day,
Returning to their tasks once more
Stronger and abler than before;
Last—may they never need again
To seek in weakness and in pain
The surgeon's skill, the sisters' care,
But—if they're wanted, these are there!

❖   ❖   ❖   ❖   ❖

From *All Clear Aft: Episodes at Sea*, published by Seamen's Hospital Society, UK, 1936, Dedication, p. v.

This poem is prefaced by the following dedication: "To the men of the Merchant Navy, who—through sickness or through injury arising out of their hazardous calling—have sought and found health and relief in the Hospitals of the Seamen's Hospital Society, this book is dedicated."

Clipper Ship *St. David*

In Prize

A ship was built in Glasgow, and oh, she looked a daisy—
Just the way that some ships do!

An' the only thing against her was she allus steered so crazy,
An' it's true, my Johnnie Bowline, true!

They sent 'er out in ballast to Oregon for lumber,
An' before she dropped 'er pilot she all but lost 'er number.

They sold 'er into Norway because she steered so funny,
An' she nearly went to glory before they drawed the money.

They sold 'er out o' Norway—they sold 'er into Chile,
And Chile got a bargain because she sailed so silly.

They chartered 'er to Germans with a bunch o' greasers forrard:
Old shellbacks wouldn't touch 'er because she steered so 'orrid.

She set a course for Bremen with contraband inside 'er,
An' she might 'ave got there sometime if a cruiser 'adn't spied 'er.

She nearly drowned the boarders because she cut such capers,
But they found she was German through inspectin' of her papers.

So they put a crew aboard 'er, which was both right an' lawful,
An' the prize crew 'ad a picnic because she steered so awful.

But they brought 'er into Kirkwall, an' then they said "Lord lumme,
If I ever see an 'ooker as steered so kind o' rummy!"

But she fetched 'er price at auction, for oh, she looks a daisy
Just the way that some ships do!

An' the chap as tops the biddin' won't know she steers so crazy,
But it's true, my Johnnie Bowline, true!

❖ ❖ ❖ ❖ ❖

From *Sea Songs and Ballads 1917-22*, edited by Cicely Fox Smith, published by Houghton Mifflin Co., New York, US, 1924, pp. 135-136. Published earlier in *Small Craft*, 1917. First published in *Punch* magazine, Volume 152, June 20, 1917, p. 404.

This WWI poem is modeled after the traditional sea shanty "Do Me Johnny Bowker, Do" and should be a real rouser to sing. The chorus lines should be incorporated in every verse.

The header graphic is a photograph titled *Raising anchor on the clipper ship "St. David,"* circa 1900, from the Detroit Publishing Co., photographer unknown.

In Sailortown

They don't sell no flash gear in Sailortown—
In Sailortown—
Where the slop shops
And the pop shops
And the sheeny dealers be
That sell caps and walking-sticks
To sailors in from sea,
Handkerchiefs with horseshoes
And shore-going suits,
Cheap yellow oilskins
And shoddy sea-boots,
Glass beads and brass rings
As cheap as bought kisses . . .
That's the stuff they sell
In a street like this is.

They don't serve no swell eats in Sailortown—
In Sailortown—

Where the Chink shops
And the slink shops
And the sausage counters are,
But there's laughter and dancing in Muldoon's Bar,
Noodles, and stewed eels,
Greasy and slippy,
And the smell of hot chestnuts
When the nights get nippy,
Coffee and cocoa
It's worth your while suppin',
Hot and sweet and thick
That a spoon 'ud stand up in . . .

They ain't got grand shop-fronts in Sailortown—
In Sailortown—
The Jew shops,
The tattoo shops,
And the junk stores and the rest . . .
But the shipchandler's window it does its blooming best
With its coils of new cable
And copper and brass,
Winking and shining
That cheerful as you pass,

And the yellow, red and blue
Of its bunting fresh and new,
And megaphones like mates' mouths
Open wide to bawl—
"Heave now and bust her,
Ye sojers, heave and pawl!" . . .
And something sets you thinking
Of things half forgotten,
Of old lost ships
Whose bones have long been rotten,
Foreign ports and far seas
And chaps you used to know,
And scraps of old shanties
That you sang long ago . . .

❖   ❖   ❖   ❖   ❖

From *Full Sail: More Sea Songs and Ballads*, edited by Cicely Fox Smith, Houghton Mifflin Co., New York, US, 1926, pp. 72-74.

Here the poet maybe thinking generally or of the dockyard areas she knew and loved so well from Victoria, British Columbia, comparing them to those back in her homeland of England.

She uses the sailor's slang of the time in characterizing what she remembers and such characterizations often grate on our more culturally sensitized ears. She shared that practice with other notable poets of her time such as Kipling and Masefield.

In the Trades

Ho, let her rip—with her royal clew a-quiver,
And the long miles reeling out behind—
For the Trade's got a hold of her and every rope's a-shiver
With the strong and steady urging of the wind.

All the gleaming white of her, all the sun and shade
Leaning, swaying to the seas,
All up the height of her the South-east Trade
Humming like a swarm of bees.

Underneath the heel of her the white wake flying,
Tumbled and trampled into snow—
Down below the keel of her the lost ships lying
In the weed and the coral, far below . . .

❖ ❖ ❖ ❖ ❖

From *Sea Songs and Ballads 1917-22*, edited by Cicely Fox Smith, published by Houghton Mifflin Co., New York, US, 1924, p. 34.

The "South-east Trade" was the prevailing wind off the eastern coast of South America, on the last leg of the voyage from the Pacific of a ship homeward bound to England.

Jim

Jim's done
Pretty near everything under the sun;
Fact, the job is to find the one
Jim's not done.

He's been a tipster, he's been a tramp,
He's been a cook in a lumber camp,
He's been a clerk, he's been a waiter,
He's walked on in a 'Frisco theayter,
He's punched cows, he's herded sheep,
He's had poultry and pigs to keep,
Busted broncos too, has Jim.
But the blamed things took and busted him!
He's dug for silver, he's dug for gold,
In places hot and places cold
From Yukon River to Broken Hill,
He's tried for rubies in Brazil,
And had a shot at some treasure hid
On Cocos Island by Captain Kidd.
You might say, mining's quite a whim with Jim.

Jim says
He don't intend to end his days
Breaking of his blinking back
At pullyhaul like a blooming black

To make a darned shipowner fat:
He knows a trick worth two o' that,
Easy money's the game for him—
Says Jim.
So off he hikes to make his pile:
But one fine morning after a while
Back 'll come, with a long heart-breaking
Yarn of the fortune he's just missed making,
Broke to the wide, without a dollar,
In a ragged shirt and a paper collar,
And a busted bowler without a brim—
Jim!

❖   ❖   ❖   ❖   ❖

From *Full Sail: More Sea Songs and Ballads*, edited by Cicely Fox Smith, published by Houghton Mifflin Co., Boston, US, 1926, pp. 22-24.

Job o' Work

A Job o' Work

"I ain't no glutton for work," said Bill, "though I done my whack in my day,
An' I'd never say 'No' to a boss's job if such was to come my way;
But many's the time I've proved this true since first I followed the sea—
A job o' work's a wonderful thing, an' you can take it from me."

"When your nine months' pay is a song that's sung an' your gear's a yarn that's spun,
An' your girl's took up with a steamboatman as soon's your cash was done,
An' you're back to the sea as plenty o' chaps 'ave been since the world began—
Both ends an' the bight of a bloomin' fool of a dead-broke sailorman;"

"An' you've shipped aboard of an outward-bound, but you can't remember when,
An' you're sick an' sorry an' ready to swear as you won't touch liquor again,
An' you've got a head like a lump o' lead an' a throat as dry as a bone,
An' you don't much care if she sinks or swims so long's they leave you alone;"

"An' a hard-case mate comes waltzin' around as ugly as he can be,
And yanks you out by the slack o' your pants, an' cusses frequent an' free—
Just bear in mind as you've come to a place where back-chat isn't allowed,
An' ketch a holt o' the tackle-fall an' tally on with the crowd!"

"An' afore the tugboat's dropping astern you'll be singin' out like the rest,
An' afore the pilot's over the side you'll pull your weight with the best,
An' afore the old dead 'orse is out an' 'oisted over the rail,
You'll be scoffin' pantiles an' 'arness-beef as if they was cakes an' ale."

"For whether it's trampin' the capstan round or whether it's shiftin' sail,
Or whether it's hangin' on by your teeth in the thick of a Cape 'Orn gale,
Or sweatin' up a t'gal'n yard, or tackin' ship with the watch,
Or sittin' makin' rovin's, maybe, in the sun on the after-hatch,
Or scrapin' cables or tarrin' down all day in the blue Trade weather,
A job o' work's a wonderful thing for pullin' a man together!"

❖ ❖ ❖ ❖ ❖

From *Rovings: Sea Songs and Ballads*, edited by Cicely Fox Smith, published by Elkin Mathews, London, UK, 1921, pp. 46-49. First published in *Punch* magazine, Volume 160, May 25, 1921, p. 409.

"Afore the old dead 'orse is out an' 'oisted over the rail" refers to the celebration held after a month at sea on many voyages on the old sailing ships. It was common practice for the sailor's first month's pay to be paid to the crimp (shipping agent) who had got him his current berth. This meant the sailor did not begin earning pay until he had worked a month at sea. The "dead horse" was typically an effigy of wood and canvas, sometimes stuffed with straw.

This is also the origin of the saying, "flogging a dead horse," since there was no use threatening to withhold a sailor's pay in the first month; it was already spoken for and the captain or mate's threats had no impact.

The header graphic titled *Job o' Work* is drawn by Phil W. Smith and illustrates this poem, from *Rovings*, frontispiece.

Joe

Joe makes models, beauties too,
Not much that way that Joe can't do.

Any ship you like to name,
Say the word, it's all the same.
Joe'll do her, true as life,
All with just his sailor's knife,
Whittle out her masts and spars,
Sheave-blocks, deadeyes, capstan bars,
To the last belaying pin,
Cut out little sails of tin,
Carve a little figurehead,
Paint her house-flag blue and red,

The Model Maker

Tinker with her half a year,
Then, the first pub he gets near,
Sell her for a pint o' beer.

❖   ❖   ❖   ❖   ❖

From *Full Sail: More Sea Songs and Ballads*, edited by Cicely Fox Smith, published by Houghton Mifflin Co., Boston, US, 1926, p. 21.

Some sailors made incredibly detailed ship models, now worth thousands of dollars, but they were lucky to get five dollars for them at the end of a voyage.

The header graphic is an illustration titled *The Model Maker* as drawn by Gordon Grant in his book *Sail Ho!*, facing p. 84.

John Company's Ships

John Company's Ships

John Company's ships, they sailed the seas—
The *Merchant's Hope* and the *Trade's Increase*,
Globe and *Dragon* and *Hector* too,
Thames and *Canning* and *Waterloo*—
With gums and ingots and spice and silk,
Blood-red rubies and pearls like milk . . .
Idols of ivory, cups of jade,
Caskets of ebony gold-inlaid,
Lacquer and crystal, gifts for kings,
Brass and filigree, beads and rings,
Rugs like the sunset, madder and gold,
John Company's ships brought home of old.

John Company's ships, they were steady and slow,
Their tops'ls came in when it started to blow,
For their hulls were roomy and round and wide,
Bluff in the bows and big in the side,
And they loaded them deep and they crammed them full
With the cargoes they bought from the Great Mogul . . .
But they held their own when it came to a scrap
With a Barbary rover or any such chap,
And many a pirate or privateer
That had smacked his lips as the prize drew near
Limped home with his wounds at the last to tell
John Company's ships could fight as well.

John Company's ships, they went their way,
They cleared and they sailed for Dead Men's Bay,
With captains gallant in blue and gold,
And bawling bosuns and seamen bold,
Bows all splendid with gilt and glitter,
Pennants streaming and pipes a-twitter,
Carven stern-ports and guns arow,
Flashing brasses and decks like snow—
They went their way: and the gulls they call
On London's river, by old Blackwall,
And the winds they blow and the tides they run
The same to-day as they've always done:
But they are gone like a tale that's told—
John Company's ships of the days of old.

❖   ❖   ❖   ❖   ❖

From *Rovings: Sea Songs and Ballads*, edited by Cicely Fox Smith, published by Elkin Mathews, London, UK, 1921, pp. 12-15. First published in *Punch* magazine, Volume 160, March 2, 1921, p. 170.

The poet sub-titles this poem "East India Docks" to indicate at which point in her rovings (or "dock walloping" as she used to say) she recalled the memories of these fine ships and cargoes.

The term "John Company" was often used to describe the East India Company. The East India Company was not actually a single corporate body, consisting as it did of a variety of individuals and other interests but it was sufficiently closely linked to be treated as such. Its ship's captains and officers were not very well paid but were allowed sufficient space on board to trade for themselves as well as "the company" and so could earn a goodly amount. The general crew had no such freedom.

The header graphic is titled *John Company's Ships* as drawn by Phil W. Smith and was used to illustrate this poem in *Rovings*, p. 13.

The Jolly Bargeman

I've put the old mare's tail in plaits—now ain't she lookin' gay,
With ribbons in 'er mane likewise, you'd think it First o' May;
For why? We're under Government, though it ain't quite plain to me
If we're in the Civil Service or the Admiralties!

An' it's "Gee hup, Mabel," an' we'll do the best we're able,
For the country's took us over an' we're 'elpin' 'er to win,
An' when the war is over, oh, we'll all lie down in clover,
With a drink all together at the Navigation Inn!

I brought the news to Missis, an' to 'er these words did say:
"Just chuck yon old broom-'andle an' a two-three nails this way:
We're bound to 'ave a flag-staff for our old red, white an' blue,
For now we're under Government we'll 'ave our ensign too."

The Navy is the Navy, an' it sails upon the sea,
The Army is the Army, an' on land it 'as to be;
There's the land an' there's the water, an' the Cut comes in between,
An' I don't know what they'll call me if it ain't an 'Orse Marine.

The Missis sits upon the barge, the same's she used to sit,
But they'll 'ave 'er in the papers now for Doin' 'er Bit:
An' I walk upon the tow-path 'ere as proud as anything,
If I 'aven't got no uniform, I'm serving of the King.

An' it's "Gee hup, Mabel," oh, we'll do the best we're able,
For the country's been an' called us, an' we've got to 'elp to win;
An' when this war is over, then we'll all lie down in clover,
With a drink all together at the Navigation Inn!

❖   ❖   ❖   ❖   ❖

From *Small Craft: Sailor Ballads and Chantys*, edited by Cicely Fox Smith, published by George H. Doran Co., New York, US, 1919, pp. 72-73. First published in *Punch* magazine, Volume 152, May 16, 1917, p. 320.

Captures a moment in WWI when the British Government has issued an order mobilizing the canal bargemen into the war effort, replete with great detail.

First adapted for singing by Michael Kennedy, 2009. Also by Charles Ipcar, as recorded on *Songs from an Old Sea Chest*, 2012.

The Navigation Inn, Bugsworth Canal Basin,
near Stockport, UK, as photographed by Charles Ipcar in 2010.

Knitting for the Troops

The Knitters

In streets that are humming
With the city's stair . . .
Or where leaves fall rustling
Through the quiet air . . .
There are women knitting
Everywhere . . .

Knitting and waiting
Through hours like years—
Not with loud grieving
Nor sighing nor tears—
In their hands the needles
Flash like spears.

Every thread a sorrow,
Every strand a prayer—
("Oh, where sleeps my dear one?
Or how does he fare?")
There are women knitting
Everywhere . . .

❖ ❖ ❖ ❖ ❖

From *Sailor Town: Sea Songs and Ballads*, edited by Cicely Fox Smith, published by George H. Doran Co., New York, US, 1919, p. 131. Earlier published in *The Naval Crown* by Elkin Mathews in 1915.

Composed during the first year of WWI in tribute to those who waited for their loved ones at home and quietly knitted.

The header graphic is a cartoon showing a lady knitting for the troops at the front as drawn by C. A. Shepperson, from *Punch* magazine, November 4, 1914, p. 377.

Sealing Schooners, Victoria Harbour, c. 1895

The Last of the Sealing Fleet

All in the slime of the stagnant Arm, the mouldering slips beside,
Where dark as sin slinks out and in the fouled and furtive tide,
There, slowly parting strake from strake, the poor old sealers lie,
And whisper to the jostling booms of a brave day gone by.

Unkept, uncaulked, their gaping decks are blistered, bleached and bare;
Along their keels the chuckling ebb mocks at their blind despair;
And ever like a ghostly tune through rotted ropes and green
Runs the shrill keening of the wind and the long sob between.

"Oh, south away to 'Frisco Bay the open seas do roll,
And north to the white bear's hunting grounds about the lonely Pole;
And at rutting time on the Pribyloffs the lusting seal do roar,
But we'll go out by Bretchie Ledge on the sealer's road no more."

"Oh, north away from 'Frisco Bay the tumbling seas do roll,
Both wide and free to Behring's Sea which laps around the Pole:
A thousand miles from 'Frisco Bay the feeding seals may fare
With never a foe but the killer whale and the brown man and the bear."

"Yestereen along the waterside I saw my captain go,
A weary and a broken man, with lagging step and slow;
Salt was his blood as the salt tide and restless as the sea,
And like the sea the wild blue eye that there did gaze on me."

"'Old ship,' he said, 'when we were young together, you and I,
A man's life I lived with men between the sea and sky;
And would to God you had sunk deep and I also had died
Who now upon the land decay as you rot in the tide.'"

"'By God, it were a kindlier thing to make an end with those
Which split upon the uncharted reef or splintered in the floes
Than to cheat death a hundred times and last to find the day
When a man's strength must fail him and a good ship decay.'"

"'And north away from 'Frisco Bay the plunging seal do go,
But never a schooner plies that way of all we used to know;
And there the spouting bowhead blows and the grey gulls do soar,
But south or north, though you go forth, you'll find us there no more.'"

❖　❖　❖　❖　❖

From *Songs and Chanties: 1914-1916*, edited by Cicely Fox Smith, published by Elkin Mathews, London, UK, 1919, pp. 80-82.

Victoria's (British Columbia) schooner sealing fleet was laid up when an International Treaty was signed in 1911 banning pelagic sealing. As the poet said later in her book *Sailor-Town Days*, 1923, p. 178:

"I daresay there are now none of those old decaying sealing schooners left which used to lie, green and rotting, in that part of Victoria's Inner Harbour known as 'The Arm'—a dismal, stagnant sort of spot, dedicated to garbage, and dead cats, and snags, and sawmill refuse, and mouldering slipways, and sinister leaning boathouses that seemed waiting for murders to be committed in them."

First adapted for singing by Michael Kennedy, 2009.

The header graphic is a photograph titled *Sealing Schooners, Victoria Harbour, c. 1895*, photographer unknown, from *Light on the Water*, p. 138.

The Last Ship

W'en the floods come down an' the *Ark* was new—
To me way-ay-i-oh!
An' Cap'n Noah signed on 'is crew—
It's a long time ago.
An' Solomon's ships come wallerin' back
With 'olds full of ivory, w'ite an' black,
An' gold as well an' a monkey or two
An' fancy birds for the Palestine Zoo,
I don't jus' know nor I don't much care
Wot sort of a crowd them 'Ebrews were,
The kind o' long splices aboard them craft,
Or if they was square-rig or fore-an'-aft,
But there's jus' one thing as it's easy to say,
You bet there was someone as talked—this—way:—

"Oh, you orter 'ave seen my las' ship,
You orter 'ave seen 'er go,
Best old 'ooker ever I've struck
An' the best as ever I'll know!
You orter 'ave scoffed the grub we got,
The bread was fresh an' the coffee was 'ot,
The scouse *was* scouse an' the duff *was* duff,
Nor the junk warn't out o' the or'nary tough,

An' the skipper an' mates was the real old kind,
An' the fo'c'sle crowd was the best you could find—
That was the way in my las' ship—my ol' ship—the bes' ship—
Which it ain't in this 'ere ol' scow,
An' I'd give the 'arf o' my nine months' pay
To be back in that ol' ship now!"

An' ever since then, both near an' far—
To me way-ay-i-oh!
From Sydney 'Eads to Astoria Bar—
It's a long time ago!
There ain't a ship as 'as gone to sea
With coal or copra or cotton or tea,
Things as smell nasty an' things as smell nice,
Cloves an' guano, blubber an' spice;
Queer old 'ookers of rum old rigs,
Yankee clippers an' coaly brigs,
Liner an' freighter, tramp an' tanker,
From the Skagerrack to the Straits o' Banka,
There ain't been a ship 'as sailed the seas,
But someone's been here as said words—like—these;—

"Oh, you orter 'ave seen my las' ship,
For she was the gal to go,
Round ol' Cape Stiff in a 'undred days
From Cali-for-ni-o!
She was a picter, she was a ship,
Fifteen knots was 'er usual clip,
None o' your bloomin' nines an' such,
The same as we do in this ol' Dutch;
You orter 'ave seen 'er carryin' sail,
W'en the eighteen knot was over the rail,
Oh, she was a beauty, my las' ship—my ol' ship—my bes' ship—
A flier from stern to bow,
An' I'd give the 'arf o' my pay, God's truth,
To be back in that ol' ship now!"

❖ ❖ ❖ ❖ ❖

From *Sailor's Delight*, edited by Cicely Fox Smith, published by Methuen & Co., London, UK, 1931, pp. 60-63; first published in the magazine *Holly Leaves*.

A sailor's memory of his last ship, once he had left her, was frequently positive, regardless of how miserable the experience was.

Lavender Pond

Lavender Pond

Never a swallow wets his wing
In Lavender Pond from Spring to Spring;
Never a lily, pure and chill,
Holds her cup for the dews to fill;
Never a willow, gnarled and hoar,
Bends his bough to a reedy shore;
Never a fragrant flower-spike blows there,
Never a lordly King-staff grows there,
Slender and straight where sedges shiver
And glistening Mayflies glance and quiver,
In Lavender Pond by London River.

But the Baltic barques the come and go
With their old pump-windmills turning slow,
And the tall Cape Horners rest and ride
Like stately swans on the murky tide,
And the ocean tramps all red and rusted,
Worn and weathered and salt-encrusted,
Gather and cluster near and far,
Derrick and funnel, mast and spar,
From many a port of old renown,
And lonely wharf where the booms float down,
To Lavender Pond by London Town.

And keen and strong is the wind that comes
To the dingy streets of the Deptford slums,
Strong and keen with the scent it steals
Off piled-up acres of Kalmar deals—
Spruce and cedar and baulks of pine;
Red with resin and drenched with brine,
Sawn from the boles that once did stand
Rank on rank in a virgin land,
Where the cougar prowls through the silent glades
In the forest depths of the far Cascades . . .
And the gulls go flying, the gulls go crying,
And the wind's sob and the water's sighing
Croon to the ships an old sea ditty
In Lavender Pond by London city.

❖ ❖ ❖ ❖ ❖

From *Rovings: Sea Songs and Ballads*, edited by Cicely Fox Smith, published by Elkin Mathews, London, UK, 1921, pp. 22-25. First published in *Punch* magazine, Volume 160, April 6, 1921, p. 278.

Lavenerder Pond was part of the Surrey Commercial Docks, a large group of interconnected docks in Rotherhithe on the south bank (the Surrey side) of the Thames in South East London. The primary purpose of Lavender Pond was to float timber to prevent it from drying out and cracking. The docks operated in one form or another from 1696 to 1969. In July 1620 the Pilgrim Fathers' ship the Mayflower sailed from Rotherhithe for Southampton.

First set to music by Michael Head (1900-1976) in 1949, as published in *Six Sea Songs*.

The header graphic is titled *Lavender Pond* as drawn by Phil W. Smith and was used to illustrate this poem in *Rovings*, p. 23.

The Steamer *Lillian* Sinking

Leave Her Johnnie

A hundred miles from the Longships Light—
Leave her, Johnnie, leave her!—
And blowing up for a dirty night—
And it's time for us to leave her!

Down by the head and settling fast—
Her name and number's up at last,
And it's time for us to leave her!

It isn't the sea she's sailed so long:
It isn't the wind that's used her wrong,
But it's time for us to leave her!

We've pumped her out with a right good will,
A day and a night, and she's sinking still,
And it's time for us to leave her!

She's smashed above and she's stove below,
And there's nothing to do but roll and go,
For it's time for us to leave her!

A hundred miles from the Longships Light—
Leave her, Johnnie, leave her!—
And blowing up for a dirty night—
It's time for us to leave her!

❖ ❖ ❖ ❖ ❖

From *Rhymes of the Red Ensign*, edited by Cicely Fox Smith, published by Hodder and Stoughton, London, UK, 1919, p. 31; first published in *The London Chronicle*.

Here we have the old shellbacks singing an update of their old pumping shanty, as they pull away from their sinking steamer, which likely has struck a mine while nearing the English coast in WWI.

First adapted for singing by Bob Zentz (US), as recorded on *Closehauled on the Wind of a Dream*, 2007.

The header graphic is a photograph of the steamer *Lillian* that was sunk off the New Jersey shore after a collision with a German freighter in February of 1939, photographer unknown, from *Shipwrecks Along the Atlantic Coast*, p. 115

Hauling on the Lee Fore Brace in a Gale

Lee Fore Brace

There was ten men haulin' on the lee fore brace
In the rain an' the drivin' hail,
And the mile-long greybeards chargin' by,
An' a thunderin' Cape Horn gale.

That dark it was, you scarce could see
Your hand before your face;
That cold it was, our fingers froze
Stiff as they gripped the brace.

An' "Christ!" says Dan, "for a night in port
An' a Dago fiddler's tune,
An' just one whiff o' the drinks again
In a Callao saloon!"

There was ten men haulin' on the lee fore brace
When the big sea broke aboard;
Like a stream in spate, a foaming flood
Right fore an' aft it poured.

The ship, she staggered an' lay still—
So deep, so dead lay she,
You'd think she could not rise again
From such a weight of sea.

There was ten men haulin' on the lee fore brace…
Seven when she rose at last;
The rest was gone to the pitch-dark night,
An' the sea an' the ice-cold blast.

An' one of them was Dago Pete,
An' one was Lars, the Dane,
An' the third was the lad whose like on earth
I shall not find again.

An' I'll heave an' haul an' stand my wheel,
An' reef an' furl wi' the rest…
For winds an' seas go on the same,
When they've took an' drowned the best.

An' it ain't no use to curse the Lord,
Nor it ain't no sense to moan,
For a man must live his life the same,
An' keep his grief his own

An' I'll drink my drink an' I'll sing my song,
An' nobody'll know but me
A lump o' my heart went down with Dan
That night in the wild Horn sea!

❖ ❖ ❖ ❖ ❖

From *Sea Songs and Ballads 1917-22*, edited by Cicely Fox Smith, published by Houghton Mifflin Co., NY, 1924, pp. 92-93.

One wonders if the sailor "Dan," whose name appears in so many Smith's poems, was a close personal friend. Certainly "Dan" was at least one of her favorite nautical informants.

Smith's description of the incident displays her familiarity with shipboard life as hauling on the lee fore brace can be one of the most dangerous jobs there in a storm, with the bow plunging and rolling in mountainous seas.

First adapted for singing by Alan Fitzsimmons, 2000, as recorded on *Sea Boot Duff & Hand Spike Gruel* by Pinch o' Salt. A subsequent recording was made by Baggyrinkle on *One More Pull*, 2000. An alternative setting by Charles Ipcar to Gerry Hallom's tune for Henry Lawson's poem "The Outside Track" is recorded on *More Uncommon Sailor Songs*, 2005.

The header graphic is a painting by Anton Otto Fischer from his book *Focs'le Days*, p. 31, and shows such a gang hauling on the lee fore brace in a gale.

A Merchantman Outward Bound

Let Her Go! (a Tramp Shanty)

'Er keel was laid in Seventy-four,
Let 'er go—let 'er go!
They built 'er cheap, an' they scamped 'er sore,
'Er rivets was putty, 'er plates was poor,
An' then come in the Plimsoll Line,
Or I wouldn't be singin' this song of mine.
Let 'er go!

She was cranky an' foul, she was stubborn an' slow
Let 'er go—let 'er go!
An' she shipped it green when it come to blow;
'Er crews was starved, an' the pay was low,
An' 'er bloomin' owners was ready to faint
At a scrape o' pitch or a penn'orth o' paint.
Let 'er go!

But she's been 'ere, an' she's been there
Let 'er go—let 'er go!
An' she's been almost everywhere;
An' whenever you went you'd see *'er,*

With 'er rust-red hawse an' 'er battered old funnel,
All muck an' dirt from 'er keel to 'er gun'le.
Let 'er go!

She's earned 'er keep in a number o' climes,
Let 'er go—let 'er go!
She's changed 'er name a number of times
Which won't fit right into these 'ere rhymes;
But the name o' 'er now is the *Sound o' Mull*—
Built on the Tyne an' sails out of 'Ull.
Let 'er go!

'Er keel was laid in Seventy-four
Let 'er go—let 'er go!
An' a breaker's price was 'er price before;
The ships was scarce an' the freights did soar;
But she's fetched 'er fourteen pound a ton
On the Baltic Exchange since the war begun.
Let 'er go!

So she's doin' 'er bit, which we all must do
Let 'er go—let 'er go!
An' whether she's old or whether she's new;
Don't make much odds to a war-time crew;
An' 'ooever's sunk, or 'ooever's drowned,
The *Sound o' Mull* keeps pluggin' around.
Let 'er go!

An' when she goes, by night or by day,
Let 'er go—let 'er go!
Either up or down, as she likely may,
I only 'ope as somebody 'll say,
"'Er keel was laid in Seventy-four,
She done 'er best, an' she couldn't do more;
She warn't no swell, nor she warn't no beauty,
But she come by 'er end in the way of 'er duty".
Let 'er go!

❖ ❖ ❖ ❖ ❖

From *Sea Songs and Ballads 1917-1922*, edited by Cicely Fox Smith, published by Houghton Mifflin Co., New York, US, 1924, pp. 132-134. Earlier published in *Sailor Town*, 1919. First published in *Punch* magazine, Volume 152, March 28, 1917, p. 205.

First adapted for singing in 1995 by Alan Fitzsimmons, as recorded on *Seaboot Duff & Handspike Gruel* by Pinch o' Salt in 2000.

The header graphic is an illustration titled *Gravesend: A Merchantman Outward Bound* drawn by Muirhead Bone, from *Merchantmen-at-Arms*, p. 3

Lieutenant Shellback, R. N. R.

He has learnt the ways of the ships at sea
In most of the sorts of ships there be,—
In most of the kinds of deepsea craft,
Steam and squaresail and fore-and-aft,
A Liverpool crack and a London barque
As bluff as a barge and as old as the *Ark*,
A tramp, a tanker, a Yankee schooner,
He 's served in all of 'em later or sooner . . .

And there isn't a build, and there isn't a rig,
Be it fast or slow or little or big,
From Chapman Light to the Bay of Bengal,
But Lieutenant Shellback knows 'em all.

He has learnt the ways of the seas that roll,
Broad or narrow or deep or shoal,
Gulf and channel and bight and strait,
From the Barrier Reef to the Golden Gate;
He has learnt the ways of the winds that blow
Off palm and coral and Polar snow,
The typhoon sweeping the China seas,
And the Trades, and the stormy westerlies . . .

And there isn't a port the wide world round
From London River to Puget Sound,
From Sand Heads Light to Vallipo Bay,
But Lieutenant Shellback's passed that way.

And some he learnt from an old-style skipper
That once cracked on in a China clipper,
And a blue-nose mate like a live cyclone,
All fist and boot and muscle and bone;
To reef and furl and hand and steer
He knew full well by his sixteenth year,
To lift a chantey, and patch and darn,
And carve a model and spin a yarn . . .

And there wasn't so much those old salts knew,
"Sails" and bosun, skipper and crew,
From trimming yards to a fancy knot,
But Lieutenant Shellback learnt the lot.

But he learnt the most, when all's been told,
Where his fathers learnt the same of old,
In the sun and storm, in the wind and rain,
Twice round the Horn and home again …

He has learnt it here, he has learnt it there,
He has learnt it foul, he has learnt it fair,
Both inside out and upside down,
'Tween the Tail o' the Bank and 'Frisco town . . .

And there isn't a death that sailors dare
From Carrick Roads to the Straits of Le Mair,
Nor a kind of a risk that seamen run,
But Lieutenant Shellback's faced each one.

That's what has made him, tried and true,
Hardened and tested and proved him too,—
Born and bred to the sailor's trade,
Hemp to the core and cable-laid,
Like the nine-strand stuff that a seaman knows
Will hold and hold till the last strand goes . . .
And whether he's fighting, or sweeping, or towing,
And whether it's hailing, or raining, or blowing,
Whether he's out on the U-boat trail,
Or saving a crew in a North Sea gale,
There isn't a job you can find him to do
But Lieutenant Shellback will carry it through.

❖   ❖   ❖   ❖   ❖

From *Rhymes of the Red Ensign*, edited by Cicely Fox Smith, published by Hodder and Stoughton, London, UK, 1919, pages 7-9. First published in *Punch* magazine, Volume 154, May 22, 1918, p. 334.

A Lift by the Way

When the road it is rough and the sun it is strong,
And the miles of the country seem long and more long,
And your spirits they flag in the heat of the day,
Oh, a wonderful thing is a lift by the way!

It may be a milk-float aglitter with cans,
It may be a tinker with kettles and pans,
A farmer's smart gig or a rattling old shay—
It won't come amiss for a lift by the way.

It may be a baker's cart fragrant with bread,
Or a farm-cart whence ordours less pleasing are shed,
A lorry with sacks or a wagon of hay—
They all come alike for a lift on the way.

The motors flash by with their noise and their smell
Assailing your eyes and your nostrils as well,
So modern their haste is, no leisure have they
For old-fashioned things like a lift by the way.

But long may there linger in England's green lanes
The jingling old shandries and creaking old wains,
And long may they lend in the heat of the day
To weary foot-farers a lift by the way!

❖ ❖ ❖ ❖ ❖

From *Punch* magazine, Volume 163, September 27, 1922, p. 294.

This is one of the few poems from 1914 to 1931 that was not re-published in any of the poet's books.

The H. M. S *Amphion,* an Old Style Light Cruiser

Light Cruisers (Old)

"Vide Naval Expert's Classification"

When you've marshalled your navies and gloried your fill
In the latest they show of invention and skill,
The lion in strength and the lizard in speed,
The watchful in waiting, the present in need—
The great Super-Dreadnaughts gigantic and grim,
The thirty-knot cruisers both subtle and slim,
The weight and the range of each wonderful gun—

Remember the cruisers, the out-of-date cruisers,
The creaky old cruisers whose day is not done,
Built some time before Nineteen Hundred and One!

You may look to the South, you may seek in the North,
You may search from the Falklands as far as the Forth,
From Pole unto Pole all the oceans between,
Patrolling, protecting, unwearied, unseen,
By night or by noonday the Navy is there,
And out-of-date cruisers are doing their share;
Yes, anywhere, everywhere under the sun—

You will find an old cruiser, an off-the-map cruiser,
An out-of-date cruiser whose work's never done,
Built some time before Nineteen Hundred and One!

It may be you'll meet with her lending a hand
In clearing the way for the soldiers to land,
Escorting an army, and feeding it too,
Or sinking a raider (and saving her crew);
Blockading by sea or attacking by dry land,
Bombarding a coast or annexing an island,
Where there's death to be daring or risk to be run—

You may look for the cruiser, the out-of-date cruiser,
The creaky old cruiser that harries the Hun,
Built some time before Nineteen Hundred and One!

In wild night of winter when warmly you sleep,
She is plugging her way through the dark and the deep,
With Death in the billows which endless do roll,
And the wind blowing cold with the kiss of the Pole;
While seas slopping over both frequent and green,
Call forth on occasion expressions of spleen,
Of all the old kettles awarding the bun—

To the out-of-date cruiser, the obsolete cruiser,
The creaky old cruiser whose work's never done.
Built some time before Nineteen Hundred and One!

And when the day breaks for whose smoke-trail afar
We scan the grey waters by sunlight and star,
The day of great glory—the splendour, the gloom,
The lightning, the thunder, the judgment, the doom,
The breaking of navies, the shaking of kings,
When the Angel of Battle makes night with his wings,
Oh, somewhere, be sure, in the thick o' the fun—

You will find an old cruiser, a gallant old cruiser,
A creaky old cruiser whose day is not done,
Built some time before Nineteen Hundred and One!

❖   ❖   ❖   ❖   ❖

From *Small Craft: Sailor Ballads and Chantys*, edited by Cicely Fox Smith, published by George H. Doran Co., New York, US, 1919, pp. 82-84. First published in *Punch* magazine, Volume 149, August 18, p. 149, 1915.

A tribute to the older light cruisers which supported England's war efforts all over the globe.

The header graphic is a photograph of such a British light cruiser that was developed in the late 19th century, with a few still in active service during WWI, photographer unknown.

Limehouse Reach

Limehouse Reach

I fell in love with a Limehouse lass,
But she has proved untrue;
She looked as fresh as a figurehead
That's just been painted new;
But she's took and married a lighterman,
So it's time for me to go:
But I would have loved you so, my dear,
I would have loved you so!

Oh, a shake o' the foresheet pays for all
That a sailor leaves behind,
For an alehouse shot, and a friend forgot,
And a sweetheart false or kind;
And the bloomin' mudhook's off the ground,
For it's time for us to go:
But I would have loved you so, my dear,
I would have loved you so!

Now a long good-bye to Limehouse Reach,
And a last good-bye to you;
A feller's a fool to die for love,

Which I don't mean to do;
There are girls as smart in every port
From here to Callao—
But I would have loved you so, my dear,
I would have loved you so!

❖ ❖ ❖ ❖ ❖

From *Full Sail: More Sea Songs and Ballads*, edited by Cicely Fox Smith, published by Houghton Mifflin Co., New York, US, pp. 59-60, 1926.

Here the deep-water sailor acknowledges losing his love to a more shallow-water man, a lighterman. The sailor is then committed to shipping out but is still wistful.

First set to music by Humprey Proctor-Gregg in 1932, and then by Michael Head (1900-1976) in 1949, as published in *Six Sea Songs*. Years later Dave Webber and Anni Fentiman (UK) adapted this poem for singing as recorded on *Constant Lovers*, 2000. An alternative musical setting was made and recorded by Charles Ipcar (US) on *More Uncommon Sailor Songs*, 2005.

The header graphic is titled *Limehouse Reach* as drawn by Phil W. Smith and which illustrates this poem in *Full Sail*, facing p. 60.

The Little Things

I used to be a peaceful chap as didn't ask for trouble,
An' as for rows an' fightin', why, I'd mostly rather not,
But now I'd charge an army single-'anded at the double,
An' it's all along o' little things I've learned to feel so 'ot.

It's 'orrid seein' burnin' farms, which I 'ave often seen 'ere,
An' fields all stinks an' shell-'oles, an' dead among the flowers,
But the thing I've 'ated seein' all the bloomin' time I've been 'ere
Is the little gardens rooted up—the same as might be ours.

It's bad to see the chattos—which means castles—gone to ruin,
An' the big cathedrals knocked to bits as used to look so fine,
But what puts me in a paddy more than all them sorts o' doin's
Is the little 'ouses all in 'eaps—the same as might be mine.

An' when the what's-it line is bust an' we go rompin' through it,
An' knock the lid off Potsdam an' the Kaiser off 'is throne,
Why, what'll get our monkey up an' give us 'eart to do it?
Just thinkin' o' them little things as might have been our own,
(An' most of all the little kids as might 'ave been our own!)

❖ ❖ ❖ ❖ ❖

From *Small Craft: Sailor Ballads and Chantys*, edited by Cicely Fox Smith, published by George H. Doran Co., New York, US, 1919, pp. 55-56. First published in *Punch* magazine, Volume 153, July 25, 1917, p. 56.

The poet does a good job of putting into words what motivates the common soldier. Sometimes it's such "little things" that gets one through, not the great cause.

The Black Ball Liner *Great Western*

The Liverpool Ship

"Liverpool on her stern and bound to go"—Old Sea Saying.

Oh, it's of a spanking clipper,
And she flew the old Black Ball,
With her staysails and her stunsails
And her Jamie Green and all;
"Sixty days to Hell or Melbourne,"
So you'd hear the old man say,
Under royals in the forties,
Romping down to Hobson's Bay.
"Crack her on with all she'll carry,
What she can't she'll have to drag!"
Was the way they used to work things
Underneath the Black Ball flag . . .

When it was "Blow, bullies, blow,
On a Circle southward ho!
You can let her rip—she's a Liverpool ship,
And you bet she's bound to go!"

Oh, it's of a tall Cape Horner
Loaded down with 'Frisco grain,
On the last lap of her voyage
Round the world and home again—
Plunging eastward through the greybeards
Where they thunder from the Pole,

Dipping deep her lee mainyard-arm
In the drink with every roll:
With her three year's rust upon her,
And her sailors sick for home
And the Fastnet's blink of welcome
Out across the lonely foam . . .

For it was "Blow, bullies, blow,
From Californ-i-o!
She's a Liverpool ship, so let her rip,
And she's surely bound to go!"

Oh, it's of a dandy liner
With her passengers and mails,
Plugging through it trim and steady
In the equinoctial gales,
With her paint and brass a-shining
And her flag of far renown,
And her ports at night-time flashing
Like a blessed floating town,
And her mighty engines pulsing,
And her white wake flowing wide,
And the parted rollers streaming
From her high and cliff-like side . . .

And it's "Blow, bullies, blow,
East and West and to and fro—
She's a Liverpool ship, so let her rip,
For you bet she's bound to go!"

❖ ❖ ❖ ❖ ❖

From *Full Sail: More Sea Songs and Ballads*, edited by Cicely Fox Smith, published by Houghton Mifflin Co., New York, US, 1926, pp. 111-113.

This is a vivid description of a tall ship running under all full sail, regardless of the danger of splitting a sail or losing a yard:

> "Crack her on with all she'll carry,
> What she can't she'll have to drag!"

There were several "Black Ball Lines" that were associated with Liverpool. The oldest was between New York and Liverpool begun in the early 19th century. A later Black Ball Line made runs from Liverpool to Australia and the Orient.

There are several traditional songs embedded in this poem including the sea shanty *Californi-O* and The *Wild Colonial Boy*.

The header graphic is a painting by Antonio Jacobsen showing the Black Ball liner *Great Western*, not to be confused with the early steam ship of the same name.

London River

Half a score o' sailormen that want to sail once more,
Cruising round the waterside with the Peter at the fore!
Half a score o' sailormen the sea will never drown—
Seven days in open boats a-drifting up and down!—
Out to find another ship and sail from London Town!

Half a score o' sailormen broke and on the rocks,
Linking down Commercial Road, tramping round the Docks,
Half a score o' sailormen, torpedoed twice before,

Once was in the Channel chops, once was off the Nore,
Last was in the open sea five hundred mile from shore!

Half a score o' sailormen that want to sail again—
And her cargo's all aboard her, and it's blowing up for rain!
Half a score o' sailormen that won't come home to tea—
For she's dropping down the river with the Duster flying free—
Down the London River on the road to the open sea!

❖ ❖ ❖ ❖ ❖

From *Rhymes of the Red Ensign*, edited by Cicely Fox Smith, published by Hodder and Stoughton, London, UK, 1919, p. 25. First published in *Punch* magazine, Volume 154, February 6, 1918, p. 92. Also published under the title "Half a Score o' Sailormen" in *War Verse*, edited by Frank Foxcroft, published by T. Y. Crowell, New York, US, 1918, p. 48.

In tribute to the merchant sailors in WWI who after being mined or torpedoed went back to sea on the next available ship.

Ladies Boarding a Thames Wherry

London Seagulls

The pigeons of the Abbey, the pigeons of Saint Paul's,
That woo in windy niches of grey and grimy walls,
The pearl-grey dawns of London, his sky that gleams and glooms,
His stately smoky sunsets are in their changing plumes.

The saucy London sparrows, their Cockney chatter tells
Their parents nested surely in earshot of Bow Bells . . .
But Oh! the London seagulls a-cruising up and down,
They're most like old-time seamen come back to London town.

Old salty swearing seadogs and tarry buccaneers,
With bacca quids and pigtails and ear-rings in their ears,
That spent their money handsome and took their ease ashore
In rowdy Ratcliff aleshops with sand upon the floor . . .

And bawled their old sea-ballads, and told their thumping lies,
In fearsome deep sea lingo to open landsmen's eyes,
And drained their brimming pewters, and spat into the tide,
In old shipboarded taverns by Wapping waterside . . .

And saw there at their moorings the Geordie colliers rock,
The latest pirate dangling at Execution Dock,
The anchored ships unloading their silks and laces fine,
And spices from the Indies, and rum, and Spanish wine . . .

And watched the busy wherries all plying with their fares,
From Globe, Jamaica, Wapping and Cherry Garden Stairs,
And the lighters and the barges a-passing to and fro
As they did on London River two hundred years ago.

❖ ❖ ❖ ❖ ❖

From *Sea Songs and Ballads 1917-1922*, edited by Cicely Fox Smith, published by Houghton Mifflin Co., New York, US, 1924, pp. 6-7. Earlier published in *Sea Songs and Ballads*, 1922. First published in *Punch* magazine, Volume 163, July 12, 1922, p. 44.

The header graphic is an illustration titled *London Seagulls* as drawn by Phil W. Smith, 1923. with a view of ladies boarding a Thames wherry, from *Sea Songs and Ballads: 1917-1922*, facing p. 6.

Collier Outward Bound

The Lone Hand

She took her tide and she passed the Bar
With the first o' the morning light;
She dipped her flag to the coast patrol
At the coming on o' the night;
She has left the lights of the friendly shore
And the smell o' the English land,
And she's somewhere South o' the Fastnet now . . .
God help her . . . South o' the Fastnet now . . .
Playing her own lone hand.

She is ugly and squat as a ship may be,
She was new when the *Ark* was new,
But she runs her risk and she takes her chance
As well as the best may do,
And it's little she heeds the lurking death
And little she gets of fame,
Out yonder South o' the Fastnet now . . .
God help her . . . South o' the Fastnet now . . .
Playing her own lone game.

She has played it once, she has played it twice,
She has played it times a score,
Her luck and her pluck are the two trump cards
That have won her the game before,
And life is the stake where the tin fish run,
And Death is the dealer's name
Out yonder South o' the Fastnet now . . .
God help her . . . South o' the Fastnet now . . .
Playing her own lone game!

❖ ❖ ❖ ❖ ❖

From *Rhymes of the Red Ensign*, edited by Cicely Fox Smith, published by Hodder and Stoughton, London, UK, 1919, pp. 13-14. First published in *Punch* magazine, Volume 154, January 2, 1918.

A WWI poem about a merchantman heading out on her own from England, without the added security of being part of a convoy.

The header graphic is an illustration by Charles Wilson showing an old collier outward bound from his book *Ships*, published by Barre Publishers, Barre, Massachusetts, US, 1971, p. 95.

Pamir in 1946 after Slipping Her Tow off Cape Flattery

The Long Road Home

There's a wind up and a sighing along the waterside,
And we're homeward bound at last on to-night's full tide:
Round the world and back again is very far to roam . . .
And San Juan Strait to England, it's a long road home!

We'll tow out to Flattery before the sun is high;
We'll shake the harbour dust away and give the land good-bye:
And singing in her topsails, O, the deep-sea wind'll come,
And lift us through it lively on the long road home.

The Old Man he goes smiling, for he's gathered in a crew:
We've various Turks and infidels, we've most things but a Jew:
He's got the pick of all the stiffs from Panama to Nome,
And we'll make them into sailors on the long road home.

The leaves that just are open now, they'll have to fade and fall,
They'll be reaping time and threshing time and ploughing time and all:
But we'll not see the harvest fields nor smell the fresh cut loam:
We'll be rolling gun'le under on the long road home.

We've waited for a cargo and we've waited for a crew,
And last we've waited for a tide, and now the waiting's through:
O don't you hear the deep-sea wind and smell the deep-sea foam,
Out beyond the harbour on the long road home?

And it's "home, dearie, home" when the anchor rattles down,
In the reek of good old Mersey fog a-rolling rich and brown:
Round the world and back again is very far to roam . . .
And all the way to England it's a long way home!

❖ ❖ ❖ ❖ ❖

From *Songs and Chanties: 1914-1916*, edited by Cicely Fox Smith, published by Elkin Mathews, London, UK, 1919, pp. 31-32. First published in *The Daily Colonist*, Victoria, Vancouver Island, British Columbia, Canada, December 17, 1912, p. 8.

This poem likely commemorates the poet leaving Victoria, British Columbia, after a stay of almost three years. However, she actually returned on the steamer *Teutonic*, not a sailing ship, on November 24, 1913, to her native England. This poem seems to form a set with "Pacific Coast" and "The Ship's Good-bye."

There are similarities in the fourth verse with the third verse in "Rosario."

"Home, dearie, home" is a reference to a traditional folk song of the same name, also known as "Ambletown."

Peter Massey (UK) first adapted this poem for singing, as recorded on *The Long Road Home*, 2005; later recorded by Charlie Ipcar on *Old Sailor-Poets*, 2007, using Massey's setting.

The header graphic is a photograph titled *Gale off Cape Flattery* by Hugh Frith taken of the four-masted barque *Pamir* in 1946 after slipping her tow, from *Light on the Water*, p. 18.

The Lost Rivers

Far down from the thunder
And rush of the street,
Flow Westbourne and Tyebourne
And Effra and Fleet,
'Neath blue skies and grey skies
Once freely that ran—
Lost rivers of London,
Forgotten of man.
Do they ever remember
Where night is like day,
Red leaves of October
And green leaves of May;
The sunshine and starshine,
The rain and the dew,
The gold of the kingcup,
The kingfisher's blue?

Do they think of the flurry
And rush of the weirs,
The mill-wheel that scattered
Drops from it like tears,
The sun-dappled shallows,
The dusk of the pool
Whose fishes bade urchins
Play truant from school?

Do they dream about cresses
And catkins in spring,
And beds of green rushes
Where reed-warblers sing,
Of willow-herb blowing
And swallows that weave,
Where the dragonfly glistens,
Their mazes at eve?

Deep under the bustle
And rush of the street
Flow Westbourne and Tyebourne
And Effra and Fleet,
In darkness and silence
Forlornly they run,
Lost rivers of London,
Forgetting the sun.

❖ ❖ ❖ ❖ ❖

From *Sailor's Delight*, edited by Cicely Fox Smith, published by Methuen & Co., London, UK, 1931, pp. 118-120.

With the rise of the cities comes the demise of the little rivers, buried beneath the new city streets as drains. This poem pays tribute to them.

East Indiaman Merchant Ship being Dismasted by a Hurricane

The Lost Ship

Come you up from southward, oh, come you there—away?
And saw you not my ship there that's late now many a day?
And touched you ne'er a port where she came a-sailing thither?
Where's the barque *Aurora* and all her people with her?

Ah, good-bye and fare you well now, ship and sailor:
Ah, good-bye, for never harbour more shall hail her:
Ask the unsleeping drift if still it lifts her westing,
Or the Tuscarora Deeps if there she's resting.

Home, come home: it is no use at all to linger:
Never will be tide so late that it will bring her:
Salt like tears the scud is, cold the sea tides streaming:
Never will you greet your man but in your dreaming,

Ask the roaring Norther: ask the berg that broke her:
Ask the growlers of the Horn where last they spoke her.
Ask the seas that, pouring through the splintered hatches,
Last relieved for good and all her labouring watches.

Ask the crazy gale that, hither-thither shifting,
Snatched the last tired chantey stave their lips were lifting.
Ask the Austral lights that in their dances reeling
Mocked across the empty skies her flares' appealing.

Ask the lonely dawn that, scarlet, silent, splendid,
Looked across the world and found the fight was ended.
Ask the wind and wave that bruised and broke and shook her . . .
And the sea's great silence at the last that took her.

❖   ❖   ❖   ❖   ❖

From *Small Craft: Sailor Ballads and Chantys*, edited by Cicely Fox Smith, published by George H. Doran Co., New York, US, 1919, pp. 109-110. Also in *Songs and Chanties: 1914-1916*, edited by Cicely Fox Smith, published by Elkin Mathews, London, UK, 1919, pp. 33-34. Earlier appeared in *Songs in Sail*, 1914.

The header graphic is a painting by Thomas Goldsworth Dutton and shows a bird's eye view of an East Indiaman merchant ship being dismasted by a hurricane in about 1846, while on a run from London to Calcutta.

Love's Marketing

Along the lanes from market
    Folk went by:
White along the river-side
    Mist did lie:
Hob rode the grey mare,
    Rob rode the roan:
Then met I a stranger lad
    Trudging alone.

"How, pray you, tell me,
    Did the market go?
Sold you your wares there
    High or low?"
All in the dusty lanes
    Tears did fall:
"Love the Fool, Love the Fool,
    Men me call!"

"Gold for the bay colt,
    Gold for the brown,
For the goodwife's dairying
    A fine new gown:
Silver for the sweet herbs
    That in the garden grow:
What for love, what for love?
    Nought but woe."

"Some sell for money,
    Some for kind:
What though your wares be
    All left behind!
Ah, me, the bare board!
    Ah, the chill morrow! . . .
Love the Fool, Love the Fool,
    Sells for sorrow!"

❖ ❖ ❖ ❖ ❖

From *Small Craft: Sailor Ballads and Chantys*, edited by Cicely Fox Smith, published by George H. Doran Co., New York, US, 1919, pp. 156-157.

The Lowland Sea

Oh, sailed you by the Goodwins,
Oh, came you by the Sound?
And saw you there my true love.
That was homeward bound?

"Oh, never will he anchor
Again in English ground;

A-sailing by the Lowlands
Your sailorman is drowned."

"They gave his ship her death-blow
As she was sailing by,
And every soul aboard her,
Oh, they left them all to die."

"They were not common pirates
Nor rovers of Sallee . . .
But gentlemen of high estate
Come out of Germanie!"

It was no worthy gentleman.
Though he were crowned King;
It was no honest seaman
That wrought so vile a thing.

But the foulest of all pirates
That ever sailed the sea . . .
And they should swing as pirates swing
Upon the gallows tree,
A-sailing by the Lowlands
That took my lad from me!

From *Sailor Town: Sea Songs and Ballads*, edited by Cicely Fox Smith, published by George H. Doran Co., New York, US, 1919, pp. 118-119. Earlier published in *The Naval Crown* by Elkin Mathews in 1915. First published in *Punch* magazine, Volume 148, March 10, 1915, p. 108.

"The Goodwins" are a reference to a large bank of shoal sands that lies 6 miles east of the coast of Kent near the entrance to the English Channel from the North Sea.

Lumber

If I'd got to choose alone
One of all the freights I've known—
All my cargoes live and dead,
Bacon pigs and pigs of lead;
Cattle, copra, rice and rails,
Pilgrims, coolies, nitrates, nails,
Lima beans and China tea—
What do you think my pick would be?

If I'd got to name the best—
Take just one and leave the rest
Out of all the ports I've known—
Coral beaches white as bone,
All the hot lands and the cold,
Nights of stars and moons like gold,
Tropic smells and Spanish wine,

Loading Lumber

Whispering palm and singing pine,
All the isles of all the sea—
Where do you think I'd want to be?

Loading lumber long ago
In a ship I used to know,
With the bow-ports open wide
In her stained and rusted side,
And the saws a-screaming shrill
At the Steveston lumber-mill;
Where the Fraser floods and flows
Green and cold with melting snows,
And the tow-boats' wailing din,
As the booms come crawling in,
Fills the echoing creeks with sound,
And there's sawdust all around,
Deep and soft like drifted snow;
Nowhere much a man can go,
Nothing much to see or do,
Mouldiest burg you ever knew!

But I'd give the years between—
All I've done and all I've seen,
All the fooling and the fun,
All the chances lost and won,
All the good times and the bad,
All the memories sweet and sad,
Far and near, by shore and sea,
I would give them all to be
Loading lumber years ago
With the lads I used to know—
Loading lumber all day long
Stacks of scented deals among—
Loading lumber at the mill
Till the screaming saws were still,
And the rose-red sunset died
From the mountains and the tide,
And the night brought out its stars,
And the wind's song in the spars
Of that ship I used to know—
Loading lumber, long ago.

From *Rovings: Sea Songs and Ballads*, edited by Cicely Fox Smith, published by Elkin Mathews, London, UK, 1921, p.p. 33-34. First published in *Punch* magazine, Volume 160, January 12, 1921, p. 30.

The poet was based in Victoria, British Columbia, for much of the time that she was on the West Coast of Canada, from 1912 to 1913. She describes in vivid detail walking the docks, watching the sunsets, admiring the sailing ships, listening to the yarns of the ship-keepers and other sailors, and nosing around the waterfront. The Village of Steveston is located in Richmond, BC, adjacent to Vancouver where she likely also visited. Curiously, there is no record of a Steveston Lumber Mill, although lumber was shipped by rail to Steveston and then shipped out by sailing ship to ports beyond.

Charles Ipcar (US) first adapted this poem for singing, as recorded on *More Uncommon Sailor Songs*, 2005.

The header graphic is a photograph of lumber being loaded into a ship with her "bow-ports open wide" at the Chemainus docks on Vancouver Island, BC, circa 1900, photographer unknown, from *Light on the Water*, p. 150.

Auctioning Off a "Dead Man's Chest."

Mainsail Haul

"I don't want none of 'is stuff," said Bill,
"Nor I don't want none of 'is gear,
I don't want things as I've known 'im use
Nor things as I've seen 'im wear:
It ain't such things as them," he said,
"An' that the truth, my son,
'Ull make me think o' Mike my pal,
Now Mike 'e's dead an' gone."

"There's Bluenose Pete 'e wants 'is palm
An' the knife 'e wouldn't sell,
An' Jake 'e wants 'is good seaboots,
'Cos 'is own they leak like hell,
An' one wants this an' one wants that,
The way chaps do at sea—
Well, let them take their pick, says I,
They can 'ave the lot for me."

"An' they can 'ave 'is teakwood chest
Wi' the paintin' as 'e did
O' the *Southern Cross* off Sydney 'Eads,
Full sail, inside the lid,
An' the marlin spike 'e always used,

An' the bottled ship 'e made,
Rollin' up to the Western Isles,
Close-hauled on the Nor' East Trade.

"For Mike an' me was pals," said he,
"An' I couldn't bring my mind
To wrangle like a greedy gull
For the gear 'e left behind:
We've sailed together rough an' smooth,
We've stuck it, sink or swim,
An' it ain't Mike's bits o' things, God knows,
'Ull make me think of 'im."

"It's sun an' stars an' fog an' frost
An' blue weather an' grey,
An' big seas curlin' green as glass
Afore they break in spray,
An' sudden dark on tropic seas
Dropped down like a blind that's drawn,
An' stormy sunsets off the capes
An' strange landfalls at dawn."

"It's drunkards shoutin' scraps o' songs
In waterfront saloons,
An' two-stringed fiddles Chink girls play
Thrum-thrumin' queer old tunes,
An' the papery noise the palm-trees make
When offshore winds are wakin',
An' the fellers singin' out on the brace,
An' the royal clew a-shakin'."

"It's things you eat an' things you drink
In all the ports you know,
An' the raspy twang o' Spanish wine,
An' mule trains tinklin' slow,
An' the steamy reek of Eastern towns
An' stuffy smoky smells
In shrines where fat pot-bellied gods sit
Smilin' to theirsels."

"It's things you see an' things you 'ear
An' things you feel an' do,
They bring the dead alive again,
They make the old years new,
An' it ain't Mike's bits o' things I'll want,
An' that's God's truth, my son,
To make me think o' Mike my pal,
Now Mike 'e's dead an' gone."

From *Sea Songs and Ballads 1917-1922*, edited by Cicely Fox Smith, published by Houghton Mifflin Co., New York, US, 1924, pp. 8-10. First published in *Punch* magazine, Volume 161, November 23, 1921, p. 417.

Some sailors formed close bonds with their shipmates, and shipped together voyage after voyage. This poem gauges the depth of such a friendship after one of the pair has died.

Gordon Morris (UK) of Marrowbones first adapted this poem for singing as recorded on *Full Sail: Inside the Lid*, 2000.

The header graphic is an illustration drawn by Gordon Grant from his book *Greasy Luck*, facing p. 122, showing the auctioning off of a "dead man's chest."

With Her White Skirts like a Flower

Mariquita

Old man Time, 'e's wrote his log up in the wrinkles on my brow,
And there ain't that much about me as a gal 'ud take to now;
For I've changed beyond all knowing from the chap I used to be,
When I can remember Mariquita . . . as was mighty fond o' me!

I can shut my eyes and see it just as plain as yesterday,
See the harbour and the mountains and the shipping in the bay,
And the town as looked like heaven to us shellbacks fresh from sea,
And I can remember Mariquita . . . as thought a deal o' me!

I can hear the chiming mule-bells, and a stave o' Spanish song,
And the blessed old guitarros as kep' tinkling all night long;
Hear the dusty palm trees stirring, taste the *vino* flat and sour,
And I can remember Mariquita, and her white skirts like a flower.

But it's years now since I seen her, if she died I never knew,
Or got old and fat and ugly same as Dagoes mostly do;
And it's maybe better that way, for there's nothing left but change,

And the ships I knew all going, and the ports I knew grown strange,
And the chaps I knew all altered, like the chap I used to be,
But I can remember Mariquita, and she's always young for me.

From *Full Sail: More Sea Songs and Ballads*, edited by Cicely Fox Smith, published by Houghton Mifflin Co., NY, 1926, pp. 108-110.

This poem reflects the memory of an old sailor for the days of his youth when he roamed the dockside of some western South American country and met a lovely young local woman that he fell in love with. But there is more than nostalgia in this poem. There's the acknowledgement that the sailor has changed through the years, as have the ships and ports he knew so well.

The reference to "Dagoes" is a little hard to take for contemporary readers but it's an accurate representation of how sailors referred to residents of South America or Spain.

First adapted for singing by Gordon Morris, as recorded on *Full Sail: Inside the Lid*, 2002. An alternative adaptation was done by Charles Ipcar, as recorded on *Uncommon Sailor Songs*, 2005.

The header graphic is a photograph of a young Peruvian girl dancing in colonial costume at a festival in Plaza de Armas, Trujillo, 1980's, as photographed by Robert Frerck, Odyssey Productions/Chicago, used with permission.

Market Day

As I rode on the limber
Through the old French market-square,
There were bricks and fallen timber
And shell-holes everywhere.

The place was blank as Sunday,
But something seemed to say:
"Today is surely Monday,
And Monday's market day."

"Oh, all along the by-road
That goes by Three Maids Down,
And the long, straight Roman high-road,
They're driving in to town."

"They drive the colt in the gig now
I'd just begun to ride,
And the setter pup's grown big now,
And maybe runs beside."

"The gentry use 'The Garter,'
The farmers use 'The Plough,'
And the rest 'The Jolly Carter,'
Or else the old 'Brown Cow.'"

"There are crowds o' horses baiting—
There's one in every stall—
And the carriers' carts stand waiting
Outside the Market Hall."

"There's a fellow selling halters,
And another hawking cloam,
For nothing ever alters
On market day at home."

Oh, I'll shake a leg and go there,
When leave time comes round once more,
And all the folks I know there
Will stand in every door.

And strolling down the street there,
On the sunny side o' the way,
There's a lass I'll maybe meet there
At home on market day.

From *Sailor Town: Sea Songs and Ballads*, edited by Cicely Fox Smith, published by George H. Doran Co., New York, US, 1919, pp. 47-48. An earlier edition of *Sailor Town* was published by Elkin Mathews in 1914.

This poem was written in the first year of WWI and portrays a soldier walking through a war-torn market square in France, while thinking back to the market day in his own home town. Compare with "Half-Past Eleven Square."

The Bucko Mate

Mate

A great big brute of a bawling bluenose—
Came through the hawse-pipe and don't care who knows!

Lives on holystones—wallows in paint—
That fond o' prayer-books you'd take him for a saint.

Voice like a foghorn, fist like a block,
First time he hits you, you think you've struck a rock.

Face like a seaboot, never seen to smile:
When he hails the topsail yard you hear him half a mile.

The sea's been his school and the wide world his college:
What he don't know of sailorin' darn well ain't knowledge!

❖ ❖ ❖ ❖ ❖

From *Full Sail: More Sea Songs and Ballads*, edited by Cicely Fox Smith, published by Houghton Mifflin Co., Boston, US, 1926, pp. 6-7.

The header graphic is an illustration titled *The Bucko Mate* drawn by Gordon Grant from his book *Sail Ho!*, facing p. 34.

A Nineteenth Century Overall View of Mejillones, Chile

Mejillones

I don't want to go back to Mejillones,
    On the dusty Chile shore;
I don't want to go back to Mejillones,
    Where they load the copper ore;
I don't want to go back to Mejillones,
    Never no more.

It ain't because there's no decent drinks there,
    Of any sort or kind;
It ain't because there's only sand and stinks there,
    And the cold snows behind.

It ain't because it's mostly hot as blazes,
    Though it's all o' that, Lord knows!
It ain't along o' the thirst a feller raises,
    In them dry winds that blows.

It ain't because I got shoved in the jug there
    To finish up a spree,
And sampled every blooming breed of bug there,
    As a man could hope to see.

It's because I don't want to mooch around alone there,
    Where the tin roofs crackle in the sun;
Thinking of the fun I've had and chaps I've known there,
    In an old ship that's gone,

Likes a blooming walking ghost in Mejillones,
    Now the ship's gone and the men . . .
And that's why I ain't going back to Mejillones,
    Never again!

From *Sailor's Delight*, edited by Cicely Fox Smith, published by Methuen & Co., London, UK, 1931, pp. 98-99.

"You can't go back!" is a common theme in many poems and if you do "go back" there is often the disquieting familiarity of some of what you see combined with the absence of what you remember. The poet never returned to Victoria, British Colombia, where she spent two of her younger years but she thought about returning there in "Pacific Coast" as well as other poems.

The header graphic is titled *A nineteenth century overall view of Mejillones, Chile*, artist unknown.

Memories

"Ships . . . they go," said Murphy, "like a spent pay-roll . . .
They're sunk in the deep water or they're wrecked in the shoal;
Burnt or scrapped in the long run, the big ships an' the small,—
An' the ships a man remembers, they're the best ships of all."

"Friends . . . they go," said Murphy, "the false an' the true,
They all go at the finish, the same as the ships do;
They go like a spree that's ended or a last year's song,
But the friends a man remembers, they're his own his life long."

"Times . . . they pass," said Murphy, "the fair and foul weather,
The good times an' the bad times, they all pass together;
Like a steersman's trick that's ended, or a blown-out squall . . .
An' the times a man remembers . . . they're the best times of all!"

❖   ❖   ❖   ❖   ❖

From *Ships and Folks,* edited by Cicely Fox Smith, published by Elkin Mathews, London, UK, 1920, p. 67.

"Murphy" is the poet's sailor philosopher; see also "Port o' Dreams."

Tower Hill Mercantile Marine Memorial

Merchantmen

These were the ships that kept on going
When the seas were thick with the War's black sowing—
Great ocean liners in white paint and gold,
Shabby little colliers, all grime and green mould,
Up-to-date cargo boats ugly as sin,
Old seven-knotters with their plates rusted thin,
Has-been clipper-ships, laid up for ages,
Fitted out and rigged new and sent to earn their wages,

Coal-ships and cotton–ships,
Sound ships and rotten ships
From Thames and Clyde and Merseyside that fetched their ports no more—
Tyne ships and Humber ships,
Grain-ships and lumber-ships—
Ships that went down in the War!

These were the men that knew no shirking
The hungry waters where death lay lurking—
Grizzled old skippers that had grown grey in ships,
Young brassbounders with the down on their lips,
White-faced black squad and tanned A. B.'s
In oil-stained boiler-suits and torn dungarees,
That dropped beside the wheel on the deck all bloodied,
That drowned in the darkness when the stokehold flooded,
That froze on the rafts in the bitter Atlantic,
That drifted in boats till the thirst drove them frantic,
Some with wives and youngsters to cry their eyes red,
Some with neither chick nor child to care that they were dead.

Not reckoned greatly daring men,
But every-day seafaring men,
Who stood their trick and earned their whack and took their fun ashore,
Until on every tide for us
They took their chance and died for us—
Men that went down in the War!

❖ ❖ ❖ ❖ ❖

From *Sailor's Delight*, edited by Cicely Fox Smith, published by Methuen & Co., London, UK, 1931, pp. 138-140.

A tribute to the WWI Mercantile Marine Memorial in Trinity Square in London. First adapted for singing in 1995 by Alan Fitzsimmons, as recorded on *Seaboot Duff & Handspike Gruel* by Pinch o' Salt in 2000.

The header graphic is a photograph of the Mercantile Marine Memorial in Trinity Square in London, photographed by Charles Ipcar, 2010.

Merchantmen (1917)

All honour be to merchantmen,
And ships of all degree,
In warlike dangers manifold
Who sail and keep the sea,—
In peril of unlitten coast
And death-besprinkled foam,
Who daily dare a hundred deaths
To bring their cargoes home.

A liner out of Liverpool—a tanker from the Clyde—
A hard-run tramp from anywhere—a tug from Merseyside—
A cattleboat from Birkenhead—a coaler from the Tyne—
All honour be to merchantmen while any star shall shine!

All honour be to merchantmen,
And ships both great and small,
The swift and strong to run their race
(And smite their foes withal),
The little ships that sink or swim,
And pay the pirates' toll,
Unarmoured save by valiant hearts
And strong in nought but soul.

All honour be to merchantmen
So long as tides shall run,
Who gave the seas their glorious dead
From rise to set of sun;
All honour be to merchantmen
While England's name shall stand,
Who sailed and fought, and dared and died,
And served and saved their land!

A sailing ship from Liverpool—a tanker from the Clyde—
A schooner from the West Countrie—a tug from Merseyside—
A fishing smack from Grimsby town—a coaler from the Tyne—
All honour be to merchantmen while sun and moon do shine!

❖ ❖ ❖ ❖ ❖

From *Rhymes of the Red Ensign*, edited by Cicely Fox Smith, published by Hodder & Stoughton, London, UK, 1919 pp. 19-20. Earlier published in *Small Craft*, 1917, pp. 68-69.

A Message

It was about the midnight hour,
I heard the wind go by:
I heard on the wet mould the shower
Beat, and the bare trees sigh.
I heard your hand upon the pane,
Your footstep at the door,
A moment lingering in the rain,
And then . . . no more!

One moment . . . then the door was wide,
Yet none there was to hark,
Nor any answer when I cried
Your name across the dark.
There was none there . . . although I knew
Your footstep, ah, so plain!—
Only the weary wind that blew,
And the driving rain!

Was there no sign you could have brought,
No word that you might say,
To tell what thing it was you sought,
And you so far away?

They say I heard but the rain fall
And the wind beat . . . yet I,
Should I not know your step, though all
The world went by?

❖ ❖ ❖ ❖ ❖

From *Small Craft: Sailor Ballads and Chantys*, edited by Cicely Fox Smith, published by George H. Doran Co., New York, US, 1919, pp. 115-116. First published in *Songs of Sail*, 1914.

The first poem in a set called "Songs of Home" published shortly after the poet's return to England after 3 years in Canada and as WWI was just beginning. These poems seem to represent an attempt by the poet to reconcile where she grew up with what she had experienced since she left England in 1911. This haunting poem might be linked with "Lee Fore Brace" in which "Dan", whom the poet knew well and loved, was lost at sea.

Mike

Mike's a Jonah, an out-and-outer
As ever signed in a Hebrew spouter;
All the kinds of misfortune trail
After Mike like a comet's tail.

Water failing and watches drowned,
Ships dismasted and ships aground,
Ships on fire at sea, or drifting
On a lee shore with the cargo shifting,
Sunken wreckage and rocks and floes,
All the worries and all the woes
Ever a ship fell foul of yet—
Mike's been into 'em all, you bet!

His life's packed full of troubles and knocks
Like a blooming What-you-may-call-her's box,
Stowed in his old sea chest he's got 'em,
With hope hid somewhere in the bottom.
For come what may and come what will
Old Mike he comes up smiling still.

Same old, game old, split-face grin
You could shove a baked potato in,
Same old wrinkling, twinkling eyes,
With the look in 'em of mild surprise
As if he was thinking, "Why in thunder
Does things turn out this way, I wonder?"

And for all he brings you the darnedest luck
Of any poor blighter ever you struck,
It's rum, a feller can't help but like Mike!

❖ ❖ ❖ ❖ ❖

From *Full Sail: More Sea Songs and Ballads*, edited by Cicely Fox Smith, published by Houghton Mifflin Co., Boston, US, 1926, pp. 19-20.

See also "The Jonah" for a precursor to this poem. First set to music by Mike Kennedy in 2009.

Ship's Cat at Ease on the Quarterdeck

Mike and the Cat

"It's a thing I never done," said Mike, "it's a thing I call queer"
(Scratching the dingy galley Tom under his starboard ear),
"To give your 'eart to a cockatoo or a bloomin' pink-eyed rat,
Which I've knowed chaps do in my time," said he, "but I likes a cat."

"Small dogs gets stole on you, big 'uns is too big;
It's only huntin' trouble to pal with a pig;
Mice and rats is vermin, an' there ain't no denyin'
Them little small birds is the divvle for dyin'."

"I've known chaps keep lizards an' snakes an' the like;
Well, them as wants crawlin' things can 'ave 'em," said Mike;
"A tortoise ain't sociable; rabbits ain't clean;
Monkeys is mischievious and parrots is mean."

"But a cat's a good shipmate as a man 'ud wish to find;
'E minds 'is own bizness an' he knows 'is own mind;
'E knows who 'is friends are as well as me or you,
And 'e sticks by 'is ship like a seaman ought to do."

"And if 'e takes a run ashore, why, 'tain't for me to blame,
For where's the sailorman alive as never done the same?
Where was ye now in Singapore, ye blagyard, tell me that?
It ain't no use to wink at me,
Ye darned old whited sepul-chree!
Ye know well enough ye was out on the spree," said Mike to the cat.

❖ ❖ ❖ ❖ ❖

From *Sailor's Delight*, edited by Cicely Fox Smith, published by Methuen & Co., London, UK, 1931, pp. 95-97.

"Mike" is another of the poet's favorite older sailor informants. Cats did adapt well to shipboard life and generally were appreciated for their help in keeping the vermin population under control.

A "Sepulchree" is a tomb or funerary monument.

The header graphic is a photograph of a ship's cat at sea, aboard the cargo steamer *Irish Poplar* bound for the Suez Canal from Geraldton, Western Australia, April 1959; photographer unknown.

Mike's Fancy

"You can 'ave your lights o' London, you can keep your great White Way:
They're well enough," said Murphy, "when you're out to burn your pay:
They're right enough for some folks, but them folks' tastes ain't mine,
For, Lord, gimme a little burg an' then I'm suited fine."

"A sawmill an' a Chink store an' a two-by-four saloon,
Where the loggers dance in couples to a cracked piano's tune,
A slashin' Clyde fourposter loadin' lumber at the quay,
An' a sailor's welcome waitin' when a ship blows in from sea."

"A big port's bitter lonesome, an' it's bitter cruel too
When you're down and out," said Murphy, "an you've wore your
                                                welcome through,
You can lie down in the dirt an' die an' who in thunder'll care?
That's why I like a little burg—a feller's someone there!"

"Just a few adobe 'ouses on a bloomin' dusty shore
With the frozen peaks be'ind 'em an' the sunset seas afore:
But the tinklin' o' the mule-bells some'ow allus seems to say:
'Ello, Mistaire Inglees sailorman, 'ow long you goin' to stay?'"

"An' when I chuck up sailin', which I some day likely will—
When I've seen the best there is to see from China to Brazil—
When there's nowheres else I want to go from Singapore to Nome—
Why, I'll find me out some little burg where I can feel at 'ome . . ."

"A street of whitewashed 'ouses and an 'arbour somewheres nigh,
Where you smell the fish an' seaweed an' the nets spread out to dry,
With a pub for winter evenin's where shellbacks' yarns are told,
An' a corner by the fireside for a bloke that's getting' old."

❖ ❖ ❖ ❖ ❖

From *Full Sail: More Sea Songs and Ballads*, edited by Cicely Fox Smith, published by Houghton Mifflin Co., New York, US, 1926, pp. 78-80.

This poem forms a set with "Mariquita" and "Port o' Dreams" as Murphy muses over where he'd like to settle when he finally quits seafaring.

Topsail Weather

Missing

I

She was spoken off Saint Vincent, outward bound . . .
Some lumber-laden barque from Puget Sound,
Heaving her sodden deck-load through the foam,
Weary of the sea-ways, climbing the hill for home . . .
Some nine-knot tramp from Melbourne or Bombay,
Wallowing deep-freighted on her homeward way,
Her grimy decks awash, her blistered funnel
Leprous with salt, sea-stained from keel to gunwale,
Rust-streaked, and battered with the Cape Horn gales,
Sighted at grey of dawn her shining sails . . .
White as a woman's breast they gleamed afar,—
Her gilded main-truck flashing like a star,—
And the first shafts of sunrise turned to gold
Her sleek side, heaving upward as she rolled . . .
So passed she by—and those who watched her go
Thought of that road they had good cause to know,
Thought how, when they were sheltered dry and warm,
She would go plunging through some night of storm,
All hands aloft, reefing the steel-hard sails,
Cursing . . . with frozen hands and bleeding nails . . .
Her yards sheeted with ice . . . her leaning deck
A seething flood of men toiled in to the neck . . .
Then thought of winking glasses, warmth and noise—
Good pay to burn—sordid seaport joys—

Saying: "Who'd change with them chaps now?"—and yet
Still felt a strange half-envy, half-regret,
Such as men may who, ease and wealth attained,
And their full measure of good fortune gained,
From the safe harbour of their middle years
Look back on youth, its burning hopes and fears,
Its unattempted capes and unsailed sea,
Landfalls unguessed, and all things yet to be,
Fond dreams, fantastic loves, and dark despair,—
Know it for ever fled—know it was fair . . .
So passed she by—her tall masts swaying, singing,
Sailors (mere specks) on dizzy foot-ropes swinging,
Whence, looking down, they saw beneath them spread
All her slim length from stern to fo'c'sle head,
The cleft wave streaming from her wedge of bow,
Where the carved warrior with his casqued brow
Leaned always out over the sea's unrest,
With arms laid crosswise on his mailed breast,
And eyes that, all unseeing, seemed to gaze
Out to the ultimate end of all men's ways . . .
Passed . . . till hull down on the horizon's rim,
Her lonely beauty lessened and grew dim ...
Passed . . . like a song unfinished, a broken rhyme . . .
And the sea's silence took her for all time.

II

She will not come . . . oh, never, never more
Shall she draw near to any earthly shore;
In storm or calm—in foul weather or fine—
Fast-hurrying wrack or watery pale sunshine—
Frost when the jackstay burns the naked hand—
Odours of forests blowing off the land—
Chill driving mist, or roar of tropic rain—
Dawn, noontide, sunset, dark ... never again!
No more at sunrise, all the winds at rest,
The sea rose-dappled like a pigeon's breast,
Shall her black tug—a dwarf leading a queen—
Bring her the lighthouse-guarded strait between . . .
No more, when folks ashore begin to stir,
And wood-smoke hangs on the sharp morning air,
Her sailormen, tramping the capstan round,
Shall wake the sleeping anchorage with sound—
Lifting some wild sea shanty of old time,
Some ancient strain wedded to rough old rhyme—

"Lowlands Away" or "Rio Grande"—unheard
Each trivial phrase, each vile and worthless word,

Only the strange wild cadences remaining,
Full of the sea's voice and the wind's complaining,
The sad old wistful melody that seems
The stuff of old men's memories, young men's dreams . . .
No more of her along the anchored tiers
Shall all the shipping ripple into cheers
Of welcome or farewell . . . no more again
On any tide her restless cables strain . . .
Nor any landlocked roadstead more behold
Her mirrored pride . . . no harbour see her fold—
After long wanderings come at last to shore—
Her weary wings at sunset any more . . .
Never again to any foul lagoon
Or fetid river in the reek of noon,
Or any lone teredo-fretted quay
Where pine-clothed ranges echo all the day
The crash of falling forests . . . bustling hong,
Or small white Spanish town its palms among . . .
Or where the gleaming Andes hold on high
Their spears in challenge to the sunset sky . . .
To any port of all the ports there be
Shall she come with her beauty from the sea.

III

Aye, all that grace and beauty, strength and speed—
All that she was—are now no more indeed—
Ropes, hard and hairy as a seaman's hand—
Planking, scoured white as bone with stone and sand—
Fife-rails with staunch belaying-pins arow—
And racks of capstan bars—and sails like snow—
Clean smells of tar and paint—and brasses bright
As gold in the sun—and darkly shining teak . . .
That little ordered world, austere and bleak
As some bare chapel of a monkish creed
That asks not pomp nor pride for its soul's need . . .
No more, that strength, that swiftness and that grace,
Than one blown foam-flake on the ocean's face—
No more than one of the millions bubbles
Beneath some proud ship's forefoot, when she troubles
The tumbled whites and blues of tropic seas
A little, and is gone—no more than these,
Less than the least small shell the ocean sweeps

Through the winds and waves and unimagined deeps,
Far from the warmth of blue West Indian seas,
And gaudy parrots screaming through the trees,
Hot tropic smells, and fireflies, and the song

Of Trade winds in the palm-trees all day long,
To the cool greys and blues of temperate skies,
Cold tide-left pools, and the strange sea-birds' cries,
And the pink sea-thrift on the headlands blooming,
And in the hollow caves the Atlantic booming.

IV

Where rests she now? . . . On what Antarctic shore
Where nothing grows but lichens, grey and hoar
As the pale lips of death . . . and nothing moves
On the long beaches, in the deep sea-coves,
But uncouth sea-beasts in their secret, strange
Matings and breedings . . . nothing seems to change

Year by slow year . . . and the fog comes, and the floe,
And the sea thunders, and the great winds blow . . .
And on still wings great birds go sailing by,
Seeking, with slantwise head and watchful eye,
Scraps for the naked nestlings . . . and the time
Comes, and the time goes, and the ocean slime
Coats her with foulness, and the seaweeds green
Clothe her, whom once men tended like a queen . . .

Let be! . . . She is one with all things that have been—
Embers of longing—ashes of desire—
And hope grown cold—passion quenched like fire—
Friendship that death or years or the rough ways
Of chance have sundered . . . all things meet for praise,
Lost yet remembered, that were ours of yore—
Things lovely and beloved, that are no more . . .

❖ ❖ ❖ ❖ ❖

From *Ships and Folks*, edited by Cicely Fox Smith, published by Elkin Mathews, London, UK, 1920, pp. 8-12.

This poem is another fine tribute to the Great Age of Sail.

The header graphic is a painting titled *Topsail Weather* as painted by Anton Otto Fischer, from *Anton Otto Fischer*, p. 165.

Queen Morgana le Fay

Morgan Le Fay

I will put by my violent days, and the ill deeds that I have wrought,
All wayward sins of a wild heart, all empty joys I sought,
I will forswear the fruitless year and the deedless day,
And the long gold tresses and false caresses of Morgan le Fay.

The songs are hollow and empty: the wine is down to the lees:
I am full sick of the witching dance and unclean mysteries:
And the palace of magic and wonder just an ill shadow seems,
Wild feats and vile faces out of evil dreams.

There shall no sleep come nigh me all through the long night,
Where I watch mine arms alone for a space ere I ride forth to fight,
Alone with the cold altar and the cross of my slain Lord,
With the stark helm and the grey mail and the cross-hilted sword.

I have bound the spur to my heel again; I have rent the past like a scroll:
In the bitter waters of sorrow will I wash clean my soul.
I have put by the worthless world and the deedless day,
And the long gold tresses and false caresses of Morgan le Fay.

❖ ❖ ❖ ❖ ❖

From *Small Craft: Sailor Ballads and Chantys*, edited by Cicely Fox Smith, published by George H. Doran Co., New York, UK, 1919, pp. 147-148; published earlier in *New York Tribune*, July 30, 1904.

The second poem in a set titled "Romance."

This unusual poem may represent a time when the poet was disillusioned with a romantic interest. However, she probably never fully escaped from the "spell" cast by Morgan le Fay. She may have had a love interest in"Dan" the shantyman in Victoria, BC, but he disappeared. She never married once she returned to England, nor is there any hint of any romantic involvement in her later life.

The header graphic is an illustration of *Queen Morgana le Fay* as drawn by Howard Pyle from his book *The Story of King Arthur and His Knights*, Charles Scribner's Sons, New York, US, 1903.

Morning Watch

The high stars grow paler—
Day comes to the sea;
The sky's rim unbroken,
The ship running free,—

White sea-birds that follow
And call on her way;
Bright flying fish gleaming
In rainbows of spray,—

Wide seas all around her,
The wide skies above,
And the long road before her
That leads to my love!

❖   ❖   ❖   ❖   ❖

From *Ships and Folks*, edited by Cicely Fox Smith, published by Elkin Mathews, London, UK, 1920, pp. 52-53.

This is from a set of poems entitled "The Way of the Ship" which were set to music by Easthope Martin, and published as *Five Chantey Songs*, Enoch & Sons, 1920.

The New Outer Wharf at Victoria, BC

Mother Carey

As late I went a-walking, a-walking by the sea,
I thought I heard men talking, I heard them call to me:
"Oh, sorrow take the city streets and the weary city stones,
It's time for you to leave them while the strength is in your bones."

Ah, shake and wake her, Johnnie, there's the ship for you,
Lying in the Royal Roads waiting for her crew,
And every brace and backstay is singing soft and low,
"Mother Carey wants you and you're all bound to go!"

As late I went a-strolling, a-strolling by the shore,
And thought of ports I'd like to see I haven't seen before,
Across the Strait the lighthouse kept winking fine and free
To show me where the road is that leads to open sea.

Ah, shake and wake her, Johnnie, yonder where she rides,
Lying in the Royal Roads swinging with the tides,
Singing with the muttering tides that past her cables flow,
"Mother Carey wants you and you're all bound to go!"

As late I went a-walking, a-walking by the tide,
I thought my love was with me and walking by my side;
So kind she did reproach me, so sweet her eyes did shine,
Yet could not hold beside her this restless heart of mine.

Ah, shake and wake her, Johnnie! . . . don't you hear them calling
Out across the Royal Roads and the dusk a-falling!
Time and time for me to leave you though I love you so;
"Mother Carey wants us and we're all bound to go!"

All bound to go, Johnnie, all bound to go,
If it's late or early, lad, if you will or no,
Sure as sun will rise, Johnnie, sure as tides do flow,
When Mother Carey wants us we're all bound to go.

❖   ❖   ❖   ❖   ❖

From Songs and Chanties: 1914-1916, edited by Cicely Fox Smith, published by Elkin Mathews, London, UK, 1919, pp. 100-102; first published in *The Bookman* (US), Vol, XLVII, No. 6, August 1918, p 688.

"Mother Carey" here can be interpreted as a benevolent but compelling spirit. This poem was probably composed near the end of the poet's stay in Victoria, British Columbia, when she was apprehensive about the fate of her beloved "shipmate" Dan who was evidently lost at sea. The "Strait" referred to in the poem is Juan de Fuca and the "lighthouse blinking" is on Race Ledge.

Since the poet was there in Victoria in 1913 the old Outer Wharf has long since rotted away and a new Breakwater has been established immediately to the West. The glorious view in the evening, however, is much the same:

"Over across the Strait of Juan de Fuca the summits of the ranges of the American mainland are flushed with faint rose, for it is only at sunset that the black bass bite . . . The light on Brotchie Ledge has just begun to wink leisurely, and far out on Race Rocks the lighthouse answers it with his occulting beam. The sun has gone down into the China Seas in a great fiery golden pomp, like the sea-burial of an old Norse king, and a splendid afterglow, slow and solemn as a funeral march, goes flooding up to the zenith like the glow of a funeral pyre; and on the edge of it hangs a lonely star. A small moon drifts like a feather dropped from an archangel's wing. A riding-light has begun to glimmer in the rigging of the anchored windjammer in the Royal Roads."

Tom Lewis (UK) first adapted this poem for singing as recorded on *Tinker Tailor Soldier Singer!*, 1995.

The header graphic is a photograph of the current Outer Wharf and Breakwater silhouetted in the sunset, as photographed by Charles Ipcar in 2005.

Harmonica Player

The Mouth-Organ

Oh, there ain't no band to cheer us up, there ain't no 'Ighland pipers
To keep our warlike ardure warm round New Chapelle an' Wipers;
So—since there's nothin' like a tune to glad the 'eart o' man—
Why, Billy with 'is mouth-organ 'e does the best 'e can.

There ain't no birds in Plug Street Wood, the guns 'ave sent 'em flyin',
An' there ain't no song to 'ear except the squealin' shells a-cryin';
The thrushes all 'ave 'ooked it, an' the blackbirds 'ad to flit . . .
So Billy with 'is mouth-organ 'e ups an' does 'is bit.

'Is notes is somewhat limited, they are not 'igh an' soary;
'E 'asn't got that many things in 'is bloomin' repertory;
But when 'e's played the lot, why, then 'is course is straight an' plain,
'E starts at the beginnin' an' 'e plays 'em all again!

'E plays 'em oft upon the march, an' likewise in the trenches;
'E plays 'em to the Gurkhas, an' 'e's played 'em to the Frenchies;
'E may be ankle-deep in dust or middle-deep in slime,
But Billy with 'is mouth-organ 'e's at it all the time.

Wet, 'ungry, thirsty, 'ot or cold, whatever may betide 'im,
'E'll play upon the 'ob of 'ell while the breath is left inside 'im;
And when we march up Potsdam Street an' goosestep through Berlin,
Why, Billy with 'is mouth-organ 'e'll play the Army in!

❖ ❖ ❖ ❖ ❖

From *Sailor Town: Sea Songs and Ballads,* edited by Cicely Fox Smith, published by George H. Doran Co., New York, US, 1919, pp. 132-133. Earlier published in *The Naval Crown* by Elkin Mathews in 1915. First published in *Punch* magazine, Volume 149, July 21, 1915, p. 70.

During WWI, the mouth-organ or harmonica was the instrument of choice for the soldier, being small enough to be stuffed in a pocket and relatively indestructible.

The header graphic titled *Harmonica Player* is a painting of a British soldier by Percy E. Syer done during WWI.

Regimental Sports—The Mule Derby

Mules

I never would 'ave done it if I'd known what it would be;
I thought it meant promotion an' some extra pay for me,
I thought I'd miss a drill or two with packs an' trenchin' tools,
So I said I'd 'andled 'orses—an' they set me 'andlin' mules.

An' 'orses they are 'orses—but a mule 'e is a mule
(Bit o' devil, bit o' monkey, bit o' bloomin' boundin' fool!).
Oh, I'm usin' all the adjectives I didn't learn at school
On the prancin', glancin', rag-time dancin' Army Transport Mule!

If I'd been Father Noah when the cargo walked aboard
I'd 'ave let the bears an' tigers in an' never spoke a word;
But I'd 'ave shoved a placard out to say the 'ouse was full,
An' shut the *Ark* up suddent when I saw the Army mule.

They buck you off when ridden, they squish your leg when led;
They're mostly sittin' on their tails or standin' on their 'ead;
They reach their yellow grinders out an' gently chew your ear,
An' their necks is India rubber for attackin' in the rear!

They're as mincin' when they're 'appy as a ladies' ridin' school,
But when the fancy takes 'em, they're like nothin' but a mule,
With the off-wheels in the gutter an' the near wheels in the air,
An' a leg acrost the traces, an' the driver Lord knows where!

They're 'orrid in the stable, they're worse upon the road,
They'll bolt with any rider, they'll jib with any load;
But soon we're bound beyond the seas, an' when we cross the foam
I don't care where we go to, if we leave the mules at 'ome!

For 'orses they are 'orses, but a mule 'e is a mule
(Bit o' monkey, bit o' devil, bit o' bloomin' fool!)
Oh, I'm usin' 'eaps o' adjectives I never learned at school
On the rampin', raw-boned, cast-steel jawboned Army Transport Mule!

From *Songs and Chanties 1914-1916*, edited by Cicely Fox Smith, published by Elkin Mathews, London, UK, 1919, p.p. 209-208. First published in *Punch* magazine, Volume 151, August 16, 1916, p. 118.

It is interesting to note that the poet was writing this in England at about the same time as "Banjo" Patterson was writing his poem "Army Mules" in Australia (1917). Two poems with a similar title but a completely different viewpoint.

The header graphic is a cartoon titled *Regimental Sports—The Mule Derby* as drawn by Lionel Edwards, from *Punch* magazine, June 5, 1918, p. 365.

New Heavens—New Earth (Christmas, 1916)

Nigh Bethlehem town poor shepherds heard
Beside their cotes a wondrous word:
"Nowell, Nowell" (the song did pour),
"Nowell, Nowell, from ship to shore,
Nowell, Nowell, the whole world o'er,
New Heavens, new Earth, for evermore!"

Is this, then, all—earth's countless dead,
Her homes whence Christmas joy is fled,
Such spilth of blood, such seas of tears—
The harvest of two thousand years?
And shall the War Star's blood-red light
Put out the Star of Bethlehem quite?
The cannon's thunder wholly drown
The Angels' song nigh Bethlehem town?

"Nowell, Nowell, from ship to shore,
For ever and for evermore!"
You Christmas bells, how shall you ring?
You Christmas choirs, how shall you sing,
When bells whose praise for centuries rung
To earth in molten heaps are flung,
And shrill the heedless bullet sings
By altars of the King of Kings,—
How shall you sing as oft of yore,

"Nowell, Nowell, the whole world o'er,
New Heavens, new Earth, for evermore?"

Be still, O doubting heart recall
How but through Death came Life for all;
The road was trod for you and me
From Bethlehem—even to Calvary:
The light which round the Manger shone
More glorious lit the rolled-back stone.

You hero souls, rejoicing bear
Your gold, your frankincense and myrrh;
More rich than gold, more sweet than spice

The fragrance of your sacrifice!
You mourners, lift your weeping eyes,
Look up, behold the rifted skies:
Lo, darkest night hath brightest morn,
The glory of the world re-born!

And all the molten bells shall ring,
And all the broken hearts shall sing,
And all the risen dead shall raise
With one accord their endless praise:
"Nowell, Nowell" (the song shall pour),
"Nowell, Nowell, from ship to shore,
New Heavens, new Earth, the whole world o'er,
For ever, yea, for evermore!"

❖ ❖ ❖ ❖ ❖

From *Small Craft: Sailor Ballads and Chantys*, edited by Cicely Fox Smith, published by George H. Doran Co., New York, US, 1919, pp. 74-76. First published in the *Brisbane Courier*, Queensland, Australia, December 19, 1916, p. 10.

Composed during the third Christmas of WWI in the hope that a new world would soon rise from the ashes of the old.

New Year

South o' Cape Stiff, an' the last night o' the year,
In the hooker *Maid o' Judah* we'd hard an' scanty cheer:
With water to the fife-rail an' a wind that cuts you through
Out went the Old Year and in come the New.

Every ship in harbour'd be strikin' her bell,
Every steamer's syren blowin' off like hell:
They'd be passin' round the bottle an' singin' "Auld Lang Syne,"
And all the young brassbounders kickin' up a shine.

But the galley fire was out, an' we'd very near forgot
The feel o' something dry an' the taste o' something 'ot:
With salt beef to bite on, an' sodden tack to chew,
Out went the Old Year and in come the New.

South o' Cape Stiff, in the darkness an' the cold,
In come the New Year and out went the Old:
Close beside my elbow I heard Mike Murphy say:
"*This* year, so 'elp me, I'm goin' to save me pay."

❖ ❖ ❖ ❖ ❖

From *Full Sail: More Sea Songs and Ballads*, edited by Cicely Fox Smith, published by Houghton Mifflin Co., New York, 1926, pp. 67-68.

Sometimes there was a Christmas celebration aboard a ship if it were good weather but most holidays were ignored as described here.

Newfoundland's Gift

Gifts from a full garner—wealth from a brimming store—
How shall these things be offered from a sea-girt land and poor?
I—who have neither gold nor jewels, cattle nor corn—
I (says Newfoundland) give the lads I have borne!

Toll o' the Banks when the white fog spins a shroud there,
Toll o' the Gulf when the Fundy gales are loud there,
Toll o' the ice-pack grinding south by Labrador—
These things I have paid . . . yet will not grudge my part in war.

Bone o' my bone—and bitter pain I bare them!
Blood o' my blood—oh, it's cruel hard to spare them!
Splendid sons of seamen—more than life to me—
No new thing is sacrifice to them which use the sea!

Salt is the sea-crust on our land's wave-fretted shore;
Salt, salt seas, they bring our seamen home no more,
Salt, salt winds, they'll blow them home no more to me—
Well we know the taste of it whose menfolk use the sea!

Bone o' my heart—and the salt sad tides roll over them;
Heart o' my heart—oh, the wide, cold seas 'll cover them!
Gold and gear I give not . . . life and love and all to me,
These I give to England . . . to England and the sea!

❖   ❖   ❖   ❖   ❖

From *Sailor Town: Sea Songs and Ballads*, edited by Cicely Fox Smith, published by George H. Doran Co., New York, US, 1919, pp. 108-109. First published in *The Naval Crown* by Elkin Mathews in 1915.

Composed during the early years of WWar I as men were volunteering for service in the war from all corners of the British Empire.

News from the North

As I went down by London Bridge
(And I not long on land),
I met a lad from the North Country,
And gripped him by the hand,

And said, "If you be late from home,
Oh, quickly tell me true
How fares it now with mine own country
And with the folks I knew?"

Oh, he looked up and he looked down,
And slow he shook his head,
And "Sure the place is not the same
This many a year," he said.

"For this one's dead, and that one's wed,
And that gone over sea:
You scarce would know the place again
So many changes be."

"Tell me no more, no more," I cried,
"This grievous news and ill:
Full well I know where'er you go
The round world stands not still.

For folks must die and folks most wive,
Since change and chance must be
Alike for those that bide at home
As those who use the sea."

"Tell me if anything I'll find
I knew and loved before:
Do the trees stand up by Oakenclough,
The winds blow off the moor?

Do magpies in our planting build,
And hares by Blackbrook run,
And at the Top o' th' Lowe the grasses blow
All ruddy in the sun?"

"Still runs the brook, the trees stand up
By yonder cloughside still:
You can see your father's barn
Look over the windy hill."

"There will I go, and there shall meet
Old ghosts of joy and pain,
And the folks I knew in the time that's gone
Shall greet me once again."

"The lad that's dead, the lad that's wed,
With me shall leap and run,
As they did when we were boys at home
Ere roving days begun."

"There is no land so lone and far,
There is no sea so wide,
There is no grave so deep that there
Shall they unheeding bide,
When the winds that blow in mine own country
Do call them to my side!"

❖ ❖ ❖ ❖ ❖

From *Small Craft: Sea Songs and Ballads*, edited by Cicely Fox Smith, published by George H. Doran Co., New York, US, 1919, pp. 117-119. First published in *Songs of Sail*, 1914. Also in *The Spectator*, July 29, 1917, p. 17.

The second poem in a set called "Songs of Home" published shortly after the poet's return to England after nearly 3 years in Canada and as WWI was just beginning. They represent an attempt by the poet to reconcile where she grew up with her later experience.

Waterfront Bar Crowd

News in Daly's Bar

In Daly's Bar, when night is come, and the lighted gas-lamps glow,
All red and gold the drinks do shine, and the glittering taps a-row,
And out and in by the swinging doors the sailors come and go.

They come with word of ship and man—with news of Trade and tide,
From nitrate port and sawmill wharf and islands far and wide,
And many a foreign sailor town and roaring waterside.

And never a tale goes round the ports from Riga to Rangoon,
And never a seaman's yarn is spun in a water-front saloon,
But the sailormen to Daly's Bar they bring it late or soon.

And old or new, and false or true, they bring it near or far,
From the Golden Gate to Sunda Strait, where ships or sailors are,
Till soon or late the tale is told at last in Daly's Bar.

And never a ship is cast away, from Leeuwin unto Line,
In ice or fog, in storm or calm, in foul weather or fine,
But they tell the tale in Daly's Bar when the flaring lamps do shine.

And there was one night, when wet and wild the puddle streets did show,
And all along the silent wharves the volleying wind did go,
I heard them speak in Daly's Bar of a man I used to know.

And "Have you spoke Jim Driscoll, then?" I cried, "And where is he?
Does he sail yet in windjammers, or has he left the sea?
Or has he taken berth in steam by now, the same as me?"

"Shipmates were we in the old *Kinsale*, and the best of pals ashore—
You mind the old *Kinsale*—Clay's ship she was in '94—
They sold her to the Dagoes since—we build her like no more."

"Shipmates and more were him and me in a time that's far away—
And for that old time's sake alone I'd give twelve month's pay
To shake Jim Driscoll by the hand and see his face today!"

Then up spoke an old shellback there that close beside did stand—
All red and blue the bright tattoo showed on each hairy hand,
And his eyes they narrowed in the glare, as he were strange to land.

And "Go you South to Sandy Point or North to Behring Sea,
And ask you news in all the ports both East and West," said he,
"But never a man you'll find has seen Jim Driscoll's face since me."

"I sailed with him from Frisco Bay with a drunken deadbeat crew
In all the crowd was hardly one could steer beside us two—
An' he was a decent sailorman—as good's I ever knew."

"There was him an' me an' Sam the Yank, there in the wild Horn weather,
That hard it blew our royals went down wind like a gull's feather—
Him an' me an' the Yank was there on the tops'l yard together."

"We hauled the blasted tackle out an' got the earing passed,
An' fisted down the frozen sail an' made the reef-points fast—
So bad a blow I never saw, but we made all snug at last."

"The worst damned night I ever knew—blowin', an' black as hell—
An' how he went, or where he went, there's no one lives can tell . . .
For the Yank an' me, we never heard nor saw when Driscoll fell."

"He was somewhere out in the thunderin' dark an' roarin' foam to lee."
"What . . . Driscoll dead?" said I . . . He laughed . . . "Ay, dead enough," said he.
"God knows the man was never born could live in such a sea."

I turned away from Daly's Bar, for I could bear no more—
The spilled drink, and the reek of breath, and the foul and slimy floor,
And the fool's din of the drunken men that sang, and laughed, and swore.

I felt the cold rain lash my cheek, and chill me to the bone,
I heard along the empty streets, the wild wind make its moan,
And I thought of Driscoll dying there in the darkness all alone.

I heard the roaring of the wind and the beating of the rain,
And the full tide lap in the dock-basins and the mooring-ropes complain,
And I thought of him whom on this earth I shall not meet again.

Music and mirth in lighted rooms I heard as I went by,
The dancers' feet upon the floor, and laughter rising high,
And I thought of him who was too strong, too full of life to die.

And still, for all I heard so clear, the words so plainly said,
And well I know that none comes back by the road he had to tread,
Still many's the time I think of him, and cannot think him dead.

Ay, still—though none knows more than I how deep, how far he lies—
If I, in some strange foreign port, should one day lift my eyes,
And see him cruising down the street, I should not feel surprise—

With a whistled tune between his teeth, the way he used to do,
And his old accordion under his arm, and a crested cockatoo,
And the roving eye and merry glance, and ready laugh I knew—

And we should meet in the old fashion, and greet as shipmates may,
And a score of tales would be to tell, and a thousand things to say,
While the day it faded into dark, and the night grew into day—

And this should be a tale to tell, when all our yarns were through,
The last and best among them all, and a laugh between us two,
The news I heard in Daly's Bar, and half believed it true . . .

❖   ❖   ❖   ❖   ❖

From *Ships and Folks*, edited by Cicely Fox Smith, published by Elkin Mathews, London, UK, 1920, pp. 28-32.

Here we learn that an old shipmate has died, and the person hearing the news just can't quite believe it, hoping that somehow the news is incorrect. The pain and shock expressed in this poem may be no idle poetic exercise and the poem may be a veiled reference to the loss of the poet's old shipmate "Dan."

First adapted for singing by Charles Ipcar in 2008, as recorded on *Sailortown Days*, 2009.

The header graphic is titled *New Bedford Whaling Types* by Anton Otto Fischer, from *Anton Otto Fischer*, p. 157.

Nitrate Barges in Chile

Nitrates

All alone I went a-walking by the London Docks one day,
For to see the ships discharging in the basins where they lay,
And the cargoes that I saw there, they were every sort of kind,
Every blessed brand of merchandise a man could bring to mind;
There were things in crates and boxes, there was stuff in bags and bales,
There were tea-chests wrapped in matting, there were Eastern-looking frails,
There were balks of teak and greenheart, there were stacks of spruce and pine,
There was cork, and frozen carcasses, and casks of Spanish wine,
There was rice and spice and coco-nuts, and rum enough was there
For to warm all London's innards up and leave a drop to spare.

But of all the freights I found there gathered in from far and wide,
All the smells both nice and nasty from the Pool to Barkingside,
All the harvest of the harbours from Bombay to Montreal,
There was one that took my fancy first and foremost of them all.

It was neither choice nor costly, it was neither rich nor rare,
And in most ways you can think of it was neither here nor there,
It was nothing over beautiful to smell nor yet to see,
Only bags of stuffy nitrates . . . but it meant a lot to me!

I forgot the swarming stevedores—I forgot the dust and din,
And the rattle of the winches hoisting cargo out and in,
And the rusty tramp before me with her hatches open wide,
And the grinding of her derricks as the sacks went overside;
I forgot the murk of London and the dull November sky;
I was far, ay, far from England in a day that's long gone by!
I forgot the thousand changes years have brought to ships and men,
And the knots on Time's old log-line that have reeled away since then,
And I saw a fast full-rigger with her swelling canvas spread,
And the steady Trade wind droning in her royals overhead,
Fleecy Trade clouds on the sky-line—high above the tropic blue—
And the curved arch of the foresail, and the ocean gleaming through;
I recalled the Cape Stiff weather, when your soul-case seemed to freeze,
And the trampling, cursing watches, and the pouring, pooping seas,
And the ice on spar and jackstay, and the cracking, volleying sail,
And the tatters of our voices blowing down the roaring gale.
I recalled those West Coast harbours just as plain as yesteryear,—
Nitrate ports all dry and dusty, where they sell fresh water dear,
Little cities white and wicked on a bleak and barren shore,
With an anchor on the cliff-side for to show you where to moor,
And the sour red wine we tasted, and the foolish songs we sung,
And the girls we had our fun with in the days that we were young,
And the dancing in the evening down at Dago Bill's saloon,
And the stars above the mountains, and the sea's eternal tune.

Only bags of stuffy nitrate from a far Pacific shore
And a dreary West Coast harbour that I'll surely fetch no more,—
Only bags of stuffy nitrate, with its faint familiar smell
Bringing back the ships and shipmates that I used to know so well . . .
Half a lifetime lies between us, and a thousand leagues of sea,
But it called the days departed and my boyhood back to me.

❖ ❖ ❖ ❖ ❖

From *Sea Songs and Ballads 1917-22*, edited by Cicely Fox Smith, published by Houghton Mifflin Co., New York, US, 1924, pp. 85-88. First published in *Punch* magazine, Volume 159, August 4, 1920, p. 86.

The header graphic is a photograph by Frank Brookesmith who sailed on the barque *Kilmallie* as a deckhand in 1925 to the West Coast of South America.

A Heavily Armed Coasting Barge

The North Atlantic Trade

As I was walking beside the docks I met a pal o' mine
I sailed with once on the Colonies' run in Thomson's White Star Line;
Said I, "What cheer—what brings you here?"—"Why, 'aven't you 'eard?" he said;
"I'm under the Windsor 'ouse-flag now in the North Atlantic trade.
We sweep a bit an' we fight a bit (an' that's what we like the best),
But a towin' job or a salvage job, it all goes in with the rest;
When we aren't too busy upsettin' old Fritz an' his frightfulness blockade,
A bit of all sorts don't come amiss in the North Atlantic trade."

"And how does old Atlantic look?" "Oh, round an' about the same;
'E 'asn't seemed to alter a lot since I've been in the game;
'E's about as big as 'e always was, an' 'e's pretty well just as wet
(Or, if there's some parts anyway dry, well, I 'aven't struck none yet!),
There's the same old bust-up, same old mess, when a green sea breaks inboard,
An' the equinoctials roarin' by the same as they've always roared,
An' the West Wind playin' the same old larks 'e's been at since the world was made,
They've a peach of a time, 'ave sailormen, in the North Atlantic trade."

"And who's your skipper, and what is he like?" "Oh, well, if you want to know,
I'm sailin' under a hard-case mate as I sailed with years ago;
'E's big an' bucko an' full o' beans, the same as 'e used to be
When I knowed 'im last in the windbag days when first I followed the sea.
'E was worth two men at the lee fore brace, an' three at the bunt of a sail;
'E'd a voice you could 'ear to the royal-yards in the teeth of a Cape 'Orn gale;
But now 'e's a full-blown lootenant an' wears the twisted braid,
Commandin' one of 'is Majesty's ships in the North Atlantic trade."

"And what is the ship you're sailin' in?" "Oh, she's a bit of a terror,
She ain't no bloomin' levvyathan, an' that's no fatal error!
She scoops the seas like a gravy-spoon when the gales are up an' blowin',
But Fritz 'e loves 'er above a bit when 'er fightin' fangs are showin'.

The liners go their 'aughty way an' the cruisers take their ease,
But where would they be if it wasn't for us, with the water up to our knees?
We're wadin' when their soles are wet, we're swimmin' when they wade,
For I tell you small craft gets it a treat in the North Atlantic trade!"

"And what is the port you're plying to?"—"When the last long trick is done
There'll some come back to the old 'ome port—'ere's 'opin' I'll be one!—
But some 'ave made a new landfall, an' sighted another shore,
An' it ain't no use to watch for them, for they won't come 'ome no more.
There ain't no 'arbour dues to pay when once they're over the bar,
Moored bow an' stern in a quiet berth where the lost three-deckers are,
An' there's Nelson 'oldin' 'is one 'and out an' welcomin' them that's made
The roads o' Glory an' the port of Death in the North Atlantic trade!"

❖ ❖ ❖ ❖ ❖

First published in *Punch* magazine, Volume 153, August 22, 1917, p. 142. Later reprinted in *Small Craft: Sailor Songs and Chantys* in 1917, pp. 25-28.

One of several WWI poems by this poet that pay tribute to the former merchant sailors who were now manning the armed trawlers and sailing barges that swept for German mines and protected incoming convoys from U-boat attacks.

The header graphic is titled *A Heavily Armed Coasting Barge* with two impressive guns in her bow as drawn by Muirhead Bone, from *Merchantmen-at-Arms*, p. 83.

WWI German mine Fished up by Trawler

The North Sea Ground

Oh, Grimsby is a pleasant town as any man may find,
An' Grimsby wives are thrifty wives, an' Grimsby girls are kind;
An' Grimsby lads have never yet been lads to lag behind
When there's men's work doin' on the North Sea ground.

An' it's "Wake up, Johnnie" . . . for the high tide's flowin',
An' off the misty waters a cold wind blowin';
Skipper's come aboard, an' it's time that we were goin',
An' there's fine fish waitin' on the North Sea ground!

Soles in the Silver Pit . . . an' there we'll let 'em lie!
Cod on the Dogger . . . oh, we'll fetch 'em by an' by!
War on the waters . . . an' it's time to serve an' die,
For there's wild work doin' on the North Sea ground.

An' it's "Wake up, Johnnie" . . . they want you at the trawlin'
(With your long sea-boots an' your tarry old tarpaulin);
All across the bitter seas duty comes a-callin',
In the winter's weather off the North Sea ground.

It's well we've learned to laugh at fear (the sea has taught us how);
It's well we've shaken hands with death—we'll not be strangers now,
With death in every climbin' wave before the trawler's bow,
And the black spawn swimmin' on the North Sea ground.

Good luck to all the fightin' ships that rule the English sea;
Good luck to our brave merchantmen wherever they may be;
The sea it is a highway, and we've got to sweep it free
For the ships passin' over on the North Sea ground.

An' it's "Wake up, Johnnie" . . . for the sea wind's cryin',
"Time an' time to go where the herrin' gulls are flyin'"—
An' down below the stormy seas the dead men lyin'
Oh, the dead lyin' quiet on the North Sea ground!

❖   ❖   ❖   ❖   ❖

From *Songs and Chanties: 1914-1916*, edited by Cicely Fox Smith, published by Elkin Mathews, London, UK, 1919, pp. 129-131. Earlier publish in *The Naval Crown*, Elkin Mathews, 1915. First published in *Punch* magazine, Volume 148, March 24, 1915, p. 230.

WWI had a huge impact on the North Sea fishing grounds, and even the Grimsby fishing trawlers were mobilized to help sweep for mines and battle the German U-boats.

Alan Fitzsimmons first adapted this poem for singing, as recorded by *The Keelers on The North Sea Ground*, 1998; Fitzsimmons also recorded this song on his solo CD *Old Wood is Best*, 1998.

The header graphic is a photograph of a WWI German mine brought back to port by Plymouth trawler *Genesta* long after the war ended, 1934, photographer unknown, from the National Maritime Museum, Greenwich.

Cheering the Outward Bound

The Old Breed

They cheered her from the waterside,
They watched her from the shore
Drop swiftly down the Mersey tide
Till she was seen no more,
Till, stately-swaying, tall and proud,
Her tower of sail grew dim,
And faded like a summer cloud
Beyond the far sea-rim.

They passed—like summer clouds they passed,
As fleeting and as fair:
The shapely hull, the soaring mast,
The speed beyond compare:
The hemp, the teak, the brasses bright,
The sunlit sails ashine,
The paint, the planking scoured and white,
The spars of glistening pine.

They passed—the ships, the men likewise,
The captains tried and bold,
The rich in lore of seas and skies,
The mates of mighty mould,
The bawling bosuns heard afar,
Sea craftsmen, Chips and Sails,
The crew whose veins ran Stockholm tar,
Big-fisted, hard as nails.

Long turned their log-book's final page!
Far South'ard now no more
Their royals dare the Forties' rage
As they were wont of yore.
No more, no more from Salthouse Dock
For lands of gold they clear,
Or, homebound, welcome off the Rock
The tugboat with a cheer.

What then remains? . . . The gulls, the breeze,
They bear from near and far
No words of *Empress of the Seas.*
Red Jacket, Shalimar,
But long as calls the Mersey gulls
And Mersey tides do run,
The breed that drove the clipper hulls
Lives on from sire to son.

Clipper and liner, steam and sail,
The old law guides them still,
The ancient, stark sea needs prevail
Of courage, foresight, skill,
As when they ran the easting down
(Oh blow, my bully boys, blow!)
In clipper ships of old renown
Threescore long years ago!

❖ ❖ ❖ ❖ ❖

From *Full Sail: More Sea Songs and Ballads*, edited by Cicely Fox Smith, published by Houghton Mifflin Co., New York, US, 1926, pp. 95-97.

The header graphic shows a dockside crowd cheering the ill-fated *Loch Achray* outward bound from Liverpool as painted by Charles Pear, from *Salt-Water Poems and Ballads,* facing p. 4.

Old Fastnet

The ships to the westward, by night and by day,
In storm and in sunshine go forth on their way,
The big ships and little ships, swift ships and slow . . .
And Fastnet—old Fastnet—he watches 'em go.

Hull down to the westward they vanish afar,
Like the waft of a wing or the flash of a star,
A feather of smoke on the rim of the sky . . .
And Fastnet—old Fastnet—he waves 'em good-bye.

Strange stars will behold them, strange harbours will know,
Strange lights for their guiding will beacon and glow,
And they'll maybe remember and maybe forget
That Fastnet—old Fastnet—he's waiting there yet.

A-waiting the day, be it distant or soon,
When the ships from the westward, by night or by noon,
In storm or in sunshine rejoicing will come . . .
And Fastnet—old Fastnet—he'll welcome them home!

❖   ❖   ❖   ❖   ❖

From *Rovings: Sea Songs and Ballads*, edited by Cicely Fox Smith, published by Elkin Mathews, London, UK, 1921, p. 50.

"Fastnet" here refers to the lighthouse at Fastnet Rock off Southern Ireland, the last land to be sighted by early Irish immigrants and the first to be sighted by returning trans-Atlantic sailors.

First adapted for singing by Richard Miles, 2012.

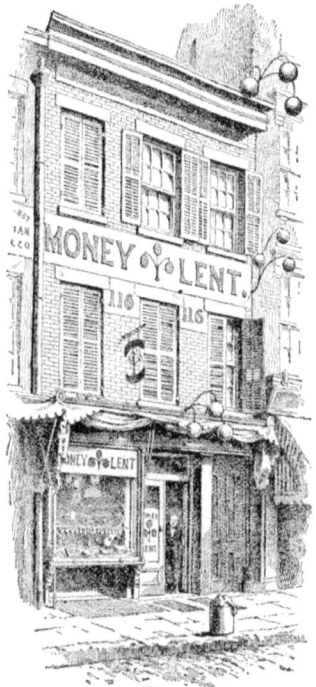

Old Pawn Shop in New York City

The Old Fiddle

By Chinese Charley's junk-store, by the Panama Saloon,
Where 'longshore loafers lean and spit, at morning, night, and noon,—
All among the keys without a lock, and locks without a key,
The old boss-eyed binoculars and sextants on the spree,
New Brummagem and old Bombay a-tumbling side by side,
A brown bald-headed idol and an "Extra Master's Guide,"—
Mouldy, musty, dumb and dusty, broken on the shelf,
I thought I heard the sailor's fiddle singing to itself.

Singing in a queer old quaver, shaky, shrill, and sad,
Like an old man singing songs he knew when he was yet a lad,

Singing of a good old time that all too fast did fly,
When the world was rather younger in the years gone by.

There were scraps of dead old choruses and snatches of old tunes,
We surely knew in other worlds and under other moons;
There was singing in the half-deck, and the sky full o' stars;
And bits o' tipsy shouting out of gaudy, glary bars;
Little tunes on Chinese fiddles in a quiet street
Full of dinky Chinee houses, where the East and West do meet;
"Ranzo, Ranzo, Reuben Ranzo"—came the sound to me
Of a chantey chorus roaring with the roaring sea.

Was it only seagulls piping faint and far away,
All in rows along the freight-sheds where they sit all day,—
Mewing round the inner harbour where the tugboats lie—
Or a song we sang together in the years gone by?

There were ships that once I sailed in, sail and steam, and great and small;
And some were good and some were bad, but, Lord, I loved 'em all;
There were rusty-red old hookers going plugging round the world,
And Clyde-built China clippers with their splendid wings unfurled;
And all the winds of all the seas came singing down the street,
With its smell of beer and harbour-mud, and tread of weary feet,
Till I heard the stormy westerlies go thrashing through the sails,
And the Trades' low thunder, and the Biscay gales.

Was I waking, was I sleeping, did the wet wind go
Thrumming in the slender tops of ships I used to know,
With the deep-sea glory on them all against a sunset sky,
On the tide o' dreams a-sailing out of years gone by?

There were faces long forgotten, friends both false and true
I sailed with once and lost again, the way that sailors do;
There were folks I loved and lost with smiling faces all a-shine,
Came and walked a while beside me with a hand in mine;
Are you dead or living, comrade, near or far away?
Do you ever think of me, lad, friend upon a day?
Late or soon, lad, night or noon, lad, you and I will meet,
All the seas and years behind us, strolling down the street.

Was it but the muttering tide that by the wharf did go,—
Or the footsteps of a comrade out of long ago?
Did I hear the wave lap and the light wind sigh,—
Or the voices of my shipmates in the years gone by?

By Chinese Charley's junk-store, by the Panama Saloon,
I walked and talked with shadows there in all the glare of noon,
Where—among the keys without a lock and locks without a key,
The old boss-eyed binoculars and sextants on the spree,

New Brummagem and old Bombay a-tumbling side by side,
A brown bald-headed idol and an "Extra Master's Guide,"—
Mouldy, musty, dumb and dusty, broken on the shelf,
I thought I heard the sailor's fiddle singing to itself.

❖   ❖   ❖   ❖   ❖

From *Small Craft*, edited by Cicely Fox Smith, published by George H. Doran Co., NY, 1920, pp. 91-95. First published in *The Spectator*, May 3, 1913, p. 18; also in *The Worker*, Brisbane, Queensland, August 14, 1913, p.5; also published in *Songs in Sail* by Cicely Fox Smith, published by Elkin Mathews 1914.

Smith was fond of poking around the waterfronts of sailortown, and one of the typical shops she loved the most was the nautical junk-store, chock-a-block with mundane and exotic artifacts from the seven seas. She described a similar junk store a block or two from where she worked on Wharf Street in Victoria, British Columbia, that she found one day in its flourishing Chinatown, and which she was never able to find again.

First adapted for singing by Charles Ipcar, as recorded on *More Uncommon Sailor Songs*, 2005.

The header graphic is an illustration from *Darkness and Daylight* in New York, published by A. D. Worthington & Co., Hartford, US, 1897, p. 605.

Old Sailor on a Spree

The Old Shellback

By Murphy's Hotel as I loitered along
I heard an old shellback a-singing his song,
A crazy old chorus, a song of no skill,
In a voice that was boozy, and broken, and shrill.

A roaring old song of the ships and the men
In fine days departed which come not again . . .
With the chink of the glasses came drifting the tune
And the smell of the drinks out o' Murphy's saloon.

I stood there to hear it, and swift as I heard
My soul like a ship was awakened and stirred,

Like a vessel becalmed when she quivers to feel
The kiss of the Trade from her truck to her keel.

Then fast fled my heart down the seas and the years,
And the winds of the world they blew loud in my ears,
The winds of the ocean recalling to me
Lost things and lovely, like dawns on the sea.

Lips that have smiled on me . . . friends who are fled . . .
All that was Life in the time that is sped . . .
Laughter of long ago . . . frolics gone by
In the ports of the West where the windjammers lie.

Nights off the Horn, and the ice on our spars . . .
Tall skysail clippers a-raking the stars . . .
With a "blow the man up, bullies, blow the man down" . . .
And a crew of hard cases from Liverpool town!

❖   ❖   ❖   ❖   ❖

From *Sea Songs and Ballads 1917-22*, edited by Cicely Fox Smith, published by Houghton Mifflin Co., New York, US, 1924, pp. 119-120. Appeared earlier in *Rhymes of the Red Ensign*, Hodder & Stoughton, 1919, pp. 67-68.

The penultimate line is a clear reference to that traditional shanty "Blow the Man Down" which in a variety of forms has been sung by sailors the world over and is still a favorite with shantysingers today. This poem can be readily sung to the tune of *The Old Orange Flute*.

The header graphic is an illustration of an old shellback drinking in a waterfront saloon, artist unknown, from *Songs of the Sea*, p. 173.

Ghost Fleet in Lake Union, Seattle

The Old Ships (1919)

They called 'em from the breakers' yards, the shores of Dead Men's Bay,
From coaling wharves the wide world round, red-rusty where they lay,
And chipped and caulked and scoured and tarred and sent 'em on their way.

It didn't matter what they were nor what they once had been,
They cleared the decks of harbour-junk and scraped the stringers clean

And turned 'em out to try their luck with the mine and submarine . . .
With a scatter o' pitch and a plate or two,
And she's fit for the risks o' war—
Fit for to carry a freight or two,
The same as she used before;
To carry a cargo here and there,
And what she carries she don't much care,
Boxes or barrels or baulks or bales,
Coal or cotton or nuts or nails,
Pork or pepper or Spanish beans,
Mules or millet or sewing-machines,
Or a trifle o' lumber from Hastings Mill . . .
She's carried 'em all and she'll carry 'em still,
The same as she's done before.

And some were waiting for a freight, and some were laid away,
And some were liners that had broke all records in their day,
And some were common eight-knot tramps that couldn't make it pay.

And some were has-been sailing cracks of famous old renown,
Had logged their eighteen easy when they ran their easting down
With cargo, mails and passengers bound South from London Town . . .

With a handful or two o' ratline stuff,
And she's fit for to sail once more;
She's rigged and she's ready and right enough,
The same as she was before;
The same old ship on the same old road
She's always used and she's always knowed,
For there isn't a blooming wind can blow
In all the latitudes, high or low,
Nor there isn't a kind of sea that rolls,
From both the Tropics to both the Poles,
But she's knowed 'em all since she sailed Sou' Spain,
She's weathered the lot, and she'll do it again,
The same as she's done before.

And sail or steam or coasting craft, the big ships with the small,
The barges which were steamers once, the hulks that once were tall,
They wanted tonnage cruel bad, and so they fetched 'em all.
And some went out as fighting-craft and shipped a fighting crew,
But most they tramped the same old road they always used to do,
With a crowd of merchant-sailormen, as might be me or you . . .
With a lick o' paint and a bucket o' tar,
And she's fit for the seas once more,
To carry the Duster near and far,
The same as she used before;
The same old Rag on the same old round,
Bar Light vessel and Puget Sound,

Brass and Bonny and Grand Bassam,
Both the Rios and Rotterdam—
Dutch and Dagoes, niggers and Chinks,
Palms and fire-flies, spices and stinks—
Portland (Oregon), Portland (Maine),
She's been there once and she'll go there again,
The same as she's been before.

Their bones are strewed to every tide from Torres Strait to Tyne—
God's truth, they've paid their blooming dues to the tin-fish and the mine,
By storm or calm, by night or day, from Longships light to Line.

With a bomb or a mine or a bursting shell,
And she'll follow the seas no more,
She's fetched and carried and served you well,
The same as she's done before—
They've fetched and carried and gone their way,
As good ships should and as brave men may . . .
And we'll build 'em still, and we'll breed 'em again,
The same good ships and the same good men,
The same—the same—the same as we've done before!

❖   ❖   ❖   ❖   ❖

First published in *Punch* magazine, Volume 156, April 9, 1919, p. 290. The poem was later expanded by four lines and slightly modified a year later when it was reprinted in *Ships and Folks*, 1920.

The header graphic is a photograph of the *Monongahela* and old ships like her which were remobilized from harbors scattered all over the world as cargo carriers during WWI, photographer unknown, from *This was Seafaring*, p. 98.

The Old Ships (1920)

They called them from the breakers' yards, the shores of Dead Men's Bay,
From coaling wharves the wide world round, red-rusty where they lay,
And chipped and caulked and scoured and tarred and sent 'em on their way.

It didn't matter what they were nor what they once had been,
They cleared the decks of harbour-junk and scraped the stringers clean,
And turned 'em out to try their luck with the mine and submarine . . .

With a scatter o' pitch and a plate or two,
And she's fit for the risks o' war . . .
Fit for to carry a freight or two,
The same as she used before;—
To carry a cargo here and there,
And what she carries she don't much care,—
Boxes or barrels or baulks or bales,
Coals or cotton or nuts or nails,
Pork or pepper or Spanish beans,
Mules or millet or sewing-machines,
Or a trifle o' lumber from Hastings Mill,—

She's carried 'em all and she'll carry 'em still,
The same as she's done before.

And some were waiting for a freight, and some were laid away,
And some were liners that had broke all records in their day,
And some were common eight-knot tramps that couldn't make it pay.

And some were has-been sailing cracks of famous old renown,
Had logged their eighteen easy when they ran their easting down
With cargo, mails and passengers bound south from London Town . . .

With a handful or two o' ratline stuff,
And she's fit for to sail once more,
She's rigged and she's ready and right enough,
The same as she was before,—
The same old ship on the same old road
She's always used and she's always knowed . . .
For there isn't a blooming wind can blow
In all the latitudes high or low,
Nor there isn't a kind of sea that rolls,
From both the Tropics to both the Poles,
But she's knowed 'em all since she sailed Sou' Spain,
She's weathered the lot, and she'll do it again,
The same as she's done before!

And foreign trade or coasting craft, the big ships with the small,
The barges which were steamers once, the hulks which once were tall,
They wanted tonnage cruel bad, and so they fetched 'em all.

And some went out as fighting craft and shipped a fighting crew,
But most just tramped the same old round they always used to do,
With a crowd o' merchant sailormen as might be me or you . . .

With a lick o' paint and a bucket o' tar,
And she's fit for the seas once more,—
To carry the Duster near and far
The same as she used before . . .
The same old Rag on the same old round,
Bar Light Vessel and Puget Sound,
Dutch and Dagoes, niggers and Chinks,
Palms and fire-flies, spices and stinks,—
Brass and Bonny and Grand Bassam,
Both the Rios and Rotterdam—
Portland, Oregon, Portland, Maine,
She's been there once and she'll go there again,
The same as she's been before.

Their bones are strewed to every tide from Torres Strait to Tyne;
By storm or calm, by night or day, from Longships light to Line,
God's truth, they've paid their blooming dues to the tin-fish and the mine . . .

With a bomb or a mine or a bursting shell,
And she'll follow the seas no more;
She's fetched and carried and served us well,
The same as she's done before—
They've fetched and carried and gone their way,
As good ships should and as brave men may,
The way of Nelson, the way of drake,
And all who have died for the old Rag's sake,
Fought and suffered and sailed and died
For England's honour and England's pride . . .
And we'll build 'em still, and we'll breed 'em again—
The same good ships and the same good men—
The same—the same—the same as we've done before!

❖ ❖ ❖ ❖ ❖

From *Ships and Folks*, edited by Cicely Fox Smith, published by Elkin Mathews, London, UK, 1920, pp. 54-57.
An earlier version of this poem was published in *Punch* magazine, Volume 156, April 9, 1919, p. 290.

Old Stormy on the Yard End

Old Stormy

"Stormy's dead," I heard them say, "he's dead and gone to rest";
Of all the skippers I have known old Stormy was the best,
His name was known on every sea, his fame on many a shore,
And Stormy's dead, that good old man, he'll sail the sea no more.

A rough old, tough old nut of an old-style hard-case skipper
As ever cracked on sail in a racing Melbourne clipper,
And hung on to his topsails in bad weather off the Horn,
And made a crew of deadbeats wish they never had been born.

In the Western Ocean packets had old Stormy served his time,
He had known the Blackwall frigates and the tea-fleet in its prime,
In the days of single topsails, stunsails, Jamie Greens and all,
Stormy'd sailed for Hell or Melbourne in the ships of the Black Ball.

He was skipper of the *Sheba*—she was one of Farlane's best,
Sister ship to *Eldorado* and *Golconda* and the rest,
"Farlane's yachts" they always called them from Blackwall to Sandridge Pier,
Slashing ships and smart as frigates—skysail yards and lots o' sheer.
"*Sheba's* luck" they used to talk of in the ports both near and far,
For he drove her like a demon, but she never lost a spar,
Roaring westward in the forties with her maindeck white with foam,
Flying light with Gippsland fleeces on the long sea road for home.

Twenty years old Stormy had her, and he loved her like his own,
But the day of steam was coming and the day of sail had flown,
And the times they kept on changing, and the freights they fell away,
And they sold the *Sheba* foreign, for they said she didn't pay.

And old Stormy heard the tidings with a sad and sorry heart,
"Twenty years," he said, "I've had her, and it's bitter hard to part,
Twenty years we've been together, but I'm getting old, I know,
And they've sold the *Sheba* foreign, and it's time for me to go."

So he left the little *Sheba* for to start her life anew,
With a whiskered Dago captain and a greasy Dago crew,
And a brand-new Dago ensign where the Duster used to be . . .
But the *Sheba's* luck had left her when old Stormy left the sea.

And she barged away down Channel in the equinoctial gales,
With a black nor'-easter blowing, and she loaded down with rails,
And the seas they pooped her cruel, and a big one broached her to,
And she couldn't seem to right herself, for all that they could do,
And the water came aboard her, and her masts went overside,
And she took and drowned herself at last, the night old Stormy died.

❖ ❖ ❖ ❖ ❖

From *Rovings: Sea Songs and Ballads*, edited by Cicely Fox Smith, published by Elkin Mathews, London, UK, 1921, pp. 35-37. First published in *Punch* magazine, Volume 161, August 31, 1921, p. 178.

A popular nickname for a skipper in poems and shanties is "Old Stormy" or often "Stormalong John."

The header graphic is an illustration showing an old sailor out at the yard end during a gale, artist unknown, from *Yankees Under Sail*, edited by Richard Heckman, Yankee Books, Dublin, New Hampshire, US, 1986, p. 177.

HMS *Vindictive* after the Raid

The Old *Vindictive*

It was the old *Vindictive* out of Dover put to sea,
And she sailed to the Lowlands low,
With cruisers and with small craft all to bear her company,
And her fighting lads on fire to sight the foe!
"St. George for Merrie England," went the word from man to man,
"Let us give the Dragon's tail a twist as British seamen can,"—
The twenty-third of April when *Vindictive* led the van,
And she sailed to the Lowlands low—
With a fighting signal flying, and a cheering crew replying,
Oh, she sailed to the Lowlands low!

It was the old *Vindictive*, and her years were turned a score
When she sailed to the Lowlands low—
For years she'd lain forgotten to her moorings at the Nore,
And they thought her day was over long ago;
But oh, they sang another song, another tale they told,
When she came as Drake and Cochrane with their fireships came of old,
In the mist and flame and darkness, all to storm the pirates' hold,
On that night by the Lowlands low—
For they caught the pirates drowsing, and they gave their nest a rousing,
In the night by the Lowlands low!

It was the old *Vindictive*, and she went to fight her last
Once again to the Lowlands low,
With her glorious scars upon her to her glorious grave she passed,
As fighting ships and men would choose to go.
With roar of many a battery, and boom of many a gun,
Her last commission's ended and her battles all are done,
For we sank her and we left her where her fighting fame was won,
And she lies by the Lowlands low,—
Still her silent watch a-keeping, with the tide above her sweeping,
There she lies by the Lowlands low!

From *Rhymes of the Red Ensign*, edited by Cicely Fox Smith, published by Hodder & Stoughton, London, UK, 1919, pp. 37-38.

Although no musical notation was included in this book the poem ended with the following note:

"Musical setting by Easthope Martin (Enoch & Sons)."

The HMS *Vindictive* was an obsolete cruiser that led a raid against Zeebrugge Harbor submarine and torpedo boat base in Belgium on April 23, 1918. The objective of the raid was to block the harbor and canal by sinking several ships. There was a desperate battle but the raid was only partially successful.

The header graphic is a photograph of the HMS *Vindictive* following the raid, photographer unknown.

Capt. J. L. Vivian Millett

The Old Whale

When I'm growing old (if I'm getting tired of sailing
Up and down the seas, and always finding something new),
When I come to feel the sight and strength of me are failing,
Maybe I'll curl up then, as the old whales do;
When I've lived on land, and never feel the fret and fever
Pull me back to seaward (as may one day be),
When I hear my old bones saying that it's time for me to leave her,
Maybe I'll curl up then ashore, and leave the sea!

I'll grow a few flowers then; I'll have a few friends nigh me,
Lie soft, and never care for all the winds that blow:
Eat, and sleep, and smoke, and let the hours go by me,
In the little easy ways that old men know;
Or sit by a winter fire, and tell the old tales over,
Listen for a shipmate's step coming to the door,
Talk of men and ships I knew, from Torres Strait to Dover,
And . . . maybe the heart of me'll be happy on the shore.

Maybe I'll forget then how, when I was younger
(Pleasant folks about me, and my girl's kiss on my lip),
When I've been a month or less on land I'd feel the hunger
Drive me through the ports again, looking for a ship;

Maybe then the shore things won't seem stale; and I won't waken
In the night and think of all my friends forgetting me,
Nor know (when it's too late to know) how sore I was mistaken
Curling up ashore there . . . with my heart at sea!

❖ ❖ ❖ ❖ ❖

From *Songs and Chanties: 1914-1916*, edited by Cicely Fox Smith, published by Elkin Mathews, London, UK, 1919, pp. 35-36.

In 1914 when this poem was written, the poet had recently returned to England from a three-year residence in Canada. England was on the verge of WWI and it likely seemed to the poet that her life was about the enter a new and uncertain phase. She was only 32 at the time but wise beyond her years.

This poem was first adapted for singing by Mike Kennedy, 2009.

The header graphic is a photograph of Capt. J. L. Vivian Millett, an old sea-faring friend of Cicely Fox Smith, from his *Yarns of an Old Shellback*, Brentano's, New York, NY, 1925, frontispiece. Capt. Millet swallowed the anchor in 1924.

The Old-Timer

Times, they say, must change, and folks must change with 'em too:
That's how it is in the West, now the old lights seem to fail:
The prairie that was is passing, and giving place to new,—
Give me again the old times, and the buffalo trail!

Give me again the great days between earth and sky,
The red roaring nights, the blood that leapt like a flame,
Men that were men, friends that were friends in the years gone by,
Life that held more than dollars to make it worthy the name.

Give me again the hot hours by the old corral,—
Bill on the pinto, and Pat on the buckskin, and me on the bay,—
The flurry of unshod hoofs, the voices,—where are they all,
Horses and men, and the good glad hours that were yesterday?
Do you remember?—but only the prairie wind replies:
"Yesterday's gone like a gleam, and here is To-day with its change:
Here with its new towns growing from nothing under your eyes,
And the scar of the settler's plough on the last of the cattle range."

"Yesterday's gone, with all that was in it of good and of bad,
Gone like the hunt that's over, a song that's sung:
Give me again laughter and life and the heart of a lad,
Give me again the old times . . . when the world was young!"

❖ ❖ ❖ ❖ ❖

From *Small Craft: Sailor Ballads and Chantys*, edited by Cicely Fox Smith, published by George H. Doran Co., New York, US, 1919, pp. 138-139.

The sixth in a set of poems entitled "Songs of the Wild."

The Oldest Thing in London

The Oldest Thing in London

A thousand landmarks perish,
A hundred streets grow strange;
With all the dreams they cherish
They go the ways of change;
But, whatso towers may tumble,
And whatso bridges fall,
And whatso statues crumble
Of folk both great and small,
The Oldest Thing in London he changes not at all.

The shoutings of the foeman,
The groanings of the slain,
The galley of the Roman,
The longship of the Dane,
The warring of the nations,
The judgment of the Lord
On heedless generations
In plague and fire and sword,
The Oldest Thing in London has known them and endured.

When London wall was builded
And London stone was new,
When first Paul's spire rose gilded
And gleaming in the blue,
Ere Holbein yet was christened,
When no one dreamed of Wren,
And clear the Ty-bourne glistened
And the Fleet was seen of men
The Oldest Thing in London was not much younger then.

New Londons rise like bubbles,
Like bubbles break and pass,
Or some dark dream that troubles
A wizard's magic glass;
A little while they hustle
And glitter in the sun,
And feast and fret and bustle
And chaffer, and have done—
The Oldest Thing in London he sees them every one.

No stones so strong to weather
Sun's heat or winter's blast
But time and man together
May tear them down at last;
The toughest rafters moulder,
The stoutest beams decay,
But he seems little older
From day to changing day—
The Oldest Thing in London that passes not away.

Each day to her, his daughter,
On each returning tide
He brings as first he brought her
Her dower of wealth and pride;
Twice daily, now as ever
At London's feet is laid
By London's ancient river
The burthen of her trade
By London's ancient river—
Way-hay, you London River!
The Oldest Thing in London, whereby was London made!

❖ ❖ ❖ ❖ ❖

From *Sailor's Delight*, Methuen & Co., London, UK, 1931. Published later in *Here and There in England with the Painter Brangwyn*, by Cicely Fox Smith, a limited edition published by F. Lewis, Leigh-on-Sea, UK, 1945, pp. 18-19, with excellent color plates and is one of her better travel books.

The words imply they were written during WWI when the London River, as the poet called the Thames, was a target for many bombs and the scene of much destruction. It is interesting to note that this book was published in large format at a time (or very soon after) of severe paper rationing.

To those unfamiliar with London, "Paul's spire" is the dome of St. Paul's cathedral designed by Sir Christopher Wren. Ty-bourne (nowadays Tyburn) and Fleet are tributary rivers of the Thames. Holbein was Court painter to the late Tudor monarchs of England.

The header graphic is an illustration titled The *Oldest Thing in London* as drawn by Phil W. Smith, from *Sailor's Delight*, frontispiece.

Worsening Weather

The Open Boat

"When this 'ere war is done (says Dan) an' all the fighting's through,
There's some will pal with Fritz again as they've been used to do . . .
But *not me* (says Dan the sailorman), *not me* (says he)—
Lord knows it's nippy in an open boat on winter nights at sea!"

"When the last battle's lost and won, an' won or lost the game,
There's some'll think no 'arm to drink with square-'eads just the same,
But *not me* (says Dan the sailorman), an' if you ask me why,
Lord knows it's thirsty in an open boat when the water breaker's dry."

"When all the bloomin' mines are swep' an' ships are sunk no more,
There's some'll set 'em down to eat with Germans as before;
But *not me* (says Dan the sailorman), *not me*, for one,—
Lord knows it's 'ungry in an open boat when the last biscuit's done."

"When peace is signed an' treaties made an' trade begins again,
There's some'll shake a German's 'and an' never see the stain,
But *not me* (says Dan the sailorman), *not me*, as God's on high,—
Lord knows it's bitter in an open boat to see your shipmates die . . ."

❖   ❖   ❖   ❖   ❖

From *Rhymes of the Red Ensign*, edited by Cicely Fox Smith, published by Hodder & Stoughton, London, UK, 1919, p. 21-22. Earlier published in *Small Craft*, 1917, pp. 70-71. Also published in *Punch* magazine, Volume 154, February 20, 1918, p. 126.

The header graphic titled *Worsening Weather* is from a WWII painting of a lifeboat crew taking in sail as wind picks up by Anton Otto Fischer, 1942, from *Anton Otto Fischer,* p. 194.

Orion's Figurehead at Whitehall

The *Orion's* Figurehead at Whitehall

All wind and rain, the clouds fled fast across the evening sky—
Whitehall aglimmer like a beach the tide has scarce left dry—
And there I saw the figurehead which once did grace the bow
Of the old bold *Orion*—
The fighting old *Orion*,
In the days that are not now.

And I wondered did he dream at all of those great fights of old,
And ships from out whose oaken sides Trafalgar's thunder rolled;
There was *Ajax, Neptune, Temeraire, Revenge, Leviathan,*
With the old bold *Orion*—
The fighting old *Orion*,
When *Victory* led the van.

Old ships, their ribs are ashes now . . . but still the names they bore
And still the hearts that manned them live to sail the seas once more—
To sail and fight, and watch and ward, and strike as stout a blow
As the old bold *Orion*—
The fighting old *Orion*,
In the wars of long ago.

They watch, the gaunt gray fighting ships, like death as bleak and stern;
They wait (not yet, not yet has dawned the day for which they burn):
They're ware and waiting for the word that sets their thunders free,
Like the old bold *Orion*—

The fighting old *Orion*,
When Nelson sailed the sea.

Oh, waiting is a weary game—but Nelson played it too!
And be it late or be it soon, such work is yet to do
Your starry namesake never saw who walked the midnight sky
(Old bold *Orion*—
Fighting old *Orion!*)
In the great old years gone by.

And be the game a waiting game we'll play it with the best;
Or be the game a watching game we'll watch and never rest;
But the fighting game it pays for all when the guns begin to play
(Ah, bold *Orion*—
Fighting old *Orion!*)
As you heard 'em yesterday!)

❖ ❖ ❖ ❖ ❖

From *Sailor Town: Sea Songs and Ballads*, edited by Cicely Fox Smith, published by George H. Doran Co., New York, US, 1919, pp. 97-99. A slightly different version was first published in *Punch* magazine, Volume 148, April 28, 1915, p. 330, and then reprinted in *War Verse*, 7th edition, 1918.

A poem composed in the early years of WWI when the British Grand Fleet was eagerly awaiting a climatic battle with the German High Seas Fleet. For years a giant HMS *Orion* figurehead, actually taken from a war ship launched in 1854, welcomed visitors at the entrance of the Royal United Service Museum in London. Unfortunately that figurehead was destroyed by bombing during WWII.

The header graphic is a photograph of HMS *Orion* figurehead, 1854, at the entrance to the Royal United Service Museum in London, from the Hunter Figurehead Archives, used with permission.

The Orkney Man

"I've sailed onst with an Orkney man,
A deal o' years ago," said Dan,
"In Clay's old packet *Kubla Khan*."

"A feller full o' quare old tales
O' singin' seals, an' stranded whales
As comes ashore in the winter gales."
"A decent shipmate, too . . . he's dead,
Lost overboard off Java Head
A deal o' years ago," Dan said.

❖ ❖ ❖ ❖ ❖

From *Full Sail: More Sea Songs and Ballads*, edited by Cicely Fox Smith, published by Houghton Mifflin Co., Boston, US, 1926, p. 54.

This is a good example of the poet attempting to illustrate the vernacular of her characters. If the words are treated phonetically it is possible to get an idea of the language as it would have been spoken by the sailors she knew.

"Onst" means once. "Quare" means queer (strange or odd).

Laid Up and Abandoned

The Ould Has-Been

All down by the harbour a-walking one day,
I saw an old hulk by the wharf-side that lay,
Her topmasts lopped off and her paint weathered bare,
Red rust flaking off her, and no one to care.

Then met I a man standing lounging beside,
Who scornful did speak as he spat in the tide:
"There lies an ould has-been which once had a name
Of a sea-going clipper, a clipper of fame!"

"Time was when her races, with grain or with wool,
Were the talk of the crews, 'tween Bombay and the Pool,
When the tales of her sailing like wildfire did fly
From Leith to Port Phillip, from Cork to Shanghai."

"But now who's a glance for her, limping her round
With coal for the ferries that ply on the Sound?
And who that now sees her would know her the same
Which once was a clipper, a clipper of fame!"

Oh, long I stood gazing there, sad to be told
How all men neglected her, now she grew old;
And my heart just to see her with pity was sore
For her, once so lovely, now lovely no more.

I marked the thick grime on her main-deck forlorn,
I marked the poor masts of her, woeful and shorn;
And all of my thought was that sure it was shame
To see such an end of that clipper of fame.

I thought of her sailing, so hopeful and proud,
The dawn of her sails like a mountain of cloud;
I thought of her battles, none stouter than she,
With the strength and the rage of her rival the sea.

Oh, better the sea that so long she did use
Should take her and break her as good ships would choose,
Some chance of the storm or some mercy of flame
Should make a brave end of that clipper of fame.

I thought of her captains, how once they would stand
So proud on the poop of their splendid command;
And all the good sailormen, each in his day
That loved her, and left her, and went on his way.

Oh, scattered the world through to-day they must be,
And some sleeping sound in the deeps of the sea;
And some will be old men grown grizzled and lame,
That were lads like myself in that clipper of fame.

But no one can steal from those stubborn old sides
The secrets she shares with the winds and the tides,
The tales that she tells of the sea and the sky
To the weed and the gulls and the ships going by.

And I took off my cap by the dingy wharf-side
To the grace and the glory, the strength and the pride,
That all were her portion who once had the name
In a day that's gone by, of a clipper of fame.

❖ ❖ ❖ ❖ ❖

From *Songs and Chanties: 1914-1916*, edited by Cicely Fox Smith, published by Elkin Mathews, London, UK, 1919, pp. 83-85. Earlier appeared in *Sailor Town*, Elkin Mathews, 1914.

This poem forms a set with "Age" and "Poor Old Ship: Regent's Canal Dock."

The header graphic is a lithograph titled *Cape Horner* by John A. Noble of the *Occidental*, laid up for years in Port Johnson, New Jersey, from *Hull and Hulks in the Tide of Time*, edited by Erin Urban, published by John A. Noble Collection, New York, US, 1993, p. 165.

Sailors Cruising Sailortown

Outward Bound

We've painted the Ratcliff Highway red
To the tune of twelvemonth's pay—
We've cruised around from the "Ship Aground"
To the shores of Tiger Bay;
We've stood our pals and we've kissed the gals
For a fortnight and a day…

For there's something gone wrong with the dance and the song,
And there ain't no bite in the beer—
So, *I'll* sail to Vallipo, and you'll sail to Maine,
Coromandel, Callao, Perim, Port o' Spain,
Baltic way, down the Bay, up the China Seas.
Pernambuco, Providence, anywhere you please,
Don't matter where if it's far enough from here!

You can git your se chest out o' pawn,
Or leave it where it lies—
You can pay your shot, or maybe not,
You can leave your gal likewise;
With a "Now my Dear, be of good cheer,
And wipe them blooming eyes"…

For we'll warp her out with a song and a shout,
And we'll give the tug a cheer—
And *I'll* sail to 'Frisco, and you to Callao,

Honolulu, Trinidad, Montevideo,
Baltic way, down the Bay, up the China Seas,
Pensacola, Palembang, anywhere you please,
Don't matter where if it's far enough from here!

❖ ❖ ❖ ❖ ❖

From *Full Sail: More Sea Songs and Ballads*, edited by Cicely Fox Smith, published by Houghton Mifflin Co., NY, 1926, pp. 69-71.

This is a classic sailortown poem where the sailors have "laid around and played around" too long and it's high time to ship out.

First adapted for singing by Charles Ipcar, as recorded on *More Uncommon Sea Songs*, 2005.

The header graphic is an illustration titled *Whorehouse District in a French Seaport* as redrawn by Stan Hugill, from his book *Sailortown*, facing p. 150.

143. Victoria Inner Harbour, c. 1900

Pacific Coast

Half across the world to westward there's a harbour that I know,
Where the ships that load with lumber and the China liners go,—
Where the wind blows cold at sunset off the snow-crowned peaks that gleam
Out across the Straits at twilight like the landfall of a dream.
There's a sound of foreign voices—there are wafts of strange perfume

And a two-stringed fiddle playing somewhere in an upstairs room;
There's a rosy tide lap-lapping on an old worm-eaten quay,
And a scarlet sunset flaming down behind the China Sea.

And I daresay if I went there I should find it all the same,
Still the same old sunset glory setting all the skies aflame,
Still the smell of burning forests on the quiet evening air,—
Little things my heart remembers nowhere else on earth but there.

Still the harbour gulls a-calling, calling all the night and day,
And the wind across the water singing just the same old way
As it used to in the rigging of a ship I used to know
Half across the world from England, many and many a year ago.

She is gone beyond my finding—gone forever, ship and man,
Far beyond that scarlet sunset flaming down behind Japan;
But I'll maybe find the dream there that I lost so long ago—
Half across the world to westward in a harbour that I know—
Half across the world from England many and many a year ago.

❖   ❖   ❖   ❖   ❖

From *Sea Songs and Ballads 1917-22*, edited by Cicely Fox Smith, published by Houghton Mifflin Co., New York, US, 1924, pp. 96-97; previously published in *Ships and Folks*, 1920, pp. 65-66.

This poem describes the poet's nostalgic feelings after leaving the Pacific Northwest and returning to England, as she thinks back on her two year residency in and around Victoria, British Columbia.

First adapted for singing by Charles Ipcar as recorded on *More Uncommon Sailor Songs*, 2005, to the tune of "Rolling Home."

The header graphic is a photograph of Victoria Harbour, circa 1900, with the floating boathouse of the Victoria Yacht Club, small sailing craft moored in front. The old Customs House is in the right background, photographer unknown, from *Light on the Water*, p. 32.

Recruiting on the Beach

The Packet Rat

When I leave this Western ocean, to the South'ard I will steer
In a tall Colonial clipper, far an' far enough from here,
Down the Channel on a bowline, through the Tropics runnin' free—
When I've done wi' the Western Ocean—an' when it's done wi' me!

An' I'll run my ship in Sydney, an' then I'll work my way
To them smilin' South Seas Islands where there's sunshine all the day,
An' I'll sell my chest an' gear there, as soon's I hit the shore,
An' sling away my last discharge an' go to sea no more.

It's a pleasant time they have there—they've easy, quiet lives—
They wear no clo'es to speak on—they've a bunch of browny wives;
An' they're bathin' all the day long, or baskin' on the sand,
All along wi' them Kanakas as naked as your hand.

An' I'll lay there in the palm shade, an' take my ease all day,
An' look across the harbour to the shippin' in the bay,
An' watch the workin' sailormen—the bloomin' same as me,
In the workin' Western Ocean, afore I left the sea.

I'll hear 'em at the capstan bars, a-heavin' good an' hard:
I'll hear 'em tallyin' on the fall, an' sweatin' up the yard,
Hear 'em lift a halliard shanty, hear the bosun swear an' shout,
An' the thrashin' of the head-sheets as the vessel goes about.

An' if the fancy takes me—as it's like enough it may—
Just to smell the old ship smells again, an' taste the salt an' spray,
I can take a spell o' pearlin' or a tradin' trip or two
Where it's none but golden weather an' a sky that's always blue.

But I'll do no sailorizin' jobs . . . I'll walk or lay at ease,
Like a blessed packet captain just as lordly as you please,
With a steward for my table an' a boy to bring my beer,
An' a score or two Kanakas for to reef an' furl an' steer.

An' when I'm tired o' cruisin' up an' down an' here an' there,
There'll be kind Kanaka women wi' the red flowers in their hair,
All a-waitin' there to welcome me when I come in from sea,
When I've done wi' this here ocean . . . but that'll never be.

For I'd hear the parrots screamin', an' the palmtrees' drowsy tune,
But I'd want the banks in winter, an the smell of ice in June,
An' the hard-case mates a-bawlin', an the strikin' of the bell,
God! I've cursed it oft an' cruel . . . but I'd miss it all like hell!

Yes I'd miss the Western Ocean where the packets come an' go,
An' the grey gulls wheelin', callin', an' the grey skies hangin' low,
An' the blessed lights of Liverpool a-winkin' in the rain,
For to welcome us poor packet rats come back to port again.

An' if I took an' died out there, my soul'd never stay
In them sunny Southern latitudes to wait the Judgment Day,
All across the seas from England I should hear the ol' life call,
An' the bloomin' Western Ocean it'd get me after all.

I'd go flyin' like a seagull, as they say dead shellbacks do,
For to see the ships I sailed in an' the shipmates that I knew,
An' the tough old North Atlantic where the winds do always blow,
An' the Western Ocean packets all a-plyin' to an' fro.

An' I'd leave the Trades behind me, an' I'd leave the Southern Cross,
An' the mollymawks an' flyin' fish an' stately albatross,
An' I'd steer through wind and weather an' the sea fogs white as wool,
Till I sighted old Point Lynas an' the Port o' Liverpool.

Then I'd fly to some flash packet when the 'ands was bendin' sail,
An' I'd set up on the main-truck doin' out my wings an' tail,
An' I'd see the tug alongside, an' the Peter flyin' free,
An' the pilot come aboard her for to take her out to sea.

An' I'd follow down to Fastnet light, an' then I'd hang around,
There to watch 'em out to Westward an' to greet 'em homeward bound . . .
For I know it's easy talkin'—an' I know when all is said,
It's the bloomin' Western Ocean what'll get me when I'm dead!

❖ ❖ ❖ ❖ ❖

From *Sea Songs and Ballads 1917-22*, by Cicely Fox Smith, published by Houghton Mifflin Co., New York, US, 1924, pp. 69-73. Earlier appeared in *Ships and Folks*, by Cicely Fox Smith, published by Elkin Mathews, 1920, pp. 13-16. First published in *Punch* magazine, Volume 158, April 7, 1920, p. 266.

This poem seems another take on sailor fantasizing; see "Port o' Dreams" and "Sailor's Farewell." With this poet such fantasy is often tempered with deeper insights.

"Run (jump) my ship in Sydney" means that the sailor plans to leave ship there rather than complete the return voyage.

First adapted by William Pint for singing as recorded on *Seven Seas*, 2004, set to the traditional song "Adieu Sweet Lovely Nancy." Also adapted for singing by John and Joy Rennie of Dogwatch as recorded on *Adventures*, 2006.

The header graphic is an illustration titled *Recruiting on the Beach* as drawn by Gordon Grant from his book *Greasy Luck*, p. 109.

Padre

'E don't go round glad-'andin' chaps nor 'it them on their backs;
'E don't deal much in pious talk an' distributin' tracks;
'E don't think decent seamen is a sort of 'eathen blacks.
But 'e'll sing an' smoke an' crack 'is joke an' use 'is fists as well;
An' the crimps along the water-front they 'ate 'im worse'n 'ell,
For the 'ottest shop in 'Frisco ain't too 'ot for Padre Fell.

❖ ❖ ❖ ❖ ❖

From *Sailor's Delight*, edited by Cicely Fox Smith, published by Methuen & Co., London, UK, 1931, p. 34; first published in *Punch* magazine, Volume 180, April 29, 1931, p. 470.

"Padre Fell" is most likely a reference to the Rev. James Fell who founded the Seamen's Institute, a social center and safe haven for sailors in San Francisco from 1892 to 1898.

"The 'ottest shop" is a reference to the many bawdy places that flourished in San Francisco's sailortown known as the Barbary Coast in the late 19th century.

Pals

"What's become o' the ship you went to sea with
A month ago or more?
And what's become o' the pal you used to be with
When you was last ashore?"

"She's made a far port an' a quiet mooring,
And a strange landfall . . .
She's where she won't heed the sea's roaring,
If she hears it there at all."

"There's no bell to strike nor watch to keep there,
An' no wind to blow . . .
It's a spell o' rest he's found an' a deep sleep there,
An' a long watch below . . ."

"An' I'll find many another ship to sign in,
For they clear with every tide,
An' I'll find plenty ports with pals o' mine in,
For the world's good an' wide . . ."

"An' I'll maybe find a ship as good as she was,
But never another friend,
Never another pal as good as he was,
Not till the world's end . . ."

❖ ❖ ❖ ❖ ❖

From *Rhymes of the Red Ensign*, edited by Cicely Fox Smith, published by Hodder & Stoughton, London, UK, 1919, p. 23.

Presumably this is a sailor thinking of a long time friend who has passed away and gone to the sailor's heaven called "Fiddler's Green."

Paradise Street

As I was a-walking down Paradise Street,
A bonny young maiden I chanced for to meet;
She gave me good-morning all as I went by,
With lips full of laughter and love in her eye;
"Here's wine in the flagon, and white bread and brown,
And a bright pretty parlour where you may sit down,
And a fiddle to dance to, and friends two or three:
Turn again, turn again, lad from the sea!"

As I was walking down Paradise Street,
The roses and posies, all blushing and sweet,
They bloomed in the gardens and breathed in the air,
A breath that smelt fine as the roses so fair;
They said, "Oh, young sailor, why go you so soon

Cruising Paradise Street

Before the flower's open that budded in June?
O stay for to-day, before faded we be:
Turn again, turn again, lad from the sea!"

As I was walking down Paradise Street,
All out of the westward I heard a wind beat,
All out of the sunset so loudly it blew,
It fluttered the flowers in the gardens that grew,
It shook the green shutters and rattled the pane,
And shrill round the gables it whistled amain,
And the smell it came blowing, yes, blowing to me,
From the white flowers that bloom on the fields of the sea.

As I was walking down Paradise Street,
So heavy my heart grew, so weary my feet,
I said, "I must go, for I hear my friends call,
From the wine and the fiddles and dancing and all;
Oh keep you your white bread and keep you your brown,
And by your fireside let some other sit down,
For I hear a ship calling, yes, calling to me:
'Turn again, turn again, lad, to the sea!'"

❖ ❖ ❖ ❖ ❖

From *Songs and Chanties: 1914-1916*, edited by Cicely Fox Smith, published by Elkin Mathews, London, UK, 1919, pp. 17-18. Published earlier in *Songs in Sail*, 1914 but first published in *Hawera & Normanby Star*, Volume 45, NZ, October 18, 1913, p. 9.

The header graphic was drawn by the team of Alice and Martin Provensen to illustrate the shanty "Blow the Man Down," from *Fireside Book of Folk Songs*, edited by Margaret Bradford Boni, published by Simon and Schuster, New York, 1947, p. 153.

Tramp Freighter at Cape Town Docks

A Parting

"I come ashore off a Cardiff tramp—the worst as ever I see:
She was all the things you could name," said Bill, "as a ship's no right to be:
She was gritty an' grimy an' smelly an' slimy, the same aloft as alow,
But it's allus 'ard at the last," said he, "when it's time for a man to go."

"There was nothin' to pleasure a seaman's eye in the blessed whole shamozzle:
She was ugly as sin from her slab of a stern to her blunt old lump of a nozzle:
She rolled like a pig an' steered like a dray, she crawled like a bloomin' 'earse,
An' the things she done in a seaway, Lord, they'd make a parson curse."

"But there I stood like a bloomin' fool on the quay in the drippin' weather
An' looked at 'er, an' thought o' the things us two 'ad seen together,
The work an' fun as was over an' done, the pals, the sprees ashore,
An' the times we'd 'ad both good an' bad as'd never come round no more."

"An' I spat in the dock, an' I turned to go with a kind of a mist in my eye,
An' a fool of an ache in my fool of an 'eart as I said, 'Ol' girl, good-bye!'
For let 'em be good uns or let 'em be bad, an' let 'em be fast or slow,
It's allus the same with a ship," said Bill, "when it's time for a man to go."

❖   ❖   ❖   ❖   ❖

From *Full Sail: More Sea Songs and Ballads*, edited by Cicely Fox Smith, published by Houghton Mifflin Co., New York, US, 1926, pp. 114-116.

Another poem describing what a sailor feels upon leaving even the most ugly duckling of a ship.

Gordon Morris (UK) first adapted this poem for singing as recorded on *The Long Road Home*, 2005.

The header graphic is an illustration titled *Cape Town Docks* as drawn by Ian Marshall, from *Sea History*, National Maritime Society, Peekskill, New York, US, Volume 129, Winter, 2009, p. 33

Parting is Such Sweet Sorrow

"Mr Cook is leaving for Russia shortly"—Daily Paper

Unlike the housewife who, aghast, surveys
The broken tenor of domestic days,
Britannia hears with joy far more than grieving
The words, for once so welcome, "Cook is leaving."

❖   ❖   ❖   ❖   ❖

From *Punch* magazine, Volume 171, January 12, 1926, London, UK, p. 601.

"Mr. Cook" is almost certainly a reference to A. J. Cook who was a member of the Communist Party and was active at that time in such areas as the mining industry.

The Passing of Sail

I often think how sad that time will be
When no wind lifts a sail on any sea—
When all that through the long slow centuries grew
From the first hollowed trunk or bark canoe
To mould that miracle of power and grace
Which made a wonder of the water's face
Must pass at last away and be no more—
All ancient skill and slow-won sailor lore
That taught hard hands with customed artifice
To shape tough hemp in many a bend and splice,

Dead eye and gasket, cunning hitch and knot,
With those that were its masters, clean forgot:
While those two sullen djinnee, Coal and Oil,
Usurp the old and honourable toil
By ships the four winds drove required of man
Since he and his sea-venturing first began.

Yet it may be that in some watery star
Beyond this earth and all its changes far,
Cetus or Capricornus, or that Ship
Which on our southern sea-rim seems to dip
Her wandering keel, or such as sailors name
Yardarm or Spanker, or the unflickering flame
Of high Polaris—there, it well may be,
Still sail the ships long fled this earthly sea:
The same, though fairer, that in days gone by
Had of their lovers faithful ministry,
Filling with toil their lives' unwritten page
From youth through manhood to neglected age,
Breaking their bodies with weariness, yet swelling
The seaman's heart with beauty past his telling . . .

There day by day a Trade that never fails
Shall fill from dawn to dark their straining sails.
There shall old tales be told, old songs by sung,
As in those years when earth and they were young:
All that was bitter and brutal, base and blind,
In the old life, for ever cast behind,
Where at the last the eternal Truth shall give
To each his dream, and only beauty live . . .

Sternview of
Square-rigged Ship

❖ ❖ ❖ ❖ ❖

From *Sailor's Delight*, edited by Cicely Fox Smith, published by Methuen & Co., London, UK, 1931, pp. 105-107; first published in the magazine *Country Life*.

The header graphic is a photograph showing the sternview of square-rigged ship, photographer unknown, from *Square Rigger Days*, edited by Charles W. Domville-Fife, Naval Institute Press, Annapolis, Maryland, US, 2007, facing p. 238

Peaceable Mister M'Gee

"Peace an' quiet's the motter for me,"
Said Mister Samuel S. M'Gee,
Otherwise known as Seaboot Sam;
"I'm a peaceable sort of a bloke, I am."
"Peace an quiet's an 'obby o' mine,
Fightin' an' suchlike ain't my line.
I tell you straight, I'm the kind of a cuss
What's got no use for trouble or fuss;
I don't want nobody makin' bother,

"And laid Bill out with a marline-spike"

No, not if he was my own born brother,
Back-chat's a thing my taste don't lean to,
But, when I get things fixed like I mean to,
Why, there ain't a peaceabler mate than me
Sails outer Frisco," said Sam M'Gee.

So he spat on his fists and he hopped off the poop
And waltzed around with a yell and a whoop;
He landed Ginger a clump on the chin
For wearing an impudent kind of a grin;
He hammered the soul-case out of Mike
And laid Bill out with a marline-spike,
And chased Jake on to the topsail yard,
And jumped on Joe with his seaboots on
And pummelled him up there good an hard
For something or other they'd been and done.

Then he fetched the helmsman a kick like a horse
For lettin' the ship get off her course,
And he rubbed his hands, and he said, said he,
"Peace an' quiet is what suits me;
I'm a peaceable sort of a bloke, I am,
And don't you forget it!" said Seaboot Sam.

From *Sailor's Delight*, edited by Cicely Fox Smith, published by Methuen & Co., London, UK, 1931, pp. 100-101.

Some might suggest that Seaboot Sam attend "anger management" training but would they dare say that to his face?

First adapted for singing in 1995 by Alan Fitzsimmons, as recorded on *Seaboot Duff & Handspike Gruel* by Pinch o' Salt in 2000.

The header graphic is an illustration by Charles Pears from *Salt-Water Poems and Ballads*, facing p. 48.

Philosophy

"Last night in the Baltic Tavern tap
I met," Mike said, "a longshore chap
And said, 'Don't sailorin' look queer
With all them mines an' such like gear?'
'If I was you,' 'e says, says 'e,
'I'd take a shore job same as me,
An' leave this trouble that's around
For them that's fond o' getting' drowned.'

"'No, no,' I says, 'I ain't a-givin'
It up for any square'ead livin'.
The way I puts it in my 'ead
Is—no man's done until 'e's dead,

An' if it comes to dyin', sure,
A man dies once, an' then no more.'

"I says, 'When ships 'as left off goin',
An' grass on London docks is growin',
(The same's it is, so I've 'eard say,
On all them 'Amburg wharves this day),
When Lloyd's is broke an' on their uppers,
An' all the owners in the scuppers,
Why, then,' I says, 'I might be lookin'
For a job o' cartin' coals, or cookin',

Or washin' pots, or sellin' tapes,
Or leadin' bears, or learnin' apes,
But since, as I 'ear tell, so far
There's still ships passin' Mersey Bar,
An' one or two comes in each day
To London Docks, so I've 'eard say,
An' ships can't sail without no crew,—
So long as they sail, I sail too.'"

"'If you, young man, 'ad followed the sea
Your 'ole life long, the same as me,
'Ad known it wakin' an' asleep,
An' seen God's wonders in the deep,
I guess you'd not be rattled much
By mines or submarines or such,
Or care a bloomin' finger snap
For no fool Kaiser or such chap…'"

"'Besides,' I says, 'when all is said,
Just think o' them poor chaps that's dead—
Poor pals o' mine as 'ad to die—
They took their chances . . . so do I!'"

❖ ❖ ❖ ❖ ❖

From *Small Craft: Sailor Ballads and Chantys*, edited by Cicely Fox Smith, published by George H. Doran Co., New York, US, 1919, pp. 44-45.

One of this poet's more explicit efforts to bolster patriotic spirit among the merchant sailors during the dark days of WWI.

Anton Otto Fischer at His Easel

Pictures

"Some likes pictures o' women," said Bill,
"An' some like 'orses best,"
As he fitted a pair of fancy shackles
On to his old sea chest,
"But I like pictures o' ships," said he,
"An' you can keep the rest.

An' if I was a ruddy millionaire
With dollars to burn that way,
Instead of a dead-broke sailorman
As never saves his pay,
I'd go to some big paintin' guy
An' this is what I'd say:

'Paint me the *Cutty Sark*,' I'd say,
'Or the old *Thermopylae*,
Or the *Star o' Peace* as I sailed in once
In my young days at sea,
Shipshape and Blackwall fashion, too,
As a clipper ought to be . . .

An' you might do 'er outward bound,
With a sky full o' clouds,
An' the tug just dropping astern,
An' gulls flyin' in crowds,
An' the decks shiny-wet with rain,

An' the wind shakin' the shrouds . . .
Or else racin' up Channel
With a sou'wester blowin',
Stuns'ls set aloft and alow,
An' a hoist o' flags showin',
An' a white bone between her teeth
So's you can see she's goin' . . .

Or you might do 'er off Cape Stiff,
In the high latitudes yonder,
With 'er main deck a smother of white,
An' her lee-rail dippin' under,
An' the big greybeards racin' by
An' breakin' aboard like thunder . . .

Or I'd like old Tuskar somewheres abound . . .
Or Sydney 'Eads maybe . . .
Or a couple o' junks, if she's tradin' East,
To show it's the China Sea. . .
Or Bar Light . . . or the Tail o' the Bank . . .
Or a glimp o' Circular Quay.

An' I don't want no dabs o' paint
As you can't tell what they are,
Whether they're shadders, or fellers' faces,
Or blocks, or blobs o' tar,
But I want gear as looks like gear,
An' a spar that's like a spar.

An' I don't care if it's North or South,
The Trades or the China Sea,
Shortened down or everything set—
Close-hauled or runnin' free—
You paint me a ship as is like a ship . . .
An' that'll do for me!'"

❖   ❖   ❖   ❖   ❖

From *Ships and Folks*, edited by Cicely Fox Smith, published by Elkin Mathews, London, 1920, p. 36-37. Later published in *Sea Songs and Ballads* 1917-22, 1924, pp. 82-84. First published in *Punch* magazine, Volume 158, February 11, 1920, p. 110.

First adapted for singing by Bob Zentz (US), as recorded on *Closehauled on the Wind of a Dream*, 2007.

The header graphic is a photograph of Nautical artist *Anton Otto Fischer at His Easel* painting a ship, from *Anton Otto Fischer,* p. 107.

Cartoon of German Pirate WWI

The Pirate's Only Delight

Hey, bullies, ho, bullies, what have ye seen,
Flying with the seagulls where the sea was green?

Oh, I saw a ship a-sinking,
And the sight it pleased me well
Says Teach the pirate drinking
Red wine in Hell.

Hey, bullies, ho, bullies, what about the crew?
There were men that watched 'em drowning as we often used to do.

A fine sport for sharing,
A rare tale to tell
Says Teach the pirate, baring
Yellow fangs in Hell.

Hey, bullies, ho, bullies, saw you aught beside?
Oh, we saw a drowned girl there drifting on the tide!

A sight to split you laughing,
A sweet thing to tell
Says Teach the pirate, quaffing
Red wine in Hell.

❖ ❖ ❖ ❖ ❖

From *Sailor Town*, edited by Cicely Fox Smith, published by George H. Doran Co., New York, US, 1919, p. 127. First published in *The Naval Crown* by Elkin Mathews in 1915.

Composed during the first year of WWI as a protest of the German's unrestricted naval campaign to blockade England, in which ships were sunk on sight without any warning or attempt to save the crews afterwards.

The header graphic is a cartoon titled *The Bread Winner* as drawn by L. Raven-Hill, from *Punch* magazine, March 3, 1915, p. 163.

The Plains of Mexico

There's a country wild and weary, and a scorching sun looks down
On the thirsty cattle ranges and a queer old Spanish town,
And it's there my heart goes roving by the trails I used to know,
Dusty trails by camps deserted where the tinkling mule-trains go,
On the sleepy sunlight ranges, and the plains of Mexico.

Is it only looking backwards that the past seems now so fair?
Was the sun then somehow brighter, was there something in the air
Made no day seem ever weary, never hour that went too slow
When we rode the dusty ranges on the plains of Mexico?

Then the low hot-scented evenings, and the fiddle's squeaky tune,
When we danced with Spanish lasses underneath the golden moon,
Girls with names all slow and splendid, hot as fire and cold as snow,
In the spicy summer night-time on the plains of Mexico.

I am growing tired and lonely, and the town is dull and strange:
I am restless for the open sky, and wandering winds that range:
I will get me forth a-roving, I will get me out and go,
But no more, no more my road is to the plains of Mexico.

For the sun is on the plateau, and dusty trails go down
By the same old cactus hedges to the sleepy Spanish town,
But I'll never find my comrade that I lost there long ago,
Never, never more (Oh, lad I loved and left a-lying low!)
Where the coward bullet took him on the plains of Mexico!

❖   ❖   ❖   ❖   ❖

From *Small Craft: Sailor Ballads and Chantys*, edited by Cicely Fox Smith, published by George H. Doran Co., New York, US, 1919, pp. 131-132. First published in *The Labor Journal*, Everett, Washington, US., February 14, 1913, p. 3.

The second of a set of poems entitled "Songs of the Wild."

There is no evidence, other than a poem or two, that this poet was ever in Mexico, but she did lose a close friend and that loss may be reflected again in the final verse. And in the next to last verse she resolves to "get me out and go" which she did in the fall of 1913 when she returned from Canada to her native England.

The Pool by the Mill

No one bathes in the pool,
The deep pool by the mill . . .

There's never a flash of a limb,
Nor a boy's form, straight and slim,
Taking off for a dive,
Making the stillness alive
Of the deep pool by the mill.

It's the best place for a swim
Up the river or down;
For it's always clear and still,
Deep and tempting and cool,
In the shadows green and brown
Of the deep pool by the mill.

When the boys come from the school
They run with laughter and cries,
Strip, and splash in the shallows
Where the minnows glance, and the swallows
Dart for the dancing flies,
But no one bathes in the pool—
The deep pool by the mill—
Because of the thing in the pool
That drags them down.

❖   ❖   ❖   ❖   ❖

From *Ships and Folks*, edited by Cicely Fox Smith, published by Elkin Mathews, London, UK, 1920, p. 75.

This is an unusual dark poem for this poet, especially so at this stage in her life. The last two lines are rather explicit! Compare this poem with her "Song of the Mill."

Merchantman Sinking

Poor Old Ship

She wasn't much to brag about, she wasn't much to see,
A rusty, crusty hooker as a merchant ship could be;
They sunk her off the Longships Light as night was coming on,
And we had to go and leave her there, and, poor old ship, she's gone!
All that was good of her, all that was bad of her,
All that we gave to her, all that we had of her,
Poor old ship, she's gone!

The times we spent aboard her, they was oftener bad than good,
But, good and bad, we'd live the lot all over if we could;
She's stood her trick the same as us, she's had her whack of fun,
She's shared it all with sailormen, and, poor old ship, she's done!
Hard times and soft times, and all times we've been with her;
Bad days and good days, and all sorts we've seen with her,
And, poor old ship, she's done!

She's stuck her crazy derricks up by half a hundred quays,
She's dipped her dingy Duster in the spray of all the seas,
Her funnel's caked with Cape Horn ice and blistered in the sun,
She's moseyed round above a bit, and, poor old ship, she's done!
North seas and South—and they've all had a go at her,
Hot winds and cold—and they've all had a blow at her,
Poor old ship, she's done!

She's trailed her smudge the wide world round in weather grey and blue,
She's churned a half-score oceans with her blooming nine-knot screw;
She's sampled all the harbour mud from Cardiff to Canton,
And she'll never fetch another port, for, poor old ship, she's gone!
Ports up and down—and she's seen many a score of 'em;
High seas and low—and she won't sail no more of 'em—
Poor old ship, she's gone!

And chaps that knowed her in their time, 'tween London and Rangoon,
In many a sailor's drinking-place and waterfront saloon,
Will set their drinks down when they hear her blooming yarn is spun,
And say, "I sailed aboard her once, and, poor old ship, she's done!
Many's the hard word I once used to spend on her
Ah, them was great days—and now there's an end on her—
Poor old ship, she's done!"

❖   ❖   ❖   ❖   ❖

From *Rhymes of the Red Ensign*, edited by Cicely Fox Smith, published by Hodder & Stoughton, London, UK, 1919, p. 27-29. First published in *Punch* magazine, Volume 154, March 27, 1918, p. 206.

Another tribute by the poet to the old tramp freighters and their sailors torpedoed or sunk by a mine within a day's return to England.

The header graphic is a photograph of a merchant ship sinking after being torpedoed in WWI, photographer unknown.

The Four-masted Barkentine *Conqueror*

Poor Old Ship (Regent's Canal Dock)

Her rigging it was once of the best a man could find;
With canvas of the stoutest her lockers they were lined;
But now from truck to keelson she's stinted shamefully,
For want of tar and seizing, a sight she is to see—
Poor old ship!

Her planking was like snow and her brasses they did shine,
Likewise with sand and canvas they kept her bulwarks fine,
But now her seams are gaping, her brass a fair disgrace,
And her teak is daubed and plastered like a painted woman's face—
Poor old ship!

Her freights were mostly clean ones, her charters they were good,
She picked them and she chose them and went just where she would,
But those good times are over and she has had her day,
And firewood and scrap-iron are all that come her way—
Poor old ship!

She had shellbacks four-and-twenty that hauled and reefed and furled,
And shantied up her mud-hook and worked her round the world,
But now a scant half-dozen are all the chaps she's got,
And hardly one's a seaman in all the blinkin' lot—
Poor old ship!

She's sailed the round world over here and there and everywhere,
She's served her masters faithfully in weather foul and fair,
And now her old age is on her it's a shame to see her so;
She's nothing left to live for; to the breaker let her go—
Poor old ship!

From *Sailor's Delight*, edited by Cicely Fox Smith, published by Methuen & Co., London, UK, 1931, pp. 102-104.

This poem forms a set with "Age (Millwall Dock)" and the poet suggests that it can be sung to the tune of the traditional forebitter "Poor Old Horse."

First adapted for singing by Mike Kennedy, as recorded on *A Dog's Life*, 2015

The header graphic is a photograph by Harry A. Kirwin of the four-masted barkentine *Conqueror* just prior to being hauled off to the breaker's dock in Seattle, 1938, from *This Was Seafaring*, p. 46.

Port Forsaken

A Port Forsaken

She sent her five fighting ships once on a day
To meet the bold Spaniard in battle array:
And a King's son brought to her in days that are done
His beauty that perished, his dream of a throne.

She had ships once in plenty from all the seven seas
That crowded her harbour and thronged at her quays,
Brown barques from the Baltic all battered with gales,
And brigs from Bilbao and schooners from Wales.

Oh, 'twas then she had traffic that stuffed her sheds full
With ropes out of Bridport and Westcountry wool,
With granite from Cornwall and seacoal from Tyne,
And rum from the Indies and Portingal wine.

Her merchants they flourished, her pilots did thrive,
Her sail lofts and rigging lofts hummed like a hive:

There was singing o' nights at the "Ship" and the "Crown,"
And a sailor apiece for the girls in the town.

But now 'tis all ended and nothing comes near
But the steamers in summer a few times a year:
A sail on the sea-line, a smudge on the sky,
She sees the ships pass her and never come nigh.

The quays are deserted, the sail lofts are bare,
The spiders spin cables where hempen rope were,
And the wind through the wharf sheds goes singing alone
His dismal old ditty of days that are done.

❖ ❖ ❖ ❖ ❖

From *Full Sail: More Sea Songs and Ballads*, edited by Cicely Fox Smith, published by Houghton Mifflin Co., New York, US, 1926, pp. 117-119.

In another poem, "Mariquita," Smith muses about the impact of time on the sailortowns she knew and loved:

> " And it's maybe better that way, for there's nothing left but change,
> And the ships I knew all going, and the ports I knew grown strange…"

The header graphic titled *Port Forsaken* is drawn by Phil W. Smith to illustrate this poem, from *Full Sail*, facing p. 116.

Port o' Dreams

Port o' Dreams

"There's a deal o' ports," said Murphy, "an' I guess I've sampled most,
Round about the Gulf o' Guinea, and up an' down the Chili coast,
In the Black Sea an' the Baltic an' the China seas I've been,
An' the North Sea an' the South Sea an' the places in between.

An' the ports as look the finest turns out some'ow worst of all,
For I lost my chum in Rio in a Dago dancin' 'all,
An' I lost my bloomin' 'eart once to a wench in Callao,
An' I lost my youth in Frisco…but that's years an' years ago.

But there's one I've never sighted out of all the ports there be;
It's a place a feller talked of as was shipmates once with me,
In the hooker *Maid of Athens*, she was one of Dunc Macneill's,
She went missin' many a year since bound from Steveston home with deals.

An' this feller said the drinks there are the best a man could find,
An' a sailor's always welcome, an' the girls are always kind,
An' there's dancin' an' there's singin' an' there's every sort o' fun,
In the plaza of an evenin' when the lazy sun is done.

An' the blessed old Pacific he keeps singin' like a psalm,
To the shippin' in the roadstead an' the firefly in the palm,
An' the days are never scorchin' an' the nights are never 'ot,
In that port 'e used to yarn of with the name I've clean forgot.

An' I'll never fetch that harbour, but it's maybe for the best,
For I daresay if I found it, it'd be like all the rest,
An' I like to think it's waitin', waitin' all the while for me,
With the red wine an' the white wine an' the dancin' an' the spree,
An' the firefly gleamin' golden in the palms I'll never see!"

❖ ❖ ❖ ❖ ❖

From *Sea Songs and Ballads 1917-22*, edited by Cicely Fox Smith, published by Houghton Mifflin Co., NY, 1924, p.p. 32-33. First published in *Punch* magazine, Volume 163, August 16, 1922, p. 163.

This poem shares a theme and imagery with "The Golden City of St. Mary" by John Masefield.

I love the pursuit of the romantic dream as told by this old salt, the recognition that the dream is an unlikely reality, but what the Hell, it's still fun to muse on!

First adapted for singing by Danny and Joyce McLeod, as recorded on *No Cross Words*, 2002. Gordon Morris also adapted this poem for singing as recorded on *Full Sail: Inside the Lid*, 2002. Another musical setting for this poem was later made by Charles Ipcar, as recorded on *Uncommon Sailor Songs*, 2005.

The header graphic is an illustration painted by Charles Pears from *Salt-Water Poems and Ballads*, facing p. 58.

Portrait of a Lady-1

Ladies a-plenty
Have painters drawn
In velvet and cramoise,
Lace and lawn;

Grave Infantas
In stiff brocades;
Nymphs that wanton
In woodland shades;

Mild Madonnas
Who gaze serene
From many a gilded
And carven screen.

Reynolds' beauties
Like country posies;

The Pilot Comes Aboard

Dames of Flanders
Like full-blown roses.

And here's a lady
Fair as them all,
Gracious to look upon,
Royally tall.

Many her lovers
Of old have been;
Men have paid court to her
As to a Queen,

Humoured her whimsies,
Watched her ways,
Lovingly chided her,
Sung her praise,

Served her in poverty,
Hunger and cold,
Spent their best years for her,
Toiled and grown old,

Lavished upon her
A loyalty true,
Ay, and, if need were,
Died for her too.

Yonder's her picture
(In oils, no less!),
The Colonies' clipper,
Good Queen Bess,
Taking her pilot
Off Dungeness.

❖ ❖ ❖ ❖ ❖

From *Sailor's Delight*, edited by Cicely Fox Smith, published by Methuen & Co., London, UK, 1931, pp. 64-66. First published in *Punch* magazine, Volume 173. December 21, 1927, p. 695.

The "Colonies' clippers" were fast passenger sailing vessels that went back and forth between England and Australia or India in the late 19th century.

The header graphic is an illustration titled *The Pilot Comes Aboard* drawn by Gordon Grant in his book *Sail Ho!*, facing p. 120.

Portrait of a Lady-2

Pilot boat, lighthouse,
Stiff green sea—
House-flag and number
Plain as can be—

Sails like the cheek
Of the cherubim—
Blackwall fashion,
Shipshape and trim—

Cottonwool clouds
In a crude blue sky—
Who owned it, I wonder
In days gone by?

What old skipper
Or mate, maybe,
Snug by his fireside,
Done with the sea,

Lovingly scanned it
With age-dimmed eyes,
Saw in his pipe-smoke
Pictures rise—

Let, by the lamplight,
Memory range
A hundred harbours
And landfalls strange:

Mast-fringed Hooghly
And junk-thronged Praya,
And mat-thatched hamlets
Of far Malaya:

The Trade exultant,
The Doldrum calm,
The long surf creaming
On shores of palm:

Channels Formosan
Typhoon-torn,
Towering, tremendous
Seas of the Horn:

Long-lost shipmates

In long-drowned ships—
Smiling, yet sadly,
With bearded lips.

To think of the laughter
And larks that he had
In the old windjammers
When he was a lad,

And the storms he weathered
And songs he sung,
In days long over,
When earth was young!

❖ ❖ ❖ ❖ ❖

From *Sailor's Delight*, edited by Cicely Fox Smith, published by Methuen & Co., London, UK, 1931, pp. 67-69.

Here the poet is musing on some crude portrait of a ship, as an old sailor might do in his retirement from the sea.

Gipsy Fortune teller

The Portsmouth Road

As I went down the Portsmouth Road,
A careless, rambling fellow,
The stormcock whistled on the bough,
A stave both loud and mellow;
To hear his song I paused awhile,
Then tossed it back with laughter,
But all along the seaward road,
I heard it follow after:

*"East—West—home is best—
You'll wander far and lone, lad,
But of all the lands you'll find on Earth,
There's none just like your own, lad."*

As I went down the Portsmouth Road
My step was light and merry;
I met a tramping gipsy wife,
As brown as any berry;
She told my fortune for a crown,
But little did it please me
To hear her speaking once again
The same old words to tease me:

*"East—West—home is best—
You'll wander far and lone, lad,
But of all the lands you'll find on Earth,
There's none just like your own, lad."*

I wandered here, I rambled there,
Since I set off that morning,
And many's the time I thought about
That gipsy's word of warning;
And many a strange far land I saw,
And gaudy foreign city,
And often enough did seem to hear
Once more the stormcock's ditty:

*"East—West—home is best—
You'll wander far and lone, lad,
But of all the lands you'll find on Earth,
There's none just like your own, lad."*

As I came up the Portsmouth Road,
My bundle on my shoulder,
The years had come, the years had gone,
And I was growing older;
The wayside fires were white and cold,
The leaves were turning yellow,
And never a gipsy crossed my path,
Nor stormcock whistled mellow:

*"East—West—home is best—
You'll wander far and lone, lad,
But of all the lands you'll find on Earth,
There's none just like your own, lad."*

But, what cared I for silent bird,
Or what for fires forsaken,
From many a land and many a sea
Whose homeward road was taken?
The gipsy's words were in my heart,
Afire to cheer and warm me,
And all the way the stormcock's tune,
Went singing on before me:

"East—West—home is best—
You'll wander far and lone, lad,
But of all the loves you'll find on Earth,
There's none just like your own, lad."

❖ ❖ ❖ ❖ ❖

From *Ships and Folks*, edited by Cicely Fox Smith, published by Elkin Mathews, London, UK, 1920, pp. 76-78.

Here the poet seems to be reconciling herself to her return home to England, after her three year stay in Canada. Do note the change in wording of the last line of the last chorus.

This poem was first adapted for singing by Bob Zentz (US), as recorded on *Closehauled on the Wind of a Dream*, 2007, using the traditional Scottish tune "Mormon Braes."

The header graphic is a photograph of a Gipsy woman on the Biddeford Beach, early 1900s, photographer unknown, from *A Day's Work*, Volume 2, W. H. Bunting, Tilbury House, Gardiner, Maine, 2000, p. 331.

The Prairie Shepherd

Baa, baa, black sheep!—whose fault but your own
That you're here on the western prairie, herding the sheep alone,—
Here in a wide and lonely land, by the stranger's fold,—
Oh, rise and go to your father; he growing weary and old.

Poets talk about the shepherds, and the wonderful times they've got
Playing tunes to Amaryllis, and all such rot!
And it might be better than nothing for passing the time away
If you'd got a girl to talk to, or a penny whistle to play.

I was a fool and I'm paying—I'm on a job that would beat
The other prodigal hollow, with the husks that the swine did eat.
Wouldn't I think I was lucky if I'd plenty of pigs to keep!
They're sociable sort of creatures—if you've ever lived among sheep.

All the way to the Rocky Mountains, nothing to see . . .
Bare and bald and droughty and dusty, and never a tree!
Never a voice to hail you, only a hawk's lone cry
Hanging there aloft like a speck in the aching sky.

Only the dry grass stirring, only the weary wind
Seeming to sigh for the people and places you left behind:
And I wonder how long I'll stand it before I'm crazy and grey,
With the sheep bleating, bleating all the night and the day.

God! Will they always be at it in the everlasting old tone,
Telling me over and over the things I have loved and known,
Keeping my heart from forgetting, no matter how hard I try,
The various kinds of a fool I was in the years gone by . . .

Baa, baa, black sheep!—no one's fault but your own
That you're here on the western prairie, herding your sheep alone,—
No one but God around to see you, and pity your tears
For the things you wish you could alter, back there in the bygone years.

From *Sailor Town: Sea Songs and Ballads*, edited by Cicely Fox Smith, published by George H. Doran Co., New York, US, 1919, pp. 66-68. An earlier edition of *Sailor Town* was published by Elkin Mathews in 1914.

This one could take some decoding. Think back on the first time you took a job which while it paid the rent it bored you to tears. I seem to remember a basement office once where I was working as a researcher for the Michigan Occupational Information Coordinating Committee. Some of my co-workers there are probably ready now to retire—baa, baa, baa!

Prairie Sunset

Where the Great Chief's sullen crest
Looks over the land,
The splendour floods from the west,
Ruddied and grand.

Like a vast Armada's wrecked
And ravaged pride,
Reeling over a flecked
And crimsoned tide.

Or a cachalot lashing the spray
In his wounded throe,
On a South sea far away
Where the whalers go.

Till the light is gone and the skies
Are cold and dree
As a blue gulf in the ice
Of a Polar sea.

❖   ❖   ❖   ❖   ❖

From *Small Craft: Sailor Ballads and Chantys*, edited by Cicely Fox Smith, published by George H. Doran Co., New York, US, 1919, p. 137.

The fifth in a set of poems entitled "Songs of the Wild." "Dree" is an archaic Lancashire word meaning monotonous. It is also archaic Scottish for "endure" or "suffer."

Prairie Wind

I looked out as the dusk fell on the prairie waste and wide,
There was no dog that barked there, nor any tree that sighed:
Silence, and nought but silence, was there on every hand,
But for the lone wind blowing over the lone land.

But for the voice of the lonely places, wandering by
Between the vast and empty earth and the star-sown sky,
From the wrinkled flanks of the mountains where the eagle rears her brood,
And screams from her wild eyrie to the barren solitude.

But for the voice from the ramparts where hasten down alone
Cold and unforded rivers flowing to seas unknown,
And the lost ranges where never a white man's foot has trod,
And lakes in deep hill-hollows look lonely up to God.

But for the ancient burthen of the long uncounted years
In far untravelled gorges where the waiting echo hears
Only the cougar hunting by night, and the eagle's cry,
And the lone wind blowing under the lone sky.

❖ ❖ ❖ ❖ ❖

From *Songs and Chanties 1914-1916*, edited by Cicely Fox Smith, published by Elkin Mathews, London, UK, 1919, pp. 50-51. First published in *Songs in Sail*, 1914.

Fourth in a set of poems called "Songs of the Wild."

Sir Francis Drake

The Queen's Delight (a Ballad of Master Mariners)

Gloriana's mood was bitter, Gloriana's brow was black,
She railed upon her ladies—there was none durst answer back;
She rapped my Lord of Leicester on the knuckles with her fan;
She tore the poets' verses up and swore they didn't scan;
She scowled on all her courtiers—"I am sick of words," said she—
When in came a Master Mariner just home from over sea.
He could turn no courtly phrases, but in words both few and plain
He spoke of golden ingots and of jewels seized from Spain;
And the Queen she ceased her frowning and the Queen she smiled instead,
"Faith! We like this seaman mightily—a sword, a sword!" she said,
Then tapped him on the shoulder as he knelt upon the floor,
Said, "Rise, Sir Master Mariner—and now go fetch some more."

Gloriana's with her fathers, and her captains bold are sped
Who sailed beyond the sunset, who bartered, fought and bled
From the Arctic to the Andes till they dipped beyond recall,
Hull down below the skyline on the last great quest of all;

But still down all the ages, as Gloriana bade,
Went forth the Master Mariners that used the seas for trade.
They went in valiant cockboats of queer and antique rig,
In flyboat, hoy and galley, in snow and pink and brig;
They plunged their high poop-lanthorns and gilt stern-galleries
Deep wallowing far to south'ard in the steep Agulhas seas;
They went in trim-built frigates and clippers swift and tall,
The pride of Clyde and Mersey and the glory of Blackwall.

They were but simple merchantmen and bred to ways of peace,
But they proved their fighting mettle on broad and narrow seas;
They fought with Turkish galleys and corsairs of Algiers,
And yelling painted savages and saucy privateers;
And when trade grew something scanty and freights were poor and few
Then peaceful British merchantmen went privateering too!

Amazed, in seas uncharted new continents they hailed,
Their leadsmen groped a fairway where never ship had sailed;
They blazed the trail for commerce to a thousand isles unknown;
They grappled with the westerlies and made their realms their own;
They thundered down the easting with the lee-rail deep in foam;
They drove the racing clippers with their tea rip-roaring home.

Gloriana's with her fathers, but the breed she knew remains,
While go the ships of Britain down all the long sea-lanes;
Though sail and spar have vanished like foam-flakes down the wind,
And gone the last Cape Horner as went the *Golden Hind*—
The men of mould unchanging, more scant of word than deed,
Staunch in their country's service as instant in her need,

Wish with the world-old wisdom of winds and skies and seas,
Schooled in the ancient ocean's eternal mysteries;
The men who late unflinching (have we ourselves not seen?)
Endured the lurking horrors of the mine and submarine;
In liner, tramp and tanker without reproach who bear
The name that Drake and Dampier bore of Master Mariner.

❖ ❖ ❖ ❖ ❖

From *Sailor's Delight*, edited by Cicely Fox Smith, published by Methuen & Co., London, UK, 1931, pp. 133-137.

The header graphic is a painting titled *Sir Francis Drake at Buckland Abbey, Devon, 1590* or later, artist unknown.

Racing Clippers

Racing Clippers: a Wool Fleet Memory

I've not made much o' my life, Lord knows; I'm a has-been through an' through,
An' meanin' 's as far as I've mostly got with the things as I've meant to do;
Of muckin' my chances and blowin' my pay I reckon I've done my share,
But—I was one of the *Clansman's* crowd when she raced the *Robin Adair.*

There was Dan an' Clancy an' Liverpool Bill—an' they were the pick of the lot—
An' a Glasgow lad as skenned like mad, but his name I've clean forgot;
A big buck nigger an' a cross-eyed Swede, an' a feller from County Clare—
Them was the chaps in the starboard watch when we raced the *Robin Adair.*

An' Dan was lost off the topsail yard o' the *Pole Star* years ago,
An' Clancy died with a knife in his side in a dive in Callao;
An' Bill he's married and livin' ashore, an' the rest of 'em's Lord knows where,
As I sailed with once in the *Clansman's* crowd hen we raced the *Robin Adair.*

Neck an' neck to the Snares we was, an' then it started to blow,
An' soon the *Clansman* was reelin' 'em off a steady seventeen or so,
An' the skipper grinned as he paced the poop, for that was the weather for her,
An' "Ah 'm thenkin' we've seen the last," says he, "O' their wonderful *Robin Adair!*"

But there come a time as we climbed the Trade, the day was just begun
When we sighted a ship hull down astern an' comin' along like fun,
An' the Old Man clapped his glass to his eye, an' you should ha' heard him swear,
For out o' the South with a bone in her mouth up romps the *Robin Adair.*

We started pilin' the canvas on, and it 'ad to stop there too;
It was breezin' up when we sighted 'er first, an' afore it was dark it *blew*!
I've seen some carryin' on in my time but I tell you he made me stare
Crackin' it on in the Biscay gales to beat the *Robin Adair.*

But we made the London river at last—it was twelve by St. George's clock,
I counted the chimes as we made her fast to the buoys in the London Dock—
An' we'd won the race from the width o' the world with the tail of a tide to spare—
That was the way of it, long ago, when we raced the *Robin Adair!*

The grand ol' ship's been gone to chips this fourteen year and more;
They sold 'er away to a Dago bunch, an' the blighters run 'er ashore;
An' somewheres round by the Ramirees an' south o' the Straits o' Le Maire,
With the fishes cruisin' among her ribs, lies drowned the *Robin Adair.*

There ain't no racin' clippers now, nor never will be again,
And most o' the ships are gone by now, the same as most o' the men,
An' nobody left but a few old shells like us in the world to care
For the great ol' skippers an' the great ol' ships an' the great ol' days they were,
And the way they had in the Wool Fleet once when we raced the *Robin Adair.*

❖   ❖   ❖   ❖   ❖

From *Sailor's Delight*, edited by Cicely Fox Smith, published by Methuen & Co., London, 1931, pp. 51-55. First published in *Punch* magazine, Volume 173, July 13, 1927, p. 36.

Also known as "Race of Long Ago" as sung through the years by a number of folk singers beginning with Bob Roberts (UK) in 1981 as recorded on his album *Breeze for a Bargeman* on Solent Records, and more recently by Dave Webber and Anni Fentiman also from the UK. Later adapted for singing by Bob Zentz (US), as recorded on *Closehauled on the Wind of a Dream*, 2007.

The graphic header titled *Racing Clippers* is drawn by Phil W. Smith and illustrated this poem in *Sailor's Delight*, facing p. 54.

Rain

"I don't 'old with grousin' about weather,
Nor never did, that's flat:
I jus' takes the good an' bad together
An' lets it go at that:
I jus' lumps it one sort with another,
An' then you can't complain:
But if there's one thing gets my goat more'n another,"
Said Bill, "it's rain."

"There's somethin' about the way the sea wets you
As a man can understand:
There's somethin' about the way them green uns gets you
As you can't 'elp feelin's grand;
There's somethin' about getting' wet with salt water—
Well, I guess I can't explain,
But it seems to me as a feller didn't oughter
Get wet with rain."

"It gets inside your soul-an'-body lashin's,
It trickles down your neck:
It ketches you with little slops an' splashin's,
It's hell on a teak deck:
I've 'ad many a wet shirt in a Cape 'Orner
When she's shipped it good an' green—
But standin' in the rain at a street corner,"
Said Bill, "That's *mean.*"

"I don't 'old with kickin' about weather,
It ain't no bloomin' good:
I jus' takes the rough an' smooth together,
Same's anybody would:
I guess I've sampled most sorts, late an' early,
O' fancy brands an' plain,
But the only kind as gets my goat fairly,"
Said Bill, "it's rain."

❖ ❖ ❖ ❖ ❖

From *Full Sail: More Sea Songs and Ballads*, edited by Cicely Fox Smith, published by Houghton Mifflin Co., New York, US, 1926, pp. 75-77.

S. S. *Teutonic* leaving Liverpool

Rathlin Head

We left the murk of Merseyside, we left the flaring town;
All smouldering red by Spanish Head the stormy sun went down;
We saw the lamp blink out and in the Mull o' Galloway,
And at dead of night to Rathlin light a long good-bye did say,

On a bitter cold night in the morning watch,
A little before the day!

Black deep of night without a star both sky and sea did fill;
So cautious crept we through the dark our engines near stood still;
All salt like tears on rope and rail the sea mist clinging grey . . .
And Rathlin Island close to port, Kintyre to starboard lay

On a bitter cold night in the morning watch,
A little before the day!

We heard across the blind black tide the lighthouse boom forlorn,
All night we heard a Glasgow barque blowing the old cow's horn;
And groping slow we passed her by a bare ship's length away—
"A near thing with the barque," was all I heard the Old Man say—

On a bitter cold night in the morning watch,
A little before the day!

All houseless stretch the unfenced fields that cold and green do roll
Where winds do herd the berg and floe which calve about the Pole;
Oh, peace be on the small green fields of a land that's far away,
And on the little farms therein where folks a-sleeping lay,

On a bitter cold night in the morning watch,
A little before the day!

And oh, good-bye the narrow seas and forelands loud wi' foam!
There's many a turning in the road that brings the sailor home;
Full speed once more our engines throbbed as faint the east grew grey,
I turned my face to Rathlin Head, a long good-bye to say,

On a bitter cold night in the morning watch,
A little before the day!

❖ ❖ ❖ ❖ ❖

From *Songs and Chanties: 1914-1916*, edited by Cicely Fox Smith, published by Elkin Mathews, London, UK, 1919, pp. 95-97.

The poet seems to be describing a young sailor experience outward bound from Liverpool on his first voyage. The seascape detail, correct in all particulars, is what separates Smith from the romantic land-based poets. This particular poem was characterized as "a great favorite" with her contemporary critics.

Compare with this poet's "The Long Road Home."

"Rathlin Light" is located on an island off Northern Ireland, while "Kintyre" is a pininsular in western Scotland, on opposite sides of the North Channel.

First adapted for singing by Mike Kennedy, as recorded on *A Dog's Life*, 2015

The header graphic titled *The White Star Liner "Teutonic" Leaving Liverpool on her Maiden Voyage*, August, 1889, is painted by William Lionel Wyllie, from *The Art of Nautical Illustration*, by Michael E. Leek, Quantum Books, London, UK, 2005, p. 143.

Recollection

Do you remember the ol' *Isle o' Skye*, Billy,
As we sailed in years ago;
The time we loaded nitrates home from Chile?
" . . . Ay, I do so."

An' how we was 'ove to in the South Atlantic
For two nights an' a day;
An' the long calm as druv the Ol' Man frantic,
An' the dustin' we 'ad in the Bay?

She was a tough ship, Bill, an' no bloomin' error,
Was that same ol' hooker,
An' for losin' 'ands from the braces a fair terror—
But a rare good-looker.

An' the skipper was the 'ardest nut I've clapped my eyes on,
'Cept the mate, an' 'e was worse;
An' the grub Slush served us out was more like p'ison,
Fit to make a bone idol curse.

There warn't none o' these 'ere curries an' calavances
Used to come our way then,
An' such-like stuff as Board o' Trade blokes fancies
Is good scoff for sailor-men.

And, Bill, it's rum, but I'd go back this minute,
I'd give the good grub an' the good pay
To be bitin' on 'ard tack with weevils in it
In that ol' ship this day . . .

To be layin' out on a yard when it's hailin' an' snowin'
Off o' the Straits o' Le Mair,
Fistin' a frozen course with big guns blowin'
So's you can't 'ear to swear . . .

Or runnin' the Eastin' down with both rails rollin'
An' burying theirselves in foam . . .
Or climbin' the Trade at a good fourteen on a bowline,
With 'er course set for 'ome . . .

Or haulin' topsail yards in the Biscay weather
When the waist's a smother o' snow—
Or settin' on the fore-hatch yarnin' together
In fine watches below . . .

Sharin' the good an' the bad, an' the rough an' the smooth of it
In the ol' *Isle o' Skye* . . .
That's where I'd be if I could, Bill, an' that's the plain truth of it . . .
" . . . And, by cripes, so would I!"

❖   ❖   ❖   ❖   ❖

From *Sailor's Delight*, edited by Cicely Fox Smith, published by Methuen & Co., London, UK, 1931, pp. 91-94; first published in the magazine *Holly Leaves*.

Just two old sailors waxing nostalgic about their favorite old ship while drinking together in a sailortown pub.

The Recruit

Bat and ball are there, lad,
And you not there to play . . .
"There's a nobler game playing
For English lads today."

And if your mates miss you
As they are like to do? . . .
"If my mates were men, lad,
They'd ha' 'listed too."

What will your dad say
That is old and grey? . . .
"Oh, he'd give life and all, lad,
To be young this day."

Was your mother not weeping
As you marched away? . . .
"Ay, weeping she kissed me
As a lad's mother may."

And what'll your girl say then
That used to walk with you? . . .
"Perhaps she'll walk lonely
For she loves me true."

"But parents both and sweetheart,
All have said the same—
'If you hadn't gone, lad,
I'd ha' died for shame!'"

❖   ❖   ❖   ❖   ❖

From *Sailor Town: Sea Songs and Ballads*, edited by Cicely Fox Smith, published by George H. Doran Co., New York, US, 1919, pp. 129-130. Earlier published in *The Naval Crown* by Elkin Mathews in 1915.

Composed during the first year of WWI to reinforce the mobilization efforts.

S.S. *Rotomahana*

The Red Duster (R. N. R. Demobilised)

Oh, some will save their Navy pay and take their ease ashore
And some will sit at an office desk and go to sea no more,
And some will follow the blooming plough and hear the skylark's song,
But oh! it's me for the old Red Duster, for that's where I belong.

I'll sign and sail in the Lord knows what—I'll go to Lord knows where—
From Hudson's Bay I'll beat my way to the Straits of old Le Mair;
From Pernambuck to Palembang, and I know I'll not go wrong
So long's I'm under the old Red Duster, for that's where I belong.

I'll take a turn in the Black Sea trade, a trick on the Gulf Ports run,
I'll feel the bite of the Cape Horn cold, and the burn o' the Perim sun;
I'll make the round of the blessed lot from the Gunfleet to Hong-Kong,
When I get back to the old Red Duster—the place where I belong.

I'll ship aboard of the first that comes, and any old thing'll do,
And I don't much care if she's sail or steam, or whether she's old or new,
There'll be never a tramp too foul for me, nor a spounter smell too strong,
So long's I'm under the old Red Duster—for that's where I belong!

For Navy chaps are Navy chaps—good luck to all and one!
And Navy ways are Navy ways—and now the fighting's done,
I'm sick at heart for a shellback's yarn my old-time pals among,
And oh! It's me for the old Red Duster, for that's where I belong!

❖ ❖ ❖ ❖ ❖

From *Ships and Folks*, edited by Cicely Fox Smith, published by Elkin Mathews, London, UK, 1920, p. 58-59.
First published in *Punch* magazine, Volume 157, August 6, 1919, p. 130.

In this poem, composed shortly after the end of WWI, the poet is focused on the naval seaman recently demobilized who is determined to return to his former life as a merchant seaman.

First adapted for singing by Bob Zentz (US), as recorded on his *Closehauled on the Wind of a Dream*, 2007.

The header graphic shows the "Red Duster" flying from the stern post of the old *S.S. Rotomahana* as painted by Charles Dickson Gregory.

Remember, Remember....

"Remember, remember the Fifth o' November' was what we used to say
When I was a nipper in Rother'ithe an' it come round Guy Fawkes Day,
With an 'andful o' squibs an' a cracker or two an' a gunny sack stuffed with 'ay."

"'Remember, remember the Fifth o' November,' bangin' an old tin can,
But I've 'ad bonfires enough, Lord knows, since them old days," said Dan;
"An' I'll remember the Fifth o' November while I'm a livin' man."

"I was in the old barque *Brig o' Doon*, Clyde-built in seventy-three;
A rare old flyer too she'd been—you'd know the ship maybe—
An' we loaded coal at Barry Dock an' sailed for the China Sea."

"An' first it started smellin' a bit an' then it got smokin',
Till we couldn't see the royal yards nor lift a stave for chokin';
An' it kep' on gainin' all the while as if Old Nick was stokin'."

"Ten mortal days we fought it, an' the tenth we 'ad to clear,
An' of all the blessed days there are in all the blessed year
The day we left was the Fifth o' November as true as I stand 'ere."

"The sun dropped sudden like a stone; the stars came out to stare
In their beastly cold off-handed way as if they didn't care
What made the sea one bloomin' flame an' the sky one bloomin' glare."

"All night we watched the old ship burn like fellers in a dream;
We saw the sparks fall far an' wide from every bubblin' seam;
Like smoke from a hundred burnin' ghauts we saw the black smoke stream."

"We saw 'er yards come crashin' down, 'er masts fall one by one;
All up 'er shrouds we watched the flames like lightnin' leap an' run,
Till the dawn come like a scarlet flower an' she was all but done."

"Nothin' left but a blackened hull of 'er as looked so fine
With decks like snow an' swellin' sails an' brasses all one shine,
An' all her flyin' kites aloft, rollin' down to the Line."

"Nothin' at all but the burnt-out shell of what she used to be;
An' me—I 'ad to turn my 'ead; I didn't want to see;
For she was a grand old ship, Lord knows, an' a good old ship to me—
An' I'll remember the Fifth o' November as long's I live," said he.

❖ ❖ ❖ ❖ ❖

From *Punch* magazine, Volume 169, November 4, 1925, p. 490.

"Dan" recalls the flaming demise of one of his favorite old ships, doomed by the spontaneous combustion of her cargo of wet coal.

Outward Bound in Square Rig

Resurrection

Down at Devine's Hotel—where night and day
The noises of the harbour find their way,
The endless stir of ships coming and going,
Rattle of cranes and winches, sirens blowing,
Racket of ships in drydock, bawled commands,
And scraps of sailor speech from many lands—
While through the breath-dimmed windows of the bar
You see the fluttering houseflags, crown and star,
Chequer and cross, chevron and prince's-feather,
And funnels, streaked and stained with grime and weather,
Buff, yellow, scarlet, black—with here and there
A big sea-going schooner, stark and bare,
In from the Nova Scotian coast with lumber . . .
And now and then one of the dwindling number
Of proud squareriggers lifts there, slim and tall,
The wonder of her spars above them all,
To stir the old shellback's heart, and loose his tongue
With old wild yarns of the years when he was young . . .

Down at Devine's Hotel the talk went round
Of all the ports from Hull to Puget Sound,
Of sprees in foreign harbours, women, wine,
Cargoes, and ships, and weather foul and fine,
And—in the jumbled talk of false and true—
My heart leapt up to greet a name I knew.

It was the *Britomart* they spoke of—she
That was most dear of all my ships to me—
She, first of many ships to which I gave

Strength, service, labour, love—a willing slave . . .
Macrae of Greenock built her—she was fine
Like all Macrae ships—fine and clean of line,
And tall—maybe a shade too heavy-sparred,
Skysails crossed, and a ninety-foot mainyard,
And yet with all that sail a boy could steer her . . .
There was none but the *Cutty Sark* that could come near her
Running the easting down . . . Her very name
In that drink-sodden place was like a flame
Lighting the heart with memories . . . ah, well
They knew that name in the Paragon Hotel,
When all the wool fleet crews blew in together
With many a shellback's yarn of wind and weather
From London to the Heads, and to and fro
Went speech of ships vanished long ago—
Mermerus, Sobraon, John o' Gaunt, Loch Sloy,
Salamis, Cimba, Torrens, Yallaroi—
Sounding and stately names of stately clippers—
And roaring reckless mates and hard-case skippers . . .
Great ships, great days . . . oh had I wealth and leisure,
Money to burn, and fortune's smiles full measure,
Comfort and ease and fame desired of men,
I would give all to live those years again!

"She run on the rocks all standing," some one said,
"Bass Point the place was, hard by Lizard Head . . .
Thick fog . . . that thick you couldn't see your hand . . .
The skipper'd thought himself well clear of land . . .
Lord knows what made him miss his reckoning so. . .
Mistook the Wolf for Saint Agnes . . . I dunno. . .
The ol' barky's back was broke, we couldn't save her . . .
A grand old ship . . . the old man cried to leave her . . ."

So, she is gone . . . oh, better, better so!
Whatever must come, this at least I know,
I shall not on some bleak and bitter day,
Walking the wharves, an old man bent and grey,
See her . . . befouled with spittle and with grime,
Battered with brutal cargo, stained with slime,
Paint-daubed and pitted, blistered and forlorn,
A thing for some to pity, most to scorn,
Like some lost Princess, lonely and unfriended,
Whom once a train of busy courtiers tended . . .
And knowing in that moment, all unwilling,
The measure of youth's dream and life's fulfilling,
Shed the slow difficult tears old eyes must know,
To see remembered beauty brought so low.

Better the winds and waves should work their will on her—
Better the rocks and reefs should feast their fill on her!

For still, while any lives that loved as I
That beauty which was hers in years gone by,
Still shall she sail at will, a gracious ghost,
Each well-known seaway, each familiar coast,
Still in the Trades the drowsy lookout hail
On the sea's rim her dawn-flushed spire of sail,
Still in the crowded harbours of the world
To staves unheard her viewless sails be furled,
Still in the high South latitudes shall she
Measure anew her might with wind and sea,
Fight her fight over with the seas that roll
Green and tremendous from the Antarctic Pole,
Still—like a mist through morning mists agleam—
Signal her pilot for the port of dream . . .
What's past can never perish—what has been
Lives, and lives on, through all the years between:
The years shall bring her beauty: lost youth lend her
His vanished gleam, lost dreams their morning splendour.
Unchanged, unchanging, in a world of change,
She shall endure, through all things else grow strange,
And, though her bones to rust and dust be gone,
Find in men's dreams her resurrection.

❖   ❖   ❖   ❖   ❖

From *Sea Songs and Ballads 1917-22*, edited by Cicely Fox Smith, published by Houghton Mifflin Co., New York, US, 1924, pp. 13-16.

This poem may well represent the poet's ultimate statement on the Great Age of Sail—the ships, the men, the work, and the dreams.

It was a rare ship that was salvaged and rebuilt after being abandoned but the *James Craig* of Australia is an inspiring exception.

The header graphic is an illustration titled *Outward Bound in Square Rig* drawn by David W. Bone from his book *Landfall at Sunset*, Gerald Duckworth & Co., London, UK, 1956, facing p. 15.

Retrospect

"Ain't it rum?" said Dan one day,
Yarning while he worked away
At his model, all but done,
Of the clipper ship *Keemun*—
Fully rigged and all to scale,
Shroud and backstay, spar and sail,
Tiny blocks and tackles fine,
Tacks and sheets of Hambro line,
Dainty skysails fairy-small,
Stunsails, Jamie Green and all—
"Ain't it sort o' rum," said he,
"Human natur, seems to be—
How a feller never knows
What he likes best—till it goes?"

"Take the ports I used to know—
How I cussed 'em years ago,
Cussed the insecks an' the stinks,
Cussed the lingo an' the drinks,
Cussed the blacks for bein' black,
Cussed the lot to—Hull an' back!
Never thought how some fine day
I'd sit yarnin' here an' say
What I'd give to see again
Just them things I hated then—
Talk and tell how nothin' else
Smells just like them Eastern smells—
Finish up with 'Seems to me
Ports ain't what they used to be!'"

"Take this ship, the old *Keemun*,
Names I've called 'er, many a one;
Called 'er cranky, stubborn, slow,
Bad aloft an' worse below,
Worst darned ship I'd set my eyes on,
Pikin' pay and grub like pison,—
Never thought I'd come to spend
All the time I've spent on end
('Alf a year's dog-watches good)
Carvin' of 'er out o' wood—
Fight a feller in a pub
Cos he called 'er 'blinkin' tub' . . .
Funny, ain't it? . . . seems to me
Ships ain't what they used to be."

"Chaps I've sailed with—thought per'aps
Pretty much like other chaps,
Maybe liked an' maybe not,
Drunk with, scrapped with, half forgot—
Never thought I'd come to say,
Thinkin' of 'em far away,
'Them was fellers, them was men,
Shipmates they was shipmates then,
Lookin' back, why, seems to me
Chaps ain't what they used to be.'"

"That's the way I've always found
Things turn out, the whole world round;
If it's gals or ships or beer
Don't much matter, ain't it queer
(Human nature, I suppose)
How a feller never knows
What he likes best—till it goes?"

From *Sea Songs and Ballads 1917-1922*, edited by Cicely Fox Smith, published by Houghton Miflin Co., New York, US, 1924, pp. 60-62. It was earlier published in *Rovings*, 1921, page 41 in the same form. First published in *Punch* magazine, Volume 160, March 30, 1921, p. 244.

Here "Dan" is waxing philosophical on the fundamentals of human nature. This poem is just another example of how Smith viewed her present through the lens of an old sailor's eyes. The Great Age of Sail was fast disappearing around her.

Mahogany Bar

The Return

"When did your ship dock, Jim Dale,
That you come so late this night?
Long since I heard the clocks strike three,
And it will soon be light."

"How did you get in, Jim Dale,
With the doors all locked and barred?
I never heard you knock nor call
Nor the dog bark in the yard."

"They told me you were drowned and dead
In the South Seas cold and far,
At Paddy's Goose the tale was told,
And the Old Mahogany Bar."

"Why do you look at me so sad,
So strange and shake your head?
They told me you were dead and drowned,
I cried my poor eyes red . . .

But it's hard for girls to walk alone
For the sake of them that's dead."

He pointed to her faithless name
On his bare breast tattooed,
And ever the dripping wet in streams
Ran from him where he stood.
One moment, and she saw him clear—
The next, and he was gone,
Like a fitful moonbeam through the room
Passing—but no moon shone.

She heard no lifting of the latch,
No footstep on the stair,
No board that creaked in the still house
To show he had been there.

And up the street and down the street
No man might she behold,
But the clocked policeman on the beat
Striking his chest for cold.

She saw the rain come slanting down,
The sheds, the high dock wall,
The masts and funnels of the ships,
The derricks gaunt and tall.

And through the darkness and the rain
The light came creeping grey,
And all along the dreary street
The gas-lamps paled to day.

❖ ❖ ❖ ❖ ❖

From *Sea Songs and Ballads 1917-22*, edited by Cicely Fox Smith, published by Houghton Mifflin Co., New York, US, 1924, pp. 29-31. Earlier published in the *London Mercury*, unknown date, p. 234.

In traditional folk songs there is a set of songs described as "night-visiting songs" where a deceased lover visits his love as a ghost in the dark of night only to disappear with the coming dawn.

"Paddy's Goose" and the "Old Mahogany Bar" were well known hangouts for sailors in the 19th century in London's sailortown along the Radcliff Highway. They were later taken over by reformers and made into sailor's temperance halls and rooming houses. The Old Mahogany Bar still survives as a Wilton's Music Hall in London today, one of the few survivors of London's "sailortown."

The header graphic is an illustration of the old *Mahogany Bar* as drawn by Phil W. Smith, 1924, from *Ship Alley*, facing p. 14.

Canada!

The Return of the Prodigal

I rode into Pincher River on an August afternoon—
The pinto's hoofs on the prairie drumming a drowsy tune—
By the shacks and the Chinks' truck-gardens to the Athabasca Saloon.

And a bunch of the boys was standing around by the old Scotch Store,
Standing and spitting and swearing by old Macallister's door,
And the name on their lips was Britain—the word that they spoke was "War"!

War! . . . Do you think I waited to talk about wrong or right
When I knew my own country was up to the neck in a fight?
I said "So long"—and I beat it—"I'm hitting the trail to-night!"

I wasn't long at my packing; I hadn't much time to dress;
And the cash I had at disposal was a ten-spot (more or less),
So I didn't wait for my ticket—I booked by the hoboes' express.

I rode the bumpers at night-time; I beat the ties in the day,
Stealing a ride and humming a ride all of the blooming way,
And . . . I left the First Contingent drilling at Valcartier!

I didn't cross in a liner (I hadn't my passage by me!)
I spotted a Liverpool cargo tramp, smelly and greasy and grimy,
And she wanted hands for the voyage, and the old man guessed he'd try me.

She kicked like a ballet dancer or a range-bred bronco mare;
She rolled till her engines rattled—she wallowed, but what did I care?
It was, "Go it, my bucking beauty, if only you'll take me there!"

Then . . . came an autumn morning, grey-blue, windy and clear,
And the fields—the little white houses—green, and peaceful, and dear—
And the heart inside o' me saying: "Take me, Mother, I'm here!"

"Here, for I thought you'd want me; I've brought you all that I own,
A lean long lump of a carcass that's mostly muscle and bone—
Six foot two in my stockings—weigh-in at fourteen stone!"

"Here, and I hope you'll have me—take me for what I'm worth,
A chap that's a bit of a waster, come from the ends of the earth,
To fight with the best that's in him for the dear old land of his birth!"

❖   ❖   ❖   ❖   ❖

From *Sailor Town: Sea Songs and Ballads*, edited by Cicely Fox Smith, published by George H. Doran Co., New York, US, 1919, pp. 100-102. First published in *Punch* magazine, Volume 147, December 30, 1914, p. 538, and subsequently in *The Naval Crown* by Elkin Mathews in 1915.

Composed in the first year of WWI as a tribute to the many young men who made their way back to England from the ends of the earth to help defend their country in the War.

Significantly this poem was the poet's first contribution to *Punch* after her own return from Canada, the first of more than 150 contributions by Smith published from 1914 to 1953 in this magazine.

The header graphic is a cartoon titled *Canada!—Ypres: April 22-24, 1915* as drawn by Barnard Partridge, from *Punch* magazine, May 5, 1915, p. 351.

James Craig Abandoned in Recherche Bay

Rhyme of the *Captive Maid*

A ship there sailed in the nitrate trade,
And she went by the name of the *Captive Maid* . . .
Built on the Clyde in sixty-nine
For Reid, Macallister's "Maiden" Line:
There was many a shellback used to praise
Her turn o' speed in the old-time days,
But the best of her years were over and done,
And the eighteen-nineties were all but run,
When they hung her up in a fog at last

On a half-tide reef both hard and fast,
Off Punta Arenas, outward bound
To load nitrates for Puget Sound.
And they took to the boats and they rowed away,
And there for a score of years she lay,
Safe and snug in a natural dock
With sandy bottom and walls of rock,
Where the biggest sea that ever did roll,
And the fiercest gale from the frozen Pole,
And the bergs and the breakers passed her by—
Passed her and left her and let her lie . . .

Nothing to hear but the wild winds crying,
Nothing to see but the grey gulls flying:
A smudge of smoke on a skyline far,
Sunset, and dawn, and a lonely star:
Frost and fog and the drifting floe,
The beating rain and the blinding snow:
An empty sea and an empty sky,
And a long, long dream of the years gone by!

A score of years—while she lay forgotten,
And her ropes decayed, and her gear grew rotten,
And her planking gaped to the sun and rain;
And her paint was tarnished with many a stain,
And the green mould caked on her idle wheel,
And the rust bit deep in her slumbering keel,
And the screaming seabirds, night and day,
Fouled with their droppings both spar and stay:
A score of years . . . while the world went round,
And thrones were shaken, and kings discrowned:
A score of years, till, every one knows,
The ships they sank and the freights they rose,
And all of a sudden somebody said:
"What about salving the *Captive Maid?*"

They came with hawsers and tugs and men,
And towed her back to the world again:
Back to the world once more—but oh,
Not the old world that she used to know!
Where were her men that served her well,
Kept her watches and struck her bell,
Learned and humoured her every whim,
Conned and steered her and watched her trim:
Scoured and painted her and kept her fine,
Her decks agleam and her yards ashine?
What of her sisters swift and tall?
Time and the sea had claimed them all—
Seas and years and the pirate Hun

Had made an end of them every one . . .
Strange new ensigns on every breeze—
Strange new craft upon all the seas—
A ghost returned to the world of men,
Does she wish herself back on her reef again? . . .

Nothing to hear but the wild winds crying,
Nothing to see but the grey gulls flying,
A smudge of smoke on a skyline far,
Sunset, and dawn, and a lonely star,
Frost and fog and the drifting floe,
The beating rain and the blinding snow,
An empty sea and an empty sky,
And a long, long dream of the days gone by!

❖   ❖   ❖   ❖   ❖

From *Sea Songs and Ballads 1917-22*, edited by Cicely Fox Smith, published by Houghton Mifflin Co., New York, US, 1924, pp. 79-81.

This poem seems less gung-ho about resurrecting old sailing ships for the war efforts than in the patriotic poems that the poet wrote at the beginning of WWI. Perhaps, she was war weary by this time and harkened for some peace herself and these old ships.

The header graphic is a photograph taken in about 1971 of the iron barque *James Craig* abandoned in Recherche Bay, Tasmania, in 1932, photographer unknown. Happily the *Craig* was towed to Sydney, Australia, in 1973 and was fully restored to sailing condition by 2000.

The *James Craig* sailing after a complete restoration, 2000, photographer unknown, from "The *James Craig* Story," by Jeff Toghill, *Maritime Life and Tradition*, Brooklin, Maine, US, #20, 2003, p. 63.

Ship Sunk by German Merchant Raider *Seeadler* in WWI

The Rhyme of the *Inisfail*

Limehouse way, the other day, as I did chance to be,
I met with a hairy sailorman was shipmates once with me,
With his short black pipe between his teeth, and his tarry dungaree.

I gripped him by the elbow then, he swung upon his heel
(And oh, that deep-sea speech to hear, that rope-hard hand to feel,
It brought once more the younger years, the look-out and the wheel,

The way of a ship in the great waters where the flying fishes are,
A creaking block, and the reef-points tapping, and a high Southern star,
And the smell of nitrates, and new lumber, and paint and Stockholm tar.)

And "What's the news now up and down?" and "Where's your ship?" I cried,
"Greenland Basin or Martin's Wharf?"—He turned and spat aside—
"She's dockin' far from here this night, on a late, long tide."

"An' I came home in steam," he said, "I never thought to do—
In a sooty, smeary cargo-tank, with a greasy steamboat crew;
An' if you'd know the why of it, I'll tell ye plain an' true."

"I sailed in June from Carrizal—no call to tell the tale
Of every bit of blow we had an' every Cape 'Orn gale—
In an old-time Clyde-built packet that was called the *Inisfail*."

"One of them ships with painted ports that Gow of Glasgow had
In the great old days of the wool-clippers when I was but a lad—
An' she was one o' the best o' them; their worst was never bad."

"All full-rigged ships in them days too, I've heard old shellbacks say;
The *Inisfail* was near the last, an' she had had her day,
When they cut the half of her sail-plan down, an' her mizzen-yards away."

"Why, well I knew the *Inisfail*," I said, "and well should know;
She lay with us in Taltal once, and once in Callao,
The time I sailed in the nitrate trade, a sight o' years ago."

"A woman with a harp she had by way of figurehead,
And shamrocks all about her dress like golden stars were spread,
A bonnier thing was never carved."—"That's her," Mike sighed and said.

"Ah, well, she's gone, the *Inisfail*; her split an' broken hull,
It doesn't lie by the Seven Stones, the Brisons or the Gull,
Where many a bumpin' cargo lies, an' many a dead man's skull."

"But fifty miles from Fastnet Light, in the wide and open sea,
Where the seagulls meet the homeward bound, close-hauled or runnin' free,
It's there I left the *Inisfail* in the place where she left me."

"A shadow like a shark, I saw the damned torpedo glide;
Like a sunken reef it jarred her ribs—it ripped her loaded side
As the killer rips the mother whale in the red Behring tide."

"We did not need the soundin' rod to try the depth below,
By the feel of her beneath our feet we could not help but know
She'd never fetch a port no more, an' 'twas time for us to go."

"So we cast the long-boat's lashin's loose, we hove her over the rail
(An' we thanked our luck as we tumbled in, it wasn't blowin' a gale),
An' we stood off an' on, to see the last o' the *Inisfail*."

"We had not got the sail off her—with all her cloths agleam
She looked as lovely as a bird, as peaceful as a dream,
As she lay with her mainyard aback an' liftin' on the stream."

"We could see the smoke from the galley-fire in little puffs that blew,
An' the brasswork winkin' in the sun, an' the gilt vane flashin' too,
An' the shark's tail at her bowsprit end, an' a score o' things we knew."

"We sat an' watched for the end o' her—we hardly spoke or stirred;
'She'll maybe float,' said someone then—he scarce had shaped the word
When she shivered an' lurched like a melting berg an' sank like a wounded bird."

"An' no one'll ever be cold or hungry, battered or sore,
Or do a job o' work aboard o' her any more,
Or lift a stave at the halliards the same as they used of yore."

"She won't know the wind an' the stars no more, the sun an' the blue,
Never the kiss of the Trade again—never the sound o' the crew
An' they chanteyin' up the anchor in one o' them ports she knew."

"No one'll sleep in the black shadows when the moon's yellow as corn
Or sing songs in the dog-watches—or wish he was never born,
Fistin' them big courses of hers, down there oft the pitch o' the Horn."

"Nor they won't sell her or scrap her now, when workin' days are done;
She won't rust in the breaker's yard, nor lie and rot in the sun
Like an old broken sailorman whose yarn is nearly spun."

"For she lies deep, the *Inisfail*—ay, deep she lies an' drowned,
Farther 'n ever a wave'll stir, deeper 'n a lead can sound,
Fifty miles from Fastnet Light, an' homeward bound."

❖ ❖ ❖ ❖ ❖

From *Songs and Chanties: 1914-1916*, edited by Cicely Fox Smith, published by Elkin Mathews, London, UK, 1919, pp. 177-182. First published in *Punch* magazine, Volume 151, September 27, 1916, p. 216.

This is a WWI poem where an aging sailing ship is torpedoed by a German U-boat when she has almost made home port.

The header graphic is a photograph of a similar ship sunk in WWI by the German merchant raider square-rigged sailing ship the *Seeadler*, photographed by Count Felix von Luckner who was captain of the raider.

Carelmapu in Distress

The Rhyme of the *Rio Grande*

In Salthouse Dock as I did pass one day not long ago,
I chanced to meet a sailorman that once I used to know;
His eye it had a roving gleam, his step was light and gay,
He looked like one just in from sea to blow a nine month's pay.
And as he passed athwart my hawse he hailed me long and loud:
"Oh, find me a full saloon where I may stand the crowd:
I'm out to rouse the town this night, as any man may be
That's just come off a salvage job, my lad, the same as me"—
"Bringin' home the *Rio Grande*, her as used to be
Crack o' Moore, Mackellar's line, back in ninety-three,—
First of all the 'Frisco fleet home in ninety-eight,
Ninety days to Carrick Roads from the Golden Gate;
Thirty shellbacks used to have all their work to do
Haulin' them big yards of hers, heavin' of her to
Down off Dago Ramierez, where the big winds blow,
Bringin' home the *Rio Grande* twenty years ago!"

"We picked her up one morning, homeward bound from Portland, Maine,
In a nine-knot gruntin' cargo tramp by name the *Crown o' Spain*.
The day was breakin' cold and dark and dirty as could be,
It was blowing up for weather, as we couldn't help but see.
Her crew was gone the Lord knows where—and Fritz had left her too,
He must have took a scare and left afore his job was through;
We tried to pass a hawser, but it wasn't no kind o' good,
So we put a salvage crew aboard, to save her if we could"—

"Bringin' home the *Rio Grande* and her freight as well,
Half-a-score o' steamboatmen cursin' her like hell,
Floundering in the flooded waist, scramblin' for a hold,
Hanging on with teeth and toes, dippin' when she rolled;
Ginger Dan the donkeyman, Joe the doctor's mate,
Loafers off the water-front, greasers from the Plate,
That's the sort of crowd we had to reef and steer and haul—
Bringin' home the *Rio Grande*, ship and freight and all."

"Our mate had served his time in sail, he was a bully boy,
It'd wake a corpse to hear him hail 'Foretopsail yard ahoy!'
He knew the way of squaresail and he knew the way to swear,
He'd got the habit of it here and there and everywhere;
He'd some samples from the Baltic and some more from Mozambique,
Chinook and Chink and double-Dutch and Mexican and Greek,
He'd a word or two in Russian, but he learned the best he'd got
Off a pious preachin' skipper—and he had to use the lot"—

"Bringin' home the *Rio Grande* in a seven days' gale,
Seven days and seven nights, the same as Jonah's whale,
Standard compass gone to bits, steering all adrift,
Courses split and mainmast sprung, cargo on the shift,
Not a chart in all the ship left to steer her by—
Not a glimpse of star or sun in the bloomin' sky . . .
Two men at the jury wheel, kickin' like a mule,
Bringin' home the *Rio Grande* up to Liverpool."

"The seventh day off South Stack Light the sun began to shine;
Up came an Admiralty tug and offered us a line;
The mate he took the megaphone and leaned across the rail,
And this, or something like it, was the answer to their hail:
He'd take it very kindly if they'd tell us where we were,
And he hoped the war was going well, he'd got a brother there,
And he thought about their offer, and he thanked them kindly too,
But since we'd brought her up so far, by God, we'd see it through"—

"Bringin' home the *Rio Grande*—and we done it too!
Courses split and mainmast sprung—half-a-watch for crew—
"Bringin' home the *Rio Grande* and her freight as well—
Half-a-score of steamboatmen cursing her like hell—

Her as led the grain fleet home back in ninety-eight—
Ninety days to Carrick Roads from the Golden Gate—
Half-a-score of steamboatmen to reef and steer and haul—
Bringin' home the *Rio Grande*—ship and freight and all!"

❖   ❖   ❖   ❖   ❖

From *Ships and Folks*, edited by Cicely Fox Smith, published by Elkin Mathews, London, UK, 1920, pp. 24-27. First published in *Punch* magazine, Volume 156, January 15, 1919, p. 34.

A WWI poem where a ship, apparently attacked and abandoned by a German merchant raider or submarine, is successfully salvaged.

The header graphic is a photograph of the square-rigged ship *Carelmapu* in distress off Vancouver Island dragging her anchor in a gale, by W. N. Kelly, 1915, from *Light on the Water*, p. 30.

The *Moshulu*, off Port Lincoln, Australia

Rio Grande

There lies a ship at her moorings out there on yonder stream;
Her lines upon the water are lovely like a dream,
And like a dream she'll slip away with the first dawning gleam,
For she's bound for Rio Grande with the morning tide.
Yes, she's bound for Rio Grande, and it's there that I would be,
And every rope aboard of her is singing to be free;
Oh, good-bye to your sweetheart dear and good-bye to your bride
If you're bound for Rio Grande with the morning tide!

I heard the seagulls piping round, and all seemed to say
Was, "Come you out, young sailorman, it's time to come away.
Oh, heave your donkey's breakfast in, there isn't time to stay
If you're bound for Rio Grande with the morning tide—
If you're bound for Rio Grande away, and oceans two or three,
And ports a plenty up and down for likely lads to see,

All across the seas, Johnnie, round the world so wide,
Going out to Rio Grande with the morning tide."

The lights in Paddy Ryan's bar they're shining on the shore;
Bid your friends good-be, Johnnie, pay you now your score,
For you don't want the sight or smell o' the harbour any more,
When you're bound for Rio Grande with the morning tide.
And "Away My Rolling River"—for the sun's put out the stars
A-tangle in her royal yards, and the frost is on her spars;
Oh, the deep sea hunger's hold of her, and not to be denied,
Going out to Rio Grande with the morning tide!

❖ ❖ ❖ ❖ ❖

From *Songs and Chanties 1914-1916*, edited by Cicely Fox Smith, published by Elkin Mathews, London, UK, 1919, pp. 86-88. Previously published in *Sailor Town*, 1914.

Another fine poem about the need to follow the sea. First adapted for singing by Charles Ipcar, as recorded on *More Uncommon Sailor Songs*, 2005.

The graphic header is a photograph by Eric Newby of a ship he sailed on called the *Moshulu*, off Port Lincoln, Australia, in January of 1939, from his book *Learning the Ropes*, published by Random House, New York, US, 1999, p. 99.

Roll Along Home!

I thought I heard the old man say—
"Aye, aye, roll along home!—
Bound home for old England we're sailing to-day—
Heave up the anchor and roll along home!
The pilot's aboard and the capstan is manned,
Blue Peter's a-waving farewell to the land,
For after long waiting our orders have come
To heave up the anchor and roll along home—
Roll—roll along home!"

The sails they are bent and the cargo is stowed—
Aye, aye, roll along home!—
And far will her way be and lonely her road—
Shake out the topsails and roll along home!
Yes, long is the road through the storm and the shine
That brings me back home to you, true love of mine;
No longer I'll wander, no further I'll roam,
But shake out my topsails and roll along home—
Roll—roll along home!"

❖ ❖ ❖ ❖ ❖

From *Ships and Folks*, edited by Cicely Fox Smith, published by Elkin Mathews, London, UK, 1920, p. 53.

From a set of poems entitled "The Way of the Ship" set to music by Easthope Martin, and published as *Five Chantey Songs*, Enoch & Sons, 1920.

Here the poet is composing some traditional style shanty verses herself.

Rolling Home

Oh, there's places up and down that are queer and quaint and pretty;
Sydney's a pleasant port, Frisco's a giddy city;
But the day's bound to come when your heart begins to weary
Of big cities and small, gay cities and dreary,
For an island in the sea, and the kind rain falling,
When you break your anchor out, with your heart in the hauling.

Heave, and wake the dead! . . . Oh, if folks would do it for me,
It's I would carry on though gales blew ne'er so stormy;
Oh, if I was a Finn I would whistle up fair weather
All the way from here to England . . . oh, heave together!

Good, ah, good it is when you're young, and all's before ye,
For to leave the things you know and the old land that bore ye,
For to know many lands and to see many places;
But the warm English hearts and the kind English faces,
But a fireside you know and a red fire there burning,
Good they are to think about when you're homeward turning.

Heave and come she must . . . for to-morrow's got to find us
Laying homeward all we know, kicking up the dust behind us;
We've a long road to travel, and the more that we linger,
Why, the longer till we're home . . . so heave and bring her!

Oh, we may be half a year or we may be rather longer,
And if but the wind blow fair, then I wish it may blow stronger;
Just a few thousand miles, or perhaps a little further,
Just a few thousand miles till at long last we berth her,
Till by harbour lights we know at the last we steer in . . .
And if Christmas Day is past, why we'll bring the New Year in!

Heave and break her out! . . . We've a little way to cover,
But we'll go all the way gay and lightly like a lover
With a posy for his lass and a ring for her finger . . .
Heave and break her out . . . heave all, and bring her!

❖ ❖ ❖ ❖ ❖

From *Songs and Chanties: 1914-1916*, edited by Cicely Fox Smith, published by Elkin Mathews, London, UK, 1919, pp. 89-91.

Here the sailor is homeward bound after many years away. Seems similar in sentiment to "The Long Road Home." The superstition that Finnish sailors had the power to control winds appears to have been a long held tradition among deep-water sailors.

Rolling Stone

I ain't a-goin' to sign in this ship, sonny,
Nor sail in 'er no more:
I'm goin' to mosey round an' spend my money
An' 'ave my run ashore,
An' then look for a ship that's bound somewheres
As I've never been afore.

It ain't as I've got anythink agin 'er
Of any sort or kind,
It ain't as I 'aven't 'ad as good times in 'er
As any I can mind;
It ain't as I 'aven't 'ad as good shipmates
As a man 'ud wish to find.

It's just that I'm fed up with things an' places,
An' all the blessed show,
An' what I want 's a fresh lot o' chaps' faces
An' a ship as I don't know,
An' different grub an' a strange berth to lie in
An' somewheres else to go.

I've always been that way since I was a nipper
An' 'ooked it off to sea,
Or I daresay by now I'd 'a' been a skipper,
Or a mate at least maybe,
But if I could I wouldn't do no different
(Which I couldn't, bein' me!)

An' I ain't a-goin' to sign again, sonny,
In this old ship no more:
I'm goin' to mosey round an' spend my money
An' 'ave my run ashore,
An' then I'll look for a ship that's goin' somewheres
As I 'aven't been afore . . .

❖ ❖ ❖ ❖ ❖

From *Full Sail: More Sea Songs and Ballads*, edited by Cicely Fox Smith, published by Houghton Mifflin Co., Boston, US, 1926, pp. 35-37.

Romance

Morn, and a world of wonder! Oh, the time
Of winds like trumpet calls, and seas that gleam,
And sounding sunlit roads that wind and climb
Far over hills of dream,—

Travelled by knight and pedlar, prince and priest,
Past many an echoing port and ringing bridge,

To some black fortress like a couchant beast
Crouched on a mountain ridge,—

Fords perilous, and haunted reach and pool,
Far-shining spires under the blaze of noon,
And twilight shrines of visions wonderful,
Dusk and an angry moon.

Glimmer of ambush—dungeons, strange escapes,
Ships swinging on the swell of darkling tides,
And faerie forests full of eerie shapes,
Long, flickering, grass-grown rides.

Dark crooked streets with lights like peering eyes,
Plotters in half-lit halls of palaces,
Orchards and gardens full of lurking spies,
And whispering passages.

Travail and bondage, battle-flags unfurled,
Earth at the prime, and God earth's wrongs above,
Honour and hope, youth and the beckoning world,
Peril and war and love!

❖ ❖ ❖ ❖ ❖

From *Small Craft: Sailor Ballads and Shanties*, edited by Cicely Fox Smith, published by George H. Doran Co., New York, US, 1919, pp. 145-146. First published in the *New-York Daily Tribune*, New York, UK., March 11, 1906, p. 6.

The first of a set of poems called "Romance."

Ronceval

O woe's me, ye people,
And woe, brave warriors all,
For the flower of all princes
Dead on Ronceval.

There lie many stark fighters
That with brave Roland rode—
Rinaldo of the White Thorn,
Ogier and Galdebode.

And Roland, ah, Roland,
That was first of them all,
Lieth among his captains
On red Ronceval.

Queens weep for Roland,
Kings go heavily:
There was none in Christendom
Better loved than he.

Prince of all courtesy,
Very true and kind:
Tears are his dwellings
Of Kaiser and of hind.

For herdsmen have hearkened,
Keeping sheep on the hill,
To a sound like the wind crying—
Yet all the winds are still.

It is the horn of Roland
Nevermore shall call—
That mourneth for slain armies
On red Ronceval.

❖ ❖ ❖ ❖ ❖

From *Small Craft: Sailor Ballads and Chantys*, edited by Cicely Fox Smith, published by George H. Doran Co., New York, US, 1919, pp. 149-150; published earlier in the *New-York Daily Tribune*, February 14, 1906., p. 5.

The third poem in a set called "Romance."

The Loading Chute at Rosario

Rosario

Early in the morning as the moon was in the sky,
Early in the morning I kissed my girl goodbye,
For kissing-time is over and it's time and time to go
When you've a long road to travel to Rosario!

Oh wake her—oh shake her!—and the Peter's flying free,
And the pilot's come aboard her, and she's hungry for the sea.
Kissing time is over; And it's time and time to go
And "a long road to travel to Rosario!"

Summer'll soon be over, the leaves'll fade and die,
And white on every furrow the winter snows'll lie,
But we're bound for the long furrows where never lies the snow,
And we've a long road to travel to Rosario!

Oh wake her—oh shake her!—and the cable surges in
To the roar of a shanty chorus as we make the handspikes spin . . .
Oh she's bound for the long furrows where never lies the snow —
And "a long road to travel to Rosario!"

And now she smells the deep sea, and now she's gathering way,
And now she meets the rollers in a white smother of spray—
Sou'west an' a half west, and steady as we go . . .
And "a long road to travel to Rosario!"

Oh, wake her—oh, shake her!—and it's good-bye to the shore,
With the north wind in her topsails, and the whole wide world before . . .
Sou'west an' a half west, and steady as you go—
And a long road to travel to Rosario!"

From *Ships and Folks*, edited by Cicely Fox Smith, published by Elkin Mathews, London, UK, 1920, pp. 50-51.

"Oh, wake her—oh, shake her!" are lines from the traditional shanty "Johnny Go Down to Hilo." There are similarities between this poem and "The Long Road Home," especially so in the third verse. A version of this poem was sent by the poet to her friend the American sea music collector Joanna Colcord.

This poem in abridged form, lacking the last verse, was set to music by Easthope Martin and published for school children in *Five Chantey Songs*, Enoch & Sons, London, UK, 1920.

Re-adapted for singing by John and Joy Rennie of Dogwatch, as recorded on *England Expects*, 2004. An alternative setting was subsequently done by Charles Ipcar as recorded on *More Uncommon Sailor Songs*, 2005.

The header graphic is a photograph of the loading wharf at Rosario, Argentina, on the Parana River as photographed by Capt. Lincoln Colcord (Joanna Colcord's father) in 1894: "The cargo, often bales of wool or hides, was slid down these long chutes to be loaded into the ship's hold." from *Letters from Sea*, edited by Parker Bishop Albee, Jr., published by Tilbury House, Gardiner, Maine, 1999, p. 30.

WWI Soldiers on the March

The Route March

We've got our foreign service boots—we've 'ad 'em 'alf a day;
If it wasn't for the Adjutant I'd sling the brutes away;
If I could 'ave my old ones back I'd give a fortnight's pay
An' chuck 'em in the pair I got this mornin'!

We've marched a 'undred miles to-day—we've 'undreds more to go,
An' if you don't believe me, why, I'll tell you 'ow I know,
I've measured out the distance by the blister on my toe,
For I've got my foreign service boots this mornin'.

We've got our foreign service boots—I wish that I was dead;
I wish I'd got the Colonel's 'orse an' 'im my feet instead;
I wish I was a nacrobat, I'd walk upon my 'ead,
For I got my foreign service boots this mornin'.

We're 'oppin' an' we're 'obblin' to a cock-eyed ragtime tune,
Not a soul as isn't limpin' in the bloomin' 'ole balloon;
But buck you up, my com-e-rades, we're off to Flanders soon,
For we got my foreign service boots this mornin'!

❖ ❖ ❖ ❖ ❖

From *Songs and Chanties 1914-1916*, edited by Cicely Fox Smith, published by Elkin Mathews, London, UK, 1919, pp. 201-202. Earlier published in *Fighting Men* by Elkin Mathews in 1916. First published in *Punch* magazine, Volume 150, June 14, 1916, p. 398.

The header graphic is a photograph from "*What a Lovely War!*", p. 123; photograph is in the private collection of Roy Palmer, photographer unknown.

Royal Naval Reserve

White Star, Cunard,
Great ships and small—
Gallant British merchantmen,
Here's to one and all!
Union Castle, Orient,
From Shanghai to Dover,
Fighting British merchantmen
All the world over!

What is the house-flag? . . .
The same that's yours and mine—
In fair weather and foul weather
The flag of the British Line!

What trade is this ye sail in? . . .
An ancient trade, and bold;
Drake's trade, Blake's trade
It was in days of old—

To mar the might of tyrants,
To keep the highway free,
And hold against all comers
The lordship of the sea!

Whence comes your right of service? . . .
By right of breed and birth!

And where had ye your schooling? . . .
In all the seas of earth;
'Tween the Lizard and Cape Leeuwin,
From Fastnet to the Horn,
We learnt the stern old lessons
None learn but seamen born.

What cargo do ye carry? . . .
Full freight of death and fame,
And the men of the White Ensign
Of the Red shall think no shame!
When the day is darkened with battle,
And the seas are sown with the dead,
The pride of the White Ensign
Shall be the pride of the Red!

Honour and pride both far and wide,
Where'er the salt tides run,
And a long sleep, the last sleep,
For them whose watch is done!

Cunard, White Star,
Great ships and small—
Gallant British merchantmen,
Here's to each and all!
Royal Mail, P. and O.,
From Shanghai to Dover,
Fighting British merchantmen
All the world over!

❖ ❖ ❖ ❖ ❖

From *Sailor Town: Sea Songs and Ballads*, edited by Cicely Fox Smith, published by George H. Doran Co., New York, US, 1919, pp. 94-96. Earlier published in *The Naval Crown* by Elkin Mathews in 1915. Also published in *The Register*, Adelaide, Australia, April 20, 1915, p 6.

A WWI poem in tribute to the various commercial shipping lines that were mobilized under the "Red Ensign" during the War. The "White Ensign" was the Royal Navy flag.

Sacramento

'Frisco City's grand and gay
Sacramento, Sacramento!
And the roaring night's as bright as day
And many ships go, small and great,
In and out by the Golden Gate,
And away O! Sacramento!
Who was it called across the night?
Sacramento, Sacramento!

What was it flashed so keen and bright?
Who is it drives down 'Frisco tide

With a six-inch blade deep in his side?
And away O! Sacramento!

O don't you see Blue Peter flying?
Sacramento, Sacramento!
O don't you hear the good wind crying?
O don't you hear the capstan chorus
And smell the open sea before us?
And away O! Sacramento!

We'll miss you, running easting down
Sacramento, Sacramento!
With a following wind from 'Frisco town;
We'll miss you beating off Cape Horn,
One man less at the pumps forlorn
And away O! Sacramento!

No more time to spend on grieving
Sacramento, Sacramento!
All because o' the man we're leaving:
The salt tides drive his drowned bones
In and out o' the Farallones
And away O! Sacramento!

❖ ❖ ❖ ❖ ❖

From *Songs and Chanties: 1914-1916*, edited by Cicely Fox Smith, published by Elkin Mathews, London, UK, 1919, pp. 28-29; first published in *The Spectator* and subsequently in *The Evening Post*, Volume 82, Issue 139, December 9, 1911, p. 17.

This is another of the few poems by Smith structured in the traditional shanty mode. Once again San Francisco's Barbary Coast has claimed another victim. See also "Shanghai Passage."

First adapted for singing by Johnny Knobbler (UK), as recorded by The Harry Browns of Bristol on *Raising Wind with The Harry Browns*, 2007.

The old "ship sailing card" below, source unknown; such sailing cards were handed out to prospective travelers on the waterfront.

The Docks at San Francisco

The Valiant Sailor

Sailor Town

Along the wharves in sailor town a singing whisper goes
Of the wind among the anchored ships, the wind that blows
Off a broad brimming water, where the summer day has died
Like a wounded whale a-sounding in the sunset tide.

There's a big China liner gleaming like a gull,
And her lit ports flashing; there's the long gaunt hull
Of a Blue-Funnel freighter with her derricks dark and still;
And a tall barque loading at the lumber mill.

And in the shops of sailor town is every kind of thing
That the sailormen buy there, or the ships' crews bring:
Shackles for a sea-chest and pink cockatoos,
Fifty-cent alarm clocks and dead men's shoes.

You can hear the gulls crying, and the cheerful noise
Of a concertina going, and a singer's voice—
And the wind's song and the tide's song, crooning soft and low
Rum old tunes in sailor town that seamen know.

I dreamed a dream in sailor town, a foolish dream and vain,
Of ships and men departed, of old days come again—
And an old song in sailor town, an old song to sing
When shipmate meets with shipmate in the evening.

From *Sailor Town: Sea Songs and Ballads*, edited by Cicely Fox Smith, published by George H. Doran Co., New York, US, 1919, pp. 11-12. An earlier edition of this book was published by Elkin Mathews, 1914. The poem was also published in *The Bookman* (US), Vol, XLVIII, No. 1, September 1918, pp 116-117.

The last verse is the important one, as this poet muses over her two year stay in Victoria, British Columbia, after returning to England in 1913. Is there regret that she tried so hard to realize a dream, only to have it slip away?

Most major ports and harbours around the world had a "sailor town" in the days of sail. It was a part of the main town or city that the sailors would go to be amongst their own type. This area had a reputation for having more bawdy houses and bars than other parts of the city. The important point from the sailor's point of view is that whatever continent or country he was in there was a good chance that he could make himself understood in such places. They spoke a common patois and the shops and taverns and boarding houses were often run by former sailors or their wives. They were a home-away-from-home that was most welcome after the hardship of a long voyage.

The poet arranged to have Alice Lee Wiley compose music for this poem so that it might be sung in the schools: published by Leonard, Gould & Bolttler, London, UK, 1930 by Paul A Schmitt Music Co.; the song is dedicated to Everton Stidham a well known singer of the day.

Later adapted for singing by Dick Miles (UK) as recorded on *Around the Harbourtown*, 1989; he first ran across this poem when a friend showed him one of this poet's books in 1987. Miles' adaptation was later recorded by Johnny Collins on *Now and Then*, 2000. and by Charles Ipcar on *Old Sailor-Poets*, 2007.

The header-graphic, the frontispiece in *Ship Alley*, is drawn by the poet's brother Phil W. Smith and may actually portray Cicely Fox Smith on the prowl in sailortown, passing The *Valiant* Sailor Tavern; this tavern still exists as a private resident on Nelson Street, Kings Lynn.

Running before the Gale

Sailor's Delight

Tall raking clipper ships driving hell-for-leather,
Swinging down the Forties in the easting weather;
Old wooden Indiamen leaking like baskets,
With half their ratlines missing and rotten slings and gaskets:
Big fourposters out of Mersey and Clyde,
Bound for grain to 'Frisco, not to be denied,
Thrashing to the westward through the great Horn seas,
With a crowd of husky reefers and a dozen A. B.'s . . .

Those were the ships Mike Murphy used to sail in,
Those were the sort he weathered many a gale in,

Handed, reefed and furled in from Timor to the Tongue
In the old days, the hard days,
The done-with mast and yard days,
('And 'ah, but they were grand days, them days when he was young!')

Seal oil, whale oil, ivory an' grain,
Lumber out of Puget Sound, an' wine out of Spain,
Deer's horns and jaggery they used to load at lost,
God-forsaken ports on the Coromandel coast . . .
Copra from the South Seas, coal out of Wales,
Copper ore, cinnamon, monkey nuts and nails:
Sweet cloves from Zanzibar, beans from Peru,
And a young white elephant consigned to the Zoo . . .

Those were the freights he sailed the world around with,
Those were the things he's been everything but drowned with,
Scorched an' soaked an' frozen from Cork to Chittagong,
In the sail days, the old days,
The hungry days, the cold days,
('And 'ah, but they were fine days, them days when he was young!')

Hard hairy sailormen with weather tanned faces,
Hands bent with hauling on sheets, tacks and braces,
Brawny forearms tattooed with strange devices,
And tough fingers skilled in cunning knots and splices . . .
Full of rum yarns and superstitious notions,
And odd bits of lingo from half a dozen oceans,
And many an old shanty, and old sailor song,
To while away a dog-watch, twenty verses long . . .

Those were the blokes Mike Murphy went to sea with,
Those were the sort of chaps he used to be with,
Shared his trick and whack with, laughed and swore and sung,
In the old days, the tough days,
Salt junk and leathery duff days,
('And 'ah but them was great days, them days when he was young!')

❖ ❖ ❖ ❖ ❖

From *Sailor's Delight*, edited by Cicely Fox Smith, published by Methuen & Co., London, UK, 1931, pp. 47-50; first published in the magazine *Holly Leaves*.

You just can't beat this poet's vivid images of the last days of sail. You can see and hear the sailors, you can even smell the cargo, and you can feel the danger implicit in the aging condition of many of these ships.

First adapted for singing in 1995 by Alan Fitzsimmons, as recorded on *Seaboot Duff & Handspike Gruel* by Pinch o' Salt, 2000.

The header graphic is a painting titled *Running before the Gale* by Anton Otto Fischer, from *Anton Otto Fischer*, p. 142.

Sailor's Farewell

Lovely is the white town, and smiling it lies
With little green gardens underneath the blue skies,
Days so full of sunshine, nights so full of glee,—
Oh, a fair place, a rare place, for sailors in from sea.

A pleasant place to come to for ships long from land,
A bright place, a light place, with mirth on every hand,
Is the white smiling city by the blue Pacific shore . . .
And I wish in my heart I may never see it more.

There's a wide white plaza where folks pass to and fro,
And a drowsy tune sounding on all the winds that blow,
Church-bells all the morning, fiddles all the night . . .
Oh, a neat place, a sweet place, for sailormen's delight!

But it's heave and break her out . . . and the best tune of all
Is the rattle of the windlass, the clicking of the pawl,
And the steady wind a-blowing, yes, blowing off the shore,
From the white smiling city that I would see no more.

For cruel is the white town for all it looks so fair,
There's a cloud upon the sunshine and there's sorrow everywhere,
And blue as Mary Mother's robe the sea is and the sky . . .
But a bitter hate I'll bear it until the day I die!

❖   ❖   ❖   ❖   ❖

From *Ships and Folks*, edited by Cicely Fox Smith, published by Elkin Mathews, London, UK, 1920, p. 68.

This haunting poem appears to be a sister to "Port o' Dreams" and "Mariquita" but something bad has gone down in this Pacific paradise. Also compare this poem with a prior one by John Masefield "The Golden City of St. Mary."

What's behind this poem may be a short story that the poet wrote called "Oranges" from her book *Tales of the Clipper Ships*, pp. 91-106; the story describes how a young sailor ashore in a Spanish port is invited by a lovely young women to join a picnic in the hills, and how later that evening she is brutally murdered by her jealous lover.

This poem was first adapted for singing by Charles Ipcar in 2006, as recorded on *Sailortown Days*, by Charles Ipcar, 2009.

The Sailor's Garden

There's a soft wind singing in the idle rigging,
High tide splashing, and a young pale moon,
Lights in a window and a fiddle jigging
Over and over there the same short tune.

Oh, was it the tide along the ship's side sighing,
Or was it the singing wind that breaths and blows,
Came like a voice across the deep crying,
Set my heart a-thinking how my garden grows?

Five years ago it was I planted roses,
Five years ago (the bush is grown a tree):
Five years ago, and once I've seen my posies,
Five years ago—and once they bloomed for me!

I was home in Spring, bloom was on the May then,
Birds all were building and buds were on the tree!
When the birds were flown, oh, I was far away then;
When the rose was open I was far at sea.

I was home in autumn; winds of cold November
Shaking the leaf that shivered on the tree;
Brown leaves that sighed of sorrow to remember
Flowers that had fallen and I far at sea.

Oh, many are the roads that lead you here and yonder,
Oh, many are the ways about the world that go;
But the longest way of all's the sailor's way to wander
To the good North Country and an isle I know.

Oh, many are the winds about the seas a-singing,
Oh, many are the songs they sing both night and noon:
But whether it be good or ill that they come bringing
The best of all's the wind that blows us home in June.

Home, home in June—and soon to be a-going;
Home, home in June—we may not long remain;
Home, home in June, just to see the garden growing,
And then fare you well till you greet us home again.

❖ ❖ ❖ ❖ ❖

From *Sailor Town: Sea Songs and Ballads*, edited by Cicely Fox Smith, published by George H. Doran Co., New York, US, 1919, pp. 45-46. An earlier edition of *Sailor Town* was published by Elkin Mathews in 1914. First published in *The Windsor Magazine*, Volume 39, December-May, 1913-1914, p. 586.

In her introduction of *Sailor-Town Days*, pp. 3-4, the poet mentions meeting a captain, while she resided on the Pacific Coast, who described the roses he had planted in his Liverpool home but had never seen bloom.

Sails

Hails from Wales,
Does Sails.

For any old thing you like to choose
From a new main course to a pair of shoes,
Or a bolt o' canvas to roll your bones
In when you voyage to Davy Jones,
Or thundering cuffers as ever you heard,
Sails is the man, you take my word!

He sits on the hatch, when it's sunny and calm,
With his specs on his nose, and his needle and palm,
Stitches and patches and yarns away
Of the ships that he knew in a bygone day,
The single topsails that once he made
For the *Fiery Cross* in the China trade,
Ringtails, watersails, Lord knows what
Old kites whose fashion is near forgot;

The Sailmaker

And many a wonderful tale he tells
Of pirate junks off the Paracels,
And the great sea serpent he once saw rolled
Asleep on the water, fold on fold,
And a craft they spoke, of an unknown rig,
Beamy and bluff as a Geordie brig,
Tearing along in the teeth of the gale,
South o' the Cape, under all plain sail,
With a bloke that stood at the wheel and steered
In old-style togs, with a long white beard,
And the eyes of him, look you, burning bright,
Like coals of fire or a ship's portlight:
And "Look you, sonnies," says Sails, "I reckon
That hooker's skipper wass—Vanderdecken!"

❖   ❖   ❖   ❖   ❖

From *Full Sail: More Sea Songs and Ballads*, edited by Cicely Fox Smith, published by Houghton Mifflin Co., Boston, US, 1926, pp. 8-10.

The sailmaker aboard a ship was often an older sailor who had a wealth of yarns to entertain his apprentices and friends.

The header graphic is from an illustration titled *The Sailmaker* drawn by Gordon Grant in his book *Sail Ho!*, facing p. 56.

Saint Andrew's Eve

The last night of November
All dreaming as I lay,
I saw a fisher toiling
In stormy seas and grey,—

A glimmering seine-net casting
In foam as white as wool . . .
And sometimes it came empty,
And sometimes it came full.

That port that fisher hailed from
Was the port of Heaven above:
The shining net he cast there
Was the net of Christ His love.

That seine it shone like silver
Or the Milky Way come down . . .
And, oh! the catch he took there
Was the souls of those who drown.

❖ ❖ ❖ ❖ ❖

From *Small Craft: Sailor Ballads and Chantys*, edited by Cicely Fox Smith, published by George H. Doran Co., New York, US, 1919, p. 77.

One of the few explicitly religious poems composed by this poet, in this case during the middle of WWI. The War drove some to question their faith, and others to re-embrace it.

Saint Andrew's Land

Cauld winds o' November, sae keenly they blaw
And the leaves o' the woodland they scattered and fa';
Oh, the swallows wi' simmer are fled o'er the faem
But the pine is aye green on the mountains of hame;
Oh, Scotland's braes are fair and Scotland's glens are bonnie
And Saint Andrew's land, Saint Andrew's land's the land
     That I lo'e best of ony.

Cauld winds o' November when simmer is fled
And ilka gay garland is withered and dead;
Though faded its bells be, its purple be sere;
Oh the heather's still sweet on the hills I lo'e dear;
Oh, Scotland's braes are fair and Scotland's glens are bonnie
And Saint Andrew's land, Saint Andrew's land's the land
     That I lo'e best of ony.

Oh, staunch as the heather and straight as the pine
Are the lads of your breeding, clear country of mine;
Like chieftains and heroes your glory of yore;

Aye, peerless an' fearless in peace and in war;
Oh, Scotland's fame is fair and Scotland's lads are bonnie
And Saint Andrew's land, Saint Andrew's land's the land
    That I lo'e best of ony.

❖ ❖ ❖ ❖ ❖

From *Saint Andrew's Land: Song*, English words by Cicely Fox Smith; Welsh words by E. Lewis; music by Charles Villiers, Stanford (1852-1924); published by Enoch & Sons, London, UK, 1918.

Transcribed at the British Library. "Cauld" is cold; "fa'" is fall; "simmer" is summer; "faem" is foam; "ony" is any; "sere" is being dried and withered; "lo'e" is love.

Saint George of England

Saint George he was a fighting man, as all the tales do tell;
He fought a battle long ago, and fought it wondrous well.
With his helmet, and his hauberk, and his good cross-hilted sword,
Oh, he rode a-slaying dragons to the glory of the Lord.
And when his time on earth was done, he found he could not rest
Where the year is always summer in the Islands of the Blest;
So he came to earth again, to see what he could do,
And they cradled him in England—
In England, April England—
Oh, they cradled him in England where the golden willows blew!

Saint George he was a fighting man, and loved a fighting breed,
And whenever England wants him now, he's ready at her need,
From Crecy field to Neuve Chapelle he's there with hand and sword,
And he sailed with Drake from Devon to the glory of the Lord.
His arm is strong to smite the wrong and break the tyrant's pride,
He was there when Nelson triumphed, he was there when Gordon died;
He sees his red-cross ensign float on all the winds that blow,
But ah! His heart's in England—
In England, April England—
Oh, his heart it turns to England where the golden willows blew!

Saint George he was a fighting man, he's here and fighting still
While any wrong is yet to right or Dragon yet to kill,
And faith! He's finding work this day to suit his war-worn sword,
For he's strafing Huns in Flanders to the glory of the Lord.
Saint George he is a fighting man, but when the fighting's past,
And dead among the trampled fields the fiercest and the last
Of all the Dragons earth has known beneath his feet lies low,
Oh, his heart will turn to England—
To England, April England—
He'll come home to rest in England where the golden willows blow!

❖ ❖ ❖ ❖ ❖

From *Songs And Chanties 1914-1916*, edited by Cicely Fox Smith, published by Elkin Mathews, London, UK, 1919, pp. 221-223. Earlier published in *Fighting Men* by Elkin Mathews in 1916. First published in *Punch* magazine, Volume 150, April 19, 1916, p. 201.

A Saint of Cornwall

I don't know who Saint Mawes was, but he surely can't have been
A stiff old stone gazebo on a carved cathedral screen,
Or a holy-looking customer rigged out in blue and red
In a sunset-coloured window with a soup-plate round his head.
But he must have been a skipper who had sailed the salt seas round
(Or at least as many of 'em as had in his time been found),
And sung his songs and kissed his girl and had his share of fun,
Till he took and got religion, when his sailing days were done.

He must have had a ruddy face, a grey beard neatly trimmed,
And eyes with crow's feet round them, neither are nor use had dimmed,
And he'd lean there on the jetty with his glass up to his eye,
And look across the Carrick Roads, and watch the ships go by,
And yarn with his old cronies of the ships he used to know,
And shipmates that he sailed with many and many a year ago,
In the West of England tin-boats on the Tyre and Sidon run,
Before he got religion or his sailing days were done.

And when he came at last to die, they'd lay him down to rest
On a green and grassy foreland sloping gently to the west,
Where the wind's cry and the gull's cry would be near him night and day,
And a rousing deep-sea shanty might come to him where he lay;
And they left him there a-sleeping, for to smell the harbour smells,
And to count the passing watches by the striking of the bells,
And listen to the sailormen a-singing in the sun,
Like a good old master mariner whose sailing days are done.

❖   ❖   ❖   ❖   ❖

From *Sea Songs and Ballads 1917-22*, edited by Cicely Fox Smith, published by Houghton Mifflin Co., New York, US, 1924, pp. 102-103. First published in *Punch* magazine, Volume 157, July 30, 1919, p. 110.

Saint Patrick's Day in the Morning

Oh, where is the lad that's far away? . . .
And what of the one who sails the sea? . . .
Oh, how will they keep Saint Patrick's Day,
Saint Patrick's Day in the morning?

There's some will hear the great guns' din
At the break o' day their tune begin.
And the snipers welcome the daylight in
On Patrick's Day in the morning.

And be they far or be they near,
Upon that day they'll keep good cheer,
And make the foe that meets them fear
On Patrick's Day in the morning.

There's some will watch the fleet that lurks
By harbour, mine and fortress works,
And some will hammer the heathen Turks
On Patrick's Day in the morning.

Oh, far and near their watch is set,
But be they cold, or be they wet,
Will there a man of them all forget
Saint Patrick's Day in the morning?

Ay, some they'll be so sound who sleep
In the fields o' France or the waters deep,
They will not know that their kinsmen keep
Saint Patrick's Day in the morning.

Sweet is the sleep of them, far away;
And how should they heed if a man should say:
"Oh, don't you remember Saint Patrick's Day,
Saint Patrick's Day in the morning?"

❖ ❖ ❖ ❖ ❖

From *Sailor Town: Sea Songs and Ballads*, edited by Cicely Fox Smith, published by George H. Doran Co., New York, US, 1919, pp. 110-111. Earlier published in *The Naval Crown* by Elkin Mathews in 1915.

Salvage

Not the encounter of navies in battle array—
The roar of salvoes—the smoke-wrack that darkens the day—
But a mined ship with her forepeak full
Off the Foreland, waiting towing . . .

Not the white flame of the searchlights, the red glare between,
The heaven-splitting thunder and roar of the struck magazine—
But a fog rolling up the Channel as white as wool,
And never a light showing . . .

Not the fierce dash of destroyers—the bow-wave like snow—
The track of the headlong torpedo launched swift on the foe—
But a ship aground off the Long Sand light,
And a hell of a gale blowing . . .

Not the stern splendour of battle, the glory, the fame,
Not the awarding of honours, the nation's acclaim,
But a crew and a cargo to take off in the night,
And the light fast going . . .

❖ ❖ ❖ ❖ ❖

From *Sailor Town: Sea Songs and Ballads*, edited by Cicely Fox Smith, published by George H. Doran Co., New York, US, 1919, pp. 123-124. First published in *The Naval Crown* by Elkin Mathews in 1915, and reprinted in *Rhymes of the Red Ensign*, p. 41, but without the final lines: (But only the duty and the deed—/ Whose reward is in no man's bestowing!)

Composed during the first year of WWI as a tribute to the sailors in the merchant marine.

A Sea Burthen

A ship swinging
As the tide swings, up and down,
And men's voices singing,—
East away O! West away!
And a very long way from London Town!

A lantern glowing
And stars looking down,
And the sea smells blowing,—
East away O! West away!
And a very long way from London Town!

Lights in wild weather
From a tavern window old and brown,
And men singing together,—
East away O! West away!
And a very long way from London Town!

❖ ❖ ❖ ❖ ❖

From *Songs and Chanties: 1914-1916*, edited by Cicely Fox Smith, published by Elkin Mathews, London, UK, 1919, pp. 27. First published in *Songs in Sail*, 1914.

The poet may be thinking back to an evening in Victoria, British Columbia, when she looked out from her bedroom window at a ship weighing anchor.

"Burthen" means here a refrain or main theme.

First set to music by Michael Head (1900-1976) in 1949, as published in *Six Sea Songs*. More recently adapted for singing by Jaqui Haigh, as recorded by the Harry Browns of Bristol on *Rolling Home to Bristol*, 2006.

Square-Rigged Ship in Trade Wind Zone

Sea Change

There was fog off the Foreland, white as wool, and Billy he says, says he.
"If ever I win the Calcutta Sweep, a thing as might easy be,
I'll build me an 'ouse down Ramsgate way, as near to the drink's I can get

Without an 'igh tide comin' inside an' makin' the doormat wet;
So's I can lay in the blankets o' nights when the Foreland fog-'orn 's goin'
And 'ear 'im blarin' the 'ole night long an' the steamers' sirens blowin',
An' think o' the bosun rousin' the watch with a voice as'd wake the dead—
'Jump now, ye sogers, rise an' shine!' . . . an' say as I turn in my bed,
'Now ain't you glad, young feller me lad, now ain't you glad you're 'ere,
As warm an' snug as a bug in a rug, with plenty o' pals an' beer,
An' not out there wi' the fog in your eyes an' the drizzle drenchin' you through,
Like them poor divvles o' sailormen wot ain't as lucky as you?'"

Off o' the Lizard she shipped 'em green, and Billy these words did say,
"When I get spliced to a wider with cash, which I mean to be some day,
We'll settle down in a snug little pub, will me and my blushin' bride,
An' where it may be don't matter to me so long as it's waterside;
So when it's blowin' a beast of a gale an' snowin' as well may be
I can lay in the sheets like a bloomin' lord and think o' the ships at sea,
An' the fellers fistin' the topsails down when they're stiff wi' the frozen spray,
Or flounderin' round in the flooded waist . . . an' just turn over and say,
'Now ain't you glad, young feller me lad, you're anchored safe ashore,
Instead o' fightin' with frozen sails the same as you used before
Instead o' haulin' on sodden ropes with a thunderin' surf alee,
Like them poor divvles o' sailormen as keeps on going to sea?'"

Down in the Tropics she logged it fine, and Billy he says, says he,
"You may talk as you like o' your berths ashore, but this is the sort for me;
Gimme a trick at the wheel," says he, "an' the flyin'-fish an' the spray,
I wouldn't swop for a fried-fish shop or a pub down Ratcliff way;
For it's grand to feel the sun on your neck an' the wheel-spokes warm to your 'and,
An' think o' fellers trampin' around in the cold an' the rain on the land,
An' 'ear the same ole steady ole Trade as he shoves the ole barkey along
In shrouds an' backstays an' topsail sheets a-singin' the same ole song,
'Now ain't you glad, young feller me lad, now ain't you glad you're 'ere,
Without no wife to trouser your pay an' leave you a bob for beer?
Now ain't you glad, young feller me lad, you signed an' sailed once more,
Instead o' trudgin' around in the wet like them poor divvles ashore?'"

❖ ❖ ❖ ❖ ❖

From *Sailor's Delight*, edited by Cicely Fox Smith, published by Methuen & Co., London, UK, 1931, pp. 82-85.

The dream of life ashore when life aboard is misery, shifts seamlessly to the delights of life a-sailing compared to misery ashore.

The header graphic is a painting of a full-rigged ship with all sails set in the zone of the trade winds by Anton Otto Fischer, from *Anton Otto Fischer*, p. 151.

A Sea Dream

Why did I dream last night, I wonder, about the ship *Ledore*
I made a passage in from China—was it 'eighty-three or—four?—
And left in the East India Basin, and after saw no more?

I thought we were off the Pescadores, waiting a breeze from the land;
There were some fishing junks becalmed there, and nets spread out on the sand;
The sun had left the sky one glory, the sea was flat as your hand.

It was just like looking at a picture, I saw it all so clear;
Little things I'd long since forgotten about her rig and her gear,
And shipmates' faces I hadn't thought of for many and many a year.

I could see them all as plain as daylight—and then some fellow spoke,
"Here comes the wind," he said, "by thunder!"—the sea all round us broke
Into a hundred thousand wrinkles, and on the word I woke.

There was nothing out of the way about her so far as I recall;
She wasn't out of common handsome or fast or smart or tall;
There was no one in the crowd to remember—they were chaps like most, that's all.

We'd nothing much in the way of weather out of the usual kind;
The times we had they were like most times, goods uns and bad combined,
And nothing ever happened on board her to make her stick in your mind.

Just the same old round of sailorizing that all us old shellbacks know,
The old hauling of sheets and braces in the doldrums to and fro,
The old jobs aloft in the Tropics when the good trade-winds blow.

Reefing and furling, wheel and lookout, shifting and bending sail,
Tallying on to the topsail halyards, snugging down in a gale,
And an old song in the dog-watches and an old seaman's tale.

I went with never a look behind me, and glad to leave her too,
When we made her fast in the dock basin and the mate said, "That'll do!"
And it's rum I should have dreamed about her, of all the ships I knew!

❖ ❖ ❖ ❖ ❖

From *Sailor's Delight*, edited by Cicely Fox Smith, published by Methuen & Co., London, UK, 1931, pp. 70-73.

An old sailor is musing over why he dreamed so vividly about a particular ship he sailed on when there was nothing remarkable about her, his crewmates, or the voyage.

"The Pescadores" are a set of islands off the northern tip of Taiwan.

First adapted for singing by Bob Zentz (US), as recorded on *Closehauled on the Wind of a Dream*, 2007.

Sea Sorrow

"Didn't you sail with Billy Riley las' v'yage—
Bloke I used to know
In the port watch o' the old *Eliza Masters?*"
Ay, I did so.

"An' could you tell me any pub where I'd be likely
To cross 'is 'awse ashore?"
You needn't look in no pub for Billy Riley,
'Cos 'e won't come back no more.

"Why, 'as 'e gone up to the South Seas then
An' lef' the sea for good,
An' set up 'ouse with a fuzzy-'eaded gal there,
Same's 'e allus said 'e would?"

'E ain't set up 'ouse with no gal, ain't Billy,
Not as I knows on . . .
For there ain't no 'ouses nor there ain't no gals neither
In the place where Bill's gone.

There was an 'ead-wind an' a cross sea runnin',
An' the day bright an' fine,
An' it breezed up so's we 'ad to get the 'ead-sails off 'er,
'Arf-way up from the Line.

An' Bill laid out on the boom with another feller,
Makin' fast the jib down-haul,
An' they didn't git done an' come back same's they would 'ave
If they'd any sense at all.

But there they stopped to watch 'er stoopin', swayin',
(I can jus' fancy 'ow)
All 'er pile o' canvas shinin', swellin',
An' the bubbles streamin' off 'er bow.

An the feller at the wheel 'e was a sodger
As warn't fit to drive an 'earse,
For 'e brought 'er up into the wind suddent,
'Cos 'e couldn't steer a curse.

So's the old gal took an' shoved 'er boom under,
Which she never done afore . . .
An' that's why I'm tellin' you as Billy Riley
Ain't comin' back no more . . .

❖ ❖ ❖ ❖ ❖

From *The Return of the "Cutty Sark,"* by Cicely Fox Smith, published by Methuen & Co., London, UK, 1924, p. 39. Also published in the same form in *Full Sail* two years later.

Second Mate

Two-and-twenty, taut and trim,
Likes the girls and the girls like him:
All the same, a fighting man,
Game to scrap whenever he can.

He's a white man through and through,
Sort of a bloke to have with you
When you're up to the neck in a Dago dive
All of a buzz like an angry hive;

Sort of a chap to have at your back
When things look ugly and bad and black
And you're taking an odds-on chance of dying
In a Rio alley when knives are flying;

Sort of a feller to have at your shoulder
Off o' the Horn when nights get colder,
When you're fighting down the bunt of a sail
On a slippery yard in a thundering gale.

For whatever the job in hand may be,
A rough house in port or rough weather at sea,
A cyclone afloat or a shindy ashore,
The tighter the place is he like it the more.

❖ ❖ ❖ ❖ ❖

From *Full Sail: More Sea Songs and Ballads*, edited by Cicely Fox Smith, published by Houghton Mifflin Co., Boston, US, 1926, pp. 15-16.

"See You in Liverpool"

The hatches are on, sonny, an' the cargo's all stowed:
Time to say "So long" now, time to take the road:
Pals we've been an' good pals, drunk an' took our fun—
An' I'll meet you in Liverpool some day, my son!

All roads lead to Rome, sonny, so the sayin' goes:
But the long road, the salt road, the road a ship knows,
'Ull lead a man to the Bar Light afore his time is done—
An' I'll see you in Liverpool some day, my son!

All the bells'll ring, sonny, all the crews'll cheer,
Watchin' of us goin', droppin' down the tier,
Shakin' of 'er topsail reefs out one by one—
An' we'll all meet in Liverpool one day, my son!

It might be a year, sonny, it might be two or three,
For the salt road's a long road for chaps like you an' me:

But fair weather or foul weather, good luck or bad,
I'll meet you in Liverpool some day, my lad!

❖ ❖ ❖ ❖ ❖

From *Full Sail: More Sea Songs and Ballads*, edited by Cicely Fox Smith, published by Houghton Mifflin Co., NY, US, 1926, pp. 98-99.

It was often the case with close shipmates that after they made their home port they would never see each other again, but there was always the hope that some day it would happen.

Gordon Morris (UK) first adapted this poem for singing as recorded on *Full Sail: Inside the Lid*, 2002.

Seeing the World

"Where I was born an' r'ared," said Clancy,
"There was pigs an' cows an' such," said he,
"House an' farm if I'd cared," said Clancy,
"They'd all have come to me.
An' if I'd stayed there," said Clancy,
"If I was there now," said he,
"I'd have moss instead of hair," said Clancy,
"An' roots the same as an ould tree."

"Where I spent my young years," said Clancy,
"There was lasses two or three,
Fit to give their ears," said Clancy,
"To go to church along o' me.
An' if I'd took a wife," said Clancy,
"An' if she'd proved a scold," said he,
"Twould have been a dog's life," said Clancy,
"So I'd just as well be free."

"But when I've seen the world," said Clancy,
"An' all there is in it," said he,
"An' my last sail's furled," said Clancy,
"An' I'm tired of goin' to sea,
I'll maybe go an' settle down there,
An' raise pigs an' cows," said he,
"An' see if there's a girl in town there
Waitin' all this time for me."

❖ ❖ ❖ ❖ ❖

From *Ships and Folks*, edited by Cicely Fox Smith, published by Elkin Mathews, London, UK, 1920, p. 45.

There's many a sea poem about old sailors thinking about the homeland they'd left. Here's another take.

Sailors being Shanghaied in 'Frisco

Shanghai Passage

"Shanghai Brown, Shanghai Brown!"
The Skipper o' the *Harvest Moon* is rampin' round the town
Looking for some sailormen to beg or steal or borrow—
Can't get a crew an' he wants to sail tomorrow!
"Prime seamen's very scarce just now—but where's his money down,
An' I'll see what I can do for him," says Shanghai Brown.

"Shanghai Brown, Shanghai Brown,"
He's sent his touts an' runners out all around the town;
He's raked in men both high an' low, he's got both black an' white;
He's got the *Lauderdale's* port watch that only berthed last night;
He's got a brace of farmhands with the hayseeds in their hair;
He's got a bridegroom and best man, for what does Shanghai care?
An' he's shipped 'em in the *Harvest Moon*, the toughest packet goin',
(That never gets a sailorman' to sign aboard her, knowin'),
With a hardcase drivin' skipper, an' a bull-voiced bucko mate,
By the Shanghai passage from the Golden Gate.

They'll be wonderin' in the mornin' what it was they drank las' night;
They'll be wonderin' what's hit 'em if they show an ounce of fight;
They'll be scoffin' seaboot duff, they'll be suppin' handspike gruel,
An' dodgin' the belayin'-pins, and cursin' Shanghai cruel;
But there's one won't wake nor wonder, nor scoff no grub at all,
Nor drag his achin' bones along to tally on the fall,
Nor jump to please the toughest mate New England ever bred,
Not stand no trick nor lookout—an' for why? Because he's dead!

"Prime seamen's very scarce just to-day!"
Says Shanghai Brown,

So he's took an' shipped a corp away,
Has Shanghai Brown,
By the Shanghai Passage, outer 'Frisco Town!

❖ ❖ ❖ ❖ ❖

From *Sailor's Delight*, edited by Cicely Fox Smith, published by Methuen & Co., London, 1931, pp. 9-10; first published in *Punch* magazine, Volume 180, May 20, 1931, p. 546.

It was not uncommon for a hired gang to roam around the back alleys and taverns in a port and secure able bodied men as crew for a skipper who couldn't get a full complement any other way. These were often delivered aboard unconscious, dead drunk or occasionally as in this poem just plain dead! "Shanghai Brown" was an infamous shipping master or crimp who plied his trade in San Francisco's Barbary Coast in the late 19th century.

First adapted for singing by Alan Fitzsimmons, as recorded by Pinch o' Salt on *Sea Boot Duff & Hand Spike Gruel*, 2000. An alternative version was fashioned by Charles Ipcar, as recorded on *Uncommon Sailor Songs*, 2004.

The header graphic is from the cover of *Shanghaied in San Francisco* by Bill Pickelhaupt, Flyblister Press, San Francisco, CA, 1996, artist unknown.

Her Spars Are Dreams

The Ship that Never Was

In Casey's Baltic Tavern Mike and I
Heard an old shellback praising to the sky,
With uncouth sailor oaths from foreign lands,
And clumsy gestures of rope-hardened hands,
A ship, the *Ladas*—praising her grace, her speed,
Beauty and strength, her handiness at need:
Telling of risks endured in fog or gale,
And hard-won triumphs snatched from queens of sail . . .

"Them was the days, my hearts, under the Duster!
No shortening sail—crack on it was an' bust 'er,
That was the game in the old *Ladas* then;
Ships was ships then, by the Lord, and men was men!"
Down crashed his fist and made the glasses chime
Some drowning sailor's knell. "That was a time,

Too good it was, by cripes, too good to last!"
Then he feel silent, brooding on the Past.

"That old man's daft," Mike said behind his hand,
"Him and his sixty days from land to land!
I knowed that *Ladas*—twenty years ago
She lay by us in the tier at Vallipo—
I was in the *Cheviot*, one o' Muir Maclean's,
She could 'ave give his ruddy *Ladas* beans!
She never beat no *Cutty Sark*, not she,
Nor done no seventeen knots, no more than me!
Such blinkin' yarns they spin, these old chaps do,
They don't know which are lies nor which are true."

Ay, so it is! Who keeps not in his heart
Some ship of vision, lovely and apart,
Some *Ladas*, *Cheviot*, call her what you will,
Passing, the years but leave more lovely still?
For she is built of joys and hopes and fears,
Passion and pain that perished with the years,
And all that foolish, fond remembrance means
Of youth and of youth's golden might-have-beens.

Oh, manned by memories, rigged with dear regret,
With tears like tropic dews her sails are wet,
Luminous as light of stars, her white wake streams
Bubbling beneath her keel—her spars are dreams.
Years shall not change her, time shall touch her never,
The ship that never was—the ship that is for ever!

❖ ❖ ❖ ❖ ❖

From *Full Sail: More Sea Songs and Ballads*, edited by Cicely Fox Smith, published by Houghton Mifflin Co., Boston, US, 1926, pp. 31-34.

The header graphic is a photograph taken of the main mast and rigging of the restored barque *James Craig* at night in Sydney, Australia, by Judy Barrows in 2005; black and white colors inverted for effect.

A Ship Picture

Pilot boat, lighthouse,
Stiff green sea,
House flag and number
Plain as can be.

Blackwall fashion,
Shipshape and trim,
Sails like the cheeks
Of a cherubim.

Cottonwool clouds
In a crude blue sky—

Who owned it, I wonder,
In days gone by?

What old grey skipper
Or mate maybe,
Snug by his fireside,
Done with the sea.

Lovingly scanned it
With age-dimmed eyes,
Saw in his pipe-smoke
Pictures rise.

Let, by the lamp's light,
Memory range
A hundred harbours
And landfalls strange.

Mast-fringed Hooghly—
And junk-thronged Praya
Mat-thatched hamlets
Of far Malaya.

The Trade exultant,
The Doldrum calm,
The long surf creaming
On shores of palm.

Channels Formosan
Typhoon-torn,
Towering, tremendous
Seas of the Horn

Long-lost shipmates
In long-drowned ships:
Smiling, yet sadly,
With bearded lips.

At thought of laughter
And larks he had
In old windjammers
When he was a lad.

And storms he weathered
And songs he sung
In days long over,
When earth was young!

From *The Lyceum Book of Verse*, edited by Mollie Stanley-Wrench, Lyceum Club, London, UK, 1931. p. 96.

"Praya" was a term used in Colonial Hong Kong to refer to a promenade by the waterfront. The name comes from the Portuguese term for the broad stone-faced road that runs parallel along the harbour in front of the city.

The first Lyceum Club was founded in London by Miss Constance Smedley in 1903 and aimed to provide a welcome and intellectually stimulating environment for educated and energetic women.

The Shipkeeper

The Ship-Keeper

When dusk comes round again
And red goes down the sun,
And all the stevedore's men
Have finished up and gone;
When silent all and dark
The tugs and lighters lie,
And derricks stand up stark
And still against the sky;

When solemn, slow as doom,
The dock policeman's tread
Wakes echoes in the gloom
Of each deserted shed—
Old Mike, his nightly tale
Of tasks at length complete,
Limps slowly to the rail
On lame rheumatic feet,
Lights his black clay, and leans
And thinks, as old men do,
Of bygone things and scenes
His lusty manhood knew;
Until, when stars begin
To gleam by two and three,
He sees the ships come in
That no one else can see—
The ships that wait no tide,
The ships that take no steam,
But to their moorings glide
As quiet as a dream;
The ships he served of old,
When blood was young and hot,
Long wrecked or scraped or sold,
Their very names forgot;
The ships that raced the wool,
The grain, the jute, the tea,
Titania beautiful,
And proud *Thermopylae;*
The "Lochs," the Irish "Stars,"
Old fleets of far renown,
Green's, Wigram's, Some's, Dunbar's,
The pride of London town.

Cold Alps of shining snow,
He knows them one and all,
The fast ships and the slow,
The big ships and the small.
Knows too each glimmering queen
Or craven king they bore,
Each dragon gold and green,
Armed knight or turbaned Moor.
Lost shipmates of old years
Along their bulwarks throng;
Old speech of theirs he hears,
Old yarns, old scraps of song.

The last rose leaves the skies;
The river breeze blows chill;
But still with age-dimmed eyes
He dreams, as old men will,

His pipe between his lips;
Still, dreaming, seems to see
The lost and lovely ships
That no one sees but he.

❖ ❖ ❖ ❖ ❖

From *Sailor's Delight*, edited by Cicely Fox Smith, published by Methuen & Co., London, UK, 1931, pp. 74-77.

The shipkeeper was typically an old retired sailor that would act as watchman on a ship in port in between cargoes. The shipkeepers along Victoria's waterfront, in the early 1900's, were the poet's chief source of yarns for her nautical poetry and short stories.

Gordon Morris (UK) first adapted this poem for singing as recorded on *Full Sail*, 2002.

The header graphic is titled *The Shipkeeper* as drawn by Phil W. Smith to illustrate this poem, from *Sailor's Delight*, facing p. 76.

Shipmate Sorrow

I was shipmates with Sorrow in a day gone by;
We shared wheel and look-out, old Sorrow and I:
Good times and bad times, foul weather and fair,
The old grey face of him was always there.

There was never shanty raised there, never song I heard,
But his voice would be in it like a crying bird;
I was dull in the dog watches when the laugh went free
Because of old Sorrow sitting down by me.

I thought I could lose him in the stir and change
Of bright wicked cities all sunlit and strange;
There came a hand at my elbow and a voice in my ear—
It was old patient Sorrow saying: "Lad, I'm here!"

And by the bustling harbour, up the busy street,
Many a time I see him, many a time I meet
The old grey face there of one I used to know . . .
And it's old shipmate Sorrow out of long ago.

And the watch at the halliards, they may sing with a will,
But the voice I used to hear, oh I think I hear it still,
Like the wind in a shroud piping, or a seabird's cry . . .
And it's old Sorrow singing out of times gone by!

❖ ❖ ❖ ❖ ❖

From *Sea Songs and Ballads* 1917-22, edited by Cicely Fox Smith, published by Houghton Mifflin Co., New York, US, 1924, pp. 116-117; also published in the same form in *Rhymes of the Red Ensign*, Hodder & Stoughton, 1919, pp. 65-66. First published in *The Windsor Magazine*, Volume 41, December-May, 1914-1915, p. 320.

It took me some time to decode this poem. It now seems to be more than a general lament for a lost shipmate. It may represent the poet's loss of a close personal friend, her shipmate "Dan" who was also a shantysinger, a loss which continued to haunt her even after returning to England. In this poem she seems reconciled to the haunting, and to even welcome it.

Changing a Jib

Shipmates (1914)

Good-bye, and fare ye well, for we'll sail no more together
Broad seas and narrow in fair or foul weather;
We'll sail no more together in foul weather or fine,
And ye'll go your own way, and I'll go mine.

Oh, the seas are very wide, and there's never any knowing
The countries we'll see or the ports where we'll be going;
All across the wide world, up and down the sea,
Before we come together, as at last may be.

Good-bye, and fare ye well; and maybe I'll be strolling,
And watching the ships there, and the crews a-coaling,
In a queer foreign city and a gay, gaudy street—
And who but yourself will I chance for to meet?

You'll blow up from Eastward and I'll blow in from the West,
And of all the times we ever had it's then we'll have the best,
Back from deep sea wanderings, back from wind and weather,
You and me from all the seas, two friends together!

Good-bye, and fare ye well. Nay, naught but good attend ye
All across the wide world where sailor's luck may send ye—
Up and down the deep seas, north and south the Line,
And ye'll go your own way and I'll go mine!

❖   ❖   ❖   ❖   ❖

From *Songs and Chanties: 1914-1916*, edited by Cicely Fox Smith, published by Elkin Mathews, London, 1919, pp. 25-26. The poem was also published in *The Bookman* (US), Vol, XLVIII, No. 1, September 1918, p 117.

The theme of this poem seems quite contemporary in theme. One wonders if this is a poem that Smith composed while parting from her sailor friend "Dan," whom she later describes as having been lost at sea. The next poem, also title "Shipmates" is an entirely different poem.

First adapted for singing by Charles Ipcar as recorded on *Old Sailor-Poets*, 2007.

The header graphic titled *Changing a Jib* is not of Smith but of another young woman Elisabeth Jacobsen who crewed aboard one of the last commercial grain carriers, the four-masted barque *Parma*, in 1933, photographed by Alan Villiers, from *Last of the Wind Ships*, p. 132.

Shipmates (Clipper Ship *Mary Ambree*)

These are the men that sailed with me
In the Colonies clipper *Mary Ambree*.
These are the men that kept her going
Through the fog and the ice and the big gales blowing:
Skipper and bosun, mates and sails,
Tough as leather and hard as nails,
Wise in the ways of seas and ships,
Soaked in brine to the finger-tips.

These are the chaps that toiled together
In Trade and Doldrum and black Horn weather:
Stood their trick on a beggarly whack
Of junk and limejuice and mouldy tack,
Scoured and holystoned, reefed and furled,
Watch and watch round the whole wet world,
Hauled and sweated at sheets and braces
With the sun in their eyes or the sleet in their faces,
Fought and fisted the frozen courses
On footropes jumping like bucking horses.

These are the men that sailed and manned,
Worked her and drove her from land to land,
Most of 'em gone, as the ships are gone,
For times must change, as the old words run,
And men change with 'em, we know full well;
For worse or for better? Time will tell.
This only is certain—ships and men,
We never shall build their likes again.

Time for us to go now it's all done and ended,
All that was beastly and all that was splendid
The rough and the smooth and the worst and the best of it
Sad times and bad times all gone with the rest of it.

Stout hearts and faint hearts, cheery blokes, glum blokes
The workers, the shirkers, the plain blokes the rum blokes.
Gone down the years like the snatch of a song—
Time for us to leave her, and—shipmates , so long!

❖ ❖ ❖ ❖ ❖

From *Full Sail: More Sea Songs and Ballads*, edited by Cicely Fox Smith, published by Houghton Mifflin Co., New York, US, 1926, prologue, pp. 1-2.,

The two italicized stanzas actually follow the descriptions of the crew but are placed here for ease of reference. The preceding poem also titled "Shipmates" is an entirely different poem.

One wonders if Smith is describing her own experiences here with a ship and its crew but there is no evidence that she sailed on such a ship. "Mary Ambree" is a reference to an alleged 16th century woman warrior who was the subject of a traditional English ballad of the same name.

Ships and Folks

"Ships are like folks," said Murphy, "the way there's good an' bad
An' weak an' strong among 'em, an' steady ones an' mad,
The way they're wild an' willing, an' kind an' cruel too,
The way there's fair an false ones, an' homely ones an' true."

"Ships are like folks," said Murphy, "the way a man can't tell
What makes him fancy one so, an' hate the next like hell,
Why some that treat him handsome he counts no more'n the rest,
An' them that use him hardest, it's them he'll like the best."

"Ships are like folks," said Murphy, "the way they come an' go,
An' some you'll sail for years with an' never seem to know . . .
An' some you'll sign just once with, an' part, an' there's an end . . .
An' some you'll first clap eyes on an' know you've found a friend."

"Ships are like folks," said Murphy, "in every kind o' way—
The way us fellers leave 'em that's knowed 'em in their day—
The way we'll chuck the best ones an' choose the worst instead—
An' curse 'em when they're livin'—an' miss 'em when they're dead."

❖ ❖ ❖ ❖ ❖

From *Ships and Folks*, edited by Cicely Fox Smith, published by Elkin Mathews, London, UK, 1920, p. 7. First published in *Punch* magazine, Volume 157, August 20, 1919, p. 166.

Murphy is another favorite shellback of the poet who always has something thoughtful to say.

First adapted for singing by Bob Zentz (US), as recorded on *Closehauled on the Wind of a Dream*, 2007, to the tune of the traditional drinking song "Three Drunken Maidens."

The Ship's Good-Bye

I leaned on the taffrail, I saw the day dying
Like a flock of gay birds round the royal yards flying;
High over the sunset I saw the young moon,
And the wind and the tide they were singing one tune.

"A hundred and fifty days out from Vancouver
(Don't you hear 'em all singing it over and over?)
A hundred and fifty days longer to roam
(Or less if you're lucky) to England and home!"

The ship took it up as she tugged at her tether,
Brace, footrope, and halliard all whistling together,
And so did the seagulls which round her did call—
But oh, my heart sang it the strongest of all!

There be many good songs we have knocked round the world to,
Manned capstan and halliard, reefed, shifted and furled to,

All round the oceans, since first we did roll
By the Straits of Le Mair for Coquimbo with coal.

All round the world, lads, to ports without number,
Chile for nitrates, the Fraser for lumber,
Where charters might offer or cargoes might call—
But the homeward-bound chantey's the best of them all.

"A hundred and fifty days out from Vancouver
Brings the ship to the land and the lad to his lover,
A hundred and fifty days longer to roam
(Or less if you're lucky) to England and home!"

❖ ❖ ❖ ❖ ❖

From *Sailor Town: Sea Songs and Ballads*, edited by Cicely Fox Smith, published by George H. Doran Co., New York, US, 1919, pp. 51-52.

Tom Lewis (UK) first adapted a version of this poem for singing titled "150 Days Out from Vancouver." He uses the 2nd verse as a chorus, as recorded on *Tinker, Tailor, Soldier, Singer!*, 1995.

The Ships He Served of Old

The ships he served of old,
When blood was young and hot,
Long wrecked or scrapped or sold;
Their very names forgot;

The ships that raced the wool,
The grain, the jute, the tea,
Titania beautiful,
And proud *Thermophylae*;

Cold Alps of shining snow,
He knows them one and all,
The fast ships and the slow,
The big ships and the small,

Knows too each glimmering queen
Or carven king they bore,
Each dragon gold and green,
Armed knight or turbaned Moor . . .

The last rose leaves the skies,
The river breeze blows chill;
But still with age-dimmed eyes
He dreams, as old men will,

His pipe between his lips;
Still, dreaming, seems to see
The lost and lovely ships
That no one sees but he.

From *Thames-Side Yesterdays*, by Cicely Fox Smith, published by F. Lewis, Leigh-On-Sea, UK, 1945, pp. 36-37.

This poem is a fragment of "The Ship-Keeper."

The poet claims to have written this with a particular ship-keeper in mind, one that she no doubt encountered while she was resident in Victoria, British Columbia. She wrote: "He was a great yarner, as most ship-keepers were. Theirs was, after all, a solitary sort of job, and memory after a while becomes a sad sort of companion."

Morning Mist

"Ships That Pass": An Episode of the Cruiser Patrol

There are ships that pass in the night-time, some poet has told us how,
But a ship that passed in the day-time is the one I'm thinking of now,
Where the seas roll green from the Artic and the wind comes keen from the Pole,
'Tween Rockall Bank and the Shetlands, up North on the long patrol.

We sighted her one day early; the forenoon watch was begun,
There was mist like wool on the water, and a glimpse of a pale, cold sun,
And she came through the dim, grey weather—a thing of wonder and gleam,
From the port o' the Past on a bowline, close-hauled on a wind of dream.

The rust of years was upon her—she was weathered by many a gale—
The flag of a Dago republic went up to her peak at our hail;
But I knew her—Lord God! I knew her, as how could I help but know
The ship that I served my time in, no matter how long ago!

I'd have climbed to her royals blindfold, I'd have known her spars in a crowd;
Aloft and alow, I knew her, brace and halliard and shroud—

From the scroll-work under her stern-ports to the paint on her figure-head—
And the shout, "All hands," on her maindeck would have tumbled me
                                                  up from the dead.

She moved like a queen on the water, with the grace that was hers of yore,
The sun on her shining canvas—what had she to do with war,
With a world that is full of trouble and seas that are stained with crime?
She came like a dream remembered, dreamt once in a happier time.

She was youth, and its sorrow that passes—the light, the laughter, the joy,
The South, and the small white cities and the carefree heart of a boy,
The farewell flash of the Fastnet to light you the whole world round,
And the hoot of the tug at parting—and the song of the homeward bound.—

The sun, and the flying-fish weather—night, and a fiddle's tune—
And palms, and the warm maize-yellow of a low West Indian moon—
Storm in the high South latitudes—and the boom of a Trade-filled sail—
And the anchor-watch in the tropics, and the old Sou' Spainer's tale.

Was it the lap of the wave I heard or the chill wind's cry,
Or a snatch of a deep-sea chanty I knew in the years gone by?
Was it the whine of the gear in the sheaves, or the seagulls' call,
Or the ghost of my shipmates' voices, tallying on to the fall?

I went through her papers duly—and no one, I hope, could see
A freight of the years departed was the cargo she bore for me!
I talked with her Dago captain while we searched her for contraband,
And...I longed for one grip of her wheel-spokes like a grip of a friend's right hand.

And I watched while her helm went over, and the sails were sheeted home,
And under her moving forefoot the bubbles broke into foam,
Till she faded from sight in the greyness—a thing of wonder and gleam,
For the port of the Past on a bowline—closehauled on a wind of dream!

❖ ❖ ❖ ❖ ❖

From *Small Craft: Sailor Ballads and Chantys*, edited by Cicely Fox Smith, published by George H. Doran Co., New York, US, 1919, pp. 33-35. Later reprinted in *Sea Songs and Ballads*, published by Hodder & Stoughton, 1922, pp. 128-131.

This kind of incident, a cruiser stopping a neutral ship to check for contraband, was quite typical for the British fleet blockading the Baltic Sea in WWI.

First adapted for singing by Bob Zentz (US), as recorded on *Closehauled on the Wind of a Dream*, 2007.

The header graphic is a painting titled *Morning Mist* with a ship materializing ghost-like as it approaches the viewer by Anton Otto Fischer, from *Anton Otto Fischer*, p. 155.

Wreck of the *Herzogin Cecilie*

Shipwreck

"She struck one night on a sunken ledge
Off the Scillies, homeward bound,
Four months out for the Surrey Docks
With deals from Puget Sound;
Her back was broke, she couldn't live,
As any man might see,
An' it's 'ard to see a good ship go
The way she went," said he.

"An' I lost my oilskins an' sea boots,
An' all my bloomin' gear,
An' my chest with fancy shackles on
I'd 'ad this many a year;
There warn't no time to think o' them,
Lord know, in such a sea,
But—it's 'ard to lose your chest an' gear
The way we done," said he.

"An' better ships then 'er maybe
I'll sign in yet, my son,
An' chest an' gear I'll get again
As good as them that's gone:
But never a chap in all the world
Like him that's drowned an' dead,
An' it's 'ard to lose a man's best pal
The way I done," he said.

❖ ❖ ❖ ❖ ❖

From *Sea Songs and Ballads 1917-22*, edited by Cicely Fox Smith, published by Houghton Mifflin Co., New York, US, 1924, pp. 27-28.

The header graphic is a photograph of the four-masted barque *Herzogin Cecilie* pounding to pieces in Starhole Bay, 1936, as photographed by *Western Morning News*, from *The Herzogin Cecilie*, by Basil Greenhill & John Hackman, Conway Maritime Press, London, UK, 1991, p. 198.

Q-Ship

The Silent Navy

Oh, it is not in the papers and we cannot always know
Where to find the Silent Service whose address is "G. P. O."
And to-day you can't be certain where to-morrow it will be
Which yesterday was "somewhere" and the day before "at sea."

You will find the Silent Navy under every star that shines;
It may be hunting submarines, it may be sweeping mines;
From Cocos Isle to Dogger Bank, the Falklands to the Bight,
You will find the Silent Navy when it gets a chance to fight.

You'll find it in the wintry seas, making heavy weather,
When the wind and the waves are playing larks together;
You'll find it cruising up and down and coming in to coal,
Then out again in mist and rain to keep its long patrol.

You will find the Silent Navy where the ships come in from sea
With wheat and meat and fighting men and sugar for our tea,
You'll find it seizing contraband in narrow seas and wide,
You'll find it near, you'll find it far, and in between beside.

It may be on the Danube, or among the Belgian dunes;
Annexing South Sea Islands or blockading hot lagoons;
Escorting armies overseas or starting out in buff
To hand a Turkish railroad-line a friendly pinch of snuff.

It's here and there and everywhere, an unexpected guest,
That is not always welcome, be its manners of the best;
You'll meet it in the Baltic and again in Riga Bay,
Or landing with its guns in Equatorial Africa.

It is not in the papers, for the Censor deems it best;
But we sometimes hear a little, and we sometimes guess the rest,
And where there's any risk to run, or any death to dare,
You may seek the Silent Navy . . . and be sure you'll find it there!

❖ ❖ ❖ ❖ ❖

From *Songs and Chanties: 1914-1916*, edited by Cicely Fox Smith, published by Elkin Mathews, London, UK, 1919, pp. 187-189. Earlier published in *Fighting Men* by Elkin Mathews in 1916.

The "Silent Navy" of WWI was a highly secret operation run out of the Admiralty which among other things directed a small fleet of innocent looking tramp steamers, trawlers, and even schooners, referred to as "mystery ships" or "Q-ships," which were fitted with concealed heavy guns and manned by select naval crews. They would cruise the regular shipping lanes in the hope of being attacked by a submarine or small commerce raider. Part of their crew would abandon ship while others manned the guns and waited for the Germans to approach closer. If the British were lucky they got a chance to sink the Germans. But as the war continued on year by year, the Germans became understandably more cautious and several of these mystery ships were sunk and their crews lost. Other operations carried out by the "Silent Navy" included landing spies, commandos and saboteurs in enemy territory.

The header graphic is an illustration of a typical Q-ship and from *War Ships & Sea Battles of WWI*, edited by Bernard Fitzsimons, published by Beekman House, New York, US, 1973, pp. 138-139.

Skipper

Skipper

A rough old nut,
A tough old nut
Of a skipper:
But the right stuff,
Sure enough,
For a racing clipper.

Stiff and sturdy and five foot seven—
Cares for nobody under heaven;

All a-taut-o from truck to keel,
Will like iron and nerves like steel:
Loves his old packet better 'n his life,
Loves her like sweetheart, or child, or wife:
Runs down the easting under all she'll carry,
Hates taking sail off her worse 'n Old Harry!
When winds are baffling, or Trades are slack,
Or she's beating to windward tack and tack,
And the most she's logging is nine or ten,
He's the devil and all to live with then.
He curses the watch and he rows the mates,
Gives steward the jumps till he smashes the plates,
And nibbles his nails, and damns the weather,
And wishes the lot at the deuce together.

But oh! it's a different sort of a tale
When the seventeenth knot is over the rail,
With the Forties roaring their blooming best,
And the big seas galloping out of the West,
And the packet rolling her lee-rail under
And shipping it green with a noise like thunder,
And the galley's swamped, and the half-deck's drowned,
And the pots and the kettles are swimming around,
And she's romping through it with all she'll stand—
Oh, everything in the garden's grand!
He'll walk the poop, and he'll whistle and sing
As happy and proud as a blooming king,
And he licks his chops, the hoary old sinner,
Like the cabin cat when there's fish for dinner,
And says, as he holds by the weather shrouds
And squints aloft at the hurrying clouds:
"Mister, I reckon it's time, about,
We shook them reefs in her topsails out!"

❖ ❖ ❖ ❖ ❖

From *Full Sail: More Sea Songs and Ballads*, edited by Cicely Fox Smith, published by Houghton Mifflin Co., New York, US, 1926, pp. 3-5.

This poem is a tribute to the skipper of the Colonies clipper *Mary Ambree* but there is no record of the poet actually sailing on such a ship.

The header graphic is titled *Skipper* as drawn by Phil W. Smith to illustrate this poem, from *Full Sail*, facing p. 4.

"Old Harry" [2nd Stanza, line 8] refers to the Devil.

"Seventh knot" [3rd Stanza, line 2] refers to the knotted line used to gauge the ship's speed.

Patrol Boat Overhauling a Suspected Blockade Runner

Small Craft

When Drake sailed out from Devon to break King Phillip's pride,
He had great ships at his bidding and little ones beside,
Revenge was there and *Lion*, and others known to fame,
And likewise he had Small Craft (which hadn't any name!).

Small Craft—Small Craft—to harry and to flout 'em!
Small Craft—Small Craft—you cannot do without 'em!
Their deeds are unrecorded, their names are never seen,
But we know that there were Small Craft—because there must have been!

When Nelson was blockading for three long years and more,
With many a bluff first-rater and oaken "seventy-four,"
To share the fun and fighting, the good chance and the bad,
Oh, he had also Small Craft—because he must have had!

Upon the skirts of battle from Sluys to Trafalgar
We know that there were Small Craft—because there always are!
Yacht, sweeper, sloop, and drifter—to-day as yesterday
The big ships fight the battles—but Small Craft clear the way!
They scout before the squadrons when mighty fleets engage,

They glean War's dreadful harvest when the fight has ceased to rage:
Too great they count no hazard, no task beyond their power;
And merchantmen bless Small Craft a hundred times an hour!

In Admirals' dispatches their names are seldom heard,
They justify their being by more than written word;
In battle, toil and tempest, and dangers manifold,
The doughty deeds of Small Craft will never all be told.

Scant ease and scantier leisure—they take no heed of these,
For men lie hard in Small Craft when storm is on the seas;
A long watch and a weary from dawn to set of sun—
The men who serve in Small Craft, their work is never done.

And if, as chance may have it, some bitter day they lie
Outclassed, out-gunned, out-numbered, with naught to do but die,
When the last gun's out of action, good-bye to ship and crew—
But men die hard in Small Craft, as they will always do!

Oh, Death comes once to each man, and the game it pays for all,
And Duty is but Duty, in great ship and in small,
And it will not vex their slumbers, or make less sweet their rest,
Though there's never a big black headline for Small Craft going west.

Great ships and mighty captains—to these their meed of praise,
For patience, skill and daring, and loud victorious days—
To every man his portion, as is both right and fair,
But oh! forget not Small Craft, for they have done their share.

Small Craft—Small Craft—from Scapa Flow to Dover;
Small Craft—Small Craft—all the wide world over;
At risk of war and shipwreck, torpedo, mine and shell,
All honour be to Small Craft, for oh, they've earned it well!

❖ ❖ ❖ ❖ ❖

From *Sea Songs and Ballads 1917-22*, edited by Cicely Fox Smith, published by Houghton Mifflin Co., New York, US, 1924, p. 121-124. Earlier published in *Small Craft*, by Elkin Mathews, 1917, also by George H. Doran Company, 1919. First published in *Punch* magazine, Volume 153, September 19, 1917, p. 242.

A tribute to the many "Small Craft" that provided such invaluable service in WWI.

The header graphic is an illustration titled *Sentinels of the Grand Fleet: Patrol boat overhauling a suspected blockade runner*, from WWI, artist unknown.

Coiling Down

So Long

All coiled down, an' it's time for us to go;
Every sail's furled in a neat harbour stow;
Another ship for me, an' for her another crew—
An' so long, sailorman … good luck to you!

Fun an' friends I wish you till the pay's all gone—
Pleasure when you spend it an' content when it's done—
An' a chest that's not empty when you go back to sea,
An' a better ship than she's been, an' a truer pal than me.

A good berth I wish you, in a ship that's well found,
With a decent crowd forrard, an' her gear all sound,
Spars a man can trust to when it's comin' on to blow,
An' no bosun bawlin' when it's your watch below.

A good Trade I wish you, an' a fair landfall,
Neither fog, nor iceberg, nor long calm, nor squall,
A pleasant port to come to, when the work's all through—
An' so long, sailorman … good luck to you.

From *Sea Songs And Ballads 1917-1922*, edited by Cicely Fox Smith, published by Houghton Mifflin Co., NY, 1924, p. 101. First published in *Punch* magazine, Volume 158, January 21, 1920, p. 44.

The last command at the end of a voyage was "All coil down," tidying up all the loose lines on deck, and then the crew was free to go ashore and get their pay. This frequently meant saying goodbye to good friends that one would never see again, the spirit of which is well captured here.

First adapted for singing by Alan Fitzsimmons in 1998 as recorded by The Keelers on *The North Sea Ground*. Subsequently recorded by Danny and Joyce McLeod on *Never a Cross Word*, 2003. Also recorded with the same tune by Roll & Go on *Rolling Down to Sailortown*, 2006, and by The Portsmouth Shantymen on *Bung Up Bilge Free*, 2006.

The header graphic is an illustration titled *Coiling Down* drawn by Gordon Grant from his book *Sail Ho!*, facing p. 8.

Sold Foreign

"Sold Foreign"

In Lady Dock, in Lady Dock, the ships from far and wide
Lay down their loads of fragrant deals the dusky sheds beside,
And there come in, a dwindling few, the old ships year by year
That bore the grain from Frisco Bay, the wool from Geelong Pier—

Swift champions of the days of sail, whose old-time far renown
Still lives in many a shellback's yarn and song of Sailortown,
Sold foreign in their latter days to drudge the years away
Till time or chance shall bring them all to berth in Dead Man's Bay.

In Lady Dock, in Lady Dock, as I was strolling by,
Among the tramps and lighters there I saw an old ship lie,
That still, for all her foreign name and foreign flag beside,
A seaman's eye might surely know a daughter of the Clyde.

The sunset light was on her spars; the sunset splendour made
A glory in her ragged gear, her rigging slack and frayed;
It fired her battered figurehead, and, passing, touched with flame
Among her scrollwork's tarnished gold her new out-landish name.

But little need had I to learn what name was hers of old
From wheel or bell or pitted brass on capstan green with mould,
Who knew it like my christened own, as any man would know
The ship's that shared his goodliest years in days of long ago.

Her mizen yards were gone, and lopped the tapering boom that bore
The threshing of her mighty jibs in many a gale of yore;

Her planking gaped at many a seam, her paint was bleached and bare,
And dull was all her burnished brass, and rust was everywhere.

But tender as a lad's first love, and brave as boy-hood's dream,
Above the Deptford lumber sheds her shining spars did gleam;
A light that was not sunset seemed about her yards to glow,
And all her freight was golden years brought out of long ago.

And there were shipmates of old time and folks that well I knew,
That looked and laughed as I went by as once they used to do;
And up and down her rutted decks, the littered gear among,
A lad went with me all the while I lost when I was young.

And through the dusty Deptford streets and noisy Rotherhithe,
With springing step and glancing eye and eager heart and blithe,
A lad walked with me all the way I knew in years gone by,
A lad I met by Lady Dock . . . and O! that lad was I!

❖ ❖ ❖ ❖ ❖

From *Rovings: Sea Songs and Ballads*, edited by Cicely Fox Smith, published by Elkin Mathews, London, UK, 1921, pp. 16-18. First published in *Punch* magazine, Volume 160, June 8, 1921, p. 450.

The poet sub-titles this poem "Lady Dock" to indicate the point she had reached in her rovings (or "dock walloping" as she called it) around the many docks alongside the Thames in and near London.

The header graphic is an illustration titled *Sold Foreign* as drawn by Phil W. Smith for this poem, from *Sea Songs and Ballads 1917-22*, facing p. 42.

The Song of the Mill

As by the pool I wandered that lies so clear and still
With tall old trees about it, hard by the silent mill
Whose ancient oaken timbers no longer creak and groan
With the roar of wheel and water, and grind of stone on stone.

The idle mill-race slumbered beneath the mouldering wheel,
The pale March sunlight glided no motes of floating meal,
But the stream went singing onward, went singing by the weir—
And this, or something like it, was the song I seemed to hear:—

"By Teviot, Tees and Avon, by Esk and Ure and Tweed,
Here's many a trusty henchmen would rally to your need;
By Itchen, Test and Waveney, by Tamar, Trent and Ouse,
Here's many a loyal servant will help you if you choose."

"Do they no longer need us who needed us of yore?
We stood not still aforetime when England marched to war;
Like those our wind-driven brothers, far seen o'er weald and fen,
We ground the wheat and barley to feed stout Englishmen."

"You call the men of England, their strength, their toil, their gold,
But us you haven't summoned, who served your sires of old;

For service high or humble, for tribute great and small,
You call them and they answer—but us you do not call."

"Yet we no hoarded fuel of mine or well require,
That drives your fleet to battle or light the poor man's fire;
We need no white-hot furnace for tending night and day,
No power of harnessed lightnings to speed us on our way."

"By Tavy, Dart and Derwent, by Wharfe and Usk and Nidd,
Here's many a trusty vassal is yours when you shall bid,
With the strength of English rivers to push the wheels along,
And the roar of many a mill-race to join the victory song."

❖ ❖ ❖ ❖ ❖

From *Small Craft: Sailor Ballads and Chantys*, edited by Cicely Fox Smith, published by George H. Doran Co., New York, US, 1919, pp. 57-59. First published in *Punch* magazine, Volume 152, March 7, 1917, p. 155.

Sou' Spain

Are you coming, Johnnie Bowline, have you had your fill of fun?
Are you ready, Johnnie Bowline, now your pay-roll's spent and done,
And your welcome's growing stale,
And your pals begin to fail,
And there's something seems to whisper that it's time to sign again—
Time to hit the trail you know,
Time to pay your shot and go,
Time to heave your donkey's breakfast in and sail Sou' Spain!

Are you coming, Johnnie Bowline, have you kissed your girl adieu?
There's a lofty skysail clipper, and I think she waits for you,
And she's ready for the sea,
And the Peter's flying free,
And the wind goes through her rigging like a ranting old refrain:—
"Time to find a ship once more,
You've been over long ashore,
Time to hump your old sea chest aboard and sail Sou' Spain!"

Hurry up now, Johnnie Bowline, for she hasn't long to stay,
Get a move on, Johnnie Bowline, if you mean to come away,
For the tide is at the flood,
And the anchor's off the mud,
And they're tramping round the capstan in the darkness and the rain,—
And when oilskins and sea chest
Go the way of all the rest,
Oh, it's time to take the pierhead jump and sail Sou' Spain!

Sou' Spain! Sou' Spain, in the grey dawn breaking chill!
Sou' Spain! Sou' Spain, give it lip, lads, with a will!
Oh don't you weep for me, for me, my lovely Liza Jane,
You'll soon forget your sailorman that's sailed Sou' Spain!

From *Sea Songs And Ballads 1917-22*, edited by Cicely Fox Smith, published by Houghton Mifflin Co., New York, US, 1924, pp. 1-2. Earlier published in *Sea Songs and Ballads*, 1922. First published in *Punch* magazine, Volume 162, February 22, p. 150.

Compare this poem with "Outward Bound" and "Rio Grande."

First adapted for singing by William Pint (US) as recorded with Felicia Dale and Tom Lewis on *Making Waves*, 1992; an alternative setting was done in 1995 by Alan Fitzsimmons as recorded on *Seaboot Duff & Handspike Gruel* by Pinch o' Salt.

The actual location of Sou' Spain is a matter of conjecture to many sea-faring people but we believe it refers to anywhere in the South Americas where Spain was the colonizing power and Spanish the mother tongue.

Speed the Plough: a Country Song

As I was a-walking on Chilbolton Down,
I saw an old farmer there driving to town,
A-jogging to market behind his old grey,
So I jumped up behind him and thus he did say:

"My boy he be fightin', a fine strappin' lad,
I gave he to England, the only boy I had;
My boy he be fightin' out over the foam,
An' here be I frettin' an' mopin' at home."

"An' if there be times when 'tis just about hard
Without his strong arm in the field an' the yard,
Why, I plucks up my heart then an' flicks the old grey,
An' this is the tune that her heels seem to say:"

"'Oh the hoof an' the horn, the roots an' the corn,
The flock in the fold an' the pigs in the pen,
Rye-grass an' clover, an' barns brimmin' over,
They feed the King's horses an' feed the King's men'"

"Then I looks at my furrows to see the corn spring,
Like little green sword-blades all drawn for the King,
An' 'tis 'Get up, old Bess, there be plenty to do,
For old chaps like me an' old horses like you.'"

"My boy be in Flanders, he's young an' he's bold,
But they will not have we, lass, for we be too old;
So step it out cheerful, an' kip up your heart,
For you an' me, Bess, we be doin' our part—"

"'Wi' the shocks an' the sheaves, the lambs an' the beeves,
The ducks an' the geese an' the good speckled hen,
Rye-grass an' clover, an' barns brimmin' over,
To feed the King's horses an' feed the King's men.'"

❖ ❖ ❖ ❖ ❖

From *Songs And Chanties 1914-1916*, edited by Cicely Fox Smith, published by Elkin Mathews, London, UK, 1919, pp. 214-215. Earlier published in *Fighting Men* by Elkin Mathews in 1916. First published in *Punch* magazine, Volume 150, May 24, 1916, p. 350.

First set to music by Mike Kennedy, 2010.

Spring in Hampshire: 1916

Blackthorn winter is over and done with
(Pale gold sunsets and brimming rivers,
And the robin's note where the bare copse shivers);
And all of a sudden is Spring begun . . .
Swallow and leaf and the south wind's breath,
And mating creatures of fur and feather
Praising alike in the golden weather
Him in whose hand are living and dying,
The maker and giver of life and death.

Blackthorn winter is over and done . . .
And May comes in with the cuckoo's crying,
Warmth in the wind and strength in the sun,
And blossom in spate on the hawthorn brake.
Kingcups' gold in the wet green places,
And daisies lifting their shining faces
Like to the sands or the stars in number,
Or the dead that have died for this sweet land's sake.

Blackthorn winter is over and done . . .
And you, dear dead, to whose splendid slumber
Summers and winters and springs are one,
Who shall repay you, who shall restore you
Your lost sweet springs in the land that bore you?
Beyond all parting, beyond all pain,
Shall God not give you your Spring again?

❖   ❖   ❖   ❖   ❖

From *Songs and Chanties 1914-1916*, edited by Cicely Fox Smith, published by Elkin Mathews, London, UK, 1919, pp. 226-227. Earlier published in *Fighting Men* by Elkin Mathews in 1916.

WWI now seems to this poet to have no end in sight and the costs of this terrible war are now more apparent.

A Strain on the Affections

Squareheads

"I never did 'ave no use for Germans" (said Bill the bosun to me,
As he sat on the after hatchway coaming, smoking and drinking his tea);
"Never did 'ave no use for square'eads, sonny, an' that's the truth,
Since I went to sea in the old *Lord Clive*, back there in the days o' my youth.

"Danes I 'ave knowed, an' Swedes I 'ave knowed, as was white men
                                          through and through,
Norwegian—nigger—yeller an' brown—an' hard-case citizens too:
I've sailed in my time with most o' the brands, Dago, Dutchman, and Finn,
But never a decent shipmate yet did I strike in a German skin.

"Never the feller a man 'd choose to be with in a watch together,
Never the feller you'd like to know was around in the worst o' weather,
Never the chap that you'd want by your side when caught aback in a gale,
Or layin' aloft in your shirt, maybe, off the Plate there shortenin' sail.

"All very well for a harbour job they are, as I make no doubt,
Or 'andin' plates in a restorong, or sweepin' the cuddy out;
But I never did 'ave no use for the beggars, though why I can 'ardly say,
An' I always used to 'ammer 'em good, which I'm glad to 'ave done to-day!

"An' I wish I may lie where the lost ships lie that never mounted a gun,
Them as was raked with shrapnel fire—they could neither fight nor run;
Them as spread the sea with their dead when the day was sunny and fine,
Or went down slow as the dark come on, with their guts ripped out by a mine.

"I wish I may lie where them ships lie, the little ships an' big,
Liner an' tank an' leaky tramp, barge an' schooner an' brig,
The smacks an' Frenchy onion boats, an' the poor crews they bore,
Murdered in sight of open day by square'eads makin' war!

"I wish I may lie where them ships lie, an' no more sail the sea,
An' drink the drink them dead men drank, poor sailormen like me,—
So let me drink if I forget, an' so for ever lie,
If ever I ship with square'eads more until the day I die.

"An' if ever I take a German's pay again, in steam or sail,
Or 'andle German cargo more, baulk or barrel or bale,
If ever I put a finger o' mine on stuff a German owns,
Or 'elp to fill a German till with workin' o' my bones.

"If ever I risk this life o' mine, as I 'ave done before,
To bring some Bremen merchant 'ome 'is nitrates or 'is ore,
I wish I may dream o' nothin' but sinkin' ships an' drownin' men,
An' wake out o' the dream, an' sleep, an' dream it all again,—

"Dead bodies liftin' on the swell,—strong seamen once like me,—
An' fellers wounded, freezin' to death in open boats at sea,—
Babies, an' girls with long wet hair, an' mothers mad with woe,
The devil's job—the square'eads' job—I seen it an' I know!

"I never did 'ave no use for Germans—an' when this war is done,
There may be those who will forget—well, I shall not be one!
And by the ships I pass my word—an' by them souls I swear—
There'll be 'ot times in sailor-town when I meet a square'ead there!"

❖   ❖   ❖   ❖   ❖

From *Small Craft: Sailor Ballads and Chantys*, edited by Cicely Fox Smith, published by George H. Doran Co., New York, US, 1919, pp. 21-24. Earlier published in *Small Craft*, Elkin Mathews, 1917.

Total war polarizes both sides, with each side demonizing the other to justify further retaliation and recrimination. Many of the claims against the Germans in WWI were later proved to be fabricated by propaganda specialists. One tragic consequence of this successful propaganda effort was that few believed the even more extreme claims 20 years later as the Nazis consolidated their power and began WWII. Many of those claims, it turned out were based on a grim reality.

The header graphic is a cartoon titled *A Strain on the Affections* as British survivor commiserates with survivor of neutral Scandinavian ship by Leonard Raven-Hill, from *Punch* magazine, Volume 151, November 1, 1916, p. 311.

The "Windsor 'ouse flag" is a sailor's slang term for sailing as a Merchant Navy ship under RN command. "... In the windbag days" refers to the days of sail. "... big and bucko" is sailor talk for big, tough, strong and fair. "...twisted braid" refers to the gold ranking braid. Straight for the Royal Navy wavy for the Merchant Navy.

Clipper Ship *Blackwall* in a Squall off New Zealand

The Stately Blackwaller

She hauled through the dock-gates when morning was young
And chill on the water the river mist hung,
And the chaps on the pierhead all shouted "Hooray"
For the stately Blackwaller bound Eastward away.

Her captain he walked on his poop like a lord,
They piped the side handsome when he came aboard:
She had mates half-a-dozen in brassbound array,
The stately Blackwaller bound Eastward away.

She had midshipmen, topmen and gunners and all,
And forty prime shellbacks to heave and to haul,
A bosun to pipe and a fiddler to play,
The stately Blackwaller bound Eastward away.

So down London River she vanished afar:
Her gallant red ensign it shone like a star,
Till she faded from sight in the river mist grey,
The stately Blackwaller bound Eastward away.

She dropped the tug's hawser and so did depart
By Dungeness and Dover, by Spithead and Start,
And headland by headland their farewells did say
To the stately Blackwaller bound Eastward away.

Then shaking her reefs out she turned to the south,
Her canvas all gleaming, a bone in her mouth,
To the warm tropic seas where the flying fish play—
The stately Blackwaller bound Eastward away.

But the years have gone by like a tale that is told,
And home through those waters that knew her of old,
By Goodwin and Girdler, by Chapman and Nore,
The stately Blackwaller comes sailing no more.

Down the river of years she has vanished afar,
With all her proud fabric of sail and of spar,
She has faded from sight as a mist in the sun—
The stately Blackwaller of days that are done.

❖ ❖ ❖ ❖ ❖

From *Sea Songs and Ballads 1917-1922*, edited by Cicely Fox Smith, published by Houghton Mifflin Co., New York, US, 1924, pp. 11-12. Reprinted from *Sea Songs and Ballads*, 1922.

Dave Webber (UK) first adapted this poem for singing as recorded by Danny & Joyce McLeod on *Never a Cross Word*, 2002. It was also recorded by Gordon Morris and Peter Massey on *Full Sail: Inside the Lid*, as adapted for singing by Gordon Morris, 2002.

The header graphic is an illustration titled *Clipper Ship "Blackwall", 1000 Tons, in a squall off New Zealand on her homeward passage December 16th, 1857*, artist unknown.

Steel Rails

She sailed out o' Sunderland with a cargo o' rails—
She sailed out o' Sunderland all among the March gales;
With a cargo o' steel rails toward the Baltic she bore . . .
An' she'll sail out o' Sunderland with steel rails no more!

An' no one'll tell us, for no one'll know,
If she went at last sudden, or if she went slow,
But for all that we don't know, oh, this much is sure,
She'll sail out o' Sunderland with steel rails no more.

An' the ships out o' Sunderland, they will put forth again,
Bearing up for the Baltic in the wind an' the rain,
In the wind an' the weather when the March gales do roar—
But she'll sail out o' Sunderland with steel rails no more.

An' one load o' steel rails, oh, it's just like another,
But there's no lad the same as her own to his mother—
No lad in the world like the one that she bore . . .
An' he'll sail out o' Sunderland with steel rails no more!

❖ ❖ ❖ ❖ ❖

From *Sea Songs And Ballads 1917-22*, edited by Cicely Fox Smith, published by Houghton Mifflin Co., New York, US, 1924, pp. 99-100.

This one seems a straightforward lament, which is brought into sharp focus in the final verse.

"The late lamented Army mule, you'll meet 'im in the stew."

Stew

If you 'ave lost your 'aversack, your kit-bag or your pipe,
Your 'ousewife, soap or oily rag with which you clean your 'ipe,
Your belt or second pair o' socks, your lanyard or pull-through,
Oh, do not be dispirited, you'll get 'em in the stew!

If from the transport lines you miss a face you used to know,
With stick-up ears and yellow teeth all in a smilin' row,
'E is not gone for evermore, though seemin' lost to view,
The late lamented Army mule, you'll meet 'im in the stew.

We get it 'ot, we get it cold, we get it in between,
We get it thick, we get it thin, we get it fat an' lean;
We get it for our day-joo-nay, our tea and luncheon too,
An' when the long day's march is done we top it off with stew.

As we go through the countryside, route marchin' in the sun,
With bandy-rolls an' clobber on, which weighs about a ton,
Oh, this is what the people shout as we go marchin' through,
"'Ere come the Loyal Whatdyecalls—I'm sure I smelt the stew!"

When we are bound for foreign shores, an' 'arf across the water
The transport starts a-rollin like a transport didn't oughter,
To cheer our faintin' spirits up when we are feelin' blue,
They'll get the dixies goin' an' they'll serve us out some stew.

So when the wicked war is done an' peace is 'ere again,
We won't forget the chaps as toiled to please our inner men,
We'll call to mind the favourite dish we found on our menu,
An' think of our Battalion cooks—an' drink their 'ealths in—stew!

From *Songs and Chanties*, edited by Cicely Fox Smith, published by Elkin Mathews, London, UK, 1919, pp. 203-204. Earlier published in *Fighting Men* by Elkin Mathews in 1916. First published in *Punch* magazine, Volume 151, August 30, 1916, p. 156.

This is another of the poet's set of WWI poems which reflects the soldier's sense of humor with regard to what they were fed.

The header graphic is a cartoon drawn by Major George Denholm Armour, from *Punch* magazine, Volume 151, September 20, 1916, p. 211.

Stormy Dusk

To-night the dark came stormy down,
The sun went red to rest;
And fleets of clouds like battleships
Filled all the burning West.
The wind was rising to a gale,
It howled in hedge and tree . . .
And it's cold, bitter cold,
Where our sailormen must be,
Oh, it's bitter cold this night
In the wild North Sea!

To-night I heard the church clock strike
Across the gusts of storm . . .
And I thought how go the hours at sea
While we are sheltered warm . . .
I prayed God guard our ships at sea
And keep them from all harm . . .
And guide them through the pitch-black tides
Where the drifting death may be,
And give them soon a safe return
And a fruitful victory . . .

And Christ our Lord who walked of old
On waves of Galilee,
Be near our men this night
In the wild North Sea!

❖   ❖   ❖   ❖   ❖

From *Sailor Town: Sea Songs and Ballads*, edited by Cicely Fox Smith, published by George H. Doran Co., New York, US, 1919, pp. 116-117. Earlier published in *The Naval Crown* by Elkin Mathews in 1915.

Two Prostitutes and a Sailor

Sweethearts and Wives

The very first voyage as ever I made
I went to sea in the East Coast trade,
And I courted a gal at Seaton Sluice—
If her name warn't Lizzie it must ha' been Luce—
So I did!

And then I signed in a Colonies clipper
With a rare old rip of a racing skipper,
And there warn't no sense nor there warn't no use
A-courting a gal at Seaton Sluice;
So I looked for another down Melbourne way—
If her name warn't Kitty it must ha' been May—
So I did!

Oh, next I sailed in a pearlin' brig
To the South Sea Isles both little and big,
Where it warn't no use, say what you may,
A-courting a gal down Melbourne way;
So I didn't worry with her no longer,

But I soon picked up with a gal in Tonger,
An' island gal as brown as a berry—
Don't know her name, but I called her "Cherry"—
So I did!
(And so on *ad lib*.)

But last I signed in a Liverpool liner—
Go where you will and you won't find a finer!
And it's time, thinks I, to be settlin' down,
So I married a widder in Monkeytown,
With a bit in the bank and a "corner-off,"
And when I'm ashore now I lives like a toff.
And as for the girl at Seaton Sluice
I 'ope she ain't waitin', for that ain't no use,
And as for the ones at Montreal
And Tanger and Taltal and Melbourne and all,
And all the whole boilin' from France to Fiji,
I 'ope they're all married and 'appy like me—
So I do!

❖ ❖ ❖ ❖ ❖

From *Sailor's Delight*, edited by Cicely Fox Smith, published by Methuen & Co., London, UK, 1931, pp. 111-113.

They say that a sailor had a girl in every port, and if you think about the implications of that, then each girl might have had several sailor lovers at sea as well.

First set to music by Michael Head (1900-1976) in 1949, as published in *Six Sea Songs*.

The header graphic is an illustration titled *British Plenty-1794* as drawn by Henry Singleton and shows a sailor ashore with a lovely "flashgirl" on either arm.

Three Ships

The Three Ships

I had tramped along through dockland till the day was all but spent,
But for all the ships I there did find I could not be content;
By the good pull-ups for car-men and the Chinese dives I passed,
And the streets of grimy houses each one grimier than the last,
And the shops whose shoddy oilskins many a sailorman has cursed

In the wintry Western ocean when it's weather of the worst . . .
All among the noisy graving docks and waterside saloons
And the pubs with punk pianos grinding out their last year's tunes,
And the rattle of the winches handling freights from near and far,
And the whiffs of oil and engines, and the smells of bilge and tar;
And of all the craft I came across, the finest for to see
Was a dandy ocean liner . . . but she wasn't meant for me!
She was smart as any lady, and the place was fair alive
With the swarms of cooks and waiters, just like bees about a hive;
It was nigh her time for sailing, and a man could hardly stir
For the piles of rich folks' dunnage here and there and everywhere.

But the stewards and the awnings and the white paint and the gold
Take a deal o' living up to for a chap that's getting old;
And the mail-boat life's a fine one . . . but a shellback likes to be
Where he feels a kind o' homelike after half his life at sea . . .

So I sighed and passed her by—"Fare you well, my dear," said I,
"You're as smart and you're as dainty as can be;
You're a lady through and through, but I know it wouldn't do—
You're a bit too much a rich man's gal for me!"

So I rambled on through dockland, but I couldn't seem to find
Out of all the craft I saw there just the one to please my mind;
There were tramps and there were tankers, there were freighters large and small,
There were concrete ships and standard ships and motor ships and all,
And of all the blessed shooting-match the one I liked the best
Was a saucy topsail schooner from some harbour in the West.
She was neat and she was pretty as a country lass should be,
And the girl's name on her counter seemed to suit her to a T;
You could almost smell the roses, almost see the red and green
Of the Devon plough and pastures where her home port must have been,
And I'll swear her blocks were creaking in a kind o' Devon drawl—
Oh, she took my fancy rarely—but I left her after all!
For it's well enough, is coasting, when the summer days are long,
And the summer hours slip by you just as sweetly as a song,
When you catch the scent of clover blowing to you off the shore,
And there's scarce a ripple breaking from the Land's End to the Nore;
But I like a bit more sea-room when the short dark days come in,
And the Channel gales and sea-fogs and the nights as black as sin,
When you're groping in a fairway that's as crowded as a town
With the whole damned Channel traffic looking out to run you down,
Or a bloody lee shore's waiting with its fierce and foaming lips
For the bones of poor drowned sailormen and broken ribs of ships.
So I sighed and shook my head—"Fare you well, my dear," I said,
"You're a bit too fond o' soundings, lass, for me;
Oh, you're Devon's own dear daughter—but my fancy's for deep water
And I think I'll set a course for open sea!"

So I tramped along through dockland, through the Isle of Dogs I went,
But for all the ships I found there still I couldn't be content . . .
Till, not far from Millwall Basin, in a dingy, dreary pond,
Mouldy wharf-sheds all around it and a breaker's yard beyond,
With its piles of rusty anchors and chain-cables large and small,
Broken bones of ships forgotten—there I found her after all!
She was foul from West Coast harbours, she was worn with wind and tide,
There was paint on all the bright work that was once her captain's pride,
And her gear was like a junk-store, and her decks a shame to see,
And her shrouds they wanted rattling down as badly as could be . . .
But she lay there on the water just as graceful as a gull,
Keeping some old builder's secret in her strong and slender hull;
By her splendid sweep of sheer-line and her clean-keen clipper bow
You might know she'd been a beauty . . . and, by God, she was one now!
And the river gulls were crying, and the sluggish river tide
Made a kind of running whisper by her red and rusted side,
And the river breeze came murmuring her tattered gear among,
Like some old shellback, known of old, that sings a sailor's song—
That whistles through his yellow teeth an old deep-water tune
(The same did make the windows shake in the Boomerang Saloon!),
Or by the steersman's elbow stays to tell a seaman's tale
About the skippers and the crews in great old days of sail!

And I said: "My dear, although you are growing old, I know,
And as crazy and as cranky as can be . . .
If you'll take me for your lover, oh we'll sail the wide seas over,
You're the ship among them all that's meant for me!"

❖ ❖ ❖ ❖ ❖

From *Sea Songs and Ballads 1917-1922*, edited by Cicely Fox Smith, published by Houghton Mifflin Co., New York, US, 1924, pp. 74-78. Earlier published in *Ships and Folks*, 1920. First published in *Punch* magazine, Volume 157, October 1, 1919, p. 298.

Here the poet is fantasizing about what ship she'd like to sail on again as she wanders the London docks.

"The Boomerang Saloon" in Victoria, British Columbia, was popular with men from the schooners and steamers. It was located at No. 4, Court Alley, off Bastion Square, and was attached to the Boomerang Hotel. The Boomerang was one of many saloons in the area which provided seamen with refreshing alcoholic beverages, entertainment and camaraderie.

The header graphic is an illustration titled *Three Ships* as drawn by Phil W. Smith for this poem, from *Sea Songs and Ballads 1917-1922*, frontispiece.

Mermaid

Told at "The Pilchards"

Tom Pascoe was a fisherman belonging to Portloe,
And when I can't just tell you, but 'tis middlin' long ago;
And overright the Manacles, a-hauling of his seine,
Tom Pascoe catched a merrymaid and let her go again.

Oh, I tell you, she was pretty, I tell you she was neat,
From her head down to the little tail she'd got instead o' feet;
She was pink and pearl and silver, like the sea at break o' day,
And the shiny, greeny eyes of her they stole Tom's heart away.

Now Tom he was a lazy chap and fonder of his beer
Than he was of mending up his nets and tending to his gear,
And that was how it came about the seine bust clean in two,
And Tom he stood there gaping while the merrymaid slipped through.

She popped between the meshes and she flipped her dainty tail,
And there wasn't so much left of her as just one shiny scale,

And Tom he hove a thumping sigh and nothing did he say
But hauled his gear in sorrowful and fished no more that day.

His girl run down to meet him when she saw his boat come in,
But he passed her like a stranger with a kind o' foolish grin,
And he sits down on the sea-wall and starts to mend his gear,
And, says he, "You don't give me the slip next time, my pretty dear!"

And any day and every day as boats could go to sea,
Why, there you'd see Tom Pascoe just as plain as plain could be,
Looking for his merrymaid, and peering overside
And calling to her tender-like to come and be his bride.

His mates they'd shake their heads sometimes and say, "Poor chap, he's queer!"
Then tap their foreheads meaning-like and finish up their beer,
And his girl she cried her eyes up till you'd think she'd never stop—
And then she married Mister Budd as kep' the general shop.

And his boat got old and leaky and his beard got long and white,
And folks got kind of used to him and said he wasn't right;
And all the little boys and girls 'ud point at him and say,
"Good morning, Mister Pascoe; any merrymaids to-day?"

And the years come and the years went, till one day a feller found
A boat with no one in her, on her lonesome drifting round;
And seeing she was Pascoe's it was plain enough to see
He'd gone to find his merrymaid as wouldn't come to he.

So all you likely fisher chaps as listens to my lay,
Don't have no truck wi' merrymaids—you'll find it doesn't pay;
And don't go yarning with your pals and sitting at your beer
Instead o' mending up your nets and tending to your gear,
But remember poor Tom Pascoe and the end what he come to . . .
Well, talking *is* a thirsty job; I don't mind if I do.

❖ ❖ ❖ ❖ ❖

From *Sailor's Delight*, edited by Cicely Fox Smith, published by Methuen & Co., London, UK, 1931, pp. 125-129. First published in *Punch* magazine, Volume 173, August 24, 1927, p. 206.

Gordon Morris (UK) first adapted this poem for singing, as recorded on *Full Sail: Inside the Lid*, 2002.

The header graphic is an engraving of a mermaid by A. Knesing, 1880, from *Songs of the Sea*, p. 155.

Torpedo Boats on Night Maneuvers

Torpedo Boats

There be poets in plenty have sung in the praise
Of the famous old names of Old Navy days,
Of *Victory, Téméraire, Ajax, Orion,*
Collossus, Caliope, Tiger and *Lion;*
But it's hard, you'll acknowledge, to rhyme you the fame
Of a craft that has never so much as a name,
But simply appears on the tale of the sea
As—"H. M. Torpedo Boat (One, Two, or Three)!"

Likewise our destroyers have names to suggest
Their fierceness, their fleetness, their daring, their zest,
The Insects, the Rivers, the Tribes and what not—
Not to mention selections from Shakespeare and Scott;
But though they should ransack the poets all through,
And exhaust every creature that's known at the Zoo,
Not a name would there be in the whole bag of tricks
To spare for Torpedo Boat Four, Five or Six!

But it matters not greatly when work's to be done
If they call you *Ark Royal or Nought-Forty-One;*
If you sound like a flagship of ancient renown,
Or more like the knapsack once worn by John Brown.
And whether your portion be number or name,
There are some things, you'll find, which are always the same,
And sisters in Duty, at risk of the sea,
Are Dreadnought, Destroyer, and humble T. B.

There be sea-fogs to blind her and tempests to batter,
There be shoals to decoy her and lee shores to shatter,
There be seas which engulf her and billows which roll,
With spray dashing high as a Dreadnought's control;
While to keep her from dullness are mines not a few

(And she knows just a bit about submarines too!),
Such lesser distractions as fall to the lot
Of H. M. Torpedo Boat—please yourself what!

And though scant be her portion on History's page,
Recounting great battles where fleets did engage,
Though the end of her day be to perish alone,
Her deeds unrecorded, her glory unknown;
Come lightning or tempest, come gale or come sleet,
She must stick to her job on the fringe of the Fleet,
Patrolling our coast round from Harwich to Humber,
H. M. Torpedo Boat—known by a number!

❖ ❖ ❖ ❖ ❖

From *Songs and Chanties 1914-1916*, edited by Cicely Fox Smith, published by Elkin Mathews, London, UK, 1919, pp. 193-195. Earlier published in *Fighting Men* by Elkin Mathews in 1916, pp. 26-27.

An eloquent tribute to these intrepid but fragile torpedo boats of WWI.

The header graphic is a painting titled *Torpedo Boats in action at the Naval Maneuvers* by Charles Dixon, from *Britannia's Bulwarks*, published by George Newnes, London, UK, 1901.

Tower of Babel

Annabel Lee
Is the name on the label,
Reckon it ought to be
Tower o' Babel,

For there ain't a lingo
That's spoke or swore in
From San Domingo
To Tuti-*cor*-in,

From the Pole or near it
To Pernambuker
But what you'll 'ear it
On board this 'ooker.

And I give you my word, in our port watch
There's English and Irish and Welsh and Scotch,
A Finn, a Swede and a Portuguee,
A Frenchy, a Bim and a heathen Chinee,
And a son of a Dutch, son of a Greek,
Son of a nigger from Martinique.

❖ ❖ ❖ ❖ ❖

From *Sailor's Delight*, edited by Cicely Fox Smith, published by Methuen & Co., London, UK, 1931, pp. 7-8; first published in *Punch* magazine, Volume 180, April 22, 1931, p. 433.

Here the poet seems intent on characterizing the diverse crew that typically sailed aboard windjammers in the early 1900's, using some of the rough language that the sailors would have used. She specifically notes that a "Bim" is a native of Barbados.

The Tow-Rope Girls

Oh, a ship in the Tropics, a-foaming along,
With every stitch drawing, the Trade blowing strong,
The white caps around her all breaking in spray,
For the girls have got hold of her tow-rope today.

An' it's "Haul away, girls, steady an' true,
Polly an' Dolly an' Sally and Sue,—
Mothers an' sisters an' sweethearts an' all,
Haul away . . . all the way . . . haul away, haul!"

She's logging sixteen as she speeds from the South,
The wind in her royals, a bone in her mouth,
With a wake like a mill-race she rolls on her way,
For the girls have got hold of her tow-rope to-day.

The Old Man he stood on the poop at high noon;
He paced fore and aft and he whistled a tune,
Then put by his sextant and thus he did say:
"The girls have got hold of her tow-rope to-day."

"Of cargoes and charters we've had our full share,
Of grain and of lumber enough and to spare.
Of nitrates at Taltal and rice for Bombay,
And the girls have got hold of our tow-rope to-day."

"She has dipped her yards under, hove to off the Horn,
In the fog and the floes she has drifted forlorn,
Becalmed in the Doldrums a week long she lay,
But the girls have got hold of her tow-rope to-day."

Oh, hear the good Trade wind a-singing aloud,
A homeward bound shanty in sheet and in shroud,
Oh, hear how he whistles in the halliard and stay,
"The girls have got hold of the tow-rope to-day!"

And it's oh! for the chops of the Channel at last,
The cheer that goes up when the tug hawser's passed—
The mate's "That'll do"—and a fourteen months' pay—
For the girls have got hold of our tow-rope to-day . . .

Then haul away, girls, steady an' true,
Polly an' Dolly an' Sally and Sue,
Mothers an' sisters an' sweethearts an' all,
Haul away—all the way—haul away—haul!

❖ ❖ ❖ ❖ ❖

From *Ships and Folks*, edited by Cicely Fox Smith, published by Elkin Mathews, London, UK, 1920, pp. 43-44.
First published in *Punch* magazine, Volume 158, May 12, 1920, p. 350.

An old belief from the Age of Sail is that of the "Tow-Rope Girls." When a ship was homeward bound at last, and running fast in the strong trade winds with all sails set, it was said that the girls at home were "pulling on the tow rope."

Alan Fitzsimmons first adapted this poem for singing, as recorded by Pinch o' Salt on *Seaboot Duff & Handspike Gruel*, 2000. The Harry Browns of Bristol also recorded this song on *Shipshape and Harry Fashion* in 2005, as arranged by Stephen Derrick. This poem was also adapted for singing by Bob Zentz (US), as recorded on *Closehauled on the Wind of a Dream*, 2007.

Tramp on the Waterfront

The Traveller

I've loops o' string in the place o' buttons,
I've mostly holes for a shirt;
My boots are bust and my hat's a goner,
I'm gritty with dust an' dirt;
An' I'm sitting here on a bollard
Watching the China ships go forth,
Seeing the black little tugs come sliding
With timber booms from the North.
Sitting and seeing the broad Pacific
Break at my feet in foam.
Me that was born with a taste for travel
In a back alley at home.

They put me to school when I was a nipper
At the Board School down in the slums,
And some of the kids was good at spelling

And some at figures and sums;
And whether I went or whether I didn't
They learned me nothing at all,
Only I'd watch the flies go walking
Over the maps on the wall,

Strolling over the lakes an' mountains,
Over the plains an' sea,—
As if they was born with a taste for travel—
Something the same as me!

If I'd been born a rich man's youngster
With lots o' money to burn,
It wouldn't ha' gone in marble mansions
And statues at every turn,
It wouldn't ha' gone in wine and women,
Or dogs an' horses an' play,
Nor yet in collecting bricks and bracks
In a harmless kind of a way;
I'd ha' paid my fare where I've beat my way
(But I couldn't ha' liked it more!),
Me that was born with a taste for travel—
The same if you're rich or poor.

I'd ha' gone bowling in yachts and rolling
In plush padded Pullman cars,—
The same as I've seen 'em when I lay resting
At night-time under the stars,
Me that have beat the ties
And rode the bumpers from sea to sea,
Me that have sweated in stokeholds
And dined off mouldy salt-horse and tea;
Me that have melted like grease at Perim
And froze like boards off the Horn,
All along of a taste for travel
That was in me when I was born.

I ain't got folks and I ain't got money,
I ain't got nothing at all,
But a sort of a queer old thirst
That keeps me moving on till I fall,
And many a time I've been short o' shelter
And many a time o' grub,
But I've got away from the rows o' houses,
The streets, an' the corner pub—
And here by the side of a sea that's shining
Under a sky like flame,
Me that was born with a taste for travel,
Give thanks because o' the same.

From *Sailor Town: Sea Songs and Ballads*, edited by Cicely Fox Smith, published by George H. Doran Co., New York, US, 1919, pp. 120-122. First appeared in *Songs in Sail* published by Elkin Mathews, 1914.

A note in *The Daily Colonist*, a newspaper in Victoria, British Columbia, May 11, 1913, lists this poem as having been entered by the poet in their poetry competition. The result of the competition, however, is evidently not recorded.

The poet describes this "traveller" in more detail in her book *Sailor-Town Days*, 1923, p. 170:

"The Pacific coast is a great place for rolling stones of every sort and description. I remember meeting what I should say was the very perfection of the type. He was sitting on the edge of the Outer Wharf—it was in Victoria (BC)—on a sort of coaming that runs along the edge, very comfortable to sit on, though given to exuding tar in very hot weather. His coat—I don't think there was a shirt underneath—was fastened together with string, being innocent of buttons. His knee showed through his trousers. His boots were ruins. But he spoke with the unmistakable accents of cultivation."

Smith was evidently quite fond of this poem. She used the last four lines in her preface of a book by the Theodore Roosevelt family titled *Cleared for Strange Ports*, 1924.

This poem was first adapted for singing by Charles Ipcar in 2008, as recorded on *Sailortown Days*, 2009.

The header graphic is an illustration titled *A Tramp's Sunday Morning Change* from *Darkness & Daylight* in New York, p. 597, artist unknown.

Traveller's Rest

When you are tired of the long road and the open sky,
I wish it may be my door that you're passing by:
I wish it may be my hearth where you will sit down
And tell your tales of the land and sea and the strange far town.

Oh, come you in from eastward or come you in from the west,
Here's good cheer to greet you and welcome of the best:
Oh come you with your pockets full or come you home poor,
Here's a place by the fireside and an open door.

You'll tell me where you were since, and the things you've seen
Up and down the wide world where so long you've been,—
All the time that I've been here and you far away,—
And then awhile be silent, as good friends may.

And then awhile listen to the wind and rain,
Moaning in the chimney-breast, beating at the pane,—
Dark and cold outside there, and the stormy skies,
And you sitting down here with the firelight in your eyes.

❖ ❖ ❖ ❖ ❖

From *Sailor Town: Sea Songs and Ballads*, edited by Cicely Fox Smith, published by George H. Doran Co., New York, US, 1919, pp. 69-70. An earlier edition of *Sailor Town* was published by Elkin Mathews in 1914.

This poem seems to be a follow-up to "Shipmates," the poet still somewhat hopeful that her sailor friend "Dan" might find his way back to her. See also "News in Daly's Bar" for when she's given up hope.

The *Tryphena's* Extra Hand

In the clipper ship *Tryphena* swingin' nor'ard from the Line,
With the Trade wind blowin' steady and her flyin' kites ashine,
Five and sixty days from Anjer with her freight of Foochow teas,
There a sailorman lay dying, and the words he spoke were these:

"Many a year I've knowed this packet, and I've got to like her well,
And I've not much hopes of heaven and I've not much use for hell:
But if so be as they'll let me, by the great hook-block I swear,
When the old *Tryphena* wants me, dead as living I'll be there."

There'll be one more at the halyards, there'll be one on the yard
Fisting down them thundering courses when they're frosted good and hard,
One more tallying on the forebrace when the waist's neck deep in foam,
One more hand to sweat the tops'ls up and sheet to'gal'n's'ls home.

So, just off the Western Islands, when he smelt the land he died,
And they laid aback the main y'rd and they dropped him overside,
Then they squared away for England, pulley-hauling with a will,
But, for all they thought they'd left him there, he sailed aboard her still.

And the chaps as was his shipmates went the way as all chaps go,
And the folks as was her owners sold the old ship long ago,
But whoever owned or sold her, and whoever went or came,
The *Tryphena's* extra hand he sailed aboard her just the same.

And he never signed no Articles, he never drawed no pay,
He never scoffed no vittles, but by night as well as day,
Though you'd never know his coming, nor you'd never see him go,
He'd be always somewheres handy and it comin' on to blow.

And he'd stand by wheel and lookout, and you'd kind o' feel him near,
Kind o' see him and not see him, kind o' hear him and not hear,
And the funny thing about it was you somehow couldn't swear
(Though you knew it sure as shooting) when the Extra Hand was there.

And in port, when all the chaps had gone ashore to take their ease,
And left the ship as lonely and as quiet as you please,
Not a blessed soul aboard her but the galley cat and you,
Then you'd hear a sort o' something—more than once I've heard it too.—

Like a feller up aloft there, puttering round among the gear,
Seizing there another ratline, putting on a mousing here,
And rum-tumming old tunes over such as shellbacks used to know
In the good old China tea trade, many and many a year ago.

❖ ❖ ❖ ❖ ❖

From *Full Sail: More Sea Songs and Ballads,* edited by Cicely Fox Smith, published by Houghton Mifflin Co., New York, US, 1926, pp. 41-45.

This is a haunting poem of an old sailor who after dying returns as a ghost to help sail his favorite ship. There are similarities in this poem to one by Masefield titled "Cape Horn Gospel."

First adapted for singing by William Pint (US) using the traditional tune from "Quare Bungle Rye" as recorded by William Pint and Felicia Dale on *Round the Corner*, 1997; later recorded by Bob Zentz on *Closehauled on the Wind of a Dream*, 2007. An alternative setting was made by Gordon Morris as recorded on *Full Sail: Inside the Lid*, 2002.

Meeting the Ocean Swells

War Risks

"Let go aft" . . . and out she slides,
Pitching when she meets the tides . . .
She for whom our cruisers keep
Lordly vigil in the deep . . .
Sink or swim, lads, war or no,
Let the poor old hooker go!

Soon, hull down, will England's shore,
Smudged and faint, be seen no more:
Soon the following gulls return
Where the friendly docklights burn . . .

Soon the cold stars, climbing high,
March across the empty sky . . .
Empty seas beyond her bow
(Lord, she's on her lonesome now!)

When the white fog, stooping low,
Folds in darkness friend and foe . . .
When the fast great liners creep
Veiled and silent through the deep . . .

When the hostile searchlight's eye
Sweeps across the midnight sky
Lord of light and darkness, then
Stretch Thy wing o'er merchantmen!

When the waters known of old
Death in dreadful shape may hold . . .
When the mine's black treachery
Secret walks the insulted sea . . .

(Lest the people wait in vain
For their cattle and their grain),
Since Thy name is mercy, then,
Lord, be kind to merchantmen!

❖ ❖ ❖ ❖ ❖

From *War Verse*, edited by Frank Foxcroft, published by T. Y. Crowell, New York, US, 1918, p. 124. First published in *The New York Tribune*, December 27, 1914, and subsequently in *The Westminster Gazette*, 1915.

Composed during the first year of WWI as a prayer for outward bound merchant ships.

The header graphic is an illustration titled *Butting Into It* as painted by Anton Otto Fischer, from *Anton Otto Fischer*, p. 174.

The Waters of Oblivion

I had ridden far from the battle, from the red wrack, and the last
Lost hope that had clung to hope till the shadow of hope was past,
From the stream that ran blood, not water, and the grief that burned like fire
For the cause lying trodden down and down in the battle-mire.

I had not washen my sweat off, nor the red stain o' the field;
I could scarce bear up my battered harness and dinted shield.
Spent was I, clean forspent, and my heart like lead in my breast,
And the very bones o' my body yearned and hungered for rest.

Then, through the dusty byways, while yet the West was aflame
Like a plundered city with sunset, at the end of even I came,
Heart-weary and body-weary, with my wounds both many and deep,
To the well that is called oblivion, to the quiet waters of sleep.

Rosy it brimmed in the twilight, redder and fairer than wine,
Cold in a grey stone hollow I saw it dimple and shine:
And of all that a man might dream and desire, then seemed it the best
To drink, and be no more thirsty, lie down and for ever rest.

I looked my last on the sunset ere my dry lips drank their fill,
I bade good-bye to the earth and sky and the windy hill:
And all I had fought and lost for, all I had loved and known,
Came back and lingered beside me where I knelt by the pool alone.

A bird cried o-er the pastures, a weak wind wakened and stirred,
Rustling the dusty wayside weed like a stealthy step half-heard:
And the well that slept in silence deep as the dreamless years
On a sudden sobbed in the stillness with a sound like human tears.

Old trumpets pealed in the twilight; lost war-cries rang as of old:
And I looked where the night mist gathered ghostly and grey, and behold!
Squadron on squadron, rank upon rank in the darkening sky,
Saw as it were my comrades muster, and heard them cry:

"You will sleep sound, our comrade: never, never again
Will you ride out for a cause forlorn, in the wind and rain.
And the din and thunder of battle shall be in your ears no more
Than the sigh of a lost wave breaking on a far-off shore."

"All that was bitter and weary, all that was grievous and hard,
You shall put off as a garment, and cast away as a shard.
All that was gallant and goodly—the splendour, the glory, the gleam,
Shall pass away as a tale forgotten, or a long past dream."

"Laid aside as a burthen, as a child's sorrow forgot,
Though morn and even clamour the trumpets: 'Why comes he not'—
He who was once our comrade—he whose slumber is deep
By the well which is called Oblivion, by the quiet waters of Sleep?"

"Win or lose, what matters at all, when the unheeding hand
Never gropes through the mist of sleep for the rusted brand?
What matter when never the dreaming heart nor the drowsy eye
Quicken because he remembers the great old days gone by?"

Ah, God, I was weary . . . weary, and wounded, and sore athirst:
But I turned from the clear cold waters, my heart knew them accurst:
And I rode in my dinted armour, with my wounds both many and deep,
From the well that is called Oblivion, from the quiet waters of Sleep.

❖   ❖   ❖   ❖   ❖

From *Small Craft: Sailor Ballads and Chantys*, edited by Cicely Fox Smith, published by George H. Doran Co., New York, US, 1919, pp. 151-155. First published in an earlier edition of *Small Craft*, 1914.

The fourth in a set of poems titled "Romance." It's possible that this poet, in 1914, was in fact in deep despair from the loss of her beloved sailor "Dan" and may even have considered suicide. But in this poem she clearly turned away.

Wales Forever

Have you heard the torrent leaping from the mountain to the sea?
Have you heard the tempest sweeping over Snowdon wild and free?
Have you seen the beacon springing over Cambria's hills and dales?
Have you heard the war-cry ringing to the dauntless heart of Wales?
Oh! A fair land, a clear land, as any far or near land—
God guard the land of Wales for evermore.

It is in the name of freedom that the harp of Wales has rung;
It is in the praise of freedom that the songs of Wales are sung;
It is in the cause of freedom, her wealth, her boast, her pride;
That the sword of Wales has triumphed and the sons of Wales have died;
Oh! A proud land, an old land, a little yet bold land—
God guard the land of Wales for evermore.

Oh, where's the man would palter with a coward word or deed?
Oh, where's the man would falter in the hour of Cambria's need?
No tyrant e'er could tame her or break her soul of yore;
No son of Wales will shame her when the trumpet calls to war;
Oh, a fine land, a fair land, the freemen claim as their land—
God bless the land of Wales for evermore.

❖ ❖ ❖ ❖ ❖

From *Wales Forever:* Song, English words by Cicely Fox Smith; Welsh words by E. Lewis; music by Charles Villiers, Stanford (1852-1924); published by Enoch & Sons, London, UK, 1918.

Transcribed at the British Library. "Palter" is to talk or act insincerely or misleadingly.

The Way of a Ship

Give me a tall barque swinging
South'ard with all she'll stand;
Give me the sea's voice singing
Far out of sight of land;
And East way or West way,
North or South of the Line,
The way of a ship is the best way—
A ship's way the way that's mine!

Give me the royals gleaming
Silver against the moon—
Give me the white wake streaming,
Give me the Trade's old tune . . .
And East Way or West way,
Up or down the sea,
The way of a ship is the best way,
A ship's way's the way for me!

❖ ❖ ❖ ❖ ❖

From *Ships and Folks*, edited by Cicely Fox Smith, published by Elkin Mathews, London, UK, 1920, p. 51. In this earlier version there are some minor spelling changes and a different last line.

Also titled as "Sea Voices:"

> Give me a tall barque swinging
>   S'uthard with all she'll stand
> Give me the sea's voice calling
>   Far out o' the sight of land
>
> And it's East or it may be West away
>   Nor'ard or South the line
> The way of a ship is the best way
>   A ship's way's the one that's mine
>
> Give me the royals gleaming
>   Silver against the moon
> Give me the white wake streaming
>   Give me the trade's old tune
>
> Give me a tall barque swinging
>   Nor'ard or South the line
> The way of a ship is the best way
>   A ship's way's the one that's mine

This is from a set of poems entitled "The Way of the Ship" which were set to music by Easthope Martin, and published as *Five Chantey Songs*, Enoch & Sons, 1920.

Dedicated to Sir Edward Elgar, O. M.

Capt. John Brander

What the Old Man Said

"Don't you take no sail off 'er," the Ol' Man said,
Wind an' sea rampagin'
Fit to wake the dead,—

Thrashin' through the Forties
In the sleet and 'ail,
Runnin' down the Eastin'
Under all plain sail

"She's loggin' seventeen
An' she's liftin' to it grand,
So I'm goin' below
For a stretch off the land.

"An' if it gits any worse, Mister,
You can come an' call me,
But—don't you take no sail off 'er,"
Said the Ol' Man,
Said 'e!

Them was the days, sonnies,
Them was the men,
Them was the ships
As we'll never see again.

Oh, but it was somethin'
Then to be alive—
Thrashin' under royals
South o' Forty-five . . .

When it was—
"Don't you take no sail off 'er"
The Ol' Man'd say,
Beard an' whiskers starin'
Stiff with frozen spray—

"She's loggin' seventeen,
An' she's liftin' to it grand,
An' I mean to keep 'er goin'
Under all she'll stand."

"An' if it gits any worse, Mister,
You can send an' call me,
But—don't you take no sail off 'er,"
Said the Ol' Man,
Said 'e!

❖ ❖ ❖ ❖ ❖

From *The Return of the "Cutty Sark,"* by Cicely Fox Smith, published by Methuen & Co, London, UK, 1924, p. 30. This poem was later published in the same form in *Full Sail* two years later. First published in *Punch* magazine, Volume 167, September 10, 1924, p. 297.

The header graphic certainly looks the part for this poem but is actually a photograph of Capt. John Brander of the ill-fated four-masted steel barque the *Wanderer*; photographer unknown.

Burial at Sea

The Wine of Life

"When I've left off carin' the way I do,
For the things that's old an' the things that's new,

For the things that's happenin' every minute,
An' all the sights as the world's got in it;

When a ship's no more than a ship to me
An' there's nowhere left as I want to see;

When the fun's all flat an' the jokes all stale,
An' there ain't no taste in the cakes an' the ale—

You can stitch me up as soon as you like
In a corner o' wore-out sail," said Mike,

"With 'olystones at my 'eels and 'ead,
An' dollop me overboard—I'll be dead!"

❖   ❖   ❖   ❖   ❖

From *Full Sail: More Sea Songs and Ballads*, edited by Cicely Fox Smith, published by Houghton Mifflin Co., New York, US, 1926, pp. 46-47.

Imagine an old time sailor in the quiet hours musing about the things he enjoys and that make his life complete. "You can stitch me up as soon as you like"—When a sailor died at sea he was sewn up into a canvas shroud, usually a scrap of old sail, with weights inside to make him sink and then he was dropped overboard.

The header graphic is a painting titled *Burial at Sea* by Anton Otto Fischer from his book *Foc's'le Days*, facing p. 48.

Wireless Room aboard the U. S. S. *Cheyenne*

Wireless

The ships call night and day,
They call both far and near . . .
And a hundred words have they,—
Warning, counsel and cheer.

They call, they call and they cry,
They call, and their words are whirled
Under the rim of the sky,
Over the edge of the world.

The ships call each to each,
They call anear and afar;
As deep unto deep their speech,
As star calling to star.

The ships call night and day,
They call both far and near,
And a hundred words have they,
But never the one word—"Fear!"

❖ ❖ ❖ ❖ ❖

From *Rhymes of the Red Ensign*, edited by Cicely Fox Smith, published by Hodder & Stoughton, London, UK, 1919, p. 39.

The header graphic is a photo of the wireless room aboard the U. S. S. *Cheyenne*, 1916, photographer unknown.

Witches

"Finns, they're witches," said Murphy, "'tis born in 'em maybe,
The same as fits, an' freckles, an' follerin' the sea,
An' ginger 'air in some folks . . . an' likin' beer in me."

"Finns, they're witches," said Murphy, "an' powerful strong ones too . . .
They'll whistle a wind from nowhere, an' a storm out o' the blue
'Ud sink this 'ere old hooker, an' all her bloomin' crew."

"Finns, they're witches," said Murphy, rubbing his hairy chin,
"An' some says witchcraft's bumkum, an' some it's deadly sin,
But . . . there ain't no 'arm as I see in standin' well with a Finn."

❖   ❖   ❖   ❖   ❖

From Sea Songs and Ballads 1917-22, edited by Cicely Fox Smith, published by Houghton Mifflin Co., New York, US, 1924, p. 91. First published in Punch magazine, Volume 158, February 25, 1920, p. 156.

The superstition that Finnish sailors had the power to control winds appears to have been a long held traditional one among deep-water sailors.

Circular Quay, Sydney, Australia—1871

A Wool Fleet Chorus

Fare you well, you Sydney girls, time for us to go!
The Peter's at the fore truck, and five thousand bales below,
We've a dozen shellbacks forrard, and a skipper hard as nails,
And we're bound for old England and the January sales!

Soon we'll leave the Snares behind, blusterous and strong,
Up'll come the Westerlies and hustle her along:
Running like a driven deer through the thundering gales,
Racing under royals for the January Sales!

Old Cape Stiff'll drop astern, like a blinking dream,
Sleet and snow and crashing seas, fog and ice'll seem,
Snoring through the Tropics with a Trade that never fails,
Nor'ard on a bowline for the January sales!

Then the girls'll get her towrope, and she'll smell the land again,
And she'll reel the knots off steady as a blessed railway train,
Till seventy days from Sydney Heads the Lizard Light she hails—
First to the Channel for the January sales!

❖   ❖   ❖   ❖   ❖

From *The Return of the "Cutty Sark,"* edited by Cicely Fox Smith, published by Methuen & Co., London, UK, 1924, p. 24. This poem was also published in *Full Sail* by Houghton Mifflin Co., 1926, in basically the same form as given here.

Barrie Temple (UK) first adapted this poem for singing, as recorded by Salt o' the Earth on *Tomorrow's Tide*, 1998.

The header graphic is a photograph of Circular Quay in Sydney, Australia as photographed by Charles Pickering, 1871, from *Sail & Steam*, pp. 34-35. According to Falconer: "In this panoramic view, clippers are moored near the wool warehouses that lined the quay. The wool clipper in the centre of this photograph is the *Duke of Sutherland*, built in 1865; it was on this ship that the novelist Joseph Conrad served as an ordinary seaman in 1878-79."

Words of Wisdom

"Come all you young seamen, take heed now to me,
A hard case old sailorman bred to the sea,
As had sailed the seas over afore you was born,
And learned 'em by heart from the Hook to the Horn . . .
Don't hold by the ratlines when going aloft
(Which I've told you afore, but I can't tell you too oft),
Or you'll strike one that's rotten as sure as you live,
And it's too late to learn when you've once felt it give;
If you don't hit the bulwarks, you'll sure hit the sea—
For them rotten ratlines—they're the devil," says he.

"Now if you should see, as you like enough may,
When tramping the docks for a ship some fine day,
A spanking full-rigger just ready for sea,
And think she looks all that a hooker should be . . .
Take heed you don't ship with a skipper that drinks—
You'd better by half play at fan-tan with Chinks!
For that stands for nothing but muddle and mess—
It may mean much more and it can't mean much less—
What with wrangling and jangling to drive a man daft,
And rank bad dis-*cip*-line both forrard and aft,
A ship that's ill-found and a crew out of hand,
It's a touch-and-go chance she may never reach land,
But sink in the gale or broach in a sea,
For them drunken skippers—they're the devil," says he.

"And if you go further and pause to admire
A ship that's as neat as your heart could desire,
As smart as a frigate aloft and alow,
Her brasswork like gold and her planking like snow . . .
Look round for the mate by whose twang it is plain
That his home port is somewhere round Boston or Maine,
With a jaw that's the cut of a square block of wood,
And . . . beat it, my son, while the going is good!
It's scouring and scraping from morning till night
To keep that brass shiny and keep them decks white,
And belaying-pin soup both for dinner and tea,
For them smart down-easters—they're the devil," says he.

"But if by good fortune you chance for to get
A ship that ain't hungry, or wicked, or wet,
That answers her hellum both a-weather and lee,
Sails well on a bowline, and well running free . . .
A skipper that's neither a fool nor a brute,
And mates not too free with the toe of their boot . . .
A "Sails" and a bosun not new to the trade,

And a "Slush" with a notion how vittles is made,
And a crowd that ain't half of 'em Dagoes or Dutch.
Or Mexican greasers, or niggers, or such,
You stick to her close as you would your wife—
She's the sort that you only find once in your life—
And ships is like women—you take it from me
That if they *are* bad 'uns, they're the devil," says he.

❖   ❖   ❖   ❖   ❖

From *Ships and Folks*, edited by Cicely Fox Smith, published by Elkin Mathews, London, UK, 1920, pp. 17-18. Also in *A Sea Chest*, edited by Cicely Fox Smith, 1927, pp. 196-199. First published in *Punch* magazine, Volume 158, January 7, 1920, p. 10.

The ethnic and racial slurs in this poem are typical of the sailor slang that unfortunately prevailed in the Great Age of Sail.

Man Overboard!

A Yarn of Dan's

"Now 'ere's a yarn as is true," said Dan, "An' you can't say that o' most:
I was in the packet *Mogador* an' bound to the Chile coast,
An' there was a chap in the watch wi' me—a greaser from Brazil—
An' 'is name it was Pedro (or Josey, maybe), but we mostly called 'im Bill.

An' 'e was the rottenest sort of a bloke in the sailorizin' line
As ever you see in your life—leastways, as ever I see in mine:

'E couldn't pull 'is weight on a rope, 'e could neither reef nor furl,
I give you my word in a gale o' wind 'e was worse nor a seasick girl.

The mate we 'ad was a down-east Yank, an' 'e was sure a terror,
'E fairly wallered in paint an' pitch, an' that's no fatal error.
It was 'olystonin' an' scourin' paint an' keepin' brasswork bright,
An' chippin' anchors an' scrapin' seams, from mornin' until night.

Well, me an' Bill we was tarrin' down on the crojick yard one day,
The packet snorin' along like fun an' shippin' dollops o' spray,
An' Bill 'e slumped 'is bucket o' tar, which was just what you might expeck,
'Arf of it over a brand-new course an' the rest on the fresh-scoured deck.

The mate 'e let a roar like a bull when 'e seen what Bill 'ad done
As fetched the 'ole o' the watch below on deck to see the fun,
An' 'e jumped for the shrouds an' started aloft with a face that was fit to kill,
An' into the drink with a flop an' a splash an' a Dago yell went Bill.

The mate 'e squinted over the rail an' saw Bill swimmin' strong,
An' 'e started kickin' 'is seaboots off, an' that didn't take him long,
An' over the rail in a brace o' shakes in all the rest of 'is gear
'E follered Bill like a streak o' light—an' you should 'ave 'eard us cheer!

The Old Man passed the word along to 'eave the packet to,
'I can't afford for to lose my mate, an' a thunderin' good mate too,
So lower away the quarter boat, an' pull, my lads, with a will,
But I'm darned if I'd lower a boat,' says he, 'for a lump o' stuff like Bill.'

Well we lowered the boat, an' we pulled away, but that ain't part o' the yarn,
An' we picked 'em off o' the buoy we'd thrown, best part of a mile astern:
The mate 'e'd got Bill's 'ead in 'is arm in a kind of a strangle 'old,
With 'is fingers twisted into 'is wool as if 'e'd been stuffed with gold.

We hauled 'em in by the slack o' their pants, an' as soon's we'd got 'em aboard
The mate 'e blew a bubble or two an' 'e got 'is breath an' roared:
'I'll larn ye spilin' my deck, ye swab,—by thunder so I will!'…
An' they give 'im a pair o' binoculars along o' savin' Bill!"

❖ ❖ ❖ ❖ ❖

From *Sea Songs and Ballads 1917-22*, by Cicely Fox Smith, published by Houghton Mifflin Co., New York, US, 1924, pp. 17-19. Previously published in *Sea Songs and Ballads,* 1922. First published in *Punch* magazine, Volume 162, April 26, 1922, p. 336.

This poem has a nice twist in it. With Smith one never quite knows how a poem will wind up.

The header graphic is an illustration titled *Man Overboard!* as drawn by Gordon Grant for his book *Sail Ho!*, p. 107

The Yarn of the Blue Star Line

When I was a lad and went to sea
In Seventy-seven or six maybe,
There was ten tall ships on Merseyside
Did sail or berth with every tide;
There was "Hills" and "Halls" and "Dales" and "Bens,"
"Counties" and "Cities" and "Lochs" and "Glens";
But none there was so fast and fine
As them that sailed in the Blue Star Line.

They had tough nut skippers as hard as nails
To crack 'em along in the Cape Horn gales,
And hard-case shellbacks thirty-two
There used to be in a Blue Star crew,—
To man the capstan, and raise the shout
At tacks and sheets when she went about,
And brassbound reefers eight or nine
In them tall ships of the Blue Star Line.

But, Lord! the names them good ships had—
Enough to drive a plain man mad!
The way them names was spelled or said
'Ud crack your jaw like Liverpool bread;
There was *Parthen-ope* and *Thucydides,*
And a whole lot more and worse besides,
And *Melpomene* and *Euphro-syne*
Was the sort o' names in the Blue Star Line.

But the steam come up and the sail went down,
And them tall ships of high renown
Was scrapped, or wrecked, or sold away
To the Dutch or the Dagoes, day by day;
They went the way o' the songs we sung,
And the girls we kissed when we all were young,
And most o' the chaps as used to sign
Along wi' me in the Blue Star Line.

The *Parthen-ope* she met her fate
Run down in a fog off the Golden Gate;
And the *Thucy-dides* kept knocking around
'Tween the Cape and Cardiff and Puget Sound,
Till a fire in her main hold burned her down
To the water's edge at Simonstown . . .
And none was left but the *Euphro-syne*—
The blooming last o' the Blue Star Line.

There isn't a cargo great or small
But that old hooker's carried 'em all;

For whether it's rubber or whether it's rice,
Coal or copra or salt or spice,
Teak or whale oil or bone manure,
Smelly guano or copper ore,
Gulf Ports cotton or B.C. pine,
All's one to the last of the Blue Star Line.

There isn't a tugboat far or near
But's took her to sea with a parting cheer,
Or picked her up off o' Lizard Head
With nine months' rust in her hawse pipes red;
There isn't a pilot near or far
From Gravesend Reach to Astoria Bar,
On Hudson or Hoogly or Thames or Tyne,
But's known the last o' the Blue Star Line.

She's been up and down, and here and there,
But there ain't no time for to tell you where;
She's been sunk and raised, and drove ashore,
A wreck, and a hulk, and a prize o' war . . .
But she's gone at the last, as I've heard tell,
In the Channel chops as she knowed so well,
On Saint Agnes light where a drifting mine
Done in the last o' the Blue Star Line.

And it's good to know as she took her bones,
When it come to the last, to Davy Jones,
With the old Red Duster flying the same
As it did in the days when she earned her fame,
When ten tall ships on Merseyside
Did sail or berth with every tide,
And none o' them all so fast and fine
As them tall ships o' the Blue Star Line.

❖ ❖ ❖ ❖ ❖

From *Rhymes of the Red Ensign,* edited by Cicely Fox Smith, published by Hodder & Stoughton, London, UK, 1919, pp. 55-57. First published in *Punch* magazine, Volume 155, September 25, 1918, p. 197.

The Blue Star Line named ships of the same type after a particular feature, hence the lines:

> There was "Hills" and "Halls" and "Dales" and "Bens,"
> "Counties" and "Cities" and "Lochs" and "Glens"

But their pronunciation was easy compared to that of the mythological names:

> There was *Parthen-ope* and *Thucydides,*
> And a whole lot more and worse besides,
> And *Melpomene* and *Euphro-syne*

One could readily sing this poem to the tune of Gilbert & Sullivan's "The Ruler of the Queen's Navee."

Whitby Harbour, 1882

Yarns

When the docks are all deserted, and the derricks all are still,
And the wind across the anchorage comes singing sad and shrill,
And the lighted lanthorns gleaming where the ships at anchor ride
Cast their quivering long reflections down the ripple of the tide,

Then the ships they start a-yarning, just the same as sailors do,
In a hundred docks and harbours from Port Talbot to Chefoo—
Just the same as deep-sea sailormen a-meeting up and down
In the bars and boarding-houses and the streets of sailortown.

Just the same old sort of ship-talk sailors always like to hear—
Just the same old harbour gossip gathered in both far and near—
In the same salt-water lingo sailors use the wide world round
From the shores of London River to the wharves of Puget Sound,—

With a gruff and knowing chuckle at a spicy yarn or so,
And a sigh for some old shipmate gone the way that all men go,
And there's little need for wonder at a grumble now and then,
For the ships must have their growl out, just the same as sailormen.

And they yarn along together just as jolly as you please,
Lordly liner, dingy freighter rusty-red from all the seas,
Of their cargoes and their charters and their harbours east and west,
And the coal-hulk at her moorings she is yarning with the best—

Telling all the same tales over, many and many a time she's told,
In a voice that's something creaky now, because she's got so old,
Like some old broken sailorman when drink has loosed his tongue,
And his ancient heart keeps turning to the days when he was young.

Is it but the chuckling mutter of the tide along the buoys,
But the creak of straining cables, but the night-wind's mournful noise,
Sighing with a rising murmur in among the ropes and spars,
Setting every shroud and backstay singing chanties to the stars?

No, the ships they all are yarning, just the same as sailors do,
Just the same as deep sea sailors from Port Talbot to Chefoo,
Yarning through the hours of darkness till the day-light comes again . . .
But oh! the things they speak of, no one knows but sailormen.

❖ ❖ ❖ ❖ ❖

From *Rovings: Sea Songs and Ballads*, edited by Cicely Fox Smith, published by Elkin Mathews, London, UK, 1921, pp. 38-40. First published in *Punch* magazine, Volume 159, November 17, 1920, p. 390.

This poem is a delightful piece of whimsy. There are many tales of horses and other animals talking together at the end of the day when work is done but this is the only one I know of about ships having such a conversation.

Mike Kennedy first adapted this poem for singing, 2009.

The header graphic is a painting titled *Whitby Harbour, 1882*, by Atkinson Grimshaw, from The Art of Nautical Illustration, p. 92.

The Yeoman's Son

It fell about the edge of dark,
Between the sun and moon,
The yeoman's son came home again
With the mire upon his shoon—

With the red clay upon his shoon
From a furrowed field afar—
The sour and bitter clod that breaks
Beneath the share of war.

"Oh, kiss me once on the brows, mother,
And hold me to your breast;
For the long day's work is over and done,
And I go glad to rest."

"And oh, good-bye, my father's house,
Good-bye to field and hill,
For I'll lie down in the red furrow
To sleep, and sleep my fill."

"I shall not rouse at the cock-crow,
I shall not wake with the sun;

I shall sleep the sleep of a strong man tired
When his day's work is done."

"Ay, deep I'll sleep in the red furrow,
Out over the Channel foam . . .
And another hand than mine, mother,
Must lead the harvest home!"

❖ ❖ ❖ ❖ ❖

From *Songs and Chanties 1914-1916*, edited by Cicely Fox Smith, published by Elkin Mathews, London, UK, 1919, pp. 229-230; also published in *Fighting Men* by Elkin Mathews in 1916. First published in *The Windsor Magazine*, Volume 42, June-November, 1915, p. 290.

The Younger Son

The Younger Son he's earned his bread in ways both hard and easy
From Parramatta to the Pole, from Yukon to Zambesi;
For young blood is roving blood, and a far road's best,
And when you're tired of roving there'll be time enough to rest!

And it's "Hello" and "How d'ye do?" "How's the world been using you?
Thought you were in Turkestan or China or Peru!"—
It's a long trail in peace-time where the roving Britons stray . . .
But in war-time, in war-time, it's just across the way!

He's left the broncos to be bust by who in thunder chooses;
He's left the pots to wash themselves in Canada's cabooses;
He's left the mine and logging camp, the peavie, pick and plough,
For young blood is fighting blood, and England needs him now!

And it's "Hello" and "How d'ye do?" "Who'd ha' thought of meeting you!
What's the news of Calgary, Quebec and Cariboo?"
It's a long trail in peace-time where the roving Britons stray,
But in war-time, in war-time, it's just across the way!

He's traveled far by many a trail, he's rambled here and yonder,
No road too rough for him to tread, no land too wide to wander;
For young blood is roving blood, and the spring of life is best,
And when all the fighting's done, lad, there's time enough to rest.

And it's good-bye, tried and true, here's a long farewell to you
(Rolling stone from Mexico, Shanghai or Timbuctoo)!
Young blood is roving blood, but the last sleep is the best,
When the fighting all is done, lad, and it's time to take a rest!

❖ ❖ ❖ ❖ ❖

From *Sailor Town: Sea Songs and Ballads*, edited by Cicely Fox Smith, published by George H. Doran Co., New York, US, 1919, pp. 88-90. Earlier published in *The Naval Crown* by Elkin Mathews in 1915. First published in *Punch* magazine, Volume 148, June 9, 1915, p. 458.

This poem is from the beginning of WWI, describing how young men scattered all over the world were returning to their native England to fight and defend the Empire from the Germans and their allies.

BOOK 3

THE LATER POEMS: 1932 TO 1953

The Three Daws Hotel, drawn by Phil W. Smith,
from *Sailor-Town Days*, facing page p. 100.

Burying the Plunder

Pirate Gold

"Pieces of eight!" sighed the palm-trees, whispering each to each;
"Pieces of eight!" screamed the seabirds, in a voice like human speech;
"Pieces of eight!" roared the long Pacific rollers, thundering up the beach. . . .

Pieces of eight that they buried long ago,
Toiling up the hillside when the moon hung low
Half-a-dozen pirates with a brass-bound chest,
Six out of twenty-four, and where were all the rest?
Nigger Joe, Manuel, Pedro from Brazil,
Hooky Sam, and Black Patch, and Crook-nosed Bill. . . .

Pillage of the Indies, plunder of the Main,
With a ghost to watch over it until they came again:
Big branched candlesticks crusted thick with gems,
Uncut diamonds for kings' diadems;
Emerald rings, silver bars, gold doubloons,
Rubies big as pigeons' eggs, and pearls like moons. . . .

Dead men's treasure waiting day by day
For the slim black schooner curtseying up the bay!
Dead men's treasure, and no one's left to know
The place where they buried it, centuries ago. . . .

❖ ❖ ❖ ❖ ❖

From *True Tales of The Sea*, by Cicely Fox Smith, published by Oxford University Press, London, UK, 1932, p. 63. Published originally in *Country Life*.

The header graphic is drawn by Rowland Hilder and was used to illustrate this poem in *True Tales of The Sea*, p. 61.

The Island

Great ports and swarming cities
There be by all the seas,
With shipping in their harbours
And bales upon the quays;
But I'd leave them all behind me
To cruise the wide world round,
And maybe find an island
(A lost and lonely island!)
That no one else has found.

If East or West I know not,
If North or South the Line,
Ringed round with whispering palm-trees,
Or crowned with singing pine;
But in some unsailed ocean
I know must surely be
An undiscovered island
(A sweet and secret island!)
That waits for none but me!

❖   ❖   ❖   ❖   ❖

From *True Tales of The Sea*, by Cicely Fox Smith, published by Oxford University Press, London, UK, 1932, p. 145. Published originally in *Country Life*.

This poem preceded a tale about the real "Robinson Crusoe's Island."

The Coast of Barbary-2

It's of a British merchantman, from London town she hailed,
She loaded figs and Spanish wine, and homeward then she sailed;
But it chanced that she was taken by a rover of Sallee—
All along the coast of Barbarie!

She was taken by a galley with a crew of turbaned Moors,
Who shave men's crowns, and scourge them, and chain them to their oars,
Till they wear their lives out at the last in hard captivity—
All along the coast of Barbarie!

But the captive English mariners each to the other said,
'We will not live in bondage, it were better to be dead!
Let us bide our time, and strike our blow for blessed liberty—
All along the coast of Barbarie!'

The wind began to thunder and the sea began to rise,
And they crept upon the captain and they took him by surprise:
They took him by the breeches and they hove him in the sea—
All along the coast of Barbarie!

The boatswain and the master's mate they served too the same,
Likewise the Moorish seamen they quickly over-came:
They clapped them under hatches where the rats and beetles be—
All along the coast of Barbarie!

Then they set a course for Naples where they changed the ship for gold,
And all the Moorish captives into slavery they sold,
And with money in both pockets they departed joyfully—
All along the coast of Barbarie!

From *True Tales of The Sea*, by Cicely Fox Smith, published by Oxford University Press, London, UK, 1932, pp. 175-176. Published originally in *Country Life*.

This poem is completely different from an earlier poem she wrote with the same title and also has marked differences from the well known folk ballad of the same name though it was probably intended to be sung in a similar fashion.

A Smuggler's Swag

A Smuggler's Song

The privateersman loves the chase,
And the smell of smoke and powder O!
He likes to hear the boarders cheer,
And the cannon thundering louder O!
But the smuggler O, the smuggler O,
He likes a craft so handy O—
A cargo of silk and a cargo of lace,
And a cargo of good French brandy O!

The poacher likes a shiny night
When the hunter's moon is soaring O!
And the wrecker's toast is 'A rockbound coast

And the winter gales a-roaring O!'
But the smuggler O, the smuggler O,
He likes a beach so sandy O!
A cargo of lace and a cargo of rum,
And a cargo of good French brandy O!

❖ ❖ ❖ ❖ ❖

From *True Tales of The Sea*, by Cicely Fox Smith, published by Oxford University Press, London, UK, 1932, p. 200. Published originally in *Country Life*.

This poem was clearly intended as a song, possibly modeled after the traditional shanty Smith collected titled "A Sailor Likes His Bottle."

The header graphic is titled *The Smuggling Trade—a night scene in a smugglers' headquarters, near Calais, Maine, assorting the "Swag,"* sketched by J. Becker, from *Frank Leslie's Illustrated Newspaper*, September 6, 1873, p. 413.

Old Ship's Logs

Loud in the chimney the wild wind blows,
But all is peace where the salt wind glows;
A green wood fire will smoulder and smell,
But an old ship's sides will serve you well;
A fire of elder brings dull and harm,
But an old ship's bones they are lucky and warm;
And a fire of pine may crackle and sing,
But an old ship's ribs are a fire for a king.

❖ ❖ ❖ ❖ ❖

From *The Western Morning News*, Plymouth, Exeter, and Truro, UK, October 3, 1932, front page.

This poem is part of an ad placed by Shipbreakers, Ltd., for selling ship's logs from the old HMS *Defiance*: "A limited supply of old ship's logs, so famous for their beautiful colour flames from the old *Defiance*."

This ship is further described at http://www.battleships-cruisers.co.uk: The twelfth *Defiance* is a 91-gun screw wooden ship, launched at Pembroke in 1861. She is of 5270 tons, 3350 horse-power, and 12 knots speed. Her length, beam, and draught were 255 ft., 56 ft., and 18 ft. This ship, however, was never commissioned until December 1884, when she was appropriated as the stationary Torpedo School Ship at Devonport.

To a Rusty Bicycle

How many times in years gone by,
My faithful grid have you and I
Sought gladly out in sun and rain
By broad highway and winding lane,
In many a well remembered ride,
The secrets of the countryside!
Who shall recount how many a time
I've pushed you up some endless climb
And breathless, as I topped the rise,
Possessed five counties with my eyes—
What long descents gone hurtling down
To river bridge or red-roofed town,
While past me, vibrant, shrill and strong,

The cleft air thrilled its heartening song?
How often in those days of yore
Hard words and undeserved you bore,
When on some upland bleak and bare,
A dozen miles from everywhere,
I heard the faint protesting sigh,
As dark came down on earth and sky,
Of punctured rubber basely torn
By lurking nail or casual thorn!

Enough old friend. The days are done
Of careless rides in rain and sun;
Too fearful are the joys they feel
Who take today the road a-wheel.
And you in attic hid must lie
While day by empty day goes by,
Your bright enamel cracked and dim,
A spider's mesh on spoke and rim,
While people urge without avail,
"*Do* give that to the jumble sale!"

Perish the thought! For old sake's sake
No hand but mine shall clutch your brake,
No alien feet awake again
Your grinding hubs and rattling chain;
Like some old hunter out at grass
You shall your life's long evening pass,
And, dreaming of brave days we've known,
Flake slowly into rust alone.

❖ ❖ ❖ ❖ ❖

From *Punch* magazine, Volume 183, November 23, 1932,

"Grid" in line 2 is old slang for bicycle.

I Have Seen

I have seen—I have seen
Beneath these dreary skies,
Beside these swamps
A greater Rome arise.

I have seen the masts
Stand close and straight as pines,
Climbing the slopes
O' the purple Apennines.

I have seen ships
With neither sail nor oar,
Crowd with their freights
From many a distant shore.

I have seen—I have seen
A thousand bustling quays
Piled with the trade
Of undiscovered seas.

I have seen—

❖   ❖   ❖   ❖   ❖

From *Anchor Lane*, by Cicely Fox Smith, published by Methuen & Co., London, UK, 1933, p. 26.

This poem is an imagined piece recited by a Finnish sailor named Balticus from about 100 AD, conveying a vision of what the London docks will look like centuries later in the 1900's.

Ham, Shem and Japhet

Ham, Shem, and Japhet went a-sailing in the *Ark*,
With all the kinds of animals that grunt and squeak and bark,
All the birds and beasts and things the world has ever known,
And Ham, Shem, and Japhet chose pets to be their own.

Ham chose an elephant, Shem chose a whale,
Japhet chose a little mouse with only half a tail;
Ham and Shem had each a bird with feathers on his forehead,
Japhet had a beetle; Mrs. Noah cried "How horrid!"

Ham got a unicorn, Shem a shiny dove,
Japhet, just a lonely toad that nobody would love;
Ham picked the white puppy, Shem picked the brown,
Japhet picked the spotty one that they were going to drown.

❖   ❖   ❖   ❖   ❖

From *All the Other Children*, by Cicely Fox Smith, published by Methuen & Co., London, UK, 1933, p. 1.

Master Brocky

Long before the Mammoth died in the ice and snow,
Master Brocky made his earth snug and warm below.

Long before the Flint Men made barrows, mounds, and rings,
Master Brocky Badger he was catching snails and things.

Long before the Legions marched down the road from Rome,
Master Brocky Badger he was very much at home.

Long before the Vikings came to kill and burn and spoil,
Master Brocky Badger had his earth in English soil.

So don't you grudge his simple meal of beetles, worms, and frogs,
And don't you go upsetting him with nasty yapping dogs!

His diet might not much appeal to folk like you and me,
But Master Brocky Badger's got a noble pedigree!

❖   ❖   ❖   ❖   ❖

From *All the Other Children*, by Cicely Fox Smith, published by Methuen & Co., London, UK, 1933, p. 2.

Wolf Cubs

If all the old stories are true that we hear
Of wolves and their doings, it's certainly queer
The only idea that they have about girls
Is to eat them up whole with their baskets and curls,
Whereas Romulus, Remus, and Mowgli, and others
Have found them, we're told, most affectionate mothers . . .
Why is it, you ask? . . . well four words are enough
To solve the whole mystery—"Boys are too tough!"

❖   ❖   ❖   ❖   ❖

From *All the Other Children*, by Cicely Fox Smith, published by Methuen & Co., London, UK, 1933, p. 8.

The Changeling

"Look!" said the hedge-sparrow, "isn't he fine?
Nobody else has a child like mine!
Look at his appetite—look at his size—
Look at his beak—and his wings—and his eyes!
Every day he keeps growing and growing,
And what he will be, well, there isn't no knowing!
Flies by the dozen and worms by the score,
Whatever he gets he keeps asking for more,
I'm sometimes afraid that he'll swallow me whole.
All the others fell out of the nest,
I was sorry, but there—it was all for the best.
Just you look at him! Isn't he fine?
Was ever a child such a whopper as mine?"

❖   ❖   ❖   ❖   ❖

From *All the Other Children*, by Cicely Fox Smith, published by Methuen & Co., London, UK, 1933, p. 22.

In the book the poet shows a picture of a cuckoo chick dwarfing a hedge sparrow and writes of the cuckoo's predilection for laying eggs in other bird's nests.

Hide and Seek

I rather think I would not wish,
If I might choose, to be a fish.

They cannot play with bat or ball.
For why? They have no hands at all!

Nor even kick each other's shins,
When all the feet they have are fins.

But little fishes, so they say,
Grand games of hide-and-seek can play

Among the lilies and the reeds
And mass of trailing water weeds;

In sunlit shoal and shadowy pool
And twinkling eddy, bright and cool.

There to and fro they dart and gleam
All up and down their native stream,

Till from the willow's twisted roots,
With fuss and fluster, out there shoots,

Roused from his nap, a cross old trout,
With "Hi! young varmints! You keep out!"

❖ ❖ ❖ ❖ ❖

From *All the Other Children*, by Cicely Fox Smith, published by Methuen & Co, London, UK, 1933, p. 25.

The Hen that has Hatched Ducks

"Dear, dear! Cluckety-cluck!
Who'd be a hen that has hatched out a duck?
Cluck-cluck! What shall I do?
Was ever a hen with such pickles as you?"

❖ ❖ ❖ ❖ ❖

From *All the Other Children*, by Cicely Fox Smith, published by Methuen & Co., London, UK, 1933, p. 34.

It is not unusual for a hen to be set to brood a clutch of duck eggs, and if there is a pond nearby the newly hatched ducklings will invariably make a bee-line for it much to the consternation of the hen.

Nests

Nests are wonderful things . . .
The rook's high house that swings
Daring the winds of March,
The loose-built home the dove
The neat mud ball that clings
Close to the sheltering eaves
The friendly martins love:
Nests that birds great and small
Fashion of grass and leaves,
Lichen and moss and wool . . .
Nests are most wonderful.

❖ ❖ ❖ ❖ ❖

From *All the Other Children*, by Cicely Fox Smith, published by Methuen & Co., London, UK, 1933, p. 42.

Master Hippo

The hippo from the banks of Nile,
How wide and winning is the smile
With which he does his simple best
In hippo language to suggest
The thought that stirs his inmost mind—

"It's time, I think, I supped or dined!"
And meals for hippopotami
Are weighty things, you can't deny;
For when they're babies you must buy 'em
Full thirty quarts of milk per diem,
And when they're older, every day
A baby hippo can enjoy
His bath like any human boy,
And splash and splash like Billy-o!

He's not—despite his name, of course—
The least bit like a river horse,
But much more like a river pig,
He is a harmless beast, and though
He is not beautiful, we know,
No doubt his mother thinks him so!

❖ ❖ ❖ ❖ ❖

From *All the Other Children*, by Cicely Fox Smith, published by Methuen & Co., London, UK, 1933, p. 56.

Mr. Prickles

Old Prickles he lives in the midst of a wood,
Where slugs, snails, and beetles abound for his food,
Himself and his wife, and their children all four,
In a snug little dwelling with ground for the vloor—
Ground for the vloor—ground for the vloor—
In a snug little nest that's got ground for the vloor!

❖ ❖ ❖ ❖ ❖

From *All the Other Children*, by Cicely Fox Smith, published by Methuen & Co., London, UK, 1933, p. 60.

Mr. Prickles is of course a hedgehog. This is Smith's adaptation of an old country song. The use of "vloor" is intended to sound like the west country dialect pronunciation of floor.

The Kingfisher

Kingfisher blue,
Was it you
Or a scrap of the sky
Flashed by,
Kingfisher blue?

❖ ❖ ❖ ❖ ❖

From *All the Other Children*, by Cicely Fox Smith, published by Methuen & Co., London, UK, 1933, p. 66.

Penguins

"Pengwengs," the bos'n said,
"They're sailors drowned an' dead—
Fellers wot went to sea
As might be you or me,

An' fell from aloft in a gale
On a dark night, shortenin' sail . . .
An' now they keep cruisin' around
Sailormen drowned an' dead"—
The bos'n said.

❖ ❖ ❖ ❖ ❖

From *All the Other Children*, by Cicely Fox Smith, published by Methuen & Co., London, UK, 1933, p. 68.

The Art of Catching Flies

Down in the shadow
Up in the sun,
Catching flies
Is wonderful fun:
Dipping, darting
From dawn to dark,
Catching flies
Is no end of a lark.

❖ ❖ ❖ ❖ ❖

From *All the Other Children*, by Cicely Fox Smith, published by Methuen & Co., London, UK, 1933, p. 78.

Little Gorilla

Little Gorilla, why do you look so sad? . . .
Are you thinking about the glorious times that you had
In the branchy nest in the boughs were you sat at your ease,
While the painted parrots screamed in the tops of the trees,
And the crocodiles basked in the mud at the river's brink
While the deer on their delicate hoofs tripped down to drink?
Do you think of the heat and the scents and the glare of the sun,
All that was Africa once in the days that are done?
Little Gorilla, is that why you look so sad?
Or have you played some prank on your hairy old dad
Which has had the effect of making him frightfully mad?
Or is it only something to eat that you have had
Of an indigestible kind that is making you bad?
Little Gorilla, tell me why you are looking so sad!

❖ ❖ ❖ ❖ ❖

From *All the Other Children*, by Cicely Fox Smith, published by Methuen & Co., London, UK, 1933, p. 86.

The Alligator's Children

The alligator is a creature
With not a single pleasing feature;
And even when it's very small,
It is not cuddlesome at all.
With countless teeth its jaws are set.
I do not want one for a pet.

❖ ❖ ❖ ❖ ❖

From *All the Other Children*, by Cicely Fox Smith, published by Methuen & Co., London, UK, 1933, p. 88.

The Bob-Cat

The puma is a puss-cat, and a thumping big one too,
But mostly when you meet one it's a deal more scared than you;
You can scat it nine times out of ten with nothing but a shout;
But if it's got a kitten—well you—just—look—out!

❖ ❖ ❖ ❖ ❖

From *All the Other Children*, by Cicely Fox Smith, published by Methuen & Co., London, UK, 1933, p. 96.

South Sea Whaler, "Scrimshaw" Model

HARPOONEER
Eliphalet Lobb
Was a crackerjack
At a scrimshaw job.

Wonderful smart,
So all hands said,
Were the bits of things
Eliphalet made—

Babies' rattles,
Thimbles and reels,
Shuttles for tatting
And pastry wheels:

But the damndest thing
That ever he done
Was the South Sea whaler
The *Midnight Sun*—

Crow's nest, tryworks
And all complete,
Carved out o' whalebone
Neat as neat;

Boats and lances
And line tubs—well
Pretty near everything
Only the smell!

* * * * *

Old-time spouter
And harpooneer,
They've gone on their way
This many a year,

With the look-out's hail
From the high crow's nest
Nantucket sleigh rides
And all the rest;

Gamming and grousing
Work and fun,
In the South Sea whaler
The *Midnight Sun*

The same that you see here,
White as snow,
Carved out of whalebone
Long ago,

By Harpooneer
Eliphalet Lobb—
A crackerjack
At a scrimshaw job.

❖ ❖ ❖ ❖ ❖

From *Punch* magazine, Volume 184, June 14, 1933.

This was a poem about a model ship that didn't make the cut for the poet's book about model ships.

Granfer Scroodle

Granfer Scroodle,
Honest soul,
Never drew no weekly dole;
He served as a hedger
To the R. D. C.
And died last week
At seventy three.

"I ain't no scollard,"
He often said,
"But I've allus earned
Me daily bread."

To a mort of things
His mind was Dark,
And he always signed
with Scroodle's "mark".

When he went west
A week ago,
We thought he'd left
No sort of dough.
He cut his cloth

Exceeding fine;
The sum in fact
Was four-and-nine.

Therewith was left
By Scroodle's whim
His club deposits
To bury him.
For he always said
"A man ain't made for
Enjoyin' things
He hasn't paid for."

Granfer Scroodle
All of grit,
Never drew no benefit;
Time held sharper
Shears than he'
And cut him down
At seventy three.

❖   ❖   ❖   ❖   ❖

From *Mr. Punch's Country Manners,* Vol XII, published by The Educational Book Company, London, UK, 1934.

Stoke Charity—a Hampshire Placename

Of all the names of ford and town,
Hamlet and bridge and furzy down.
That makes sweet music to the ear
By troutful Test and Itchen clear,
The Clatfords and the Sombornes twain,
Freefolk and Farley Chamberlayne,
Shy Bransbury and St. Mary Bourne,
The ford dead Rufus passed forlorn,
The Candovers, the Worthys three,
The sweetest is Stoke Charity.

"Stoke Charity" The tall elms shade
The grey old church the Normans made;
The yew-tree lifts its noon-dark head
By mounds where sleep the quiet dead;
Through mellowed pains the sunlight passes
To splash with gold the graven brasses
Of knight and lady, son and daughter,
Who went their ways as went the water
That turned, years past, the vanished mill
Whose mouldering wheel has long stood still.
A kindly name—a kindly place,

Where life still keeps its peaceful pace,
Where nothing day by day is found
But man's and nature's homely round,
But joys and sorrows, hopes and fears
And passing of unstoried years,
Toil, rest and slumber—all the same
As when old furious Corbett came
This way, with generous heart aflame,
Drew rein and paused awhile to see
How faired it with Stoke Charity.

To-day, as then, the willows shiver
All green and grey along the river
Where in the pools Jack Heron fishes
And through the weeds the moorhen swishes,
And in the bank the bright-eyed vole
Peers shy and watchful from his hole;
The whole wide valley fills and glows
With dawn-fires and with sunset rose;
In meadows bare to wind and sun
The mad March hares rejoicing run
And gathering plovers flock and fly,
Soar, turn and gleam with plaintive cry;
Season by season brings again
The farmer and the latter rain,
And Spring's first swallow oversea
To England—and Stoke Charity.

❖ ❖ ❖ ❖ ❖

From *Punch* magazine, Volume 186, January 10, 1934, p. 41.

The final 4 lines are repeated in "Cicely Fox Smith of Bow," by A. B. Blackmore, published in *Devon Life*, May, 1977, No. 131, pp. 28-29.

This poem was composed in 1934 while the poet was living at Stoke Charity, not far from Winchester, England. The first verse contains a litany of village names from the area.

"Rufus" probably refers to King William II (1056-1100) who was nicknamed Rufus and whose body passed nearby on its journey to Winchester Cathedral.

"Cobbett" refers to William Cobbett. He was an "anti-Corn Law" campaigner and the author of *Rural Rides* published in 1820.

A Beached Collier Unloading into Carts

Geordie Collier Brig

Here's the likeness of the *Betsy*: sometime in the eighteen thirties
They built her in Newcastle where the coaly dust and dirt is.

She'd a "come home" like a frigate, she was chubby as an apple;
Her old man was religious and he used to preach in chapel.

And when anything upset him, such as contraries or calms
He'd often ease his feelings, like, with bits out of the Psalms.

The mate he hailed from canny Shields, he went to sea in clogs;
He used to raise big gooseberries and little whippet dogs;

And for fighting and for drinking and for courting lassies plenty
You'd hardly find another one to match him out of twenty.

They'd neither of 'em sextants, for they ne'r learned the trick of it;
They shut their eyes and chanced their luck and barged into the thick of it.

And, call it luck or what you like, there isn't any doubt of it
That when they made their landfall they were mostly not far out of it.

Well, the years they kept on going and the preaching skipper died,
And the mate died, and his gooseberries and running dogs besides;

And still the stout old *Betsy* plodded on the same old track
From the Wooden Dolly Landing down to Wapping Wall and back.

But she did it once too often, for one night in late October,
With a north-east gale a-blowing and the skipper not quite sober,

He put her on the Middens 'cos he saw the shore lights double,
And she smashed herself to smithereens to save the breakers trouble.

❖ ❖ ❖ ❖ ❖

From *Punch* magazine, Volume 186, January 24, 1934, p. 97.

This was a ship model poem that also didn't make it into the poet's book titled *Ship Models*.

"Wooden Dolly . . . to Wapping Wall" refers to trade between London and Newcastle via the North Sea. The "Middens" refers to rocks in the river Tyne, Newcastle, covered at high tide and the cause of many shipwrecks, notable in 1864 when 5 ships were wrecked in 3 days, with many deaths.

The header graphic is a painting titled *A Beached Collier Unloading into Carts*, circa 1790, by Julius Caesar Ibbetson, from the National Maritime Museum, Greenwich, England.

New Orleans Waterfront—1840's

Mobile Bay

There's a song has gone through my mind all day,
As a song will sometimes do;
It takes me back to the years of youth
And the men and the ways I knew—
To the men I knew in a time that's gone
And a ship of old renown,
When I sailed on a day to Mobile Bay,
Where they roll the cotton down!

I remember the feel of the noonday sun
And the warm West Indian smells—
Rum and sugar, niggers and mud,
And the dear Lord knows what else:
The shuffle and stamp of the naked feet
On the levees once again:
They all come back from the years that were
To the sound of that old refrain.

"Roll the cotton down, bullies,
Roll the cotton down!"
I am far away from the dingy street
And the drab grey Northern town:
I remember the yarns my shipmates spun
And the great old songs we sung,
The way of a ship at a twelve-knot clip
In the years when the world was young.

It's the width of a world from here, worse luck,
It's the half of my life since then,
And it's ill to tread, so I've heard said,
A trail you've left again;
And I may sail east, or I may sail west,
Where the folks are yellow or brown,
But I'll sail no more to Mobile Bay
Where they roll the cotton down.

❖ ❖ ❖ ❖ ❖

From *Punch* magazine, Volume 186, February 28, 1934, p. 248.

This poem is prefaced with the note "An Old Song Re-sung." It contains phrases from the traditional stevedore/halliard shanty "Roll the Cotton Down," a version of which the poet collected and published in *A Book of Shanties*, 1927. The cotton bales were wrapped with burlap and then rolled down the dock to the ship.

This poem was first adapted for singing by Charles Ipcar in 2008, as recorded on *Sailortown Days*, 2009.

The header graphic is an illustration titled *New Orleans Waterfront—1840's*, as drawn by Stan Hugill from his book *Sailortown*, p. 185.

The Misanthrope

I think some spiteful fairy
My natal day did grace
And leave me for dowry
A sympathetic face.

Or why do people tell me,
Whenas by train I go,
The things I do not ask them
And do not care to know?

They tell me of their troubles,
They tell me of their mirth,
Of funerals and of feastings,
Of marriage and birth.

They speak about their in-laws
And cousins twice removed,
And disagreeable neighbours
And loves inconstant proved—

Smart quips of loathsome children
I inly yearn to smack,
And what is in the parcels
They balance on the rack.

Their lives' most secret moment
From me are seldom hid
The men they might have married,
The wretched wights they did.

They talk about diseases
And will not be denied,
And what they take to cure them
And how they feel inside;

Or leaving mundane matters
For themes more strange and high,
How Millions now Living
Will never need tot die

And large and stout the volume
That yet would scarce contain
The things that total strangers
Have told me in the train.

❖ ❖ ❖ ❖ ❖

From *Punch* magazine, Volume 184, March 14, 1934, p. 289.

Old Wood is Best

A fire that's made of green wood—
Of greenwood—
A fire that's made of greenwood
Is nought but smoke and smell;
So light your fire of old wood—
Of old wood—
See your fire be old wood
And it will warm you well.

A ship that's built of new wood—
Of new wood—
A ship that's built of new wood
Will let the salt sea through;
So look your planks be seasoned—
Well seasoned—
Build of wood well seasoned
Or you shall surely rue.

A house that's built of green wood—
Of green wood—
The roof that's built of green wood
Will only warp and fall;
So look your beams be old wood—
Be old wood—
Look you build with old wood
Or never build at all.

Oak and elm and chestnut—
Sweet chestnut—
Oak and elm and chestnut
That grow on English ground;
And best if you can get 'em—
Can get 'em—
Ship's ribs if you can get 'em
That have sailed the world around.

For old wine's the best wine—
The best wine—
The oldest wine's the best wine
And best the oldest friend.
 And an old ship's timbers—
Old timbers—
An old ship's timbers
Will serve you to the end.

❖ ❖ ❖ ❖ ❖

From *Punch* magazine, Volume 184, March 21, 1934, p. 313.

The tune that the poet may have had in mind for this poem is the old folk song "Go Tell Aunt Rhodie."

Odyssey

"It's all very well these 'ere blessed flim-flammers—
These 'ere bloomin' Omers an' suchlike
Writin' books about the ol' windjammers,
Same as I used to know," said Mike;
"All about the wonderful sort o' things as goes on
Or as used to go on at sea;
But nothin' ever used to 'appen as I know on—
Leastways, it never did to me.

I've been follerin' the sea since I was a nipper
An' sailed in a billyboy from Humber way
With a real old 'ard case of a preachin' skipper
As wrung my ear-'ole ten times a day.
An' I've done nothin' much else but roam about
In all sorts o' ships the whole world round,
But I never seed nothin' in it to write 'ome about—
Leastways, nothin' as I ever found.

You turnin' in to a wet bunk after 'arf the night haulin'
On ropes as stiff as bars in a freezin' gale,
An' as soon as you'd shut an eye there'd be the bosun bawlin';
'Turn out all hands, an' shorten sail!'
You could grumble an' grouse, but you just had to do it;
When the mate said 'Go.' You'd *got* to go;
'Ard work an' rotten grub an' there weren't much else to it,
You can take that from me—for why? I *know*.

You signed on an' you paid off an' you drawed your pay an' blowed it,
An' when you got down to your last pence
You took an' signed on again afore you knowed it
(Because you 'adn't got no more sense).
The tack was full o' weevils an' the beef was stinkin',
What bit of it you got;
An' you went to all sorts o' foreign ports where the beer weren't worth drinkin'
(An' when you'd seen one you'd seen the lot).

Some weather was good an' some was mucky,
The same as it is anywhere you go;
An' your pay was three-poun'-ten a month if you was lucky;
An' some ships was fast an' some was slow,
You might get a kicking mate or a crazy cap'n,
For you never quite know your luck at sea;
But as for anythin' 'appenin'—wot you might call *'appen*,
Well, it didn't, that's all." Said he.

❖ ❖ ❖ ❖ ❖

From *Punch* magazine, Volume 186, April 4, 1934, p. 386.

"'Omers"—refers to Homer's *Odyssey*.

"Smith-with-a-Hi"

Signing on in the *Emerald Isle*
Up comes a bloke in the shellback style,
All fish hooks, spunyarn and Stockholm tar,
Fist like a block and wrist like a spar,
And he shifts his quid and he says to the clerk,
"I ain't no scholar; I makes my mark;
but I spells my name with a Hi,"
Says he,
"I spells my name with a Hi!"

"There's lots o' monikers twice as fancy,
Such as Fitzmedoodles and Montmorency;
There's plenty as there's a grander sound with,
An' chaps that's got 'em I wouldn't be found with
I was shipmates once with a bloke called Percy
De Burgh de Bewfort de Lordamercy,
And I give you my word at sailorisin'
He was no more use than a jug o' pisin
So write me Smith with a Hi,"
Says he,
"Just write me down with a Hi!"

"It's a name as 'as served me near and far,
From the Tail o' the Bank to Astoria Bar;
It's a name as I've carried both far and near,
From old Point Lynas to Sandridge Pier,
And I've got no use for, I don't give a darn
For your *y's* amidship an' *e's* astern,
Nor yet no syphons nor nothink o' that;
I spells myself with a Hi—that's flat.
I'm just plain Smith with a Hi,"
Says he,
"You write me down with a Hi!"

❖   ❖   ❖   ❖   ❖

From *Punch* magazine, Volume 186, April 18, 1934, p. 441.

Sailor's Pleasure

When the time comes, as it will, that I go to sea no longer—
Though maybe, please the Lord, that day'll not be yet—
I don't want to forget the years when I was younger
The way a lot of old men seem to forget.

I want to have it all there as plain as writing,
To keep and turn over again in my mind—
All the work and play, the fun and the fighting,
And maybe a woman or two that was kind.

I want to recall my shipmates and the look of their faces,
Folk I liked or didn't, afloat and ashore,
And the loveliness of ships and the queerness of foreign places;
I want to think about them after I see them no more.

I want to remember it all—like some fellow hauling his chest out
For a spell of sailor's pleasure in the South-East Trade,
Turning his gear, his bottled ships and the rest out,
Calling to mind how he got them or when they were made.

I want to think about things like the dawn scarlet and splendid
After a night of storm; the wind and the rain and the sun;
Good times or bad times—what's the odds when they're ended?
They're all good to remember when they're finished and done.

❖ ❖ ❖ ❖ ❖

From *Punch* magazine, Volume 187, September 5, 1934, p. 254.

"Sailor's pleasure" means setting sail with a favoring wind.

Elegy

"So the Ol' Man's gone," said Bill—"ol' Cap'n Warren
I signed with onst in the clipper *Rathlin Head;*
'E give up the sea after they sold 'is ship foreign.
An' he lived to be eighty-odd, an' now 'e's dead.

'E was an 'ard ol' case, a tough ol' terror,
W'en you felt 'is fist it was like a kick from an 'orse;
But one thing I'll tell you, an' no fatal error:
'E was a grand seaman as ever set a course.

An 'ard-'ittin', 'ard-livin', 'ard-swearin' ol' sinner—
That was 'im," said Bill. And struck his palm on the bar;
"But nobody never passed 'is ship while 'e was in 'er,
An' 'e drove 'er for twenty years an' never lost a spar.

'E was a tough ol' nut an 'ard ol' devil
As ever walked the weather side of a poop," Bill said,
"A cross-grained ol' cuss as didn't know 'ow to be civil
Either to God or man—an' I'm kind o' sorry 'e's dead."

❖ ❖ ❖ ❖ ❖

From *Punch* magazine, Volume 188, January 16, 1935, p. 68

This is a poem which drives a modern spell check crazy but it has been checked!!

The abab rhyme scheme is an aid to punctuation also. For example "devil" is pronounced "divil" to rhyme with civil.

Sailors' Waterfront Pub

The Rendezvous

A pub there is of far renown,
A pub that seamen know
In every street of Sailortown
Or sea where they in ships go down
From Clyde to Callao.

And there they say if a man should wait
A twelvemonth and a day
That all his shipmates soon or late
Would surely pass that way.

Both night and noon the door swings wide
To the noisy dockside's din,
Both night and noon with every tide
The sailormen blow in.

They come with talk of ships and men
And lean upon the bar
And yarn and drink and yarn again
Of ports both near and far.

But theirs are ships I never spoke
And trades to me unknown,
And all they see is a grizzled bloke
That drinks his drink alone.
They neither pause nor listen when
From all the oceans home
Between the tides the sailormen
I wait alone for come—

Come in with laughter on their lips
And names I used to know
And speech of men and speech of ships
Forgotten long ago.

No door swings wide to let them through,
No eye but mine can see
That all the shipmates ever I knew
Blow in to drink with me.

❖ ❖ ❖ ❖ ❖

From *Punch* magazine, Volume 188, February 27, 1935, p. 250.

This poem shares certain elements with "The News in Daly's Bar" and "Old Fiddle."

The header graphic is a painting titled In *The Red Lion* by Anton Otto Fischer, 1937, from Anton Otto Fischer, p. 219.

Liftboatman - 1900

The Lifeboatman

Helmeted, knightwise, booted to the knee,
Cuirassed to meet the charging cavalry
Of seas wind-generated, medalled from no fight
Save that men wage with eternal Ocean's might –
The Farnes, the Forelands know him; outer isles,
Beaches where the North Sea breaks for miles,
Cliffs at whose feet the Atlantic surges shatter
Wave upon irresistible wave, and scatter
The coves with shards once ships; bird-haunted nesses,
Pools where the long weed trails like mermaids' tresses
Round snarling reefs, and siren sands whose lips
Batten on bones of men, on ribs of ships …
They know his skill, his courage, his sea lore,
His hard-learned craft of tiller, sail and oar,
Sometimes his end, who, at the call of duty
Forsaking all life's colour and warmth and beauty,
Goes forth to risks none better knows than he,
To snatch men's lives at peril of the sea…

❖ ❖ ❖ ❖ ❖

From The Times, London, UK, April 25, 1935.

The poem was included in a full page advertisement for the Lifeboat Service which included four photographs of lifeboats, a short article by H. M. Tomlinson, and two short pieces by Admiral of the Fleet Sir Henry Oliver, Chairman of the Boat Committee, and Sir John Cumming, Chairman of the Finance Committee.

The header graphic is a photo of a lifeboatman, circa 1900, by an unidentified photographer.

Boy at the Wheel

Romance and Reality

A boy there was and he went to sea
With a head as full as a head could be
Of all the yarns that ever he'd read
By an inch of candle at night in bed . . .
He thought a sailor had nothing to do
When the wind was fair and the skies were blue
But sit in the sun and watch the ship
Sailing herself at a twelve-knot clip,
With a song and a yarn and a hornpipe or so
To liven him up when things got slow.
He thought it sounded a first-rate notion
To be cast away in the Southern Ocean
And rig himself in a home-made trousseau
And ramble round like Robinson Crusoe,
With plenty of turtles' eggs to scoff
Till a ship chanced by and took him off.
He often dreamed about digging up gold

The pirates hid in the days of old,
Though why in thunder they went and hid it
Nobody knows but the blokes that did it.

But—there's not much time for hornpipe-dancing
With a-hard-case mate that's always prancing
And bawling round in a voice like thunder,
"Jump now, ye sojers, or stand from under!"
And a length of rope's-end neatly planted
Was all the livening-up he wanted.
And the only island the ship went smash on
It hadn't been furnished Crusoe fashion;
There weren't any turtles' eggs on the beaches,
Nor goats with skins to make into breeches;
And after they'd lived a month or more
On things they found on the rocks and the shore,
Winkles and weed as salt as the dickens
And penguins' eggs that were nearly chickens;
Talk about islands—well, no one reckoned
He ever wanted to sample a second . . .
And he never had time nor he never had leisure
For little matters like hunting treasure,
So all the treasure ever he found
While he was sailing the wide seas round
Was a handful or two of pay to burn—
Easy to spend but the devil to earn!—
And a head as full as a head could be
Of an old man's dreams of the ships and the sea.

❖   ❖   ❖   ❖   ❖

From *Punch* magazine, Volume 188, May 15, 1935 p. 582.

The header graphic is a photograph titled *John A. Noble at the wheel of the "Anna Sophia"*, circa 1928, while the schooner is safely moored, from *Hulls and Hulks in the Tide of Time*, p. 4, photographer unknown.

The Clock with One Finger

The clock with one finger
Was made in the days
When time used to linger
By leisurely ways—

When nobody reckoned
(Or so we are told)
Each fugitive, second
More precious than gold,

But the clocks, like the people,
Took things as they came,
And the chimes in the steeple
Said mostly the same:—

"Some day—no day—
Maybe—one, day—
Come day—go day—
God—send—Sunday!"

No moral didactic
Is borne on the sound
Of its slow-footed tack-tick
The thirty hours round.

It strikes just for pastime
As chance may befall,
Be it slow time or fast time
Or no time at all.

And the crooked old hand on
Its countrified face
Keeps on and on *and* on
Its countrified pace,

And, scorning all worry.
Announces each day:
"There bain't no such hurry
As some folk do say;

For bring the day pleasure
Or bring the day sorrow,
I be certain to measure
Another to-morrow . . .

Some day—no day—
Maybe—one day—
Come day—go day—
God—send—Sunday!"

❖ ❖ ❖ ❖ ❖

From *Punch* magazine, Volume 188, June 26, 1935, p. 742.

Once upon a time, not so long ago, time passed at a more gracious pace than it does today.

Offa's Dyke

Down in the dyke of the ancient folk,
Hard by the rampart crowned with oak,
My foot sank deep in the drift of years,
Of buried battles and hates and fears,
And fights none reckons who lost or won,
Long won, long lost in the time that's done.

Deep in the dyke of the ancient folk,
Something stirred in its sleep and woke,
Something rose to the light of day,
Something followed me all the way,
Something dogged me that came not nigh,
Loitered and hastened and stopped as I.

Out of the dyke I came at last,
Where the drift lay high of the ages past,
From the following thing that lingered there
To the sun and the sky and the lark in air,
And the wind in the bents that, strong and fleet,
Ran like flame on its unseen feet . . . .

Deep in the dyke of the ancient men
Something turned to its rest again.

❖ ❖ ❖ ❖ ❖

From *Punch* magazine, Volume 189, September 18, 1935, p. 319.

Sheep Fair on the Marches

When gorse-pods are popping
And heather's in bloom
And nuts begin dropping
In coppice and cwm,

Then down through the valleys
That echoed of yore
The clashes and rallies
Of borderland war,

Where saplings, wind-shaken,
Are blowing like flags
From castles forsaken
That cling to their crags,

With many-hued fleeces
Come wethers and ewes

Of Jenkins and Rhyses
And Griffiths and Pughs,

And young lambs a-larking
And leaping for fun.
And wall-eyed dogs barking
Behind as they run.

Then tap-room and stable
And steep winding street
Are busy as Babel
When farmer folk meet,

And loud with the noises
Of auction and pen
And high-pitched Welsh voices
Of women and men;

Till night brings the stars out
On valley and hill,
With turning of bars out
(Each man with his fill),

And after the riot
The darkness comes down
On sheep-pens grown quiet,
On castle and town,

On a man like a log
By the roadside asleep.
And a wise wall-eyed dog
Going home with the sheep.

❖ ❖ ❖ ❖ ❖

From *Punch* magazine, Volume 189, October 16, 1935, p. 430.

An unusual setting (Wales) for a Smith poem but she's lost nothing of her feel for new locations and her ability to depict a place in a few well crafted lines.

"Cwm" is Welsh for hill. "Tap-room" is today a room in a Public House (Pub) but was originally used to refer to any building (or room) where alcoholic drinks were bought over the counter.

The Figurehead

The Figurehead

In the days when every seaport had its figureheads to show—
Queens, princesses, sea-nymphs, witches, girls of all sorts, row on row,
With their faintly smiling faces and their outstretched pointing hands
Reaching out across the water-lanes that lead to far-off lands—

There was once a ship a-building on the slips down Black-wall way
(Yard and builder, ship and owner, long ago they had their day),
And it chanced one summer morning when the work was nearly done
The Owner came to look at her and see how things went on.

Now this Owner, I must tell you, was a pious sort of bloke
That didn't know the way to smile and never cracked a joke:
He'd an "Albert" on his waistcoat and a whisker on each cheek,
And his face was like a sea-boot or the wettest kind of week.

Well, he looked the ship all over and he'd got no fault to find,
But, says he, "There is a point on which I've quite made up my mind;
I will not have this ship o' mine called after one of those
Outrageous heathen goddesses with hardly any clo'es.

It's not a good example to the people where we trade
To see upon our vessels' bows such things as those displayed;
So let her name be Enterprise or Thrift or Industry,
And I think we can't do better than a figurehead of ME."

So the carver carved his likeness, though he said it was a job
To make a decent showing of that hammick-faced old swab;
And they launched the ship and christened her with homemade rhubarb-wine,
For he said he'd have no dealings with the product of the vine.

They named her Perseverance, and they sent her out to sea
To show the folks in foreign parts a figurehead of HE,
With a go-to-meeting topper of the real stove-pipe sort
And the kind of stick-up collar Mr. Gladstone used to sport.

And when she got to forty South up comes old Davy Jones
From his house below the water that's all built of sailors' bones,
To see the latest vessel and her figurehead to scan,
For he likes, a nice young female, just like any sailor-man.

But when he clapped his eyes on her it made him fair disgusted;
He cussed like any bucko mate until he nearly busted,
And looked and looked and looked again, and said, "Well, strike me pink!"
Then took and yanked the Owner off and slung him in the drink.

And he drifted and he lifted as the winds and currents chose.
With the seabirds sitting on him from his waistcoat to his nose,
And he lifted and he drifted many a month and many a mile,
Till he fetched up at the finish on a South Pacific isle.

And there the natives found him, high and dry upon the shore,
And they gathered round and stared at him till they could stare no more;
Then they set him on a heap of stones and hung him round with flowers
And said, "Now where's the island that can show a god like ours?"

And fuzzy-headed damsels wearing hardly any clo'es
But wisps of grass and feathers—and uncommon few of those—
Used to come and dance for him o' nights beneath the golden moon
To the singing of the palm-trees and the tide in the lagoon.

And there he sat and scowled at them; and so the years went on
Till, what with time and weather, all the paint off him was gone,
And his whiskers and his collar had got worn so flat and small
That you couldn't recognise him for the Owner's self at all.

Well, at last there came a schooner cruising round the Southern Seas
With a learned bloke on board collecting curiosities,
And when he saw the figurehead he cried, "Now here's a find;
This here's a tribal totem of a most unusual kind."

And the island folks were thinking that he couldn't be much good
Because he hadn't made it rain just when they thought it should;
So they swopped him for a gramophone as willing as you please,
And he travelled back to England wrapped up careful like a cheese.

He's in Blankby Town Museum now for all the world to see,
With a label underneath him, "Heathen Idol from Fiji";
And if there is a moral in this story strange but true,
Well, I only hope you see it—I'll be jiggered if I do!

❖   ❖   ❖   ❖   ❖

From *Punch* magazine, Volume 189, November 13, 1935, pp. 540-541.

The header graphic depicts the figurehead floating on the ocean, as drawn by Charles Grave for this poem and published in *Punch* magazine above.

Animal House

In Animal House (by which title I call
A dwelling whose true name is not that at all)
There are dogs on the sofas and cats on the chairs;
Wherever you sit you get covered with hairs;
While your progress is marked by the yelps and miaous
Of beasts you have walked on in Animal House.

There's an Old English bantam that welcomes the dawn,
There's a cat that sings love-songs all night on the lawn,
There's a bachelor turtle-dove making sweet moan
And a puppy lamenting because it's alone;
The rowdiest tavern where topers carouse
Is a meeting of Quakers to Animal House.

There's a tortoise asleep in the strawberry bed
(They say it's asleep but it smells a bit dead);
There are rabbits—they tell me they pluck them alive—
And ferrets in hutches and bees in a hive,
And goats, male and female, that merrily browse
On the stockings they hang out at Animal House.

There's a little green parrot like old Uncle Ned
Without any feathers on the top of its head,
He's eighty years old and he's just laid an egg;
There's a toad and a newt and a thrush with one leg,
A hedgehog, an owl and a Japanese mouse,
But . . . people are nowhere at Animal House.

❖ ❖ ❖ ❖ ❖

From *Punch* magazine, Volume 189, December 25, 1935, page 723.

The poet intentionally spelt "miaous" in that fashion.

The Salt Road

As I went by the waterside
I met a man I knew.
Said I, "Before you take the tide
I'll sign and sail with you;
I'm sick of loafing up and down,
As lonely as can be;
I want to leave this weary town
And bear away to sea."

"I want to meet old friends a few
I've known by sea and shore,
And maybe fetch a port or two
I haven't seen before.
I know there's many a house of call
Stands open yet for me,
And I think I'd like to see them all
Before I quit the sea."

"I'll watch on South Pacific seas
The old Horn greybeards curled,
And greet the stormy Westerlies
That blow around the world.
Old stars'll swim into my sight
With a hundred yarns to tell,
Old lights'll wink across the night
As if they knew me well."

"I'll pass the time with all that floats
At chance of wind and tide;
I'll smell the smell of the cattle boats
With all their hatches wide.
I'll see the tramps ply to and fro,
Like hoboes of the foam,
And see the big lime-juicers go
By the old road roaring home."

"I'll steer in sunshine, calm and rain,
From Bluff to Nootka sound,
Then when I've done I'll start again
The same old blooming round;
From Barrier Reef to Bantry Bay,
From White to Tasman Sea,
Till I grow grey I'll beat my way
Nor want for company."

"Ship, harbour, coast-line, light and star
Will bring back all I've seen,

The things that were, the things that are,
The things that might have been;
The things I've had, and loved, and lost,
And the songs that don't grow staler;
The good old game that's worth the cost,
The life of a deepsea sailor!"

"Oh fare you well, for the Peter's flying,
And it's time for us to go
Where the winds are up and the grey gull's crying
On the old salt road we know;
We are bound away to Lord knows where,
But you'll see us—Lord knows when! —
Come back some day with a pocketful of pay
By the old salt road again!"

❖   ❖   ❖   ❖   ❖

From *The Oxford Annual for Boys*, Volume 28, 1935; the poem is accompanied by drawings in the margins by Philip Wilson Smith.

"And that ghost's mine!"

The Haunted Ship

Houses have ghosts they say; well, like enough they may have—
Folks that have lived within their walls in the bygone days;
And why should not ships have their ghosts also, even as they have—
Men that have hated or loved them, served them and gone their ways,

Sweated and shivered, know hunger and thirst and been weary,
Slept, waked, worked their traverses well or ill?
I know of one that walks in the old barque *Kashmiri*,
If she's floating still.

Here and there on the familiar decks he lingers,
Watching the crowd at their work, making or furling sail;
Pausing now and then to touch with remembering fingers
Wheel-spoke and capstan-bar, or handle rope and rail.
He stands at the half-deck door awhile, smiling to see there
The notched table, the bunk where he used to lie—
Nothing changed at all since the time he used to be there
But the old faces he knew in the years gone by.

In tropic dog-watches he stays a little to hearken
The hands lounging and yarning as of old on the fore-hatch;
He hears the "one-two, one-two" of the bells and, as evening darkens,
The hoarse voice of the bosun rousing out the watch;
He catches the whiff of the mate's pipe, he hears him tramping
Fore and aft, fore and aft, steady and slow;
He sees the warm yellow of the binnacle light lamping
The intent face of the steersman over its glow.

He stands at his elbow, hearing the night-wind singing
Up aloft, far aloft in the sheave-blocks and spars,
Watching the lift of the royal leech and the high trucks swinging,
Swaying their ceaseless arc against the sky and the stars . . .
North, South, East, West—sunny weather or dreary,
Cold in the high South latitudes, steamy hot on the line—
There's a ghost walks I know, in the old barque *Kashmiri*—
And that ghost's mine.

❖ ❖ ❖ ❖ ❖

From *Punch* magazine, Volume 190, March 4, 1936, p. 266.

See also "The *Trythena's* Extra Hand."

The header graphic is an illustration titled *"There was a ship—"* as drawn by Phil W. Smith, from *There Was A Ship*, by Cicely Fox Smith, Edwin Valentine Mitchell, Hartford, US, 1930, facing p. 10.

Sic Transit…

Bundy and Son
In days that are done
Used to build coaches for everyone;
Manor and hall
Great folk and small,
Bundys built carriages once for 'em all.

Coaches and gigs
And thingummyjigs
For people in patches and full-bottomed wigs
That highwaymen stopped
Who long ago dropped
To dust on the gibbet where downland sheep cropped;

Cabriolets
And family shays
Of George's and Anne's and Victoria's days—
Slow wheels and fast
All have at last
Rattled away down the road of the Past.

Bundy is dead;
Pumps green and red
Stand in a row in his carriage works' stead;
And, dappled with mire,
By the didakai's fire
You may see the smart dog-cart he built for the squire,
With a skinny-ribbed gry
A-grazing hard by
And the didakai's duds hung about it to dry.

❖ ❖ ❖ ❖ ❖

From *Punch* magazine, Volume 190, March 18, 1936, p. 321.

The title is taken from a longer Latin phrase "Sic transit gloria mundi" that means "Thus passes the glory of the world." The double entendre of the title also includes the various methods of transportation, which have disappeared (or passed).

Launching the *Queen Mary*

A Sea Queen

Queen among ships, and named for a well-loved queen,
Fair be her landfalls, and her years serene,
Such uneventful and unstoried years
As in passing, clean of blood and tears,
Make ships, like nations, blessed. May she be
A happy ship for such use the sea—
The day she heralds be that of all our dreaming,
With shipyards once more clanging, seaports-teeming
With flags and funnels and derricks as of yore.
Such be her happy fortune—aye, and more,
This be her mission and her task,to bind
As by a bridge invisible, mind to mind,
Sharers of kindred knowledge, kindred speech,
In knowledge and in friendship each with each;
And so foreshadow some far brighter day
When fear and hate shall pass at last away
And all men harvest the good earth's increase,
Labour and traffic, sow and reap in peace. . . .

❖ ❖ ❖ ❖ ❖

From *Country Life,* Volume 190, March 28, 1936, in the archives of the National Maritime Museum, Greenwich, UK.

This poem is likely a tribute to the launching of the ocean liner *Queen Mary*.

The header graphic is a photograph of the launching of the ocean liner *Queen Mary* in 1934 from Brown Shipyard on the Clyde in Scotland.

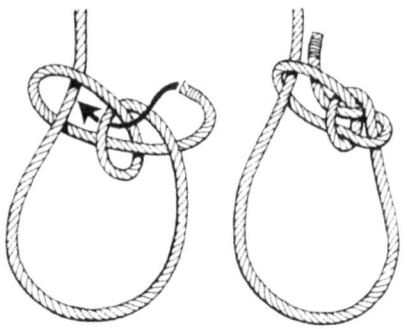
How to Tie a Running Bowline

Knots

"There's a lot
In a knot,"
Bill'd say
While working away
With fingers as hard
As the tarred
Rough hemp that he'd fashion and splice
With handiwork nice
And precise
Into many a seaman's device—
Turk's Head, stopper and wall,
Mathew Walker and all.
"There's a lot
In a knot . . .

There's hitches and bends
Good enough for their ends
You make shift
With and cast 'em adrift
And they're done . . .
There's others just fancy fal-lals
Like the dollied-up gals
A man courts
In the ports
For his fun . . .
And there's some like the one
(Or two, if he's lucky enough!)
Best pal a man finds in his puff,
That'll hold on and hold
Till Hell's cold
And beyond . . . There's a lot
In a knot."

❖   ❖   ❖   ❖   ❖

From *Punch* magazine, Volume 191, November 25, 1936, p. 609.

The header graphic is an illustration of how to tie a running bowline, artist unknown.

When the Ports Were Filled with Loveliness . . .

These were the ships—the flying hell-for-leather ships—
That ran their gunwales under with the wool and jute and tea;
Teak and oak and iron, close-hauled and easting weather ships,
That filled the ports with beauty when sails were on the sea.

Proud ships, tall ships—frigate-built Blackwall ships—
Brasses all a-glitter, planking white as foam;
Fast Calcutta clippers with their hardy racing skippers
Reeling out the log-line from the James and Mary home . . .

Carry-on-an'-break-her ships—shake-her-up-and-wake-her ships—
Crammed with Southern fleeces for the Sou' West India Dock—
The westerlies to hustle 'em and the steady Trades to bustle 'em
Eighty days from Melbourne to the chime of Limehouse clock!

Auckland frozen meat ships—slashing Clyde-built wheat ships,
Out with coal and general to sail the world around,
Loaded deep with corn again by the wintry Horn again,
From 'Frisco and Astoria and ports of Puget Sound.

Beating to the westward days and weeks together—
Plunging through the fog and snow off the Ramirees—
Fisting frozen canvas down in the black Horn weather—
That was once the way of it when sail was on the seas!

These were the ships—the fine ships, the fair ships,
Golden Fleece and *Cutty Sark* and swift *Thermopylae*;
Sailors they were sailors then—ay, and ships they were ships,
When the ports were filled with loveliness and sails were on the sea . . .

❖   ❖   ❖   ❖   ❖

From *Blue Peter*, May, Volume XVI, # 170, 1936, p. 227. Prefatory poem to Volume III of *Sail* edited by Basil Lubbock.

This poem seems loosely based on an earlier poem by Cicely Fox Smith, "Sailor's Delight," that was published in the book of that same name.

Alongshore

Oh, some the broad highways desire
By hill and plain that go;
And some the winding country lanes
That country people know;
And some the wide and lighted streets
Where wealth and fashion shine—
Well, let them have their choice, but oh,
The waterfront is mine!

What though the streets of Sailortown
Be dingy, poor, and mean?
The salt breath of the ocean blows
Its jumbled roofs between.
And what though cheap and tawdry wares
Be all its shops display?
The wealth and wonder of the seas
Are spilt there day by day.

Now, some are all for aeroplanes
To soar towards the stars,
And others find their hearts' desire
In high-powered racing cars;
And some on Western plains would choose
To gallop far and free,
A sea of tossing horns beside—
But oh, a ship for me!

I like them all, both sail and steam,
The little ships and big,
The craft of every trade and flag,
Of every build and rig,
The liner bright with brass and paint
The tramp with rusted side,
The sturdy tugs that sit in rows
Like seagulls on the tide.

I like the good ship-smells as well,
The honest hard ship-feels,
The paint and pitch and Stockholm tar,
The tang of Baltic deals,
The touch of bunting, rough and harsh,
The satin smooth of teak,
And hemp as hairy and as brown
As some old shellback's cheek.

I like their cargoes, one and all,
The boxes, bags, and bales,
The rice and spice and cinnamon,
The cloves in plaited frails,
The sugar and the Spanish wine,
Tobacco, treacle, tea,
And narwhals' horns and walrus tusks
And mammoth ivory.

So some the open road may choose,
By hill and dale that goes,
And some the shady lanes prefer
Where scent of hawthorn blows.

But I will take the road that leads
To dock, and wharf, and quay;
Let others have their choice, but still
The waterside for me!

❖ ❖ ❖ ❖ ❖

From The Oxford Annual for Boys, Volume 29, 1936, p. 51; the poem is accompanied by drawings in the margins by Philip Wilson Smith.

"Alongshore" means along the shore or coast.

"Frails" are rush baskets for holding fruit, especially dried fruit.

Sale by Auction

I went to an auction
To bid for a chair;
I bought a stuffed pheasant
Because it was there.

I went to an auction
To buy a divan;
I bought a piano
That wouldn't pian.

I went to an auction
For curtains and things;
I bought an old fiddle
Without any strings.

I went to an auction
To buy me a bed;
I bought an old bundle
Of music instead—

All twiddly old "pieces"
And ancient quadrilles;
Once played by young ladies
In flounces and frills.

While gallants Victorian
Turned over the leaves,
Bewhiskered as tom cats
That court on the eaves.

I went to an auction
Equipped with a list:
Of bargains desirable
Not to be missed.

Of the things that I went for
I didn't get one;
But what did it matter?—
I'd plenty of fun!

❖   ❖   ❖   ❖   ❖

From *Punch* magazine, Volume 192, January 27, 1937, p. 95.

Ceres

The Ketch *Ceres* 1811-1936

A century and a quarter, full of chance and change had passed
Since they built her, down in Devon, where they mostly build to last,
And sent her out to earn her keep at risk of wave and war,
And dodge the nimble privateer along the Biscay shore.

And war went out and peace came in and time it went and came,
And brought new changes every year but her it left the same;
The privateers they vanished and the Indiamen likewise,
And the first steam-kettle trailed her smoke across the affronted skies.

The tea fleet and the wool fleet, in their turn they had their day;
She marked them in their beauty as she plied upon her way,
Their canvas piled like summer clouds, . . . like summer clouds they passed,
But—she was built in Devon and they build 'em there to last.

She loaded nuts and oranges, she carried coal and props,
And bricks and hay and china-clay and barley-malt and hops;

She traded north to Derry and she traded south to Spain,
And east about to Wells and Lynn and back to Bude again.

She knew the rips and overfalls from London to the Lizard,
And once she nearly left her bones off Padstow in a blizzard,
But when winter fogs were thickest she could mostly smell her way
By the old familiar sea-marks into Bude or Watchett Bay.

And peace went out and war came in and forth she went once more
To dodge the nimble submarines along the English shore,
And war went out and peace came in and still she held together
Spite of floating mine and tin fish and the good old Channel weather.

She loaded salt and timber and she carried slate from Wales,
Cement and corn and cattle-cake and paving-stones and nails;
She worked her way to Liverpool and down the coast for cloam,
Across the war to Swansea Bay and then with slag for home.

But a time it comes to ships and men when sailing days are past,
Even such as hail from Devon, where they mostly build to last,
And her seams began to open and the Severn tide came through,
And the water kept on gaining spite of all that they could do.

They did their best to beach her but they couldn't do no more,
And she foundered at the finish there in sight of Appledore;
And her bones'll never flicker blue on any longshore fire,
For she'll lie there and she'll moulder as an old ship might desire,
And hear the vessels passing by and dream about the past,
And the great old times in Devon, where they built her once to last.

❖   ❖   ❖   ❖   ❖

From *The Western Morning News*, Plymouth, Exeter, and Truro, UK, March 13,1937, p. 13; reproduced from the *Blue Peter* magazine, February, 1937.

"Cloam" is a collective word for clay or earthenware pots.

"Ceres," in ancient Roman religion, was a goddess of agriculture, grain crops, fertility and motherly relationships.

The header graphic is a photo of the *Ceres* entering the seaside resort town of Bude in north Cornwall, England, circa 1920, photographer unknown.

The Optimist

"Ships—they're all right," said Murphy, "for all you hear folks tell.
There's some shoves their bows under in a seaway, and there's some rolls like hell;
There's some as can't wear nor stay, and some won't steer a course
Without pullin' the arms out of you like a bad tempered horse;
And some's wet and some's wicked—but taking them all together
And allowing for things like bad crews an' contrary weather,
And owners that skinny they'd die afore they'd bust a farden on paint—
Why ships ain't bad," said Murphy—"not to my thinkin' they ain't."

"The sea's all right," said Murphy, "if it's took as it comes—
Good an' bad, rough an' smooth, Trade an' Doldrums.
There's pamperos and southerly busters, and maybe a hurricane
Or a typhoon or such little diversion just now and again;
But takin' the high with the low latitudes and all the way round,
Why, the sea ain't that bad," said Murphy—"leastways not as I've found."
"Chaps, they're all right," said Murphy, "took one with another—
There's some as'd slit your throat for a nickel if you was their born brother;
There's them as never earn their whack or work a traverse or pull their weight;
And some's that crooked they'd make a dog's hind-leg look straight;
Some'd pinch the pennies of a man's eyes and he lyin' dead;
But look at 'em wholesale and in the lump, why chaps is mostly decent," he said.

❖ ❖ ❖ ❖ ❖

From *Punch* magazine, Volume 192, June 6, 1937, p. 662.

Thoughts in a Garden

Why, where erstwhile I sowed my choicest seeds,
Come up but weeds?
Why do large docks
Appear where should be stocks
And phlox?
Why flaunts the dandelions brazen face
In zinnia's place?
What makes the groundsel flourish
In patches which should nourish
The useful parsnip and the onion mild?
Why does the thistle (child
By rights of Caledonia stern and wild)
Invade the peaceful South?
Why do all these defy
Both frost and drouth
When dahlias die?
Why does the buttercup
Incessantly come up,
And things like salvias perish at a touch
But not the scutch?

Alas! What boots it with incessant care
To importune thus the air?
Full well I know
I'll rout
These growths detested out
With toil and pain—
And next week with a hoe
I'll do it again!

❖ ❖ ❖ ❖ ❖

From *Punch* magazine, Volume 193, July 7, 1937, p. 1.

Tea in the Garden

I will not go to tea with you, Mrs. Arden,
Yourself, your house, your tea,
These three
Are all acceptable to me;
But oh!
Too well I know
That if I go
You will say
Brightly
How pleasant it will be
To-day
To have tea
In the garden . . . .
And I—poor fool!—politely
Shall agree

Then will my tea be tepid
And into it will things
Descend on strings
Like acrobats intrepid,
Ants with fierce gallop, wasps with eager wings
Will to the jam resort,
And in the cream the game-some earwig sport.
My chair will be so low
(That too I know)
I'll scarce be able
To reach the table—
Its scones
And buttered buns,
And sandwiches with bits of green inside,
The sun have somewhat dried . . . .

Pardon
Me therefore, Mrs. Arden,
And think me not ungrateful

Because I deem most hateful
Tea in the garden.

❖   ❖   ❖   ❖   ❖

From *Punch* magazine, Volume 193, July 21, 1937, p. 77.

Sailor's Tavern in Helsinger, Denmark

Sailor, Sailor—

"Sailor, Sailor, why did you go—
Why did you go for a sailor?
Why didn't you choose to cobble folk's shoes,
Or live at your ease as a tailor?"
"I stayed out all night at Michaelmas fair
And blowed my week's wages on the roundabouts there,
And I knew my old dad 'ud be waiting for me
With a face like a foot and his belt on his knee,
And I thinks, thinks I, 'Well it can't be as bad
To run off to sea as be belted by Dad'—
And that's why I went for a sailor—a sailor—
That's why I went for a sailor."

"Sailor, Sailor, why did you go—
Why did you go for a sailor?
Why didn't you learn good money to earn
As a beer or a whisky retailer?"
"I wheeled a wheelbarrow when I was a boy
In and out o' the cowshed where I got employ;
I wheeled it and wheeled it from morning to night,

And sometimes 'twas heavy and sometimes 'twas light;
I wheeled it six months and I'm willing to bet
That if I'd stayed there I'd be wheeling it yet—
And that's why I went for a sailor."

"Sailor, Sailor, why did you go—
Why did you go for a sailor?
Why aren't you a star of Bench or of Bar
A judge, a K. C., or a jailor?"
"I courted a girl and she gave me the chuck;
I thought my poor heart was most certainly bruk;
So I went to the docks, for I thought it was better
To travel the world round and try to forget her.
We were bound out to Sidney, and—well, to be candid
I was courting another as soon as we landed—
But that's why I went for a sailor."

"Sailor, Sailor, why did you go—
Why did you go for a sailor?"
"Why does the earth keep on turning around?
Why do the trees have their roots underground?
Why does the sun rise—and what makes it set?
Why is the snow cold, and why is the rain wet?
Why do the rivers run down to the sea?
Answer me these things—and after ask me
To tell why I went for a sailor—a sailor."

❖ ❖ ❖ ❖ ❖

From *Punch* magazine, Volume 193, August 4, 1937, p. 125.

The header graphic is titled *Tavern in Helsinger, Denmark, circa 1850* and is from a woodcut from *Illustreret Tidende*, Copenhagen, 1877, artist unknown.

Country Pleasures

I always rather bar
A Bazaar.

I simply cannot bear
A Fancy Fair.

I'm not keen
On Dancing on the Green.

An Olde Englyshe Revel
Is the very devil.

I just won't go
To a Baby Show.

I particularly dislike
A decorated bike.

But the thing I absolutely hate
Is a Common or Garden Fète.

❖   ❖   ❖   ❖   ❖

This poem first appeared in *Punch* magazine, Volume 193, September 1, 1937, p. 243.

Although, given the fact that it was written for *Punch* and was clearly meant as a humorous piece, the overall message is in keeping with what we know of Smith's own tastes.

Galloping Horses (After the Flower Show)

Come for the prizes
All are allotted,
Leaving the ranks of
Cut flowers and potted,
Leaving the marrows,
Monstrous, incredible,
Turnips and carrots,
Vast but inedible,
Leaving the honey
(Bottle and section),
Leaving the conquering
Queen-wasp collection,
Leaving the fruit-cakes
(Underdone, mostly)
Lone in the show-tent
Vacant and ghostly.
Come—on the common
Where golden the gorse is
Wait the Original
Galloping Horses!

Listen—the organ's
Just about starting!
Who could resist
That imperative blarting?
Hark to the voice of it,
Clamant, compelling,
Blaring down even
The ballyhoos' yelling.
Hamelin's pipers
Advertised playing
Never could charm like that
Resonant braying.
Which horse will you have,
The chestnut—the bay one?
Pick where you like, but
Mine is the grey one.

What though his mane
And tail have been slightly
Thinned by equestrians
Clutching them tightly?
Still must his crinion
Command admiration
(That I believe, is
the right designation).
Look at his nostril,
Redly distended,
Mark too his action,
Spirited, splendid.

Shriek goes the organ,
Lustily blowing;
Get to your saddles;
Now we are going!
Up and then down
Like the waves on the ocean—
Where cou'd be found more
Inspiring motion?

Down and then up
Like a gale in the Channel—
Cook from the Manor
Is whiter than flannel!
Up again, down again,
Quicker and quicker—
"Stick to 'im, 'arold"—
Look at the vicar!
Over the elm-trees
Climbs the moons crescent,
Thin as a shaving,
Pale opalescent;
Flits the white owl by,
Who as he passes
Mingles his hoots
With the squealing of lasses,
While in the zenith
The stars in their courses
Wink at their brothers
The Galloping Horses!

❖ ❖ ❖ ❖ ❖

From *Punch* magazine, Volume 193, September 15, 1937, p. 289.

Might Have Been

"If I was a bloke as could paint,"
Bill said, "which I ain't,
Lord! The pictures I'd do
Of ships runnin' free
In the Tropics, or flyin' like stags
Down the Forties; an' seas, white an' blue,
In the Trades, or like cliffs in a blow
Off the Leeuwin, or calm
After storm, an' the dawn comin' solemn an' slow
Like a psalm . . . .
Ports too,
Full o' funnels an' flags,
I'd do,
If I was a chap as could paint,"
Said Bill, "but I ain't.

Or if I'd the knack of the pen"
(Bill said) "like some men,
Lord! The yarns I could spin
About the queer places I've bin
To an' the queer things as I've seen an' I've done
'Most everywhere under the sun:
A picnic we 'ad
In a copper ore barque
Out o' Bristol,
When the skipper went mad
An' started in pickin' the watch
For a lark
Off the yard with a pistol,
Till the second mate managed to catch
Him a clout
With a handspike, an' that laid him out
Good an' proper, an' ended his bother . . .
Then the time when we roasted an' froze
Both together
In a ship with her cargo alight
Off Cape Stiff in the worst of his weather;
For it snowed
An' it blowed
A fair fright
An' the deck got
That 'ot
We was 'oppin' around like a hen
On a griddle—an' then
Come a ship by as tuk us off just
In time, 'fore she blowed up an' bust . . .

An' yarns about cannibal isles,
Where they sharpen their teeth up with files
'Case they dish up for tea
Some hard-cased old shellback like me;
An' shipwrecks an' shangha-ing too
I could tell—and a few
Of 'em true,
If I had the trick o' the pen,"
Bill said, "like some men.

But all as I done wi' the brush
In my puff
Ain't been much
Only touching up bulwarks and such,
Or slung overside in the sun
Or aloft with a bucket o' slush,
An' the mate comin' sneakin' be'ind
An' growlin', 'No holidays, mind,
Ye sons o' sea-cooks!' . . . .
An' the schoolin' I 'ad
As a lad
Was enough
For to learn me to sign
Ships' articles, forty-odd year
Far an' near
'Stead o' makin' my mark . . . . An' that's 'ow
It is there'll be nobody now
To read all them books,
Or to see
Them pictures as might ha' been mine—
Only me . . . ."

❖   ❖   ❖   ❖   ❖

From *Punch* magazine, Volume 193, October 27, 1937, p. 453.

Meet at Eleven

They were here on the side
Of the downs a few minutes ago . . .

Hounds dappled and pied,
And riders pink-coated and black,
And people on foot holding back
Their bobbery pack
On leads,
All sizes and breeds,
The laughter and chatter
As neighbour greets neighbour, the sound
Of the whip's voice berating a hound—
"Hi, Raffle!

Hi, Ranger!"—
That has strayed into danger
From the ribbon-tailed kicker;
The creaking of leather,
The clink of a snaffle,
A whiff of cigar smoke, a whicker
From a fidgety mare, then the chatter
Of a late-coming rider. And so
They moved off and were gone
Altogether.

And there's only
The lonely
And brown
Long curve of the down,
Rabbit-pitted, sheep-shorn,
Crescent cut where the horses have passed
And anon
The distant
Insistent
Thin blast
Of the horn . . .

❖ ❖ ❖ ❖ ❖

From *Punch* magazine, Volume 193, December 8, 1937, p. 623.

Winter Morning

Five teams at plough,
All at plough together . . .
Red the beechen bough,
Crisp and cold the weather.
Bright shares cleaving
Through the frosty clods,
Strong flanks heaving
While the ploughman plods.

Whistling loud and clear
Up the field's long shoulder,
Starlings flocking near
Chilly days make bolder.

Bare the copses now,
Brisk and keen the weather;
Bright-eyed on the bough
Robin puffs a feather . . .
And there are five teams at plough,
All at plough together.

❖ ❖ ❖ ❖ ❖

From *Punch* magazine, Volume 193, December 22, 1937, p. 693.

Pirate Schooner

Deep Sea Plunderings

If one could be mine for the asking
Of all the ships there be,
The great and small and swift and tall
That sail the salty sea,
No battleship or mailboat,
No clipper fair and fine,
No yacht bescrolled with white and gold
Is the one I'd ask for mine.
For some are too big for my fancy,
And some are too grand for me,
But a schooner smart is the ship of my heart,
Or a saucy brig maybe;
I'd fit her out with all things needful,
And then I would sign a crew
Of shipmates tried to stand by my side,
A cat, and a cockatoo.

We'd wave good-bye to the lighthouse,
And the buoy on the leaping bar,
At the wind's sweet will our sails we'd fill,
We'd steer by a wandering star.
We'd follow the southbound swallow
To the coasts of sun and sand,
Where the desert drowns the ancient towns
In the heart of a thirsty land.

We'd take a slant to the northward
To the ice and the Arctic snows;
Then south again to the West Wind's reign
And the seas where the White Whale blows.
We'd bask on the tropic beaches,
And watch where the bright fish pass
In the pools sand-strewn of the still lagoon,
Through the water as clear as glass.

We'd sail to the South Sea islands,
We'd call on a cannibal chief,
We'd fish for pearls where the long tide curls
On the fringe of the Barrier Reef;
We'd land on an isle uncharted,
Forgotten, far and lone,
And seek the hoard by a pirate stored
In a secret place unknown.

We'd ravage the coasts of wonder,
We'd plunder the ports of dream,
We'd store our hold with the Tropics' gold,
And the spoil of the spray-bow's gleam.
Till—weary at last from sailing,
And tired of the wind and foam—
We'd steer once more for a well-loved shore,
And the open door of home!

❖ ❖ ❖ ❖ ❖

From *The Oxford Book for Boys*, 1938

This romantic pirate poem is aimed at entertaining children.

The header graphic illustrated the pirate poem in this book and was drawn by Phil W. Smith.

Lower Pool

"Where are you bound for,
Sailorman, sailorman
With the missis and the dog
And your big spreets'l flopping?"
"Maldon, Manningtree,
West as far's the Wight, maybe,
With bricks, hay,
China-clay,
Bit o' that or
Bit o' this,
Don't much matter
What it is—
Here, there
Everywhere,
And back again to Wapping . . . ."

"Where are you bound for,
Sailorman, sailorman
Up and down the coast
For a little bit o' shopping?"
"Shields, Tyne, Grimsby, Goole,
Hull, Hell an' Hartlepool,
With salt, soap,

Coals and rope,
Bit o that or
Bit o' this
Don't much matter
What it is—
Here, there
Everywhere,
And back again to Wapping . . . ."

"Where are you bound for,
Sailorman, sailorman
Down from Lower Pool
On the late tide dropping?"
"'Cross the bay and Sou' Spain,
Round the world and home again,
With motor-cars, steel rails
Worcester sauce and bags o' nails,
Cloves, cork, cotton seed,
Soya beans and parrot-feed,
Bit o' that or
Bit o' this
Don't much matter
What it is—
Here, there
Everywhere,
And back again to Wapping . . . ."

❖ ❖ ❖ ❖ ❖

From *Punch* magazine, Volume 194, June 29, 1938, p. 712.

Most of the place names mentioned are either on the Thames or served by boats sailing from the Thames.

"The Pool" could be either the upper or lower pool which are sections of the River itself.

Places

Some people collect
Stamps and Old Masters,
Queen Anne pepper-casters
Pistols and kreeses,
And orchids, all blotchy and flecked
Like diseases,
And China and Chippendale chairs,
And stuffed heads of bison and bears,
And fiddles
And butterflies stuck through their middles,
And Lord knows what
Rot . . . .
And others, of course, collect
Money . . .

But it's funny
I don't
Collect even plain £.s.d.—
It won't
Stick to me,
And I don't expect
Ever it will;
So let those that can have their fill
Collecting things—I collect
Places . . .

You don't need glass cases
To keep them in,
Nor museums and strong rooms to heap them in;
You don't have to be for ever worrying about
Whether the rot's rotting them or the damp's rusting them;
You don't have to pay anyone for hurrying about
Dusting them;
You don't have to be always finding a fly in the ointment
The way these collecting blokes do,
And eating your insides out with rage and disappointment
Because someone else has got a bigger and better one than you . . .

Yes, even if you can't spend them
Or lend them,
It's rather a jolly sort of a notion
That you've got
The Atlantic and the Pacific and the Indian Ocean
And the Rockies and the Andes,
And Ascension and Trinidad and Juan Fernandez,
And the veld and the pampas and the prairie,
And the Sahara and the Kalahari,
The heights and the deeps . . .
And no matter how old you may get,
Or how hungry and cold you may get,
Or whether your coat's full of holes
And your boots haven't got any soles,
They're your own, all the lot
And for keeps . . . .

❖ ❖ ❖ ❖ ❖

From *Punch* magazine, Volume 195, August 10, 1938, p. 159.

A Ballad of Blue Water

Three sons there are of my father's house,
The youngest I of three,
And two he left both gold and gear,
But a rambling heart to me.
He willed to me no gold or gear,
No beast or byre or hall,
For I was born to blue water
(Blue water, deep water!),

I was born to blue water,
And that is best of all.

The eldest minds his crops and kine
And walks his acres wide,
He goes in dread of drought and rain
And a hundred ills beside:
So let him keep his flocks and herds,
His store of garnered sheaves,
And his heart as heavy as the clay,
His painful ploughshare cleaves.

The second plies the merchant's trade,
A rich man him they call;
He hires himself poor sailormen
To sail his ships withal;
I would not change with him for all
The stuff his ships can hold;
And a heart as hard and heavy
As his silver and his gold.

They plough a weary furrow,
They pile a weary hoard,
They have no joy to spend the wealth
Which they with pain have stored.
They never bring to pleasuring
So light a heart as we
That win our scanty livelihood
In hardship on the sea.

They served their long apprenticeship
To plough and desk and stool,
But we were tossing on the seas
When they were fast in school;
Forth from our childhood's play we went,
And from our mother's knee,
To learn the ways of life and death
At peril of the sea.

A man may save his whole life long,
Yet always lack a friend;
And all the hoarded gold on earth
Will fail him at the end.
But when all the pay's spent, dear lad,
And the last song is sung,
We'll turn once more to blue water —
(Blue water, deep water!)
Go back once more to blue water,
True shipmates among!

❖ ❖ ❖ ❖ ❖

From The Oxford Annual for Boys, Volume 31, 1938. p. 131; the poem is accompanied by drawings in the margins by Philip Wilson Smith.

Everything is Different in Africa

Everything is different in Africa.
Strange stars by night look down,
And threepence is called a tickey
And a florin's like half-a-crown.

Everything is different in Africa;
Hardly a thing's the same,
And any that are are mostly
Called by a different name.

"Everything is different in Africa,"
I thought—till my gaze did roam
By chance to some words familiar
That seemed like a voice from Home.

And still as the train rolled onward
They sang through my brain all night,
While the dust of the Kalahari
Sat on me, fine and white.
For they spoke of a strap I clung to
In a train I used to know,
And Waterloo in the rush-hour
In a time that's long ago.

"Do not throw out of the window"—
Thus went the haunting tune,
Like a magical incantation,
Like a druid's mystic rune—

"Bottles or other articles"—
Never such deed be mine!—
"Likely to injure anyone
Working on the line!"

❖ ❖ ❖ ❖ ❖

From *Punch* magazine, Volume 195, August 17, 1938, p. 172.

The poet had just returned from a steamer trip around Africa, stopping at ports along the way.

Winter Pleasures

I hate
To skate.

Ski
Are not for me.

Lugeing
I do not find amusing.

I would go a long way
Rather than sleigh.

I will construct an abominable snowman
For no man.

In short, though I am told
It is very healthy to be cold,

I consider ice
Far from nice.

And to the question, "Do you like snow?"
My answer is definitely "No!"

❖   ❖   ❖   ❖   ❖

From *Punch* magazine, Volume 196, February 1, 1939, p. 135.

Going for 'ard with the food

Departure

When I was a lad
No more than a nipper
I signed in a packet
Called the *Highland Maid*
To pay out my dad
'Cos he dusted my jacket
For some sort o' trick
As I'd been and gone and played. . . .

She'd a mate as could kick
An' a boozing skipper;
She rolled like a pig an' she steered like a hearse,
An' the pork was rotten an' the beef was worse;
So afore so long, as you may fancy,
I was sick an' sorry, or my name ain't Clancy.
It blew like hell when we sunk the Foreland
Night comin' on an' a cold rain fallin',
The poor old barkey with her lee rail under,
An' a great big darkey with a voice like thunder
Settin' a tune to the halliard chorus
An' our homes astern an' the seas afore us,
An' I says to myself, "When I'm once ashore
I'll quit the sea an' I'll sail no more,"
As I watched an' watched till there warn't no more land—
Nothin' to see of the home I was leavin'
Only the rain an' the grey waves heavin',
 An' a few gulls astern of us a-callin'
An' a-hollerin';
"Here's another young silly
Young billy
Of a sailor chap wot's took to follerin'
The sea. . . ."

It's a divil of a while since then, Lord knows,
An' the years they comes an' the years they goes,
An' my old dad's dead long since wot licked me,
An' the boozy skipper an' the mate as kicked me;
An' the shantying darkey
His singin' 's past,
An' the poor old barkey
She's leaked her last,
An' the world's as wide an' the sea's as wet
As they was when I started—but I ain't quit yet!
An' the same old gulls they're a-callin' an' a-hollerin';
"Here's another young silly
Young billy
Of a sailorchap as can't quit follerin'
The sea. . . ."

❖ ❖ ❖ ❖ ❖

From *Punch* magazine, Volume 196, March 15, 1939, p. 301.

In terms of the mores and manners of the day the term "darkey" was used for anyone with a dark coloured skin tone and was not necessarily interpreted as insulting.

The header graphic is a photograph of a ship's boy titled *Going for 'ard* with the food by Alan Villiers aboard the four-masted barque *Parma* during a gale, from *Last of the Wind Ships*, #78

Swallows at Zimbabwe

Great Zimbabwe in the sun,
Far away
Dreams all day
Of his riddle solved of none,
Where just now the swallows muster,
Cling and cluster,
Chestnut breasts and cloven tails,
On the wires and on the rails,
Soon to fly
Straight and high,
Following still the airy blue
Roads they knew
Centuries ere Zimbabwe grew
Under those dead builders' hands,
Over bush and swamp and range,
Lake and jungle lost and strange,
Lone and lion-coloured lands
Of sun and sands.
So they fly
Straight and high,
Far and fast,
Till at last
Looking out beneath the thatch
On the church, the elms, the green,
Budding hedgerow, cressy brook,
Springing wheat and fresh turned loam—
All the quiet old serene
English scene,
Somebody may chance to catch
A sudden flash of wings and cry;
"Look—Look—
The swallows have come home!"

❖ ❖ ❖ ❖ ❖

From *Punch* magazine, Volume 196, April 12, 1939, p. 399.

In this context the name Zimbabwe does not refer to the country we know today, which had not yet been formed. Zimbabwe (zihm-BAHB-way) which means "House of Stone" refers to the 900-year-old stone ruins left by the Shona people which is still a mystery and major tourist attraction.

Luck

"Luck"
Said Dan,
"Never no luck
Come my way, sonny!
None o' them widders with a nice little pile
Lookin' for a sailor man
Looked at me—

Not she!
Money
Never stuck
To me the way it does to some folks;
Fortune never 'ad no smile
For me the way she 'as for some blokes;
An' the only thing as ever I found
Was one 'arf-crownd,
An' then I was 'ad—
It was bad.

Luck—I never 'ad none,
But what's the odds when you've done . . . ?
Say you marry a rich wider and she turns out a terror
(Which plenty do, an' no fatal error)
Life ain't no catch with somebody shrieking:
'Dan, wipe
Them boots on the mat!'
An' 'Dan, put out that filthy pipe!'
An' 'Dan, this' an' 'Dan, that,'
Until you're that fed up you go sneakin'
Downstairs in your socks
An' off to the docks
An' sign in the first
An' maybe the worst
Sort o' packet as comes along
To get out o' reach o' the old woman's tongue.

Or say you win a nice packet
In a sweep, an' whack it
With your pals, or booze it,
Or put the blessed lot on an 'orse an' lose it
Well, I reckon you're an 'ole lot
Worse off than if you'd never got
No
Bloomin' packet to blow.

Me,
Forty years now I've been follerin' the sea;
Forty years I've been moseyin' round,
An' I've earned my pint an' I've earned my pound,
The ships I've served in, small an' large,
They've mostly give me a good discharge,
I've stood my trick an' I've pulled my weight
From Sand'eads Light to the Golden Gate,
An' takin'
In a manner o' speakin',
The rough an' the smooth an' the fair an' the foul weather
All together,

Why, I reckon the times I've 'ad
Ain't been bad.
I ain't been no outsize sinner, nor yet no plaster saint;
But as for bein' a lucky man,"
Said Dan,
"Well, I ain't."

❖   ❖   ❖   ❖   ❖

From *Punch* magazine, Volume 197, September 13, 1939, p. 306.

WWII Poster

What Bill Said

"So Fritz 'e's at 'is tricks," Bill said,
"'Is dirty sinkin' game:
We thought we'd learned 'im better—
Well it seems 'e's still the same,
But there ain't no 'Ans-medoodle
In the blessed 'ole caboodle
As'll stop me
Goin' to sea."
Bill said, said he.

"I've known 'is little ways last war,
First was off the Lizard
In a seven-knot rusty cargo tramp
By name the *Northern Wizard*;
I left 'er in my singlet
In a January blizzard
Which wasn't the best o' fun—
And that was Number One,"
Bill said, said he.

"Next was south the Fastnet
In the tanker *Panama*;
'E peppered us with shrapnel
Just afore he said 'Ta-ta!'
We was seven days driftin'
With our dead and dyin' crew—
An' that was Number Two,"
Bill said, said he.

"Last was west of Ushant,
The Old Man up an' damned 'em;
'E shoved the 'elm 'ard over
And 'e went for 'em and rammed 'em,
That was Number Three,"
Bill said, said he.

"And now 'e's at 'is tricks," Bill said,
"The same old game again.
Well, let 'im do 'is darnedest,
And 'e'll find as 'e found then
I ain't met
The square-'ead yet
As'll stop me
Goin' to sea,"
Bill said, said he.

❖ ❖ ❖ ❖ ❖

From *Punch* magazine, Volume 197, October 4, 1939, p. 367.

The poet is reviving some of her poetic nautical dialogue begun in WWI for WWII.

The header graphic is a WWII poster by nautical artist Anton Otto Fischer, 1942.

The Shantyman

Now the pilot's come aboard us,
And the Peter's down at last,
And the last "So-long" 's been shouted
From the pier head as we passed;
Now the old familiar sea marks
Drop behind us one by one —
And our bows are turning seaward
Where the wild white horses run. . . .

And it's "Pipe up, Shantyman!"
Lift a deep-sea chorus,
All the blooming seas to sail,
All the world before us.
Far astern in mist and twilight
Fade from sight the lights o' land—
"Bound away—bound away—
For the rolling—Rio—Grand!"

Dips the northern Plough behind us—
Climbs ahead the starry Cross—
Soon the blowing whale will greet us,
And the lordly albatross.
Mad with glee the dolphins topple
In the turmoil of our wake,
While the flying fish like silver
Skim the bubbles as they break. . . .

And it's "Pipe up, Shantyman!"
Barefoot days are come—
Every shroud is singing loud,
Every rope a-thrum,
Fog and cold and Biscay gales
Now are far behind—
"Rolling down to St Helena
On the brave Trade Wind!"

South, far below the Forties
Race the rollers round the world,
With their crested manes in thunder
High above our bulwarks curled;
Loud above the wind's commotion
Claps the thrashing bellying sail—
And the shout's "Aloft and furl it!"
In the darkness and the gale. . . .

And it's "Pipe up, Shantyman!"
Down the wind away
Go the tatters of our voices
Blown to leeward with the spray,
Where the mile-long foaming greybeards
Gallop furious from the west—
"Stormy's gone, that good old skipper,
Stormy's dead and gone to rest!"

We have wallowed, lumber laden,
Both rails under off the Horn,
We have hobbled into harbour
With our canvas split and torn,
We have moseyed round for cargoes
From the Nicobars to Nome—
But our orders came this morning,
And I think the word is home. . . .

So it's "Pipe up, Shantyman!"
Tramp the capstan round,
Give it lip and with a will, lads,
Till the anchor leaves the ground,
And the sleeping anchorage echoes—
"Rolling home across the sea,
Rolling home to dear old England,
Rolling home, dear land, to thee!"

❖ ❖ ❖ ❖ ❖

From *The Oxford Annual for Boys*, Volume 32, 1939. p. 71; note there is a small illustration by Phil W. Smith.

Wapping: Conversation Piece

'Lo, Ginger . . . 'Lo, Mike . . .
Where you been this long while
Since you an' me was in the ol' *Mona's Isle?* . . .
Oh, jus' moseyin' around like. . . .

Ever see anything o' the ol' ship? . . .
Aye, sailed in her myself las' trip . . .
You did? . . . Aye. She's gone, Fritz sunk 'er;
Shoved a tin fish in 'er starboard bunker
An' down she went like a stone—
Quickest thing I ever known. . . .

Was there any more o' the ol' crowd in 'er? . . . A few—
You'd remember the mate, ol' Mister Bell? . . .
Aye, I do. . . .
Well—
An' all them little birds he used to keep

(Nice little singers they was, it was a treat to 'ear 'em
When you was anywhere near 'em)—
Remember 'ow the Ol' Man used to raise merry 'ell
'Cause they sung that loud they sp'iled 'is sleep? . . .
Aye . . . Well, 'e's gone too. . . .

Well, reckon I'll be pushin' along, Mike, Tootle-oo. . . .
Me too . . .
Time I was lookin' out for another berth . . . Same 'ere
Ain't goin' to stop at 'ome to please Jerry, like . . . ?
No bloomin' fear . . .
Well s' long, Ginger . . . S' long, Mike . . .

❖ ❖ ❖ ❖ ❖

From *Punch* magazine, Volume 198, April 17, 1940, p. 420.

Withdrawal from Dunkirk

The Day of Little Ships

Long after the shadow of war is fled
And the last battle is fought
Men will remember the Little Ships
And the great things they wrought.
We shall tell over with laughter and tears
The homely names they bore—
They, not meant for the baptism of fire
And the grim uses of war.

Paddler, dinghy and sailing barge
Eagle and *Queen* and *Belle*,

And the humble Marthas of the ports
That have no name to tell.

Let us remember them and their men
Who asked not fee nor fame,
But all they knew was a job to do,
And they spat on their palms and they came.

They dared the hell of the shell-swept dunes,
The hell of the bomb-torn tide,
They cared not a damn if they sank or swam,
Nor yet if they lived or died.

Home they came from that coast of death,
Each with her tale of men,
Stayed but to set them ashore—and so
Back to hell's mouth again. . . .

Therefore, while England's cliffs shall stand,
And the Channel tides do roll,
Let us remember the Little Ships—
How on the Day of the Little Ships
They saved an army whole.

From *Punch* magazine, Volume 198, June 19, 1940, p. 664.

The evacuation of Dunkirk took place between May 27th and June 4th, 1940, with a diverse fleet of civilian ships assisting in the rescue of 366,162 British and Allied troops.

First adapted for singing by Charles Ipcar, as recorded on *Never Turn a Blind Eye to the Storm,* 2015

The header graphic is a drawing titled *The Evacuation at Dunkirk*, from *The Illustrated London News*, June 8, 1940, pp. 766-767. The small print under the headline said it was drawn by their "special war artist," John A. Bryan de Grineau "from descriptions furnished by eye-witnesses."

The Ghost of Sir Francis Drake

Drake's Breed

Drake looked out to the English shore
From the port of Dead Man's Bay;
He heard the din and the thunder of war
Come to him from far away.
He said "Is it well with the isle we knew?
Is her heart still sound? Are her lads still true?
Do they flutter her foes as we used to do
In the old Armada's day?"

Drake looked out to the sea and the ships,
To mark how the fight went on;
With a smile that twitched at his bearded lips,
As it did when he sighted the Don,
Said he "It is well—though the foe be strange,
And the craft be new, and the old ways change,
In the same old fashion the seas we range
As we did in the time that's gone."

Drake looked out to the sea and the sky
From the port of Dead Man's Bay;
And he cried aloud as he smote his thigh,
"Is it well with old England? Yea!

Though never we knew such craft as these,
That ride the clouds as we rode the seas,
They harry the foe as we harried him then,
They hustle and harry him, one to ten,
As it was when we harried the might of Spain,
Down the Channel and round by the Main,
In the old Armada's day."

❖ ❖ ❖ ❖ ❖

From *Punch* magazine, Volume 199, September 4, 1940, p. 251.

There is a legend that if Britain is ever in great need then Sir Francis Drake will come back to fight (usually said to be summoned by Drake's Drum) and here the poet is playing on that myth and effectively comparing the Armada of Luftwaffe planes with the Armada of Spanish ships so long ago. The phrase "one to ten" refers to the alleged odds of one British craft for every ten Spanish ships (or German planes).

The header graphic is a cartoon titled *Drake's Way* commemorating the British raid on the German submarine base at Zeebrugge on St. George's Day as drawn by Bernard Partridge, from *Punch* magazine, May 1, 1918, p. 281.

Supermarine Spitfire Fighter Plane

Everybody's Doing It

We're all buying Spitfires
As fast as we can buy
Spitfires and Hurricanes
For battles in the sky . . .

The girls whose names are this or that,
The folk who keep a dog or cat,
The darts clubs and the foxhound packs,
The chimney-sweeps and steeplejacks,
The men who work in mine or mill,
Who milk our cows, our fields who till,
The rich and poor, the great and small,
The towns and counties one and all—

They're all buying Spitfires
(Hurricanes and Spitfires)
As fast as they can buy.

They're all buying Spitfires
The people near and far
Hurricanes and Spitfires
To help to win the war . . .

In Port of Spain and Singapore,
And Chequerbent and Cockey Moor,
In Burma, Bluff and Table Bay,
And tiny islands far away,
In Durban, Malta and Fiji,
From John o' Groats to Tasman Sea,
In all the ends of all the earth
They're writing cheques for all they're worth—

And they're all buying Spitfires
(Hurricanes and Spitfires)
To help us win the war . . .

They're all buying fighters,
And as soon as they have done
They'll all be buying bombers
To go and bust the Hun . . .

❖ ❖ ❖ ❖ ❖

From *Punch* magazine, Volume 199, September 25, 1940, p. 316.

September 1940, when this poem was written, was the turning point of what became known as the Battle of Britain. The RAF (and allied forces) were defending London and southern England from the German Luftwaffe. Throughout Britain ordinary people were collecting and organizing events for "The Spitfire Fund" to help purchase fighters for the RAF.

The header graphic is a photograph of a Supermarine Spitfire fighter plane, photographer unknown.

Salute to Sailor Town

The little streets of Sailor Town
They are not fair nor fine,
That struggle with their sooty slates
By Mersey, Thames and Tyne,
By Humber and by Severn sea,
From Hull to Solent side,
The little streets of Sailor Town—
The shabby streets of Sailor Town
That know not wealth nor pride.
The little streets of Sailor Town
This day they mourn their dead
That give their lives in death-sown seas
To bring a people bread;
No day that adds not to the tale
Of those that come no more
To little homes in Sailor Town
In grimy streets of Sailor Town

That suffer and endure.
The little streets of Sailor Town
They are not rich nor grand,
But death and glory walk this day
Their pavements hand in hand.
Come fire, come steel—they cannot break
The courage proud and high
Of humble folk in Sailor Town
In little streets of Sailor Town
In gallant streets of Sailor Town
That know the way to die.

❖   ❖   ❖   ❖   ❖

From *Punch* magazine, Volume 199, December 18, 1940, p. 587.

At this time the "Battle of Britain" between the RAF and the Luftwaffe had just reached its height and there was an immense amount of praise for the airmen concerned. This is Smith's way of pointing out that sailors, especially Merchant Seamen, were just as committed and suffering heavy casualties.

A Question

Women wear trousers
To trail round the shops;
Women in trousers
Wield brushes and mops.

Women wear trousers
For sleeping and sitting
And pouring out tea in
And doing their knitting.

For cleaning the windows
And filling the shells,
And taking round letters,
And answering bells.

Women in trousers,
(Or leastways in breeches)
Are planting potatoes
And scrapping out ditches

They wear them for punching
Our tickets in trams,
Or pushing their babies
Abroad in their prams.

In fact nearly everything
Under the sun
But—why don't they wear them
For manning a gun!

From *Punch* magazine, Volume 201, December 3, 1941, p. 483.

Not a question anyone would even think about in the 21st Century but when this was first published during WWII it was perfectly valid. Trousers were in fashion for women for all sorts of reasons but the military lagged far behind civvy street.

Post-War Plans

"When this 'ere war's finished," Bill said,
"If we ain't all dead,
Most of the crowd's all for quittin' the sea.
Joe's goin' in for a chip shop or fish maybe;
Young Charlie's talkin' about a motor garage,
And Bert's idea's mate of a cement barge
So's he can get 'ome once in a while for tea;
Ginger says 'e's goin' in for a little place down Essex way
Where 'e can set back quiet an' watch the 'ens lay . . .
But me—well, I'm going on sixty-six,
And you can't learn an old dog new tricks,
So I'm goin' to find
The first Jerry I can and kick his be'ind,
And then—well, seems to me
I can't do much better than go back to sea.

❖   ❖   ❖   ❖   ❖

From *Punch* magazine, Volume 204, March 18, 1942, p. 211.

"Cement Barge" it is not clear if the poet meant a barge made out of cement or a barge carrying cement. It is my opinion she meant the former.

A Lament

It induces a sensation
Of irritation
(Not to mention frustration
And even indignation)
When one makes humble solicitation
For employment in some useful occupation
In this crisis in the affairs of the nation
And receives in reply a communication
To the effect that in relation
To the aforesaid application
It will receive due consideration
After further amplification
Explanation
And elucidation
And of course the most careful investigation
And filling up of forms in duplication,
Triplification,
And quadruplification,
And that the said application

Will be open for further—
Oh, blast—
Procrast-ination!

❖ ❖ ❖ ❖ ❖

From *Punch* magazine, Volume 204, April 22, 1942, p. 335.

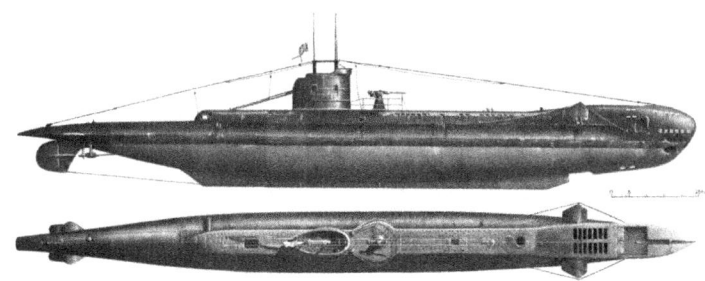

HMS *Upholder*

Submarines

"I take off my 'at to them blokes in the submarines," said Murphy,
"It ain't no picnic for none of us fellers at sea;
What with mines and bombs, there's always something to worry you,
But I reckon theirs is the toughest traverse of the whole lot," said he.

"If you're sunk, well, you've got a chance of your life maybe,
You've got the sea round you and the sky overhead,
And if you've got to go I'd as soon that way as any other—
But if they die, they die in the dark," he said.

"Down there in the dark, and nobody seein' them,
Nobody ever to know how the end come,
How or when, or slow or sudden, or anything at all about it,
Only that the days go by, an' they don't come 'ome . . ."

❖ ❖ ❖ ❖ ❖

From *Punch* magazine, Volume 206, January 27, 1943, p. 68.

The poet prefaced this poem with: "H. M. Submarine—is now much overdue, and must be considered lost."

The header graphic is an illustration of a famous WWII British submarine the HMS *Upholder* which was sunk by enemy action in April of 1942, from *The Encyclopedia of Sea Warfare*, published by Thomas Y. Crowell Co., New York, US, 1975, pp. 106-107.

Epitaph on an Unfortunate Lady

In day's ere war's despite had used her ill,
Tireless she sped o'er valley, plain and hill;
To-day—how sad her plight, her fate how hard!—
Tireless she sits, and cannot move a yard.

From *Punch* magazine, Volume 206, April 7, 1943, p. 285.

Although it doesn't state which vehicle the poet is referring to, I suspect it is her trusty bicycle that she wrote about in other poems.

Homecoming at Dawn

Over the white cliffs, over the downlands whirring,
Out of the dappled east with dawn aflame,
The moon pale in the sky, and the first birds stirring,
Homeward the war-scarred battle squadrons came.

Came . . . all but those who shall see no more below them
Mapwise the small green chequered countryside,
Places greatly loved that shall never again know them—
All that was England—all for which they died.

❖ ❖ ❖ ❖ ❖

From *Punch* magazine, Volume 206, May 5, 1943, p. 368.

A Thought for Gardeners

The Russians, so we lately learned,
Are fighting on the Slucz—
A piece of news which cannot fail
An answering chord to tucz,
Since how you spell it, after all,
Can't really matter mucz,
And we who dig for victory
Are toiling—in the slucz.

❖ ❖ ❖ ❖ ❖

From *Punch* magazine, Volume 208, January 26, 1944, p. 81

The "Slucz" is a river in Poland, the scene of heavy fighting in 1944. Here the poet is delivering a heavy pun on the pronunciation, which to English ears would sound like slush or sluch.

The Windmill

High on its curving hillside
The windmill stands and sees
Below it copse and pasture
And hamlet bowered in trees.
It sees the white road winding
From London to the sea,
That saw the laurelled coaches
Bear news of victory.
It sees the Hundred Acre
Where now the plough teams go,
The striving steaming horses,
The ploughman trudging slow.
The gulls that scream and wrangle
The shining share behind
That cleaves the turf, unbroken
Since time nigh out of mind.
Where soon the green wheat springing

A Sussex Windmill

Like spears in rest shall come,
And soon again the reaping
And day of harvest home.
Turn, turn, you sails triumphant,
Grind surely, stones, and well—
So turned they, and so ground they,
The year Napoleon fell.

❖   ❖   ❖   ❖   ❖

From *Here and There in England with the Painter Brangwyn*, by Cicely Fox Smith, published by F. Lewis, Leigh-on-Sea, UK, 1945, p. 46.

The header graphic is titled *A Sussex Windmill* by the painter Brangwyn and illustrates this poem in this book on p. 47.

The Bridge

Over the bridge when the moon is high
There comes a horseman galloping by,
Like one that has ridden both fast and far,
That bears great tidings of peace or war—
Whither . . . whither . . . ?

Over the bridge he gallops amain,
The sparks from the cobbles they shower like rain,
The arches ring as he thunders o'er,
And into the dark he goes once more—
Whither . . . whither . . . ?

Over the bridge and into the night,
Till the sound is lost of his furious flight,
And nothing is left but the wind that moans,
And the river hastening over its stones—
Whither . . . whither . . . ?

❖   ❖   ❖   ❖   ❖

From *Here and There in England with the Painter Brangwyn*, by Cicely Fox Smith, published by F. Lewis, Leigh-on-Sea, UK, 1945, p. 55.

Dogs

Spaniels are all very well,
But they smell.

Sealyhams deposit white hairs
On the chairs.

Wire-hairs are all right,
But they fight.

(Which also applies to the Irish variety,
Such charming society.)

A Dalmatian is no good, of course,
Without a carriage or a horse.

And hounds are nice, but you've got
To have such a lot.
Dashshunds are capital fun,
But slightly Hun.

Very large breeds, such as St. Bernards eat
Quantities of meat,

While very small ones, unhappily,
Bark so much and so yappily.

But please don't jump to the conclusion that I dislike
A tyke.

It's simply that I prefer
An honest-to-goodness Cur.

❖ ❖ ❖ ❖ ❖

From *Punch* magazine, Volume 210, January 24, 1945, p. 78.

The Unchanged

When all this maniac dream is overpast,
And earth from her nightmare wakes at last,
Marred beyond thinking, seamed by many a scar—
Where shall we turn to find no trace of war,
No age-old beauty shattered in an hour
(Grey wall and traceried arch and soaring tower),
No sanctuary despoiled or tumbled spire,
No splintered woodland swept and seared by fire,
Or ravaged beach, or crater-pitted down,
Or last remotest isle mourning her fronded crown?

The sea—the sea remains; through all the same,
Eternal, cold, unchanged, whence all life came,
Her chill indifferent beauty takes no heed
Of faith and valour, anger and fear and greed,
Tossing aside as unconsidered things
The pride of navies and the pomp of kings,
Yet bearing safe through whatso storms may batter
The frail small shell a finger's touch might shatter . . .

Still shall her tides wherever tides shall run
Darken and gleam in shadow and in sun,
Still to the south her charging squadrons roll
In endless crested splendour round the Pole,

And still her bergs from the cold north set free
Melt in the Gulf Stream, mingle with the sea;
Still, still her tropic bird with vigilant eye
Scan the wide emptiness of sea and sky,
And find between the twain nor less nor more
Of last night's tempest than of six years' war;
And all the nations' grief and the world's trouble
Pass like a bird's passing . . . a cloud's shadow . . . a breaking bubble . . .

Still, as through countless centuries, come and go
Sunsets and dawns . . . and only memory know
How lost, how loved, the dead who sleep below.

❖ ❖ ❖ ❖ ❖

From *Punch* magazine, Volume 210, June 27, 1945, p. 548.

The poet's musings near the end of WWII.

The House-Hunter

I have been looking at a hovel
At the back o' behind;
It was like something out of a Welsh novel
Of the grimly realistic kind.
It clung to a mountain-side sternly and sadly
As a fly clings to the wall,
It had a tin shed or two, and the roof leaked badly,
And there was no road to it at all.

I have been looking at a pig-sty
(Though they didn't call it so),
It wasn't a very nice or a very big sty
Even as sties go;
Its walls were as wet as the inside of a cistern,
I nearly broke my neck in the "grounds,"
There was a rat-hole in the dinning room floor you could put your fist in,
And the price was fifteen hundred pounds.

I have been looking at a shanty
At the end of a long lane;
There wasn't a bath, and anyway the water was scanty,
It depended entirely on the rain;
The chimney smoked like the dickens when it was gusty,
You couldn't swing the smallest size of cat;
There was nowhere to keep the coals and kitchen stove was rusty,
And they wanted two thousand for that.

* * * * * * *

I have looked at very many hovels,
I have seen pig-sties galore;

I have looked at them until my spirit grovels
And my heart is sick and sore;
I cannot find a decent roof to cover me,
Be it large or be it small;
I will sit down in a ditch with an umbrella over me
And live nowhere at all.

❖   ❖   ❖   ❖   ❖

From *Punch* magazine, Volume 211, December 5, 1945, p. 484.

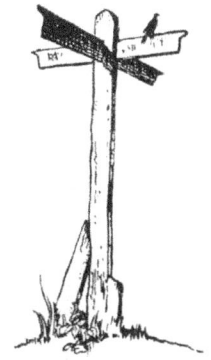
The Finger Post

The Finger Post

Across the field, beyond the church.
You see the sign post stand.
And towards the highway lean and lurch.
With crazy outstretched hand.
Faint marks upon whose surface show
Where letters once were traced;
Which wind and weather, long ago,
Have more than half effaced.
What matters it if near or far
The place whose name was writ?
The course the sign post bids you steer
Will never lead to it.
One moonless night (I sometimes think)
When all the cats were grey,
Some homebound reveller, filled with drink,
Came rolling up this way.
Who, pixy led, through wind and shower
Went rambling all night long,
And whiled away the passing hour
With staves of hiccuped song.

All night he tumbled out and in
Of thicket, ditch and mire,
Bestuck with burrs from heel to chin

And scratched by many a brier.
They led him round till dawn almost,
And last, in playful mood,
They changed him to a Finger Post
And left him there for good.
And still he stands and leans about
As he must surely fall,
And points the Road to Nowhere out
Where is no road at all.
He points the way through ditch and hedge,
And over field and furrow,
And water meadow speared with sedge
And banks where rabbits burrow.
By dale and down he points you still,
And on the skylines rim
The scarecrow from the windy Hill
Waves blithely back to him.

❖   ❖   ❖   ❖   ❖

From *Country Days and Country Ways: Trudging Afoot in England*, by Cicely Fox Smith, published by F. Lewis, Ltd., Leigh-on-Sea, UK, 1947, p. 12.

Here the poet is describing the perils of country walking in England.

The header graphic is titled *The Finger Post* as drawn by E. A. Cox, R. B. A., and illustrates this poem in the above book.

The Plovers' Wind

The Plovers' Wind

The plovers' wind is blowing—
A lusty wind and strong
In viewless torrents going
The leafless boughs among.

It shakes, it fills with riot
The bent and groaning pine,
And stirs a pulse unquiet
In nature's veins and mine.

The plovers' wind is blowing,
It fills the brimming springs,
And sets the hot life flowing
In all created things.

To all it brings renewing—
The sap to bush and tree—
The plover to his wooing,
And the ghost of love to me . . .

❖   ❖   ❖   ❖   ❖

From *Country Days and Country Ways: Trudging Afoot in England,* by Cicely Fox Smith, published by F. Lewis, Ltd., Leigh-on-Sea, UK, 1947, p. 26.

The header graphic is drawn by E. A. Cox, R. B. A., and is the one that accompanies the poem in the above book.

Pretty Meadow

In the field the farm-folk call,
        One and all,
Pretty Meadow—if you look
        Domesday Book
Very likely gives its name
        Just the same—
Once a great house used to stand,
        Bravely planned,
Brick and stone, accounted sure
        To endure,
Clustered chimneys—windows too
        Not a few
Flashing back the sunset light
        Night by night.

So it stood till—who may know
        By what foe?
War that wasted many a shire,
        Tempest, fire,
Or by time and slow decay
        Worn away,
Beam from beam, and stone from stone,
        Down were thrown.
Fretted cornice, pillared hall,
        Vanished all—
And of all the countless panes
        None remains
Where the sunset, night by night,
        Used to light
All his mimic fires aglow
        Row on row.

Only on some mounded heaps
              Cinquefoil creeps,
By whose line you still may pace
              Out the place
Where a great house, bravely planned,
              Used to stand . . .
And I doubt if ever there
              Sight more fair
Pretty meadow had to show
              Long ago
Than the lapwing's clutch of young,
              Diamond hung
On their backs of dappled down,
              Golden brown,
Hurrying through the dewy grass
              As you pass—
So I saw them, but to-day,
              Here in May!

❖ ❖ ❖ ❖ ❖

From *Country Days and Country Ways: Trudging Afoot in England*, by Cicely Fox Smith, published by F. Lewis, Ltd., Leigh-on-Sea, UK, 1947, pp. 31-32.

The Old Bellringer

The Old Bellringer

"Don't sound," old Job, the ringer, said,
"No muffled peal for I,
But pull your lustiest, lads, instead,
When I do come to die,"

'Till chaps at plough ten mile away,
So loud the music swells,
Do hear and stop their teams and say,
"There goes Long Barton bells."

"For look, when they do show their powers
And swing and shake the spire,

There hain't a peal can match wi' ours,
No, not in all the shire."

"I've rung they bells year in, year out,
Since I was but a boy,
And loved 'em best when they did shout
Like marning stars for joy."

"So toll, when I to churchyard go,
No knell wi' mournful sound,
But ring 'em high an' ring 'em low
An' ring 'em round an' round."

"An' send out all your j'yfullest notes
When I do come to die;
But never let they tuneful throats
Be sad along of I!"

❖ ❖ ❖ ❖ ❖

From *Country Days and Country Ways: Trudging Afoot in England*, by Cicely Fox Smith, published by F. Lewis, Leigh-on-Sea, UK, 1947, p. 45. Earlier published by *Punch* magazine.

The header graphic is drawn by E. A. Cox, R. B. A., and illustrates this poem in the above book.

A Complaint

Why—can anybody say?—
Has upon my natal day
Nothing ever taken place
Of importance to the race?

Why has no one great or glorious,
Famous, or at least notorious—
Author, actor, or highwayman,
Poet, prophet, priest or layman,
Ever chosen to appear
Then on this sublunary sphere?

Battles have been lost or won,
Kingdoms fallen, reigns begun,
People been decapitated,
Shipwrecked, crowned, assassinated,
Every day, it seems, but one—
One by fickle fame passed by,
No one's anniversary,
One round which no splendours cluster
Such as shed a borrowed luster
On the birthdays of my friends . . .
Only—"Partridge Shooting Ends."

❖ ❖ ❖ ❖ ❖

From *Punch* magazine, Volume 214, January 22, 1947, p. 103.

Upon Julia, Playing the Oboe

When as I hear my Julia play
Upon the oboe, oft I say
Well pleased were I if I might sit
Hour-long by her and hark to it,
So sweet the strains, so true the note
She charmeth from its well-tuned throat.

But, oh! When I do see her face,
How grievously doth she grimace,
How both her cheeks do swell and puff,
Like Boreas when his breath is rough!
Her cheery lips, how they are pursed,
The while she blows as she would burst;
Her eyes, too, from her head are seen
To start as she had strangled been,
And all her face doth take the shape
Most like a gargoyle or an ape.

Thus, while she plays, am I resigned
To be awhile, like Cupid, blind.

❖   ❖   ❖   ❖   ❖

From *Punch* magazine, Volume 214, February 5, 1947, p. 149.

Old Shipmates on a Spree

Should Auld Acquaintance . . . ?

Fancy you knowin' old Bill Barley—
I haven't seen 'im since I don't know when;
Him an' me made a voyage or two together—
Nine years ago, was it, or ten?
Terrible argumentative sort of bloke Bill was;
'E'd quarrel with his own toenails;
If he was adrift in the Atlantic Ocean

'E'd raise a row with the sharks and whales.
Last time him and me met
It was in this here bar;
We was havin' a pint and a yarn
Same as what you an' me are,
And Bill up and started something,
I don't just remember how,
Anyway, before you could say knife
We was having a first class row,
And they took and chucked us outside
For to finish our chat,
And I shoved Bill through a plate-glass winder,
And that was the end o' that . . .

But taking Bill all round
He wasn't a bad sort of chap,
Not a bad old scout, wasn't Bill,
If he hadn't been so fond of a scrap,
So if you run across him anywhere
You might say "How do" for me and shake,
And tell him I'd like to see his ugly dial again,
Just for old time's sake . . .

From *Punch* magazine, Volume 214, May 7, 1947, p. 392.

Sometimes our fondness for an old memory, in this case a brawl, outweighs our aversion to the participants over time.

The header graphic is an illustrations of two old shipmates drawn by Charles Pears, from *Salt-Water Poems and Ballads*, facing p. 40.

HMS *Warspite*

In Memoriam: HMS *Warspite*

"So the old ship's gone, Ginger" . . .
"Ay, so they say,
Piled herself up on the rocks somewhere" . . .
"Well, it was the best way."

"Rummy, isn't it, how an old ship always seems to know
When she's bound for the knacker's yard" . . .
"Ay, it is so."

"Well, she was a good old ship.
I knew her many a year,
And I'm glad she's cheated the breakers at the finish" . . .
"Same here . . ."

❖ ❖ ❖ ❖ ❖

From *Punch* magazine, Volume 214, May 14, 1947, p. 411.

In 1947 HMS *Warspite*, originally a WWI *Queen Elizabeth* class battleship but rebuilt for WWII, en route to the breakers yard was wrecked. She had broken free from her tugs near the Wolf Rock and was the largest wreck ever to occur on the Cornish coast. Her boilers still lie off St. Michael's Mount, near Penzance.

The header graphic is a photograph of the HMS *Warspite* during WWII in the Indian Ocean by Lieutenant D. C. Oulds, a Royal Navy official photographer.

Domestic Problem

I don't aspire to be a person of wealth and leisure,
Such as one sees on the screen.
With lackeys in livery ready to do my pleasure
With a skilled and attentive mien;
Gallant gay domestics and all the rest of it
Ain't anything in my line—
But if somebody came now and again and cleaned the place up a bit
It would be fine.

I don't mind turning on my own bath-water,
Though in the best circles of course it isn't done;
I can run a house and arrange flowers, and take the place of a daughter,
I can also use the phone.
Sitting about all day being a perfect lady
Is not written in my fate—
But if someone else once in a way got a meal ready
It would be great.

I always do my own hair and tie my own shoe-laces,
I should really rather hate to have a maid;
Footmen, I always think, have such supercilious faces,
And butlers simply make me afraid.
I don't want a housemaid, either under or upper'
If I did, I couldn't pay the price—
But if somebody once in a blue moon washed up after supper
It *would* be nice. . . .

❖ ❖ ❖ ❖ ❖

From *Punch* magazine, Volume 214, May 18, 1947, p. 465.

The poet never lost her perspective or her sense of humor.

"Screen" means cinema screen. "Under" or "upper" presumably means below stairs or above stairs maids. Above stairs maids were usually better trained and more presentable.

Casuarina Tree

The Casuarina Tree

Whence came you,
Wind from the sea,
Singing through
The casuarina tree?

Across what lands forlorn
Where your breath passes
Over granite and gnarled thorn
And bending grasses . . .

Ranges aloof, alone,
By man's foot untrod,
And pools none has known
But the stars and God . . .

Grey forsaken kraals
Of the ancient races,
Where the past's shadow falls
On their vacant places . . .

Streams where the duiker drink
In deep secret kloofs,
Stepping down to the brink
On slim delicate hoofs . . .

Uplands empty and bare
To the rain and the sun,
Where the bright lizards here and there
Flash and are gone . . .

With your restless voice waking
The wandering heart once more,

Like the sound of surf breaking
On a far-off shore,

Why come you,
Wind from the sea,
Singing through
The casuarina tree?

❖ ❖ ❖ ❖ ❖

From *Punch* magazine, Volume 215, August 13, 1947, p. 161.

The poet visited what was then called Rhodesia in her trip around Africa in 1938, trekking far inland to pay homage to the graves of her youthful heroes Cecil John Rhodes and Leander Starr Jameson. During her journey ashore she also spent some time visiting with an old German settler in a nearby settlement, in *All the Way Round,* p. 226:

"I don't think I shall ever hear a casuarina tree stir in the wind without thinking of old Peter Falk in his garden, with his kindly blue eyes and his weathered face that wrinkles into smiles as he says: 'Now I bring you to my seaside!'"

The header graphic is titled *Casuarina Tree, Endeavour Strait*, Australia, from Dickinson & Co., London, 1849, artist unknown.

Getting Off

I have taken to cycling again after a lapse of a generation,
How long I hardly care to tell,
And on the whole, taking everything into consideration,
I am getting on fairly well;
Getting on, in fact, I don't find at all harassing,
I can stick on too, easily enough,
But the thing that I do find rather embarrassing
Is that I can't get off.

All kinds of things happen when I take my feet off the pedals;
Sometimes I stand on one leg like a goose;
Sometimes I plunge head-first into a bed of nettles,
Which is not just what one would choose;
Now and then I fetch up all standing
Against a bank or a wall,
And occasionally I execute an out-and-out pancake landing
Which is not nice at all.

I seem to remember hopping off easily and lightly,
I can't imagine how,
With a kind of curtseying motion, most graceful and sprightly,
But I can't do it now.
Still, I keep on trying with grim desperation,
Though the going's rather rough,
And thinking all the time how I shall enjoy the sensation
When I remember how to get off.

❖ ❖ ❖ ❖ ❖

From *Punch* magazine, Volume 215, August 20, 1947, p. 177.

Finance

It's funny,
But I can never understand about
Money.

Sterling
Sets my brain whirling.

I am completely downed
By the Pound.

As for the Dollar
It makes me all hot under the collar.

My mind is a complete blank
About what goes on in the Bank.

In fact, all I know about the stuff
Is that there is never enough.

❖ ❖ ❖ ❖ ❖

From *Punch* magazine, Volume 215, September 3, 1947, p. 231.

Les Champignons (Conversation Exercise)

Let us go now and seek mushrooms
For supper. Stewed with milk
They will provide a nourishing meal.
Shall we require our ration-books?
No. mushrooms are not yet rationed.
Where shall we find them?
In the meadow.
Shall we not require a bag or a basket?
Perhaps. Here is one.
Is that large enough?
Let us hope we shall fill it.
Look, there I think is a mushroom.
Do not hurry. It will not run away.
It is a white stone.
That is a pity.
Here at last is one.
It is rather small. It will not make a very large dish.
Never mind, It is a beginning.
Here is another.
Throw it away. It is a toadstool.
It is nevertheless very handsome.
Many people, I believe, eat toadstools.
Many people also die of eating them.

We will perhaps throw it away.
Here, however, is another mushroom.
It is somewhat worm-eaten. A mushroom
Which is worm-eaten is even more poisonous than a toadstool.
We will throw that one away also.
Let us go in.
Yes, it is growing late.
Have you the mushroom?
Yes, it is in the basket.
We did not require such a large basket. I do not see the mushroom.
It was there a minute ago.
It is not there now.
That is strange. I saw it when I put down the basket to climb the fence.
See, that chicken is eating something.
It is eating the mushroom.
That is a pity. We shall not now have mushrooms for supper.

❖ ❖ ❖ ❖ ❖

From *Punch* magazine, Volume 215, November 5, 1947, p. 453.

Second Fiddle

Old Jan Riddle
So I've heard tell,
He played the viddle
Uncommon well.

Master player
Was old Jan Riddle,
But all he played
Was second viddle.

And when folk said,
As folk they would,
Play first viddle
They thought Jan should,

He'd only smile
And say he reckoned
Somebody's got
To play the second,

And if he played
So well's he could,
Why, first or second
'Twas just as good.

And now old Jan
In chirchyard lays,

And his old viddle
Nobody plays.

But old Jan Riddle,
So I've heard tell,
He played that viddle
Uncommon well—

Master player
Was old Jan Riddle,
For all he played
But second viddle.

❖ ❖ ❖ ❖ ❖

From *Punch* magazine, Volume 216, May 10, 1948, p. 361.

Great Zimbabwe (Southern Rhodesia)

Who were the builders of Great Zimbabwe?
No man knows . . .
Who were those
That quarried, chiseled, hewed,
Laid stone on stone,
Till the high wall stood
And their task was done?
Who and when
No man knows
Only that many men
In a time long gone—
Hundreds of years, thousands of years,
It is all one—
Under the terrible, fierce
African sun,
Sweated and wrought in their day,
And went their way . . .
But to what end they fashioned
High wall, strong tower,
Altar and citadel,
By what urge impassioned,
Desire of gold or power,
No man can tell.

Who were the dwellers in Great Zimbabwe?
No man can say
What manner of folk were they,
Nor what dark dynasties
Of blood and fear
Held, as they should not cease,
Dominion here,

Before—how swiftly, how slowly
No man can say,
Famine, pestilence or the foe,
No man can know—
The doom swept them wholly
And for ever away,
Leaving to time and decay
And the years' slow silt,
The gods to whom they prayed
And the strong places they had built
And everything they had made . . .

Empty as a bleached skull
Of the loud life,
The voices and the trafficking and the strife
That fills it full . . .
Empty and alone,
Empty of life, empty of memory, empty of all—
Only the wild fig, self-sown,
Clings with knotted fingers to the wall,
And the bright lizards on the sun-baked stone
Flicker, gleam for a moment, flash and are gone . . .

❖ ❖ ❖ ❖ ❖

From *Punch* magazine, Volume 217, September 29, 1948, p. 299.

The poet visited these ruins in her trip around Africa in 1938.

The Old Cob Wall

Old cob wall
Have fell at last;
Us knowed he might
A good while past.

Great-grandad he
Built thickly wall
With maiden earth
And oaten strawl.

He built en in
The good old way,
And there he've stood
Until to-day.
But wind and rain
And frost and snow
Have all combined
To lay en low.

Us propped en up

With stones and 'ood,
Us done our best,
But t'weren't no good.

He gived a bit
And then a lot,
And at the finish
Down he squat.

And now, since barns
Has got to be,
Us'll build another
'Stead of he.

But not the same
He was afore,
'Cos no one builds
Cob walls no more.

❖ ❖ ❖ ❖ ❖

From *West Country Book*—No. 1, edited by J. C. Trewin, published by Westaway Books, London, UK, 1949.

A "Cob wall" is a wall made out of sand, clay, straw, and water that has been thoroughly mixed together. From the old English word cob meaning a ball of clay. The use of this word and the general use of dialect point to this having been written some time after Smith's return to England and taking up residence in South Western England. The language is definitely of that area.

My Lawn

My garden has a lawn—
Green and withdrawn,
Shaded by trees
Wherein the breeze
And—need I add?—the bees
Make soothing melodies . . .

And on a day
It may
Befall,
When I have pulled up all
The various kinds of weed
That seed,
Blithe and unbidden—
The groundsel, fat hen, chickweed, ragwort,
milk thistle, nettles (dead and otherwise)
and the rest—
And hurled them on the midden,
And dealt with every conceivable brand of
garden pest—
The ant, the leatherjacket, the palmer, the earwig
(which I am told is an excellent mother)

As well as the aphides which smother
The rose trees—
And, after coping with all these,
Tackled the wasps that generally get to the ripe pears first,
And shooed away the blackbird that regularly comes
And eats the plums
Till he is ready to burst . . .
When that day,
As I say,
Shall dawn,
I shall lay down the shovel and the hoe
(Like Poor Old Joe),
Not to mention the trowel and shears
And the secateurs,
And go
And fetch a garden-chair
On to the lawn
And there
I'll sit
On it . . .

❖ ❖ ❖ ❖ ❖

From *Punch* magazine, Volume 219, July 13, 1949, p. 52.

The Best Days

"Your old days 'll be your best days,"
The gypsy woman said,
A patched old soldier's coat she wore,
And a bright scarf round her head,
Her face was tanned like an old saddle,
Her lips were close and wise,
And the knowledge of the ancient East
Was in her sloe dark eyes.

"Oh, youth it is a pleasant time
When the blood's quick in the veins
But ah! its grief is cruel hard,
Its pains they're bitter pains;
Its sorrow clouds the brightest day,
Its tears put out the sun,
For there's no trouble like young trouble,
Since this old world began."

"But the years they bring forgetting,
The years they cure your woes,
For time it is a healing herb
As any herb that grows,
So, spend your youth, my lucky lad,
Go spend it how you will,
But your old days 'll be your best days,
When you have spent your fill."

❖ ❖ ❖ ❖ ❖

From Punch magazine, Volume 219, July 13, 1949, p. 52.

Islands

Islands

When the days of creation
Were all but done,
And earth lay drowsing
Under the sun—

Forest and desert
Aching and vast,
Rivers unforded,
Ranges unpassed—

Yet, ere the sunset
Faded to night,
The Lord wrought islands
For man's delight.

Flung them, a skein
On the sea's calm breast,
Set them, a ledge
For the sea-bird's nest;

Ringed them with coral,
Crowned them with palm,
Bade them be singing
Their endless psalm;

Wreathed them with mist-wrack,
Crested with cloud,
Fronting the sunsets,
Royally browed.

Virginal, nameless,
Lone in the sea,

Waiting the voyagers
Yet to be—

Tawny as lions,
Or fleeced like sheep,
Sleek as a whale's back
Cleaving the deep,

Sea-swept skerries
And sun-drenched cays . . .
The Lord wrought islands
For which be praise!

❖   ❖   ❖   ❖   ❖

From *Punch* magazine, Volume 219, August 3, 1949, p. 127.

The header graphic is an illustration drawn by Ernest Shepard to accompany this poem in the above magazine.

Mad about Music

I'm mad about music,
As mad as can be;
There's no one much madder
On music than me.

I'm nuts about Chopin,
I'm crackers on Strauss;
On Bach and Beethoven
I'm simply bughouse.

I'm crazy on Delius,
Holst and Scarlatti;
On Mozart and Verdi
I'm out-and-out batty.

I'm dotty on everything
Rubbra has written,
And I'm barmy, yes, barmy
On Benjamin Britten.

❖   ❖   ❖   ❖   ❖

From *Punch* magazine, Volume 219, August 10, 1949, p. 112.

The poet prefaced this poem with this quote: "I'm nuts on Chopin"—President Truman.

HMS *Implacable*

Deep Water

Sink her in deep water
Where her proud sisters lie,
Wrecked in storm or sunk in fight
In the times gone by;
Far from the tides' turmoil,
From the wind and sun,
Sink her in deep water,
Now her day is done.

All the brave memories
Of her eight-score years—
The thrill of the chase, the capture,
The boarders' cheer,
The riddled ensign flying
In the cannon's hot breath,
And the fierce grapeshot crying
Its thin song of death;

The decks once reddened
With the blood she saw flow
For the dreams of an emperor,
Dust long ago—

All she wrought for, all she fought for,
In her great days past—
Let the sea's salt oblivion
Take at last!

From *Punch* magazine, Volume 219, August 17, 1949, p. 180.

The poet prefaced this poem with these remarks:

"The Implacable, ex-*Duguay-Trouin*, last survivor of the French fleet which fought at Trafalgar, is to be sunk in deep water to save the cost of preservation." She was in fact towed out to sea and blown up.

The header graphic is a painting of the HMS *Implacable* being used as a training ship in Devonport, by Charles Dixon, 1900, from *Britannia's Bulwarks* published by George Newnes, London, UK, 1901.

Apples

The old apple-tree at the top of the orchard
Lies flat
On its back . . .
It's been like that
Since it came down smack
In a big blow
Four or five years ago.

It lies there
With half its roots in the air;
It's full of American blight, and canker, and weevils,
And all the rest of evils
That afflict apple-trees . . .
It's all elbows and knees,
Like an old man with the screws . . .
And yet, to be perfectly fair
To the old apple-tree that lies flat
At the top of the orchard with its roots in the air,
It does produce
Apples . . .

Nothing at all out of the way,
Just apples . . . Nobody's ever bothered to prune it, or lime it, or spray
It with DDT or XYZ or ABC . . .
In short, it's just an old apple-tree
Somebody's great-grandfather planted
Lord knows when—
Might be fourscore and ten,
Might be more years ago . . .
And wiseacres look at it and say
"You should do away
With that old thing,
It's no good
For anything but firewood . . ."
And you say "Yes, I suppose I should—
Perhaps next year" . . . And then
The spring comes again,
And it's still there
With its roots in the air,

And there's a blossom on the old thing,
And the birds come and sing
And build nests in it just where they built them before,

And you say "May as well let it go a year or more" . . .
So the old apple-tree at the top of the orchard
Goes on lying on its back doing just what it chooses
And produces
Apples . . .

❖   ❖   ❖   ❖   ❖

From *Punch* magazine, Volume 219, August 24, 1949, p. 213.

HMS *Foudroyant*

The Survivor

"So they couldn't save the old Frenchie at the finish,"
Bill said, "an' now she's gone—
Gone, an' left the little old *Foudroyant*
Keepin' her watch alone.

They been chummy ships in one port and another
A long while, them two,
An' I wouldn't wonder somehow if they miss each other,
Ginger, would you?

But there ain't a much better place after all than old Pompey
For an old ship to lay,
An' there ain't a much better job for an old ship or an old sailorman
Than learning the young uns the old sea way.

She can look across to the old *Victory* yonder
From her moorings where she rides,
She can feel the sun an' the rain, the wind an' the weather,
An' the tug o' the double tides.

She can see the Hard, an' the Point, an' the White Ensign flying,
An' the ships goin' by . . .
Well, good luck and long life to you, little *Foudroyant* . . ."
"Ay, an' so say I . . ."

❖   ❖   ❖   ❖   ❖

From *Punch* magazine, Volume 220, May 17, 1950, p. 556.

As the poet prefaced this poem:

"With the *Implacable* gone, the *Foudroyant* is the last frigate of the old sailing navy left in this country. She is used as a holiday training ship for boys and girls ..."

In 1987, the *Foudroyant* was taken by a huge seagoing barge to Hartlepool, where she was refloated, beautifully restored, renamed *Trincomalee* and is now preserved as a museum piece.

The header graphic is a photograph of the *Foudroyant* while still serving as a training ship for sea scouts, photographer unknown.

The Old Rectory

They are going to pull down the old rectory next year,
So I hear,
And put up an ugly little red
Brick one instead . . .

Which, of course, as you say,
Is the sensible thing to do,
Since who
Wants those great rambling places to-day . . .
That great drawing-room with the tall
Gracious windows that let in the sun and show all
The worn bits on the carpet and chairs . . .
The stairs
With the slender Queen Anne balustrades,
And the bedrooms—how many? Nine, I suppose,
Not counting nurseries—and the schoolroom whose paper still shows
Where the tinkling old Broadwood
Once stood
And was practiced on year after year by girls
In crinolines, ringlets and curls;
Then the kitchens, immense, beetle-haunted and bleak,
And the vast yawning range that would swallow
Your coal for a year in a week . . .
The stabling, too, built long ago by some parson
Or squarson
Whose delight was to follow
The hounds every day (except Sunday, of course,
When he preached two dull sermons perforce) . . .
And all on four hundred a year,
And *no* maids . . .

So the days will go by, and the lawn will be knee-deep in grass,
Where you scatter the seeds
Of the weeds
As you pass
On the borders once fragrant with flowers . . .
And the warm sunny hours
Bring no laughter, no flutter of muslins, no cries of
"Oh. Oh,
You pig—just look—he's sent me to Jericho!"

And the mallets are broken and rotten,
And the balls all lost and forgotten . . .

Ah well! . . . Yes, as you say,
No one wants these great places to-day . . .

❖   ❖   ❖   ❖   ❖

From *Punch* magazine, Volume 221, July 9, 1950, p. 87.

Man Polling Log

The First Ship

This is the ship the Man built . . .
In time's grey dawn, by the unsailed sea,
Hairy and lonely and wild stood he.
Deep in his darkling soul there woke
Something that stirred him, something that spoke
Of lands to find in the burning west;
And the vision grew, and troubled his rest
With strange new dreams of the waters wide . . .
Till he launched a Log on the sunset tide.
But the Log it rolled till it rolled him under

And the loud surf roared in his ears like thunder,
Battered and bruised him, whirled him round,
Smothered and choked him, all but drowned,
And tossed him up on the beach again . . .

He took the Log, and with care and pain
He hollowed it out with axe and fire
And shaped it at last to his heart's desire;

Called it his Woman, his Love, his Pride,
And launched it again on the sunset tide.

But all it did was to drift unsteered
Wherever the tides and the currents veered,
A night and a day till they flung it at last
High on the beach again, hard and fast . . .
So he took a branch and he made him an Oar.

He toiled all day till his hands were sore,
Then glanced and saw how over his head
The seabirds sailed with their wide wings spread,
And clapped his hands with a shout and a cry,
"I too, I too will have wings and fly,
I too will steer like a gull down gale!"
So he wove a mat and he made him a Sail.

Into the sunset he sailed away,
And what became of them none can say,
The Log and the Oar and the Hairy Man—
But that was the way the Ship began.
And all the ships there ever have been
Go back and back through the years between
To the Hairy Man on the lone seashore
That hollowed the Log, and shaped the Oar,
And spread the Sail on the unsailed sea
(First of the countless sails to be)
In the Ship—the Ship the Man built.

❖ ❖ ❖ ❖ ❖

From *Ship Models*, by Cicely Fox Smith, published by Conway Maritime Press in 1972. First published by *Country Life*, Limited, London, UK, 1951, pp. 17-18.

The header graphic is an illustration titled *Man Polling Log* from *Oars, Sail And Steam*, p. 12.

Ex-Voto Breton Church Model

Ex-Voto **Breton Church Model**

Once on a day a Paimpol man
Promised a ship to the good St. Anne . . .

Name of a name! How the great seas roared,
Tossing their manes as they crashed aboard!
So large the ocean, the ship so small,
There seemed no hope she could live at all;
So in his need did the Paimpol man
Promise a ship to the good St. Anne.

Ah, such a ship! No thing of botches
A man might make in a couple of watches,
But his own ship, see you, the staunch goelette,
Named for St. Yves, with all sail set,
Her hull to scale and her rigging to plan—
A credit to him and to good St. Anne.

And the gale went down and the peril was past,
And ship and seaman came home at last;
And when "Pardon" dawned in the spring of the year,
Barefoot, bareheaded, in fisherman's gear,
True to his word came the Paimpol man
Bringing a ship to the good St. Anne.

What was the end of him? Who shall tell
Whether his fishing fared ill or well?
Whether he sleeps among churchyard graves
Or far from home in the restless waves,
Fathoms deep where the cold seas roll
From Rockall Bank to the rim of the Pole?

And his ship—did she moulder at last away
On a peaceful beach in some Breton bay,
Where the fishermen's bairns would climb and hide
The long day through round her weed-hung side,
Or pound to chips in a flurry of foam
On St. Gildas Isle within hail of home?

But here is the ship that a Paimpol man
Vowed on a day to the good St. Anne.

❖   ❖   ❖   ❖   ❖

From *Ship Models* by Cicely Fox Smith, re-published by Conway Maritime Press in 1972. Earlier published by Country Life Limited, London, UK, 1951, pp. 25-26; first published in *Punch* magazine, Volume 183, November 16, 1932, p. 539

Many early sailors were both religious and superstitious and would not dream of setting out on a voyage without visiting their favorite shrine. In some of these shrines there were models of the ships they would sail. These models (those that still remain) are the clearest descriptions of the earliest boats. This poem was composed by the poet after a visit to such a sailor's church in San Telmo in Las Palmas.

The header graphic is a photograph from the above book, p. 97, and shows this early model ship, photographer unknown.

Royal Yacht *Mary*

Royal Yacht

Samuel Pepys, as all men know,
Loved ladies and ships in the long ago;
A rounded bosom, an ankle trim
Were toys that came not amiss to him;
And yet his soul took an equal joy
In frigate and first-rate, ketch and hoy—
*Sweepstakes, Orange-Tree, Garland, Hope,
Unicorn, Phoenix* and *Antelope.*

Samuel Pepys, on the Sabbath Day,
When St. Olave's chime called folk to pray
Forth from his house in Seething Lane
Churchward would pace with wig and cane,
Sober, sedate and dignified,
To his wonted seat by his lady's side.
And it well might be that once in a while,
When the preacher was dull and his matter was vile,
Good Master Samuel's thoughts would wander
From the parson's droning, now here, now yonder—
To last night's music and dance and laughter,
To kisses he stole (and repented after),
To the fine new suit that so much became him,
And its cost, wherefor his wife did blame him,

And the sound of voices singing together
On the sunlit Pool in the summer weather
That day they rowed from the Tower in wherries
To kiss ripe lips and eat ripe cherries.
And then it might chance his mind would turn
On public matters of grave concern,

Like the latest trouble afoot—Od rat 'em!—
With the master-shipwrights down at Chatham,
And the plaguey waste of carving and gilding
On Old Rowley's yacht, just then a-building . . .
Till the periwigged pate drooped more and more
And Samuel Pepys began to snore.

Samuel Pepys-God rest his bones!—
Sleeps soundly under St. Olave's stones;
Folly, finery, feasting and fun,
The good and the bad of him all are done.
But here's the model he may have pondered
In his oaken pew while his fancy wandered
Of the new yacht building at Chatham Yard,
Curved like a lady, slender-sparred,
With her garlanded ports and her gilded galleries,
And her figurehead with its carved fallaleries,
Her smirking Leves with their chubby paunches,
And Tritons blowing on fluted conches,
Just as they were in that vanished heyday
When Samuel Pepys loved ship and lady
Tall ship, fair lady, now long since passed
Where ships and ladies all wend at last.

❖ ❖ ❖ ❖ ❖

From *Ship Models*, by Cicely Fox Smith, published by Conway Maritime Press, 1972, p. 39. Earlier published by Country Life Limited, London, UK, 1951. First published in *Punch* magazine, Volume 183, October 5, 1932, p. 378.

Charles II was called "Old Rowley" by his subjects; the model would have been one of his royal yachts. Samuel Pepys, the noted diarist, was an English naval administrator. As Clerk of the Acts to the Navy Board, Seething Lane was his official lodgings. The entrance to St. Olave's Church is in Seething Lane and it is there that Pepys was buried.

The header graphic is a photograph of a full hull model of the Royal Yacht *Mary*, circa 1660, from the collection of the National Maritime Museum at Greenwich, UK, photographer unknown.

The phrase "od rat 'em" is actually a deliberate typo by *Punch* and others and should be read "Oh drat them" a mild expletive now (and then) but frowned on in print. Possible derivation of Drat, Darn, or Damn.

The Fighting *Téméraire*

The Fighting *Téméraire*—Bone "Prisoner" Model

No tusk from trackless jungle brought,
No bone of slaughtered whale
Her wreathed and Tritoned sternports wrought
And bulwarks eggshell frail.
No warm dog-watch her building whiled
Away in tropic seas,

For no shore-anchored salt beguiled
His unaccustomed ease.
Mellow as ancient ivory
And fine as carven jade,
From beef-bones of captivity
The shapely hull was made,
Whose making helped upon their way
Such limping hours and slow
As measure out the leaden day
That none but prisoners know.
Old wars, old woes, old wasted years,
Old causes lost and won,
Old bitterness of captives' tears
As dreams-as dreams are done.
As dreams the stubborn hulls, the pride
Of masts that raked the sky,

Sea-shattering bows and oaken side
Of fighting fleets gone by.
Yet still, though thrones and systems shake
And pass and are no more,
The spars a casual touch might break
Unharmed by Time endure.

Still, though the world in change be whelmed,
From these small mimic bows
The antique warrior, mailed and helmed,
Looks out with frowning brows,
Like those beneath whose sightless stare
The sullen smoke-drift rolled
Round her, well-named the *Téméraire,*
In famous fights of old.
What of her builder? Did he sail
Home to his France at last,
To tell in happier times the tale
Of wars and prisons past?
Or is, upon some gravestone hoar,
The legend plain to see:
"He was a Prisoner of War,
But Death has set him free"?

❖ ❖ ❖ ❖ ❖

From *Ship Models*, by Cicely Fox Smith, published by Conway Maritime Press, 1972, pp. 49-50. Earlier published by Country Life Limited, London, UK, 1951, pp. 49-50. First published in *Punch* magazine, Volume 184, April 26, 1933, p. 462.

The *Téméraire* was second to the *Victory* in line of battle at Trafalgar and tried to shield Nelson's flagship by sailing in front only to be called back unceremoniously by Nelson himself.

Many prisoners-of-war seamen in those days would while away their time carving models of ships. In this case out of cattle bones.

The epitaph quoted in the final lines is to be read upon a stone in the churchyard at Odiham, Hampshire, England.

The header graphic is a photograph of this ship model as it appeared in *Ship Models*, p. 104, photographer unknown.

Sailor's Picture Model—Unnamed

Yonder she sails on her paper sea—
Masts just a trifle too tall, maybe—
Chain-plates and whiskers, all, in short,
That proves her one of the grand old sort—
Frame that must surely have graced some day
The *Christian Martyr* or *Stag at Bay*
The little model (none knows her name,
Whose flag she flew, from what yard she came)
Some shellback fashioned with calloused, twisted
Fingers that many a sail had fisted,
Giving to make her such scanty ease
As sailors snatched from the winds and seas
In long bright hours when the hooker snored
Down the sunlit Trade with her tacks aboard.

Was she wet or hungry, speedy or slow,
Whose likeness this was in the long ago?

Was she tight or leaky, happy or hard,
Lucky, I wonder, or evil-starred?

What other cargoes, captains, crews?
What trade did she sail in, what harbours use?
Did time or fire or the chance of weather
Make an end of story and ship together?

What of her maker? Did his bones
Find rest at the last with Davy Jones?
Or did he live till he came to be
A broken seaman, done with the sea,
Who sometimes, gazing with rheumy eyes
On the model he made under Tropic skies,

Saw ships long vanished and shipmates dead,
All that was life in the long years sped,
The grace, the glory, the pride again
God lends for a little to ships and men?

It may be. We know not. This alone,
This and no more of them both is known—
That someone once, in a ship forgotten,
Whose name is lost and whose bones are rotten,

Saw, knew and laboured with halting skill
(Yet, since he loved her, not wholly ill)
To hold a moment the fleeting dream,
The flying beauty, the foam-bow gleam,
Sculptor and painter, craftsman, sage,
Follow and find not, age by age . . .

Tall and lovely beyond all telling,
Her dimpled sails in the sunlight swelling,
Her bow-wave piling like drifted snow . . .
Some shellback fashioned her, long ago.

❖ ❖ ❖ ❖ ❖

From *Ship Models*, by Cicely Fox Smith, published by Conway Maritime Press, 1972, p. 65. Originally published by Country Life Limited, London, UK, 1951.

The title is that of the Chapter it opens in *Ship Models*.

Coasting Brigantine—Unnamed

I rather think they built her in some good old-fashioned yard
That smelt of pitch and sawdust and of hemp rope newly tarred,
Where they changed their ways but little as the centuries rolled along,
And they built a trifle slowly, but they built uncommon strong.

I think her little model used to grace some homely shelf,
Where a brace of pop-eyed poodles flanked the gaily-painted delf,
And the harbour's pleasant bustle through the open window came
With the mewing of the seagulls and the scent of gorse in flame.

I think her name was *Good Intent*, or *Peggy, New Revived*,
Or *John and Sarah's Venture*—well, I trust, their venture thrived—
Or *Gipsy Bride* or *Farmer's Lass*, or something sweet and dainty
To match her little figurehead that looks so prim and painty.

I think she never loaded things like gold mohurs and spice
And China tea and narwhals' teeth and monkey-nuts and rice,
And ivory, apes and peacocks out of Africa that come,
And Eastern frails and cotton bales and right Jamaica rum.

But she got her honest living out of homelier kinds of freights,
Such as salt and malt and china clay and blue Bethesda slates,
With perhaps a voyage foreign once in every good long while
For a fragrant load of oranges from far St. Michael's Isle.

I think she knew no distant lands, all sun and glare and smells,
And illy-ollying coolie gangs and chiming temple bells;
No lumber, grain or nitrate ports from Yukon to Peru,
No lone palm-girdled atolls in the false Pacific blue.

But the saltings and the maltings round from Lymington to Lynn,
And a hundred creeks and harbours from the Solent to the Swin,
From Eddystone to Lizard Head and round the Land to Wales
Knew her dipping in from seaward with the sunlight on her sails.

I think her little figurehead, all weathered, worn and bare,
With its valiant faded simper and its sad forsaken stare,
Gazes out across the water where the long tides break in snow
On the cruel hidden ledges where a ship sank long ago.

And the sand has choked the slipways where they built stout ships of old,
And the painted delf is broken and the pop-eyed dogs are sold;
And the little model—Lord knows how she found at last her way
To the dingy Thames-side junk-shop where I bought her yesterday.

❖ ❖ ❖ ❖ ❖

From *Ship Models*, by Cicely Fox Smith, published by Conway Maritime Press, London, UK, 1972, p. 77, from an original Country Life publication of 1951. The title is that of the Chapter it opens. First published in *Punch* magazine, Volume 184, February 1, 1933, p. 120.

This model was part of the poet's personal collection.

The "mohur" was an Indian coin, some of which were made of gold and were of considerable size and value.

A Ship in a Bottle

A Ship in a Bottle

In a sailormen's restaurant Rotherhithe way,
Where the din of the docksides is loud all the day,
And the breezes come bringing off basin and pond
And all the piled acres of lumber beyond,
From the Oregon ranges the tang of the pine
And the breath of the Baltic as bracing as wine …
Among the stale odours of hot food and cold,
In a fly-spotted window I there did behold
A ship in a bottle some sailor had made
In watches below, swinging South with the Trade,
When the fellows were patching old dungaree suits,
Or mending up oilskins and leaky sea-boots,
Or whittling a model, or painting a chest,
Or smoking and yarning and watching the rest.

In fancy I saw him—all weathered and browned,
Deep crows'-feet and wrinkles his eyelids around,
A pipe in the teeth that seemed little the worse
For Liverpool pantiles and stringy salt horse …
The hairy forearm with its gaudy tattoo
Of a bold-looking female in scarlet and blue …
The fingers all roughened and toughened and scarred,
With hauling and hoisting so calloused and hard,
So crooked and stiff you would wonder that still
They could handle with cunning and fashion with skill
The tiny full-rigger predestined to ride
To its cable of thread on its green-painted tide,
In its wine-bottle world while the old world went on,
And the sailor who made it was long ago gone.

And still as he worked at the toy on his knee
He would spin his old yarns of the ships and the sea,

Thermopylae, Lightning, Lothair and *Red Jacket*,
And many another such famous old packet—
And many a tough bucko and daredevil skipper
In Liverpool blood-boat and Colonies clipper—
The sail that they carried aboard the *Black Ball*,
Their skysails and stunsails and ringtail and all,
And storms that they weathered, and races they won,
And records they broke in the days that are done.

Or else he would sing you some droning old song,
Some old sailor's ditty both mournful and long,
With queer little curleycues, twiddles and quavers,
Of smugglers and privateers, pirates and slavers,
"The Brave Female Smuggler," the "packet of fame
That sails from New York, an' the *Dreadnought's* her name."
And "All on the coast of the High Barbaree,"
And "The flash girls of London were the downfall of he."

In fancy I listened, in fancy could hear
The thrum of the shrouds and the creak of the gear,
The patter of reef-points on tops'ls a-shiver—
The song of the jibs when they tauten and quiver—
The cry of the frigate-bird following after—
The bow-wave that broke with a gurgle like laughter—
And I looked on my youth with its pleasure and pain,
And the shipmate I loved was beside me again ...
In a ship in a bottle a-sailing away
In the flying-fish weather through rainbows of spray,
Over oceans of wonder by headlands of gleam
To the harbours of youth on the wind of a dream!

❖ ❖ ❖ ❖ ❖

From *Ship Models*, by Cicely Fox Smith, published by Conway Maritime Press in 1972, p. 87, from an earlier edition published by *Country Life*, London, UK, 1951. It earlier appeared in *Rovings*, edited by Cicely Fox Smith, published by Elkin Mathews, London, 1921, pp. 19-21. First published in *Punch* magazine, Volume 159, September 22, 1920, p. 230.

The lines:

> "And I looked on my youth with its pleasure and pain,
> And the shipmate I loved was beside me again"

are of particular interest, reinforcing evidence that the poet had been in love with a sailor she had met while in Victoria, British Columbia.

First adapted for singing by Charles Ipcar as recorded on *Old Sailor-Poets*, 2007.

The header graphic is a photograph of a ship in a bottle model at the China Sea Marine Trading Company in Portland, Maine, as photographed by Charles Ipcar in 2007.

Old Boatbuilding Yard

They Built Ships

Nigh the mouldering staithe
Where the lads came to bathe,
And the tidal river as it passes
Licks with salty lips
The wiry grasses
Where the cattle graze,
There, in the old days,
They built ships . . .

Staunch little ships they built here,
Craft with coastwise rigs,
Schooners, ketches, brigs,
That sailed many a year
With their homely freights—
Cornish clay, granite, Bethesda slates—
To and fro between Fowey and Falmouth, Runcorn and Wales,
Dipping both rails under in the Channel gales,
Beating up to wind'ard with the sunlight on their sails . . .

There were bustle and noise then,
Voices of boys and men,
And the clean shipyard smells
Of sawdust, paint and tar;
You could hear from far

Late and soon
The anvil's clang,
And the caulkers' mallets as they rang
All in time and tune,
Like a peal of bells . . .

But now it's ended and done;
Thirty years a gone
The last ship left the ways,

With her bunting flying,
And the gulls crying
All around her, and the folks cheering from the riverside
To see her take her tide . . .
And by the rotting staithe,
Where the lads came to bathe,
No stir of life is seen
And over the old slips
Where they used to build ships
The grass grows green . . .

❖   ❖   ❖   ❖   ❖

From *Punch* magazine, Volume 222, January 21, 1951, p. 127.

The header graphic drawn by cartoonist Ernest Shepard accompanied this poem in Punch.

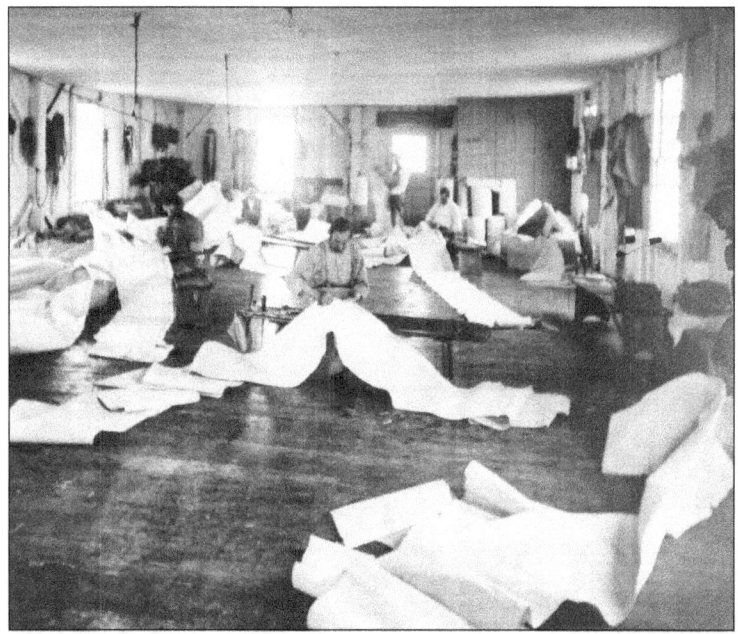

They Made Sails

They Made Sails

In the old raftered loft
Where the winds blow
Like thin querulous voices
Out of long ago,
And the cobwebs sway
To and fro, to and fro,
Like the fine top-hamper
Etching out the sky
Of a tall square-rigger
In a time gone by . . . .

In the old raftered loft
They made sails . . . .

Moonsails, skysails
(To deck a new-built clipper),
Stunsails, trysails
(To suit a racing skipper),
Mainsails, to'gans'ls,
Great sails and small,
In the old raftered loft
They made them all . . . .

Yonder where the sun strikes
On the rutted floor,
Old Sails used to sit
Forty years or more,
Like an old bald Buddha,
Squatting on his throne,
Where the girls come with garlands
And the yellow monks intone.
There he'd sit and yarn
Hour by hour
About the Blackwall frigate
Owen Glendower,
Where he learned his trade
A dog watch ago,
Striding down the Tropic
With her tacks boarded
And a wake like snow . . . .

In the old raftered loft
He made sails . . . .

They drooped in the Doldrums
Dark with tropic dew;
They stooped in the Forties
When the West winds blew;
They flushed like Alps at sunrise
In the dawn's first glow;
They took the last daylight,
Tall towers of snow . . . .
When it was "Watch, aloft and furl it"
In the black Horn night;
And "Shake another reef out"
At the first gleam of light;
Give her all she'll carry
Through the Trade Wind foam,
By the great Lord Harry
Crack it on for home . . . .

Outer jibs, flying jibs
(Killers of men),
Ringtail and Jamie Green
(They will not come again).
Stunsails, skysails
(To dress a flying clipper),
Every sort of handkercher
To suit a racing skipper . . . .
Big sails and little sails
For ships great and small,
In the old raftered loft
They made them all . . . .

❖ ❖ ❖ ❖ ❖

From *Punch* magazine, Volume 222, February 21, 1951, pp. 240-241.

There are not many contemporary sailors who could name all these sails, or would know their function.

The header graphic is a photograph of the Washburn Sail Loft in Rockland, Maine, 1892, photographer unknown.

Sailortown

Streets

Many streets have the cities
Near and far,
Underneath the tropic sun
And Northern star . . .
Wide streets and narrow streets,
Grim streets and gay,

Boulevards with bright trees
Both sides the way,
Some full of pushing crowds
And busy as a fair,
Some paved with broken dreams
And drab with despair.
Many streets have the cities,
But the best streets for me
Are the long streets of Sailortown
Going down to the sea.
There are the cheap dives

Full of flyblown grub,
And the slop shops and the pop shops
And the corner pub.
The cliff-sided warehouses
And the high dock walls,
And the mean secret alleys
Where no sun falls,
The stale smells of harbour mud
And bilge and beer,
And the shops with their foreign names
Exotic and queer,
The wailing of the sirens,
The tide lapping the hulls,
The grinding of the derricks,
And the mewing of the gulls.
The wide sky and the free wind
And the masts and flags of ships
And the old spell of the waterside
And the salt on the lips . . .

Many streets have the cities
Where men go to and fro,
Seeking each the things he wants
High and low . . .
Gold, painted women.
Pleasure and power,
And fame like a bright bloom
That dies in an hour . . .
Many streets have the cities,
But of all the streets there be
The long streets of Sailortown
Are the best streets for me,
Where shipmate meets shipmate
Coming in from the sea . . .

❖   ❖   ❖   ❖   ❖

From *Punch* magazine, Volume 223, September 5, 1951, pp. 266-267.

A last tribute by the poet to the streets of Sailortown.

The header graphic drawn by cartoonist Ernest Shepard appeared with this poem in *Punch*.

Dover Street

Do you recall those times gone by—
How long ago?—when you and I
Trod, day by day, with eager feet
The well known stones of Dover Street?

How far they seem, those vanished years,
The hopes, ambitions, joys and fears,
The secret dreams, so strange and sweet,
We dreamed in humdrum Dover Street.

Yet some things change not—still, be sure,
The same while earth and time endure,
Shall youth salute the morning skies
With fresh and forward-looking eyes,
And take life's road with eager feet—
As we did—once—in Dover Street.

The Manchester High School for Girls

❖   ❖   ❖   ❖   ❖

From *The Magazine of the Manchester High School*, Souvenir Issue, Manchester, UK, 1952, p. 8.

This Souvenir Issue commemorated the opening of the new buildings at Grangethorpe. The poet dedicated this poem "To an old school friend." Smith wrote several articles for her old school magazine.

The header graphic depicts *The Manchester High School for Girls* on Dover Street which the poet attended from 1894 to 1897, artist unknown, from the above magazine.

Old Tom Hubbard

Old Tom Hubbard
To Trentisbeare,
He brewed cider
For many a year.

He brewed cider
In his old pound
You couldn't match
The country round.

Queer old sample
Was old Tom Hubbard,
So red and hard's
A Winter Stubbard,

But master cider
And no mistake,
Old Tom Hubbard
Did used to make.

And in summer time
When a chap was workin'!

Adolph Ipcar pressing cidar, 1953.

He'd ask nought better
To fill his firkin.

When cider-making
Time come round,
He'd carry his apples
Home to pound.

And in 'd come
Tom's old grey mare,
What done the job
For fifteen year.

And round and round
'Ud go old Bess,
Till all the apples
Was ready for press.

Old mare's dead,
But the track she wore
Be plain to see
On the pound-house floor.

Old Tom's dead,
And now the spider
Spins his webs
Where he made his cider;

And all folks get
To wet their throttles
Is gassy old trade
In fancy bottles.

For cider now,
Seem so to me,
Ain't what cider
Did used to be.

And the finest cider
I ever did take
Old Tom Hubbard
He used to make.

❖ ❖ ❖ ❖ ❖

From The West Country Magazine, Spring, 1952, p.34.

"Stubbard" is a variety of cider apple. "Firkin" is a measure of ale/cider equal to 9 imperial gallons.

The header graphic is a photo of Adolph Ipcar pressing cider in the front barnyard, Robinhood Farm, Georgetown, Maine, 1953, photographer unknown.

The Queen's Ships

The Queen's Ships

Queens' ships—Queens' ships…
Gloriana's mariners,
    Putting forth to sea
Afire to beard the Spaniard
    Wherever he may be…

Hanging on the Plate fleets' flanks
    Like hounds upon the deer,
Roving, raiding, voyaging
    Year on weary year. . .

Leaking, reeking, nail-sick,
    Rolling home again
With their scurvy-rotten seamen
    And the plunder of the Main.

Queens' ships, Queens' ships…
Stately first rates
    Of Good Queen Anne's day,
Plunging deep their gilded bows
    In the trampled spray—

With their fighting ship's companies
    That well the Frenchmen knew
And their brave bewigged admirals
    Of the white, red and blues—

Rooke that gained Gibraltar,
    And gallant Leake also,
Myngs and stout old Shovell
    And honest Benbow. . .

Queens' ships—Queens' ships. . .
Little ships and great ships,
    The seven seas over,
Keeping up the long patrol
    From Davis Straits to Dover.

(Franklin in the Arctic,
    Gunboats at Rangoon—
Calliope at Apia
    Fighting the Typhoon)—

Cruising, sounding, searching,
    Keeping clear the seas,
Through the little wars of Britain
    And the piping times of peace. . .

Queens' ships—Queens' ships. . .
Great ships, small ships,
    From the wide seas beckoned,
Gather to salute
    Elizabeth the Second. . .

Ships pass, men pass,
    The old ways grow strange,
All but the old faith
    That knows not any change—

The old love that alters not
    Through all the years between
Valiant Tudor cockleshell
    And sleek grey submarine. . .
Love and faith to England
    And to England's Queen!

❖ ❖ ❖ ❖ ❖

From *Punch* magazine, Volume 226, June 17, 1953, p. 715.

This is the last poem published in *Punch* by this poet, and commemorated the coronation of England's Queen Elizabeth II.

The header graphic is an illustration of how this last poem was published in *Punch*, as drawn by Ernest Shepard.

BOOK 4

UNPUBLISHED POEMS

View of the first incarnation of the Imperial War Museum, Crystal Palace,
London, England, early 1920s, from Imperial War Museum.

INTRODUCTION

With the exception of one poem, which was found at the National Maritime Museum in Greenwich, UK, all of the unpublished poems in Book 4, were found in five hand-written folders. Four of which were donated to the Imperial War Museum by Margaret Smith after her sister's death in 1954, and one, which was sent to a family friend, was later acquired by Danny McLeod from a bookseller in Sydney, Australia. These folders include both published and unpublished poems by Cicely Fox Smith. One might assume that the unpublished poems included here were never published because the poet decided they did not merit publication. Regrettably she made no such statement. Clearly some of these poems are in fact alternative forms of poems that were published, as noted. Of course there is the possibility that some poems may have been published in magazines, which we have yet to locate and review. We are making them available now to complete the inventory of the poems Smith composed, so that readers may better judge her evolution as a poet.

All the Way Home

As by Shadwell Basin I chanced for to be,
I met there a sailorman in from the sea,
I met there a shellback, a shellback I know
In a shirt that was borrowed and trousers also.

Oh boys, ay boys, all the way home!

"Oh where is your kit now and where is your chest?"
"They're somewheres down Channel along wi' the rest;
They're somewheres down Channel deep under the foam
With a cargo of grain as'll never reach 'ome."

Oh boys, ay boys, all the way home!

"I sailed in a steamer from Portland in Maine,
And she was chock-full to the coamings wi' grain;
She was loaded that deep we was glad it was fine,
And we got our fair rations o' tin-fish and mine."

Oh boys, ay boys, all the way home!

"We slipped into port an' we lifted a cheer,—
But all as they said was 'You're not wanted 'ere;
We 'aven't no berths nor we 'aven't no men;
So you set about gettin' your mud'ook again."

Oh boys, ay boys, all the way home!

"So we got up our anchor; we couldn't do more,
For it's no use to talk to them fat-'eads ashore,
An' when darkness was fallin' an' Dungeness past,
Just off the South Foreland they sunk us at last."

Oh boys, ay boys, all the way home!

❖ ❖ ❖ ❖ ❖

Unpublished poem transcribed from a Cicely Fox Smith hand-written manuscript, courtesy of Danny and Joyce McLeod, who believe it was probably never meant to be published as drafted.

Après La Guerre

There's an office back in London, and the dusty sunlight falls
With its swarms of dancing motes across the floor,
On the piles of books and papers and the drab distempered walls,
And the bowlers on their pegs behind the door.
There's a row of clerks a-sitting at their desks there day by day,
While the muffled roar of London thunders by;
With their eyes upon their ledgers they are growing bald and grey,
And if something hadn't happened—so would I!

But après la guerre—après la guerre—
They'll have to find another chap to hang his hat up there;
They'll have to get some other lad to climb that office stair,
For I'm going to ramble round a bit—après la guerre!

There's an office-stool in London where a fellow used to sit
(But the chap that used to sit there's oversea!)
There's a job they're keeping open till that fellow's done his bit
(And the chap that job is waiting for is—Me!)

There's a spotty fly-blown window and a dusty dim wire blind,
There's a view of dingy bricks and smoky sky;
But I've cut the whole connection and I've left the lot behind,
And I'm never going back there—no, not I!

For après la guerre—après la guerre—
They'll have to get some other chap to fill that vacant chair,
For there's something waked up in me that I never knew was there
And I'm going to let it rip a bit —après la guerre!

There's a chap in the Canadians, a clinking good chap too,
And he hails from back o' nowhere in B. C.,
And he says it's sure some country, and I wonder if it's true,
And I rather think I'm going—just to see!
Just to see the mountain gorges where the glacier meets the pine,
And the hosts of heaven go marching star by star,
Over leagues of silent ranges where the lone lakes gloom and shine,
Out beyond the survey—up in Cassiar!

And après la guerre—après la guerre—
There's a trail I mean to follow and a camp I mean to share,
Through the passes to the Westward, by the Smoky and the Bear,
Oh, it's there you'll have to look for me—après la guerre!

For it may be black ingratitude, but oh, good Lord, I know
I could never stick the office life again,
With the coats and cuffs and collars, and the long hours crawling slow,
And the quick lunch, and the same old morning train;
I have looked on Life and Death, and seen the naked soul of man,
And the heart of things is other than it seemed,
And the world is somehow larger than the good old office plan,
And the ways of earth are wider than I dreamed.

And après la guerre—après la guerre—
Though a thousand jobs await me, by my living soul I swear,
If the God of Battles spares me I'll be anywhere but there
When the boys go marching home again—après la guerre!

❖ ❖ ❖ ❖ ❖

Unpublished poem transcribed from a Cicely Fox Smith hand-written manuscript, courtesy of Danny and Joyce McLeod, who believe it was probably never meant to be published as drafted.

This is even a longer version of the published poem "The Call-2."

The Auxiliary

I saw her last a year ago, or maybe it was more
Discharging general cargo by some far Pacific shore
There was whiskey, steel and paving stones, and sewer pipes and string—
But now she's in the Navy List, a-serving of the King!

Yes, now she's in the Navy List, which used to tramp around
A hundred ports both large and small from here to Puget Sound
She's carried, wheels, nuts and nails and every kind of thing
And now she's in the Navy List, a-serving of the King!

The next I saw in summertime sail o'er the Irish Sea,
With all her passengers aboard so full of mirth and glee
(Six hundred seasick trippers bound from Liverpool to Isle of Man!)
But now she's in the Navy List and doing what she can!

Yes, now she's in the Navy List, she's HMS *Seaspray*
She's left her passengers behind, she's painted warlike grey
No more about her crowded decks you hear the trippers sing
For now she's in the Navy List, a-serving of the King!

The next I saw she casts her nets and takes full many a weighty haul
But never market sees the catch that comes into her trawl
A black and bitter catch she draws from waters cold and grey
For now she's in the Navy List—she trawls for death today!

Yes now she's in the Navy List, you'll find her name beside
The Dreadnoughts and the Cruisers there, which are old England's pride
A smelly North Sea trawler once, plain, common everyday
But now she's in the Navy List—and Lord she earns her pay!

❖   ❖   ❖   ❖   ❖

Transcribed at the Imperial War Museum from *The China Sea and Other Poems*, a hand-written manuscript by Cicely Fox Smith.

The Bare Boughed Forest

Hay the Bare-boughed forest beside the sounding sea!
Where neither woodland fathers nor untried saplings be—
Which strong against the storm-wind stands up, a host of spars
Which strikes no roots down, deeply through mounded mould of years.

No thrush in this storm forest comes home to nest and sing
No dove makes gentle wooing with each returning spring
For these, God's roving singers make wilder melody—
The cry of gull and petrel, the song of winds at sea.

No sun casts golden bounty on green moss banks below
High driven by April breezes no blossoms lie like snow

From springtime unto springtime the white foam flying free
From sunrise unto sunset the green fields of the sea.

❖   ❖   ❖   ❖   ❖

Transcribed at the Imperial War Museum from *Steel Rails and Other Poems*, a hand-written manuscript by Cicely Fox Smith.

Bitter Sweet

All in a dream I saw God's cupbearer
That stands forever by the judgement seat
Bearing the cup where of must all men share
Which God's hand filleth with the Wine of Life
The Wine of laughter and love and tears and strife
Bitter and sweet.

The cup wherein the angel Azrael
Hath steeped his sword: full of the salt of tears
Earth's age long travail since the morn-star fell
Passion and sin, and pain of Calvary—
Cold as the grave and bitter as the sea
Sad as lost years.

O let me drain the cup even to the last
Lest shrinking from the gall, I shall not gain
Honey of heaven—ah me, when all is past
Shall I not, with my cold lips at the brim
See in the bitter dregs God's pure pearl swim
And death himself be slain?

❖   ❖   ❖   ❖   ❖

Transcribed at the Imperial War Museum from *Retrude's Child: a Christmas Legend and Other Poems*, a hand-written manuscript by Cicely Fox Smith.

"Azrael" is the Archangel of Death in some extrabiblical traditions. He is also the angel of death in Islamic theology and Sikhism. It is an English form of the Arabic name Azra'eil the name traditionally attributed to the angel of death in some sects of Islam and Sikhism, as well as some Hebrew lore.

The Chanteyman

I heard a wind at sunset come calling from the sea;
It was like a friend's voice singing a song well known to me
To a tune the creaking blocks make with the whistling ropes a-straining,
(Chanteyman, chanteyman, sing a song again!)

Gustily, lustily down the drift of time,
Many a crashing chorus came, many a rough old rhyme;
Sun and shadow, fun and folly, dreams forgotten long,
From the full tide blowing like a far faint song.

I heard the yard mast-headed with "Rolling Rio Grande,"
Beating up against the Westerlies with every rag she'd stand;

I heard the great Horn greybeards go plunging on their way,
And the big Northers sweeping down Valparaiso Bay.

I heard it all like echoes from other days than these,
The tramping cursing watches, the pouring pooping seas;
The shrill wind past us shrieking, the cracking volleying sail,
And the tatters of our voices flying down the roaring gale.

I heard the pumps clanking all a bitter night and day
When, rolling rails under, like a half tide rock she lay,
And the old man swore, if sing we must, we'd sing some other song
For we drove him stamping crazy with the tune of "Stormalong."

Chanteyman, chanteyman, gone are ships and men;
Gone as went the days and years we spent so careless then;
If you sail the high seas over from shore to farthest shore
You may meet with ships a-plenty, but her like you'll find no more.

For she's gone with all aboard her and gone the lads we knew;
Yes, she's gone beyond our knowing, as ships and sailors do;
And nothing but a dream left of days we used to know,
(Chanteyman, chanteyman, was it long ago?)

And sometimes we went hungry, and mostly we went poor,
But the lives we've lived already are those we'd live once more;
Fair weather and foul weather, the shine with the rain,
(Chanteyman, chanteyman, just the same again!)

❖　❖　❖　❖　❖

Transcribed at the Imperial War Museum from *The China Sea and Other Poems*, a hand-written manuscript by Cicely Fox Smith.

First adapted for singing by Charles Ipcar and recorded on Never Turn a Blind Eye to the Storm, 2015, as recorded on *Never Turn a Blind Eye to the Storm*.

Gathergold

All under the wintry sky
Gathergold goes wearily.

His gnarled hands are nipt and blue:
His tattered coat the winds blow through.

Always he scans with rheumy eyes
The spilth o' gold in glittering skies.

He looked up from the miser's hoard
Whereon year long his eyes had pored.

He did not see the shipman's star
Swing high his lamp for ships afar.

Nor that great Hunter and his Hounds
Stride glimmering o'er the heaven's voids bounds.

But "So!" he said, "what wondrous mint
Pours forth these coins that gleam and glint

As all the wealth of all the world
In one vast shower were broadcast hurled?"

Still he walks, and still he weeps
Through the world when the world sleeps

He gets no rest, he seeks no slumber,
For the gold he cannot number,

And yet must count the whole night long
All for his ancient wrong.

Shivering through the bitter night,
And cannot get the tale aright.

Still he walks, still he wails
When in the dawn the gold gleam pales,

And cock crows, and night is run
And the stars are molten by the sun,
Or ever half his task is done.

❖ ❖ ❖ ❖ ❖

Transcribed at the Imperial War Museum from *The China Sea and Other Poems,* a hand-written manuscript by Cicely Fox Smith.

"Spilth" is something spilled or the act of spilling.

The Grand Banks of Newfoundland

Sunday is a pleasant time when all the bells do ring
And lovers in the lanes do walk to hear the sweet birds sing;
Small heart have I for the Sabbeth bells, or the blackbird's courting tune;
The Grand Banks o' Newfoundland they call me night and noon.

And oh! Ring loud, you pealing bells, you cannot ring so clear
But still the sound is never drowned which night and noon I hear—
But still the voice of ship bells comes across the world to me,
From the Grand Banks o' Newfoundland, about the fog bound sea.

Sailor lads from near and far upon the banks are found,
And schooners out of Gloucester town which use the deep sea ground;
And long as shines the cold North Star or the cold tides do roll,
The Grand Banks o' Newfoundland of these shall take their toll.

They take their toll by mist and storm, by the blind unhearing floe,
A hidden sea, a hidden shore, a doom that none may know;
A silent and a fog bound tide and a barren land thereby,
And the Grand Banks o' Newfoundland they call me till I die.

❖ ❖ ❖ ❖ ❖

Transcribed at the Imperial War Museum from *The China Sea and Other Poems*, a hand-written manuscript by Cicely Fox Smith.

The Greatest of These

Over the bleak moorland
The snow lieth white:
Masters will ye let me in
To the warm firelight?
Ye bar your door against me
Out on the bare wold
Christ Jesu pity you
When ye are old!

Will ye fill me a cool beaker?
Will ye break me a crust?
Will ye give me shade in your garden?
I have trudged long in the dust
Ye drove me on footsore
Ye scorned me and cursed:
Christ Jesu pity you
When ye are a-thirst.

Gentles, will ye greet me?
Will ye not behold
My soul that goes thirsting
And my heart that is a-cold?
Ye turned not from your feasting:
Ye heard not my moan:
Christ Jesu pity you
In the dark alone!

❖ ❖ ❖ ❖ ❖

Transcribed at the Imperial War Museum from *Retrude's Child: a Christmas Legend and Other Poems*, a hand-written manuscript by Cicely Fox Smith.

"Gentles" are considerate or kindly in disposition/of good family, wellborn.

Hell's Market

Where so are builded cities, where so Earth's Kingdom's be
In the reek of the wine and the perfume, the lamps and the revelry
Go in their gauds and glories the sons and daughters of vice
Up and down in Hell's Market buying souls for a price.

To uses of all uncleaness, lust and lying and greed
At the world's price they will buy them for the world's daily need
Neither stinting no haggling, neither with stroke of pen
After the world's old fashion they buy the souls of men.

When the price you got, O my brothers, has brought you hunger and drouth—
Is turned dry leaves in your coffers, and a bitterness in your mouth
Shaking by your cold hearthstone, hungry by your bare board
Will you not rue the bargain and hold the wage abhorred.

In your naked halls ye shall curse them—the mad wild pleasures that pass
Ye shall wring your hands to a steely sky and wail to a heaven like brass
Not lightly shall ye buy back now, what was so light to sell
Ye who have sold your birthright in the open mart of Hell.

There none shall heed your sorrow, there shall none number your tears.
In blood and in bondage and a tote of weary years
Ye shall eat bread of affliction and drink of a bitter well
'Ere ever ye win your souls back from the Hungry Lords of Hell.

❖ ❖ ❖ ❖ ❖

Transcribed at the Imperial War Museum from *Retrude's Child: a Christmas Legend and Other Poems*, a handwritten manuscript by Cicely Fox Smith.

His Majesty's Trawler

His Majesty's Trawler

As I was walking beside the water, as I was walking by Grimsby quay
I chanced to meet with a bearded sailor and asked him what might his business be.
"Oh, I've not been in a fancy line, or sailed with cargoes the world around
For I serve in a trawler, His Majesty's trawler, shootin' her nets on the North Sea ground."

"Oh we were out on the Cemetery when nights were long and the North
    winds blew
Blew with the breath o' the Pole behind them on the Dogger Bank as they
    mostly do
And we've weather an' plenty of it, the worst of weather that ever was found—
(As we mostly do in the Grimsby trawlers, shootin' our nets on the North
    Sea ground)."

And what o' the fish you took out yonder? . . . "Oh some we drew from the
    Silver Pit
And some we had at the Long Forties, but never a scale brought home of it—
And foul was the fish that we went seeking—as ragged a beggar as ever
    was found
In the gear of a trawler, a Grimsby trawler,—shootin' her nets on the North
    Sea ground."

"Oh was it a shark or a murderin' conger—Oh was it a dogfish toothed
    so keen?"
"These be bad, but a net for mendin' such a catch the less is the worst
    they mean"
Spawn of hate in the stormy waters, eggs of iron rusted and round;
These are the haul of His Majesty's trawler—sweeping for mines in the
    North Sea ground!

As I was walking beside the harbour, as I was walking by Grimsby quay
I heard a wind of the high tide blowing and this was the song it sang to me:—
"Goodbye to the husband, goodbye to the lover, a long Goodbye to the lost
    and drowned
And Goodbye to the trawler—His Majesty's trawler, that comes no more
    from the North Sea ground!"

❖ ❖ ❖ ❖ ❖

Transcribed at the Imperial War Museum from *The China Sea and Other Poems*, a hand-written manuscript by Cicely Fox Smith.

"Dogger Bank" is a shallow area of the southern North Sea about 60 miles off the east coast of England. (54° 50'N 2° 20'E).

"Long Forties" lies between the NE coast of Scotland and SE Norway. (57°N 0° 30'E).

The header graphic is a photo of a WWI German mine brought back to port by Plymouth trawler *Genesta* long after the war, 1934, from National Maritime Museum, Greenwich, UK, photographer unknown.

Holiday

O to leave the whirlpool where so many ships go down
The stale smells and the faintness and the rank dust of the town!
O to steep one's soul in peace, far and far away,
Eight miles from everywhere and two trains a day!

There in burnished splendour all the long day through
On some grey old manor roof pigeons strut and coo;
Gently o'er the dial 'mid the sun drowned grass,
Slowly to their golden close the golden moments pass.

Memory hath her home there—kind, familiar, clear,
Memories of the centuries as of yesteryear;
Dreams the rough world scared away, gentle-eyed and shy,
Linger there to greet us from the years gone by.

Not to feel the stress and strain, not to hear the din,
Not to look on ancient wrong, lust, and shameless sin!
Not to feel the world's pain and the ceaseless fray,
Eight miles from everywhere, and two trains a day!

❖ ❖ ❖ ❖ ❖

Transcribed at the Imperial War Museum from *The China Sea and Other Poems*, a hand-written manuscript by Cicely Fox Smith.

Hunter's Croft

By Hunter's Croft when moon hung low
I saw the hounds and the huntsmen go
I heard the hollo die down the morn
And the faint far cry of a ghostly horn.
I saw them all, when the east grew grey
Fade into mist ere the break of day.

"Good luck to your hunting" was all I said
I had no fear of the harmless dead;
For if wrong they wrought when they had the ground,
It was not to the music of horn and hound
And since sorrow and pain are the wages of sin
This was not the coin it was paid them in.

What wonder, I say, if the hounds and men
Come back at the call o' the earth again,
If the good grass fields they used to know
Tug hard at the hearts that loved them so,—
And bring them back, till the night be done
To the well-known ways where the brown hares run?
Ah, hunters all, when we come to die
God deal with us no harder fate, say I!

❖ ❖ ❖ ❖ ❖

Transcribed at the Imperial War Museum from *Steel Rails and Other Poems*, a hand-written manuscript by Cicely Fox Smith.

In Manus Tuas Domine

God who breathed in our nostrils, God who numbers our years
Fashioned our limb for labour, moulded our eyes for tears
He hath set our feet on a hard road, He hath drawn a mist o'er our ways
He hath made a Law for our sojourn and an end to our days

Wheat in the barren places and tares in the tilled field
The seed goes to the four winds and we know not what it shall yield
Where we dreaded dearth there is plenty; we reap not where we have sown
And the tares and the wheat together at last are mown

Tho' we eat bread in sorrow all thro' the troubled years
The bitter bread of affliction that is sodden as with tears
The God of death is the God of life, he shall quicken tho' he destroy
We who lie down in sorrow shall rise up in joy.

❖   ❖   ❖   ❖   ❖

Transcribed at the Imperial War Museum from *Retrude's Child: a Christmas Legend and Other Poems*, a handwritten manuscript by Cicely Fox Smith.

"In Manus Tuas Domine" can be translated as "In Your Hands Lord" or "Into Your Hands Lord."

Jack All Alone

Walking on the causeway, very lone was I:
I leaned upon the wall there and saw the folk go by:
In all this town so full of folk, no friend to call my own,
Walking on the causeway I was all alone.

Lonesome as a seagull and all the rest away,
Nesting in the islands, diving in the spray ......
Walking on the causeway I wished that luck would send
A hand to clap my shoulder, a voice to call me friend.

I went beside the sawmills, where the rotting sealers lie
But there I saw no topmasts stand up against the sky
And by the outer harbour, O nothing could I hear
But the waves lap, lapping on the brown pier.

So then I fell a-thinking, what this and that would say
If they by chance should meet me at this hour of the day,
If I should chance to meet them, as any time might be,
Walking on the causeway, with not a thought of me!

It might be soon or later, it might be night or noon,
In China ship or 'Frisco ship or sailing round the Horn
In a little coasting freighter or whaling ships that go
To the cold Northern waters where the right whales blow.

I would be "Ah, is it you, lad" and "Lad, is it you?"
And half I'd think it dreaming and half believe it true;
There'll be old tales telling then and old songs sung
When friends meet together that were friends when they were young.

Walking on the causeway, I thought o' friends o' mine
And just to think about them it warmed my heart like wine;
As if they too were thinking of one that's far away,
Walking on the causeway, about the end of day.

❖   ❖   ❖   ❖   ❖

Transcribed at the Imperial War Museum from *The China Sea and Other Poems*, a hand-written manuscript by Cicely Fox Smith.

Jennifer

As I went down to ferry
With my gun beneath my arm,
I saw the stile was broken
That leads to Julian's farm.

As I came up from ferry—
'Tis maybe half a mile—
Who should I meet but Jennifer
Steppin' over the stile?

An' when she saw me comin',
She smiled where she did stand;
Says I, "The stile is broken,
So won't you take my hand?"

She took the hand I gave her,
She stole my heart the while,
The day that I met wi' Jennifer
Steppin' over the stile.

No one saw but the daisies,
Only the blackbird heard,
No one could tell but the hart's tongue
That never can speak a word.

Who should I meet but Jennifer,
What should she do but smile,
An' how could I keep from kissin' her,
Steppin' over the stile?

❖   ❖   ❖   ❖   ❖

Unpublished poem transcribed from a Cicely Fox Smith hand-written manuscript, courtesy of Danny and Joyce McLeod, who believe it was probably never meant to be published as drafted.

"Hart's Tongue" is a kind of fern and very quiet.

King Cormac to Rand Conall

What dost thou here, O singer, with this song,
What dost thou here? Our life is not so long,
That we have space therein for rhymes of woe
Or strange old tales of unremembered wrong;
We will not hear thy music, soft and low
That makes all streams of frozen sorrow flow
That brings old faces in a glimmering throng
From graves our own hands hollowed years ago.

Yet if thou wilt, O singer, thou shalt stay
Close by our throne to while long hours away
Tickles our ears with praises of our might
And wake remembrance of our last fought fray,
And sometimes in the dark of the night
Shalt tune thy harp when full cup brims bright
Raise 'mid the laughter and lamps a drinkers lay,
Touch a lascivious chord to wake delight.

Then, if thou wilt, when dumb is all the earth
And we grow deaf to praises of our worth,
Go tell thy sorrows to the cold grey sea
Let the loud beaches hear of the heart's dearth;
The dim bare fields will hear thine agony;
Thy pain that makes not merry minstrelsy,
Drop thy warm tears on the brown bosomed earth,
Gasp out thy grief that jars upon our glee.

We cannot share this sorrow song of thine
We who must die, why need we to repine —
To hear thy sad tears falling, salt and slow,
Or see thy hearts blood dripping like red wine?
O singer, suffer not thy tears to flow —
Lest thy sweet harp take on the use of woe
And call our hearts to some foresaken shrine,
Echo again some grief of long ago.

❖ ❖ ❖ ❖ ❖

Transcribed at the Imperial War Museum from *Retrude's Child: a Christmas Legend and Other Poems,* a handwritten manuscript by Cicely Fox Smith.

King Cormac Mac Art, ruled in Tara, County Meath, in the third century A.D. He is credited with streamlining the Army of the Fianna, which was set up with troops from many different clans around Ireland to guard the country against invasions.

Kites

At the top end of Elgin Street
An open space there lies
A cindered waste of bricks and shards
Of every sort and size
Where prowling cats make loud the night
With secret jungle cries …..

At the top end of Elgin Street
When day draws to it's close,
And smokey sunsets spread afar
Their plumes of gold and rose

The women gossip at their doors
And the cobbler's blackbird sings
And little boys, they fly their kites
In summer evenings.

They shout, they run, to see the kites
Climb gaily in the breeze
With upturned gaze and parted lips
Like cherubs in a frieze.

They run, they shout, their laughter peals
They watch with wondering eyes
The paper things that tug their strings
And wander in the skies.

Above, above the crowded roofs
The houses mean and small
The public and the picture house
And the mill that looks so tall
And the weathercock upon the spire—
They fly above them all …….

❖   ❖   ❖   ❖   ❖

Transcribed at the Imperial War Museum from *Lady Dock—Sold Foreign and Other Poems*, a hand-written manuscript by Cicely Fox Smith.

The Lifting of the Latch

When the wind's in the chimney, and the stars are in the sky,
I turn the key, I shoot the bolt, for fear you might go by;
You're long away in the foreign towns that are across the foam …
But the door'll be on the latch, lad, when you come home!

And some day I'll be sitting late in the firelight's glow,
And lift my head, and turn my head, to hear a step I know;

There's grand towns in the far countries where all this time you roam,
But … the door'll be on the latch, lad, when you come home.

There's a fire that's never cold upon my heart's hearthstone,
And a lamp always burning that's lit for you alone;
There's a room in this heart o' mine where no one else can come,
And the door'll be on the latch, lad, when you come home!

❖ ❖ ❖ ❖ ❖

Unpublished poem transcribed from a Cicely Fox Smith hand-written manuscript, courtesy of Danny and Joyce McLeod, who believe it was probably never meant to be published as drafted.

This poem belongs in a set with "Traveller's Rest," "The Coast of Barbary," and "The Message."

The Losers

Did you win or lose, O ye dead where you lie low.
You who lived your life in deeds, you who struck your good blow?
You who flung your lives like foam on a hopeless, helpless shore.
Does the ruin of it all rend your brave hearts anymore?

These which the world counts loser, these which the world says won.
How shall it all avail them when winning and losing are done
When the deed is tried for the deeds sake, and the word for the word's worth
Far from the clouded judging and the faulty barter of earth?

Neither Kingship nor honour, neither praising nor blame
Neither love of fair women, nor forgetting, nor fame
Any more shall they care for, any more shall they heed
They are weighed in a true balance, very just is their need

You who lost—O what lost you?—a draught of laughter and tears
A handful of gold and glory, a little measure of years
You who won ere death took you—won you your long work's worth?
Does the gold in your dead fingers lie more lightly then the earth?

"Is it peace or war?" Say the dead where they lie low
(Turn and rest, turn and rest, what avails it friend or foe?)
Is it wind in the long grasses that grow rank overhead,
Or the crying of the trumpets down the highway where we led?

❖ ❖ ❖ ❖ ❖

Transcribed at the Imperial War Museum from *The China Sea and Other Poems*, a hand-written manuscript by Cicely Fox Smith.

Lost

A weary road in Elfinland,
And a long road to roam!
And where are the hills of mine own country
And the good grey walls of home?
Was it yestereen, or yesteryear
Or a score o' years gone by
That I came over the little hill
Whence the elfin riders hie?

The weary road winds down and up,
It winds by brake & briar,
But never again to mine own country,
Which is my soul's desire,
Never again from the shuddering waste
Wherein I walk forlorn,
In twilight of Elfinland
Where is not night or morn.

The weary road winds down and up
It winds by moss & mire
How far, how far to mine own country
And the hills o' my desire?

❖ ❖ ❖ ❖ ❖

Transcribed at the Imperial War Museum from *The China Sea and Other Poems*, a hand-written manuscript by Cicely Fox Smith.

Love at Layrock Fold

At the coming on of Lady Day
When pussy willows blow
By Four Lane Ends to Layrock Fold
Came Love a-limping slow.

His eyes were like two moorland pools
So brown they were and clear;
"Now, thee begone," the goodwife cried
"We want no trampers here!"

"We want no buttons nor no silk,
Nor laces—no, for sure!
We've work eno' to keep our sels
'Bout buying stuff at door."

"I've naught to sell," Love said, and smiled,
"I ask no alms or fee . . ."

"Well, get thee gone," she scolded shrill,
"I've nowt for folk like thee."

Old Rover from his kennel crept
And licked Love's felted shoon . . . .
Yon dog's a soft dog" (Gaffer said)
"So heed yon trampin' loon."

Late the night, when darkness kind
Came down on dale and hill
And all things slept but the moorland birds
That called and were not still.

All but the boughs that sighing stirred
And the strong wind that blew,—
I heard Love, homeless on the moor,
Sobbing the long night through.

❖ ❖ ❖ ❖ ❖

Transcribed at the Imperial War Museum from *The China Sea and Other Poems*, a hand-written manuscript by Cicely Fox Smith.

Love the Loiterer

O Love, be fleet upon the road,
Nor linger by the wayside fires
Nor dally with an hour's desires,
Lest thou shalt find the doors that glowed
Against thy coming, closed and stark,
And all the lighted casements dark,
And all the dulcet viols dumb
And all the strange sweet harmonies
Upon the singers lips that hung
To waken but when thou shouldst come
O Loiterer with the dreaming eyes
Forgotten, never to be sung.

O Love, be fleet upon the way
Lest, on some bleak and bitter day
Coming, thou, thou comest all too late
And, beating on the bolted gate
Hear but the dreary echoes ring
Along the empty corridor,
Hear but the thin-voiced winds that sing
Of feasts made ready once before
Minstrels that filled these halls of yore
Yet wearied of thy tarring.

❖ ❖ ❖ ❖ ❖

Transcribed at the Imperial War Museum from *Retrude's Child: a Christmas Legend and Other Poems*, a hand-written manuscript by Cicely Fox Smith.

Magic

I went picking mushrooms—I went all alone;
I saw a big mushroom—turn into a stone;
I ran up to pick it as quick as could be,
And I found a white stone sitting laughing at me.

The dark was just coming—the trees all said "Hush"—
I saw a tall rider—turn into a bush;
I crept by the hedge, never making a sound,
And a twisty old hawthorn was all that I found.

But when the moon's shining and nurse is asleep,
Downstairs in the moonlight so softly I'll creep,
Past all the queer shadows that hide in the house
And come out when it's quiet, I'll run like a mouse.

I'll cross the cold oilcloth without any shoes;
Then out through the orchard all shiny with dews;
I'll run down the meadow as fast as I can,
And I'll pick that mushroom, and I'll catch that man!

❖ ❖ ❖ ❖ ❖

Unpublished poem transcribed from a Cicely Fox Smith hand-written manuscript, courtesy of Danny and Joyce McLeod, who believe it was probably never meant to be published as drafted.

A Meeting

In from the sea
Lone as could be,
Who should I meet with but Billy Magee—
Billy Magee
As was shipmates with me
Once on a time in the *Mary Ambree*?
Just like old times it was, Billy and me!

I dunno how
We started the row—
I might have known once, but I couldn't say now;
Maybe 'twas me—
More likely 'twas he—
Contrary divil was Billy Magee—
But—just like old times it was, Billy and me!

We've had little rubs
In dance-halls and pubs
And teetotal concerts in sailormen's clubs;
Ashore and at sea
From the Start to Fiji

We've fought one another both frequent and free—
Just like old times it was, Billy and me!

In fo'c's'les and bars
Or sprawling on spars
Of tall skysail yarders a-scraping the stars,
Shortening sail
In a fifty-knot gale
South o' Cape Stiff in the frost and the hail—
Wherever we be
Fact is that we
Can't meet without scrapping, can't Billy and me,
And—just like old times it was, Billy and me!

❖   ❖   ❖   ❖   ❖

This is an unpublished poem composed by Smith while resident at Stoke Charity, Sutton Scotney, Hampshire between 1933 and 1938, from the archives of the National Maritime Museum, Greenwich, UK.

There is another similar "Billy Magee" poem in this collection entitled "Follow The Sea." Smith may not have thought this one was good enough to have published. There is also another published poem here with "Billy" in a more reflective mood "The Eternal Feminine."

On a Tramcar

I climb the stair, to crush and crowd
In stifling shelter and crowding
And meet with leaping heart the loud,
Glad greeting of the morning.

Adown the town ways drab and stale,
A wind comes piping rarely,—
The wind that fills the rover's sail,
The wind that shakes the barley.

Say not, the air of street and slum
Shall choke my soul's ambition,
Or these confining roofs become
The skyline of my vision.

A voice is in this rustling breeze
That streams exultant by me,
Of wider skies, and stormy seas,
Beyond these vistas dree.

The ocean calls the rover yet,
And still, though earth be hoary,
Strong tides of dauntless vision set
To shores of hope and glory.

O joyful wind! O good world made,
For neither fool nor craven!
God steer his stalwarts unafraid
To some triumphant haven!

❖   ❖   ❖   ❖   ❖

Transcribed at the Imperial War Museum from *The China Sea and Other Poems* ,a hand-written manuscript by Cicely Fox Smith.

"Dree" is archaic Scottish for "endure" or "suffer."

On Horrel Hill

An aeroplane's down on Horrel Hill
And all the rabbits in a fright…
Gold leaves are on the beech-clump stile,
And traveller's-joy on the hedge is white.

Where from the steep road's crest you see
Road, stream and railway winding far
From England, peaceful, calm and free,
Toward the Channel and the War,—

The wise old English countryside,
King's forest and cloud-dappled wold,
The rushy common wet and wide,
Village and spire and clinking fold.

An aeroplane's down on Horrel Hill;
Old Stock (?) the ploughman plods to see,
From guiding of his Bess and Jill
With ancient lore of "Ray" and "Ree."

A stooped old man with blue bright eyes,
Like some old badger grizzly-grey,
And "My boy Jack in France" (he sighs)
"Do see a smartish lot o' they . . ."

Twelve strikes, and from the schoolhouse near
The children scamper, calling shrill:
"Come, come! Run quick! Come look what's here,
An aeroplane down on Horrel Hill!"

❖   ❖   ❖   ❖   ❖

Unpublished poem transcribed from a Cicely Fox Smith hand-written manuscript, courtesy of Danny and Joyce McLeod, who believe it was probably never meant to be published as drafted.

One More Day

One more day for Johnnie . . . coming up like fire
On the storm littered decks, and the water rising higher
In the hold . . . mps at their everlasting clanking . . .
And the God o' the sailormen pity us
Sixty days out from Carrizal
and sinking . . . .

One more day for Johnnie, one more day to wonder
Why in mercy's name the sea doesn't come and roll her under . . .
All the day the hot sun burning us,
All the night the cold stars blinking
And the God o' the sailormen pity us
Sixty days out from Carrizal
and sinking . . . .

One more day for Johnnie, one more day a-waking
On the wide empty sea and the hearts within us breaking
And the thoughts that keep crowding in the silence
Of the things you can never mend wi' thinking . . .
And the God o' the sailormen pity us
Sixty days out from Carrizal
And sinking . . . .

❖ ❖ ❖ ❖ ❖

Transcribed at the Imperial War Museum from *The China Sea and Other Poems*, a hand-written manuscript by Cicely Fox Smith.

See also "Copper Ore."

The Pack of Feathers

From the gusty rain and the twilight
With the last gleam of day
There came in a stranger man
That was wet as sea-spray.

"I come from a far country
I come from a lone land.
Of winds song and waves song
And spindrift and sand;
From a down and an upland pasture
And a skyline far and free,
From a grey cliff and a bleak beach
And an island of the sea."

"In the pack on my shoulders
Are neither ribbons gay

Neither silks nor satins
For fair maids array;
It is not filled with sweetmeats
Nor honey from the comb
But with soft grey feathers
From the place of my home—
Neither from the dovecot,
Nor the grey goose's breast
From any man's farmstead,
Nor any woodland nest.

Where the gulls call to the surf's sound
And the great tides come and go
On ledges of mine ownland
They are drifted like snow
Smell!—the sea is in them
Fresh and keen and clean
You will need o perfume
To lay your sheets between
Put your arms among them
As deep as you may—

They are soft as the cloud-wrack;
They are fine as the sea-spray
They will make you pillows
Such as Kings might lay
Your sleep shall be sweeter
Than Queens in Babylon
Pillow full of magic
They will surely be
Full of strange Island stories
And dreams of the sea.

❖   ❖   ❖   ❖   ❖

Transcribed at the Imperial War Museum from *The China Sea and Other Poems*, a hand-written manuscript by Cicely Fox Smith.

Paladin

I know not if Caerleon knew
The face I dreamed of yesternight
Or underneath fierce alien blue
His crest at Acre led the fight
Or if 'mid Charles' chivalry
He rode with Roland knee to knee.

I know not if some sculptured face
Or painters dream of nobleness
Galahad's whiteness, Arthur's grace

St George's pity for distress
Out of the ruck of memories came
And lit the dark with steadfast flame.

Only I saw a little while—
Ah strong, ah sure to dare and bear—
The gracious eyes and grave sweet smile
That one might dream God's angels wear
The face of one who, sprung from death,
Looks earthward and remembereth.

Strong Angel glorious in thy seers,
Dream—Bayard of the stainless soul
Stoop to me from the sleeping stars
Touch thou my hurts and make them whole
Thy war-worn arms have clashed with sin —
Christ's gentle conquering Paladin.

❖ ❖ ❖ ❖ ❖

Transcribed at the Imperial War Museum from *Retrude's Child: a Christmas Legend and Other Poems*, a handwritten manuscript by Cicely Fox Smith.

"Paladin" the Paladins, sometimes known as the Twelve Peers, were the foremost warriors of Charlemagne's court and have come to refer to any chivalrous hero.

"Bayard" may be, Pierre Terrail, seigneur de Bayard (Chevalier de Bayard) (1473–1524), French soldier, known as *"le chevalier sans peur et sans reproche."*

The Rebel

I cannot hear the howling crowd
Nor yet the death bell booming loud;
I hear the hoofs drum down the sward,
The blown bugle and drawn sword
By red moorside and purpled ford,
Where, the wild roads of war along,
Winning and losing, weak and strong,
In fair weather and foul weather,
My King and I rode close together.

We saw the Kingly hope lie dead
Where loyal blood ran deep and red;
We heard the hounds bay down the trail;
We heard the chase sweep moor and dale;
From ditch to barn, from bog to byre,
In sweat and chill, in rags and mire,
In fair weather or foul weather,
They chased my King and me together.

If I might lie on couch of down
And drive my coach through London town,

I would not change my dungeon damp.
The hurdles and the bonds that clamp
This hempen cord for a rich order
Or half the wealth both sides the border;
I hold my shame no shameful thing;
I wear it for my rightful King.*

And you great Lords who watch me die
When in your graves you too shall lie,
The gallows tree above my bones
Shall be more proud than your tomb stones;
Nor all the gems and gold there be
Unmake a lifetime's treachery;
So come what may, as come what must,
Tho' the four winds receive my dust
In fair weather or foul weather,
My King and I were men together.

❖   ❖   ❖   ❖   ❖

Transcribed at the Imperial War Museum from *Retrude's Child: a Christmas Legend and Other Poems*, a handwritten manuscript by Cicely Fox Smith.

* The following verse was written on the opposite page of the manuscript; it's unclear if it represents a revision or addition to the poem:

> And leave unlived the ringing years
> Of hope and grief and soldiers' tears
> And lose the gallant memories worth,
> Most treasured things men find on Earth,
> Though I might change these rags I wear
> For silk and lace and velvet rare.

The Recall

As up the street and down the street and through the town I went
For all the folk I there did meet I could not be content:
A tune kept going in my head—a song I used to know
That had a roaring old refrain, "It's time for us to go!"

Ay, time and time it is" (said I) "and has been long before;
There's more than leather soles wore out with tramping round ashore;
I'm sick of loafing up and down as lonely as can be,
And a man that has no friend ashore may find a friend at sea."

"I will go down to the mean streets to the grimy waterside
Where ships of all the world do come and go with every tide;
I'll hear the creak of mooring-ropes, and the river gulls calling,
And the drone and click of the windlass pawls, and the crews a-hauling."

"I will go down by the dock basins, along the silent quays
When all's still but the clucking tide and the cold river-breeze;
And through the web of rope and shroud I'll see a mast-light gleam
And know, above the dingy sheds, the vessel of my dream."

"I'll see and know her where she lies—a bird with folded wings,
Asleep and waiting for her tide, a live and lovely thing,
With speed and strength in every sweeping line of stem and hull;
Oh the soul of me's aboard her looking seaward like a gull."

"But times are changed, as change they must for all beneath the sun,
And all, they say must have their day—the day of sail is done;
The pride of many a shipyard once—far famed from shore to shore,
They pass, the tall and lovely ships, we build their like no more."

"They pass, their names pass, year by year, the famous ships of old;
And some are wrecked and some are scrapped and many more are sold;
And these the cursed Dutchmen own, and those the Porteugese,
And some the black Chilenos in the South Pacific seas."

"Yes, times are changed, from dock to dock this day a man may go,
And find no more the ships and crews that once he used to know,
And find among a hundred keels no thing of grace and speed,
But a reeking, leaking Cardiff tramp—well she must serve my need."

And lurching past the leading lights—and sheering with the swell
We'll leave the plunging bar-buoy and the clanging braying bell,
And meet once more the deep-sea wind a-blowing salt and strong
Like some old shellback, known of old, that sings a sailor's song.—

That whistles through his yellow teeth an old saltwater tune,
(The same did make the windows shake in the Boomerang Saloon)
Or by the steersman's elbow stays to tell a seaman's tale,
About the skippers and the crews in brave old days of sail.

❖   ❖   ❖   ❖   ❖

Transcribed at the Imperial War Museum from *The China Sea and Other Poems*, a hand-written manuscript by Cicely Fox Smith.

Retrude's Child: a Christmas Legend

Nowell! Nowell!
Christmas-tide is here!
Now are old things remembered
And far things near;
Angels have told it
To a world forlorn,
Nowell! Nowell!
A child is born!

Nowell! Nowell!
The stars are cold o'er head;
It is the night when Christ was born

All in the oxen's shed;
Retrude in her room apart
Watches beside her dead.

She hath put on her festal dress
And braided her bright hair;
There is no grief in her white face
As she sits watching there—
No madness born of misery,
Nor dullness of despair.

She saith: "I will not weep tonight
For my child's short sweet years,
Lest that my grief should reach in heaven
The ear which all things hears—
Lest through Earth's triumph song should sound
The dropping of my tears."

She saith: "I will not go tonight
In mourning guise forlorn,
Nor shut mine ears to the glad sound
Of fife and lute and horn."
Nowell! Nowell!
A child is born!

Surely she keeps this Christmas-tide
'Mid the Archangels seven
And all who rightiously on earth
Have loved and lost and striven—
There my child's spirit blooms, among
The whitest flowers of heaven.

This hour the oxen bow the knee
For it is Christ his morn:
This hour it is mystic blossoming
Breaketh the midnight thorn—
Nowell! Nowell!
A child is born!

O by that star the wise men saw
Move onward strangely bright,
And by that heaven where in to-day
My lost child's soul is white,
Nowell! Nowell!
I will not weep to-night.

Nowell! Nowell!
Christmas-tide is here!
Now are old things remembered

And far things near;
Sing, men and angels,
Welcoming the morn:
"Nowell! Nowell!
A child is born!"

❖ ❖ ❖ ❖ ❖

Transcribed at the Imperial War Museum from *Retrude's Child: a Christmas Legend and Other Poems*, a handwritten manuscript by Cicely Fox Smith.

The Return of Sir Jasper

Sir Jasper rideth from Faerie Land
Weeds for a crown and a rush in his hand.

Ragged he goeth and hath no heed
Words he speaketh that none may rede.

He saith: "There are no birds that sing
Like those in the land where I was King."

He saith: "No flowers on the broad down
Smell sweet as these that are my crown."

His own dogs bark and his child cries,
As he goes by with his empty eyes.

His lady clings about his neck:
For all her weeping he takes no reck.

She saith: "And is thy heart a stone,
Thou wilt not hear thy true-love's moan?"

Low he laugheth and wearily:
"My heart I left in Faerie."

"I have forgot, yet well I ween,
In Faerie Land a turf is green."

❖ ❖ ❖ ❖ ❖

Transcribed at the Imperial War Museum from *Retrude's Child: a Christmas Legend and Other Poems*, a handwritten manuscript by Cicely Fox Smith.

A Rime of Three Dead Knights

I   Sir Gawain

How fares it with you, now the lights are out
Such as you knew, and all the noisy rout
Goes on, forgetting you, O false and gay,
Who naked on your uncompanioned way
Wander, and can no merrier minstrel find
Than the bird's cry, and the thin piping wind?

What will you say, how answer, light and gay,
When a stern Angel meets you on the way
Whose grave accusing eyes you cannot blind
Nor stop her mouth with kisses, nor make kind
With glittering gifts, nor with a posyed ring
Buy her silence,—nay, not anything
Out of thy matchless store,—not quips nor lies,
Nor vows, nor baits such as light women prize,
Can woo away the anger from her eyes.
Chaff o' the earth, from the last threshing thrown,
Dead leaf o' life along the starways blown,
How fares it with you in the dark alone?

II   Sir Lancelot

This was as brave a knight as e'er drew sword
In battle for the Cross and his liege lord,
And fell through love of woman; can it be
There is no hope of heaven for such as he?
Must the fair shield be utterly defaced
And all its proud devices clean erased,
And all the deep and honourable scars
Which tell the record of a life of wars,
Wherein he had no shame from friend or foe,
Forgotten?—nay, we know not, nor shall know.
Yet haply it may be,—remembering
Her beauty which betrayed him to this thing,—
His sin shall perish with that peerless clay
Which was Queen Guinevere upon a day,
And marred innocency of his soul
Whence sprang his flower of courage, white and whole
Shine in a sunlight brighter far than were
Her eyes, and the gold glory of her hair.

III   a certain knight whose name the
chronicles telleth not.

This knight, (whose name and lineage are not told
Nor his coat-armour anywhere enrolled)

Drank deeds like wine; though his words were rough
And few, his many blows spoke loud enough
To men, by him and by his like the host
Won victory after victory, coast to coast.
Calm in the face of death, he made good cheer
For such as flagged: he had not looked on fear.
I think he thought not much on Heaven or Hell,
(Save when, a child, he heard his mother tell);
And simply—for he used not much the court,—
Drank and made merry, in the English sort:
And being called, put his scant pleasures by
Gladly, as e'er he heard his good hounds cry,
And died, as Christ saith men do best to die.

His name, I said, men tell not but they say
A grey old Northland woman far away
Looks for his home returning, day by day,
And of his simpleness and hard head,
More than of greater, be it said
Earth is the poorer, seeing he is dead.

❖   ❖   ❖   ❖   ❖

Transcribed at the Imperial War Museum from *The China Sea and Other Poems* a hand-written manuscript by Cicely Fox Smith.

The poet wrote "posied" which means "having a composed and self-assured manner." However, I think she means "posyed;" "posy" has two meanings, a small bunch of flowers, or a short motto or line of verse inscribed inside a ring. (archaic). I think she means the second older meaning.

"Baits" means an enticement, a temptation or lure.

The Roman Road

The moon hangs o'er the town tonight
And all the roofs are silver-bright:
Yet I have hailed her with no spell,
No warlock charm remote and rare,
That thus, like mist that morning clears,
This ruck of caged humanity
Meets in the moon's strange alchemy,—
The crucible of light and air
And all her long remembered years,—
Meets till the fields are fields once more
Green to the clean calm rivers shore,
And here a bridge, and there a cot,
Or moated manor, long forgot,
In their slow world of yesterday
Stand, as before this alien sway
Wiped out the long and hoarded store
Of tale, and name, and legend-lore,
With all their landmarks clean away,—

Meets till time present is no more,
And all these chimnied deserts seem
But memories of a monstrous dream.

Chink of bridle, lift of rein!
Who rides upon the moonlit road? . . . .
It is the road the Romans made
Ages gone, when the dawn-star glowed
Across the dusk of trackless time;
And out of all the ghostly train
That have plied thereon for war or trade,
On flight or journey, robbing or raid
Comes to me, like a snatch of rhyme
From a song heard once, and long forgot,
The sound of a horse's hoofs that trot
As I heard it once—what lives away—
On some companion'd yesterday.

O why?—from all the agelong-piled
Stardust and sand-drift time hath swirled
On this as on all roads there be
Comes this lost echo strange and wild
To stir the restless soul of me
With a broken tale of wonderous things
Of far, undreamed of wanderings,
A wide hope and a younger world.

Who rides? Who rides? What wanton hand
Blurred out the half-told tale in blood?
What shameful death in the wayside wood
Lurked as one rode there undismayed—
What discord, on dark fate's command
Into some brave life's harmony
Broke—and the rest was never played?

No answer from the veiled Past;
No answer from the dark To-be;
To say that—sure one day again
(Since God hath ordered nought in vain)
The chords to which in Life's high noon
Hoof-beat and spur-clink rang in time
Shall crash once more to the destined end;
No answer but the hoofs that wend
With their nameless burthen of hopes and fears,
Echoing over the empty years
Along the blank and moonlit way
From some companion'd yesterday.

❖ ❖ ❖ ❖ ❖

Transcribed at the Imperial War Museum from *The China Sea and Other Poems* a hand-written manuscript by Cicely Fox Smith.

Saint David of the Daffodils

As down the valley Saint David did go,
He saw by the river the daffodils blow,
When March like a lion came in with his gales;
And "Mine be the daffodil" (said David of Wales).

He heard the glad tinkle of snow-swollen rills;
He heard the young lambs bleating low on the hills;
He saw the green promise of mountains and dales,
And "Lo, the brave daffodil!" (said David of Wales).

"Though oft on his traces cold Winter returns,
The flame of its courage unquenched shall burn;
The hope of the spring-time undaunted it hails,—
So mine be the daffodil" (said David of Wales).

"Saint George hath his rose, of all gardens the queen,
Our Lady her lily, so pure to be seen;
Saint Patrick his shamrock in Ireland's green vales,
But mine be the daffodil" (said David of Wales).

"It is fearless and proud as the heart of the free;
It is brave as the little land dearest to me;
Its faith never falters; its hope never fails;
Then mine be the daffodil" (said David of Wales).

❖ ❖ ❖ ❖ ❖

Unpublished poem transcribed from a Cicely Fox Smith hand-written manuscript, courtesy of Danny and Joyce McLeod, who believe it was probably never meant to be published as drafted.

Sailing Ships

"It's 'ard on them old sailin' ships as never come to land,"
Said Murphy, whittling a leathery plug in a brown and calloused hand,
"They takes their chanst, does ships there, with these 'ere times at sea,
But it's 'ard on them old sailin' ships, an' so it is," said he.

"There's been a sight of good uns gone since this 'ere war come on,
An' some was rotten bad, God knows, but—well, poor things, they've gone!
An' good or fair or rotten bad as was the name they bore,
It's 'ard on them old sailin' ships—they wasn't meant for war."

"There ain't so many steamers now but mount a handy gun,
An' some there are can stand an' fight, an' some can fight an' run;
At least they's got a sportin' chanst, the big uns an' the small,
But it's 'ard on them old sailin' ships—they've got no chanst at all."

"An' fast as go the old ships down, the new uns take the tide,
They're buildin' 'em o' concrete now, an' the Lord knows what beside—

But, build they better craft or worse than those that went before,
It's 'ard on those old sailin' ships—they build their likes no more."

"It's long since I was in 'em now when first I sailed the Main,
But I'd give 'arf my livin' life to 'ave them years again;
It's a lord's life, is steamboatin', to what sail used to be—
But it's 'ard on them old sailin' ships, an' that's God's truth," said he.

❖   ❖   ❖   ❖   ❖

Unpublished poem transcribed from a Cicely Fox Smith hand-written manuscript, courtesy of Danny and Joyce McLeod, who believe it was probably never meant to be published as drafted.

The Shepherd's Dream

Brother, by my flocks as I lay drowsing yonder,
I ha' dreamed a dream that has wet my cheek with tears;
I saw the lost lambs through all the earth that wander;
I heard their sad voices crying down the years.

Frightened in a flock they huddled lost and dreary,
Far from the innocence and cleaness of their birth;
I heard their tired tread, footsore, oh and weary,
Patter on their way down the paven roads of dearth.

Thin and torn and worn with their squalid pastures leanness,
Wi' the dust of strange roads and usage hard and cold,
Dumbly athirst for a far hill's cool and greenness,
Dazed and unshepherded, knowing not their fold.

To them as they lie there, shrinking from this brightness,
Yea, fearful of his step who fed them oft of old,
Cometh the shepherd which remembering their whiteness
Saith: "These be my sheep which were strayed from the fold."

❖   ❖   ❖   ❖   ❖

Transcribed at the Imperial War Museum from *The China Sea and Other Poems*, a hand-written manuscript by Cicely Fox Smith.

The Ships of Biorn

From the broken altars, from the trodden corn,
From the smouldering homesteads smoking to the morn,
Full of slaves and plunder sailed the ships of Biorn
Biorn o' the Strong Sword,
Grey wolf o' war.

The Prior with his brethren, they left full cold and stark;
They left the shrines foresaken and the chapels dark,
And they took the grey-eyed singing lads with voices like the lark
To sing at the feast of Biorn,
Grey wolf o' war.

The children crept as closely as their bonds would let them lie;
They said: "There's none to help us since we saw our kindred die;
We shall ne'er see the fields we knew under the good grey sky."
Slaves in the hall of Biorn,
Grey wolf o' war.

Then softly spoke the youngest: "By fire and sword they died;
The Danes spared not the mothers, nor their babes that clung and cried,
And we, who carry flint and steel close hid till need betide,
Shall we spare the Strong Sword,
Grey wolf of war?"

They said: "We shall burn also!": they wept: "We fear the flame!"
Quoth he: "There is no ruddy fire that brands so deep as shame,
And the whips mark upon our back is all that we can claim,
Such is the hire of Biorn,
Grey wolf of war."

"The wolf is red with slaughter; his claws have rent our kin;
Therefore may God forgive us if this we do be sin,—
For ere night the wolf shall know full well how the pup's teeth sink in!"
Biorn of the red sword,
Grey wolf of war.

Redder than the skies sunset, redder than April morn,
With a smoke greater than fired farms among the trampled corn;
Heaven high on a sea like heaven flared up the ships of Biorn,
Biorn of the strong sword,
Grey wolf of war.

❖ ❖ ❖ ❖ ❖

Transcribed at the Imperial War Museum from *Retrude's Child: a Christmas Legend and Other Poems*, a handwritten manuscript by Cicely Fox Smith.

The Ships of Spain

Merry men all, why stand we wondering
What the world holds for a man's desire?
There's seas to sweep and there's ships for plundering,
War to the death wi' the sack and the fire.

Ho, for the deep sea lustily leaping;
Ho, for the Isles of the Western Main!
Ho, for the ports where wait for the reaping,
Glory and gold from the ships of Spain!

English lads be merry mariners;
English hearts were born to be free;
Rat's work, mole's work, leave we to foreigners
Ours be the sky and the windy sea.

Hey, for the wealth that was dug full drearily—
Theirs the getting and ours the gain—
Hey, for the path where the fleets plunge wearily,
Heavy with gold from the mines of Spain.

Ransoms for Kings in rubies and pearls there be,
Bars o' silver, pieces of eight;
Silks and satins for English girls there be—
Here's for a cast o' the dice with fate!

Up the mainsail! So, all together!
Here's goodbye till we meet again!
Send us good fortune, send us fair weather!
Send us a grip wi' the Ships of Spain!

❖ ❖ ❖ ❖ ❖

Transcribed at the Imperial War Museum from *The China Sea and Other Poems*, a hand-written manuscript by Cicely Fox Smith.

South Wind

Spring with her wild passion and her hot head is here;
Spears of daffodils gleaming anew in the van of the year;
Quick earth and breaking blossom and the swift swallow again,
South wind, South wind shaking at the pane!

The West wind, the rover, knoweth ships and the sea,
Armed comes the East, his brother and a bitter heart hath he,
And the North, the loud fighter, hath white wings of storm,
South wind, South wind blowing soft and warm.

Many songs have the four winds, and many dreams they bring;
Wisdom and grief of ages are in the songs they sing,
Roving and home returning and love and friends that part,
South wind, South wind and a hand at my heart

Where gleaned you last years gamer-blossom, tang and sweet,
That you bring now in your warm hands and lay down at my feet?
Where found you the key so long lost, where got the strange sweet smell?
South wind, South wind, singing thro' my soul!

❖ ❖ ❖ ❖ ❖

Transcribed at the Imperial War Museum from *Retrude's Child: a Christmas Legend and Other Poems*, a hand-written manuscript by Cicely Fox Smith.

Spaniards Isle

In the midnight, in the murk-night, at dark o' the moon,
When the stars are drowned in sea mist, and still the winds tune;
When the tide like a sleeping serpent heaves silent mile on mile,
The grey ghosts come creeping over Spaniards Isle.

Creeping like the mist wrack, like the white sea-spray,
Round the gold they garnered, once upon a day;
(Is it a sigh of the sea-wind, is it a sob o' the tide?
Was it a hungry spirit or a bird that cried?)

Gold for a snowy bosom, gold for a white neck—
Gold and the spending of it, gone together to wreck;
They weep for their lost bodies—O riotous days they planned,
Sifting through lifeless fingers God's gold of the sand.

When the hands heed not what matter if they hold
Such gems as men lose heaven for, or the sea's lavished gold;
Any joy of the body, any pleasure at all,
Gold cannot buy for them, souls in thrall!

❖ ❖ ❖ ❖ ❖

Transcribed at the Imperial War Museum from *The China Sea and Other Poems*, a hand-written manuscript by Cicely Fox Smith.

Spanish Girls

Spanish girls, goodbye for ever—
Aye, aye, roll an' go—
For we are bound for the London River—
An' a girl at home is the girl for me!

Girls in Rio—girls in Spain—
Val-a-paraiso to Vancouver—
A girl at home is the girl for me!

Be they brown or be they yellow—
I'll leave them all for some other fellow—
An' a girl at home is the girl for me!

Oh, my love's bright an' my love's bonny
An' my love's lips are sweet as honey—
An' a girl at home is the girl for me!

Blow, you winds, an' blow for ever,
An' blow me home to the London River—
For a girl at home is the girl for me!

❖ ❖ ❖ ❖ ❖

Transcribed at the Imperial War Museum from *Steel Rails and Other Poems*, a hand-written manuscript by Cicely Fox Smith.

The Spendthrift

What will be thine when all is done
O, spendthrift autumn, scattering gold—
What, save the watery wintry sun

The limbs that shudder in the cold
And scent of last years mould?

(Ah, leafless bough and driving sleet
Ah, silent bird and frozen fount)
"I shall have memory bitter sweet—
I shall have known both good and ill—
The which is life's account;
I shall have grief enow—and yet—
Blows there not through the bare woods still
Soft rain of sorrow and regret
And hope of next year's spring?"

❖ ❖ ❖ ❖ ❖

Transcribed at the Imperial War Museum from *The China Sea and Other Poems*, a hand-written manuscript by Cicely Fox Smith.

Tyburn Tree

This was a place where long ago
Great throngs of eager folk would flow.
Got wot, no goodly sight to see!
Therefore; for his dear sake who died,
Yea, who with thieves was crucified,—
Tread softly! this was Tyburn Tree.

Cut-throat and cut-purse, knave and jade,
A bitter price it was they paid,
A bitter weird was theirs to dree:
Whether they did in tears repent,
Or, loud in vain defiance, went
Beyond the grave and Tyburn Tree.

Upon this earth be many roads
Whereon men stagger with their loads
And earn of men their various fee:
And none more easy nor more wide,—
Nor harder whence to turn aside
Than that which led to Tyburn Tree.

We know not, we, to what vile thing
Sin, want and wrong ourselves might bring
Were Heaven less kind to you and me:
On earth their piteous lives are null!—
Lord, be to sinners merciful
E'en such as died at Tyburn Tree!

❖ ❖ ❖ ❖ ❖

Transcribed at the Imperial War Museum from *The China Sea and Other Poems*, a hand-written manuscript by Cicely Fox Smith.

One trickey looking word here, "dree" or so I thought. But, "dree" is archaic Scottish for "endure" or "suffer," which fits in.

As for "Got wot," in line three, we believe it means "God knows," not necessarily to imply that God is all-knowing but merely to emphasize the truth of the statement it follows.

The Web of Dreams

All in the soft starshine between dark and day
Kind-eyed or gentle-spoken, in a mantle grey,
Singing to your swift shuttle a song like summer streams,
Weave soft your web about me, O weaver o'dreams.

Shuttle o'faeries making the dream, weaver wielded,
Her web is spun of the sheeny grey flax o' the magic fields
O glinting gold and silver! o skein o' flying yarn,
Swishing with lost laughter and appeals.

Weave wide your web about me, o weaver of dreams
That I may walk thro' dead summers by beloved streams,
Till hot-foot over the mountains comes up the strong morn,
And the shuttle is silent and the web is torn.

❖   ❖   ❖   ❖   ❖

Transcribed at the Imperial War Museum from *Retrude's Child: a Christmas Legend and Other Poems*, a handwritten manuscript by Cicely Fox Smith.

The Well at the World's End

Three heads float where the rushes bend
O'er the well that is at the World's End,
Weary heads with crowns of gold,
Bound above their foreheads cold.

"O comb and dry me and lay me down;
Take off the weight of my weary crown
That my true love may see me lie
And kiss my lips as she passes by,
As she goes by to heavens gate
And leaves me here all desolate,
Singing where the rushes bend,
O'er the well that is at the World's End."

"Kings were we upon the earth;
Kings by right of power and birth,
And we wrought ill from our high thrones
Till wrath and sorrow and pain and groans
Dragged us down beyond the grave,
To float upon the lilied wave,
Singing where the rushes bend,
O'er the well that is at the World's End."

O our true loves shall soon or late
Pass on their way to heaven's gate;
Our true loves that wrought no wrong
Shall pass and listen to our song,
Shall kiss our lips ere on they wend,
And leave us where the rushes bend,
O'er the well that is at the World's End.

For this we wait the year's end long;
For this we sing our weary song:
"Wash me and comb me and lay me down;
Take off the weight of my weary crown
That my true love may see me lie
And kiss my lips ere she goes by,
And I hear the gates of heaven clang to
Where my true love at last goes through,
And leaves me where the rushes bend,
O'er the well that is at the World's End."

❖ ❖ ❖ ❖ ❖

Transcribed at the Imperial War Museum from *Retrude's Child: a Christmas Legend and Other Poems,* a handwritten manuscript by Cicely Fox Smith.

The "Well at the World's End" is a fantasy novel by the British artist, poet, and author William Morris, first published in 1896. This fantasy/romance bears no relation to the poem by the poet.

The Wrecker

What hear you in the night-wind?
"Brother, drowning men—
Years gone, they sank there
Full threescore an' ten;
Ships an' men by the cliff there;
Down under the hill
When the tides at full, brother,
They are calling still"

What hear you at the door latch?
"Brother, drowned men—
Come up from the cold tides, brother,
Threescore an' ten;
All in the dark night-time,
Up the dunes they come,
White as drifts o' sea-fog,
Silent an' dumb."

What makes you start an' shudder?
"Brother, drowned men,
Feeling round the room, brother,
Threescore an' ten,

For their rings an' their jewels
An' their good red gold—
But the gold's all spent, brother,
The gems all sold."

"All spent an' gone, brother,
Nothin' left at all
But the dead ash on the hearthstone,
The long hours that crawl,
But the ghost of a wanton's kisses
The tang of last night's wine,
And the grip of a cold hand, brother,
Closing fast on mine."

❖ ❖ ❖ ❖ ❖

Transcribed at the Imperial War Museum from *Retrude's Child: a Christmas Legend and Other Poems*, a handwritten manuscript by Cicely Fox Smith.

A Year Ago

Oh was it all a year ago
    Or only yesterday,
The bugles blew through our town—
    Through our town, through our town—
The bugles blew through our town
    And called the lads away?

Springtime, and sowing time,
    And mowing time have been,
Since the lads went out from our town—
    From our town, from our town—
Since the lads went out from our town
    When last year's leaves were green.

And over all the place now
    There's something sad and strange,
Though a man might walk through our town—
    Through our town, through our town—
A man might walk through our town
    And see no sign of change.

He would not see the heart-break,
    He would not see the pain,
Nor the lonely hearts in our town,
    In our town, in our town—
The breaking hearts in our town
For the lads that went from our town,
    And will not come again.

❖ ❖ ❖ ❖ ❖

Unpublished poem transcribed from a Cicely Fox Smith hand-written manuscript, courtesy of Danny and Joyce McLeod, who believe it was probably never meant to be published as drafted.

Young Bartram

Young Bartram in the springtime went thro' the fields at morn;
The fields wherein his joy had been since the day that he was born,
And it was the newest of new days and strangest of all springs
For one walked with him all the day who spoke of wonderous things
(His eyes were brimming pools of light between his folded wings).

Put by thee now thy boyhood's toys, put by thy heedless life
O heart for valiant breaking made, O spirit born to strife,
Not for the sheltered byways, where thou till now hast played
Thy soul came from the lips of God or ever Earth was made.

Yea, I am fain of a wilder sky and a lordlier battle ground;
Yea, for I hear the armies meet and the mad trumpets sound!
Am I not strong of sinew—hath not my right hand might?
Fain would I range me with my peers along the field of fight.

Neither with sound of trumpet nor charging chivalry
Silent and sole and helpless shall thy contending be;
With pitfall and dark ambush and foemen undeclared
Thou shalt be taken in the toils and in a net be snared.

In softness of great cities, there doth thy peril dwell
Whose halls are halls of magic, whose streets go down to hell;
In days when faith seems folly and hope a burntout flame
Thou shalt be toilmate of despair and bedfellow of shame.

Thou shalt lie down foresaken, thou shalt wake up forlorn,
With the memory of thy trampled soul and of thy faith forsworn,
Dust of Earth shall be thy bread, thy drink thine own salt tears,
Barren the empty threshing floor of thy unfruitful years.

Yet hope like a strong hunter and the sharp spur of love
And memory with her falling tears and voice like a crooning dove
Out of the pit of misery wherein Earth's wrecks are cast
These three, with thine own living soul, shall save thee at the last.

Thee—made of flame and foulness, of stardust and the clod
Which, blind, for daylight yearneth,
Which, drenched, still dimly burneth,
Which, earthy, to earth turneth and godlike came from God.

❖ ❖ ❖ ❖ ❖

Transcribed at the Imperial War Museum from *Retrude's Child: a Christmas Legend and Other Poems*, a handwritten manuscript by Cicely Fox Smith.

APPENDIX A:
REVIEWS (1899-1931)

Manchester High School Magazine: **Review** *Songs of Greater Britain, and other Poems.*
June 1899; page 20.

Those of us who can remember the political atmosphere of the earlier seventies realise what a change in national sentiment has since then occurred, under the influence of the new wave of patriotic and imperial feeling which has so widely influenced our literature. Of this new spirit the work above-mentioned is a manifestation, inspired doubtless, as is the work of all young poets, by the poets who have gone before—Kipling, Longfellow, and Kingsley in this case—but, nevertheless, a pure spring of heroic and heart-stirring song. Poetry, as distinct from verse making, has its own true ring, when the thought and the phrase are musical and strong in their harmony; something of this precious metal is found here, though as yet but in snatches and fragments. As thus, of the new ships and the old, "Then and Now."

> "Sped forward by their hearts' fierce palpitations,
>   White foam from these resistless bows far-hurled,
> They watch upon the highway of the nations."

Of the "Norseman."
> "Gleam reatless eyes of steely grey,
> That look out calmly, unafraid,
>   from brows deep-tanned by salt sea spray,
> Thro' many a year of sun and breeze,
>   Spent toiling over unknown seas."

And again, of the Witch Wife, who dwells by the Northern Sea.

> "and she wears on her brow a golden crown,
> for she rules the seals from the North Cape down
>   To the coast of Noroway."

Here, if we mistake not, is the note of the old ballads, as again in "Rosalie."

> "She combed his locks of ruddy god,—
>   Ah, Rosalie!
> She kissed his cheek so lily cold:
>   Ah, Rosalie!

> And lapped him in her mantle's fold;
> Alas, alas for rosalie!"

It is, indeed, in this simplicity and directness, as of one whose eye is fixed on the object, and renders its impression straightway into words, that the great merit and the real promise of these poems consist. The work of a young girl must needs have its limitations and its inadequacies; the question is whether the power is there. Our own opinion coincides with that of several journals of repute, in the affirmative. Freshness, grip, music, sympathy with nature, individuality, force,—such are the qualities of the verse; one who has gone so far may well go farther.

"How we took the Great Galleon," and "The Fight of the Caroline," are two of the longer ballad poems in this slim little volume. Then follow some patriotic songs, more properly so-called, which suffer perhaps because, as one reads them, the echoes of the "Seven Seas" sound in the ears. "The Vanguard" is, we think, the best; and the occasional poems, like those on Dargai and Omdurman, the least worth preserving. In the miscellaneous verses the true not rings out strongest. "The Grey Wolf," "The Witch wife," and "Ultima Thule," are real poetry. How the charm and mystery and weird horror of Northern Seas come into verse written 'mid our smoky vistas of red brick boxes, is a strange question; but there they are.

Manchester High School Magazine: **Review *The Foremost Trail*.**
February 1900; page 52.

We have to congratulate the author of *Songs of Greater Britain* on the publication of this, her second volume of poems, by so well-known a house and under such happy auspices. It is an advance on the first in a literary sense also, though it has naturally the same characteristics, and its contents deal with similar themes. The title poem gives the key-note of adventurous wanderings in far lands by the pioneers of the Empire, Kipling's "legion that never was 'listed."

> "We're outward bound for action—
> To tread the Foremost Trail."

The finest poem in the book is, we think, the "saint Paul's" which we reproduce, by permission, in this number. It has the dignity and restraint, the melody and simplicity, of the best English masters. A fine poem, with much the same intention, as "Sons of the English."

> "When will ye cease to roam, Sons of the English
> Out over perilous seas no longer forth faring?"

Some of the patriotic songs are a little commonplace or forced, such as "Lords of the Sea," or "True Blue," but it is given to few writers to make *all* their verse poetry. On the other hand, the true note sounds in "Man, the Conqueror," and "The men who may not sleep," "Out and Away," with its moor and woodland music, and the "Last Trek."

Throughout the volume we are impressed, even more than in the earlier work by the extraordinary power the author has of rendering some aspects of Nature. English poetry, as Matthew Arnold points out, has always had this gift, this natural magic, as in the passages:—

> "Stood dido with a willow in her hand
> Upon the wide sea banks, and waft her love
> To come again to Carthage."

> "Opening on the foam
> Of perilous seas in faery lands forlorn."

Something of this magic charm, which penetrates our old ballads, echoes through the great dramatists, and sounds sweetest perhaps in Shelley, Keats, and Tennyson, our author has, and it is her best possession. Witness "The Four Buglers," a song of the winds:—

> "In the high halls or morning,
>   Where the red dawn-lights glow"

or the "Lament of Maeldune":—

> "And it's oh for the scent of the sea-weed,
>   In the land that I loved of yore,
> In the island of Inisfalen,
>   grey billow and shingled shore;"

and of the clouds:—

> "All day the clouds sail by,
> Out of the west, where tears are scarcely dried,
> Where the veiled sun, 'reft of his crimson pride,
>   Glows gold athwart the sky."

We have said enough, perhaps, to make readers go to the book and enjoy it themselves, and that is, or should be, the purpose of all reviews.

The Manchester Evening News: Review "A Literary Curiosity"
January, 10, 1899, p. 5.

Songs of Greater Britain and Other Poems is the title of a little volume recently issued. The venture is a bold one. In the first part are found "the songs of Greater Britain;" these are mostly jingoic. Coming to the public notice just at this time, it is not difficult to believe that the first edition has been speedily exhausted.

The "Apotheosis of the British Flag" would more fittingly have described these twenty-two heroics as more than half of them mark out for glorification the national banner. The verse which opens up the volume reads as follows:—

> Sons of the sea-girt land
> Strong round the banner stand
> Steadfast and true!
> Honour and loyalty
> Ever our watchword be!
> Flutter o'er land and sea
> Red, white and blue.

The author is up to date. The "Gordons at Dargai" come in for a spirited panegyric. "Omdurman" is commemorated in five verses, which are, however, spoilt by the unworthy refrain, "… avenged is Gordon slain." It reminds us of the style of the present Poet Laureate, as indeed do several of the poems. "The Vanguard" is perhaps the most striking selection in this portion of the book. It opens—

> We, the vanguard of a nation in the lands of desolation;
> We who live and die unknown;
> We who spend our days in sorrow for the people of to-morrow
> And the land we call our own.

For easily flowing rhyme an extract from "Our Country" may be worth quoting—

> O England, merry England!
> The whole wide world can show
> No land so sweet as England
> Where're the four winds blow
> The sweep of English uplands
> The sigh of English trees
> The laugh of English rivers
> Or breath of English breeze.

Under the heading "Miscellaneous Verses" are arranged twenty-one short poems. Even here we come across some stanzas entitled "The Rally Round the Flag" but otherwise this latter half of the volume contains many pleasing verses. There might be specially mentioned "Guido Sebaldi," "The Skylark," "Mariners Born." We quote from the last named—

> I had three sons and I loved them dear,
> Ruddy and strong and tall;
> And I cherished them well for many a year,

> But the deep sea took them all!
> For one by one they would yearn to roam,
> As they grew from childhood's days,
> And one by one they went from our home
> To go on their seabound ways.

The extraordinary fact concerning this volume remains to be told. The poems are the production of one who is but in her early teens Miss Cicely Fox Smith, a Manchester schoolgirl. Herein lies much of the interest which the booklet will call forth. As the efforts of so very youthful an author some of the verses are little short of marvellous. If Miss Fox Smith will for a few years think, read, and work there is a good hope that she may one day rise to eminence as a writer of English verse. A word of praise is due to Messrs. Sherratt and Hughes for the manner in which they have set forth this neat little book, the first edition of which may some day be sought after as a value.

The Bookman, review: "Sea songs by a Woman" by Martha Plaisted
Volume 60, August, 1919, pp. 708-710

Most readers affect to be very scornful of the jacket which swathes a new book. Indignantly they tear off the gaudily illuminated sheet, declaring its scarehead encomiums to be one more deadly affront offered to their intelligence by the money-motivated publisher. But if I had thrown away unread the covers of "Sailor Town" and "Small Craft," I should have missed half my pleasure in reading these books, for I should never have suspected C. Fox-Smith was a woman.

This does not mean that my zest in reading varies with the sex of the author; but to a person who has been brought up, rebelling, on the text-book formula that a writer's success depends entirely on his persistence in keeping his "eye on the object," it is gratifying to find, at last, an instance of an author who can write with glamour about a subject necessarily outside the range of her experience. And Miss Fox-Smith does write with glamour about the life before the mast.

To be sure, the poems in the two little volumes are not great in the sense that Masefield's sea poems and some of the descriptive prose-poetry in Conrad are great. The range of the theme is too narrow. Roughly the subjects can be classed into a very few groups; the tragedy of the degraded old age of once proud ships; the longing of the sailor ashore for his bunk; his homesickness when on the deep for his English fireside, his English garden and his English lass; and his indomitable British valor when faced by the new danger of the submarine. Then too there is the ballad, direct descendant of "Sir Patrick Spens," about the cruelty of the sea, which must always have its toll of blood and tears. By confining herself largely to the seaman's vocabulary and point of view, Miss Fox-Smith cuts herself off irreparably from the rich, imaginative diction which distinguishes such poems as Masefield's "Quinquereme of Ninevah" and Flecker's "I have seen old ships sail like swans asleep." Moreover, these chanteys are not entirely innocent of imitation. One recognizes rather too often the familiar lilt of a haunting Kipling or Masefield rhythm.

These are the faults which prevent the collection from being great sea poetry. But they are faults of scope rather than of ability. What the writer has succeeded in reproducing with undeniable convincingness, is the melancholy, humorous, reckless resignation with which the sailorman accepts his obsession for the sea; the paradoxical discontent with which he longs for and abhors the safety of his home:

> Maybe then the shore things won't seem stale and I won't waken
> In the night and think of all my friends forgetting me.
> Nor know (when it's too late to know) how sore I was mistaken,
> Curling up ashore there with your heart at sea.

She is able to convey the feeling of a ship with the wild sea beneath it, the keen zest of battle for life against famine, cold, and shipwreck:

> But it's ah, fare you well, the deep sea's calling
> Back to cold and hunger and heaving and hauling.
> To decks awash and frozen yards, as very well you know,
> But ah, Deep-water Johnnie, kiss your girl and go.

Her senses are quick to the sights and sounds of harbors, the beauty of ships straining at their anchors to be gone, the pathos of old boats sinking into decay,—

> Oh, better that so long she did use,
> Should take her and break her as good ships would choose,
> Some chance of the storm or some mercy of flame
> Should make a brave end of that clipper of fame.

She knows the smell of tarry ropes and dock mud and beer: the tantalizing suggestiveness of the ship-chandler's shelves; the revelry and profanity and cheer of the longshore saloon:

> By Chinese Charlie's junk shop, by the Panama saloon,
> Where longshore loafers lean and spit at morning, night and noon,
> Mouldy, musty, dumb, and dusty, broken on the shelf,
> I thought I heard the sailor's fiddle singing to itself.

And all these things she gives with such an absence of affectation, such a free, swinging rhythm, such a lusty singing quality, that the sailorman himself would not be ashamed to roar them out on a gala night with such favorite chanteys as "Home, dearie, home" and "Ah, fare you well."

The Literary World, Review of *Men of Men*
Volume 63, January 8, 1901, p. 217.

An examination of Mr. C. Fox Smith's *Men of Men* leads us to believe that the author is hurrying rather too quickly, thus committing a fault that is painfully common among versifiers. It is a very short time, comparatively speaking, since Mr. Smith made his first appeal to the public by means of a book of songs, and already he has signed his name to no less than three volumes. In our opinion he does not improve; indeed, it would be really remarkable were he to do so under the circumstances. We shall be sorry if Mr. Smith falls into that pit which is ever gaping for those who force the Muse, as if she were an exotic plant in Kew Gardens. We think any acute judge of verse who may have time and inclination to compare *Men of Men* with Mr. Smith's "The Foremost Trial" will agree with us in declaring that there is no increase of worth in the later volume. But to stand still is to go back. War has a good deal to do with the contents of this little book, in which there is a section devoted to "Peninsular Ballads," as well as several pieces dealing with strife and prospects in South Africa. We have here one more proof that England is barren of singers able to write warlike verse of splendid quality. Mr. Smith is by no means original in his way of employing the stock-in-trade of the warrior bard. He should remember the benefits to be gained by lying fallow for a season.

Critical and Biographical Essay, by Alfred H. Miles.
Women Poets of the Nineteenth Century: Joanna Baillie to Katharine Tynan, 1907.

The publication of four successive volumes of verse by a writer who has not attained to twenty-four years of age is surely phenomenal, and one naturally looks for signs of haste and immaturity in work produced so early and with so much rapidity. The work, however, if not perfect, will bear the scrutiny, and its examination only increases one's wonder at both the quantity and the quality of the output. Cicely Fox-Smith was born at Lymm, in Cheshire, in 1882, and was educated at home. Her father, who died in 1905, was a barrister on the Northern Circuit, an old Balliol man—a pupil of Jowett, and the Arnold prize-winner of his year; her mother, a clergyman's daughter. Her publications are *Songs of Greater Britain* (1899), *The Foremost Trail* (1900), *Men of Men* (1901), and *Wings of the Morning* (1904).

Songs of Greater Britain appeared at the outbreak of the South African War, and the time spirit is well represented in its pages. But nature is not forgotten amid the blaze and fury of strife; the poet has still time to listen to the skylark's song and note the falling of the autumn leaf. *The Foremost Trail* appeared in the following year, while the war was still raging far afield, and its echoes found rhythmic expression in its numbers. *Wings of the Morning* was issued in 1904, when peace was once more smiling on the country, and, though the patriotic note is not absent, sweeter notes prevail.

The selections given here fairly represent the several volumes, and show an advance from first to last from which something may be expected in future volumes. These will be awaited with interest,—hopeful interest not perhaps unattended by anxiety. The poet is so young, and the world is so jealous of its best, that both can afford to wait, if by waiting betterment can be achieved.

The Bookman, "Miss Cicely Fox-Smith" review by W. A. F.
Volume 64, September, 1923, pp. 273-274.

Miss Cicely Fox-Smith has almost imperceptibly made her way into the front rank of those who sing of seamen and shipping. Her progress has been as unobtrusive as the rising of the tide. Readers of *Punch* and other periodicals are accustomed to expect something breezy, something with "the tar and seaweed smell," from a poem over the signature of "C. F. S." But with too many that is the limit of their acquaintance. A few have ventured further and bought one or two of the dainty little volumes of poems by C. Fox-Smith. Had they suspected a feminine authorship it might have added piquancy to their venture, and lent wings to her fame. But the author was obviously a man. What woman would talk about "Rusty red old hookers, going plugging round the world"? Besides, nautical journals found nothing in the poems to quarrel with; all the details were quite correct. Obviously a woman.

Seamen wrote many letters to "C. F. S." testifying that here at last was the genuine thing, something worth reading.

Miss Fox-Smith owes nothing to Masefield. In fact to some extent she is prior to Masefield. *Sailor Town*, which includes some of her best and most characteristic work—for example, "The Ballad of the *Matterhorn*," her own favourite, and "Rathlin Head," a great favourite with her critics—was written two years before *Salt Water Ballads* appeared. Nor, when her Muse leaves the sea for the dry land, does she owe anything to Kipling, as far as she knows, though the perusal of her "Prairie Shepherd" with its refrain, "Baa, baa, black sheep, no one's fault but your own," is not likely to recall Kipling. "The Route March," with its imprecations on the foreign service boot—"We're 'oppin' and we're 'obblin' to a cock-eyed ragtime tune"—has really nothing in common with Kipling's "Boots." But the same cannot be said of her treatment of the mule—"the late lamented army mule, you'll meet him in the stew"—which has a strong smack of the verses on the "Commissariat Camuel."

Having said that, you have said all there is to say. The vast majority of Miss Fox-Smith's poems are inspired directly by the living fact, the actual experience.

The "Prairie Shepherd" was connected with an important chapter in Miss Fox-Smith's life. A brother had settled in Alberta, and three years before the war she and other members of her family went out to join him. Twelve months of that western prairie were enough for them. "Bare and bald and droughty and dusty" it was in summer, and during the interminable winter "the fierce Keewatin whistled over the waste like a flight of geese from the Pole, and the strong breath of the Chinook thundered across the plains." Anyone who wants an unvarnished picture of a settler's life in Alberta should read her story, *The City of Hope*.

From Alberta to Victoria, B. C., was a pleasant change, and her old enthusiasm for the sea re-awoke as she wandered through "Sailor-Town," got glimpses into the interior of "Chinese Charley's junk store" and listened to

> "Little tunes on Chinese fiddles in a quiet street,
> Full of dinky Chinese houses."

In due time a return was made to London, and henceforward the ballads introduce themselves familiarly with such phrases as "Limehouse way, the other day" or "Down by Millwall Basin." The singer was in fact haunting the docks and the lower river, gathering that knowledge which she turned to such good account in *Sailor Town Days*. Loyalty to actual fact makes her introduce the chantey but sparingly into her ballads. "Sacramento" may be accounted one exception and "Heave all together" of "Rolling Home" another. The chantey has gone out with the going of the sailing ship. The few of these that are left are nearly all foreigners, and foreigners don't sing chanteys. But the spirit of the chantey, its rollicking breeziness, pervades her song, mingling with and often overcoming the melancholy of the seaman's ballad, sung, not round the capstan, but "in the tavern window old and brown," the long ballad, as she terms it, "that they generally sing through their noses," the "doleful, sentimental bawl" imitated by Kingsley in "The Last Buccaneer." In her words it is "a queer old quaver, shaky, shrill and sad, with queer little curly cues, twiddles and quavers," sung to the accompaniment of "a creaky old leaky concertina underneath the great gold moon." But this pathos wages a losing fight not only against her prevailing humour, the humour of "The Ballad of the Ressurection Packet of the Salt 'Orse Line," for instance, but against her high spirits, which insist on embarking on a good swinging rhythm.

Such musical verse, such singable ballads which retain their quality even when chanting of the

> "Rampin', raw-boned, cast-steel-jawboned
> Any transport smile,"

ought to proceed from a musician or the daughter of a musician. But she can put forward no such claim. Nor does she owe to heredity her great feeling for the music of the sea. You would imagine her father an old sea captain. But he was a solicitor. How then did the love of the sea come to her, living on those Lancashire wolds? "By intuition," she says. It is a riddle. Perhaps the explanation may be found in the way of her life on those wolds. She lived an open-air life, following on foot the Holcombe Harriers, whose huntsman, John Jackson, she celebrates in "For'ard on!" And roaming over the hillsides she got wide views of cloudland and plain down to the distant sea. Remember that Coleridge was similarly soaking himself in moorland air when he wrote the greatest of all sea poems.

Here on these Lancashire hills must have begun that love of the sea which was confirmed when she came south and haunted the London Docks, and steeped herself in sea-lore. She learned the heart of the sailor, his golden visions of lazying at home or in South Seas lotus lands, and his deep-seated mistrust of these visions.

> "I'd want the hard-case mates a-bawlin', an' the strikin' o' the bell;
> I've cursed it oft and cruel—but I miss it all like hell."

"Ain't it queer," another of her sailors says, "how a feller never knows what he likes best till it goes?" Happier the Tommy of the "Grand Tour," undistracted by any sea longings, who has seen just as much as he wanted. "I've seen the Perramids and Spink, which I 'ad oft desired."

We suspect that Miss Fox-Smith has no longing for South Sea beaches or "Spinks," but is content with her own world, limited but inexhaustible, of docks and seamen and coasting vessels. Her senses are almost unconsciously on the alert to catch every little point of interest:

> "The patter of reef-points on tops'ls a-shiver;
> The song of the jibs when they tauten and quiver."

come as natural, unsought music to the ears of this true poet of the sea.

Notes:

This *Bookman* 1923 review of Cicely Fox Smith is the most comprehensive review that exists, demonstrating as it does a deep appreciation of her work, and was found by us among the papers she deposited at the National Maritime Museum Archives at Greenwich, England. The true identity of "W. A. F." remains an intriguing mystery.

Daily Mail, "Legends," review by Joseph Conrad
August, 15, 1924

In her I verily believe the quintessence of the collective soul of the latter-day seaman has found its last resting-place, and a poignant voice before taking its flight forever from the earth.

Spectator

"No one, not even Mr. Mansfield, has written finer sea ballads or come closer to the heart of those who go down to the great waters. In any anthology of the sea Miss Fox Smith's 'The Ballad of the *Matterhorn*,' 'Bill the Dreamer,' 'The Last of the Sealing Fleet' and 'Rathlin Head' must occupy a high place."

"Miss Fox Smith is one of the few people living who can write a real 'chanty' combining a mastery of sea-lingo with perfect command of sea rhythms."

The Times

It is not likely that many lovers of sea-songs have missed the voice of Miss Fox Smith, but if they do not know her *Songs in Sail* let them read *Sailor Town*—the dancing colours and fresh scents of the harbour, the rush of the sea and wind, the cheery pathos of the outward-bound, the sailor's homesickness—all this is carried on the rhythm of her verses with a vividness hardly equaled by any other verse writer of the day.

"These are the right stuff."

Miss C. Fox Smith's naval verse … shows here, as in her former collection, her exceptional métier for apt metrical celebration of the spirit, the humour of the pathos of war and of the fighting man.

Evening Standard

Ballads and songs of the war, reeking of spindrift and spume, breezy and direct as those who go down to the sea in ships.

Nautical Magazine

Mr. C. Fox Smith must be congratulated on his dainty little volume of poems, *The Naval Crown*. We remember how well we enjoyed the author's *Sailor Town* and can say that the enjoyment and high opinion we then formed of the author have been in no way lessened by the present volume.

Navy

The writer's vocabulary of sea phrases is striking and characteristic; the technicalities proclaim a real sea lover, and the tone and colour are only excelled by the lilt of the verses.

Syren

An excellent little collection of ballads referring to various phases of the war, some of which our readers have doubtless made the acquaintance of in the pages of *Punch*. "The Rhyme of the *Inisfail*" … is the gem, and an excellent one, of the collection. The author has a capital vein of humour.

Manchester City News

The sea songs have the breath and the sound and the motion of the waters in them.

Punch

Small Craft ... contains several poems that have appeared in *Punch* over the initials "C. F. S." They should receive a fresh welcome from all who share her understanding of the ways of seafaring men, and from the larger public that is beginning to appreciate the gallantry and devotion of our Merchant Service.

Those who appreciate Miss C. Fox Smith's familiarity with the ways and moods of sailormen and her flair for the true sea-tang will welcome the new collection of poems which she has brought out under the title, *Ships and Folks* . . . Most of these verses have appeared in *Punch*, and no further commendation is here needed.

APPENDIX B
SELECT DISCOGRAPHY: CICELY FOX SMITH POEMS RECORDED AS SONGS

From the North, by Gary & Vera Aspey, (1975):— "From the North," and "The Parting."
Breeze for a Bargeman, by Bob Roberts, (1981)— "Race of Long Ago (Racing Clippers)."
Bread & Roses, by Sarah Morgan of Bread and Roses, (1987):— "Homeward."
Port of Dreams, by William Pint & Felicia Dale, (1991):— "The Tow-Rope Girls."
Making Waves, by Tom Lewis, William Pint & Felicia Dale, (1992):— "Sou' Spain."
Seaboot Duff & Handspike Gruel, by Pinch o' Salt, (1995):— "Sou' Spain," "Cooper Ore," "Eight Bells," "Hoodoo," "The Tow-Rope Girls," "Let Her Go (a Tramp Shanty)," "Lee Fore Brace," "Shanghai Passage," "The Cape Horner," "Peaceable Mister M'Gee," "Home for Christmas—Old Style," "A Sailor's Delight," "Follow the Sea," "The Half Loaf," and "Merchantmen."
Tinker Tailor Soldier Singer, by Tom Lewis, (1995):— "150 Days Out from Vancouver [version of: 'The Ship's Good-Bye']."
Round the Corner, by William Pint and Felicia Dale, (1997):— "The Tow-Rope Girls," "Tryphena's Extra Hand," and "Blue Peter."
Old Wood is Best, by Alan Fitzsimmons, (1998):— "North Sea Ground."
On the North Sea Ground, by The Keelers, (1998):— "North Sea Ground," and "So Long."
Tomorrow's Tide, by Salt of the Earth, (1998):— "A Wool Fleet Chorus," and "Copper Ore."
Where Seagulls Dare, by Landlocked, (1999):— "Lee Fore Brace."
When Our Ship Comes Home, by Bob Walser & Friends, (1999):— "Shanghai Passage."
Just for the Record, by Marrowbones (Gordon Morris and Peter Massey), (1999):— "Port o' Dreams."
Old Swansea Town, by Baggyrinkle, (2000):— "150 Days Out from Vancouver" [version of: 'The Ship's Good-Bye'].
One More Pull, by Baggyrinkle, (2000):— "Lee Fore Brace."
Bank Trollers, by Bob Webb, (2000):— "150 Days Out from Vancouver" [version of: 'The Ship's Good-Bye'].
Constant Lovers, by Dave Webber and Anni Fentiman, (1998):— "Limehouse Reach."
Sailing Bye, by Derek Gifford, (2001):— "Shanghai Passage."
Away from It All, by Dave Webber and Anni Fentiman, (2002):— "Race of Long Ago (Racing Clippers)."
Full Sail: Inside the Lid, by Gordon Morris, (2002):— "Port o' Dreams," "Racing Clippers," "Mainsail Haul," "The Convalescent," "Tom Pascoe (Told at the Pilchards)," "Sea Change," "The Extra Hand," "Admiral Dugout," "Stately Blackwaller," "Mariquita," "The Shipkeeper," and "See You in Liverpool."
Rare Thing, by Marrowbones (Gordon Morris and Peter Massey), (2002):— "Port o' Dreams," "The Shipkeeper," "Racing Clippers," and "The Convalescent."
Never a Cross Word, by Danny & Joyce McLeod, (2002):— "The Capehorner," "Tryphena's Extra Hand," "The Stately Blackwaller," "Port o' Dreams," "Lee Fore Brace," and "So Long."

Now and Then, by Johnny Collins, (2002):— "Sailor Town."
Around the Harbour Town, by Dick Miles & Friends, (2003):— "Sailor Town."
Tom Lewis 360°, by Tom Lewis, (2003):— "The Tow-Rope Girls."
England Expects, by Dogwatch, (2004):— "A Dog's Life," "Casey's Concertina," and "Rosario."
Bung Up Bilge Free, by the Portsmouth Shantymen, (2004):— "All Coiled Down (So Long)," and "Tow-Rope Girls."
Seven Seas, William Pint and Felicia Dale, (2004):— "The Packet Rat."
Uncommon Sailor Songs, by Charlie Ipcar, (2004):— "Flying-Fish Sailor," "Outward Bound," "Shanghai Passage," "Limehouse Reach," "Port o' Dreams," and "Mariquita."
More Uncommon Sailor Songs, by Charlie Ipcar, (2005):— "Rio Grande," "Lee Fore Brace," "Lumber," "Hastings Mill," "Old Fiddle," "Rosario," "Pacific Coast," and "All Coiled Down (So Long)."
Shipshape and Harry Fashion, by The Harry Browns, (2005):— "The Tow-Rope Girls."
Across a Starry Heaven, by Di Franklin, (2005):— "By the Old Pagoda Anchorage."
Adventures, by Dogwatch, (2006):— "The Packet Rat, Bill's Enemy."
The Long Road Home, by Peter Massey, (2006):— "Conversation Book," "The Long Road Home."
Rolling Down to Sailortown, by Roll & Go, (2006):— "Outward Bound," "All Coiled Down (So Long)," "Mariquita," "Port o' Dreams."
Rolling Home to Bristol, by The Harry Browns, (2006):— "A Sea Burthen," "Home Boys Home (Homeward)."
Sing the Sun into the Sky, by Two Black Sheep & a Stallion, (2006):— "Homeward (Home, Boys, Home)."
Closehauled on the Wind of a Dream, by Bob Zentz, (2007):— "Ships & Folks," "A Dog's Life," "The Eternal Feminine," "The Blue Peter," "Pictures," "Sea Dream," "Casey's Concertina," "Ice: The Bosun's Story," "The Tryphena's Extra Hand," "The Portsmouth Road," "Ships that Pass," "The Red Duster," "The Ballad of the Eastern Crown," "Racing Clippers," "The Tow-Rope Girls," "Bill's Christmases, Eight Bells," "Leave Her Johnny."
Extra Rough Tracks, by John Hills et al of Elsie's Band, (2007):— "Gerrans Churchtown."
Old Sailor-Poets, by Charlie Ipcar, (2007):— "Sailor Town," "Shipmates (1914)," "A Ship in a Bottle," "The Long Road Home."
Raising Wind with The Harry Browns, by The Harry Browns, (2007):— "Sacramento."
Life of Brine, by The Roaring Forties, Australia, (2008):— "Wool Fleet Chorus," "Lee Fore Brace," "Mainsail Haul," "The Day's Work," "A Channel Rhyme."
Sailortown Days, by Charlie Ipcar, (2009):— "Leave Her Johnnie," "Mobile Bay," "News in Daly's Bar," "By the Old Pagoda Anchorage," "Sailor's Farewell," "The Traveller."
Cutaway Mike, by John Hills et al of Elsie's Band, (2009):— "Limehouse Reach."
Eight Bells, by William Pint and Felicia Dale, (2009):— "Bill's Christmases," "Eight Bells."
Look Out, by Roll & Go, (2010):— "Mobile Bay," "Shipmates," "Lumber," "The Long Road Home."
Back to You, by Martyn Wyndham-Read & No Man's Band, (2010):— "Farewell to ANZAC"
Michael Head: Songs, by Hyperion, (2012):— "Limehouse Reach,"
Songs from an Old Sea Chest, by Charlie Ipcar, (2012):— "A Parting," "Farewell to ANZAC," "The Jolly Bargeman," and "Rathlin Head."

A Dog's Life, by Mike Kennedy, (2015):— "A Dog's Life," "Fiddler John," "An Ocean Tramp," "High Noon in the Tropics," "Messmates All," "Poor Old Ship," and "Rathlin Head."

Never Turn a Blind Eye to the Storm, by Charlie Ipcar, (2015):— "Christmas Night," "High Noon in the Tropics," and "Day of Little Ships," and "The Chanteyman."

APPENDIX C
CICELY FOX SMITH BIBLIOGRAPHY

Cicely Fox Smith's poetry books include:

Songs of Greater Britain, Sherratt & Hughes, Manchester, UK, 1899.
The Foremost Trail, Sampson Low, Marston & Co., London, UK, 1899.
Men of Men, Sampson Low, Marston & Co., London, UK, 1900.
Wings of the Morning, Elkin Mathews, London, UK, 1904.
Lancashire Hunting Songs & Other Moorland Lays, J. E. Cornish, Manchester, UK, 1909.
Songs in Sail, Elkin Mathews, London, UK, 1914.
Sailor Town: Sea Songs and Ballads, Elkin Mathews, London, UK, 1914 & George H. Doran Co., New York, US, 1919.
The Naval Crown, Elkin Mathews, London, UK, 1915.
Fighting Men, Elkin Mathews, London, UK, 1916.
Small Craft, Elkin Mathews, London, UK, 1917 & George H. Doran Co., New York, US, 1919.
Rhymes of the Red Ensign, Hodder & Stoughton, London, UK, 1919.
Songs and Chanties: 1914-1916, Elkin Mathews, London, UK, 1919.
Ships and Folks, Elkin Mathews, London, UK, 1920.
Rovings, Elkin Mathews, London, UK, 1921.
Sea Songs and Ballads 1917-22, Houghton Mifflin, London, UK, 1923 & Houghton Mifflin, New York, US, 1924.
Full Sail: More Sea Songs and Ballads, Houghton Mifflin, London, UK, 1926.
Sailor's Delight, Methuen & Co., London, UK, 1931.
All the Other Children, Methuen & Co., London, UK, 1933.
Here and There in England with the Painter Brangwyn, F. Lewis, Publishers, Ltd., Leigh-on-Sea, UK, 1945.
Country Days and Country Ways Trudging Afoot in England, F. Lewis, Publishers, Ltd., Leigh-on-Sea, UK, 1947.
Ship Models, Country Life, London, UK, 1951.

Note, many of these books overlap in terms of poems included, and there are sometimes slight differences between poems of the same title from book to book.

Other books written, co-authored, or edited by Cicely Fox Smith include:

The City of Hope (novel set in Alberta), Sidgewick & Jackson, London, UK, 1914.
Singing Sands (novel set in Vancouver Island, BC), Hodder & Stoughton, London, UK, 1918.
Peregrine in Love (novel set in Victoria, BC), Hodder & Stoughton, London, UK, 1920.
Sailor Town Days, Methuen & Co., London, UK, 1923.
A Book of Famous Ships, Houghton Mifflin, New York, US, 1924.
The Return of the Cutty Sark, Methuen & Co., London, UK, 1924.
Ship Alley: More Sailor Town Days, Houghton Mifflin, New York, US, 1925.

Tales of the Clipper Ships, Houghton Mifflin, New York, US, 1926.
A Book of Shanties (traditional sea songs), Methuen & Co., London, UK, 1927.
A Sea Chest: An Anthology of Ships and Sailormen, Methuen & Co., London, UK, 1927.
Ancient Mariners, Methuen & Co., London, UK, 1928.
There Was a Ship: Chapters from the History of Sail, Methuen & Co., London, UK, 1929.
Ocean Racers, Philip Allan, London, UK, 1931.
The Thames, Methuen & Colk London, UK, 1931
True Tales of the Sea, Oxford University Press, London, UK, 1932.
Anchor Lane, Methuen & Co., London, UK, 1933.
Peacock Pride (with Madge S. Smith), Frederick Muller, London, UK, 1934.
Adventures and Perils, Michael Joseph, London, UK, 1936.
Three Girls in a Boat (with Madge S. Smith), Oxford University Press, London, UK, 1938.
All the Way Round: Sea Roads to Africa (travel), Michael Joseph, London, UK, 1938.
The Ship Aground: A Tale of Adventure, Oxford University Press, London, UK, 1940, 1942, 1958.
The Voyage of the "Trevessa's" Boats, Oxford University Press, London, UK, 1940.
The Story of Grace Darling (biography), Oxford University Press, London, UK, 1940.
Thames Side Yesterdays, F. Lewis, Publishers, Ltd., Leigh-on-Sea, UK, 1945.
Painted Ports (with Madge S. Smith), Oxford University Press, London, UK, 1948, 1965.
Knave-Go-By: The Adventures of Jacky Nameless (with Madge S. Smith), Oxford University Press, London, UK, 1951.
Seldom Seen (with Madge S. Smith), Oxford University Press, London, UK, 1954.
The Valiant Sailor (with Madge S. Smith), Oxford University Press, London, UK, 1951, 1955, 1959.

APPENDIX D
BIBLIOGRAPHY OF NAUTICAL ARTWORK

Anton Otto Fischer Marine Artist, edited by Katrina Sigsbee Fischer, Mill Hill Press, Nantucket, Massachusetts, US, 1984.

The Art of Nautical Illustration, by Michael E. Leek, Quantum Books, London, UK, 2005.

Darkness and Daylight in New York, A. D. Worthington & Co., Hartford, US, 1897.

Dibdin's Sea Songs, edited by Thomas Dibdin, Henry G. Bohn, London, UK, 1854.

Focs'cle Days, by Anton Otto Fischer, Charles Scribner's Sons, New York, US, 1947.

Greasy Luck, by Gordon Grant, William Farquhar Payson, New York, US, 1932.

The Last of the Wind Ships, by Alan J. Villiers, George Routledge & Sons, London, UK, 1935.

Learning the Ropes, by Eric Newby, Random House, New York, US, 1999.

Light on the Water, by Keith McLaren, Douglas & McIntyre, Vancouver, 1998.

Merchantmen-at-Arms, by David Bone, Chatto & Windus, London, UK, 1919.

Punch, Project Gutenberg Online Serial Archive/British Library, various issues from 1914-1954.

Sail Ho!, by Gordon Grant, William Farquhar Payson, New York, US, 1931.

Sailing Vessels in Authentic Early Nineteenth-Century Illustrations, reprinted by Dover Publications, New York, US, 1989.

Sailor-Painter, by Robert Lloyd Webb, Flat Hammock Press, Mystic, Connecticut, US, 2005.

Sailortown, by Stan Hugill, E. P. Dutton & Co., New York, US, 1967.

Salt-Water Poems and Ballads, by John Masefield, The Macmillan Co., New York, US, 1914.

Sea Songs and Shanties, by Captain W. B. Whall, Brown, Son & Ferguson, Glasgow, UK, 1927.

Shanties from the Seven Seas, by Stan Hugill, Mystic Seaport Museum, Mystic, Connecticut, US, 1987.

Ships, by Charles Wilson, Barre Publishers, Barre, Massachusetts, US, 1971.

Songs of American Sailormen, by Joanna C. Colcord, Bramhall House, New York, NY, 1938.

Songs of the Sea, by Stan Hugill, McGraw-Hill Book Co., New York, US, 1977.

This Was Seafaring, by Ralph W. Andrews and Harry A. Kirwin, Bonanza Books, New York, US, 1955.

APPENDIX E
GRAPHIC ARTISTS

A good faith effort has been made to identify and appropriately credit all the photographers, illustrators, cartoonists and other artists whose work has been used to illustrate the poems in this book.

George Denholm Armour (1864-1949)
Judith M. Barrows (1950-present)
Sir David W. Bone (1873-1959)
Sir Muirhead Bone (1876-1953)
Frank Brookesmith (1901-1991?)
John A. Bryan de Grineau (1883-1957)
Gustave Adolf Closs (1864-1938)
Capt. Lincoln Alden Colcord (1857-1913)
Edward William Cooke (1811-1880)
George Cruikshank (1745-1814)
Kathryn L. Darnell (present)
Montague Dawson (1895-1973)
Charles Dixon (1872-1934)
Edward Duncan (1803-1882)
Thomas Goldsworth Dutton (1819-1891)
Lionel Edwards (1878-1966)
Sydenham Edwards (1768-1819)
Hugh Frith (present?)
Anton Otto Fischer (1882-1962)
Alison Lee Freeman (present)
Robert Frerck (present)
Gordon Grant (1875-1962)
Charles Grave (1886-1944)
Charles Dickson Gregory (1850-1920)
Atkinson Grimshaw (1836-1893)
Emil Otto Hoppé (1878-1972)
Stan Hugill (1906-1992)
Julius Caesar Ibbetson (1759-1817)
Charles Ipcar (1942-present)
Robert W. Ipcar (1939-present)
Antonio Jacobsen (1850-1921)
Maurice Ernest Jessop (deceased)
Harry A. Kirwin (1891-deceased)
Count Felix von Luckner (1881-1966)
George Morrow (1869-1955)
Eric Newby (1919-2006)
John A. Noble (1913-1983)
Lieutenant D. C. Oulds (deceased)
Sir Bernard Partridge (1861-1945)

Charles Robert Patterson (1878-1958)
Charles Pears (1873-1958)
Charles Pickering (1867-1921)
Jean François Portaels (1818-1895)
Alice Provensen (1917-present)
Martin Provensen (1916-1987)
Howard Pyle (1853-1911)
Leonard Raven-Hill (1867-1942)
Ernest Shepard (1879-1976)
Claude Allin Shepperson (1867-1921)
Henry Singleton (1766-1839)
Philip Wilson Smith (1880-194?)
Francis Smitherman (1879-1972)
George L. Stampa (1875-1951)
Percy E. Syer (deceased)
Bert Thomas (1883-1966)
F. H. Townsend (1868-1920)
Edwin Tunis (1897-1973)
Alan Villiers (1903-1982)
Denys Watkins-Pitchford (1905-1990)
Veronica Whall (1887-1967)
Charles J. A. Wilson (1880-1965)
William Lionel Wyllie (1851-1931)

APPENDIX F
AUTOBIOGRAPHICAL AND BIOGRAPHICAL REFERENCES (CHRONOLOGICAL ORDER)

British Census, 1891, 1911.
1908 Passenger List (Montreal/Quebec).
1913 Passenger Lists (Liverpool).
Victoria, B. C., 1889, bird's-eye view map published by Ellis & Co., Victoria, BC.
Henderson's Greater Victoria City Directory, 1913.
Peregrine in Love, Cicely Fox Smith, published by Hodder & Stoughton, London, UK, 1920, pp. 86-87.
Later English Poems 1901-1922, J. E. Wetherell, published by B. A., McClelland & Stewart, Limited, Toronto, Canada, 1922, pp. 35-36.
Sailor Town Days, Cicely Fox Smith, published by Methuen & Co., London, UK, 1923, pp. 13-14, pp. 163-182.
"Cicely Fox Smith," by W. A. F., *The Bookman*, published by Hodder & Stoughton, London, UK, Volume 64, September, 1923, pp. 273-274.
A Book of Famous Ships, Cicely Fox Smith, published by Houghton Mifflin Co., New York, 1924, p. 160.
Ship Alley, Cicely Fox Smith, published by Houghton Mifflin, New York, US, 1925, pp. 65-66, pp. 72-78, pp. 126-127.
There Was a Ship, Cicely Fox Smith, published by Edwin Valentine Mitchell, Hartford, Connecticut, 1930, pp. 168-169.
Anchor Lane, Cicely Fox Smith, published by Methuen & Co., London, UK, 1933, p. 8.
Who Was Who in Literature: 1906-1934, UK, p. 1059.

All the Way Round, Cicely Fox Smith, published by Michael Joseph, London, UK, 1938.
"Miss C. Fox Smith—Obituary," *The Times of London*, UK, April 9, 1954.
Who Was Who in Literature: 1951-1960, UK, p. 1013.
"Books by Miss C. Fox Smith," W. H. Webb, *Sea Breeze*s, UK, November, 1966, pp. 818-819.
"Cicely Fox Smith of Bow," A. B. Blackmore, in *Devon Life*, UK, May, 1977, #131, pp. 28-29.
"Cicely Fox Smith," Danny McLeod, in *Seaboot Duff & Handspike Gruel*, UK, 1995.
"Cicely Fox Smith: Hampshire Resident and Poet of the Sea and Sailors," John Edgar Mann, *Folk on Tap*, UK, July-September, 1999, #80, pp. 17-18.

GLOSSARY

All My Eye: This is British slang for nonsense.

Allus: This is British dialect for "always."

'Ans-Medoodle: This is a mock Germanic name.

Bandogs: A massive spirit-world mastiff with huge jaws from which flames appeared. (The name is now also used for a breed of real large mastiffs).

Barguest: This is a phantom black dog, as large as a calf and with long sharp fangs and claws. It is an unwelcome guest at best!

Barkey: This is a sailor's pronunciation of barque, a type of sailing ship.

Beat the Ties: This means "hoboing" or making one's way along the rail line.

Belayin'-Pins: These are large wooden pegs for tying off sails but often used as weapons by irate sailors.

Benefit: This refers to the national assistance as it was then known.

Billyboy: This refers to a type of ship.

Blackwall: This refers to the Blackwall Docks in London as well as the Blackwall shipping line to India, Australia and points east. The Blackwall ships were typically well-made, well-armed, virtual cargo-carrying frigates that reigned supreme until supplanted by the clipper ships of the 1850's.

Blowed It: In this case "blowed" means spending your money quickly (and probably unwisely).

Blue Peter: This is nautical slang for the blue and white signal flag flown to warn sailors ashore that they should report on board for their ship is about to proceed to sea.

Bluenose: This is sailor's slang for someone from Nova Scotia. Also refers to a person who advocates a rigorous moral code.

Board School: This is an early British school run by a Board of Education.

Bollard: This is a large post, wood or iron, on the dock to which a ship would be moored while in port.

Bottled Ships: This refers to a model ship contained within an ordinary bottle that a sailor would build in his leisure time.

Brassbounder: This is sailor's slang for an apprentice, someone who was training to become an officer.

The Breaker: This is a reference to the salvage yard where old ships were broken up for their useful parts.

Bust a Farden: This means to spend a farthing (one quarter of an old penny or 1/960 of a pound sterling).

Cape Stiff: This is sailor's slang for Cape Horn.

C.B.: This is soldier's slang for being "confined to barracks" as punishment.

Charley Brown's: This was a favorite sailor's tavern along Ratcliffe Highway in London.

Came through the Hawse-Pipe: This phrase means he has worked his way up to mate from his initial status as a common sailor, not through any nautical training institution; "hawse-pipe" literally means a conduit for the anchor cable.

Channel Chops: These are heavy short waves in the English Channel.

Casuarina tree: Is a small tree or shrub that is considered one of the most versatile tree species in the tropics. (*C. equisetifolia*). It is used for boomerangs, building construction and fire wood amongst other things.

Coaches, Gigs, Cabriolets, Shays, Dog-Carts: These are all various types of wheeled carriage from the era before automobiles.

Coppice: This is a thicket or grove of small trees or shrubs.

Corp: This is slang for corpse.

Crossed 'Awse: This literally means crossed hawse or bowline, crossed paths in plainer English.

Cuffer: This is old English slang for lies.

Cwm: This means "valley" in the Welsh language (pronounced "coom").

Deadheads: Refers to the novice or poor sailors who were seasick at the start of a voyage and unfit for work. This nickname ceased when they stopped "groaning" or being sick.

Didakai: This was the name that used to be given to caravan-dwelling roadside people who live like Gypsies but are not true Romany.

Divil: This is a colloquialism for "devil."

Dixies: This is a military slang for the huge cooking vats.

Doctor: This is sailor's slang for the ship's cook, when they were being polite.

Dogwatches: These are a pair of two-hour watches, half the duration of a normal four-hour watch, from 4 to 8 pm. The suggestion by some that these watches were called "dogwatches" because they were "curtailed" while amusing appears to have no foundation in fact.

Doldrums: This zone is roughly located along the Equator and is generally where prevailing winds cannot be counted on.

Donkey's Breakfast: This is sailor's slang for his straw mattress.

Dree: Archaic Scottish for "endure" or "suffer." Also archaic word in Lancashire for "monotonous."

Drifter: A kind of commercial fishing craft in the early 20th century.

Duiker: These are various small African antelopes of the genera Cephalophus or Sylvicapra, having short, backward-pointing horns.

Dugout: This is old Royal Navy slang for a retired officer.

Dusted My Jacket: This implies he was beaten.

The 'Eads: This is most likely a reference to Sydney Harbour's two headlands.

Fairleads: This is a ring or block of wood with a hole in it through which rigging is passed, implying a deck cargo has been loaded as well.

Fastnet: This would be the Fastnet Rock landmark off the southwest coast of Ireland, also capped with a lighthouse.

Flyin' Kites: These are small extra sails such as "skysails" that are only deployed in moderate winds to pick up a little exra speed.

Flying-Fish Sailor: This was a nickname for those sailors who sailed regularly from England to the Orient.

The Forties: This is the zone in the Southern Hemisphere around 40 degrees latitude South.

Fritz: This is a nickname for a member of the German Armed Forces.

Fust: This means "first."

Gam: An exchange of visits between ships at sea.

Good Discharge: This means a good testimonial from the captain upon leaving a ship.

Granfer: This is old English dialect term meaning grandfather.

Greybeards: These are those long surging waves that ships would encounter as they ran their "easting down" in the roaring forties of the Great Southern Ocean.

Gry: This is Romany for a "horse."

Guerdon: Means reward.

Halliard Chorus: This is a reference to how many of the jobs on board a sailing ship would have been done with the help of a work-song or "shanty" and there were different types of shanties for different types of job.

Handspike Gruel: This is a euphemism for blood.

Harpooner: This would be a strong sailor who could throw the harpoon accurately, a skilled trade.

Hauling His Chest Out: This means a sailor's sea-chest containing all his earthly possessions.

Hawse-pipe: A figure of speech meaning to work your way up the ranks and not coming straight in as an officer.

Hawse or 'Awse: Hawse pipes are actually at the bows of a ship; so to cross someone's "hawse" means to pass in front of them. In the context of a poem, CFS uses it to describe bumping into an old shipmate.

He Cut His Cloth Exceeding Fine: This is a polite way of saying he was very careful with his money.

Hen-and-chickens: Is the name of a flower that grows close to the ground.

Hellom: This is sailor's slang for "helm."

His Club Deposits: This refers to the common practice in many areas to pay a given amount a week into a burial fund (or club) as a sort of insurance scheme to ensure you did not end up in a pauper's grave. Such schemes still exist today.

Holy Office: Refers to the Spanish Inquisition.

Holystones: These are large flat sandstones that are used for sanding down the deck, sometimes referred to as "bibles."

Hooker: This is sailor's slang for any old ship.

Humble Marthas: This is a reference to inconsequential people or things; see the story of Martha and Mary in Luke 10:38-42.

I Makes My Mark: This is when an illiterate sailor signed on with a symbol of some sort. In this case the sailor wants the shipping clerk to spell "Smith" with an "i" in the middle.

Jamie Green: This is one of the extra sails or "kites" a captain would add in the hope of gaining a little more speed.

Jerry: This is slang for a German serviceman.

Junk: This is sailor's slang for salt beef or salt pork, a major staple for the crew.

K.C.: This is an abbreviation for King's Council, a well respected barrister.

Kicking Mate: Discipline could be hard on board a ship and a "kicking mate" was an officer who enforced his orders with his boots.

Killick: This is another term for anchor.

Kloof: This is a Southern African mountain pass, a gorge or mountain pass, usually wooded. It is similar to the English dialect word clough for the same features.

Knacker: This is the old name for the tradesman who would buy up old beasts and render them down for horsemeat, horsehair, skin and even glue. If a horse were knackered it would be thoroughly recycled.

Kraal: This is a rural village in Southern Africa, typically consisting of round thatched houses surrounded by a stockade or an enclosure for livestock.

Kreese: Another spelling of Kris, a mallay knife.

Left 'Er in Me Singlet: This implies that he was shipwrecked and had little time to dress properly.

Lighter: This is a watercraft for transporting freight from ship to shore, or vice versa.

Limber: This is an old military term referring to a detachable part of a gun carriage consisting of two wheels, an axle and a pole.

The Line: This would be the Equator.

Lizard: This is a prominent peninsular on the Cornish Coast with a lighthouse.

Lurry: This could be a lorry but is more likely the old Lancashire dialect term for hauling.

Merrymaids: These are what we think of as mermaids, and one should steer clear of such creatures.

To a Mort of Things: This refers to a number of things.

Mudhook: This is sailor's slang for the anchor.

My Pint and My Pound: A merchant sailor was once upon a time entitled to a pound of meat and a pint of drinking water per day whilst at sea according to the Navigation Acts.

Nantucket Sleigh Ride: The towing of a boat in the wake of a harpooned whale.

A Nice Packet: This means a lot of money in a sweep, as in winning a raffle or sweepstake.

The Ninth Wave: This is traditionally the last and final wave beyond which lies the land of death and/or magic (Celtic Lore).

Offa's Dyke: A man made structure to separate England and Wales.

Onst: This is English dialect for "once."

Packet: This means a sailing ship on a regular schedule.

Pierhead Jump: This phrase describes how some tardy sailors would join the ship's crew at the last minute by literally leaping from the dock to the deck as the mooring lines were cast loose.

Pilchards: These are small fish related to herring and it's also a common name for a tavern in a sea-side town.

Pisin: This means poison.

Plimsoll Line: This is a reference to an official waterline indicating the maximum limit that a ship could be legally loaded to.

Preachin' Skipper: Many of the skippers were very religious and would hold compulsory services on deck almost daily.

Pullyhaul: This literally means working with pullies to haul up the yards or sails of a ship, usually requiring a team of sailors hauling on a line together.

Rampin': This is an archaic English slang word which means rampaging.

R.D.C.: This is probably a reference to Rural District Council, a local government body one of whose duties would be to keep the roadside hedges in good order.

Red Duster: This is a nickname for the Red Ensign flown by ships of the British Merchant Marine Service since 1864.

Ricks: They are large stacks of hay.

R.N.R.: This is an abbreviation for the Royal Naval Reserve.

Rode the Bumpers: This is a way of hitching unofficial rides on early railways.

Running Her Eastern Down: This is when a sailing ship is running before a westerly wind in the "roaring forties."

Sailor-Town: This is the part of town adjacent to the waterfront filled with bars, dance halls, and shops that catered to the needs and desires of sailors.

Sandy Point: This is a prominent landmark located in South Australia.

Scollard: This is another English dialect word meaning scholar.

Scrimshaw: This is the art of carving and engraving of whalebone artifacts and the finished product; many whalermen would while away their time on long trips in this way and produce both utilitarian and decorative pieces.

Scroodle's Mark: This would have been a mark made by Scoodle in place of a signature as he was not literate.

Seaboot Duff: This is a euphemism for a good kicking.

Seagirt: Surrounded by sea.

Sennet: A method to shorten rope. Also know as Square Sennet. Often worked into a mat sailors would make from old rope.

Sent Their Pannikins Afloat: This is a reference to the common practice by sailors of tossing their straw mattresses over the side at the end of a voyage.

Set: This means sit, as in set back quiet.

Seventy-Four: This is a reference to a warship mounting 74 guns in its broadsides, a major class of fighting ships in the Napoleonic period.

Shanghai: This was to force someone to ship-out by drugging them or knocking them on the head.

Shellback: This is the nickname for an old time sailor who has spent so much time at sea that when he takes his shirt off you would expect to see sea shells clinging to his back.

Shindy: This is old English slang for a commotion or uproar, which later came to mean more of a festive party.

Sign In: This means to join the crew.

Skinny or Skint: This is old waterfront slang for being tight fisted, miserly.

Slashin' Clyde Fourposter, A: This is a reference to one of the clipper-like four-masted steel barques built by the Clyde shipbuilding company in Scotland.

Slushy: This is sailor's slang for another nickname for the ship's cook.

Slutch: This is a North England dialect word for mud.

Sodger: This is sailor's slang for "soldier" and to be called such aboard ship was considered a great insult.

Sou' Spain: This is evidently a reference to sailors who have traveled south of the Equator.

Spouter: This refers to a whaling ship.

Square-'eads: This is sailor's slang for Germans.

Stave: This is an archaic word for song or verse.

The Tack: In this case "tack" refers to the food.

Taffrail: This is the rail at the stern of a ship.

Tally on the Fall: This means to grab hold of a line that is hanging down and haul away.

Tootle-oo: This is cockney equivalent of the French "À tout à l'heure!" (See you later!).

Trade: This is a reference to the Trade Winds, the prevailing winds in various areas of the earth which sailing ship captains took advantage of in plotting their voyages.

Trampin': This is sailor's slang for the practice of cargo ships delivering cargo to a port where they have no prior contract for return cargo and where they would then have to negotiate from scratch or sail in ballast to another port for cargo.

Trick: This is a reference to a two-hour period of time when a sailor is manning the helm.

Tryworks: This is a brick fireplace for rendering whale blubber into whale oil on board ship.

"Ultima Thule": In ancient times the northernmost region of the habitable world—hence, any distant, unknown or mysterious land.

Vanderdecken: This was the captain of the mythical "Flying Dutchman" which if you ever saw her, you knew that you and your ship were doomed.

Water Breaker: A nautical term for a small emergency water cask in a lifeboat.

Weekly Dole: This is a reference to the subsistence allowance paid by the parish or the state to indigent people at the time.

W'en: This is "when" pronounced without the "h" cockney fashion.

Whack: This is a reference to what a sailor was supposed to get every day for rations according to the current shipping regulations. It is still a common term in the England for one's allotted portion.

Whack It: This means spend it.

When He Went West: A colloquial expression meaning when he died.

Whizz-Bangs: This is WWI soldier's slang for incoming artillery shells.

With a Bone in Her Teeth: This is an old nautical expression referring to the appearance of the bow wave that a sailing ship makes as she cuts through the water powered by a brisk breeze.

INDEX OF POEM TITLES

Admiral Dugout	204
Afoot	158
After Dark	205
After Preston Fight	189
After the Storm	36
Afterglow	172
Age (Millwall Dock)	206
All Hallows	207
All Sorts	208
All the Way Home	689
Alligator's Children, The	575
Along the Prairie Trail	209
Alongshore	605
Anchor Watch, The	209
Anchors	210
Ancient Singer, The	169
Angel Unawares, An	167
Animal House	598
Apples	664
Après La Guerre	689
Armed Merchantmen: an Old Song Re-Sung	212
Art of Catching Flies, The	575
At Eventide	41
At the Dawning of the Day	183
Autumn	27
Auxiliary, The	691
Back to Hilo	213
Ballad of Blue Water	622
Ballad of Old and New, A	214
Ballad of Rosalie, The	30
Ballad of the *Dinkinbar*, The	216
Ballad of the *Eastern Crown*, The	219
Ballad of the Hun King's Dream, The	221
Ballad of the *Matterhorn*, The	223
Ballad of the Only Love, The	225
Ballad of the Resurrection Packet, The	226
Ballad of the Time, A	198
Bare Boughed Forest, The	691
Barguest	191
Basaco	88
Beauty	228
Beside the Pool	2
Best Days, The	660
Bewitched	151
Bill	229
Bill Brewster	230

Bill the Dreamer	232
Bill's Choice	232
Bill's Christmases	233
Bill's Enemy	235
Billy's Yarn	236
Bird's Call, A	159
Birthday Greeting, A	5
Bitter Sweet	692
Blue Anchor Lane	237
Blue Peter, The	238
Boats of the *Albacore*, The	239
Bob-Cat, The	576
Bond of Brotherhood, The	103
Boot and Saddle	95
Bosun	240
Boys	241
Brandan's Isle	124
Bride of Leith, The	122
Bridge, The	642
Britannia Africana	20
Britannia Triumphans	14
British Merchant Service - 1915	242
British-Born, The	12
Broken Brigade, The	109
Bugle-Call, The	20
Bugle, The	59
Builders, The	243
Bullington	244
Burial of General Craufurd at Ciudad Rodrigo, The	92
By the Old Pagoda Anchorage [1924]	245
By the Old Pagoda Anchorage [1926]	246
Caesar's Camp	146
Caged Monarch, The	37
Call 2, The	247
Call, The	247
Calling of the Birds, The	125
Calm before Storm	34
Cape Horner, The	249
Cape Stiff	250
Captain Joseph Johnson	251
Captain Paul Jones	251
Casey an' Me	252
Casey's Concertina	253
Castle in Spain, A	31
Casuarina Tree, The	653
Cavalry Soldier, A	52
Changeling, The	572
Channel Rhyme, A	254
Chanteyman, The	692

Charge of the 21st Lancers, The	59
Charge of the 23rd Light Dragoons at Talavera, The	87
China Sea, The	255
Chips	257
Christmas Night	258
Circus in the West, The	260
Ciudad Rodrigo	91
Clare's Brigade	261
Clock with One Finger, The	592
Clouds, The	76
Clough Among the Hills, The	188
Clyde-Built Clipper, The	262
Coast of Barbary-2, The	567
Coast of Barbary, The	264
Coasting Brigantine - Unnamed	674
Coastwise	264
Colonists, The	13
Commodore (North Atlantic Mail Service)	266
Complaint, A	649
Comrade, The	139
Conall's Daughter	123
Contrast, A	33
Convalescent, The	267
Conversation Book, The	268
Cook	270
Copper Ore	271
Coral Island, A	70
Country Pleasures	613
Crown of Gold, The	130
Curios	272
Cutty Comes Back (1924), The	273
Cutty Comes Back (1926), The	274
Dan	276
Dan's Dream	277
Dan's Epitaph	278
Dan's Fortune	279
Dan's Odyssey	280
Davy Jones's Locker	169
Day of Little Ships, The	633
Day's Work, The	282
Dead for England, The	283
Dead Man's Bay	284
Death of Galahad, The	150
Declaration of War, A	286
Deep Sea Plunderings	619
Deep Water	663
Deep Water Jack	287
Defaulter, The	288
Departure	625

Derelict, The	289
Diamond Jubilee	28
Die-Hards: Albuera, The	90
Dog's Life, A	290
Dogs	642
Doldrums: One of Murphy's Yarns	291
Domestic Problem	652
Dover Street	683
Dr Clark's 'Plaint	129
Drake's Breed	635
Ducklington	293
Dust of the Way, The	144
Duty	40
Early Spring	75
Eight Bells	294
Elegy	587
Elf-Child, The	177
Empire-Makers	58
Enchanted Forest, The	164
England in China: 1897-98	15
Epilogue: Cape Horn Days	295
Epitaph on an Unfortunate Lady	640
Eternal Feminine, The	296
Eve of Battle, The	97
Everybody's Doing It	636
Everything is Different in Africa	624
Ex-Voto Breton Church Model	668
Fair Hills of Ireland, The	296
Fairies' Child, The	119
Fairy Shepherd, The	152
False Colours	128
Farewell (1900)	94
Farewell (1904), A	144
Farewell to Anzac	297
Fata Morgana	174
Faugh-A-Ballagh (Clear the Way!)	100
Fiddler John: a Country Tale	298
Fife and Drum	110
Fight of the *Caroline*, The	8
Fight on the Island, The	161
Fighting Merchantmen, The	300
Fighting *Téméraire*—Bone "Prisoner" Model, The	672
Figurehead, The	596
Figureheads	302
Finance	655
Finger Post, The	645
First Ship, The	667
First Voyage	303
Five Ricks, The	305

Flanders' Woods	306
Flying Kites	307
Flying-Fish Sailor, The	308
Follow the Sea	310
For England	61
For'ard On!	178
Foremost Trail, The	41
Four Buglers, The	72
Franklin	61
Fraser River	311
From the North	185
From the Sea	165
Fuentes D'Onor	89
Fulfilment	311
Furrow, The	312
Galloping Horses (After the Flower Show)	614
Garden in the North, A	313
Gathergold	695
Geordie Collier Brig	580
Gerrans Churchtown	313
Getting Off	654
Ghosts in Deptford	314
Ghosts in the Garden	316
Gift, The	108
Gilly	197
Gipsy Soldier, The	316
Glory of the Marne, The	317
God's Gift	113
Good Hope	60
Good Intent, The	318
Good Luck	320
Gordon Avenged!	4
Gordons at Dargai, The	16
Grand Banks of Newfoundland, The	694
Grand Tour, The	321
Granfer Scroodle	577
Great Zimbabwe	657
Greatest of These, The	695
Green Ribands	155
Green Thicket, The	322
Grey Comrades, The	192
Grey Grisold	194
Grey Wolf, The	24
Guido Sebaldi	26
Half Loaf, The	323
Half-Past Eleven Square	324
Hallowe'en	193
Ham, Shem and Japhet	571
Hans Dans an' Me	325

Happy Dead, The	106
Happy Warrior (April 23rd), The	326
Hastings Mill	327
Haunted Ship, The	600
Hay Harvest: 1916	328
Hell's Market	695
Hen that has Hatched Ducks, The	573
Her Majesty's Forces	49
Hesperus	160
Hic(ks) Jacet	126
Hide and Seek	572
High Noon	328
His Going Forth is from the End of Heaven	78
His Majesty's Trawler	696
Hodson of Hodson's Horse	172
Holiday	697
Hollinshead Hall	187
Home Along	329
Home for Christmas—Old Style	330
Homecoming at Dawn	641
Homeward	332
Honour the Brave!	100
Hoodoo	333
Horn Weather	334
Horseman in the Night, The	193
House-Hunter, The	644
How We Took the Great Galleon	6
Hunter's Croft	698
Hunting of the Witch, The	182
Hunting the Hare	181
Hymn of Thanksgiving after Victory	106
I Have Seen	570
Ice: the Bosun's Story	335
Image, The	173
Implacable, The	336
In Drydock	337
In Great Waters	163
In Manus Tuas Domine	699
In Memoriam: H. M. S. *Warspite*	651
In Prize	337
In Sailortown	338
In the Museum of the Royal United Service Institution	43
In the Trades	340
Isandula-1	3
Isandula-2	155
Island, The	567
Islands	661
Jack All Alone	699
Jack Ashore—Ladysmith	98

Jacko' Lanthorn	157
Jennifer	700
Jim	340
Job o' Work, A	341
Joe	342
John Company's Ships	343
Jolly Bargeman, The	344
Jonah, The	160
Journey's End	177
Ketch *Ceres* 1811-1936, The	608
King Cormac to Rand Conall	701
King's Grief, The	116
King's Jester, The	174
King's Kraal, The	48
King's Shame, The	135
Kingfisher, The	574
Kites	702
Knitters, The	346
Knots	604
Lament of Maeldune, The	74
Lament, A	639
Lancashire from the Hills	159
Lancashire Hare, A	186
Lancashire Sunset, A	148
Last of the Sealing Fleet, The	347
Last Post: "Death is swallowed up in victory"	154
Last Race, The	35
Last Ship, The	348
Last Trek, The	56
Lavender Pond	350
Lay of the White Heifer, The	120
Leave Her Johnnie	351
Lee Fore Brace	352
Les Champignons (Conversation Exercise)	655
Lessons of Manchester North, The	127
Let Her Go! (a Tramp Shanty)	354
Lieutenant Shellback, R. N. R.	356
Lifeboatman	590
Lift by the Way, A	357
Lifting of the Latch, The	702
Light Cruisers (Old)	358
Lighthouse Builders, The	156
Limehouse Reach	360
Little Gorilla	575
Little Serving-Boy, The	121
Little Things, The	361
Little Waxy	179
Liverpool	168
Liverpool Ship, The	362

London Pool	149
London River	363
London Seagulls	364
Lone Hand, The	365
Long Road Home, The	366
Lords of the Sea	47
Losers, The	703
Loss of the *Birkenhead*, The	54
Lost	704
Lost Galleon, The	176
Lost Land, The	164
Lost Rivers, The	368
Lost Ship, The	369
Love at Layrock fold	704
Love Lies Bleeding	175
Love the Loiterer	705
Love's Marketing	370
Lower Pool	620
Lowland Sea, The	370
Luck	627
Lumber	371
Mad about Music	662
Mafeking (May 16th, 1900)	102
Magic	706
Maids of the Northern Lights, The	76
Mainsail Haul	373
Majuba Day	101
Man the Conqueror	53
Mariners Born	39
Mariquita	375
Market Day	376
Master Brocky	571
Master Hippo	573
Mate	377
Meet at Eleven	617
Meeting, A	706
Mejillones	378
Memories	379
Men of the Marches	107
Men Who May Not Sleep, The	57
Merchant Men (1904)	142
Merchantmen	379
Merchantmen (1917)	380
Message, A	381
Messmates All	110
Might Have Been	616
Mighty Hunter before the Lord, A	145
Mike	382
Mike and the Cat	383

Mike's Fancy	384
Minden Day	23
Misanthrope, The	583
Missing	385
Mist	184
Mobile Bay	581
Morgan Le Fay	389
Morning Watch	390
Mother Carey	390
Mouth-Organ, The	392
Mr. Prickles	574
Mules	393
My Lawn	659
Nec Aspera Terrent	109
Nests	573
New Heavens – New Earth (Christmas, 1916)	394
New Year	395
Newfoundland's Gift	396
News from the North	396
News in Daly's Bar	398
Nitrates	400
No Surrender	151
Norseman, A	24
North Atlantic Trade, The	402
North Country Hound (Old Style), A	185
North Sea Ground, The	403
Ocean Tramp, An	114
Odyssey	585
Offa's Dyke	594
Old Bellringer, The	648
Old Breed, The	405
Old Cob Wall, The	658
Old Fastnet	406
Old Fiddle, The	407
Old Graybeard	196
Old Love and the New, The	129
Old Rectory, The	666
Old Shellback, The	409
Old Ship's Logs	569
Old Ships (1919), The	410
Old Ships (1920), The	412
Old Stormy	414
Old Tom Hubbard	683
Old *Vindictive*, The	416
Old Whale, The	417
Old Wood is Best	584
Old-Timer, The	418
Oldest Thing in London, The	419
Omdurman	18

On a Tramcar	707
On Horrel Hill	708
One More Day	709
One Summer's Day	37
Oom Paul's Hat	79
Open Boat, The	421
Optimist, The	610
Orion's Figurehead at Whitehall, The	422
Orkney Man, The	423
Otter Hunting in Ribblesdale	183
Ould Has-Been, The	424
Our Colonial Troops	4
Our Country	21
Our Distant Kin	65
Our Jubilee Visitors	17
Out and Away	62
Outposts, The	112
Outward Bound	426
Pacific Coast	427
Pack of Feather, The	709
Packet Rat, The	428
Padre	430
Paladin	710
Pals	431
Paradise Street	431
Parting is Such Sweet Sorrow	433
Parting, A	432
Parting: The Eve of the Puppy Show	180
Passing of Sail, The	433
Path of the English, The	50
Peaceable Mister M'Gee	434
Penguins	574
Peninsular Ballads: Prologue	86
Penmaenmawr	40
Philosophy	435
Pictures	437
Piper, The	195
Pirate Gold	566
Pirate's Only Delight, The	439
Pixie-Led	170
Place of Dreams, A	194
Places	621
Plains of Mexico, The	440
Plovers' Wind, The	646
Pool by the Mill, The	440
Poor Old Ship	441
Poor Old Ship (Regent's Canal Dock)	443
Port Forsaken, A	444
Port o' Dreams	445

Portrait of a Lady-1	446
Portrait of a Lady-2	448
Portsmouth Road, The	449
Post-War Plans	639
Prairie Shepherd, The	451
Prairie Sunset	452
Prairie Wind	452
Pretty Meadow	647
Pro Patria	44
Queen Radegund	141
Queen's Delight (a Ballad of Master Mariners), The	453
Queen's Ships, The	685
Quest (Horses for the Army), The	199
Quest of the Queen, The	80
Question, A	638
Racing Clippers: a Wool Fleet Memory	455
Rain	456
Rally Round the Flag, The	27
Rathlin Head	457
Rebel, The	711
Recall, The	712
Recollection	459
Recruit, The	460
Red Duster (R. N. R. Demobilised), The	461
Red Rose, The	200
Red, White, and Blue	6
Remember, Remember....	462
Rendezvous, The	588
Resurrection	463
Resurrexit (June, 1900)	104
Retrospect	465
Retrude's Child: a Christmas Legend	713
Return of Sir Jasper, The	715
Return of the Prodigal, The	469
Return, The	467
Rhodalind	125
Rhodesia	99
Rhyme of the *Captive Maid*	470
Rhyme of the Four Strong Men, The	66
Rhyme of the *Inisfail*, The	473
Rhyme of the *Rio Grande*, The	475
Rime of Three Dead Knights, A	716
Ring o' Bells	166
Rio Grande	477
Rock, The	78
Roll Along Home!	478
Roll-Call, The	55
Rolling Home	479
Rolling Stone	480

Roman Road, A	717
Romance	480
Romance and Reality	581
Ronceval	481
Rosario	482
Rosemary	178
Route March, The	483
Roving Men	45
Royal Music	179
Royal Naval Reserve	484
Royal Yacht	670
Sacramento	485
Sailing Ships	719
Sailor Town	487
Sailor, Sailor—	612
Sailor's Delight	488
Sailor's Farewell	490
Sailor's Garden, The	491
Sailor's Picture Model – Unnamed	673
Sailor's Pleasure	586
Sails	492
Saint Andrew's Eve	493
Saint Andrew's Land	493
Saint David of the Daffodils	719
Saint George of England	494
Saint of Cornwall, A	495
Saint Patrick's Day in the Morning	495
Saint Paul's	42
Sale by Auction	607
Salt Road, The	599
Salute to Sailor Town	637
Salvage	496
School	173
Sea Burthen, A	497
Sea Change	497
Sea Dream, A	499
Sea Queen, A	603
Sea Sorrow	500
Search-Light, Kimberley, 1899-1900, The	97
Seaside Church, A	119
Second Fiddle	656
Second Mate	501
See You in Liverpool	501
Seeing the World	502
Shadow, The	162
Shanghai Passage	503
Shantyman, The	631
Sheep Fair on the Marches	594
Shepherd's Dream, The	720

Ship in a Bottle, A	676
Ship of State, The	63
Ship Picture	505
Ship that Never Was, The	504
Ship-Keeper, The	507
Ship's Good-Bye, The	512
Shipmate Sorrow	509
Shipmates (1914)	510
Shipmates (Clipper Ship *Mary Ambree*)	511
Ships and Folks	512
Ships He Served of Old, The	513
Ships of Biorn, The	720
Ships of Spain, The	721
Ships that Pass: an Episode of the Cruiser Patrol	514
Shipwreck	516
Should Auld Acquaintance . . . ?	650
Sic Transit	602
Silent Navy, The	517
Siren, The	153
Skipper	518
Skylark, The	32
Sleep	171
Small Craft	520
Smell of the Sea, The	171
"Smith-with-a-Hi"	586
Smuggler's Song, A	568
"Sold Foreign"	523
So Long	522
Song for Saint George's Day	64
Song of the Day, A	19
Song of the Greatest Isle, The	15
Song of the Mill, The	524
Song of the Open, A	111
Song of the Sword, The	13
Songs of the City	73
Sons of the English	48
Sou' Spain	525
South Africa—1899	93
South Sea Whaler, "Scrimshaw" Model	576
South Wind	722
Spaniards Isle	722
Spanish Girls	723
Speed the Plough: a Country Song	526
Spendthrift, The	723
Spring in Hampshire: 1916	527
Squareheads	528
Stand Firm!	51
Stand of Wilson's Patrol, The	10
Stately Blackwaller, The	530

Stave at Parting, A	186
Steel Rails	531
Stew	432
Stoke Charity—a Hampshire Placename	578
Stormy Dusk	433
Streets	681
Submarines	640
Survivor, The	665
Swallows at Zimbabwe	627
Sweethearts and Wives	534
Tea in the Garden	611
Then and Now	11
They Built Ships	678
They Made Sails	679
Thought for Gardeners, A	641
Thoughts in a Garden	610
Three Ships, The	535
To a Rusty Bicycle	569
To Arms	22
To the Mac Cailen More, Duke of Argyll	80
To the South African Guild of Loyal Women	105
Told at "The Pilchards"	538
Torpedo Boats	540
Tow-Rope Girls, The	542
Tower of Babel	541
Traveller, The	543
Traveller's Rest	545
Troll's Gold	196
True Blue (Song for Music)	63
Tryphena's Extra Hand, The	546
Twelve Tree Barrow	168
Tyburn Tree	724
Ultima Thule	34
Unchanged, The	643
Upon Julia, Playing the Oboe	650
Vanguard, The	22
Victoria the Well-Belowed	130
Voices of the Hills	201
Wales Forever	520
Wapping: Conversation Piece	632
War Risks	547
Waters of Oblivion, The	548
Way of a Ship, The	530
Wayfarers, The	134
Web of Dreams, The	725
Well at the World's End, The	725
Westminster Boys	114
Westminster Tower	65
What Bill Said	629

What the Old Man Said	531
When the Ports Were Filled with Loveliness . . .	605
Whom the Gods Love	96
Windmill, The	641
Wine of Life, The	523
Winter Morning	618
Winter Pleasures	624
Wireless	534
Witch of Mull, The	126
Witch-Wife, The	29
Witches	534
Wolf Cubs	572
Wool Fleet Chorus, A	555
Wool-Gatherer, The	191
Word of the English, The	94
Words of Wisdom	556
Workers, The	38
World's Way, The	167
Worshipper, A	77
Wrecker, The	726
Yarn of Dan's, A	557
Yarn of the Blue Star Line, The	559
Yarns	561
Year Ago, A	727
Yeoman's Son, The	562
York and Lancaster	190
Young Bartram	728
Younger Son, The	563

ABOUT THE EDITORS

Charles Ipcar

Charles is a singer of traditional and contemporary sea music who has toured from coast to coast in the States as well as in Canada, Australia, and the United Kingdom. Ipcar has also been featured as a solo performer and workshop leader at the prestigious Mystic Sea Music Festival in Connecticut, and has performed with his band Roll & Go at that same Festival. He is professionally trained as an Urban Geographer, with a Ph.D. from Michigan State University. He has also taught geography as a Peace Corps volunteer in the secondary schools of Ethiopia. In addition to his interest in the nautical poems of Cicely Fox Smith, Ipcar has also adapted poems for singing by John Masefield, Burt Franklin Jenness, William McFee, Edwin J. Brady, Angus Cameron Robertson, Bill Adams, and Harry Kemp. He also has composed original songs and is the author of three songbooks and five solo recordings. He resides with his wife Judy, along with their two cats, in the Kennebec River town of Richmond, Maine.

James Saville

James Saville is a former RAF officer and mathematics teacher from the UK. He became interested in folk music in his 40s and performed in various clubs in the North of England whilst still teaching and it was during this time that he heard the group Pinch of Salt singing some Fox Smith songs and was moved by the lyrics to search out more of her work. Jim also began writing his own poetry and also reciting poetry until he was better known for that than singing although he did spend 8 years with one of Britain's premier shanty crews, The Shellback Chorus. Now retired Jim spends his time performing and helping out at various folk clubs and festivals and doing freelance newspaper articles and reviews as well as writing his own prose and poetry. In his spare time he is Secretary and a Trustee of a local Children's Charity.

www.ingramcontent.com/pod-product-compliance
Lightning Source LLC
Chambersburg PA
CBHW082017300426
44117CB00015B/2259